CU00950191

THE ART OF
COMPUTER PROGRAMMING

VOLUME 4, FASCICLE 1

Bitwise Tricks & Techniques

Binary Decision Diagrams

DONALD E. KNUTH *Stanford University*

ADDISON–WESLEY

Upper Saddle River, NJ · Boston · Indianapolis · San Francisco
New York · Toronto · Montréal · London · Munich · Paris · Madrid
Capetown · Sydney · Tokyo · Singapore · Mexico City

The author and publisher have taken care in the preparation of this book, but make no expressed or implied warranty of any kind and assume no responsibility for errors or omissions. No liability is assumed for incidental or consequential damages in connection with or arising out of the use of the information or programs contained herein.

For sales outside the U.S., please contact:

> International Sales
> international@pearsoned.com

Visit us on the Web: www.informit.com/aw

Library of Congress Cataloging-in-Publication Data
Knuth, Donald Ervin, 1938-
  The art of computer programming / Donald Ervin Knuth.
  viii,261 p. 24 cm.
  Includes bibliographical references and index.
  Contents: v. 4, fascicle 1. Bitwise tricks & techniques; binary
decision diagrams.
  ISBN 0-321-58050-8 (pbk. : alk. papers : volume 4, fascicle 1)
1. Computer programming. 2. Computer algorithms. I. Title.
  QA76.6.K64 2005
  005.1--dc22

             2005041030

Internet page http://www-cs-faculty.stanford.edu/~knuth/taocp.html contains current information about this book and related books.

See also http://www-cs-faculty.stanford.edu/~knuth/sgb.html for information about *The Stanford GraphBase*, including downloadable software for dealing with the graphs used in many of the examples in Chapter 7.

And see http://www-cs-faculty.stanford.edu/~knuth/mmix.html for basic information about the MMIX computer.

Copyright © 2009 by Pearson Education, Inc.

All rights reserved. Printed in the United States of America. This publication is protected by copyright, and permission must be obtained from the publisher prior to any prohibited reproduction, storage in a retrieval system, or transmission in any form or by any means, electronic, mechanical, photocopying, recording, or likewise. For information regarding permissions, write to:

> Pearson Education, Inc.
> Rights and Contracts Department
> 501 Boylston Street, Suite 900
> Boston, MA 02116

ISBN 0-321-58050-8

Text printed in the United States, on recycled paper, at the Courier Corporation plant in Stoughton, Massachusetts

First printing, March 2009

PREFACE

These unforeseen stoppages,
which I own I had no conception of when I first set out;
— but which, I am convinced now, will rather increase than diminish as I advance,
— have struck out a hint which I am resolved to follow;
— and that is, — not to be in a hurry;
— but to go on leisurely, writing and publishing two volumes of my life every year;
— which, if I am suffered to go on quietly, and can make a tolerable bargain
with my bookseller, I shall continue to do as long as I live.

— LAURENCE STERNE, *The Life and Opinions of*
Tristram Shandy, Gentleman (1760)

THIS BOOKLET is Fascicle 1 of *The Art of Computer Programming*, Volume 4: *Combinatorial Algorithms*. As explained in the preface to Fascicle 1 of Volume 1, I'm circulating the material in this preliminary form because I know that the task of completing Volume 4 will take many years; I can't wait for people to begin reading what I've written so far and to provide valuable feedback.

To put the material in context, this fascicle contains Sections 7.1.3 and 7.1.4 of a long, long chapter about combinatorial searching. Chapter 7 is planned to be by far the longest single chapter of *The Art of Computer Programming*; it will eventually fill at least three volumes (namely Volumes 4A, 4B, and 4C), assuming that I'm able to remain healthy. It begins with a short review of graph theory, with emphasis on some highlights of significant graphs in the Stanford GraphBase, from which I will be drawing many examples. Then comes Section 7.1: Zeros and Ones, which is another sort of introduction, at a different level. Subsection 7.1.1, "Boolean basics," attempts to erect a solid foundation of theoretical and practical ideas about Boolean functions. Subsection 7.1.2, "Boolean evaluation," considers how to compute such functions with maximum efficiency. These opening pages of Chapter 7 have already been published as Volume 4, Fascicle 0; they set the scene for the material in the present fascicle.

This part of *The Art of Computer Programming* has probably been more fun to write than any other so far. Indeed, I've spent more than 30 years collecting material for subsection 7.1.3, "Bitwise tricks and techniques"; finally I'm able to assemble these goodies together and segue through them. And subsection 7.1.4, "Binary decision diagrams," was a real eye-opener, a fascinating learning experience, as explained below.

Most of Volume 4 will deal with abstract concepts, and there will be little or no need to say much about a computer's machine language. Volumes 1–3 have already dealt with most of the important ideas about programming at that level. But Section 7.1.3 is a notable exception: Here we often want to see the very pulse of the machine. Section 7.1.3 explains how to make many critical programs run considerably faster, by using supposedly low-level techniques that actually fit nicely into high-level methods, and by developing an attitude toward programming that I like to call *broadword computing.*

Therefore I strongly recommend that readers become familiar with the basics of the MMIX computer, explained in Volume 1 Fascicle 1, in order to fully appreciate the bitwise tricks and techniques described here. Cross references to Sections 1.3.1′ and 1.3.2′ in the present booklet refer to that fascicle. I've reprinted the basic MMIX opcode-and-timing chart, Table 1.3.1′–1, at the end of this booklet for convenience, together with a list of ASCII codes.

Section 7.1.4, in turn, has given me many more surprises than anything else so far. It deals with a topic that burst on the scene in 1986, long after old-timers like me thought that we had already seen all of the basic data structures that would ever prove to be of extraspecial importance. I didn't actually learn about binary decision diagrams until 1995 or so, because I was preoccupied with other things; at that time I wrote some experimental programs and realized that my existing draft of Section 7.1, originally written in 1977, was woefully out of date. I finally began to write Section 7.1.4 in May of 2007, thinking that it would eventually fill roughly 35 pages, and that I could easily complete it in three months. Now, more than a year later, I'm looking at more than four times as many pages — including answers to the exercises — even though I've constantly had to cut, cut, cut! Every week I've been coming across fascinating new things that simply cry out to be part of *The Art.*

Binary decision diagrams (BDDs) are wonderful, and so are the related structures called ZDDs. They have become the data structures of choice for Boolean functions and for families of sets, and the more I play with them the more I love them. For eighteen months I've been like a child with a new toy, being able now to solve problems that I never imagined would be tractable. Every time I've tried a new application, I've learned more. I suspect that many readers will have the same experience, and that there will always be more to learn about such a fertile subject. Already I know that I could easily teach a one-semester college course about binary decision diagrams, at either the undergraduate or graduate level, with more than enough important material to discuss in class. Many aspects of this topic are still ripe for further investigation and improvement.

Most of the theory and practice related to BDDs is due to researchers in the areas of hardware design, testing, and verification. I have, however, tried to present it from the standpoint of a programmer who is primarily interested in combinatorial algorithms. The experimental toolkits that I wrote for working with BDDs and ZDDs while writing this section are available (in unpolished form) on the Internet from my "downloadable programs" page.

In summary, both of the main topics treated in this booklet — broadword computation and the use of BDDs/ZDDs — are important concepts that are ready to become mainstream, after having been nurtured by comparatively small segments of the community of programmers.

Special thanks are due to Guy Steele and Hank Warren for their comments on my early drafts of Section 7.1.3. Similarly, I owe a great debt of gratitude to Randy Bryant, Rick Rudell, and Fabio Somenzi, who helped me significantly at several crucial stages as I was preparing Section 7.1.4. And as usual I thank dozens of others who have patiently read what I've written and corrected dozens of dozens of mistakes.

I happily offer a "finder's fee" of $2.56 for each remaining error in this draft when it is first reported to me, whether that error be typographical, technical, or historical. The same reward holds for items that I forgot to put in the index. And valuable suggestions for improvements to the text are worth 32¢ each. (Furthermore, if you find a better solution to an exercise, I'll actually do my best to give you immortal glory, by publishing your name in the eventual book:–)

Cross references to yet-unwritten material sometimes appear as '00'; this impossible value is a placeholder for the actual numbers to be supplied later.

Happy reading!

Stanford, California   D. E. K.
20 December 2008

I at last deliver to the world a Work which I have long promised,
and of which, I am afraid, too high expectations have been raised.
The delay of its publication must be imputed, in a considerable degree,
to the extraordinary zeal which has been shown by distinguished persons
in all quarters to supply me with additional information.
— JAMES BOSWELL, *The Life of Samuel Johnson, LL.D.* (1791)

A note on notation. Several formulas in this booklet use the notation $\langle xyz \rangle$ for the median function (aka majority function), which is discussed extensively in Section 7.1.1. Other formulas use the notation $x \mathbin{\dot{-}} y$ for the monus function (aka dot-minus or saturating subtraction), which was defined in Section 1.3.1′. Hexadecimal constants are preceded by a sharp sign: $^{\#}123$ means $(123)_{16}$. If you run across other notations that appear strange, please look at the Index to Notations at the end of Volumes 1, 2, or 3, and/or the entries under "Notation" in the index to the present fascicle. Of course Volume 4 will some day contain its own Index to Notations.

A note on references. References to *IEEE Transactions* include a letter code for the type of transactions, in boldface preceding the volume number. For example, '*IEEE Trans.* **C-35**' means the *IEEE Transactions on Computers*, volume 35. The IEEE no longer uses these convenient letter codes, but the codes aren't too hard to decipher: '**EC**' once stood for "Electronic Computers," '**IT**' for "Information Theory," '**SE**' for "Software Engineering," and '**SP**' for "Signal Processing," etc.; '**CAD**' meant "Computer-Aided Design of Integrated Circuits and Systems."

An external exercise. This fascicle refers to exercise 6.4–78, which did not appear in the second edition of Volume 3 until the 24th printing. Here is a copy of that exercise and its answer. (Please don't peek at the answer until you've worked on the exercise.)

▶ **78.** [*M26*] (P. Woelfel.) If $0 \leq x < 2^n$, let $h_{a,b}(x) = \lfloor (ax + b)/2^k \rfloor \bmod 2^{n-k}$. Show that the set $\{h_{a,b} \mid 0 < a < 2^n, a \text{ odd, and } 0 \leq b < 2^k\}$ is a universal family of hash functions from n-bit keys to $(n - k)$-bit keys. (These functions are particularly easy to implement on a binary computer.)

78. Let $g(x) = \lfloor x/2^k \rfloor \bmod 2^{n-k}$ and $\delta(x, x') = \sum_{b=0}^{2^k-1} [g(x + b) = g(x' + b)]$. Then $\delta(x + 1, x' + 1) = \delta(x, x') + [g(x + 2^k) = g(x' + 2^k)] - [g(x) = g(x')] = \delta(x, x')$. Also $\delta(x, 0) = (2^k \dot- (x \bmod 2^n)) + (2^k \dot- ((-x) \bmod 2^n))$ when $0 < x < 2^n$, where $a \dot- b = \max(a - b, 0)$. Therefore $\delta(x, x') = (2^k \dot- ((x - x') \bmod 2^n)) + (2^k \dot- ((x' - x) \bmod 2^n))$ when $x \not\equiv x'$ (modulo 2^n).

Now let $A = \{a \mid 0 < a < 2^n, a \text{ odd}\}$ and $B = \{b \mid 0 \leq b < 2^k\}$. We want to show that $\sum_{a \in A} \sum_{b \in B} [g(ax + b) = g(ax' + b)] \leq R/M = 2^{n-1+k}/2^{n-k} = 2^{2k-1}$ when $0 \leq x < x' < 2^n$. And indeed, if $x' - x = 2^p q$ with q odd, then we have

$$\sum_{a \in A} \sum_{b \in B} [g(ax + b) = g(ax' + b)] = \sum_{a \in A} \delta(ax, ax') = 2 \sum_{a \in A} (2^k \dot- ((2^p aq) \bmod 2^n))$$

$$= 2^{p+1} \sum_{j=0}^{2^{n-p-1}-1} (2^k \dot- 2^p(2j+1)) = 2^{p+1} \sum_{j=0}^{2^{k-p-1}-1} (2^k - 2^p(2j+1))[p < k] = 2^{2k-1}[p < k].$$

[See *Lecture Notes in Computer Science* **1672** (1999), 262–272.]

CONTENTS

[These techniques] are instances of general mathematical principles
waiting to be discovered, if an appropriate setting is created.
Such a setting would be a calculus of bitmap operations, so one can learn
to use these operations just as naturally as arithmetic operations on numbers.
— L. J. GUIBAS and J. STOLFI, *ACM Transactions on Graphics* (1982)

A nice mixture of boolean and numeric functions —
a suitable exercise for biturgical acolytes.
— R. W. GOSPER (1996)

CHAPTER SEVEN

COMBINATORIAL SEARCHING

COMBINATORICS is the study of the ways in which discrete objects can be arranged into various kinds of patterns. ...

7.1. ZEROS AND ONES

COMBINATORIAL ALGORITHMS often require special attention to efficiency, and the proper representation of data is an important way to gain the necessary speed. ... As bit players on the world's stage, we'd better have a thorough understanding of the low-level properties of binary quantities before we launch into a study of higher-level concepts and techniques. Therefore we shall start by investigating basic ways to combine individual bits and sequences of bits.

7.1.1. Boolean Basics

There are 16 possible functions $f(x, y)$ that transform two given bits x and y into a third bit $z = f(x, y)$, since there are two choices for each of $f(0,0)$, $f(0,1)$, $f(1,0)$, and $f(1,1)$. ... Such functions are often called "Boolean operations" in honor of George Boole. ...

7.1.2. Boolean Evaluation

Our next goal is to study the efficient evaluation of Boolean functions, much as we studied the evaluation of polynomials in Section 4.6.4. ...

 Complete texts of the opening sections of Chapter 7 appear in Volume 4, Fascicle 0, first published in April 2008.

Lady Caroline.   *Psha! that's such a hack!*
Sir Simon.   *A hack, Lady Caroline, that*
the knowing ones have warranted sound.
— GEORGE COLMAN, *John Bull*, Act 3, Scene 1 (1803)

7.1.3. Bitwise Tricks and Techniques

Now comes the fun part: We get to use Boolean operations in our programs.

People are more familiar with arithmetic operations like addition, subtraction, and multiplication than they are with bitwise operations such as "and," "exclusive-or," and so on, because arithmetic has a very long history. But we will see that Boolean operations on binary numbers deserve to be much better known. Indeed, they're an important component of every good programmer's toolkit.

Early machine designers provided fullword bitwise operations in their computers primarily because such instructions could be included in a machine's repertoire almost for free. Binary logic seemed to be potentially useful, although only a few applications were originally foreseen. For example, the EDSAC computer, completed in 1949, included a "collate" command that essentially performed the operation $z \leftarrow z + (x \,\&\, y)$, where z was the accumulator, x was the multiplier register, and y was a specified word in memory; it was used for unpacking data. The Manchester Mark I computer, built at about the same time, included not only bitwise AND, but also OR and XOR. When Alan Turing wrote the first programming manual for the Mark I in 1950, he remarked that bitwise NOT can be obtained by using XOR (denoted '≢') in combination with a row of 1s. R. A. Brooker, who extended Turing's manual in 1952 when the Mark II computer was being designed, remarked further that OR could be used "to round off a number by forcing 1 into its least significant digit position." By this time the Mark II, which was to become the prototype of the Ferranti Mercury, had also acquired new instructions for sideways addition and for the position of the most significant 1.

Keith Tocher published an unusual application of AND and OR in 1954, which has subsequently been reinvented frequently (see exercise 85). And during the ensuing decades, programmers have gradually discovered that bitwise operations can be amazingly useful. Many of these tricks have remained part of the folklore; the time is now ripe to take advantage of what has been learned.

A *trick* is a clever idea that can be used once, while a *technique* is a trick that can be used at least twice. We will see in this section that tricks tend to evolve naturally into techniques.

Enriched arithmetic. Let's begin by officially defining bitwise operations on integers so that, if $x = (\ldots x_2 x_1 x_0)_2$, $y = (\ldots y_2 y_1 y_0)_2$, and $z = (\ldots z_2 z_1 z_0)_2$ in binary notation, we have

$$x \,\&\, y = z \quad \Longleftrightarrow \quad x_k \wedge y_k = z_k, \qquad \text{for all } k \geq 0; \tag{1}$$

$$x \mid y = z \quad \Longleftrightarrow \quad x_k \vee y_k = z_k, \qquad \text{for all } k \geq 0; \tag{2}$$

$$x \oplus y = z \quad \Longleftrightarrow \quad x_k \oplus y_k = z_k, \qquad \text{for all } k \geq 0. \tag{3}$$

(It would be tempting to write '$x \wedge y$' instead of $x \,\&\, y$, and '$x \vee y$' instead of $x \mid y$; but when we study optimization problems we'll find it better to reserve the notations $x \wedge y$ and $x \vee y$ for $\min(x, y)$ and $\max(x, y)$, respectively.) Thus, for example,

$$5 \,\&\, 11 = 1, \qquad 5 \mid 11 = 15, \qquad \text{and} \qquad 5 \oplus 11 = 14,$$

since $5 = (0101)_2$, $11 = (1011)_2$, $1 = (0001)_2$, $15 = (1111)_2$, and $14 = (1110)_2$. Negative integers are to be thought of in this connection as infinite-precision numbers in two's complement notation, having infinitely many 1s at the left; for example, -5 is $(\ldots 1111011)_2$. Such infinite-precision numbers are a special case of *2-adic integers*, which are discussed in exercise 4.1–31, and in fact the operators $\&$, $\mid$, $\oplus$ make perfect sense when they are applied to arbitrary 2-adic numbers.

Mathematicians have never paid much attention to the properties of $\&$ and $\mid$ as operations on integers. But the third operation, $\oplus$, has a venerable history, because it describes a winning strategy in the game of nim (see exercises 8–16). For this reason $x \oplus y$ has often been called the "nim sum" of the integers x and y.

All three of the basic bitwise operations turn out to have many useful properties. For example, every relation between $\wedge$, $\vee$, and $\oplus$ that we studied in Section 7.1.1 is automatically inherited by $\&$, $|$, and $\oplus$ on integers, since the relation holds in every bit position. We might as well recap the main identities here:

$$x \mathbin{\&} y = y \mathbin{\&} x, \qquad x \mid y = y \mid x, \qquad x \oplus y = y \oplus x; \tag{4}$$

$$(x \mathbin{\&} y) \mathbin{\&} z = x \mathbin{\&} (y \mathbin{\&} z), \quad (x \mid y) \mid z = x \mid (y \mid z), \quad (x \oplus y) \oplus z = x \oplus (y \oplus z); \tag{5}$$

$$(x \mid y) \mathbin{\&} z = (x \mathbin{\&} z) \mid (y \mathbin{\&} z), \qquad (x \mathbin{\&} y) \mid z = (x \mid z) \mathbin{\&} (y \mid z); \tag{6}$$

$$(x \oplus y) \mathbin{\&} z = (x \mathbin{\&} z) \oplus (y \mathbin{\&} z); \tag{7}$$

$$(x \mathbin{\&} y) \mid x = x, \qquad (x \mid y) \mathbin{\&} x = x; \tag{8}$$

$$(x \mathbin{\&} y) \oplus (x \mid y) = x \oplus y; \tag{9}$$

$$x \mathbin{\&} 0 = 0, \qquad x \mid 0 = x, \qquad x \oplus 0 = x; \tag{10}$$

$$x \mathbin{\&} x = x, \qquad x \mid x = x, \qquad x \oplus x = 0; \tag{11}$$

$$x \mathbin{\&} -1 = x, \qquad x \mid -1 = -1, \qquad x \oplus -1 = \bar{x}; \tag{12}$$

$$x \mathbin{\&} \bar{x} = 0, \qquad x \mid \bar{x} = -1, \qquad x \oplus \bar{x} = -1; \tag{13}$$

$$\overline{x \mathbin{\&} y} = \bar{x} \mid \bar{y}, \qquad \overline{x \mid y} = \bar{x} \mathbin{\&} \bar{y}, \qquad \overline{x \oplus y} = \bar{x} \oplus y = x \oplus \bar{y}. \tag{14}$$

The notation $\bar{x}$ in (12), (13), and (14) stands for bitwise *complementation* of x, namely $(\ldots \bar{x}_2 \bar{x}_1 \bar{x}_0)_2$, also written $\sim x$. Notice that (12) and (13) aren't quite the same as 7.1.1–(10) and 7.1.1–(18); we must now use $-1 = (\ldots 1111)_2$ instead of $1 = (\ldots 0001)_2$ in order to make the formulas bitwise correct.

We say that x is *contained in* y, written $x \subseteq y$ or $y \supseteq x$, if the individual bits of x and y satisfy $x_k \leq y_k$ for all $k \geq 0$. Thus

$$x \subseteq y \quad \Longleftrightarrow \quad x \mathbin{\&} y = x \quad \Longleftrightarrow \quad x \mid y = y \quad \Longleftrightarrow \quad x \mathbin{\&} \bar{y} = 0. \tag{15}$$

Of course we needn't use bitwise operations only in connection with each other; we can combine them with all the ordinary operations of arithmetic. For example, from the relation $x + \bar{x} = (\ldots 1111)_2 = -1$ we can deduce the formula

$$-x = \bar{x} + 1, \tag{16}$$

which turns out to be extremely important. Replacing x by $x - 1$ gives also

$$-x = \overline{x - 1}; \tag{17}$$

and in general we can reduce subtraction to complementation and addition:

$$\overline{x - y} = \bar{x} + y. \tag{18}$$

We often want to shift binary numbers to the left or right. These operations are equivalent to multiplication and division by powers of 2, with appropriate rounding, but it is convenient to have special notations for them:

$$x \ll k = x \text{ shifted left } k \text{ bits} = \lfloor 2^k x \rfloor; \tag{19}$$

$$x \gg k = x \text{ shifted right } k \text{ bits} = \lfloor 2^{-k} x \rfloor. \tag{20}$$

Here k can be any integer, possibly negative. In particular we have

$$x \ll (-k) = x \gg k \qquad \text{and} \qquad x \gg (-k) = x \ll k, \tag{21}$$

for every infinite-precision number x. Also $(x \mathbin{\&} y) \ll k = (x \ll k) \mathbin{\&} (y \ll k)$, etc.

When bitwise operations are combined with addition, subtraction, multiplication, and/or shifting, extremely intricate results can arise, even when the formulas are quite short. A taste of the possibilities can be seen, for example, in Fig. 11. Furthermore, such formulas do not merely produce purposeless, chaotic behavior: A famous chain of operations known as "Gosper's hack," first published in 1972, opened people's eyes to the fact that a large number of useful and nontrivial functions can be computed rapidly (see exercise 20). Our goal in this section is to explore how such efficient constructions might be discovered.

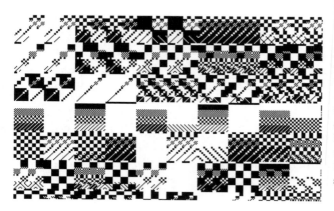

Fig. 11. A small portion of the patchwork quilt defined by the bitwise function $f(x, y) = ((x \oplus \bar{y}) \mathbin{\&} ((x - 350) \gg 3))^2$; the square cell in row x and column y is painted white or black according as the value of $((f(x, y) \gg 12) \mathbin{\&} 1)$ is 0 or 1. (Design by D. Sleator, 1976; see also exercise 18.)

Packing and unpacking. We studied algorithms for multiple-precision arithmetic in Section 4.3.1, dealing with situations where integers are too large to fit in a single word of memory or a single computer register. But the opposite situation, when integers are significantly *smaller* than the capacity of one computer word, is actually much more common; D. H. Lehmer called this "fractional precision." We can often deal with several integers at once, by packing them into a single word.

For example, a date x that consists of a year number y, a month number m, and a day number d, can be represented by using 4 bits for m and 5 bits for d:

$$x = (((y \ll 4) + m) \ll 5) + d. \tag{22}$$

We'll see below that many operations can be performed directly on dates in this packed form. For example, $x < x'$ when date x precedes date x'. But if necessary the individual components (y, m, d) can readily be unpacked when x is given:

$$d = x \bmod 32, \qquad m = (x \gg 5) \bmod 16, \qquad y = x \gg 9. \tag{23}$$

And these "mod" operations do not require division, because of the important law

$$x \bmod 2^n = x \mathbin{\&} (2^n - 1) \tag{24}$$

for any integer $n \geq 0$. We have, for instance, $d = x \mathbin{\&} 31$ in (22) and (23).

Such packing of data obviously saves space in memory, and it also saves time: We can more quickly move or copy items of data from one place to another when they've been packed together. Moreover, computers run considerably faster when they operate on numbers that fit into a cache memory of limited size.

The ultimate packing density is achieved when we have 1-bit items, because we can then cram 64 of them into a single 64-bit word. Suppose, for example, that we want a table of all odd prime numbers less than 1024, so that we can easily decide the primality of a small integer. No problem; only eight 64-bit numbers are required:

$P_0 = 0111011011010011001011010010011001011001010010001011011010000001,$
$P_1 = 0100110000110010010100100110000110110000010000010110100110000100,$
$P_2 = 1001001100101100001000000101101000000100100001101001000100100101,$
$P_3 = 0010001010001000011000011001010010001011010000010001010001010010,$
$P_4 = 0000110000000010010000100100110010000100100110010010110000010000,$
$P_5 = 1101001001100000101001000100001000100001000100100101000100101000,$
$P_6 = 1010000001000010000011000011011100001000000101101000001011010000,$
$P_7 = 0000010100010000100010100100100000001010010010001001000001010110.$

To test whether $2k + 1$ is prime, for $0 \le k < 512$, we simply compute

$$P_{\lfloor k/64 \rfloor} \ll (k \mathbin{\&} 63) \tag{25}$$

in a 64-bit register, and see if the leftmost bit is 1. For example, the following MMIX instructions will do the job, if register pbase holds the address of P_0:

SRU	$0,k,3	$0 \leftarrow \lfloor k/8 \rfloor$ (i.e., $k \gg 3$).
LDOU	$1,pbase,$0	$1 \leftarrow P_{\lfloor \$0/8 \rfloor}$ (i.e., $P_{\lfloor k/64 \rfloor}$).
AND	$0,k,#3f	$0 \leftarrow k \bmod 64$ (i.e., $k \mathbin{\&} {}^{\#}\mathtt{3f}$).
SLU	$1,$1,$0	$1 \leftarrow (\$1 \ll \$0) \bmod 2^{64}$.
BN	$1,PRIME	Branch to PRIME if $s(\$1) < 0$. ∎

(26)

Notice that the leftmost bit of a register is 1 if and only if the register contents are negative.

We could equally well pack the bits from right to left in each word:

$Q_0 = 1000000101101101000100101001101001100100101101001100101101101110,$
$Q_1 = 0010000110010110100000100000110110000110010010100100110000110010,$
$Q_2 = 1010010010001001011000010010000001011010000001000011010011001001,$
$Q_3 = 0100101000101000100000101101000100101001100001100001000101000100,$
$Q_4 = 0000100000110100100110010010000100110010010000100100000000110000,$
$Q_5 = 0001010010001010010010001000010001000010001001010000011001001011,$
$Q_6 = 0000101101000000101101000000100001101100001100000100001000000101,$
$Q_7 = 0110010100000100100100100101000000100100101000100001000101000000;$

here $Q_j = P_j^R$. Instead of shifting left as in (25), we now shift right,

$$Q_{\lfloor k/64 \rfloor} \gg (k \mathbin{\&} 63), \tag{27}$$

and look at the *rightmost* bit of the result. The last two lines of (26) become

SRU	$1,$1,$0	$1 \leftarrow \$1 \gg \$0$.
BOD	$1,PRIME	Branch to PRIME if $1 is odd. ∎

(28)

(And of course we use qbase instead of pbase.) Either way, the classic *sieve of Eratosthenes* will readily set up the basic table entries P_j or Q_j (see exercise 24).

Table 1

THE BIG-ENDIAN VIEW OF A 32-BYTE MEMORY

octa 0							
tetra 0				tetra 4			
wyde 0		wyde 2		wyde 4		wyde 6	
byte 0	byte 1	byte 2	byte 3	byte 4	byte 5	byte 6	byte 7
$a_0 \ldots a_7$	$a_8 \ldots a_{15}$	$a_{16} \ldots a_{23}$	$a_{24} \ldots a_{31}$	$a_{32} \ldots a_{39}$	$a_{40} \ldots a_{47}$	$a_{48} \ldots a_{55}$	$a_{56} \ldots a_{63}$

octa 8							
tetra 8				tetra 12			
wyde 8		wyde 10		wyde 12		wyde 14	
byte 8	byte 9	byte 10	byte 11	byte 12	byte 13	byte 14	byte 15
$a_{64} \ldots a_{71}$	$a_{72} \ldots a_{79}$	$a_{80} \ldots a_{87}$	$a_{88} \ldots a_{95}$	$a_{96} \ldots a_{103}$	$a_{104} \ldots a_{111}$	$a_{112} \ldots a_{119}$	$a_{120} \ldots a_{127}$

octa 16							
tetra 16				tetra 20			
wyde 16		wyde 18		wyde 20		wyde 22	
byte 16	byte 17	byte 18	byte 19	byte 20	byte 21	byte 22	byte 23
$a_{128} \ldots a_{135}$	$a_{136} \ldots a_{143}$	$a_{144} \ldots a_{151}$	$a_{152} \ldots a_{159}$	$a_{160} \ldots a_{167}$	$a_{168} \ldots a_{175}$	$a_{176} \ldots a_{183}$	$a_{184} \ldots a_{191}$

octa 24							
tetra 24				tetra 28			
wyde 24		wyde 26		wyde 28		wyde 30	
byte 24	byte 25	byte 26	byte 27	byte 28	byte 29	byte 30	byte 31
$a_{192} \ldots a_{199}$	$a_{200} \ldots a_{207}$	$a_{208} \ldots a_{215}$	$a_{216} \ldots a_{223}$	$a_{224} \ldots a_{231}$	$a_{232} \ldots a_{239}$	$a_{240} \ldots a_{247}$	$a_{248} \ldots a_{255}$

Big-endian and little-endian conventions. Whenever we pack bits or bytes into words, we must decide whether to place them from left to right or from right to left. The left-to-right convention is called "big-endian," because the initial items go into the most significant positions; thus they will have bigger significance than their successors, when numbers are compared. The right-to-left convention is called "little-endian"; it puts the first items where little numbers go.

A big-endian approach seems more natural in many cases, because we're accustomed to reading and writing from left to right. But a little-endian placement has advantages too. For example, let's consider the prime number problem again; let $a_k = [2k+1 \text{ is prime}]$. Our table entries $\{P_0, P_1, \ldots, P_7\}$ are big-endian, and we can regard them as the representation of a single multiple-precision integer that is 512 bits long:

$$(P_0 P_1 \ldots P_7)_{2^{64}} = (a_0 a_1 \ldots a_{511})_2. \tag{29}$$

Similarly, our little-endian table entries represent the multiprecise integer

$$(Q_7 \ldots Q_1 Q_0)_{2^{64}} = (a_{511} \ldots a_1 a_0)_2. \tag{30}$$

The latter integer is mathematically nicer than the former, because it is

$$\sum_{k=0}^{511} 2^k a_k = \sum_{k=0}^{511} 2^k [2k+1 \text{ is prime}] = \left(\sum_{k=0}^{\infty} 2^k [2k+1 \text{ is prime}] \right) \bmod 2^{512}. \tag{31}$$

Table 2

THE LITTLE-ENDIAN VIEW OF A 32-BYTE MEMORY

octa 24

tetra 28				tetra 24			
wyde 30		wyde 28		wyde 26		wyde 24	
byte 31	byte 30	byte 29	byte 28	byte 27	byte 26	byte 25	byte 24
$a_{255}\ldots a_{248}$	$a_{247}\ldots a_{240}$	$a_{239}\ldots a_{232}$	$a_{231}\ldots a_{224}$	$a_{223}\ldots a_{216}$	$a_{215}\ldots a_{208}$	$a_{207}\ldots a_{200}$	$a_{199}\ldots a_{192}$

octa 16

tetra 20				tetra 16			
wyde 22		wyde 20		wyde 18		wyde 16	
byte 23	byte 22	byte 21	byte 20	byte 19	byte 18	byte 17	byte 16
$a_{191}\ldots a_{184}$	$a_{183}\ldots a_{176}$	$a_{175}\ldots a_{168}$	$a_{167}\ldots a_{160}$	$a_{159}\ldots a_{152}$	$a_{151}\ldots a_{144}$	$a_{143}\ldots a_{136}$	$a_{135}\ldots a_{128}$

octa 8

tetra 12				tetra 8			
wyde 14		wyde 12		wyde 10		wyde 8	
byte 15	byte 14	byte 13	byte 12	byte 11	byte 10	byte 9	byte 8
$a_{127}\ldots a_{120}$	$a_{119}\ldots a_{112}$	$a_{111}\ldots a_{104}$	$a_{103}\ldots a_{96}$	$a_{95}\ldots a_{88}$	$a_{87}\ldots a_{80}$	$a_{79}\ldots a_{72}$	$a_{71}\ldots a_{64}$

octa 0

tetra 4				tetra 0			
wyde 6		wyde 4		wyde 2		wyde 0	
byte 7	byte 6	byte 5	byte 4	byte 3	byte 2	byte 1	byte 0
$a_{63}\ldots a_{56}$	$a_{55}\ldots a_{48}$	$a_{47}\ldots a_{40}$	$a_{39}\ldots a_{32}$	$a_{31}\ldots a_{24}$	$a_{23}\ldots a_{16}$	$a_{15}\ldots a_{8}$	$a_{7}\ldots a_{0}$

Notice, however, that we used $(Q_7 \ldots Q_1 Q_0)_{2^{64}}$ to get this simple result, not $(Q_0 Q_1 \ldots Q_7)_{2^{64}}$. The other number,

$$(Q_0 Q_1 \ldots Q_7)_{2^{64}} = (a_{63}\ldots a_1 a_0 a_{127}\ldots a_{65} a_{64} a_{191}\ldots a_{385} a_{384} a_{511}\ldots a_{449} a_{448})_2$$

is in fact quite weird, and it has no really nice formula. (See exercise 25.)

Endianness has important consequences, because most computers allow individual bytes of the memory to be addressed as well as register-sized units. MMIX has a big-endian architecture; therefore if register x contains the 64-bit number #0123456789abcdef, and if we use the commands 'STOU x,0; LDBU y,1' to store x into octabyte location 0 and read back the byte in location 1, the result in register y will be #23. On machines with a little-endian architecture, the analogous commands would set y ← #cd instead; #23 would be byte 6.

Tables 1 and 2 illustrate the competing "world views" of big-endian and little-endian aficionados. The big-endian approach is basically top-down, with bit 0 and byte 0 at the top left; the little-endian approach is basically bottom-up, with bit 0 and byte 0 at the bottom right. Because of this difference, great care is necessary when transmitting data from one kind of computer to another, or when writing programs that are supposed to give equivalent results in both cases. On the other hand, our example of the Q table for primes shows that we can perfectly well use a little-endian packing convention on a big-endian computer like `MMIX`, or vice versa. The difference is noticeable only when data is loaded and stored in different-sized chunks, or passed between machines.

Working with the rightmost bits. Big-endian and little-endian approaches aren't readily interchangeable in general, because the laws of arithmetic send signals leftward from the bits that are "least significant." Some of the most important bitwise manipulation techniques are based on this fact.

If x is almost any nonzero 2-adic integer, we can write its bits in the form

$$x = (\alpha\, 01^a10^b)_2; \tag{32}$$

in other words, x consists of some arbitrary (but infinite) binary string α, followed by a 0, which is followed by $a + 1$ ones, and followed by b zeros, for some $a \geq 0$ and $b \geq 0$. (The exceptions occur when $x = -2^b$; then $a = \infty$.) Consequently

$$\bar{x} = (\bar{\alpha}\, 10^a01^b)_2, \tag{33}$$
$$x - 1 = (\alpha\, 01^a01^b)_2, \tag{34}$$
$$-x = (\bar{\alpha}\, 10^a10^b)_2; \tag{35}$$

and we see that $\bar{x} + 1 = -x = \overline{x - 1}$, in agreement with (16) and (17). With two operations we can therefore compute relatives of x in several useful ways:

$$x\, \&\, (x{-}1) = (\ \alpha\ 01^a00^b)_2 \quad \text{[remove the rightmost 1];} \tag{36}$$
$$x\, \&\, {-}x = (0^\infty00^a10^b)_2 \quad \text{[extract the rightmost 1];} \tag{37}$$
$$x\, |\, {-}x = (1^\infty11^a10^b)_2 \quad \text{[smear the rightmost 1 to the left];} \tag{38}$$
$$x \oplus {-}x = (1^\infty11^a00^b)_2 \quad \text{[remove and smear it to the left];} \tag{39}$$
$$x\, |\, (x{-}1) = (\ \alpha\ 01^a11^b)_2 \quad \text{[smear the rightmost 1 to the right];} \tag{40}$$
$$x \oplus (x{-}1) = (0^\infty00^a11^b)_2 \quad \text{[extract and smear it to the right];} \tag{41}$$
$$\bar{x}\, \&\, (x{-}1) = (0^\infty00^a01^b)_2 \quad \text{[extract, remove, and smear it to the right].} \tag{42}$$

And two further operations produce yet another variant:

$$((x|(x{-}1)){+}1)\, \&\, x = (\ \alpha\ 00^a00^b)_2 \quad \text{[remove the rightmost run of 1s].} \tag{43}$$

When $x = 0$, five of these formulas produce 0, the other three give -1. [Formula (36) is due to Peter Wegner, *CACM* **3** (1960), 322; and (43) is due to H. Tim Gladwin, *CACM* **14** (1971), 407–408. See also Henry S. Warren, Jr., *CACM* **20** (1977), 439–441.]

The quantity b in these formulas, which specifies the number of trailing zeros in x, is called the *ruler function* of x and written ρx, because it is related to the lengths of the tick marks that are often used to indicate fractions of an inch: '⊢ᵀᵀᵀᵀᵀᵀᵀᵀᵀᵀᵀᵀᵀᵀᵀ⊣'. In general, ρx is the largest integer k such that 2^k divides x, when $x \neq 0$; and we define $\rho 0 = \infty$. The recurrence relations

$$\rho(2x + 1) = 0, \qquad \rho(2x) = \rho(x) + 1 \tag{44}$$

also serve to define ρx for nonzero x. Another handy relation is worthy of note,

$$\rho(x - y) = \rho(x \oplus y). \tag{45}$$

The elegant formula $x \mathbin{\&} -x$ in (37) allows us to *extract* the rightmost 1 bit very nicely, but we often want to identify exactly which bit it is. The ruler function can be computed in many ways, and the best method often depends heavily on the computer that is being used. For example, a two-instruction sequence due to J. Dallos does the job quickly and easily on MMIX (see (42)):

$$\text{SUBU t,x,1; \quad SADD rho,t,x.} \tag{46}$$

(See exercise 30 for the case $x = 0$.) We shall discuss here two approaches that do not rely on exotic commands like SADD; and later, after learning a few more techniques, we'll consider a third way.

The first general-purpose method makes use of "magic mask" constants μ_k that prove to be useful in many other applications, namely

$$\mu_0 = (\ldots 1010101010101010101010101010101)_2 = -1/3,$$
$$\mu_1 = (\ldots 1001100110011001100110011001)_2 = -1/5, \tag{47}$$
$$\mu_2 = (\ldots 10000111100001111000011110000111)_2 = -1/17,$$

and so on. In general μ_k is the infinite 2-adic fraction $-1/(2^{2^k} + 1)$, because $(2^{2^k} + 1)\mu_k = (\mu_k \ll 2^k) + \mu_k = (\ldots 11111)_2 = -1$. On a computer that has 2^d-bit registers we don't need infinite precision, of course, so we use the truncated constants

$$\mu_{d,k} = (2^{2^d} - 1)/(2^{2^k} + 1) \qquad \text{for } 0 \le k < d. \tag{48}$$

These constants are familiar from our study of Boolean evaluation, because they are the truth tables of the projection functions x_{d-k} (see, for example, 7.1.2–(7)).

When x is a power of 2, we can use these masks to compute

$$\rho x = [x \mathbin{\&} \mu_0 = 0] + 2[x \mathbin{\&} \mu_1 = 0] + 4[x \mathbin{\&} \mu_2 = 0] + 8[x \mathbin{\&} \mu_3 = 0] + \cdots, \tag{49}$$

because $[2^j \mathbin{\&} \mu_k = 0] = j_k$ when $j = (\ldots j_3 j_2 j_1 j_0)_2$. Thus, on a 2^d-bit computer, we can start with $\rho \leftarrow 0$ and $y \leftarrow x \mathbin{\&} -x$; then set $\rho \leftarrow \rho + 2^k$ if $y \mathbin{\&} \mu_{d,k} = 0$, for $0 \le k < d$. This procedure gives $\rho = \rho x$ when $x \ne 0$. (It also gives $\rho 0 = 2^d - 1$, an anomalous value that may need to be corrected; see exercise 30.)

For example, the corresponding MMIX program might look like this:

```
m0 GREG #5555555555555555  ;m1 GREG #3333333333333333;
m2 GREG #0f0f0f0f0f0f0f0f  ;m3 GREG #00ff00ff00ff00ff;
m4 GREG #0000ffff0000ffff  ;m5 GREG #00000000ffffffff;
 NEGU y,x;  AND y,x,y;  AND q,y,m5;  ZSZ rho,q,32;
 AND q,y,m4;  ADD t,rho,16;  CSZ rho,q,t;
 AND q,y,m3;  ADD t,rho,8;   CSZ rho,q,t;
 AND q,y,m2;  ADD t,rho,4;   CSZ rho,q,t;
 AND q,y,m1;  ADD t,rho,2;   CSZ rho,q,t;
 AND q,y,m0;  ADD t,rho,1;   CSZ rho,q,t;
```
$$\tag{50}$$

total time $= 19\upsilon$. Or we could replace the last three lines by

$$\text{SRU y,y,rho; \quad LDB t,rhotab,y; \quad ADD rho,rho,t} \tag{51}$$

where **rhotab** points to the beginning of an appropriate 129-byte table (only eight of whose entries are actually used). The total time would then be $\mu + 13\upsilon$.

The second general-purpose approach to the computation of ρx is quite different. On a 64-bit machine it starts as before, with $y \leftarrow x \,\&\, -x$; but then it simply sets

$$\rho \leftarrow decode\big[((a \cdot y) \bmod 2^{64}) \gg 58\big], \tag{52}$$

where a is a suitable multiplier and $decode$ is a suitable 64-byte table. The constant $a = (a_{63} \ldots a_1 a_0)_2$ must have the property that its 64 substrings

$$a_{63}a_{62}\ldots a_{58}, \; a_{62}a_{61}\ldots a_{57}, \; \ldots, \; a_5 a_4 \ldots a_0, \; a_4 a_3 a_2 a_1 a_0 0, \; \ldots, \; a_0 00000$$

are distinct. Exercise 2.3.4.2–23 shows that many such "de Bruijn cycles" exist; for example, we can use M. H. Martin's constant $^\#$03f79d71b4ca8b09, which is discussed in exercise 3.2.2–17. The decoding table $decode[0], \ldots, decode[63]$ is then

$$\begin{aligned}
&00, 01, 56, 02, 57, 49, 28, 03, 61, 58, 42, 50, 38, 29, 17, 04,\\
&62, 47, 59, 36, 45, 43, 51, 22, 53, 39, 33, 30, 24, 18, 12, 05,\\
&63, 55, 48, 27, 60, 41, 37, 16, 46, 35, 44, 21, 52, 32, 23, 11,\\
&54, 26, 40, 15, 34, 20, 31, 10, 25, 14, 19, 09, 13, 08, 07, 06.
\end{aligned} \tag{53}$$

[This technique was devised in 1997 by M. Läuter, and independently by C. E. Leiserson, H. Prokop, and K. H. Randall a few months later (unpublished). David Seal had used a similar method in 1994, with a larger decoding table.]

Working with the leftmost bits. The function $\lambda x = \lfloor \lg x \rfloor$, which is dual to ρx because it locates the *leftmost* 1 when $x > 0$, was introduced in Eq. 4.6.3–(6). It satisfies the recurrence

$$\lambda 1 = 0; \qquad \lambda(2x) = \lambda(2x + 1) = \lambda(x) + 1 \quad \text{for } x > 0; \tag{54}$$

and it is undefined when x is not a positive integer. What is a good way to compute it? Once again MMIX provides a quick-but-tricky solution:

$$\texttt{FLOTU y,ROUND\_DOWN,x; SUB y,y,fone; SR lam,y,52} \tag{55}$$

where $\texttt{fone} = {}^\#$3ff0000000000000 is the floating point representation of 1.0. (Total time $6v$.) This code floats x, then extracts the exponent.

But if floating point conversion is not readily available, a binary reduction strategy works fairly well on a 2^d-bit machine. We can start with $\lambda \leftarrow 0$ and $y \leftarrow x$; then we set $\lambda \leftarrow \lambda + 2^k$ and $y \leftarrow y \gg 2^k$ if $y \gg 2^k \neq 0$, for $k = d - 1$, $\ldots$, 1, 0 (or until k is reduced to the point where a short table can be used to finish up). The MMIX code analogous to (50) and (51) is now

```
SRU y,x,32;  ZSNZ lam,y,32;
ADD t,lam,16;  SRU y,x,t;  CSNZ lam,y,t;
ADD t,lam,8;  SRU y,x,t;  CSNZ lam,y,t;
SRU y,x,lam;  LDB t,lamtab,y;  ADD lam,lam,t;
```
$$\tag{56}$$

and the total time is $\mu + 11v$. In this case table $\texttt{lamtab}$ has 256 entries, namely λx for $0 \le x < 256$. Notice that the "conditional set" (CS) and "zero or set" (ZS) instructions have been used here and in (50) instead of branch instructions.

There appears to be no simple way to extract the leftmost 1 bit that appears in a register, analogous to the trick by which we extracted the rightmost 1 in (37). For this purpose we could compute $y \leftarrow \lambda x$ and then $1 \ll y$, if $x \neq 0$; but a binary "smearing right" method is somewhat shorter and faster:

$$\text{Set } y \leftarrow x, \text{ then } y \leftarrow y \mid (y \gg 2^k) \text{ for } 0 \leq k < d. \tag{57}$$
$$\text{The leftmost 1 bit of } x \text{ is then } y - (y \gg 1).$$

[These non-floating-point methods have been suggested by H. S. Warren, Jr.]

Other operations at the left of a register, like removing the leftmost run of 1s, are harder yet; see exercise 39. But there is a remarkably simple, machine-independent way to determine whether or not $\lambda x = \lambda y$, given unsigned integers x and y, in spite of the fact that we can't compute λx or λy quickly:

$$\lambda x = \lambda y \qquad \text{if and only if} \qquad x \oplus y \leq x \,\&\, y. \tag{58}$$

[See exercise 40. This elegant relation was discovered by W. C. Lynch in 2006.] We will use (58) below, to devise another way to compute λx.

Sideways addition. Binary n-bit numbers $x = (x_{n-1} \ldots x_1 x_0)_2$ are often used to represent subsets X of the n-element universe $\{0, 1, \ldots, n-1\}$, with $k \in X$ if and only if $2^k \subseteq x$. The functions λx and ρx then represent the largest and smallest elements of X. The function

$$\nu x = x_{n-1} + \cdots + x_1 + x_0, \tag{59}$$

which is called the "sideways sum" or "population count" of x, also has obvious importance in this connection, because it represents the cardinality $|X|$, namely the number of elements in X. This function, which we considered in 4.6.3–(7), satisfies the recurrence

$$\nu 0 = 0; \qquad \nu(2x) = \nu(x) \quad \text{and} \quad \nu(2x+1) = \nu(x) + 1, \quad \text{for } x \geq 0. \tag{60}$$

It also has an interesting connection with the ruler function (exercise 1.2.5–11),

$$\rho x = 1 + \nu(x-1) - \nu x; \qquad \text{equivalently,} \qquad \sum_{k=1}^{n} \rho k = n - \nu n. \tag{61}$$

The first textbook on programming, *The Preparation of Programs for an Electronic Digital Computer* by Wilkes, Wheeler, and Gill, second edition (Reading, Mass.: Addison–Wesley, 1957), 155, 191–193, presented an interesting subroutine for sideways addition due to D. B. Gillies and J. C. P. Miller. Their method was devised for the 35-bit numbers of the EDSAC, but it is readily converted to the following 64-bit procedure for νx when $x = (x_{63} \ldots x_1 x_0)_2$:

Set $y \leftarrow x - ((x \gg 1) \,\&\, \mu_0)$. (Now $y = (u_{31} \ldots u_1 u_0)_4$, where $u_j = x_{2j+1} + x_{2j}$.)
Set $y \leftarrow (y \,\&\, \mu_1) + ((y \gg 2) \,\&\, \mu_1)$. (Now $y = (v_{15} \ldots v_1 v_0)_{16}$, $v_j = u_{2j+1} + u_{2j}$.)
Set $y \leftarrow (y + (y \gg 4)) \,\&\, \mu_2$. (Now $y = (w_7 \ldots w_1 w_0)_{256}$, $w_j = v_{2j+1} + v_{2j}$.)
Finally $\nu \leftarrow ((a \cdot y) \bmod 2^{64}) \gg 56$, where $a = (11111111)_{256}$. $\tag{62}$

The last step cleverly computes $y \bmod 255 = w_7 + \cdots + w_1 + w_0$ via multiplication, using the fact that the sum fits comfortably in eight bits. [David Muller had programmed a similar method for the ILLIAC I machine in 1954.]

If x is expected to be "sparse," having at most a few 1-bits, we can use a faster method [P. Wegner, *CACM* **3** (1960), 322]:

Set $\nu \leftarrow 0$, $y \leftarrow x$. Then while $y \neq 0$, set $\nu \leftarrow \nu + 1$, $y \leftarrow y \,\&\, (y - 1)$.   (63)

A similar approach, using $y \leftarrow y \,|\, (y+1)$, works when x is expected to be "dense."

Bit reversal. For our next trick, let's change $x = (x_{63} \ldots x_1 x_0)_2$ to its left-right mirror image, $x^R = (x_0 x_1 \ldots x_{63})_2$. Anybody who has been following the developments so far, seeing methods like (50), (56), (57), and (62), will probably think, "Aha—once again we can divide by 2 and conquer! If we've already discovered how to reverse 32-bit numbers, we can reverse 64-bit numbers almost as fast, because $(xy)^R = y^R x^R$. All we have to do is apply the 32-bit method in parallel to both halves of the register, then swap the left half with the right half."

Right. For example, we can reverse an 8-bit string in three easy steps:

Given	$x_7 x_6 x_5 x_4 x_3 x_2 x_1 x_0$
Swap bits	$x_6 x_7 x_4 x_5 x_2 x_3 x_0 x_1$
Swap nyps	$x_4 x_5 x_6 x_7 x_0 x_1 x_2 x_3$
Swap nybbles	$x_0 x_1 x_2 x_3 x_4 x_5 x_6 x_7$

$$(64)$$

And six such easy steps will reverse 64 bits. Fortunately, each of the swapping operations turns out to be quite simple with the help of the magic masks μ_k:

$$
\begin{aligned}
y &\leftarrow (x \gg 1) \,\&\, \mu_0, & z &\leftarrow (x \,\&\, \mu_0) \ll 1, & x &\leftarrow y \,|\, z; \\
y &\leftarrow (x \gg 2) \,\&\, \mu_1, & z &\leftarrow (x \,\&\, \mu_1) \ll 2, & x &\leftarrow y \,|\, z; \\
y &\leftarrow (x \gg 4) \,\&\, \mu_2, & z &\leftarrow (x \,\&\, \mu_2) \ll 4, & x &\leftarrow y \,|\, z; \\
y &\leftarrow (x \gg 8) \,\&\, \mu_3, & z &\leftarrow (x \,\&\, \mu_3) \ll 8, & x &\leftarrow y \,|\, z; \\
y &\leftarrow (x \gg 16) \,\&\, \mu_4, & z &\leftarrow (x \,\&\, \mu_4) \ll 16, & x &\leftarrow y \,|\, z; \\
\end{aligned}
$$
$$x \leftarrow (x \gg 32) \,|\, ((x \ll 32) \bmod 2^{64}).$$

$$(65)$$

[Christopher Strachey foresaw some aspects of this construction in *CACM* **4** (1961), 146, and a similar *ternary* method was devised in 1973 by Bruce Baumgart (see exercise 49). The mature algorithm (65) was presented by Henry S. Warren, Jr., in *Hacker's Delight* (Addison–Wesley, 2002), 102.]

But MMIX is once again able to trump this general-purpose technique with less traditional commands that do the job much faster. Consider

    rev GREG #0102040810204080; MOR x,x,rev; MOR x,rev,x;   (66)

the first MOR instruction reverses the bytes of x from big-endian to little-endian or vice versa, while the second reverses the bits within each byte.

Bit swapping. Suppose we only want to interchange two bits within a register, $x_i \leftrightarrow x_j$, where $i > j$. What would be a good way to proceed? (Dear reader, please pause for a moment and solve this problem in your head, or with pencil and paper—without looking at the answer below.)

Let $\delta = i - j$. Here is one solution (but don't peek until you're ready):

$$y \leftarrow (x \gg \delta) \,\&\, 2^j, \quad z \leftarrow (x \,\&\, 2^j) \ll \delta, \quad x \leftarrow (x \,\&\, m) \,|\, y \,|\, z, \quad \text{where } \overline{m} = 2^i \,|\, 2^j. \quad (67)$$

It uses two shifts and five bitwise Boolean operations, assuming that i and j are given constants. It is like each of the first lines of (65), except that a new mask m is needed because y and z don't account for all of the bits of x.

We can, however, do better, saving one operation and one constant:

$$y \leftarrow (x \oplus (x \gg \delta)) \ \& \ 2^j, \qquad x \leftarrow x \oplus y \oplus (y \ll \delta). \tag{68}$$

The first assignment now puts $x_i \oplus x_j$ into position j; the second changes x_i to $x_i \oplus (x_i \oplus x_j)$ and x_j to $x_j \oplus (x_i \oplus x_j)$, as desired. In general it's often wise to convert a problem of the form "change x to $f(x)$" into a problem of the form "change x to $x \oplus g(x)$," since the bit-difference $g(x)$ might be easy to calculate.

On the other hand, there's a sense in which (67) might be preferable to (68), because the assignments to y and z in (67) can sometimes be performed simultaneously. When expressed as a circuit, (67) has a depth of 4 while (68) has depth 5.

Operation (68) can of course be used to swap several pairs of bits simultaneously, when we use a mask θ that's more general than 2^j:

$$y \leftarrow (x \oplus (x \gg \delta)) \ \& \ \theta, \qquad x \leftarrow x \oplus y \oplus (y \ll \delta). \tag{69}$$

Let us call this operation a "δ-swap," because it allows us to swap any non-overlapping pairs of bits that are δ places apart. The mask θ has a 1 in the rightmost position of each pair that's supposed to be swapped. For example, (69) will swap the leftmost 25 bits of a 64-bit word with the rightmost 25 bits, while leaving the 14 middle bits untouched, if we let $\delta = 39$ and $\theta = 2^{25} - 1 = {}^\#\mathtt{1ffffff}$.

Indeed, there's an astonishing way to reverse 64 bits using δ-swaps, namely

$$
\begin{aligned}
y &\leftarrow (x \gg 1) \ \& \ \mu_0, \quad z \leftarrow (x \ \& \ \mu_0) \ll 1, \quad x \leftarrow y \mid z, \\
y &\leftarrow (x \oplus (x \gg 4)) \ \& \ {}^\#\mathtt{0300c0303030c303}, \quad x \leftarrow x \oplus y \oplus (y \ll 4), \\
y &\leftarrow (x \oplus (x \gg 8)) \ \& \ {}^\#\mathtt{00c0300c03f0003f}, \quad x \leftarrow x \oplus y \oplus (y \ll 8), \\
y &\leftarrow (x \oplus (x \gg 20)) \ \& \ {}^\#\mathtt{00000ffc00003fff}, \quad x \leftarrow x \oplus y \oplus (y \ll 20), \\
x &\leftarrow (x \gg 34) \mid ((x \ll 30) \bmod 2^{64}),
\end{aligned}
\tag{70}
$$

saving two of the bitwise operations in (65) even though (65) looks "optimum."

*Bit permutation in general. The methods we've just seen can be extended to obtain an *arbitrary* permutation of the bits in a register. In fact, there always exist masks $\theta_0, \ldots, \theta_5, \hat\theta_4, \ldots, \hat\theta_0$ such that the following operations transform $x = (x_{63} \ldots x_1 x_0)_2$ into any desired rearrangement $x^\pi = (x_{63\pi} \ldots x_{1\pi} x_{0\pi})_2$ of its bits:

$$
\begin{aligned}
x &\leftarrow 2^k\text{-swap of } x \text{ with mask } \theta_k, \text{ for } k = 0, 1, 2, 3, 4, 5; \\
x &\leftarrow 2^k\text{-swap of } x \text{ with mask } \hat\theta_k, \text{ for } k = 4, 3, 2, 1, 0.
\end{aligned}
\tag{71}
$$

In general, a permutation of 2^d bits can be achieved with $2d - 1$ such steps, using appropriate masks θ_k and $\hat\theta_k$, where the swap distances are respectively 2^0, 2^1, $\ldots, 2^{d-1}, \ldots, 2^1, 2^0$.

To prove this fact, we can use a special case of the permutation networks discovered independently by A. M. Duguid and J. Le Corre in 1959, based on earlier work of D. Slepian [see V. E. Beneš, *Mathematical Theory of Connecting Networks and Telephone Traffic* (New York: Academic Press, 1965), Section 3.3].

Figure 12 shows a permutation network $P(2n)$ for $2n$ elements constructed from two permutation networks for n elements, when $n = 4$. Each '$\updownarrow$' connection between two lines represents a *crossbar module* that either leaves the line contents unaltered or interchanges them, as the data flows from left to right. Every setting of the individual crossbars therefore causes $P(2n)$ to produce a permutation of its inputs; conversely, we wish to show that any permutation of the $2n$ inputs can be achieved by some setting of the crossbars.

The construction of Fig. 12 is best understood by considering an example. Suppose we want to route the inputs $(0,1,2,3,4,5,6,7)$ to $(3,2,4,1,6,0,5,7)$, respectively. The first job is to determine the contents of the lines just after the first column of crossbars and just before the last column, since we can then use a similar method to set the crossbars in the inner $P(4)$'s. Thus, in the network

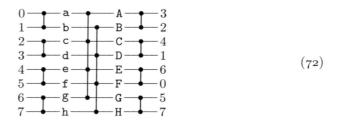

$$(72)$$

we want to find permutations abcdefgh and ABCDEFGH such that $\{\mathtt{a},\mathtt{b}\} = \{0,1\}$, $\{\mathtt{c},\mathtt{d}\} = \{2,3\}$, ..., $\{\mathtt{g},\mathtt{h}\} = \{6,7\}$, $\{\mathtt{a},\mathtt{c},\mathtt{e},\mathtt{g}\} = \{\mathtt{A},\mathtt{C},\mathtt{E},\mathtt{G}\}$, $\{\mathtt{b},\mathtt{d},\mathtt{f},\mathtt{h}\} = \{\mathtt{B},\mathtt{D},\mathtt{F},\mathtt{H}\}$, $\{\mathtt{A},\mathtt{B}\} = \{3,2\}$, $\{\mathtt{C},\mathtt{D}\} = \{4,1\}$, ..., $\{\mathtt{G},\mathtt{H}\} = \{5,7\}$. Starting at the bottom, let us choose $\mathtt{h} = 7$, because we don't wish to disturb the contents of that line unless necessary. Then the following choices are *forced*:

$$\mathtt{H}=7;\ \mathtt{G}=5;\ \mathtt{e}=5;\ \mathtt{f}=4;\ \mathtt{D}=4;\ \mathtt{C}=1;\ \mathtt{a}=1;\ \mathtt{b}=0;\ \mathtt{F}=0;\ \mathtt{E}=6;\ \mathtt{g}=6. \quad (73)$$

If we had chosen $\mathtt{h} = 6$, the forcing pattern would have been similar but reversed,

$$\mathtt{F}=6;\ \mathtt{E}=0;\ \mathtt{a}=0;\ \mathtt{b}=1;\ \mathtt{D}=1;\ \mathtt{C}=4;\ \mathtt{e}=4;\ \mathtt{f}=5;\ \mathtt{H}=5;\ \mathtt{G}=7;\ \mathtt{g}=7. \quad (74)$$

Options (73) and (74) can both be completed by choosing either $\mathtt{d} = 3$ (hence $\mathtt{B} = 3$, $\mathtt{A} = 2$, $\mathtt{c} = 2$) or $\mathtt{d} = 2$ (hence $\mathtt{B} = 2$, $\mathtt{A} = 3$, $\mathtt{c} = 3$).

In general the forcing pattern will go in cycles, no matter what permutation we begin with. To see this, consider the graph on eight vertices $\{\mathtt{ab},\ \mathtt{cd},\ \mathtt{ef},\ \mathtt{gh},\ \mathtt{AB},\ \mathtt{CD},\ \mathtt{EF},\ \mathtt{GH}\}$ that has an edge from $\mathtt{uv}$ to $\mathtt{UV}$ whenever the pair of inputs connected to $\mathtt{uv}$ has an element in common with the pair of outputs connected to $\mathtt{UV}$. Thus, in our example the edges are $\mathtt{ab}$ — $\mathtt{EF}$, $\mathtt{ab}$ — $\mathtt{CD}$, $\mathtt{cd}$ — $\mathtt{AB}$, $\mathtt{cd}$ — $\mathtt{AB}$, $\mathtt{ef}$ — $\mathtt{CD}$, $\mathtt{ef}$ — $\mathtt{GH}$, $\mathtt{gh}$ — $\mathtt{EF}$, $\mathtt{gh}$ — $\mathtt{GH}$. We have a "double bond" between $\mathtt{cd}$ and $\mathtt{AB}$, since the inputs connected to $\mathtt{c}$ and $\mathtt{d}$ are exactly the outputs connected to $\mathtt{A}$ and $\mathtt{B}$; subject to this slight bending of the strict definition of a graph, we see that each vertex is adjacent to exactly two other vertices, and lowercase vertices are always adjacent to uppercase ones. Therefore the graph

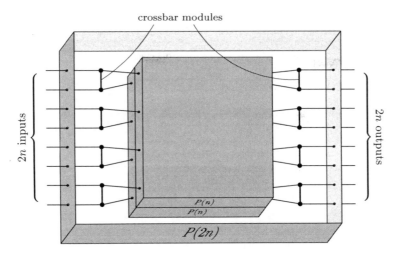

crossbar modules

$2n$ inputs

$2n$ outputs

$P(n)$
$P(n)$

$P(2n)$

Fig. 12. The inside of a black box $P(2n)$ that permutes $2n$ elements in all possible ways, when $n > 1$. (Illustrated for $n = 4$.)

always consists of disjoint cycles of even length. In our example, the cycles are

$$\text{ab} \underset{\text{CD} - \text{ef}}{\overset{\text{EF} - \text{gh}}{<\quad>}} \text{GH} \qquad \text{cd} = \text{AB}, \tag{75}$$

where the longer cycle corresponds to (73) and (74). If there are k different cycles, there will be 2^k different ways to specify the behavior of the first and last columns of crossbars.

To complete the network, we can process the inner 4-element permutations in the same way; and *any* 2^d-element permutation is achievable in this same recursive fashion. The resulting crossbar settings determine the masks θ_j and $\hat{\theta}_j$ of (71). Some choices of crossbars may lead to a mask that is entirely zero; then we can eliminate the corresponding stage of the computation.

If the input and output are identical on the bottom lines of the network, our construction shows how to ensure that none of the crossbars touching those lines are active. For example, the 64-bit algorithm in (71) could be used also with a 60-bit register, without needing the four extra bits for any intermediate results.

Of course we can often beat the general procedure of (71) in special cases. For example, exercise 52 shows that method (71) needs nine swapping steps to transpose an 8×8 matrix, but in fact three swaps suffice:

Given	7-swap	14-swap	28-swap
00 01 02 03 04 05 06 07	00 **10** 02 **12** 04 **14** 06 **16**	00 10 **20 30** 04 14 **24 34**	00 10 20 30 **40 50 60 70**
10 11 12 13 14 15 16 17	**01** 11 **03** 13 **05** 15 **07** 17	01 11 **21 31** 05 15 **25 35**	01 11 21 31 **41 51 61 71**
20 21 22 23 24 25 26 27	20 **30** 22 **32** 24 **34** 26 **36**	**02 12** 22 32 **06 16** 26 36	02 12 22 32 **42 52 62 72**
30 31 32 33 34 35 36 37	**21** 31 **23** 33 **25** 35 **27** 37	**03 13** 23 33 **07 17** 27 37	03 13 23 33 **43 53 63 73**
40 41 42 43 44 45 46 47	40 **50** 42 **52** 44 **54** 46 **56**	40 50 **60 70** 44 54 **64 74**	**04 14 24 34** 44 54 64 74
50 51 52 53 54 55 56 57	**41** 51 **43** 53 **45** 55 **47** 57	41 51 **61 71** 45 55 **65 75**	**05 15 25 35** 45 55 65 75
60 61 62 63 64 65 66 67	60 **70** 62 **72** 64 **74** 66 **76**	**42 52** 62 72 **46 56** 66 76	**06 16 26 36** 46 56 66 76
70 71 72 73 74 75 76 77	**61** 71 **63** 73 **65** 75 **67** 77	**43 53** 63 73 **47 57** 67 77	**07 17 27 37** 47 57 67 77

The "perfect shuffle" is another bit permutation that arises frequently in practice. If $x = (\dots x_2 x_1 x_0)_2$ and $y = (\dots y_2 y_1 y_0)_2$ are any 2-adic integers, we define $x \ddagger y$ ("x zip y," the *zipper function* of x and y) by interleaving their bits:

$$x \ddagger y = (\dots x_2 y_2 x_1 y_1 x_0 y_0)_2. \tag{76}$$

This operation has important applications to the representation of 2-dimensional data, because a small change in either x or y usually causes only a small change in $x \ddagger y$ (see exercise 86). Notice also that the magic mask constants (47) satisfy

$$\mu_k \ddagger \mu_k = \mu_{k+1}. \tag{77}$$

If x appears in the left half of a register and y appears in the right half, a perfect shuffle is the permutation that changes the register contents to $x \ddagger y$.

A sequence of $d-1$ swapping steps will perfectly shuffle a 2^d-bit register; in fact, exercise 53 shows that there are several ways to achieve this. Once again, therefore, we are able to improve on the $(2d-1)$-step method of (71) and Fig. 12.

Conversely, suppose we're given the shuffled value $z = x \ddagger y$ in a 2^d-bit register; is there an efficient way to extract the original value of y? Sure: If the $d-1$ swaps that do a perfect shuffle are performed in reverse order, they'll undo the shuffle and recover both x and y. But if only y is wanted, we can save half of the work: Start with $y \leftarrow z \,\&\, \mu_0$; then set $y \leftarrow (y + (y \gg 2^{k-1})) \,\&\, \mu_k$ for $k = 1$, $\dots$, $d-1$. For example, when $d = 3$ this procedure goes $(0 y_3 0 y_2 0 y_1 0 y_0)_2 \mapsto (00 y_3 y_2 00 y_1 y_0)_2 \mapsto (0000 y_3 y_2 y_1 y_0)_2$. "Divide and conquer" conquers again.

Consider now a more general problem, where we want to extract and compress an *arbitrary* subset of a register's bits. Suppose we're given a 2^d-bit word $z = (z_{2^d-1} \dots z_1 z_0)_2$ and a mask $\chi = (\chi_{2^d-1} \dots \chi_1 \chi_0)_2$ that has s 1-bits; thus $\nu\chi = s$. The problem is to assemble the compact subword

$$y = (y_{s-1} \dots y_1 y_0)_2 = (z_{j_{s-1}} \dots z_{j_1} z_{j_0})_2, \tag{78}$$

where $j_{s-1} > \dots > j_1 > j_0$ are the indices where $\chi_j = 1$. For example, if $d = 3$ and $\chi = (10110010)_2$, we want to transform $z = (y_3 x_3 y_2 y_1 x_2 x_1 y_0 x_0)_2$ into $y = (y_3 y_2 y_1 y_0)_2$. (The problem of going from $x \ddagger y$ to y, considered above, is the special case $\chi = \mu_0$.) We know from (71) that y can be found by δ-swapping, at most $2d-1$ times; but in this problem the relevant data always moves to the right, so we can speed things up by doing *shifts* instead of swaps.

Let's say that a δ-shift of x with mask θ is the operation

$$x \leftarrow x \oplus \big((x \oplus (x \gg \delta)) \,\&\, \theta\big), \tag{79}$$

which changes bit x_j to $x_{j+\delta}$ if θ has 1 in position j, otherwise it leaves x_j unchanged. Guy Steele discovered that there always exist masks $\theta_0, \theta_1, \dots, \theta_{d-1}$ so that the general extraction problem (78) can be solved with a few δ-shifts:

> Start with $x \leftarrow z$; then do a 2^k-shift of x with mask θ_k, for $k = 0, 1, \dots, d-1$; finally set $y \leftarrow x$. $\qquad$ (80)

In fact, the idea for finding appropriate masks is surprisingly simple. Every bit that wants to move a total of exactly $l = (l_{d-1} \dots l_1 l_0)_2$ places to the right should be transported in the 2^k-shifts for which $l_k = 1$.

For example, suppose $d = 3$ and $\chi = (10110010)_2$. (We must assume that $\chi \neq 0$.) Remembering that some 0s need to be shifted in from the left, we can set $\theta_0 = (00011001)_2$, $\theta_1 = (00000110)_2$, $\theta_2 = (11111000)_2$; then (80) maps

$$(y_3x_3y_2y_1x_2x_1y_0x_0)_2 \mapsto (y_3x_3y_2y_2y_1x_1y_0y_0)_2 \mapsto (y_3x_3y_2y_2y_1y_2y_1y_0)_2 \mapsto (0000y_3y_2y_1y_0)_2.$$

Exercise 69 proves that the bits being extracted will never interfere with each other during their journey. Furthermore, there's a slick way to compute the necessary masks θ_k dynamically from χ, in $O(d^2)$ steps (see exercise 70).

A "sheep-and-goats" operation has been suggested for computer hardware, extending (78) to produce the general unshuffled word

$$z \cdot\!\!\mid\cdot \chi = (x_{r-1} \ldots x_1 x_0 y_{s-1} \ldots y_1 y_0)_2 = (z_{i_{r-1}} \ldots z_{i_1} z_{i_0} z_{j_{s-1}} \ldots z_{j_1} z_{j_0})_2; \quad (81)$$

here $i_{r-1} > \cdots > i_1 > i_0$ are the indices where $\chi_i = 0$. Any permutation of 2^d bits is achievable via at most d sheep-and-goats operations (see exercise 73).

Shifting also allows us to go beyond permutations, to arbitrary *mappings* of bits within a register. Suppose we want to transform

$$x = (x_{2^d-1} \ldots x_1 x_0)_2 \quad \mapsto \quad x^\varphi = (x_{(2^d-1)\varphi} \ldots x_{1\varphi} x_{0\varphi})_2, \quad (82)$$

where φ is any of the $(2^d)^{2^d}$ functions from the set $\{0, 1, \ldots, 2^d - 1\}$ into itself. K. M. Chung and C. K. Wong [*IEEE Transactions* **C-29** (1980), 1029–1032] discovered an attractive way to do this in $O(d)$ steps by using *cyclic δ-shifts*, which are like (79) except that we set

$$x \leftarrow x \oplus \big((x \oplus (x \gg \delta)) \oplus (x \ll (2^d - \delta))\big) \,\&\, \theta). \quad (83)$$

Their idea is to let c_l be the number of indices j such that $j\varphi = l$, for $0 \leq l < 2^d$. Then they find masks $\theta_0, \theta_1, \ldots, \theta_{d-1}$ with the property that a cyclic 2^k-shift of x with mask θ_k, done successively for $0 \leq k < d$, will transform x into a number x' that contains exactly c_l copies of bit x_l for each l. Finally the general permutation procedure (71) can be used to change $x' \mapsto x^\varphi$.

For example, suppose $d = 3$ and $x^\varphi = (x_3x_1x_1x_0x_3x_7x_5x_5)_2$. Then we have $(c_0, c_1, c_2, c_3, c_4, c_5, c_6, c_7) = (1, 2, 0, 2, 0, 2, 0, 1)$. Using masks $\theta_0 = (00011100)_2$, $\theta_1 = (00001000)_2$, and $\theta_2 = (01100000)_2$, three cyclic 2^k-shifts now take $x = (x_7x_6x_5x_4x_3x_2x_1x_0)_2 \mapsto (x_7x_6x_5x_5x_4x_3x_1x_0)_2 \mapsto (x_7x_6x_5x_5x_5x_3x_1x_0)_2 \mapsto (x_7x_3x_1x_5x_5x_3x_1x_0)_2 = x'$. Then, some δ-swaps: $x' \mapsto (x_3x_7x_5x_1x_3x_5x_1x_0)_2 \mapsto (x_3x_1x_5x_7x_3x_5x_1x_0)_2 \mapsto (x_3x_1x_1x_0x_3x_5x_5x_7)_2 \mapsto (x_3x_1x_1x_0x_3x_7x_5x_5)_2 = x^\varphi$; we're done! Of course any 8-bit mapping can be achieved more quickly by brute force, one bit at a time; the method of Chung and Wong becomes much more impressive in a 256-bit register. Even with MMIX's 64-bit registers it's pretty good, needing at most 96 cycles in the worst case.

To find θ_0, we use the fact that $\sum c_l = 2^d$, and we look at $\Sigma_{\text{even}} = \sum c_{2l}$ and $\Sigma_{\text{odd}} = \sum c_{2l+1}$. If $\Sigma_{\text{even}} = \Sigma_{\text{odd}} = 2^{d-1}$, we can set $\theta_0 = 0$ and omit the cyclic 1-shift. But if, say, $\Sigma_{\text{even}} < \Sigma_{\text{odd}}$, we find an even l with $c_l = 0$. Cyclically shifting into bits $l, l+1, \ldots, l+t$ (modulo 2^d) for some t will produce new counts $(c'_0, \ldots, c'_{2^d-1})$ for which $\Sigma'_{\text{even}} = \Sigma'_{\text{odd}} = 2^{d-1}$; so $\theta_0 = 2^l + \cdots + 2^{(l+t) \bmod 2^d}$. Then we can deal with the bits in even and odd positions separately, using the same method, until getting down to 1-bit subwords. Exercise 74 has the details.

Working with fragmented fields. Instead of extracting bits from various parts of a word and gathering them together, we can often manipulate those bits directly in their original positions.

For example, suppose we want to run through all subsets of a given set U, where (as usual) the set is specified by a mask χ such that $[k \in U] = (\chi \gg k) \,\&\, 1$. If $x \subseteq \chi$ and $x \neq \chi$, there's an easy way to calculate the next largest subset of U in lexicographic order, namely the smallest integer $x' > x$ such that $x' \subseteq \chi$:

$$x' = (x - \chi) \,\&\, \chi. \tag{84}$$

In the special case when $x = 0$ and $\chi \neq 0$, we've already seen in (37) that this formula produces the rightmost bit of χ, which corresponds to the lexicographically smallest nonempty subset of U.

Why does formula (84) work? Imagine adding 1 to the number $x \mid \bar{\chi}$, which has 1s wherever χ is 0. A carry will propagate through those 1s until it reaches the rightmost bit position where x has a 0 and χ has a 1; furthermore all bits to the right of that position will become zero. Therefore $x' = ((x \mid \bar{\chi}) + 1) \,\&\, \chi$. But we have $(x \mid \bar{\chi}) + 1 = (x + \bar{\chi}) + 1 = x + (\bar{\chi} + 1) = x - \chi$ when $x \subseteq \chi$. QED.

Notice further that $x' = 0$ if and only if $x = \chi$. So we'll know when we've found the largest subset. Exercise 79 shows how to go back to x, given x'.

We might also want to run through all elements of a *subcube* — for example, to find all bit patterns that match a specification like $*10*1*01$, consisting of 0s, 1s, and $*$s (don't-cares). Such a specification can be represented by asterisk codes $a = (a_{n-1} \ldots a_0)_2$ and bit codes $b = (b_{n-1} \ldots b_0)_2$, as in exercise 7.1.1–30; our example corresponds to $a = (10010100)_2$, $b = (01001001)_2$. The problem of enumerating all subsets of a set is the special case where $a = \chi$ and $b = 0$. In the more general subcube problem, the successor of a given bit pattern x is

$$x' = ((x - (a + b)) \,\&\, a) + b. \tag{85}$$

Suppose the bits of $z = (z_{n-1} \ldots z_0)_2$ have been stitched together from two subwords $x = (x_{r-1} \ldots x_0)_2$ and $y = (y_{s-1} \ldots y_0)_2$, where $r + s = n$, using an arbitrary mask χ for which $\nu\chi = s$ to govern the stitching. For example, $z = (y_2 x_4 x_3 y_1 x_2 y_0 x_1 x_0)_2$ when $n = 8$ and $\chi = (10010100)_2$. We can think of z as a "scattered accumulator," in which alien bits x_i lurk among friendly bits y_j. From this viewpoint the problem of finding successive elements of a subcube is essentially the problem of computing $y + 1$ inside a scattered accumulator z, without changing the value of x. The sheep-and-goats operation (81) would untangle x and y; but it's expensive, and (85) shows that we can solve the problem without it. We can, in fact, compute $y + y'$ when $y' = (y'_{s-1} \ldots y'_0)_2$ is *any* value inside a scattered accumulator z', if y and y' both appear in the positions specified by χ: Consider $t = z \,\&\, \chi$ and $t' = z' \,\&\, \chi$. If we form the sum $(t \mid \bar{\chi}) + t'$, all carries that occur in a normal addition $y + y'$ will propagate through the blocks of 1s in $\bar{\chi}$, just as if the scattered bits were adjacent. Thus

$$((z \,\&\, \chi) + (z' \mid \bar{\chi})) \,\&\, \chi \tag{86}$$

is the sum of y and y', modulo 2^s, scattered according to the mask χ.

Tweaking several bytes at once. Instead of concentrating on the data in one field within a word, we often want to deal simultaneously with two or more sub-words, performing calculations on each of them in parallel. For example, many applications need to process long sequences of bytes, and we can gain speed by acting on eight bytes at a time; we might as well use all 64 bits that our machine provides. General multibyte techniques were introduced by Leslie Lamport in *CACM* **18** (1975), 471–475, and subsequently extended by many programmers.

Suppose first that we simply wish to take two sequences of bytes and find their sum, regarding them as coordinates of vectors, doing arithmetic modulo 256 in each byte. Algebraically speaking, we're given 8-byte vectors $x = (x_7 \ldots x_1 x_0)_{256}$ and $y = (y_7 \ldots y_1 y_0)_{256}$; we want to compute $z = (z_7 \ldots z_1 z_0)_{256}$, where $z_j = (x_j + y_j) \bmod 256$ for $0 \le j < 8$. Ordinary addition of x to y doesn't quite work, because we need to prevent carries from propagating between bytes. So we extract the high-order bits and deal with them separately:

$$z \leftarrow (x \oplus y) \mathbin{\&} h, \qquad \text{where } h = {}^{\#}8080808080808080;$$
$$z \leftarrow ((x \mathbin{\&} \bar{h}) + (y \mathbin{\&} \bar{h})) \oplus z. \tag{87}$$

The total time for MMIX to do this is 6υ, plus $3\mu + 3\upsilon$ if we also count the time to load x, load y, and store z. By contrast, eight one-byte additions (LDBU, LDBU, ADDU, and STBU, repeated eight times) would cost $8 \times (3\mu + 4\upsilon) = 24\mu + 32\upsilon$. Parallel *subtraction* of bytes is just as easy (see exercise 88).

We can also compute bytewise *averages*, with $z_j = \lfloor (x_j + y_j)/2 \rfloor$ for each j:

$$z \leftarrow ((x \oplus y) \mathbin{\&} \bar{l}) \gg 1, \qquad \text{where } l = {}^{\#}0101010101010101;$$
$$z \leftarrow (x \mathbin{\&} y) + z. \tag{88}$$

This elegant trick, suggested by H. G. Dietz, is based on the well-known formula

$$x + y = (x \oplus y) + ((x \mathbin{\&} y) \ll 1) \tag{89}$$

for radix-2 addition. (We can implement (88) with four MMIX instructions, not five, because a single MOR operation will change $x \oplus y$ to $((x \oplus y) \mathbin{\&} \bar{l}) \gg 1$.)

Exercises 88–93 and 100–104 develop these ideas further, showing how to do mixed-radix arithmetic, as well as such things as the addition and subtraction of vectors whose components are treated modulo m when m needn't be a power of 2.

In essence, we can regard the bits, bytes, or other subfields of a register as if they were elements of an array of independent microprocessors, acting independently on their own subproblems yet tightly synchronized, and communicating with each other via shift instructions and carry bits. Computer designers have been interested for many years in the development of parallel processors with a so-called SIMD architecture, namely a "Single Instruction stream with Multiple Data streams"; see, for example, S. H. Unger, *Proc. IRE* **46** (1958), 1744–1750. The increased availability of 64-bit registers has meant that programmers of ordinary sequential computers are now able to get a taste of SIMD processing. Indeed, computations such as (87), (88), and (89) are called SWAR methods — "SIMD Within A Register," a name coined by R. J. Fisher and H. G. Dietz [see *Lecture Notes in Computer Science* **1656** (1999), 290–305].

Of course bytes often contain alphabetic data as well as numbers, and one of the most common programming tasks is to search through a long string of characters in order to find the first appearance of some particular byte value. For example, strings are often represented as a sequence of nonzero bytes terminated by 0. In order to locate the end of a string quickly, we need a fast way to determine whether all eight bytes of a given word x are nonzero (because they usually are). Several fairly good solutions to this problem were found by Lamport and others; but Alan Mycroft discovered in 1987 that *three* instructions actually suffice:

$$t \leftarrow h \mathbin{\&} (x - l) \mathbin{\&} \bar{x}, \tag{90}$$

where h and l appear in (87) and (88). If each byte x_j is nonzero, t will be zero; for $(x_j - 1) \mathbin{\&} \bar{x}_j$ will be $2^{\rho x_j} - 1$, which is always less than ${}^\#80 = 2^7$. But if $x_j = 0$, while its right neighbors $x_{j-1}, \ldots, x_0$ (if any) are all nonzero, the subtraction $x - l$ will produce ${}^\#\mathtt{ff}$ in byte j, and t will be nonzero. In fact, ρt will be $8j + 7$.

Caution: Although the computation in (90) pinpoints the *rightmost* zero byte of x, we cannot deduce the position of the *leftmost* zero byte from the value of t alone. (See exercise 94.) In this respect the little-endian convention proves to be preferable to the corresponding big-endian behavior. An application that needs to locate the leftmost zero byte can use (90) to skip quickly over nonzeros, but then it must fall back on a slower method when the search has been narrowed down to eight finalists. The following 4-operation formula produces a completely precise test value $t = (t_7 \ldots t_1 t_0)_{256}$, in which $t_j = 128[x_j = 0]$ for each j:

$$t \leftarrow h \mathbin{\&} {\sim}(x \mathbin{|} ((x \mathbin{|} h) - l)). \tag{91}$$

The leftmost zero byte of x is now x_j, where $\lambda t = 8j + 7$.

Incidentally, the single MMIX instruction 'BDIF t,l,x' solves the zero-byte problem immediately by setting each byte t_j of t to $[x_j = 0]$, because $1 \mathbin{\dot{-}} x = [x = 0]$. But we are primarily interested here in fairly universal techniques that don't rely on exotic hardware; MMIX's special features will be discussed later.

Now that we know a fast way to find the first 0, we can use the same ideas to search for *any* desired byte value. For example, to test if any byte of x is the newline character (${}^\#\mathtt{a}$), we simply look for a zero byte in $x \oplus {}^\#\mathtt{0a0a0a0a0a0a0a0a}$.

And these techniques also open up many other doors. Suppose, for instance, that we want to compute $z = (z_7 \ldots z_1 z_0)_{256}$ from x and y, where $z_j = x_j$ when $x_j = y_j$ but $z_j = \mathtt{'*'}$ when $x_j \neq y_j$. (Thus if $x = \mathtt{"beaching"}$ and $y = \mathtt{"belching"}$, we're supposed to set $z \leftarrow \mathtt{"be*ching"}$.) It's easy:

$$\begin{aligned} &t \leftarrow h \mathbin{\&} ((x \oplus y) \mathbin{|} (((x \oplus y) \mathbin{|} h) - l)); \\ &m \leftarrow (t \ll 1) - (t \gg 7); \\ &z \leftarrow x \oplus ((x \oplus \mathtt{"********"}) \mathbin{\&} m). \end{aligned} \tag{92}$$

The first step uses a variant of (91) to flag the high-order bits in each byte where $x_j \neq y_j$. The next step creates a mask to highlight those bytes: ${}^\#\mathtt{00}$ if $x_j = y_j$, otherwise ${}^\#\mathtt{ff}$. And the last step, which could also be written $z \leftarrow (x \mathbin{\&} \overline{m}) \mathbin{|} (\mathtt{"********"} \mathbin{\&} m)$, sets $z_j \leftarrow x_j$ or $z_j \leftarrow \mathtt{'*'}$, depending on the mask.

Operations (90) and (91) were originally designed as tests for bytes that are zero; but a closer look reveals that we can more wisely regard them as tests for bytes that are less than 1. Indeed, if we replace l by $c \cdot l = (cccccccc)_{256}$ in either formula, where c is any positive constant ≤ 128, we can use (90) or (91) to see if x contains any bytes that are less than c. Furthermore the comparison values c need not be the same in every byte position; and with a bit more work we can also do bytewise comparison in the cases where $c > 128$. Here's an 8-step formula that sets $t_j \leftarrow 128[x_j < y_j]$ for each byte position j in the test word t:

$$t \leftarrow h \mathbin{\&} {\sim}\langle x\bar{y}z\rangle, \qquad \text{where } z = (x \mid h) - (y \mathbin{\&} \bar{h}). \tag{93}$$

(See exercise 96.) The median operation in this general formula can often be simplified; for example, (93) reduces to (91) when $y = l$, because $\langle x(-1)z\rangle = x \mid z$.

Once we've found a nonzero t in (90) or (91) or (93), we might want to compute ρt or λt in order to discover the index j of the rightmost or leftmost byte that has been flagged. The problem of calculating ρ or λ is now simpler than before, since t can take on only 256 different values. Indeed, the operation

$$j \leftarrow table[((a \cdot t) \bmod 2^{64}) \gg 56], \quad \text{where } a = \frac{2^{56} - 1}{2^7 - 1}, \tag{94}$$

now suffices to compute j, given an appropriate 256-byte table. And the multiplication here can often be performed faster by doing three shift-and-add operations, "$t \leftarrow t + (t \ll 7)$, $t \leftarrow t + (t \ll 14)$, $t \leftarrow t + (t \ll 28)$," instead.

Broadword computing. We've now seen more than a dozen ways in which a computer's bitwise operations can produce astonishing results at high speed, and the exercises below contain many more such surprises.

Elwyn Berlekamp has remarked that computer chips containing N flip-flops continue to be built with ever larger values of N, yet in practice only $O(\log N)$ of those components are flipping or flopping at any given moment. The surprising effectiveness of bitwise operations suggests that computers of the future might make use of this untapped potential by having enhanced memory units that are able to do efficient n-bit computations for fairly large values of n. To prepare for that day, we ought to have a good name for the concept of manipulating "wide words." Lyle Ramshaw has suggested the pleasant term *broadword*, so that we can speak of n-bit quantities as broadwords of width n.

Many of the methods we've discussed are *2-adic*, in the sense that they work correctly with binary numbers that have arbitrary (even infinite) precision. For example, the operation $x \mathbin{\&} -x$ always extracts $2^{\rho x}$, the least significant 1 bit of any nonzero 2-adic integer x. But other methods have an inherently broadword nature, such as the methods that use $O(d)$ steps to perform sideways addition or bit permutation of 2^d-bit words. Broadword computing is the art of dealing with n-bit words, when n is a parameter that is not extremely small.

Some broadword algorithms are of theoretical interest only, because they are efficient only in an asymptotic sense when n exceeds the size of the universe. But others are eminently practical even when $n = 64$. And in general, a broadword mindset often suggests good techniques.

One fascinating-but-impractical fact about broadword operations is the discovery by M. L. Fredman and D. E. Willard that $O(1)$ broadword steps suffice to evaluate the function $\lambda x = \lfloor \lg x \rfloor$ for any nonzero n-bit number x, no matter how big n is. Here is their remarkable scheme, when $n = g^2$ and g is a power of 2:

$$
\begin{aligned}
&t_1 \leftarrow h\,\&\,(x \mid ((x \mid h) - l)), \quad \text{where } h = 2^{g-1}l \text{ and } l = (2^n - 1)/(2^g - 1);\\
&y \leftarrow (((a \cdot t_1) \bmod 2^n) \gg (n - g)) \cdot l, \quad \text{where } a = (2^{n-g} - 1)/(2^{g-1} - 1);\\
&t_2 \leftarrow h\,\&\,(y \mid ((y \mid h) - b)), \quad \text{where } b = (2^{n+g} - 1)/(2^{g+1} - 1);\\
&m \leftarrow (t_2 \ll 1) - (t_2 \gg (g-1)), \ m \leftarrow m \oplus (m \gg g); \qquad\qquad (95)\\
&z \leftarrow (((l \cdot (x\,\&\,m)) \bmod 2^n) \gg (n - g)) \cdot l;\\
&t_3 \leftarrow h\,\&\,(z \mid ((z \mid h) - b));\\
&\lambda \leftarrow ((l \cdot ((t_2 \gg (2g - \lg g - 1)) + (t_3 \gg (2g - 1)))) \bmod 2^n) \gg (n - g).
\end{aligned}
$$

(See exercise 106.) The method fails to be practical because five of these 29 steps are multiplications, so they aren't really "bitwise" operations. In fact, we'll prove later that multiplication by a constant requires at least $\Omega(\log n)$ bitwise steps.

A multiplication-free way to find λx, with only $O(\log \log n)$ bitwise broadword operations, was discovered in 1997 by Gerth Brodal, whose method is even more remarkable than (95). It is based on a formula analogous to (49),

$$
\lambda x = [\lambda x = \lambda(x\,\&\,\bar{\mu}_0)] + 2[\lambda x = \lambda(x\,\&\,\bar{\mu}_1)] + 4[\lambda x = \lambda(x\,\&\,\bar{\mu}_2)] + \cdots, \quad (96)
$$

and the fact that the relation $\lambda x = \lambda y$ is easily tested (see (58)):

Algorithm B (*Binary logarithm*). This algorithm uses n-bit operations to compute $\lambda x = \lfloor \lg x \rfloor$, assuming that $0 < x < 2^n$ and $n = d \cdot 2^d$.

B1. [Scale down.] Set $\lambda \leftarrow 0$. Then set $\lambda \leftarrow \lambda + 2^k$ and $x \leftarrow x \gg 2^k$ if $x \geq 2^{2^k}$, for $k = \lceil \lg n \rceil - 1, \lceil \lg n \rceil - 2, \ldots, d$.

B2. [Replicate.] (At this point $0 < x < 2^{2^d}$; the remaining task is to increase λ by $\lfloor \lg x \rfloor$. We will replace x by d copies of itself, in 2^d-bit fields.) Set $x \leftarrow x \mid (x \ll 2^{d+k})$ for $0 \leq k < \lceil \lg d \rceil$.

B3. [Change leading bits.] Set $y \leftarrow x\,\&\,\sim(\mu_{d,d-1} \cdots \mu_{d,1} \mu_{d,0})_{2^{2d}}$. (See (48).)

B4. [Compare all fields.] Set $t \leftarrow h\,\&\,(y \mid ((y \mid h) - (x \oplus y)))$, where $h = (2^{2^d-1} \ldots 2^{2^d-1} 2^{2^d-1})_{2^{2d}}$.

B5. [Compress bits.] Set $t \leftarrow (t + (t \ll (2^{d+k} - 2^k))) \bmod 2^n$ for $0 \leq k < \lceil \lg d \rceil$.

B6. [Finish.] Finally, set $\lambda \leftarrow \lambda + (t \gg (n - d))$. ∎

This algorithm is almost competitive with (56) when $n = 64$ (see exercise 107).

Another surprisingly efficient broadword algorithm was discovered in 2006 by M. S. Paterson and the author, who considered the problem of identifying all occurrences of the pattern 01^r in a given n-bit binary string. This problem, which is related to storage allocation, is equivalent to computing

$$
q = \bar{x}\,\&\,(x \ll 1)\,\&\,(x \ll 2)\,\&\,(x \ll 3)\,\&\, \cdots \,\&\,(x \ll r) \qquad (97)
$$

when $x = (x_{n-1} \ldots x_1 x_0)_2$ is given. For example, when $n = 16$, $r = 3$, and $x = (1110111101100111)_2$, we have $q = (0001000000001000)_2$. One might expect intuitively that $\Omega(\log r)$ bitwise operations would be needed. But in fact the following 20-step computation does the job for all $n > r > 0$: Let $s = \lceil r/2 \rceil$, $l = \sum_{k \geq 0} 2^{ks} \bmod 2^n$, $h = (2^{s-1}l) \bmod 2^n$, and $a = (\sum_{k \geq 0}(-1)^{k+1}2^{2ks}) \bmod 2^n$.

$$
\begin{aligned}
&y \leftarrow h \mathbin{\&} x \mathbin{\&} ((x \mathbin{\&} \bar{h}) + l); \\
&t \leftarrow (x + y) \mathbin{\&} \bar{x} \mathbin{\&} -2^r; \\
&u \leftarrow t \mathbin{\&} a, \; v \leftarrow t \mathbin{\&} \bar{a}; \hspace{3cm} (98)\\
&m \leftarrow (u - (u \gg r)) \mid (v - (v \gg r)); \\
&q \leftarrow t \mathbin{\&} ((x \mathbin{\&} m) + ((t \gg r) \mathbin{\&} \sim(m \ll 1))).
\end{aligned}
$$

Exercise 111 explains why these machinations are valid. The method has little or no practical value; there's an easy way to evaluate (97) in $2\lceil \lg r \rceil + 2$ steps, so (98) is not advantageous until $r > 512$. But (98) is another indication of the unexpected power of broadword methods.

*Lower bounds. Indeed, the existence of so many tricks and techniques makes it natural to wonder whether we've only been scratching the surface. Are there many more incredibly fast methods, still waiting to be discovered? A few theoretical results are known by which we can derive certain limitations on what is possible, although such studies are still in their infancy.

Let's say that a *2-adic chain* is a sequence $(x_0, x_1, \ldots, x_r)$ of 2-adic integers in which each element x_i for $i > 0$ is obtained from its predecessors via bitwise manipulation. More precisely, we want the steps of the chain to be defined by binary operations

$$
x_i = x_{j(i)} \circ_i x_{k(i)} \quad \text{or} \quad c_i \circ_i x_{k(i)} \quad \text{or} \quad x_{j(i)} \circ_i c_i, \hspace{1.5cm} (99)
$$

where each $\circ_i$ is one of the operators $\{+, -, \mathbin{\&}, \mid, \oplus, \equiv, \subset, \supset, \bar{\subset}, \bar{\supset}, \wedge, \triangledown, \ll, \gg\}$ and each c_i is a constant. Furthermore, when the operator $\circ_i$ is a left shift or right shift, the amount of shift must be a positive integer constant; operations such as $x_{j(i)} \ll x_{k(i)}$ or $c_i \gg x_{k(i)}$ are *not* permitted. (Without the latter restriction we couldn't derive meaningful lower bounds, because *every* 0–1 valued function of a nonnegative integer x would be computable in two steps as "$(c \gg x) \mathbin{\&} 1$" for some constant c.)

Similarly, a *broadword chain* of width n, also called an n-bit broadword chain, is a sequence $(x_0, x_1, \ldots, x_r)$ of n-bit numbers subject to essentially the same restrictions, where n is a parameter and all operations are performed modulo 2^n. Broadword chains behave like 2-adic chains in many ways, but subtle differences can arise because of the information loss that occurs at the left of n-bit computations (see exercise 113).

Both types of chains compute a function $f(x) = x_r$ when we start them out with a given value $x = x_0$. Exercise 114 shows that an mn-bit broadword chain is able to do m essentially simultaneous evaluations of any function that is computable with an n-bit chain. Our goal is to study the *shortest* chains that are able to evaluate a given function f.

Any 2-adic or broadword chain $(x_0, x_1, \ldots, x_r)$ has a sequence of "shift sets" $(S_0, S_1, \ldots, S_r)$ and "bounds" $(B_0, B_1, \ldots, B_r)$, defined as follows: Start with $S_0 = \{0\}$ and $B_0 = 1$; then for $i \geq 1$, let

$$S_i = \begin{cases} S_{j(i)} \cup S_{k(i)}, \\ S_{k(i)}, \\ S_{j(i)}, \\ S_{j(i)} + c_i, \\ S_{j(i)} - c_i, \end{cases} \quad \text{and} \quad B_i = \begin{cases} M_i B_{j(i)} B_{k(i)}, & \text{if } x_i = x_{j(i)} \circ_i x_{k(i)}, \\ M_i B_{k(i)}, & \text{if } x_i = c_i \circ_i x_{k(i)}, \\ M_i B_{j(i)}, & \text{if } x_i = x_{j(i)} \circ_i c_i, \\ B_{j(i)}, & \text{if } x_i = x_{j(i)} \gg c_i, \\ B_{j(i)}, & \text{if } x_i = x_{j(i)} \ll c_i, \end{cases} \quad (100)$$

where $M_i = 2$ if $\circ_i \in \{+, -\}$ and $M_i = 1$ otherwise, and these formulas assume that $\circ_i \notin \{\ll, \gg\}$. For example, consider the following 7-step chain:

x_i	S_i	B_i	
$x_0 = x$	$\{0\}$	1	
$x_1 = x_0 \,\&\, -2$	$\{0\}$	1	
$x_2 = x_1 + 2$	$\{0\}$	2	
$x_3 = x_2 \gg 1$	$\{1\}$	2	(101)
$x_4 = x_2 + x_3$	$\{0, 1\}$	8	
$x_5 = x_4 \gg 4$	$\{4, 5\}$	8	
$x_6 = x_4 + x_5$	$\{0, 1, 4, 5\}$	128	
$x_7 = x_6 \gg 4$	$\{4, 5, 8, 9\}$	128	

(We encountered this chain in exercise 4.4–9, which proved that these operations will yield $x_7 = \lfloor x/10 \rfloor$ for $0 \leq x < 160$ when performed with 8-bit arithmetic.)

To begin a theory of lower bounds, let's notice first that the high-order bits of $x = x_0$ cannot influence any low-order bits unless we shift them to the right.

Lemma A. *Given a 2-adic or broadword chain, let the binary representation of x_i be $(\ldots x_{i2} x_{i1} x_{i0})_2$. Then bit x_{ip} can depend on bit x_{0q} only if $q \leq p + \max S_i$.*

Proof. By induction on i we can in fact show that, if $B_i = 1$, bit x_{ip} can depend on bit x_{0q} only if $q - p \in S_i$. Addition and subtraction, which force $B_i > 1$, allow any particular bit of their operands to affect all bits that lie to the left in the sum or difference, but not those that lie to the right. ∎

Corollary I. *The function $x \doteq 1$ cannot be computed by a 2-adic chain, nor can any function for which at least one bit of $f(x)$ depends on an unbounded number of bits of x.* ∎

Corollary W. *An n-bit function $f(x)$ can be computed by an n-bit broadword chain without shifts if and only if $x \equiv y$ (modulo 2^p) implies $f(x) \equiv f(y)$ (modulo 2^p) for $0 \leq p < n$.*

Proof. If there are no shifts we have $S_i = \{0\}$ for all i. Thus bit x_{rp} cannot depend on bit x_{0q} unless $q \leq p$. In other words we must have $x_r \equiv y_r$ (modulo 2^p) whenever $x_0 \equiv y_0$ (modulo 2^p).

Conversely, all such functions are achievable by a sufficiently long chain. Exercise 119 gives shift-free n-bit chains for the functions

$$f_{py}(x) = 2^p [x \bmod 2^{p+1} = y], \qquad \text{when } 0 \leq p < n \text{ and } 0 \leq y < 2^{p+1}, \quad (102)$$

from which all the relevant functions arise by addition. [H. S. Warren, Jr., generalized this result to functions of m variables in *CACM* **20** (1977), 439–441.] ∎

Shift sets S_i and bounds B_i are important chiefly because of a fundamental
lemma that is our principal tool for proving lower bounds:

Lemma B. *Let $X_{pqr} = \{x_r \mathbin{\&} \lfloor 2^p - 2^q \rfloor \mid x_0 \in V_{pqr}\}$ in an n-bit broadword chain,
where*

$$V_{pqr} = \{x \mid x \mathbin{\&} \lfloor 2^{p+s} - 2^{q+s} \rfloor = 0 \text{ for all } s \in S_r\} \tag{103}$$

and $p > q$. Then $|X_{pqr}| \le B_r$. (Here p and q are integers, possibly negative.)

This lemma states that at most B_r different bit patterns $x_{r(p-1)} \ldots x_{rq}$ can occur
within $f(x)$, when certain intervals of bits in x are constrained to be zero.

Proof. The result certainly holds when $r = 0$. Otherwise if, for example, $x_r = x_j + x_k$, we know by induction that $|X_{pqj}| \le B_j$ and $|X_{pqk}| \le B_k$. Furthermore
$V_{pqr} = V_{pqj} \cap V_{pqk}$, since $S_r = S_j \cup S_k$. Thus at most $B_j B_k$ possibilities for
$(x_j + x_k) \mathbin{\&} \lfloor 2^p - 2^q \rfloor$ arise when there's no carry into position q, and at most
$B_j B_k$ when there is a carry, making a grand total of at most $B_r = 2B_j B_k$
possibilities altogether. Exercise 122 considers the other cases. ∎

We now can prove that the ruler function needs $\Omega(\log \log n)$ steps.

Theorem R. *If $n = d \cdot 2^d$, every n-bit broadword chain that computes ρx for
$0 < x < 2^n$ has more than $\lg d$ steps that are not shifts.*

Proof. If there are l nonshift steps, we have $|S_r| \le 2^l$ and $B_r \le 2^{2^l - 1}$. Apply
Lemma B with $p = d$ and $q = 0$, and suppose $|X_{d0r}| = 2^d - t$. Then there are t
values of $k < 2^d$ such that

$$\{2^k, 2^{k+2^d}, 2^{k+2 \cdot 2^d}, \ldots, 2^{k+(d-1)2^d}\} \not\subseteq V_{d0r}.$$

But V_{d0r} excludes at most $2^l d$ of the n possible powers of 2; so $t \le 2^l$.

If $l \le \lg d$, Lemma B tells us that $2^d - t \le B_r \le 2^{d-1}$; hence $2^{d-1} \le t \le 2^l \le d$. But this is impossible unless $d \le 2$, when the theorem clearly holds. ∎

The same proof works also for the binary logarithm function:

Corollary L. *If $n = d \cdot 2^d > 2$, every n-bit broadword chain that computes λx
for $0 < x < 2^n$ has more than $\lg d$ steps that are not shifts.* ∎

By using Lemma B with $q > 0$ we can derive the stronger lower bound
$\Omega(\log n)$ for bit reversal, and hence for bit permutation in general.

Theorem P. *If $2 \le g \le n$, every n-bit broadword chain that computes the
g-bit reversal x^R for $0 \le x < 2^g$ has at least $\lfloor \frac{1}{3} \lg g \rfloor$ steps that are not shifts.*

Proof. Assume as above that there are l nonshifts. Let $h = \lfloor \sqrt[3]{g} \rfloor$ and suppose
that $l < \lfloor \lg(h+1) \rfloor$. Then S_r is a set of at most $2^l \le \frac{1}{2}(h+1)$ shift amounts s.
We shall apply Lemma B with $p = q+h$, where $p \le g$ and $q \ge 0$, thus in $g-h+1$
cases altogether. The key observation is that $x^R \mathbin{\&} \lfloor 2^p - 2^q \rfloor$ is independent of
$x \mathbin{\&} \lfloor 2^{p+s} - 2^{q+s} \rfloor$ whenever there are no indices j and k such that $0 \le j, k < h$
and $g - 1 - q - j = q + s + k$. The number of "bad" choices of q for which such

indices exist is at most $\frac{1}{2}(h+1)h^2 \leq g-h$; therefore at least one "good" choice of q yields $|X_{pqr}| = 2^h$. But then Lemma B leads to a contradiction, because we obviously cannot have $2^h \leq B_r \leq 2^{(h-1)/2}$. ∎

Corollary M. *Multiplication by certain constants, modulo* 2^n, *requires* $\Omega(\log n)$ *steps in an* n-*bit broadword chain.*

Proof. In Hack 167 of the classic memorandum HAKMEM (M.I.T. A.I. Laboratory, 1972), Richard Schroeppel observed that the operations

$$t \leftarrow ((ax) \bmod 2^n) \,\&\, b, \quad y \leftarrow ((ct) \bmod 2^n) \gg (n-g) \qquad (104)$$

compute $y = x^R$ whenever $n = g^2$ and $0 \leq x < 2^g$, using the constants $a = (2^{n+g} - 1)/(2^{g+1} - 1)$, $b = 2^{g-1}(2^n - 1)/(2^g - 1)$, and $c = (2^{n-g} - 1)/(2^{g-1} - 1)$. (See exercise 123.) ∎

At this point the reader might well be thinking, "Okay, I agree that broadword chains sometimes have to be asymptotically long. But programmers needn't be shackled by such chains; we can use other techniques, like conditional branches or references to precomputed tables, which go beyond those restrictions."

Right. And we're in luck, because broadword theory can also be extended to more general models of computation. Consider, for example, the following idealization of an abstract reduced-instruction-set computer, called a *basic RAM*: The machine has n-bit registers $r_1, \ldots, r_l$, and n-bit memory words $\{M[0], \ldots, M[2^m - 1]\}$. It can perform the instructions

$$r_i \leftarrow r_j \pm r_k, \quad r_i \leftarrow r_j \circ r_k, \quad r_i \leftarrow r_j \gg r_k, \quad r_i \leftarrow c,$$
$$r_i \leftarrow M[r_j \bmod 2^m], \quad M[r_j \bmod 2^m] \leftarrow r_i, \qquad (105)$$

where $\circ$ is any bitwise Boolean operator, and where r_k in the shift instruction is treated as a signed integer in two's complement notation. The machine is also able to branch if $r_i \leq r_j$, treating r_i and r_j as unsigned integers. Its *state* is the entire contents of all registers and memory, together with a "program counter" that points to the current instruction. Its program begins in a designated state, which may include precomputed tables in memory, and with an n-bit input value x in register r_1. This initial state is called $Q(x, 0)$, and $Q(x, t)$ denotes the state after t instructions have been performed. When the machine stops, r_1 will contain some n-bit value $f(x)$. Given a function $f(x)$, we want to find a lower bound on the least t such that r_1 is equal to $f(x)$ in state $Q(x, t)$, for $0 \leq x < 2^n$.

Theorem R′. *Let* $\epsilon = 2^{-e}$. *A basic* n-*bit RAM with memory parameter* $m \leq n^{1-\epsilon}$ *requires at least* $\lg \lg n - e$ *steps to evaluate the ruler function* ρx, *as* $n \to \infty$.

Proof. Let $n = 2^{2^{e+f}}$, so that $m \leq 2^{2^{e+f} - 2^f}$. Exercise 124 explains how an omniscient observer can construct a broadword chain from a certain class of inputs x, in such a way that each x causes the RAM to take the same branches, use the same shift amounts, and refer to the same memory locations. Our earlier methods can then be used to show that this chain has length $\geq f$. ∎

A skeptical reader may still object that Theorem R′ has no practical value, because $\lg \lg n$ never exceeds 6 in the real world. To this argument there is no rebuttal. But the following result is slightly more relevant:

Theorem P′. *A basic n-bit RAM requires at least* $\frac{1}{3} \lg g$ *steps to compute the g-bit reversal* x^R *for* $0 \le x < 2^g$, *if* $g \le n$ *and*

$$\max(m, 1 + \lg n) \; < \; \frac{h+1}{2\lfloor \lg(h+1)\rfloor - 2}, \qquad h = \lfloor \sqrt[3]{g} \rfloor. \tag{106}$$

Proof. An argument like the proof of Theorem R′ appears in exercise 125. ∎

Lemma B and Theorems R, P, R′, P′ and their corollaries are due to A. Brodnik, P. B. Miltersen, and J. I. Munro, *Lecture Notes in Comp. Sci.* **1272** (1997), 426–439, based on earlier work of Miltersen in *Lecture Notes in Comp. Sci.* **1099** (1996), 442–451.

Many unsolved questions remain (see exercises 126–130). For example, does sideways addition require $\Omega(\log n)$ steps in an n-bit broadword chain? Can the parity function $(\nu x) \bmod 2$, or the majority function $[\nu x > n/2]$, be computed substantially faster than νx itself, broadwordwise?

An application to directed graphs. Now let's use some of what we've learned, by implementing a simple algorithm. Given a digraph on a set of vertices V, we write $u \longrightarrow v$ when there's an arc from u to v. The *reachability problem* is to find all vertices that lie on oriented paths beginning in a specified set $Q \subseteq V$; in other words, we seek the set

$$R \; = \; \{v \mid u \longrightarrow^* v \text{ for some } u \in Q\}, \tag{107}$$

where $u \longrightarrow^* v$ means that there is a sequence of t arcs

$$u = u_0 \longrightarrow u_1 \longrightarrow \cdots \longrightarrow u_t = v, \qquad \text{for some } t \ge 0. \tag{108}$$

This problem arises frequently in practice. For example, we encountered it in Section 2.3.5 when marking all elements of Lists that are not "garbage."

If the number of vertices is small, say $|V| \le 64$, we may want to approach the reachability problem in quite a different way than we did before, by working directly with subsets of vertices. Let

$$S[u] \; = \; \{v \mid u \longrightarrow v\} \tag{109}$$

be the set of successors of vertex u, for all $u \in V$. Then the following algorithm is almost completely different from Algorithm 2.3.5E, yet it solves the same abstract problem:

Algorithm R (*Reachability*). Given a simple directed graph, represented by the successor sets $S[u]$ in (109), this algorithm computes the elements R that are reachable from a given set Q.

R1. [Initialize.] Set $R \leftarrow Q$ and $X \leftarrow \emptyset$. (In the following steps, X is the subset of vertices $u \in R$ for which we've looked at $S[u]$.)

R2. [Done?] If $X = R$, the algorithm terminates.

R3. [Examine another vertex.] Let u be an element of $R \setminus X$. Set $X \leftarrow X \cup \{u\}$, $R \leftarrow R \cup S[u]$, and return to step R2. ∎

The algorithm is correct because (i) every element placed into R is reachable; (ii) every reachable element u_j in (108) is present in R, by induction on j; and (iii) termination eventually occurs, because step R3 always increases $|X|$.

To implement Algorithm R we will assume that $V = \{0, 1, \ldots, n-1\}$, with $n \le 64$. The set X is conveniently represented by the integer $\sigma(X) = \sum\{2^u \mid u \in X\}$, and the same convention works nicely for the other sets Q, R, and $S[u]$. Notice that the bits of $S[0], S[1], \ldots, S[n-1]$ are essentially the *adjacency matrix* of the given digraph, as explained in Section 7, but in little-endian order: The "diagonal" elements, which tell us whether or not $u \in S[u]$, go from right to left. For example, if $n = 3$ and the arcs are $\{0 \to 0, 0 \to 1, 1 \to 0, 2 \to 0\}$, we have $S[0] = (011)_2$ and $S[1] = S[2] = (001)_2$, while the adjacency matrix is $\left(\begin{smallmatrix}110\\100\\100\end{smallmatrix}\right)$.

Step R3 allows us to choose any element of $R \setminus X$, so we use the ruler function $u \leftarrow \rho(\sigma(R) - \sigma(X))$ to choose the smallest. The bitwise operations require no further trickery when we adapt the algorithm to MMIX:

Program R (*Reachability*). The input set Q is given in register q, and each successor set $S[u]$ appears in octabyte $\mathrm{M}_8[\mathtt{suc} + 8u]$. The output set R will appear in register r; other registers s, t, tt, u, and x hold intermediate results.

01	1H	SET	r,q	1	*R1. Initialize.* $\mathtt{r} \leftarrow \sigma(Q)$.
02		SET	x,0	1	$\mathtt{x} \leftarrow \sigma(\emptyset)$.
03		JMP	2F	1	To R2.
04	3H	SUBU	tt,t,1	$\|R\|$	*R3. Examine another vertex.* $\mathtt{tt} \leftarrow \mathtt{t} - 1$.
05		SADD	u,tt,t	$\|R\|$	$\mathtt{u} \leftarrow \rho(\mathtt{t})$ [see (46)].
06		SLU	s,u,3	$\|R\|$	$\mathtt{s} \leftarrow 8u$.
07		LDOU	s,suc,s	$\|R\|$	$\mathtt{s} \leftarrow \sigma(S[u])$.
08		ANDN	tt,t,tt	$\|R\|$	$\mathtt{tt} \leftarrow \mathtt{t}\ \&\ {\sim}\mathtt{tt} = 2^u$.
09		OR	x,x,tt	$\|R\|$	$X \leftarrow X \cup \{u\}$; that is, $\mathtt{x} \leftarrow \mathtt{x} \mid 2^u$, since $\mathtt{x} = \sigma(X)$.
10		OR	r,r,s	$\|R\|$	$R \leftarrow R \cup S[u]$; that is, $\mathtt{r} \leftarrow \mathtt{r} \mid \mathtt{s}$, since $\mathtt{r} = \sigma(R)$.
11	2H	SUBU	t,r,x	$\|R\|+1$	*R2. Done?* $\mathtt{t} \leftarrow \mathtt{r} - \mathtt{x} = \sigma(R \setminus X)$, since $X \subseteq R$.
12		PBNZ	t,3B	$\|R\|+1$	To R3 if $R \ne X$. ∎

The total running time is $(\mu + 9\upsilon)|R| + 7\upsilon$. By contrast, exercise 131 implements Algorithm R with linked lists; the overall execution time then grows to $(3S + 4|R| - 2|Q| + 1)\mu + (5S + 12|R| - 5|Q| + 4)\upsilon$, where $S = \sum_{u \in R} |S[u]|$. (But of course that program is also able to handle graphs with millions of vertices.)

Exercise 132 presents another instructive algorithm where bitwise operations work nicely on not-too-large graphs.

Application to data representation. Computers are binary, but (alas?) the world isn't. We often must find a way to encode nonbinary data into 0s and 1s. One of the most common problems of this sort is to choose an efficient representation for items that can be in exactly three different states.

Suppose we know that $x \in \{a, b, c\}$, and we want to represent x by two bits $x_l x_r$. We could, for example, map $a \mapsto 00$, $b \mapsto 01$, and $c \mapsto 10$. But there are many other possibilities — in fact, 4 choices for a, then 3 choices for b, and 2 for c, making 24 altogether. Some of these mappings might be much easier to deal with than others, depending on what we want to do with x.

Given two elements $x, y \in \{a, b, c\}$, we typically want to compute $z = x \circ y$, for some binary operation $\circ$. If $x = x_l x_r$ and $y = y_l y_r$ then $z = z_l z_r$, where

$$z_l = f_l(x_l, x_r, y_l, y_r) \qquad \text{and} \qquad z_r = f_r(x_l, x_r, y_l, y_r); \qquad (110)$$

these Boolean functions f_l and f_r of four variables depend on $\circ$ and the chosen representation. We seek a representation that makes f_l and f_r easy to compute.

Suppose, for example, that $\{a, b, c\} = \{-1, 0, +1\}$ and that $\circ$ is multiplication. If we decide to use the natural mapping $x \mapsto x \bmod 3$, namely

$$0 \mapsto 00, \qquad +1 \mapsto 01, \qquad -1 \mapsto 10, \tag{111}$$

so that $x = x_r - x_l$, then the truth tables for f_l and f_r are respectively

$$f_l \leftrightarrow 000{*}001{*}010{*}{*}{*}{*}{*} \qquad \text{and} \qquad f_r \leftrightarrow 000{*}010{*}001{*}{*}{*}{*}{*}. \tag{112}$$

(There are seven "don't-cares," for cases where $x_l x_r = 11$ and/or $y_l y_r = 11$.) The methods of Section 7.1.2 tell us how to compute z_l and z_r optimally, namely

$$z_l = (x_l \oplus y_l) \wedge (x_r \oplus y_r), \qquad z_r = (x_l \oplus y_r) \wedge (x_r \oplus y_l); \tag{113}$$

unfortunately the functions f_l and f_r in (112) are independent, in the sense that they cannot both be evaluated in fewer than $C(f_l) + C(f_r) = 6$ steps.

On the other hand the somewhat less natural mapping scheme

$$+1 \mapsto 00, \qquad 0 \mapsto 01, \qquad -1 \mapsto 10 \tag{114}$$

leads to the transformation functions

$$f_l \leftrightarrow 001{*}000{*}100{*}{*}{*}{*}{*} \qquad \text{and} \qquad f_r \leftrightarrow 010{*}111{*}010{*}{*}{*}{*}{*}, \tag{115}$$

and three operations now suffice to do the desired evaluation:

$$z_r = x_r \vee y_r, \qquad z_l = (x_l \oplus y_l) \wedge \bar{z}_r. \tag{116}$$

Is there an easy way to discover such improvements? Fortunately we don't need to try all 24 possibilities, because many of them are basically alike. For example, the mapping $x \mapsto x_r x_l$ is equivalent to $x \mapsto x_l x_r$, because the new representation $x'_l x'_r = x_r x_l$ obtained by swapping coordinates makes

$$f'_l(x'_l, x'_r, y'_l, y'_r) = z'_l = z_r = f_r(x_l, x_r, y_l, y_r);$$

the new transformation functions f'_l and f'_r defined by

$$f'_l(x_l, x_r, y_l, y_r) = f_r(x_r, x_l, y_r, y_l), \quad f'_r(x_l, x_r, y_l, y_r) = f_l(x_r, x_l, y_r, y_l) \tag{117}$$

have the same complexity as f_l and f_r. Similarly we can complement a coordinate, letting $x'_l x'_r = \bar{x}_l x_r$; then the transformation functions turn out to be

$$f'_l(x_l, x_r, y_l, y_r) = \bar{f}_l(\bar{x}_l, x_r, \bar{y}_l, y_r), \quad f'_r(x_l, x_r, y_l, y_r) = f_r(\bar{x}_l, x_r, \bar{y}_l, y_r), \tag{118}$$

and again the complexity is essentially unchanged.

Repeated use of swapping and/or complementation leads to eight mappings that are equivalent to any given one. So the 24 possibilities reduce to only three, which we shall call classes I, II, and III:

Class I	Class II	Class III

$a \mapsto$ 00 01 10 11 00 10 01 11 00 01 10 11 00 10 01 11 00 01 10 11 00 10 01 11;
$b \mapsto$ 01 00 11 10 10 00 11 01 01 00 11 10 10 00 11 01 11 10 01 00 11 01 10 00; (119)
$c \mapsto$ 10 11 00 01 01 11 00 10 11 10 01 00 11 01 10 00 01 00 11 10 10 00 11 01.

To choose a representation we need consider only one representative of each class. For example, if $a = +1$, $b = 0$, and $c = -1$, representation (111) belongs to class II, and (114) belongs to class I. Class III turns out to have cost 3, like class I. So it appears that representation (114) is as good as any, with z computed by (116), for the 3-element multiplication problem we've been studying.

Appearances can, however, be deceiving, because we need not map $\{a, b, c\}$ into *unique* two-bit codes. Consider the one-to-many mapping

$$+1 \mapsto 00, \qquad 0 \mapsto 01 \text{ or } 11, \qquad -1 \mapsto 10, \tag{120}$$

where both 01 and 11 are allowed as representations of zero. The truth tables for f_l and f_r are now quite different from (112) and (115), because all inputs are legal but some outputs can be arbitrary:

$$f_l \leftrightarrow 0{*}1{*}{*}{*}{*}{*}1{*}0{*}{*}{*}{*}{*} \qquad \text{and} \qquad f_r \leftrightarrow 0101111101011111. \tag{121}$$

And in fact, this approach needs just two operations, instead of the three in (116):

$$z_l = x_l \oplus y_l, \qquad z_r = x_r \vee y_r. \tag{122}$$

A moment's thought shows that indeed, these operations obviously yield the product $z = x \cdot y$ when the three elements $\{+1, 0, -1\}$ are represented as in (120).

Such nonunique mappings add 36 more possibilities to the 24 that we had before. But again, they reduce under "2-cube equivalence" to a small number of equivalence classes. First there are three classes that we call IV_a, IV_b, and IV_c, depending on which element has an ambiguous representation:

$$
\overbrace{\qquad\qquad\qquad}^{\text{Class } IV_a} \qquad \overbrace{\qquad\qquad\qquad}^{\text{Class } IV_b} \qquad \overbrace{\qquad\qquad\qquad}^{\text{Class } IV_c}
$$

$a \mapsto$ 0* 0* 1* 1* *0 *0 *1 *1 11 10 01 00 11 01 10 00 10 11 00 01 01 11 00 10;

$b \mapsto$ 10 11 00 01 01 11 00 10 0* 0* 1* 1* *0 *0 *1 *1 11 10 01 00 11 01 10 00; (123)

$c \mapsto$ 11 10 01 00 11 01 10 00 10 11 00 01 01 11 00 10 0* 0* 1* 1* *0 *0 *1 *1.

(Representation (120) belongs to class IV_b. Classes IV_a and IV_c don't work well for $z = x \cdot y$.) Then there are three further classes with only four mappings each:

$$
\overbrace{\qquad\qquad\qquad}^{\text{Class } V_a} \qquad \overbrace{\qquad\qquad\qquad}^{\text{Class } V_b} \qquad \overbrace{\qquad\qquad\qquad}^{\text{Class } V_c}
$$

| $a \mapsto$ | tt | $t\bar{t}$ | $t\bar{t}$ | tt | 10 | 11 | 00 | 01 | 01 | 00 | 11 | 10; |
| $b \mapsto$ | 01 | 00 | 11 | 10 | tt | $t\bar{t}$ | $t\bar{t}$ | tt | 10 | 11 | 00 | 01; |
| $c \mapsto$ | 10 | 11 | 00 | 01 | 01 | 00 | 11 | 10 | tt | $t\bar{t}$ | $t\bar{t}$ | tt. | (124)

These classes are a bit of a nuisance, because the indeterminacy in their truth tables cannot be expressed simply in terms of don't-cares as we did in (121). For example, if we try

$$+1 \mapsto 00 \text{ or } 11, \qquad 0 \mapsto 01, \qquad -1 \mapsto 10, \tag{125}$$

which is the first mapping in class V_a, there are binary variables $pqrst$ such that

$$f_l \leftrightarrow p01q000010r1s01t \qquad \text{and} \qquad f_r \leftrightarrow p10q111101r0s10t. \tag{126}$$

Furthermore, mappings of classes V_a, V_b, and V_c almost never turn out to be better than the mappings of the other six classes (see exercise 138). Still, representatives of all nine classes must be examined before we can be sure that an optimal mapping has been found.

In practice we often want to perform several different operations on ternary-valued variables, not just a single operation like multiplication. For example, we might want to compute $\max(x, y)$ as well as $x \cdot y$. With representation (120), the best we can do is $z_l = x_l \wedge y_l$, $z_r = (x_l \wedge y_r) \vee (x_r \wedge (y_l \vee y_r))$; but the "natural" mapping (111) now shines, with $z_l = x_l \wedge y_l$, $z_r = x_r \vee y_r$. Class III turns out to have cost 4; other classes are inferior. To choose between classes II, III, and IV_b in this case, we need to know the relative frequencies of $x \cdot y$ and $\max(x, y)$. And if we add $\min(x, y)$ to the mix, classes II, III, and IV_b compute it with the respective costs 2, 5, 5; hence (111) looks better yet.

The ternary max and min operations arise also in other contexts, such as the three-valued logic developed by Jan Łukasiewicz in 1917. [See his *Selected Works*, edited by L. Borkowski (1970), 84–88, 153–178.] Consider the logical values "true," "false," and "maybe," denoted respectively by 1, 0, and ∗. Łukasiewicz defined the three basic operations of conjunction, disjunction, and implication on these values by specifying the tables

$$
x \begin{cases} \begin{array}{c|ccc} & 0 & * & 1 \\ \hline 0 & 0 & 0 & 0 \\ * & 0 & * & * \\ 1 & 0 & * & 1 \end{array} \end{cases}, \qquad
x \begin{cases} \begin{array}{c|ccc} & 0 & * & 1 \\ \hline 0 & 0 & * & 1 \\ * & * & * & 1 \\ 1 & 1 & 1 & 1 \end{array} \end{cases}, \qquad
x \begin{cases} \begin{array}{c|ccc} & 0 & * & 1 \\ \hline 0 & 1 & 1 & 1 \\ * & * & 1 & 1 \\ 1 & 0 & * & 1 \end{array} \end{cases}. \qquad (127)
$$

$$x \wedge y \qquad\qquad\qquad x \vee y \qquad\qquad\qquad x \Rightarrow y$$

For these operations the methods above show that the binary representation

$$0 \mapsto 00, \qquad * \mapsto 01, \qquad 1 \mapsto 11 \qquad (128)$$

works well, because we can compute the logical operations thus:

$$
\begin{aligned}
x_l x_r \wedge y_l y_r &= (x_l \wedge y_l)(x_r \wedge y_r), & x_l x_r \vee y_l y_r &= (x_l \vee y_l)(x_r \vee y_r), \\
x_l x_r \Rightarrow y_l y_r &= ((\bar{x}_l \vee y_l) \wedge (\bar{x}_r \vee y_r))(\bar{x}_l \vee y_r).
\end{aligned}
\qquad (129)
$$

Of course x need not be an isolated ternary value in this discussion; we often want to deal with ternary *vectors* $x = x_1 x_2 \ldots x_n$, where each x_j is either a, b, or c. Such ternary vectors are conveniently represented by two binary vectors

$$x_l = x_{1l} x_{2l} \ldots x_{nl} \qquad \text{and} \qquad x_r = x_{1r} x_{2r} \ldots x_{nr}, \qquad (130)$$

where $x_j \mapsto x_{jl} x_{jr}$ as above. We could also pack the ternary values into two-bit fields of a single vector,

$$x = x_{1l} x_{1r} x_{2l} x_{2r} \ldots x_{nl} x_{nr}; \qquad (131)$$

that would work fine if, say, we're doing Łukasiewicz logic with the operations $\wedge$ and $\vee$ but not $\Rightarrow$. Usually, however, the two-vector approach of (130) is better, because it lets us do bitwise calculations without shifting and masking.

Applications to data structures. Bitwise operations offer many efficient ways to represent elements of data and the relationships between them. For example, chess-playing programs often use a "bit board" to represent the positions of pieces (see exercise 143).

In Chapter 8 we shall discuss an important data structure developed by Peter van Emde Boas for representing a dynamically changing subset of integers between 0 and N. Insertions, deletions, and other operations such as "find the largest element less than x" can be done in $O(\log \log N)$ steps with his methods; the general idea is to organize the full structure recursively as $\sqrt{N}$ substructures for subsets of intervals of size $\sqrt{N}$, together with an auxiliary structure that tells which of those intervals are occupied. [See *Information Processing Letters* **6** (1977), 80–82; also P. van Emde Boas, R. Kaas, and E. Zijlstra, *Math. Systems Theory* **10** (1977), 99–127.] Bitwise operations make those computations fast.

Hierarchical data can sometimes be arranged so that the links between elements are implicit rather than explicit. For example, we studied "heaps" in Section 5.2.3, where n elements of a sequential array implicitly have a binary tree structure like

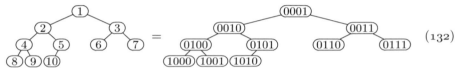

$$(132)$$

when, say, $n = 10$. (Node numbers are shown here both in decimal and binary notation.) There is no need to store pointers in memory to relate node j of a heap to its parent (which is node $j \gg 1$ if $j \neq 1$), or to its sibling (which is node $j \oplus 1$ if $j \neq 1$), or to its children (which are nodes $j \ll 1$ and $(j \ll 1) + 1$ if those numbers don't exceed n), because a simple calculation leads directly from j to any desired neighbor.

Similarly, a *sideways heap* provides implicit links for another useful family of n-node binary tree structures, typified by

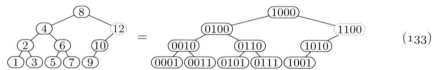

$$(133)$$

when $n = 10$. (We sometimes need to go beyond n when moving from a node to its parent, as in the path from 10 to 12 to 8 shown here.) Heaps and sideways heaps can both be regarded as nodes 1 to n of *infinite* binary tree structures: The heap with $n = \infty$ is rooted at node 1 and has no leaves; by contrast, the sideways heap with $n = \infty$ has infinitely many leaves 1, 3, 5, ..., but no root(!).

The leaves of a sideways heap are the odd numbers, and their parents are the odd multiples of 2. The grandparents of leaves, similarly, are the odd multiples of 4; and so on. Thus the ruler function ρj tells how high node j is above leaf level.

The parent of node j in the infinite sideways heap is easily seen to be node

$$(j - k) \mid (k \ll 1), \qquad \text{where } k = j \& -j; \qquad (134)$$

this formula rounds j to the nearest odd multiple of $2^{1+\rho j}$. And the children are

$$j - (k \gg 1) \qquad \text{and} \qquad j + (k \gg 1) \tag{135}$$

when j is even. In general the descendants of node j form a closed interval

$$[j - 2^{\rho j} + 1 \mathrel{..} j + 2^{\rho j} - 1], \tag{136}$$

arranged as a complete binary tree of $2^{1+\rho j} - 1$ nodes. The ancestor of node j at height h is node

$$(j \mid (1 \ll h)) \mathbin{\&} {-}(1 \ll h) = ((j \gg h) \mid 1) \ll h \tag{137}$$

when $h \geq \rho j$. Notice that the symmetric order of the nodes, also called inorder, is just the natural order $1, 2, 3, \ldots$.

Dov Harel noted these properties in his Ph.D. thesis (U. of California, Irvine, 1980), and observed that the *nearest* common ancestor of any two nodes of a sideways heap can also be easily calculated. Indeed, if node l is the nearest common ancestor of nodes i and j, where $i \leq j$, there is a remarkable identity

$$\rho l \;=\; \max\{\rho x \mid i \leq x \leq j\} \;=\; \lambda(j \mathbin{\&} {-}i), \tag{138}$$

which relates the ρ and λ functions. (See exercise 146.) We can therefore use formula (137) with $h = \lambda(j \mathbin{\&} {-}i)$ to calculate l.

Subtle extensions of this approach lead to an asymptotically efficient algorithm that finds nearest common ancestors in *any* oriented forest whose arcs grow dynamically [D. Harel and R. E. Tarjan, *SICOMP* **13** (1984), 338–355]. Baruch Schieber and Uzi Vishkin [*SICOMP* **17** (1988), 1253–1262] subsequently discovered a much simpler way to compute nearest common ancestors in an arbitrary (but fixed) oriented forest, using an attractive and instructive blend of bitwise and algorithmic techniques that we shall consider next.

Recall that an oriented forest with m trees and n vertices is an acyclic digraph with $n - m$ arcs. There is at most one arc from each vertex; the vertices with out-degree zero are the roots of the trees. We say that v is the *parent* of u when $u \longrightarrow v$, and v is an *ancestor* of u when $u \longrightarrow^* v$. Two vertices have a common ancestor if and only if they belong to the same tree. Vertex w is called the nearest common ancestor of u and v when we have

$$u \longrightarrow^* z \text{ and } v \longrightarrow^* z \quad \text{if and only if} \quad w \longrightarrow^* z. \tag{139}$$

Schieber and Vishkin preprocess the given forest, mapping its vertices into a sideways heap S of size n by computing three quantities for each vertex v:

πv, the rank of v in preorder $(1 \leq \pi v \leq n)$;

βv, a node of the sideways heap S $(1 \leq \beta v \leq n)$;

αv, a $(1 + \lambda n)$-bit routing code $(1 \leq \alpha v < 2^{1+\lambda n})$.

If $u \longrightarrow v$ we have $\pi u > \pi v$ by the definition of preorder. Node βv is defined to be the nearest common ancestor of all sideways-heap nodes πu such that v is an ancestor of vertex u. And we define

$$\alpha v \;=\; \sum \{2^{\rho \beta w} \mid v \longrightarrow^* w\}. \tag{140}$$

For example, here's an oriented forest with ten vertices and two trees:

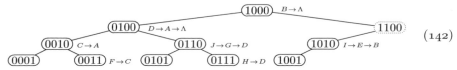

$$(141)$$

Each node has been labeled with its preorder rank, from which we can compute the β and α codes:

$$
\begin{array}{lllllllllll}
v = & A & B & C & D & E & F & G & H & I & J \\
\pi v = & 0001 & 1000 & 0010 & 0100 & 1001 & 0011 & 0101 & 0111 & 1010 & 0110 \\
\beta v = & 0100 & 1000 & 0010 & 0100 & 1010 & 0011 & 0110 & 0111 & 1010 & 0110 \\
\alpha v = & 0100 & 1000 & 0110 & 0100 & 1010 & 0111 & 0110 & 0101 & 1010 & 0110
\end{array}
$$

Notice that, for instance, $\beta A = 4 = 0100$ because the preorder ranks of the descendants of A are $\{1, 2, 3, 4, 5, 6, 7\}$. And $\alpha H = 0101$ because the ancestors of H have β codes $\{\beta H, \beta D, \beta A\} = \{0111, 0100\}$. One can prove without difficulty that the mapping $v \mapsto \beta v$ satisfies the following key properties:

i) If $u \longrightarrow v$ in the forest, then βu is a descendant of βv in S.

ii) If several vertices have the same value of βv, they form a path in the forest.

Property (ii) holds because exactly one child u of v has $\beta u = \beta v$ when $\beta v \neq \pi v$.

Now let's imagine placing every vertex v of the forest into node βv of S:

$$(142)$$

If k vertices map into node j, we can arrange them into a path

$$v_0 \longrightarrow v_1 \longrightarrow \cdots \longrightarrow v_{k-1} \longrightarrow v_k, \qquad \text{where } \beta v_0 = \beta v_1 = \cdots = \beta v_{k-1} = j. \quad (143)$$

These paths are illustrated in (142); for example, $J \longrightarrow G \longrightarrow D$ is a path in (141), and '$J \to G \to D$' appears with node $0110 = \beta J = \beta G$.

The preprocessing algorithm also computes a table τj for all nodes j of S, containing pointers to the vertices v_k at the tail ends of (143):

$$
\begin{array}{lllllllllll}
j = & 0001 & 0010 & 0011 & 0100 & 0101 & 0110 & 0111 & 1000 & 1001 & 1010 \\
\tau j = & \Lambda & A & C & \Lambda & \Lambda & D & D & \Lambda & \Lambda & B
\end{array}
$$

Exercise 149 shows that all four tables πv, βv, αv, and τj can be prepared in $O(n)$ steps. And once those tables are ready, they contain just enough information to identify the nearest common ancestor of any two given vertices quickly:

Algorithm V (*Nearest common ancestors*). Suppose πv, βv, αv, and τj are known for all n vertices v of an oriented forest, and for $1 \leq j \leq n$. A dummy vertex Λ is also assumed to be present, with $\pi \Lambda = \beta \Lambda = \alpha \Lambda = 0$. This algorithm computes the nearest common ancestor z of any given vertices x and y, returning $z = \Lambda$ if x and y belong to different trees. We assume that the values $\lambda j = \lfloor \lg j \rfloor$ have been precomputed for $1 \leq j \leq n$, and that $\lambda 0 = \lambda n$.

V1. [Find common height.] If $\beta x \leq \beta y$, set $h \leftarrow \lambda(\beta y \,\&\, -\beta x)$; otherwise set $h \leftarrow \lambda(\beta x \,\&\, -\beta y)$. (See (138).)

V2. [Find true height.] Set $k \leftarrow \alpha x \,\&\, \alpha y \,\&\, -(1 \ll h)$, then $h \leftarrow \lambda(k \,\&\, -k)$.

V3. [Find βz.] Set $j \leftarrow ((\beta x \gg h) \mid 1) \ll h$. (Now $j = \beta z$, if $z \neq \Lambda$.)

V4. [Find $\hat{x}$ and $\hat{y}$.] (We now seek the lowest ancestors of x and y in node j.) If $j = \beta x$, set $\hat{x} \leftarrow x$; otherwise set $l \leftarrow \lambda(\alpha x \,\&\, ((1 \ll h) - 1))$ and $\hat{x} \leftarrow \tau(((\beta x \gg l) \mid 1) \ll l)$. Similarly, if $j = \beta y$, set $\hat{y} \leftarrow y$; otherwise set $l \leftarrow \lambda(\alpha y \,\&\, ((1 \ll h) - 1))$ and $\hat{y} \leftarrow \tau(((\beta y \gg l) \mid 1) \ll l)$.

V5. [Find z.] Set $z \leftarrow \hat{x}$ if $\pi\hat{x} \leq \pi\hat{y}$, otherwise $z \leftarrow \hat{y}$. ∎

These artful dodges obviously exploit (137); exercise 152 explains why they work.

Sideways heaps can also be used to implement an interesting type of priority queue that J. Katajainen and F. Vitale call a "navigation pile," illustrated here for $n = 10$:

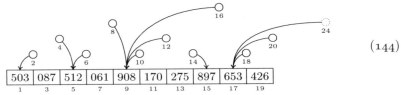

(144)

Data elements go into the leaf positions $1, 3, \ldots, 2n - 1$ of the sideways heap; they can be many bits wide, and they can appear in any order. By contrast, each branch position $2, 4, 6, \ldots$ contains a pointer to its largest descendant. And the novel point is that these pointers take up almost no extra space — fewer than two bits per item of data, on average — because only one bit is needed for pointers 2, 6, 10, $\ldots$, only two bits for pointers 4, 12, 20, $\ldots$, and only ρj for pointer j in general. (See exercise 153.) Thus the navigation pile requires very little memory, and it behaves nicely with respect to cache performance on a typical computer.

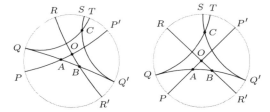

Fig. 13. Two views of five lines in the hyperbolic plane.

*Cells in the hyperbolic plane. Hyperbolic geometry suggests an instructive implicit data structure that has a rather different flavor. The *hyperbolic plane* is a fascinating example of non-Euclidean geometry that is conveniently viewed by projecting its points into the interior of a circle. Its straight lines then become circular arcs, which meet the rim at right angles. For example, the lines PP', QQ', and RR' in Fig. 13 intersect at points O, A, B, and those points form a triangle. Lines SQ' and QQ' are *parallel*: They never touch, but their points get closer and closer together. Line QT is also parallel to QQ'.

We get different views by focusing on different center points. For example, the second view in Fig. 13 puts O smack in the center. Notice that if a line passes through the very center, it remains straight after being projected; such diameter-spanning chords are the special case of a "circular arc" whose radius is infinite.

Most of Euclid's axioms for plane geometry remain valid in the hyperbolic plane. For example, exactly one line passes through any two distinct points; and if point A lies on line PP' there's exactly one line QQ' such that angle PAQ has any given value θ, for $0 < \theta < 180°$. But Euclid's famous fifth postulate does *not* hold: If point C is *not* on line QQ', there always are exactly *two* lines through C that are parallel to QQ'. Furthermore there are many pairs of lines, like RR' and SQ' in Fig. 13, that are totally disjoint or *ultraparallel*, in the sense that their points never become arbitrarily close. [These properties of the hyperbolic plane were discovered by G. Saccheri in the early 1700s, and made rigorous by N. I. Lobachevsky, J. Bolyai, and C. F. Gauss a century later.]

Quantitatively speaking, when points are projected onto the unit disk $|z| < 1$, the arc that meets the circle at $e^{i\theta}$ and $e^{-i\theta}$ has center at $\sec\theta$ and radius $\tan\theta$. The actual distance between two points whose projections are z and z' is $d(z, z') = \ln(|1 - \bar{z}z'| + |z - z'|) - \ln(|1 - \bar{z}z'| - |z - z'|)$. Thus objects far from the center appear dramatically shrunken when we see them near the circle's rim.

The sum of the angles of a hyperbolic triangle is always *less* than 180°. For example, the angles at O, A, and B in Fig. 13 are respectively 90°, 45°, and 36°. Ten such 36°-45°-90° triangles can be placed together to make a regular pentagon with 90° angles at each corner. And four such pentagons fit snugly together at their corners, allowing us to tile the entire hyperbolic plane with right regular pentagons (see Fig. 14). The edges of these pentagons form an interesting family of lines, every two of which are either ultraparallel or perpendicular; so we have a grid structure analogous to the unit squares of the ordinary plane. We call it the *pentagrid*, because each cell now has five neighbors instead of four.

There's a nice way to navigate in the pentagrid using Fibonacci numbers, based on ideas of Maurice Margenstern [see F. Herrmann and M. Margenstern, *Theoretical Comp. Sci.* **296** (2003), 345–351]. Instead of the ordinary Fibonacci sequence $\langle F_n \rangle$, however, we shall use the *negaFibonacci* numbers $\langle F_{-n} \rangle$, namely

$$F_{-1} = 1, \ F_{-2} = -1, \ F_{-3} = 2, \ F_{-4} = -3, \ \ldots, \ F_{-n} = (-1)^{n-1}F_n. \qquad (145)$$

Exercise 1.2.8–34 introduced the Fibonacci number system, in which every non-negative integer x can be written uniquely in the form

$$x = F_{k_1} + F_{k_2} + \cdots + F_{k_r}, \qquad \text{where } k_1 \ggg k_2 \ggg \cdots \ggg k_r \ggg 0; \qquad (146)$$

here '$j \ggg k$' means '$j \geq k+2$'. But there's also a *negaFibonacci number system*, which suits our purposes better: *Every integer x, whether positive, negative, or zero, can be written uniquely in the form*

$$x = F_{k_1} + F_{k_2} + \cdots + F_{k_r}, \qquad \text{where } k_1 \lll k_2 \lll \cdots \lll k_r \lll 1. \qquad (147)$$

For example, $4 = 5 - 1 = F_{-5} + F_{-2}$ and $-2 = -3 + 1 = F_{-4} + F_{-1}$. This representation can conveniently be expressed as a binary code $\alpha = \ldots a_3 a_2 a_1$,

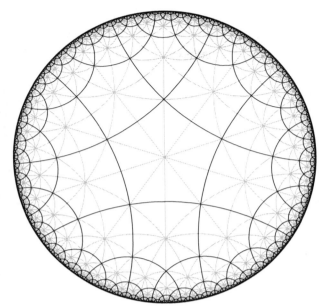

Fig. 14. The pentagrid,
in which identical pentagons
tile the hyperbolic plane.

A circular regular tiling, confined on all sides
by infinitely small shapes, is really wonderful.
— M. C. ESCHER, letter to George Escher (9 November 1958)

standing for $N(\alpha) = \sum_k a_k F_{-k}$, with no two 1s in a row. For example, here are
the negaFibonacci representation codes of all integers between -14 and $+15$:

$-14 = 10010100$	$-8 = 100000$	$-2 = 1001$	$4 = 10010$	$10 = 1001000$
$-13 = 10010101$	$-7 = 100001$	$-1 = 10$	$5 = 10000$	$11 = 1001001$
$-12 = 101010$	$-6 = 100100$	$0 = 0$	$6 = 10001$	$12 = 1000010$
$-11 = 101000$	$-5 = 100101$	$1 = 1$	$7 = 10100$	$13 = 1000000$
$-10 = 101001$	$-4 = 1010$	$2 = 100$	$8 = 10101$	$14 = 1000001$
$-9 = 100010$	$-3 = 1000$	$3 = 101$	$9 = 1001010$	$15 = 1000100$

As in the negadecimal system (see 4.1–(6) and (7)), we can tell whether x is
negative or not by seeing if its representation has an even or odd number of digits.

The predecessor $\alpha-$ and successor $\alpha+$ of any negaFibonacci binary code α
can be computed recursively by using the rules

$$(\alpha01)- = \alpha00, \quad (\alpha000)- = \alpha010, \quad (\alpha100)- = \alpha001, \quad (\alpha10)- = (\alpha-)01,$$
$$(\alpha10)+ = \alpha00, \quad (\alpha00)+ = \alpha01, \quad (\alpha1)+ = (\alpha-)0. \qquad (148)$$

(See exercise 157.) But ten elegant 2-adic steps do the calculation directly:

$$y \leftarrow x \oplus \bar{\mu}_0, \ z \leftarrow y \oplus (y \pm 1), \ \text{where } x = (\alpha)_2;$$
$$z \leftarrow z \mid (x \,\&\, (z \ll 1)); \qquad (149)$$
$$w \leftarrow x \oplus z \oplus ((z+1) \gg 2); \ \text{then } w = (\alpha\pm)_2.$$

We just use $y-1$ in the top line to get the predecessor, $y+1$ to get the successor.

And now here's the point: A negaFibonacci code can be assigned to each cell of the pentagrid in such a way that the codes of its five neighbors are easy to compute. Let's call the neighbors n, s, e, w, and o, for "north," "south," "east," "west," and "other." If α is the code assigned to a given cell, we define

$$\alpha_n = \alpha \gg 2, \quad \alpha_s = \alpha \ll 2, \quad \alpha_e = \alpha_s+, \quad \alpha_w = \alpha_s-; \qquad (150)$$

thus $\alpha_{sn} = \alpha$, and also $\alpha_{en} = (\alpha 01)_n = \alpha$. The "other" direction is trickier:

$$\alpha_o = \begin{cases} \alpha_n+, & \text{if } \alpha \,\&\, 1 = 1; \\ \alpha_w-, & \text{if } \alpha \,\&\, 1 = 0. \end{cases} \qquad (151)$$

For example, $1000_o = 101001$ and $101001_o = 1000$. This mysterious interloper lies between north and east when α ends with 1, but between north and west when α ends with 0.

If we choose any cell and label it with code 0, and if we also choose an orientation so that its neighbors are n, e, s, w, and o in clockwise order, rules (150) and (151) will assign consistent labels to every cell of the pentagrid. (See exercise 160.) For example, the vicinity of a cell labeled 1000 will look like this:

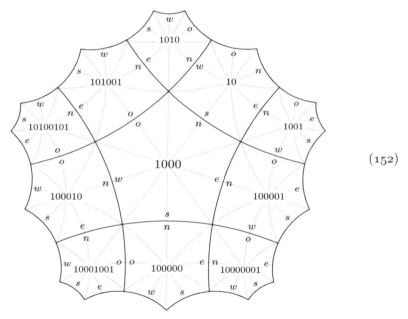

$$(152)$$

The code labels do not, however, identify cells uniquely, because infinitely many cells receive the same label. (Indeed, we clearly have $0_n = 0_s = 0$ and $1_w = 1_o = 1$.) To get a unique identifier, we attach a second coordinate so that each cell's full name has the form (α, y), where y is an integer. When y is constant and α ranges over all negaFibonacci codes, the cells (α, y) form a more-or-less hook-shaped strip whose edges take a 90° turn next to cell $(0, y)$. In general, the five neighbors of (α, y) are $(\alpha, y)_n = (\alpha_n, y + \delta_n(\alpha))$, $(\alpha, y)_s = (\alpha_s, y + \delta_s(\alpha))$,

$(\alpha, y)_e = (\alpha_e, y + \delta_e(\alpha))$, $(\alpha, y)_w = (\alpha_w, y + \delta_w(\alpha))$, and $(\alpha, y)_o = (\alpha_o, y + \delta_o(\alpha))$, where

$$\delta_n(\alpha) = [\alpha = 0], \quad \delta_s(\alpha) = -[\alpha = 0], \quad \delta_e(\alpha) = 0, \quad \delta_w(\alpha) = -[\alpha = 1];$$

$$\delta_o(\alpha) = \begin{cases} \text{sign}(\alpha_o - \alpha_n)[\alpha_o \mathbin{\&} \alpha_n = 0], & \text{if } \alpha \mathbin{\&} 1 = 1; \\ \text{sign}(\alpha_o - \alpha_w)[\alpha_o \mathbin{\&} \alpha_w = 0], & \text{if } \alpha \mathbin{\&} 1 = 0. \end{cases} \quad (153)$$

(See the illustration below.) Bitwise operations now allow us to surf the entire hyperbolic plane with ease. On the other hand, we could also ignore the y coordinates as we move, thereby wrapping around a "hyperbolic cylinder" of pentagons; the α coordinates define an interesting multigraph on the set of all negaFibonacci codes, in which every vertex has degree 5.

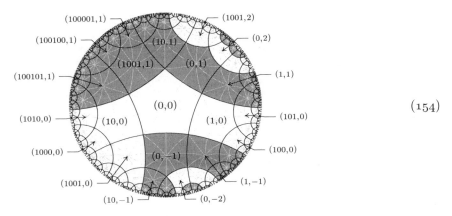

$$(154)$$

Bitmap graphics. It's fun to write programs that deal with pictures and shapes, because they involve our left and right brains simultaneously. When image data is involved, the results can be engrossing even if there are bugs in our code.

The book you are now reading was typeset by software that treated each page as a gigantic matrix of 0s and 1s, called a "raster" or "bitmap," containing millions of square picture elements called "pixels." The rasters were transmitted to printing machines, causing tiny dots of ink to be placed wherever a 1 appeared in the matrix. Physical properties of ink and paper caused those small clusters of dots to look like smooth curves; but each pixel's basic squareness becomes evident if we enlarge the images tenfold, as in the letter 'A' shown in Fig. 15(a).

With bitwise operations we can achieve special effects like "custering," in which the black pixels disappear when they are surrounded on all sides:

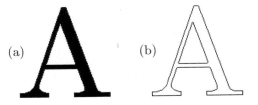

Fig. 15. The letter A, before and after custering.

This operation, introduced by R. A. Kirsch, L. Cahn, C. Ray, and G. H. Urban [*Proc. Eastern Joint Computer Conf.* **12** (1957), 221–229], can be expressed as

$$\text{custer}(X) \;=\; X \mathbin{\&} {\sim}\big((X \mathbin{\forall} 1) \mathbin{\&} (X \gg 1) \mathbin{\&} (X \ll 1) \mathbin{\&} (X \mathbin{\wedge\!\!\!\wedge} 1)\big), \qquad (155)$$

where '$X \mathbin{\forall} 1$' and '$X \mathbin{\wedge\!\!\!\wedge} 1$' stand respectively for the result of shifting the bitmap X down or up by one row. Let us write

$$X_{\text{N}} = X \mathbin{\forall} 1, \quad X_{\text{W}} = X \gg 1, \quad X_{\text{E}} = X \ll 1, \quad X_{\text{S}} = X \mathbin{\wedge\!\!\!\wedge} 1 \qquad (156)$$

for the 1-pixel shifts of a bitmap X. Then, for example, the symbolic expression '$X_{\text{N}} \mathbin{\&} (X_{\text{S}} \mid \overline{X_{\text{E}}})$' evaluates to 1 in those pixel positions whose northern neighbor is black, and which also have either a black neighbor on the south side or a white neighbor to the east. With these abbreviations, (155) takes the form

$$\text{custer}(X) \;=\; X \mathbin{\&} {\sim}(X_{\text{N}} \mathbin{\&} X_{\text{W}} \mathbin{\&} X_{\text{E}} \mathbin{\&} X_{\text{S}}), \qquad (157)$$

which can also be expressed as $X \mathbin{\&} (\overline{X}_{\text{N}} \mid \overline{X}_{\text{W}} \mid \overline{X}_{\text{E}} \mid \overline{X}_{\text{S}})$.

Every pixel has four "rook-neighbors," with which it shares an edge at the top, left, right, or bottom. It also has eight "king-neighbors," with which it shares at least one corner point. For example, the king-neighbors that lie to the northeast of all pixels in a bitmap X can be denoted by X_{NE}, which is equivalent to $(X_{\text{N}})_{\text{E}}$ in pixel algebra. Notice that we also have $X_{\text{NE}} = (X_{\text{E}})_{\text{N}}$.

A 3 × 3 *cellular automaton* is an array of pixels that changes dynamically via a sequence of local transformations, all performed simultaneously: The state of each pixel at time $t + 1$ depends entirely on its state at time t and the states of its king-neighbors at that time. Thus the automaton defines a sequence of bitmaps $X^{(0)}, X^{(1)}, X^{(2)}, \ldots$ that lead from any given initial state $X^{(0)}$, where

$$X^{(t+1)} \;=\; f(X_{\text{NW}}^{(t)}, X_{\text{N}}^{(t)}, X_{\text{NE}}^{(t)}, X_{\text{W}}^{(t)}, X^{(t)}, X_{\text{E}}^{(t)}, X_{\text{SW}}^{(t)}, X_{\text{S}}^{(t)}, X_{\text{SE}}^{(t)}) \qquad (158)$$

and f is any bitwise Boolean function of nine variables. Fascinating patterns often emerge in this way. For example, after Martin Gardner introduced John Conway's game of Life to the world in 1970, more computer time was probably devoted to studying its implications than to any other computational task during the next several years — although the people paying the computer bills were rarely told! (See exercise 167.)

There are 2^{512} Boolean functions of nine variables, so there are 2^{512} different 3 × 3 cellular automata. Many of them are trivial, but most of them probably have such complicated behavior that they are humanly impossible to understand. Fortunately there also are many cases that do turn out to be useful in practice — and much easier to justify on economic grounds than the simulation of a game.

For example, algorithms for recognizing alphabetic characters, fingerprints, or similar patterns often make use of a "thinning" process, which removes excess black pixels and reduces each component of the image to an underlying skeleton that is comparatively simple to analyze. Several authors have proposed cellular automata for this problem, beginning with D. Rutovitz [*J. Royal Stat. Society* **A129** (1966), 512–513] who suggested a 4 × 4 scheme. But parallel algorithms are notoriously subtle, and flaws tended to turn up after various methods had

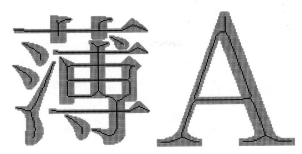

Fig. 16. Example results of Guo and Hall's 3×3 automaton for thinning the components of a bitmap. ("Hollow" pixels were originally black.)

been published. For example, at least two of the black pixels in a component like ▦ should be removed, yet a symmetrical scheme will erroneously erase all four.

A satisfactory solution to the thinning problem was finally found by Z. Guo and R. W. Hall [*CACM* **32** (1989), 359–373, 759], using a 3×3 automaton that invokes alternate rules on odd and even steps. Consider the function

$$f(x_{\mathrm{NW}}, x_{\mathrm{N}}, x_{\mathrm{NE}}, x_{\mathrm{W}}, x, x_{\mathrm{E}}, x_{\mathrm{SW}}, x_{\mathrm{S}}, x_{\mathrm{SE}}) = x \wedge \neg g(x_{\mathrm{NW}}, \ldots, x_{\mathrm{W}}, x_{\mathrm{E}}, \ldots, x_{\mathrm{SE}}), \quad (159)$$

where $g = 1$ only in the following 37 configurations surrounding a black pixel:

Then we use (158), but with $f(x_{\mathrm{NW}}, x_{\mathrm{N}}, x_{\mathrm{NE}}, x_{\mathrm{W}}, x, x_{\mathrm{E}}, x_{\mathrm{SW}}, x_{\mathrm{S}}, x_{\mathrm{SE}})$ replaced by its 180° rotation $f(x_{\mathrm{SE}}, x_{\mathrm{S}}, x_{\mathrm{SW}}, x_{\mathrm{E}}, x, x_{\mathrm{W}}, x_{\mathrm{NE}}, x_{\mathrm{N}}, x_{\mathrm{NW}})$ on even-numbered steps. The process stops when two consecutive cycles make no change.

With this rule Guo and Hall proved that the 3×3 automaton will preserve the connectivity structure of the image, in a strong sense that we will discuss below. Furthermore their algorithm obviously leaves an image intact if it is already so thin that it contains no three pixels that are king-neighbors of each other. On the other hand it usually succeeds in "removing the meat off the bones" of each black component, as shown in Fig. 16. Slightly thinner thinning is obtained in certain cases if we add four additional configurations

$$\qquad\qquad\qquad\qquad (160)$$

to the 37 listed above. In either case the function g can be evaluated with a Boolean chain of length 25. (See exercises 170–172.)

In general, the black pixels of an image can be grouped into segments or components that are *kingwise connected*, in the sense that any black pixel can be reached from any other pixel of its component by a sequence of king moves through black pixels. The white pixels also form components, which are *rookwise connected*: Any two white cells of a component are mutually reachable via rook moves that touch nothing black. It's best to use different kinds of connectedness for white and black, in order to preserve the topological concepts of "inside" and "outside" that are familiar from continuous geometry [see A. Rosenfeld, *JACM* **17** (1970), 146–160]. If we imagine that the corner points of a raster are black, an infinitely thin black curve can cross between pixels at a corner, but a white curve cannot. (We could also imagine white corner points, which would lead to rookwise connectivity for black and kingwise connectivity for white.)

time = 0   time = 1   time = 3

(a)   (b)   (c)

Fig. 17. The shrinking of a Cheshire cat

An amusing algorithm for shrinking a picture while preserving its connectivity, except that isolated black or white pixels disappear, was presented by S. Levialdi in *CACM* **15** (1972), 7–10; an equivalent algorithm, but with black and white reversed, had also appeared in T. Beyer's Ph.D. thesis (M.I.T., 1969). The idea is to use a cellular automaton with the simple transition function

$$f(x_{\mathrm{NW}}, x_{\mathrm{N}}, x_{\mathrm{NE}}, x_{\mathrm{W}}, x, x_{\mathrm{E}}, x_{\mathrm{SW}}, x_{\mathrm{S}}, x_{\mathrm{SE}}) = (x \wedge (x_{\mathrm{W}} \vee x_{\mathrm{SW}} \vee x_{\mathrm{S}})) \vee (x_{\mathrm{W}} \wedge x_{\mathrm{S}}) \quad (161)$$

at each step. This formula is actually a 2×2 rule, but we still need a 3×3 window if we want to keep track of the cases when a one-pixel component goes away.

For example, the 25×30 picture of a Cheshire cat in Fig. 17(a) has seven kingwise black components: the outline of its head, the two earholes, the two eyes, the nose, and the smile. The result after one application of (161) is shown in Fig. 17(b): Seven components remain, but there's an isolated point in one ear, and the other earhole will become isolated after the next step. Hence Fig. 17(c) has only five components. After six steps the cat loses its nose, and even the smile will be gone at time 14. Sadly, the last bit of cat will vanish during step 46.

At most $M + N - 1$ transitions will wipe out any $M \times N$ picture, because the lowest visible northwest-to-southeast diagonal line moves relentlessly upward each time. Exercises 176 and 177 prove that different components will never merge together and interfere with each other.

Of course this cubic-time cellular method isn't the fastest way to count or identify the components of a picture. We can actually do that job "online," while looking at a large image one row at a time, not bothering to keep all of the previously seen rows in memory if we don't wish to look at them again.

While we're analyzing the components we might as well also record the relationships between them. Let's assume that only finitely many black pixels are present. Then there's an infinite component of white pixels called the *background*. Black components adjacent to the background constitute the main *objects* of the image. And these objects may in turn have *holes*, which may serve as a background for another level of objects, and so on. Thus the connected components of any finite picture form a hierarchy — an oriented tree, rooted at the background. Black components appear at the odd-numbered levels of this tree, and white components at the even-numbered levels, alternating between

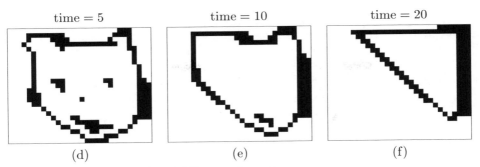

time = 5　　　　　　time = 10　　　　　　time = 20

(d)　　　　　　　　(e)　　　　　　　　(f)

by repeated application of Levialdi's transformation.

kingwise and rookwise connectedness. Each component except the background is *surrounded* by its parent. Childless components are said to be *simply connected.*

For example, here are the Cheshire cat's components, labeled with digits for white pixels and letters for the black ones, and the corresponding oriented tree:

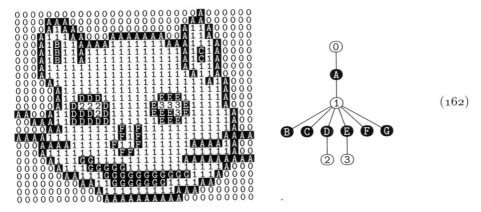

(162)

During the shrinking process of Fig. 17, components disappear in the order ⓒ, {Ⓑ,②,③} (all at time 3), Ⓕ, Ⓔ, Ⓓ, Ⓖ, ①, Ⓐ.

Suppose we want to analyze the components of such a picture by reading one row at a time. After we've seen four rows the result-so-far will be

(163)

and we'll be ready to scan row five. A comparison of rows four and five will then show that Ⓑ and ⓒ should merge into Ⓐ, but that new components Ⓑ and ③ should also be launched. Exercise 179 contains full details about an instructive algorithm that properly updates the current tree as new rows are input. Additional information can also be computed on the fly: For example, we could determine the area of each component, the locations of its first and last pixels, the smallest enclosing rectangle, and/or its center of gravity.

*Filling. Let's complete our quick tour of raster graphics by considering how to fill regions that are bounded by straight lines and/or simple curves. Particularly efficient algorithms are available when the curves are built up from "conic sections" — circles, ellipses, parabolas, or hyperbolas, as in classical geometry.

In keeping with geometric tradition, we shall adopt Cartesian coordinates (x, y) in the following discussion, instead of speaking about rows or columns of pixels: An increase of x will signify a move to the right, while an increase of y will move upward. More significantly, we will focus on the *edges* between square pixels, instead of on the pixels themselves. Edges run between integer points (x, y) and (x', y') of the plane when $|x - x'| + |y - y'| = 1$. Each pixel is bounded by the four edges (x, y) — $(x{-}1, y)$ — $(x{-}1, y{-}1)$ — $(x, y{-}1)$ — (x, y). Experience has shown that algorithms for filling contours become simpler and faster when we concentrate on the edge transitions between white and black, instead of on the black pixels of a custerized boundary. (See, for example, the discussion by B. D. Ackland and N. Weste in *IEEE Trans.* **C-30** (1981), 41–47.)

Consider a continuous curve $z(t) = \big(x(t), y(t)\big)$ that is traced out as t varies from 0 to 1. We assume that the curve doesn't intersect itself for $0 \le t < 1$, and that $z(0) = z(1)$. The famous Jordan curve theorem [C. Jordan, *Cours d'analyse* **3** (1887), 587–594; O. Veblen, *Trans. Amer. Math. Soc.* **6** (1905), 83–98] states that every such curve divides the plane into two regions, called the inside and the outside. We can "digitize" $z(t)$ by forcing it to travel along edges between pixels; then we obtain an approximation in which the inside pixels are black and the outside pixels are white. This digitization process essentially replaces the original curve by the sequence of integer points

$$\text{round}(z(t)) \; = \; \big(\lfloor x(t) + \tfrac{1}{2} \rfloor, \lfloor y(t) + \tfrac{1}{2} \rfloor\big), \qquad \text{for } 0 \le t \le 1. \qquad (164)$$

The curve can be perturbed slightly, if necessary, so that $z(t)$ never passes exactly through the center of a pixel. Then the digitized curve takes discrete steps along pixel edges as t grows; and a pixel lies inside the digitization if and only if its center lies inside the original continuous curve $\{z(t) \mid 0 \le t \le 1\}$.

For example, the equations $x(t) = 20\cos 2\pi t$ and $y(t) = 10\sin 2\pi t$ define an ellipse. Its digitization, $\text{round}(z(t))$, starts at $(20, 0)$ when $t = 0$, then jumps to $(20, 1)$ when $t \approx .008$ and $10\sin 2\pi t = 0.5$. Then it proceeds to the points $(20, 2)$, $(19, 2)$, $(19, 3)$, $(19, 4)$, $(18, 4)$, $\ldots$, $(20, -1)$, $(20, 0)$, as t increases through the values .024, .036, .040, .057, .062, $\ldots$, .976, .992:

$$(165)$$

The horizontal edges of such a boundary are conveniently represented by bit vectors $H(y)$ for each y; for example, $H(10) = \ldots 00000011111111111111000000 \ldots$ and $H(9) = \ldots 01111100000000000111110 \ldots$ in (165). If the ellipse is filled with black to obtain a bitmap B, the H vectors mark transitions between black and white, so we have the symbolic relation

$$H = B \oplus (B \wedge 1). \tag{166}$$

Conversely, it's easy to obtain B when the H vectors are given:

$$
\begin{aligned}
B(y) &= H(y_{\max}) \oplus H(y_{\max-1}) \oplus \cdots \oplus H(y+1) \\
&= H(y_{\min}) \oplus H(y_{\min+1}) \oplus \cdots \oplus H(y). \tag{167}
\end{aligned}
$$

Notice that $H(y_{\min}) \oplus H(y_{\min+1}) \oplus \cdots \oplus H(y_{\max})$ is the zero vector, because each bitmap is white at both top and bottom. Notice further that the analogous *vertical* edge vectors $V(x)$ are redundant: They satisfy the formulas $V = B \oplus (B \ll 1)$ and $B = V^{\oplus}$ (see exercise 36), but we need not bother to keep track of them.

Conic sections are easier to deal with than most other curves, because we can readily eliminate the parameter t. For example, the ellipse that led to (165) can be defined by the equation $(x/20)^2 + (y/10)^2 = 1$, instead of using sines and cosines. Therefore pixel (x,y) should be black if and only if its center point $(x-\frac{1}{2}, y-\frac{1}{2})$ lies inside the ellipse, if and only if $(x-\frac{1}{2})^2/400 + (y-\frac{1}{2})^2/100 - 1 < 0$.

In general, every conic section is the set of points for which $F(x,y) = 0$, when F is an appropriate quadratic form. Therefore there's a quadratic form

$$Q(x,y) = F(x-\tfrac{1}{2}, y-\tfrac{1}{2}) = ax^2 + bxy + cy^2 + dx + ey + f \tag{168}$$

that is negative at the integer point (x,y) if and only if pixel (x,y) lies on a given side of the digitized curve.

For practical purposes we may assume that the coefficients $(a, b, \dots, f)$ of Q are not-too-large integers. Then we're in luck, because the exact value of $Q(x,y)$ is easy to compute. In fact, as pointed out by M. L. V. Pitteway [*Comp. J.* **10** (1967), 282–289], there's a nice "three-register algorithm" by which we can quickly track the boundary points: Let x and y be integers, and suppose we've got the values of $Q(x,y)$, $Q_x(x,y)$, and $Q_y(x,y)$ in three registers (Q, Q_x, Q_y), where

$$Q_x(x,y) = 2ax + by + d \quad \text{and} \quad Q_y(x,y) = bx + 2cy + e \tag{169}$$

are $\frac{\partial}{\partial x}Q$ and $\frac{\partial}{\partial y}Q$. We can then move to any adjacent integer point, because

$$
\begin{aligned}
Q(x\pm1, y) &= Q(x,y) \pm Q_x(x,y) + a, & Q(x, y\pm1) &= Q(x,y) \pm Q_y(x,y) + c, \\
Q_x(x\pm1, y) &= Q_x(x,y) \pm 2a, & Q_x(x, y\pm1) &= Q_x(x,y) \pm b, \\
Q_y(x\pm1, y) &= Q_y(x,y) \pm b; & Q_y(x, y\pm1) &= Q_y(x,y) \pm 2c. \tag{170}
\end{aligned}
$$

Furthermore we can divide the contour into separate pieces, in each of which $x(t)$ and $y(t)$ are both monotonic. For example, when the ellipse (165) travels from $(20, 0)$ to $(0, 10)$, the value of x decreases while y increases; thus we need only move from (x, y) to $(x-1, y)$ or to $(x, y+1)$. If registers (Q, R, S) respectively hold $(Q, Q_x - a, Q_y + c)$, a move to $(x-1, y)$ simply sets $Q \leftarrow Q - R$, $R \leftarrow R - 2a$, and $S \leftarrow S - b$; a move to $(x, y+1)$ is just as quick. With care, this idea leads to a blindingly fast way to discover the correctly digitized edges of almost any conic curve.

For example, the quadratic form $Q(x, y)$ for ellipse (165) is $4x^2 + 16y^2 - (4x + 16y + 1595)$, when we integerize its coefficients. We have $Q(20, 0) = F(19.5, -0.5) = -75$ and $Q(21, 0) = +85$; therefore pixel $(20, 0)$, whose center is $(19.5, -0.5)$, is inside the ellipse, but pixel $(21, 0)$ isn't. Let's zoom in closer:

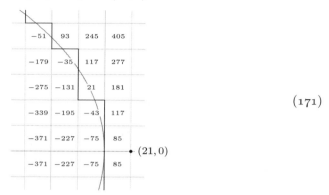

$$(171)$$

The boundary can be deduced without examining Q at very many points. In fact, we don't need to look at $Q(21, 0)$, because we know that all edges between $(20, 0)$ and $(0, 10)$ must go either upwards or to the left. First we test $Q(20, 1)$ and find it negative (-75); so we move up. Also $Q(20, 2)$ is negative (-43), so we go up again. Then we test $Q(20, 3)$, and find it positive (21); so we move left. And so on. Only the Q values -75, -43, 21, -131, -35, 93, -51, ... actually need to be examined, if we've set the three-register method up properly.

Algorithm T (*Three-register algorithm for conics*). Given two integer points (x, y) and (x', y'), and an integer quadratic form Q as in (168), this algorithm decides how to digitize a portion of the conic section defined by $F(x, y) = 0$, where $F(x, y) = Q(x + \frac{1}{2}, y + \frac{1}{2})$. It creates $|x' - x|$ horizontal edges and $|y' - y|$ vertical edges, which form a path from (x, y) to (x', y'). We assume that

i) Real-valued points (ξ, η) and (ξ', η') exist such that $F(\xi, \eta) = F(\xi', \eta') = 0$.

ii) The curve travels from (ξ, η) to (ξ', η') monotonically in both coordinates.

iii) $x = \lfloor \xi + \frac{1}{2} \rfloor$, $y = \lfloor \eta + \frac{1}{2} \rfloor$, $x' = \lfloor \xi' + \frac{1}{2} \rfloor$, and $y' = \lfloor \eta' + \frac{1}{2} \rfloor$.

iv) If we traverse the curve from (ξ, η) to (ξ', η'), we see $F < 0$ on our left.

v) No edge of the integer grid contains two roots of Q (see exercise 183).

T1. [Initialize.] If $x = x'$, go to T11; if $y = y'$, go to T10. If $x < x'$ and $y < y'$, set $Q \leftarrow Q(x+1, y+1)$, $R \leftarrow Q_x(x+1, y+1)+a$, $S \leftarrow Q_y(x+1, y+1)+c$, and go to T2. If $x < x'$ and $y > y'$, set $Q \leftarrow Q(x+1, y)$, $R \leftarrow Q_x(x+1, y) + a$, $S \leftarrow Q_y(x+1, y) - c$, and go to T3. If $x > x'$ and $y < y'$, set $Q \leftarrow Q(x, y+1)$, $R \leftarrow Q_x(x, y+1) - a$, $S \leftarrow Q_y(x, y+1) + c$, and go to T4. If $x > x'$ and $y > y'$, set $Q \leftarrow Q(x, y)$, $R \leftarrow Q_x(x, y) - a$, $S \leftarrow Q_y(x, y) - c$, and go to T5.

T2. [Right or up.] If $Q < 0$, do T9; otherwise do T6. Repeat until interrupted.

T3. [Down or right.] If $Q < 0$, do T7; otherwise do T9. Repeat until interrupted.

T4. [Up or left.] If $Q < 0$, do T6; otherwise do T8. Repeat until interrupted.

T5. [Left or down.] If $Q < 0$, do T8; otherwise do T7. Repeat until interrupted.

T6. [Move up.] Create the edge (x, y) —— $(x, y+1)$, then set $y \leftarrow y+1$. Interrupt to T10 if $y = y'$; otherwise set $Q \leftarrow Q + S$, $R \leftarrow R + b$, $S \leftarrow S + 2c$.

T7. [Move down.] Create the edge (x, y) —— $(x, y-1)$, then set $y \leftarrow y - 1$. Interrupt to T10 if $y = y'$; otherwise set $Q \leftarrow Q - S$, $R \leftarrow R - b$, $S \leftarrow S - 2c$.

T8. [Move left.] Create the edge (x, y) —— $(x-1, y)$, then set $x \leftarrow x - 1$. Interrupt to T11 if $x = x'$; otherwise set $Q \leftarrow Q - R$, $R \leftarrow R - 2a$, $S \leftarrow S - b$.

T9. [Move right.] Create the edge (x, y) —— $(x+1, y)$, then set $x \leftarrow x + 1$. Interrupt to T11 if $x = x'$; otherwise set $Q \leftarrow Q + R$, $R \leftarrow R + 2a$, $S \leftarrow S + b$.

T10. [Finish horizontally.] While $x < x'$, create the edge (x, y) —— $(x+1, y)$ and set $x \leftarrow x + 1$. While $x > x'$, create the edge (x, y) —— $(x-1, y)$ and set $x \leftarrow x - 1$. Terminate the algorithm.

T11. [Finish vertically.] While $y < y'$, create the edge (x, y) —— $(x, y+1)$ and set $y \leftarrow y + 1$. While $y > y'$, create the edge (x, y) —— $(x, y-1)$ and set $y \leftarrow y - 1$. Terminate the algorithm. ∎

For example, when this algorithm is invoked with $(x, y) = (20, 0)$, $(x', y') = (0, 10)$, and $Q(x, y) = 4x^2 + 16y^2 - 4x - 16y - 1595$, it will create the edges $(20, 0)$ —— $(20, 1)$ —— $(20, 2)$ —— $(19, 2)$ —— $(19, 3)$ —— $(19, 4)$ —— $(18, 4)$ —— $(18, 5)$ —— $(17, 5)$ —— $(17, 6)$ —— $\cdots$ —— $(5, 9)$ —— $(5, 10)$, then make a beeline for $(0, 10)$. (See (165) and (171).) Exercise 182 explains why it works.

Movement to the right in step T9 is conveniently implemented by setting $H(y) \leftarrow H(y) \oplus (1 \ll (x_{\max} - x))$, using the H vectors of (166) and (167). Movement to the left is similar, but we set $x \leftarrow x - 1$ first. Step T10 could set

$$H(y) \leftarrow H(y) \oplus ((1 \ll (x_{\max}+1-\min(x, x'))) - (1 \ll (x_{\max}-\max(x, x')))); \quad (172)$$

but one move at a time might be just as good, because $|x' - x|$ is often small. Movement up or down needs no action, because vertical edges are redundant.

Notice that the algorithm runs somewhat faster in the special case when $b = 0$; circles always belong to this case. The even more special case of straight lines, when $a = b = c = 0$, is of course faster yet; then we have a simple *one-register* algorithm (see exercise 185).

Fig. 18. Pixels change from white to black and back again, at the edges of digitized circles.

When many contours are filled in the same image, using H vectors, the pixel values change between black and white whenever we cross an odd number of edges. Figure 18 illustrates a tiling of the hyperbolic plane by equilateral $45°$-$45°$-$45°$ triangles, obtained by superimposing the results of several hundred applications of Algorithm T.

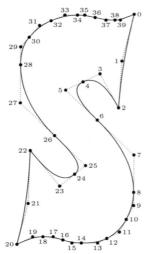

Fig. 19. Squines that define the outline contour of an '**S**'.

Algorithm T applies only to conic curves. But that's not really a limitation in practice, because just about every shape we ever need to draw can be well approximated by "piecewise conics" called quadratic Bézier splines or *squines*. For example, Fig. 19 shows a typical squine curve with 40 points $(z_0, z_1, \ldots, z_{39}, z_{40})$, where $z_{40} = z_0$. The even-numbered points $(z_0, z_2, \ldots, z_{40})$ lie on the curve; the others, $(z_1, z_3, \ldots, z_{39})$, are called "control points," because they regulate local bending and flexing. Each section $S(z_{2j}, z_{2j+1}, z_{2j+2})$ begins at point z_{2j}, traveling in direction $z_{2j+1} - z_{2j}$. It ends at point z_{2j+2}, traveling in direction $z_{2j+2} - z_{2j+1}$. Thus if z_{2j} lies on the straight line from z_{2j-1} to z_{2j+1}, the squine passes smoothly through point z_{2j} without changing direction.

Exercise 186 defines $S(z_{2j}, z_{2j+1}, z_{2j+2})$ precisely, and exercise 187 explains how to digitize any squine curve using Algorithm T. The region inside the digitized edges can then be filled with black pixels.

Incidentally, the task of *drawing* lines and curves on a bitmap turns out to be much more difficult than the task of *filling* a digitized contour, because we want diagonal strokes to have the same apparent thickness as vertical and horizontal strokes do. An excellent solution to the line-drawing problem was found by John D. Hobby, *JACM* **36** (1989), 209–229.

*Branchless computation. Modern computers tend to slow down when a program contains conditional branch instructions, because an uncertain flow of control can interfere with predictive lookahead circuitry. Therefore we've used `MMIX`'s conditional-set instructions like `CSNZ` in programs like (56). Indeed, four instructions such as 'ADD z,y,1; SR t,u,2; CSNZ x,q,z; CSNZ v,q,t' are probably faster than their three-instruction counterpart

$$\text{BZ q,@+12;   ADD x,y,1;   SR v,u,2} \qquad (173)$$

when the actual running time is measured on a highly pipelined machine, even though the rule-of-thumb cost of (173) is only $3v$ according to Table 1.3.1'–1.

Bitwise operations can help diminish the need for costly branching. For example, if MMIX didn't have a CSNZ instruction we could write

$$\begin{array}{llll}
\texttt{NEGU m,q;} & \texttt{OR m,m,q;} & \texttt{SR m,m,63;} & \\
\texttt{ADD t,y,1;} & \texttt{XOR t,t,x;} & \texttt{AND t,t,m;} & \texttt{XOR x,x,t;} \\
\texttt{SR t,u,2;} & \texttt{XOR t,t,v;} & \texttt{AND t,t,m;} & \texttt{XOR v,v,t;}
\end{array} \qquad (174)$$

here the first line creates the mask $\texttt{m} = -[q \neq 0]$. On some computers these eleven branchless instructions would still run faster than the three instructions in (173).

The inner loop of a merge sort algorithm provides an instructive example. Suppose we want to do the following operations repeatedly:

> If $x_i < y_j$, set $z_k \leftarrow x_i$, $i \leftarrow i+1$, and go to x_done if $i = i_{\max}$.
>
> Otherwise set $z_k \leftarrow y_j$, $j \leftarrow j+1$, and go to y_done if $j = j_{\max}$.
>
> Then set $k \leftarrow k+1$ and go to z_done if $k = k_{\max}$.

If we implement them in the "obvious" way, four conditional branches are involved, three of which are active on each path through the loop:

```
1H CMP   t,xi,yj; BNN t,2F      Branch if xi ≥ yj.
   STO   xi,zbase,kk            zk ← xi.
   ADD   ii,ii,8                i ← i + 1.
   BZ    ii,X_Done              To x_done if i = imax.
   LDO   xi,xbase,ii            Load xi into register xi.
   JMP   3F                     Join the other branch.
2H STO   yj,zbase,kk            zk ← yj.
   ADD   jj,jj,8                j ← j + 1.
   BZ    jj,Y_Done              To y_done if j = jmax.
   LDO   yj,ybase,jj            Load yj into register yj.
3H ADD   kk,kk,8                k ← k + 1.
   PBNZ  kk,1B                  Repeat if k ≠ kmax.
   JMP   Z_Done                 To z_done. ∎
```

(Here $\texttt{ii} = 8(i - i_{\max})$, $\texttt{jj} = 8(j - j_{\max})$, and $\texttt{kk} = 8(k - k_{\max})$; the factor of 8 is needed because x_i, y_j, and z_k are octabytes.) Those four branches can be reduced to just one:

```
1H CMP   t,xi,yj                t ← sign(xi − yj).
   CSN   yj,t,xi                yj ← min(xi, yj).
   STO   yj,zbase,kk            zk ← yj.
   AND   t,t,8                  t ← 8[xi < yj].
   ADD   ii,ii,t                i ← i + [xi < yj].
   LDO   xi,xbase,ii            Load xi into register xi.
   XOR   t,t,8                  t ← t ⊕ 8.
   ADD   jj,jj,t                j ← j + [xi ≥ yj].
   LDO   yj,ybase,jj            Load yj into register yj.
   ADD   kk,kk,8                k ← k + 1.
   AND   u,ii,jj; AND u,u,kk    u ← ii & jj & kk.
   PBN   u,1B                   Repeat if i < imax, j < jmax, and k < kmax. ∎
```

When the loop stops in this version, we can readily decide whether to continue at x_done, y_done, or z_done. These instructions load both x_i and y_j from memory each time, but the redundant value will already be present in the cache.

*More applications of MOR and MXOR. Let's finish off our study of bitwise
manipulation by taking a look at two operations that are specifically designed for
64-bit work. MMIX's instructions MOR and MXOR, which essentially carry out matrix
multiplication on 8×8 Boolean matrices, turn out to be extremely flexible and
powerful, both by themselves and in combination with other bitwise operations.

If $x = (x_7 \ldots x_1 x_0)_{256}$ is an octabyte and $a = (a_7 \ldots a_1 a_0)_2$ is a single byte,
the instruction MOR t,x,a sets $t \leftarrow a_7 x_7 \mid \cdots \mid a_1 x_1 \mid a_0 x_0$, while MXOR t,x,a sets
$t \leftarrow a_7 x_7 \oplus \cdots \oplus a_1 x_1 \oplus a_0 x_0$. For example, MOR t,x,2 and MXOR t,x,2 both set
$t \leftarrow x_1$; MOR t,x,3 sets $t \leftarrow x_1 \mid x_0$; and MXOR t,x,3 sets $t \leftarrow x_1 \oplus x_0$.

In general, of course, MOR and MXOR are functions of octabytes. When $y =
(y_7 \ldots y_1 y_0)_{256}$ is a general octabyte, the instruction MOR t,x,y produces the
octabyte t whose jth byte t_j is the result of MOR applied to x and y_j.

Suppose $x = -1 = {}^\#\texttt{ffffffffffffffff}$. Then MOR t,x,y computes the
mask t in which byte t_j is ${}^\#\texttt{ff}$ whenever $y_j \neq 0$, while t_j is zero when $y_j = 0$. This
simple special case is quite useful, because it accomplishes in just one instruction
what we previously needed seven operations to achieve in situations like (92).

We observed in (66) that two MORs will suffice to reverse the bits of any 64-bit
word, and many other important bit permutations also become easy when MOR
is in a computer's repertoire. Suppose π is a permutation of $\{0, 1, \ldots, 7\}$ that
takes $0 \mapsto 0\pi$, $1 \mapsto 1\pi$, $\ldots$, $7 \mapsto 7\pi$. Then the octabyte $p = (2^{7\pi} \ldots 2^{1\pi} 2^{0\pi})_{256}$
corresponds to a permutation matrix that makes MOR do nice tricks: MOR t,x,p
will *permute the bytes* of x, setting $t_j \leftarrow x_{j\pi}$. Furthermore, MOR u,p,y will
permute the bits of each byte of y, according to the *inverse* permutation; it sets
$u_j \leftarrow (a_7 \ldots a_1 a_0)_2$ when $y_j = (a_{7\pi} \ldots a_{1\pi} a_{0\pi})_2$.

With a little more skullduggery we can also expedite further permutations
such as the perfect shuffle (76), which transforms a given octabyte $z = 2^{32}x + y =
(x_{31} \ldots x_1 x_0 y_{31} \ldots y_1 y_0)_2$ into the "zippered" octabyte

$$w = x \ddagger y = (x_{31} y_{31} \ldots x_1 y_1 x_0 y_0)_2. \tag{175}$$

With appropriate permutation matrices p, q, and r, the intermediate results

$$t = (x_{31} x_{27} x_{30} x_{26} x_{29} x_{25} x_{28} x_{24} y_{31} y_{27} y_{30} y_{26} y_{29} y_{25} y_{28} y_{24} \cdots$$
$$x_7 x_3 x_6 x_2 x_5 x_1 x_4 x_0 y_7 y_3 y_6 y_2 y_5 y_1 y_4 y_0)_2, \tag{176}$$
$$u = (y_{27} y_{31} y_{26} y_{30} y_{25} y_{29} y_{24} y_{28} x_{27} x_{31} x_{26} x_{30} x_{25} x_{29} x_{24} x_{28} \cdots$$
$$y_3 y_7 y_2 y_6 y_1 y_5 y_0 y_4 x_3 x_7 x_2 x_6 x_1 x_5 x_0 x_4)_2 \tag{177}$$

can be computed quickly via the four instructions

$$\texttt{MOR t,z,p; MOR t,q,t; MOR u,t,r; MOR u,r,u;} \tag{178}$$

see exercise 204. So there's a mask m for which 'PUT rM,m; MUX w,t,u' completes
the perfect shuffle in just six cycles altogether. By contrast, the traditional
method in exercise 53 requires 30 cycles (five δ-swaps).

The analogous instruction MXOR is especially useful when binary linear algebra is involved. For example, exercise 1.3.1′–37 shows that XOR and MXOR directly
implement addition and multiplication in a finite field of 2^k elements, for $k \leq 8$.

The problem of *cyclic redundancy checking* provides an instructive example of another case where MXOR shines. Streams of data are often accompanied by "CRC bytes" in order to detect common types of transmission errors [see W. W. Peterson and D. T. Brown, *Proc. IRE* **49** (1961), 228–235]. One popular method, used for example in MP3 audio files, is to regard each byte $\alpha = (a_7 \ldots a_1 a_0)_2$ as if it were the polynomial

$$\alpha(x) = (a_7 \ldots a_1 a_0)_x = a_7 x^7 + \cdots + a_1 x + a_0. \tag{179}$$

When transmitting n bytes $\alpha_{n-1} \ldots \alpha_1 \alpha_0$, we then compute the remainder

$$\beta = \left(\alpha_{n-1}(x) x^{8(n-1)} + \cdots + \alpha_1(x) x^8 + \alpha_0(x)\right) x^{16} \bmod p(x), \tag{180}$$

where $p(x) = x^{16} + x^{15} + x^2 + 1$, using polynomial arithmetic mod 2, and append the coefficients of β as a 16-bit redundancy check.

The usual way to compute β is to process one byte at a time, according to classical methods like Algorithm 4.6.1D. The basic idea is to define the partial result $\beta_m = \left(\alpha_{n-1}(x) x^{8(n-1)} + \cdots + \alpha_m(x) x^{8m}\right) x^{16} \bmod p(x)$ so that $\beta_n = 0$, and then to use the recursion

$$\beta_m = ((\beta_{m+1} \ll 8) \mathbin{\&} {}^{\#}\mathtt{ff00}) \oplus crc\_table[(\beta_{m+1} \gg 8) \oplus \alpha_m] \tag{181}$$

to decrease m by 1 until $m = 0$. Here $crc\_table[\alpha]$ is a 16-bit table entry that holds the remainder of $\alpha(x) x^{16}$, modulo $p(x)$ and mod 2, for $0 \le \alpha < 256$. [See A. Perez, *IEEE Micro* **3**, 3 (June 1983), 40–50.]

But of course we'd prefer to process 64 bits at once instead of 8. The solution is to find 8×8 matrices A and B such that

$$\alpha(x) x^{64} \equiv (\alpha A)(x) + (\alpha B)(x) x^{-8} \quad (\text{modulo } p(x) \text{ and } 2), \tag{182}$$

for arbitrary bytes α, considering α to be a 1×8 vector of bits. Then we can pad the given data bytes $\alpha_{n-1} \ldots \alpha_1 \alpha_0$ with leading zeros so that n is a multiple of 8, and use the following efficient reduction method:

Begin with $c \leftarrow 0$, $n \leftarrow n - 8$, and $t \leftarrow (\alpha_{n+7} \ldots \alpha_n)_{256}$.
While $n > 0$, set $u \leftarrow t \cdot A$, $v \leftarrow t \cdot B$, $n \leftarrow n - 8$, $\qquad$ (183)
$\quad t \leftarrow (\alpha_{n+7} \ldots \alpha_n)_{256} \oplus u \oplus (v \gg 8) \oplus (c \ll 56)$, and $c \leftarrow v \mathbin{\&} {}^{\#}\mathtt{ff}$.

Here $t \cdot A$ and $t \cdot B$ denote matrix multiplication via MXOR. The desired CRC bytes, $(t x^{16} + c x^8) \bmod p(x)$, are then readily obtained from the 64-bit quantity t and the 8-bit quantity c. Exercise 213 contains full details; the total running time for n bytes comes to only $(\mu + 10\nu) n/8 + O(1)$.

The exercises below contain many more instances where MOR and MXOR lead to substantial economies. New tricks undoubtedly remain to be discovered.

For further reading. The book *Hacker's Delight* by Henry S. Warren, Jr. (Addison–Wesley, 2002) discusses bitwise-operations in depth, emphasizing the great variety of options that are available on real-world computers that are not as ideal as MMIX.

EXERCISES

▶ **1.** [*15*] What is the net effect of setting $x \leftarrow x \oplus y$, $y \leftarrow y \oplus (x \,\&\, m)$, $x \leftarrow x \oplus y$?

2. [*16*] (H. S. Warren, Jr.) Are any of the following relations valid for all integers x and y? (i) $x \oplus y \leq x \mid y$; (ii) $x \,\&\, y \leq x \mid y$; (iii) $|x - y| \leq x \oplus y$.

3. [*M20*] If $x = (x_{n-1} \ldots x_1 x_0)_2$ with $x_{n-1} = 1$, let $x^M = (\bar{x}_{n-1} \ldots \bar{x}_1 \bar{x}_0)_2$. Thus we have 0^M, 1^M, 2^M, 3^M, $\ldots = -1, 0, 1, 0, 3, 2, 1, 0, 7, 6, \ldots$, if we let $0^M = -1$. Prove that $(x \oplus y)^M < |x - y| \leq x \oplus y$ for all $x, y \geq 0$.

▶ **4.** [*M16*] Let $x^C = \bar{x}$, $x^N = -x$, $x^S = x+1$, and $x^P = x-1$ denote the complement, the negative, the successor, and the predecessor of an infinite-precision integer x. Then we have $x^{CC} = x^{NN} = x^{SP} = x^{PS} = x$. What are x^{CN} and x^{NC}?

5. [*M21*] Prove or disprove the following conjectured laws concerning binary shifts:
a) $(x \ll j) \ll k = x \ll (j+k)$;
b) $(x \gg j) \,\&\, (y \ll k) = ((x \gg (j+k)) \,\&\, y) \ll k = (x \,\&\, (y \ll (j+k))) \gg j$.

6. [*M22*] Find all integers x and y such that (a) $x \gg y = y \gg x$; (b) $x \ll y = y \ll x$.

7. [*M22*] (R. Schroeppel, 1972.) Find a fast way to convert the binary number $x = (\ldots x_2 x_1 x_0)_2$ to its negabinary counterpart $x = (\ldots x_2' x_1' x_0')_{-2}$, and vice versa. *Hint:* Only two bitwise operations are needed!

▶ **8.** [*M22*] Given a finite set S of nonnegative integers, the "minimal excludant" of S is defined to be

$$\operatorname{mex}(S) = \min\{\, k \mid k \geq 0 \text{ and } k \notin S \,\}.$$

Let $x \oplus S$ denote the set $\{x \oplus y \mid y \in S\}$, and let $S \oplus y$ denote $\{x \oplus y \mid x \in S\}$. Prove that if $x = \operatorname{mex}(S)$ and $y = \operatorname{mex}(T)$ then $x \oplus y = \operatorname{mex}((S \oplus y) \cup (x \oplus T))$.

9. [*M26*] (*Nim.*) Two people play a game with k piles of sticks, where there are a_j sticks in pile j. If $a_1 = \cdots = a_k = 0$ when it is a player's turn to move, that player loses; otherwise the player reduces one of the piles by any desired amount, throwing away the removed sticks, and it is the other player's turn. Prove that the player to move can force a victory if and only if $a_1 \oplus \cdots \oplus a_k \neq 0$.

10. [*HM40*] (*Nimbers*, also known as *Conway's field.*) Continuing exercise 8, define the operation $x \otimes y$ of "nim multiplication" recursively by the formula

$$x \otimes y = \operatorname{mex}\{(x \otimes j) \oplus (i \otimes y) \oplus (i \otimes j) \mid 0 \leq i < x,\, 0 \leq j < y\}.$$

Prove that $\oplus$ and $\otimes$ define a *field* over the set of all nonnegative integers. Prove also that if $0 \leq x, y < 2^{2^n}$ then $x \otimes y < 2^{2^n}$, and $2^{2^n} \otimes y = 2^{2^n} y$. (In particular, this field contains subfields of size 2^{2^n} for all $n \geq 0$.) Explain how to compute $x \otimes y$ efficiently.

▶ **11.** [*M26*] (H. W. Lenstra, 1978.) Find a simple way to characterize all pairs of positive integers (m, n) for which $m \otimes n = mn$ in Conway's field.

12. [*M26*] Devise an algorithm for *division* of nimbers. *Hint:* If $x < 2^{2^{n+1}}$ then we have $x \otimes (x \oplus (x \gg 2^n)) < 2^{2^n}$.

13. [*M32*] (*Second-order nim.*) Extend the game of exercise 9 by allowing two kinds of moves: Either a_j is reduced for some j, as before; or a_j is reduced and a_i is replaced by an arbitrary nonnegative integer, for some $i < j$. Prove that the player to move can now force a victory if and only if the pile sizes satisfy either $a_2 \neq a_3 \oplus \cdots \oplus a_k$ or $a_1 \neq a_3 \oplus (2 \otimes a_4) \oplus \cdots \oplus ((k-2) \otimes a_k)$. For example, when $k = 4$ and $(a_1, a_2, a_3, a_4) = (7, 5, 0, 5)$, the only winning move is to $(7, 5, 6, 3)$.

14. [*M30*] Suppose each node of a complete, infinite binary tree has been labeled with 0 or 1. Such a labeling is conveniently represented as a sequence $T = (t, t_0, t_1, t_{00}, t_{01}, t_{10}, t_{11}, t_{000}, \dots)$, with one bit t_α for every binary string α; the root is labeled t, the left subtree labels are $T_0 = (t_0, t_{00}, t_{01}, t_{000}, \dots)$, and the right subtree labels are $T_1 = (t_1, t_{10}, t_{11}, t_{100}, \dots)$. Any such labeling can be used to transform a 2-adic integer $x = (\dots x_2 x_1 x_0)_2$ into the 2-adic integer $y = (\dots y_2 y_1 y_0)_2 = T(x)$ by setting $y_0 = t$, $y_1 = t_{x_0}$, $y_2 = t_{x_0 x_1}$, etc., so that $T(x) = 2T_{x_0}(\lfloor x/2 \rfloor) + t$. (In other words, x defines an infinite path in the binary tree, and y corresponds to the labels on that path, from right to left in the bit strings as we proceed from top to bottom of the tree.)

A *branching function* is the mapping $x^T = x \oplus T(x)$ defined by such a labeling. For example, if $t_{01} = 1$ and all of the other t_α are 0, we have $x^T = x \oplus 4[x \bmod 4 = 2]$.

   a) Prove that every branching function is a permutation of the 2-adic integers.

   b) For which integers k is $x \oplus (x \ll k)$ a branching function?

   c) Let $x \mapsto x^T$ be a mapping from 2-adic integers into 2-adic integers. Prove that x^T is a branching function if and only if $\rho(x \oplus y) = \rho(x^T \oplus y^T)$ for all 2-adic x and y.

   d) Prove that compositions and inverses of branching functions are branching functions. (Thus the set $\mathcal{B}$ of all branching functions is a permutation group.)

   e) A branching function is *balanced* if the labels satisfy $t_\alpha = t_{\alpha 0} \oplus t_{\alpha 1}$ for all α. Show that the set of all balanced branching functions is a subgroup of $\mathcal{B}$.

▶ **15.** [*M26*] J. H. Quick noticed that $((x+2) \oplus 3) - 2 = ((x-2) \oplus 3) + 2$ for all x. Find all constants a and b such that $((x+a) \oplus b) - a = ((x-a) \oplus b) + a$ is an identity.

16. [*M31*] A function of x is called *animating* if it can be written in the form

$$((\dots ((((x + a_1) \oplus b_1) + a_2) \oplus b_2) + \cdots) + a_m) \oplus b_m$$

for some integer constants $a_1, b_1, a_2, b_2, \dots, a_m, b_m$, with $m > 0$.

   a) Prove that every animating function is a branching function (see exercise 14).

   b) Furthermore, prove that it is balanced if and only if $b_1 \oplus b_2 \oplus \cdots \oplus b_m = 0$. *Hint:* What binary tree labeling corresponds to the animating function $((x \oplus c) - 1) \oplus c$?

   c) Let $\lfloor x \rceil = x \oplus (x - 1) = 2^{\rho(x)+1} - 1$. Show that every balanced animating function can be written in the form

$$x \oplus \lfloor x \oplus p_1 \rceil \oplus \lfloor x \oplus p_2 \rceil \oplus \cdots \oplus \lfloor x \oplus p_l \rceil, \qquad p_1 < p_2 < \cdots < p_l,$$

for some integers $\{p_1, p_2, \dots, p_l\}$, where $l \geq 0$, and this representation is unique.

   d) Conversely, show that every such expression defines a balanced animating function.

17. [*HM36*] The results of exercise 16 make it possible to decide whether or not any two given animating functions are equal. Is there an algorithm that decides whether *any* given expression is identically zero, when that expression is constructed from a finite number of integer variables and constants using only the binary operations $+$ and $\oplus$? What if we also allow $\&$?

18. [*M25*] The curious pixel pattern shown here has $(x^2 y \gg 11) \& 1$ in row x and column y, for $1 \leq x, y \leq 256$. Is there any simple way to explain some of its major characteristics mathematically?

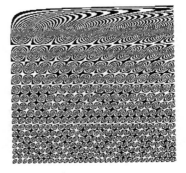

▶ **19.** [*M37*] (*Paley's rearrangement theorem.*) Given three vectors $A = (a_0, \ldots, a_{2^n-1})$, $B = (b_0, \ldots, b_{2^n-1})$, and $C = (c_0, \ldots, c_{2^n-1})$ of nonnegative numbers, let

$$f(A, B, C) = \sum_{j \oplus k \oplus l = 0} a_j b_k c_l.$$

For example, if $n = 2$ we have $f(A, B, C) = a_0 b_0 c_0 + a_0 b_1 c_1 + a_0 b_2 c_2 + a_0 b_3 c_3 + a_1 b_0 c_1 + a_1 b_1 c_0 + a_1 b_2 c_3 + \cdots + a_3 b_3 c_0$; in general there are 2^{2n} terms, one for each choice of j and k. Our goal is to prove that $f(A, B, C) \le f(A^*, B^*, C^*)$, where A^* denotes the vector A sorted into nonincreasing order: $a_0^* \ge a_1^* \ge \cdots \ge a_{2^n-1}^*$.

    a) Prove the result when all elements of A, B, and C are 0s and 1s.
    b) Show that it is therefore true in general.
    c) Similarly, $f(A, B, C, D) = \sum_{j \oplus k \oplus l \oplus m = 0} a_j b_k c_l d_m \le f(A^*, B^*, C^*, D^*)$.

▶ **20.** [*21*] (*Gosper's hack.*) The following seven operations produce a useful function y of x, when x is a positive integer. Explain what this function is and why it is useful.

$$u \leftarrow x \mathbin{\&} -x; \qquad v \leftarrow x + u; \qquad y \leftarrow v + (((v \oplus x)/u) \gg 2).$$

21. [*22*] Construct the *reverse* of Gosper's hack: Show how to compute x from y.

22. [*21*] Implement Gosper's hack efficiently with MMIX code, assuming that $x < 2^{64}$, without using division.

▶ **23.** [*27*] A sequence of nested parentheses can be represented as a binary number by putting a 1 in the position of each right parenthesis. For example, '(())()' corresponds in this way to $(001101)_2$, the number 13. Call such a number a *parenthesis trace*.

    a) What are the smallest and largest parenthesis traces that have exactly m 1s?
    b) Suppose x is a parenthesis trace and y is the next larger parenthesis trace with the same number of 1s. Show that y can be computed from x with a short chain of operations analogous to Gosper's hack.
    c) Implement your method on MMIX, assuming that $\nu x \le 32$.

▶ **24.** [*M30*] Program 1.3.2′P instructed MMIX to produce a table of the first five hundred prime numbers, using trial division to establish primality. Write an MMIX program that uses the "sieve of Eratosthenes" (exercise 4.5.4–8) to build a table of all odd primes that are less than N, packed into octabytes $Q_0, Q_1, \ldots, Q_{N/128-1}$ as in (27). Assume that $N \le 2^{32}$, and that it's a multiple of 128. What is the running time when $N = 3584$?

▶ **25.** [*15*] Four volumes sit side by side on a bookshelf. Each of them contains exactly 500 pages, printed on 250 sheets of paper 0.1 mm thick; each book also has a front and back cover whose thicknesses are 1 mm each. A bookworm gnaws its way from page 1 of Volume 1 to page 500 of Volume 4. How far does it travel while doing so?

26. [*22*] Suppose we want random access to a table of 12 million items of 5-bit data. We could pack 12 such items into one 64-bit word, thereby fitting the table into 8 megabytes of memory. But random access then seems to require division by 12, which is rather slow; we might therefore prefer to let each item occupy a full byte, thus using 12 megabytes altogether.

    Show, however, that there's a memory-efficient approach that avoids division.

27. [*21*] In the notation of Eqs. (32)–(43), how would you compute (a) $(\alpha 10^a 01^b)_2$? (b) $(\alpha 10^a 11^b)_2$? (c) $(\alpha 00^a 01^b)_2$? (d) $(0^\infty 11^a 00^b)_2$? (e) $(0^\infty 01^a 00^b)_2$? (f) $(0^\infty 11^a 11^b)_2$?

28. [*16*] What does the operation $(x+1) \mathbin{\&} \bar{x}$ produce?

29. [*20*] (V. R. Pratt.) Express the magic mask μ_k of (47) in terms of μ_{k+1}.

30. [20] If $x = 0$, the MMIX instructions (46) will set $\rho \leftarrow 64$ (which is a close enough approximation to ∞). What changes to (50) and (51) will produce the same result?

▶ **31.** [20] A mathematician named Dr. L. I. Presume decided to calculate the ruler function with a simple loop as follows: "Set $\rho \leftarrow 0$; then while $x \& 1 = 0$, set $\rho \leftarrow \rho + 1$ and $x \leftarrow x \gg 1$." He reasoned that, when x is a random integer, the average number of right shifts is the average value of ρ, which is 1; and the standard deviation is only $\sqrt{2}$, so the loop almost always terminates quickly. Criticize his decision.

32. [20] What is the execution time for ρx when (52) is programmed for MMIX?

▶ **33.** [26] (Leiserson, Prokop, and Randall, 1998.) Show that if '58' is replaced by '49' in (52), we can use that method to identify *both* bits of the number $y = 2^j + 2^k$ quickly, when $64 > j > k \geq 0$. (Altogether $\binom{64}{2} = 2016$ cases need to be distinguished.)

34. [M23] Let x and y be 2-adic integers. True or false: (a) $\rho(x \& y) = \max(\rho x, \rho y)$; (b) $\rho(x \mid y) = \min(\rho x, \rho y)$; (c) $\rho x = \rho y$ if and only if $x \oplus y = (x-1) \oplus (y-1)$.

▶ **35.** [M26] According to Reitwiesner's theorem, exercise 4.1–34, every integer n has a unique representation $n = n^+ - n^-$ such that $\nu(n^+) + \nu(n^-)$ is minimized. Show that n^+ and n^- can be calculated quickly with bitwise operations. *Hint:* Prove the identity $(x \oplus 3x) \& ((x \oplus 3x) \gg 1) = 0$.

36. [20] Given $x = (x_{63} \ldots x_1 x_0)_2$, suggest efficient ways to calculate the quantities
   i) $x^\oplus = (x_{63}^\oplus \ldots x_1^\oplus x_0^\oplus)_2$, where $x_k^\oplus = x_k \oplus \cdots \oplus x_1 \oplus x_0$ for $0 \leq k < 64$;
   ii) $x^\& = (x_{63}^\& \ldots x_1^\& x_0^\&)_2$, where $x_k^\& = x_k \wedge \cdots \wedge x_1 \wedge x_0$ for $0 \leq k < 64$.

37. [16] What changes to (55) and (56) will make $\lambda 0$ come out -1?

38. [17] How long does the leftmost-bit-extraction procedure (57) take when implemented on MMIX?

▶ **39.** [20] Formula (43) shows how to remove the rightmost run of 1 bits from a given number x. How would you remove the *leftmost* run of 1 bits?

▶ **40.** [21] Prove (58), and find a simple way to decide if $\lambda x < \lambda y$, given x and $y \geq 0$.

41. [M22] What are the generating functions of the integer sequences (a) ρn, (b) λn, and (c) νn?

42. [M21] If $n = 2^{e_1} + \cdots + 2^{e_r}$, with $e_1 > \cdots > e_r \geq 0$, express the sum $\sum_{k=0}^{n-1} \nu k$ in terms of the exponents $e_1, \ldots, e_r$.

▶ **43.** [20] How sparse should x be, to make (63) faster than (62) on MMIX?

▶ **44.** [23] (E. Freed, 1983.) What's a fast way to evaluate the *weighted* bit sum $\sum j x_j$?

▶ **45.** [20] (T. Rokicki, 1999.) Explain how to test if $x^R < y^R$, without reversing x and y.

46. [22] Method (68) uses six operations to interchange two bits $x_i \leftrightarrow x_j$ of a register. Show that this interchange can actually be done with only *three* MMIX instructions.

47. [10] Can the general δ-swap (69) also be done with a method like (67)?

48. [M21] How many different δ-swaps are possible in an n-bit register? (When $n = 4$, a δ-swap can transform 1234 into 1234, 1243, 1324, 1432, 2134, 2143, 3214, 3412, 4231.)

▶ **49.** [M30] Let $s(n)$ denote the fewest δ-swaps that suffice to reverse an n-bit number.
   a) Prove that $s(n) \geq \lceil \log_3 n \rceil$ when n is odd, $s(n) \geq \lceil \log_3 3n/2 \rceil$ when n is even.
   b) Evaluate $s(n)$ when $n = 3^m$, $2 \cdot 3^m$, $(3^m + 1)/2$, and $(3^m - 1)/2$.
   c) What are $s(32)$ and $s(64)$? *Hint:* Show that $s(5n+2) \leq s(n) + 2$.

50. [M37] Continuing exercise 49, prove that $s(n) = \log_3 n + O(\log \log n)$.

51. [*23*] Let c be a constant, $0 \le c < 2^d$. Find all sequences of masks $(\theta_0, \theta_1, \ldots, \theta_{d-1}, \hat{\theta}_{d-2}, \ldots, \hat{\theta}_1, \hat{\theta}_0)$ such that the general permutation scheme (71) takes $x \mapsto x^\pi$, where the bit permutation π is defined by either (a) $j\pi = j \oplus c$; or (b) $j\pi = (j + c) \bmod 2^d$. [The masks should satisfy $\theta_k \subseteq \mu_{d,k}$ and $\hat{\theta}_k \subseteq \mu_{d,k}$, so that (71) corresponds to Fig. 12; see (48). Notice that reversal, $x^\pi = x^R$, is the special case $c = 2^d - 1$ of part (a), while part (b) corresponds to the cyclic right shift $x^\pi = (x \gg c) + (x \ll (2^d - c))$.]

52. [*22*] Find hexadecimal constants $(\theta_0, \theta_1, \theta_2, \theta_3, \theta_4, \theta_5, \hat{\theta}_4, \hat{\theta}_3, \hat{\theta}_2, \hat{\theta}_1, \hat{\theta}_0)$ that cause (71) to produce the following important 64-bit permutations, based on the binary representation $j = (j_5 j_4 j_3 j_2 j_1 j_0)_2$: (a) $j\pi = (j_0 j_5 j_4 j_3 j_2 j_1)_2$; (b) $j\pi = (j_2 j_1 j_0 j_5 j_4 j_3)_2$; (c) $j\pi = (j_1 j_0 j_5 j_4 j_3 j_2)_2$; (d) $j\pi = (j_0 j_1 j_2 j_3 j_4 j_5)_2$. [Case (a) is the "perfect shuffle" (175) that takes $(x_{63} \ldots x_{33} x_{32} x_{31} \ldots x_1 x_0)_2$ into $(x_{63} x_{31} \ldots x_{33} x_1 x_{32} x_0)_2$; case (b) transposes an 8×8 matrix of bits; case (c), similarly, transposes a 4×16 matrix; and case (d) arises in connection with "fast Fourier transforms," see exercise 4.6.4–14.]

▶ **53.** [*M25*] The permutations in exercise 52 are said to be "induced by a permutation of index digits," because we obtain $j\pi$ by permuting the binary digits of j. Suppose $j\pi = (j_{(d-1)\psi} \ldots j_{1\psi} j_{0\psi})_2$, where ψ is a permutation of $\{0, 1, \ldots, d-1\}$. Prove that if ψ has t cycles, the 2^d-bit permutation $x \mapsto x^\pi$ can be obtained with only $d - t$ swaps. In particular, show that this observation speeds up all four cases of exercise 52.

54. [*22*] (R. W. Gosper, 1985.) If an $m \times m$ bit matrix is stored in the rightmost m^2 bits of a register, show that it can be transposed by doing $(2^k(m-1))$-swaps for $0 \le k < \lceil \lg m \rceil$. Write out the method in detail when $m = 7$.

▶ **55.** [*26*] Suppose an $n \times n$ bit matrix is stored in the rightmost n^2 bits of an n^3-bit register. Prove that $18d + 2$ bitwise operations suffice to multiply two such matrices, when $n = 2^d$; the matrix multiplication can be either Boolean (like MOR) or mod 2 (like MXOR).

56. [*24*] Suggest a way to transpose a 7×9 bit matrix in a 64-bit register.

57. [*22*] The network $P(2^d)$ of Fig. 12 has a total of $(2d - 1)2^{d-1}$ crossbars. Prove that any permutation of 2^d elements can be realized by some setting in which at most $d2^{d-1}$ of them are active.

▶ **58.** [*M32*] The first d columns of crossbar modules in the permutation network $P(2^d)$ perform a 1-swap, then a 2-swap, $\ldots$, and finally a 2^{d-1}-swap, when the wires of the network are stretched into horizontal lines as shown here for $d = 3$. Let $N = 2^d$. These N lines, together with the $Nd/2$ crossbars, form a so-called "Omega router." The purpose of this exercise is to study the set Ω of all permutations φ such that we can obtain $(0\varphi, 1\varphi, \ldots, (N-1)\varphi)$ as outputs on the right of an Omega router when the inputs at the left are $(0, 1, \ldots, N - 1)$.

a) Prove that $|\Omega| = 2^{Nd/2}$. (Thus $\lg |\Omega| = Nd/2 \sim \frac{1}{2} \lg N!$.)

b) Prove that a permutation φ of $\{0, 1, \ldots, N - 1\}$ belongs to Ω if and only if

$$i \bmod 2^k = j \bmod 2^k \quad \text{and} \quad i\varphi \gg k = j\varphi \gg k \quad \text{implies} \quad i\varphi = j\varphi \qquad (*)$$

for all $0 \le i, j < N$ and all $0 \le k \le d$.

c) Simplify condition $(*)$ to the following, for all $0 \le i, j < N$:

$$\lambda(i\varphi \oplus j\varphi) < \rho(i \oplus j) \quad \text{implies} \quad i = j.$$

d) Let T be the set of all permutations τ of $\{0, 1, \ldots, N - 1\}$ such that $\rho(i \oplus j) = \rho(i\tau \oplus j\tau)$ for all i and j. (This is the set of branching functions considered in exercise 14, modulo 2^d; so it has 2^{N-1} members, $2^{N/2+d-1}$ of which are the animating functions modulo 2^d.) Prove that $\varphi \in \Omega$ if and only if $\tau\varphi \in \Omega$ for all $\tau \in T$.

e) Suppose φ and ψ are permutations of Ω that operate on different elements; that is, $j\varphi \neq j$ implies $j\psi = j$, for $0 \leq j < N$. Prove that $\varphi\psi \in \Omega$.

59. [*M30*] Given $0 \leq a < b < N = 2^d$, how many Omega-routable permutations operate only on the interval $[a \mathinner{.\,.} b]$? (Thus we want to count the number of $\varphi \in \Omega$ such that $j\varphi \neq j$ implies $a \leq j \leq b$. Exercise 58(a) is the special case $a = 0$, $b = N - 1$.)

60. [*HM28*] Given a random permutation of $\{0, 1, \ldots, 2n-1\}$, let p_{nk} be the probability that there are 2^k ways to set the crossbars in the first and last columns of the permutation network $P(2n)$ when realizing this permutation. In other words, p_{nk} is the probability that the associated graph has k cycles (see (75)). What is the generating function $\sum_{k\geq 0} p_{nk} z^k$? What are the mean and variance of 2^k?

61. [*46*] Is it NP-hard to decide whether a given permutation is realizable with at least one mask $\theta_j = 0$, using the recursive method of Fig. 12 as implemented in (71)?

▶ **62.** [*22*] Let $N = 2^d$. We can obviously represent a permutation π of $\{0, 1, \ldots, N-1\}$ by storing a table of N numbers, d bits each. With this representation we have instant access to $y = x\pi$, given x; but it takes $\Omega(N)$ steps to find $x = y\pi^-$ when y is given.

Show that, with the same amount of memory, we can represent an arbitrary permutation in such a way that $x\pi$ and $y\pi^-$ are both computable in $O(d)$ steps.

63. [*19*] For what integers w, x, y, and z does the zipper function satisfy (i) $x\ddagger y = y\ddagger x$? (ii) $(x\ddagger y) \gg z = (x \gg \lceil z/2 \rceil) \ddagger (y \gg \lfloor z/2 \rfloor)$? (iii) $(w\ddagger x) \mathbin{\&} (y\ddagger z) = (w \mathbin{\&} y) \ddagger (x \mathbin{\&} z)$?

64. [*22*] Find a "simple" expression for the zipper-of-sums $(x + x') \ddagger (y + y')$, as a function of $z = x \ddagger y$ and $z' = x' \ddagger y'$.

65. [*M16*] The binary polynomial $u(x) = u_0 + u_1 x + \cdots + u_{n-1} x^{n-1} \pmod 2$ can be represented by the integer $u = (u_{n-1} \ldots u_1 u_0)_2$. If $u(x)$ and $v(x)$ correspond to integers u and v in this way, what polynomial corresponds to $u \ddagger v$?

▶ **66.** [*M26*] Suppose the polynomial $u(x)$ has been represented as an n-bit integer u as in exercise 65, and let $v = u \oplus (u \ll \delta) \oplus (u \ll 2\delta) \oplus (u \ll 3\delta) \oplus \cdots$ for some integer δ.

a) What's a simple way to describe the polynomial $v(x)$?

b) Suppose n is large, and the bits of u have been packed into 64-bit words. How would you compute v when $\delta = 1$, using bitwise operations in 64-bit registers?

c) Consider the same question as (b), but when $\delta = 64$.

d) Consider the same question as (b), but when $\delta = 3$.

e) Consider the same question as (b), but when $\delta = 67$.

67. [*M31*] If $u(x)$ is a polynomial of degree $< n$, represented as in exercise 65, discuss the computation of $v(x) = u(x)^2 \bmod (x^n + x^m + 1)$, when $0 < m < n$ and both m and n are odd. *Hint:* This problem has an interesting connection with perfect shuffling.

68. [*20*] What three MMIX instructions implement the δ-shift operation, (79)?

69. [*25*] Prove that method (80) always extracts the proper bits when the masks θ_k have been set up properly: We never clobber any of the crucial bits y_j.

▶ **70.** [*31*] (Guy L. Steele Jr., 1994.) What's a good way to compute the masks θ_0, θ_1, $\ldots$, θ_{d-1} that are needed in the general compression procedure (80), given $\chi \neq 0$?

71. [*17*] Explain how to *reverse* the procedure of (80), going from the compact value $y = (y_{r-1} \ldots y_1 y_0)_2$ to a number $z = (z_{63} \ldots z_1 z_0)_2$ that has $z_{j_i} = y_i$ for $0 \leq i < r$.

72. [*10*] Simplify the expression $(x\ddagger y) \mathbin{\cdot\!|\cdot} \mu_0$, when $x, y < 2^{2^{d-1}}$. (See Eqs. (76) and (81).)

73. [*22*] Prove that d sheep-and-goats steps will implement any 2^d-bit permutation.

74. [*22*] Given counts $(c_0, c_1, \ldots, c_{2^d-1})$ for the Chung–Wong procedure, explain why an appropriate cyclic 1-shift can always produce new counts $(c'_0, c'_1, \ldots, c'_{2^d-1})$ for which $\sum c'_{2l} = \sum c'_{2l+1}$, thus allowing the recursion to proceed.

▶ **75.** [*32*] The method of Chung and Wong replicates bit l of a register exactly c_l times, but it produces results in scrambled order. For example, the case $(c_0, \ldots, c_7) = (1, 2, 0, 2, 0, 2, 0, 1)$ illustrated in the text produces $(x_7 x_3 x_1 x_5 x_5 x_3 x_1 x_0)_2$. In some applications this can be a disadvantage; we might prefer to have the bits retain their original order, namely $(x_7 x_5 x_5 x_3 x_3 x_1 x_1 x_0)_2$ in that example.

Prove that the permutation network $P(2^d)$ of Fig. 12 can be modified to achieve this goal, given any sequence of counts $(c_0, c_1, \ldots, c_{2^d-1})$, if we replace the $d \cdot 2^{d-1}$ crossbar modules in the right-hand half by general 2×2 *mapping modules*. (A crossbar module with inputs (a, b) produces either (a, b) or (b, a) as output; a mapping module can also produce (a, a) or (b, b).)

76. [*47*] A *mapping network* is analogous to a sorting network or a permutation network, but it uses 2×2 mapping modules instead of comparators or crossbars, and it is supposed to be able to output all n^n possible mappings of its n inputs. Exercise 75, in conjunction with Fig. 12, shows that a mapping network for $n = 2^d$ exists with only $4d-2$ levels of delay, and with $n/2$ modules on each level; furthermore, this construction needs general 2×2 mapping modules (instead of simple crossbars) in only d of those levels.

To within $O(n)$, what is the smallest number $G(n)$ of modules that are sufficient to implement a general n-element mapping network?

77. [*26*] (R. W. Floyd and V. R. Pratt.) Design an algorithm that tests whether or not a given standard n-network is a sorting network, as defined in the exercises of Section 5.3.4. When the given network has r comparator modules, your algorithm should use $O(r)$ bitwise operations on words of length 2^n.

78. [*M27*] (*Testing disjointness.*) Suppose the binary numbers $x_1, x_2, \ldots, x_m$ each represent sets in a universe of $n - k$ elements, so that each x_j is less than 2^{n-k}. J. H. Quick (a student) decided to test whether the sets are disjoint by testing the condition

$$x_1 \mid x_2 \mid \cdots \mid x_m = (x_1 + x_2 + \cdots + x_m) \bmod 2^n.$$

Prove or disprove: Quick's test is valid if and only if $k \geq \lg(m-1)$.

▶ **79.** [*20*] If $x \neq 0$ and $x \subseteq \chi$, what is an easy way to determine the largest integer $x_, < x$ such that $x_, \subseteq \chi$? (Thus $(x_,)' = (x')_, = x$, in connection with (84).)

80. [*20*] Suggest a fast way to find all maximal proper subsets of a set. More precisely, given χ with $\nu\chi = m$, we want to find all $x \subseteq \chi$ such that $\nu x = m - 1$.

81. [*21*] Find a formula for "scattered difference," to go with the "scattered sum" (86).

82. [*21*] Is it easy to shift a scattered accumulator to the left by 1, for example to change $(y_2 x_4 x_3 y_1 x_2 y_0 x_1 x_0)_2$ to $(y_1 x_4 x_3 y_0 x_2 0 x_1 x_0)_2$?

▶ **83.** [*33*] Continuing exercise 82, find a way to shift a scattered 2^d-bit accumulator to the *right* by 1, given z and χ, in $O(d)$ steps.

84. [*25*] Given n-bit numbers $z = (z_{n-1} \ldots z_1 z_0)_2$ and $\chi = (\chi_{n-1} \ldots \chi_1 \chi_0)_2$, explain how to calculate the "stretched" quantities $z \leftharpoondown \chi = (z_{(n-1)\leftharpoondown\chi} \cdots z_{1\leftharpoondown\chi} z_{0\leftharpoondown\chi})_2$ and $z \rightharpoondown \chi = (z_{(n-1)\rightharpoondown\chi} \cdots z_{1\rightharpoondown\chi} z_{0\rightharpoondown\chi})_2$, where

$$j \leftharpoondown \chi = \max\{k \mid k \leq j \text{ and } \chi_k = 1\}, \qquad j \rightharpoondown \chi = \min\{k \mid k \geq j \text{ and } \chi_k = 1\};$$

we let $z_{j\leftarrow\chi} = 0$ if $\chi_k = 0$ for $0 \le k \le j$, and $z_{j\to\chi} = 0$ if $\chi_k = 0$ for $n > k \ge j$. For example, if $n = 11$ and $\chi = (01101110010)_2$, then $z \leftarrow \chi = (z_9 z_9 z_8 z_6 z_6 z_5 z_4 z_1 z_1 z_1 0)_2$ and $z \to \chi = (0 z_9 z_8 z_8 z_6 z_5 z_4 z_4 z_4 z_1 z_1)_2$.

85. [22] (K. D. Tocher, 1954.) Imagine that you have a vintage 1950s computer with a drum memory for storing data, and that you need to do some computations with a $32 \times 32 \times 32$ array $a[i, j, k]$, whose subscripts are 5-bit integers in the range $0 \le i, j, k < 32$. Unfortunately your machine has only a very small high-speed memory: You can access only 128 consecutive elements of the array in fast memory at any time. Since your application usually moves from $a[i, j, k]$ to a neighboring position $a[i', j', k']$, where $|i - i'| + |j - j'| + |k - k'| = 1$, you have decided to allocate the array so that, if $i = (i_4 i_3 i_2 i_1 i_0)_2$, $j = (j_4 j_3 j_2 j_1 j_0)_2$, and $k = (k_4 k_3 k_2 k_1 k_0)_2$, the array entry $a[i, j, k]$ is stored in drum location $(k_4 j_4 i_4 k_3 j_3 i_3 k_2 j_2 i_2 k_1 j_1 i_1 k_0 j_0 i_0)_2$. By interleaving the bits in this way, a small change to i, j, or k will cause only a small change in the address.

Discuss the implementation of this addressing function: (a) How does it change when i, j, or k changes by ± 1? (b) How would you handle a random access to $a[i, j, k]$, given i, j, and k? (c) How would you detect a "page fault" (namely, the condition that a new segment of 128 elements must be swapped into fast memory from the drum)?

86. [M27] An array of $2^p \times 2^q \times 2^r$ elements is to be allocated by putting $a[i, j, k]$ into a location whose bits are the $p + q + r$ bits of (i, j, k), permuted in some fashion. Furthermore, this array is to be stored in an external memory using pages of size 2^s. (Exercise 85 considers the case $p = q = r = 5$ and $s = 7$.) What allocation strategy of this kind minimizes the number of times that $a[i, j, k]$ is on a different page from $a[i', j', k']$, summed over all i, j, k, i', j', and k' such that $|i - i'| + |j - j'| + |k - k'| = 1$?

▸ **87.** [20] Suppose each byte of a 64-bit word x contains an ASCII code that represents either a letter, a digit, or a space. What three bitwise operations will convert all the lowercase letters to uppercase?

88. [20] Given $x = (x_7 \ldots x_0)_{256}$ and $y = (y_7 \ldots y_0)_{256}$, compute $z = (z_7 \ldots z_0)_{256}$, where $z_j = (x_j - y_j) \bmod 256$ for $0 \le j < 8$. (See the addition operation in (87).)

89. [23] Given $x = (x_{31} \ldots x_1 x_0)_4$ and $y = (y_{31} \ldots y_1 y_0)_4$, compute $z = (z_{31} \ldots z_1 z_0)_4$, where $z_j = \lfloor x_j/y_j \rfloor$ for $0 \le j < 32$, assuming that no y_j is zero.

90. [20] The bytewise averaging rule (88) always rounds downward when $x_j + y_j$ is odd. Make it less biased by rounding to the nearest odd integer in such cases.

▸ **91.** [26] (*Alpha channels.*) Recipe (88) is a good way to compute bytewise averages, but applications to computer graphics often require a more general blending of 8-bit values. Given three octabytes $x = (x_7 \ldots x_0)_{256}$, $y = (y_7 \ldots y_0)_{256}$, $\alpha = (a_7 \ldots a_0)_{256}$, show that bitwise operations allow us to compute $z = (z_7 \ldots z_0)_{256}$, where each byte z_j is a good approximation to $((255 - a_j)x_j + a_j y_j)/255$, *without* doing any multiplication. Implement your method with MMIX instructions.

▸ **92.** [21] What happens if the second line of (88) is changed to '$z \leftarrow (x \mid y) - z$'?

93. [18] What basic formula for subtraction is analogous to formula (89) for addition?

94. [21] Let $x = (x_7 \ldots x_1 x_0)_{256}$ and $t = (t_7 \ldots t_1 t_0)_{256}$ in (90). Can t_j be nonzero when x_j is nonzero? Can t_j be zero when x_j is zero?

95. [22] What's a bitwise way to tell if all bytes of $x = (x_7 \ldots x_1 x_0)_{256}$ are distinct?

96. [21] Explain (93), and find a similar formula that sets test flags $t_j \leftarrow 128[x_j \le y_j]$.

97. [23] Leslie Lamport's paper in 1975 presented the following "problem taken from an actual compiler optimization algorithm": Given octabytes $x = (x_7 \ldots x_0)_{256}$ and $y =$

$(y_7 \ldots y_0)_{256}$, compute $t = (t_7 \ldots t_0)_{256}$ and $z = (z_7 \ldots z_0)_{256}$ so that $t_j \neq 0$ if and only if $x_j \neq 0$, $x_j \neq$ '*', and $x_j \neq y_j$; and $z_j = (x_j = 0?\ y_j: (x_j \neq$ '*' $\wedge x_j \neq y_j?$ '*': $x_j))$.

98. [20] Given $x = (x_7 \ldots x_0)_{256}$ and $y = (y_7 \ldots y_0)_{256}$, compute $z = (z_7 \ldots z_0)_{256}$ and $w = (w_7 \ldots w_0)_{256}$, where $z_j = \max(x_j, y_j)$ and $w_j = \min(x_j, y_j)$ for $0 \leq j < 8$.

▶ **99.** [28] Find hexadecimal constants a, b, c, d, e such that the six bitwise operations

$$y \leftarrow x \oplus a, \quad t \leftarrow ((((y \mathbin{\&} b) + c) \mid y) \oplus d) \mathbin{\&} e$$

will compute the flags $t = (f_7 \ldots f_1 f_0)_{256} \ll 7$ from any bytes $x = (x_7 \ldots x_1 x_0)_{256}$, where

$$f_0 = [x_0 = \text{'!'}], \quad f_1 = [x_1 \neq \text{'*'}], \quad f_2 = [x_2 < \text{'A'}], \quad f_3 = [x_3 > \text{'z'}], \quad f_4 = [x_4 \geq \text{'a'}],$$
$$f_5 = [x_5 \in \{\text{'0'}, \text{'1'}, \ldots, \text{'9'}\}], \quad f_6 = [x_6 \leq 168], \quad f_7 = [x_7 \in \{\text{'<'}, \text{'='}, \text{'>'}, \text{'?'}\}].$$

100. [25] Suppose $x = (x_{15} \ldots x_1 x_0)_{16}$ and $y = (y_{15} \ldots y_1 y_0)_{16}$ are *binary-coded decimal* numbers, where $0 \leq x_j, y_j < 10$ for each j. Explain how to compute their sum $u = (u_{15} \ldots u_1 u_0)_{16}$ and difference $v = (v_{15} \ldots v_1 v_0)_{16}$, where $0 \leq u_j, v_j < 10$ and

$$(u_{15} \ldots u_1 u_0)_{10} = ((x_{15} \ldots x_1 x_0)_{10} + (y_{15} \ldots y_1 y_0)_{10}) \bmod 10^{16},$$
$$(v_{15} \ldots v_1 v_0)_{10} = ((x_{15} \ldots x_1 x_0)_{10} - (y_{15} \ldots y_1 y_0)_{10}) \bmod 10^{16},$$

without bothering to do any radix conversion.

▶ **101.** [22] Two octabytes x and y contain amounts of time, represented in five fields that respectively signify days (3 bytes), hours (1 byte), minutes (1 byte), seconds (1 byte), and milliseconds (2 bytes). Can you add and subtract them quickly, without converting from this mixed-radix representation to binary and back again?

102. [25] Discuss routines for the addition and subtraction of polynomials modulo 5, when (a) 16 4-bit coefficients or (b) 21 3-bit coefficients are packed into a 64-bit word.

▶ **103.** [22] Sometimes it's convenient to represent small numbers in *unary* notation, so that $0, 1, 2, 3, \ldots, k$ appear respectively as $(0)_2$, $(1)_2$, $(11)_2$, $(111)_2$, $\ldots$, $2^k - 1$ inside the computer. Then max and min are easily implemented as $\mid$ and $\&$.

Suppose the bytes of $x = (x_7 \ldots x_0)_{256}$ are such unary numbers, while the bytes of $y = (y_7 \ldots y_0)_{256}$ are all either 0 or 1. Explain how to "add" y to x or "subtract" y from x, giving $u = (u_7 \ldots u_0)_{256}$ and $v = (v_7 \ldots v_0)_{256}$ where

$$u_j = 2^{\min(8, \lg(x_j + 1) + y_j)} - 1 \quad \text{and} \quad v_j = 2^{\max(0, \lg(x_j + 1) - y_j)} - 1.$$

104. [22] Use bitwise operations to check the validity of a date represented in "year-month-day" fields (y, m, d) as in (22). You should compute a value t that is zero if and only if $1900 < y < 2100$, $1 \leq m \leq 12$, and $1 \leq d \leq max\_day(m)$, where month m has at most $max\_day(m)$ days. Can it be done in fewer than 20 operations?

105. [30] Given $x = (x_7 \ldots x_0)_{256}$ and $y = (y_7 \ldots y_0)_{256}$, discuss bitwise operations that will *sort* the bytes into order, so that $x_0 \leq y_0 \leq \cdots \leq x_7 \leq y_7$ afterwards.

106. [27] Explain the Fredman–Willard procedure (95). Also show that a simple modification of their method will compute $2^{\lambda x}$ without doing any left shifts.

▶ **107.** [22] Implement Algorithm B on MMIX when $d = 4$, and compare it with (56).

108. [26] Adapt Algorithm B to cases where n does not have the form $d \cdot 2^d$.

109. [20] Evaluate ρx for n-bit numbers x in $O(\log \log n)$ broadword steps.

▶ **110.** [*30*] Suppose $n = 2^{2^e}$ and $0 \le x < n$. Show how to compute $1 \ll x$ in $O(e)$ broadword steps, using only shift commands that shift by a constant amount. (Together with Algorithm B we can therefore extract the most significant bit of an n-bit number in $O(\log \log n)$ such steps.)

111. [*23*] Explain the 01^r pattern recognizer, (98).

112. [*46*] Can all occurrences of the pattern 1^r0 be identified in $O(1)$ broadword steps?

113. [*23*] A *strong broadword chain* is a broadword chain of a specified width n that is also a 2-adic chain, for all n-bit choices of x_0. For example, the 2-bit broadword chain (x_0, x_1) with $x_1 = x_0 + 1$ is not strong because $x_0 = (11)_2$ makes $x_1 = (00)_2$. But $(x_0, x_1, \ldots, x_4)$ is a strong broadword chain that computes $(x_0 + 1) \bmod 4$ for all $0 \le x_0 < 4$ if we set $x_1 = x_0 \oplus 1$, $x_2 = x_0 \;\&\; 1$, $x_3 = x_2 \ll 1$, and $x_4 = x_1 \oplus x_3$.
    Given a broadword chain $(x_0, x_1, \ldots, x_r)$ of width n, construct a strong broadword chain $(x'_0, x'_1, \ldots, x'_{r'})$ of the same width n, such that $r' = O(r)$ and $(x_0, x_1, \ldots, x_r)$ is a subsequence of $(x'_0, x'_1, \ldots, x'_{r'})$.

114. [*16*] Suppose $(x_0, x_1, \ldots, x_r)$ is a strong broadword chain of width n that computes the value $f(x) = x_r$ whenever an n-bit number $x = x_0$ is given. Construct a broadword chain $(X_0, X_1, \ldots, X_r)$ of width mn that computes $X_r = (f(\xi_1) \ldots f(\xi_m))_{2^n}$ for any given mn-bit value $X_0 = (\xi_1 \ldots \xi_m)_{2^n}$, where $0 \le \xi_1, \ldots, \xi_m < 2^n$.

▶ **115.** [*24*] Given a 2-adic integer $x = (\ldots x_2 x_1 x_0)_2$, we might want to compute $y = (\ldots y_2 y_1 y_0)_2 = f(x)$ from x by zeroing out all blocks of consecutive 1s that (a) are not immediately followed by two 0s; or (b) are followed by an odd number of 0s before the next block of 1s begins; or (c) contain an odd number of 1s. For example, if x is $(\ldots 01110111001101000110)_2$ then y is (a) $(\ldots 00000111000001000110)_2$; (b) $(\ldots 00000111000000000110)_2$; (c) $(\ldots 00000000001100000110)_2$. (Infinitely many 0s are assumed to appear at the right of x_0. Thus, in case (a) we have

$$y_j = x_j \wedge ((\bar{x}_{j-1} \wedge \bar{x}_{j-2}) \vee (x_{j-1} \wedge \bar{x}_{j-2} \wedge \bar{x}_{j-3}) \vee (x_{j-1} \wedge x_{j-2} \wedge \bar{x}_{j-3} \wedge \bar{x}_{j-4}) \vee \cdots)$$

for all j, where $x_k = 0$ for $k < 0$.) Find 2-adic chains for y in each case.

116. [*HM30*] Suppose $x = (\ldots x_2 x_1 x_0)_2$ and $y = (\ldots y_2 y_1 y_0)_2 = f(x)$, where y is computable by a 2-adic chain having no shift operations. Let L be the set of all binary strings such that $y_j = [x_j \ldots x_1 x_0 \in L]$, and assume that all constants used in the chain are rational 2-adic numbers. Prove that L is a regular language. What languages L correspond to the functions in exercise 115(a) and 115(b)?

117. [*HM46*] Continuing exercise 116, is there any simple way to characterize the regular languages L that arise in shift-free 2-adic chains? (The language $L = 0^*(10^*10^*)^*$ does not seem to correspond to any such chain.)

118. [*30*] According to Lemma A, we cannot compute the function $x \gg 1$ for all n-bit numbers x by using only additions, subtractions, and bitwise Boolean operations (no shifts or branches). Show, however, that $O(n)$ such operations are necessary and sufficient if we include also the "monus" operator $y \mathbin{\dot-} z$ in our repertoire.

119. [*20*] Evaluate the function $f_{py}(x)$ in (102) with four broadword steps.

▶ **120.** [*M25*] There are $2^{n2^{mn}}$ functions that take n-bit numbers $(x_1, \ldots, x_m)$ into an n-bit number $f(x_1, \ldots, x_m)$. How many of them can be implemented with addition, subtraction, multiplication, and nonshift bitwise Boolean operations (modulo 2^n)?

▶ **121.** [*M25*] By exercise 3.1–6, a function from $[0 \mathbin{..} 2^n)$ into itself is eventually periodic.

a) Prove that if f is any n-bit broadword function that can be implemented without shift instructions, the lengths of its periods are always powers of 2.

b) However, for every p between 1 and n, there's an n-bit broadword chain of length 3 that has a period of length p.

122. [*M22*] Complete the proof of Lemma B.

123. [*M23*] Let a_q be the constant $1 + 2^q + 2^{2q} + \cdots + 2^{(q-1)q} = (2^{q^2} - 1)/(2^q - 1)$. Using (104), show that there are infinitely many q such that the operation of multiplying by a_q, modulo 2^{q^2}, requires $\Omega(\log q)$ steps in any n-bit broadword chain with $n \geq q^2$.

124. [*M38*] Complete the proof of Theorem R$'$ by defining an n-bit broadword chain $(x_0, x_1, \ldots, x_f)$ and sets $(U_0, U_1, \ldots, U_f)$ such that, for $0 \leq t \leq f$, all inputs $x \in U_t$ lead to an essentially similar state $Q(x, t)$, in the following sense: (i) The current instruction in $Q(x, t)$ does not depend on x. (ii) If register r_j has a known value in $Q(x, t)$, it holds $x_{j'}$ for some definite index $j' \leq t$. (iii) If memory location $M[z]$ has been changed, it holds $x_{z''}$ for some definite index $z'' \leq t$. (The values of j' and z'' depend on j, z, and t, but not on x.) Furthermore $|U_t| \geq n/2^{2^t - 1}$, and the program cannot guarantee that $r_1 = \rho x$ when $t < f$. *Hint:* Lemma B implies that a limited number of shift amounts and memory addresses need to be considered when t is small.

125. [*M33*] Prove Theorem P$'$. *Hint:* Lemma B remains true if we replace '$= 0$' by '$= \alpha_s$' in (103), for any values α_s.

126. [*M46*] Does the operation of extracting the most significant bit, $2^{\lambda x}$, require $\Omega(\log \log n)$ steps in an n-bit basic RAM? (See exercise 110.)

127. [*HM40*] Prove that at least $\Omega(\log n/\log \log n)$ broadword steps are needed to compute the parity function, $(\nu x) \bmod 2$, using the theory of circuit complexity. [*Hint:* Every boardword operation is in complexity class AC_0.]

128. [*M46*] Can $(\nu x) \bmod 2$ be computed in $O(\log n/\log \log n)$ broadword steps?

129. [*M46*] Does sideways addition require $\Omega(\log n)$ broadword steps?

130. [*M46*] Is there an n-bit constant a such that the function $(a \ll x) \bmod 2^n$ requires $\Omega(\log n)$ n-bit broadword steps?

▶ **131.** [*23*] Write an MMIX program for Algorithm R when the graph is represented by arc lists. Vertex nodes have at least two fields, called LINK and ARCS, and arc nodes have TIP and NEXT fields, as explained in Section 7. Initially all LINK fields are zero, except in the given set of vertices Q, which is represented as a circular list. Your program should change that circular list so that it represents the set R of all reachable vertices.

▶ **132.** [*M27*] A *clique* in a graph is a set of mutually adjacent vertices; a clique is *maximal* if it's not contained in any other. The purpose of this exercise is to discuss an algorithm due to J. K. M. Moody and J. Hollis, which provides a convenient way to find every maximal clique of a not-too-large graph, using bitwise operations.

Suppose G is a graph with n vertices $V = \{0, 1, \ldots, n-1\}$. Let $\rho_v = \sum \{2^u \mid u \,—\, v \text{ or } u = v\}$ be row v of G's reflexive adjacency matrix, and let $\delta_v = \sum \{2^u \mid u \neq v\} = 2^n - 1 - 2^v$. Every subset $U \subseteq V$ is representable as an n-bit integer $\sigma(U) = \sum_{u \in U} 2^u$; for example, $\delta_v = \sigma(V \setminus v)$. We also define the bitwise intersection

$$\tau(U) = \mathop{\&}_{0 \leq u < n} (u \in U? \; \rho_u : \delta_u).$$

For example, if $n = 5$ we have $\tau(\{0, 2\}) = \rho_0 \& \delta_1 \& \rho_2 \& \delta_3 \& \delta_4$.

a) Prove that U is a clique if and only if $\tau(U) = \sigma(U)$.

b) Show that if $\tau(U) = \sigma(T)$ then T is a clique.

c) For $1 \le k \le n$, consider the 2^k bitwise intersections

$$C_k = \left\{ \underset{0 \le u < k}{\&} (u \in U? \, \rho_u : \delta_u) \;\middle|\; U \subseteq \{0, 1, \ldots, k-1\} \right\},$$

and let C_k^+ be the maximal elements of C_k. Prove that U is a maximal clique if and only if $\sigma(U) \in C_n^+$.

d) Explain how to compute C_k^+ from C_{k-1}^+, starting with $C_0^+ = \{2^n - 1\}$.

▶ **133.** [*20*] Given a graph G, how can the algorithm of exercise 132 be used to find (a) all maximal independent sets of vertices? (b) all minimal vertex covers (sets that hit every edge)?

134. [*15*] Nine classes of mappings for ternary values appear in (119), (123), and (124). To which class does the representation (128) belong, if $a = 0$, $b = *$, $c = 1$?

135. [*22*] Łukasiewicz included a few operations besides (127) in his three-valued logic: $\neg x$ (negation) interchanges 0 with 1 but leaves $*$ unchanged; $\diamond x$ (possibility) is defined as $\neg x \Rightarrow x$; $\square x$ (necessity) is defined as $\neg \diamond \neg x$; and $x \Leftrightarrow y$ (equivalence) is defined as $(x \Rightarrow y) \wedge (y \Rightarrow x)$. Explain how to perform these operations using representation (128).

136. [*29*] Suggest two-bit encodings for binary operations on the set $\{a, b, c\}$ that are defined by the following "multiplication tables":

$$\text{(a)} \begin{pmatrix} a & b & c \\ b & c & c \\ c & c & c \end{pmatrix}; \qquad \text{(b)} \begin{pmatrix} a & c & b \\ c & b & a \\ b & a & c \end{pmatrix}; \qquad \text{(c)} \begin{pmatrix} a & b & a \\ a & a & c \\ a & b & c \end{pmatrix}.$$

137. [*21*] Show that the operation in exercise 136(c) is simpler with packed vectors like (131) than with the unpacked form (130).

138. [*24*] Find an example of three-state-to-two-bit encoding where class V_a is best.

139. [*25*] If x and y are signed bits 0, $+1$, or -1, what 2-bit encoding is good for calculating their sum $(z_1 z_2)_3 = x + y$, where z_1 and z_2 are also required to be signed bits? (This is a "half adder" for balanced ternary numbers.)

140. [*27*] Design an economical *full adder* for balanced ternary numbers: Show how to compute signed bits u and v such that $3u + v = x + y + z$ when $x, y, z \in \{0, +1, -1\}$.

▶ **141.** [*30*] The *Ulam numbers* $\langle U_1, U_2, \ldots \rangle = \langle 1, 2, 3, 4, 6, 8, 11, 13, 16, 18, 26, \ldots \rangle$ are defined for $n \ge 3$ by letting U_n be the smallest integer $> U_{n-1}$ that has a *unique* representation $U_n = U_j + U_k$ for $0 < j < k < n$. Show that a million Ulam numbers can be computed rapidly with the help of bitwise techniques.

▶ **142.** [*33*] A subcube such as $*10*1*01$ can be represented by asterisk codes 10010100 and bit codes 01001001, as in (85); but many other encodings are also possible. What representation scheme for subcubes works best, for finding prime implicants by the consensus-based algorithm of exercise 7.1.1–31?

143. [*20*] Let x be a 64-bit number that represents an 8×8 chessboard, with a 1 bit in every position where a knight is present. Find a formula for the 64-bit number $f(x)$ that has a 1 in every position reachable in one move by a knight of x. For example, the white knights at the start of a game correspond to $x = {}^\#42$; then $f(x) = {}^\#\text{a51800}$.

144. [*16*] What node is the sibling of node j in a sideways heap? (See (134).)

145. [*17*] Interpret (137) when h is *less* than the height of j.

▶ **146.** [*M20*] Prove Eq. (138), which relates the ρ and λ functions.

▶ **147.** [*M20*] What values of πv, βv, αv, and τj occur in Algorithm V when the forest is
a) the empty digraph with vertices $\{v_1, \ldots, v_n\}$ and no arcs?
b) the oriented path $v_n \longrightarrow \cdots \longrightarrow v_2 \longrightarrow v_1$?

148. [*M21*] When preprocessing for Algorithm V, is it possible to have $\beta x_3 \longrightarrow^*$ $\beta y_2 \longrightarrow^* \beta x_2 \longrightarrow^* \beta y_1 \longrightarrow^* \beta x_1$ in S when $x_3 \longrightarrow x_2 \longrightarrow x_1 \longrightarrow \Lambda$ and $y_2 \longrightarrow y_1 \longrightarrow \Lambda$ in the forest? (If so, two different trees are "entangled" in S.)

▶ **149.** [*23*] Design a preprocessing procedure for Algorithm V.

▶ **150.** [*25*] Given an array of elements $A_1, \ldots, A_n$, the *range minimum query* problem is to determine $k(i, j)$ such that $A_{k(i,j)} = \min(A_i, \ldots, A_j)$ for any given indices i and j with $1 \le i \le j \le n$. Prove that Algorithm V will solve this problem, after $O(n)$ steps of preprocessing on the array A have prepared the necessary tables $(\pi, \beta, \alpha, \tau)$. *Hint:* Consider the binary search tree constructed from the sequence of keys $(p(1), p(2), \ldots, p(n))$, where p is a permutation of $\{1, 2, \ldots, n\}$ such that $A_{p(1)} \le A_{p(2)} \le \cdots \le A_{p(n)}$.

151. [*22*] Conversely, show that any algorithm for range minimum queries can be used to find nearest common ancestors, with essentially the same efficiency.

152. [*M21*] Prove that Algorithm V is correct.

▶ **153.** [*M20*] The pointers in a navigation pile like (144) can be packed into a binary string such as

0	1	0	0	1	0	0	0	0	1	0	1	0	0	0	0	0	0	0	0
2		4		6		8			10	12	14		16			18	20	22		24

At what bit position (from the left) does the pointer for node j end?

154. [*20*] The gray lines in Fig. 14 show how each pentagon is composed of ten triangles. What decomposition of the hyperbolic plane is defined by those gray lines alone, without the black pentagon edges?

▶ **155.** [*M21*] Prove that $(x\phi) \bmod 1 = (\alpha 0)_{1/\phi}$ when α is the negaFibonacci code for x.

156. [*21*] Design algorithms (a) to convert a given integer x to its negaFibonacci code α, and (b) to convert a given negaFibonacci code α to $x = N(\alpha)$.

157. [*M21*] Explain the recursion (148) for negaFibonacci predecessor and successor.

158. [*M26*] Let $\alpha = a_n \ldots a_1$ be the binary code for $F(\alpha 0) = a_n F_{n+1} + \cdots + a_1 F_2$ in the standard Fibonacci number system (146). Develop methods analogous to (148) and (149) for incrementing and decrementing such codewords.

159. [*M34*] Exercise 7 shows that it's easy to convert between the negabinary and binary number systems. Discuss conversion between negaFibonacci codewords and the ordinary Fibonacci codes in exercise 158.

160. [*M29*] Prove that (150) and (151) yield consistent code labels for the pentagrid.

161. [*20*] The cells of a chessboard can be colored black and white, so that neighboring cells have different colors. Does the pentagrid also have this property?

▶ **162.** [*HM37*] Explain how to draw the pentagrid, Fig. 14. What circles are present?

163. [*HM41*] Devise a way to navigate through the triangles in the tiling of Fig. 18.

164. [*23*] The original definition of custerization in 1957 was not (157) but

$$\text{custer}'(X) = X \mathbin{\&} \sim(X_{\text{NW}} \mathbin{\&} X_{\text{N}} \mathbin{\&} X_{\text{NE}} \mathbin{\&} X_{\text{W}} \mathbin{\&} X_{\text{E}} \mathbin{\&} X_{\text{SW}} \mathbin{\&} X_{\text{S}} \mathbin{\&} X_{\text{SE}}).$$

Why is (157) preferable?

165. [*21*] (R. A. Kirsch.) Discuss the computation of the 3×3 cellular automaton with
$$X^{(t+1)} = \text{custer}(\overline{X}^{(t)}) = {\sim}X^{(t)} \mathrel{\&} (X_{\text{N}}^{(t)} \mid X_{\text{W}}^{(t)} \mid X_{\text{E}}^{(t)} \mid X_{\text{S}}^{(t)}).$$

166. [*M23*] Let $f(M,N)$ be the maximum number of black pixels in an $M \times N$ bitmap X for which $X = \text{custer}(X)$. Prove that $f(M,N) = \frac{4}{5}MN + O(M+N)$.

167. [*24*] (*Life.*) If the bitmap X represents an array of cells that are either dead (0) or alive (1), the Boolean function
$$f(x_{\text{NW}},\dots,x,\dots,x_{\text{SE}}) = [2 < x_{\text{NW}}+x_{\text{N}}+x_{\text{NE}}+x_{\text{W}}+\tfrac{1}{2}x+x_{\text{E}}+x_{\text{SW}}+x_{\text{S}}+x_{\text{SE}} < 4]$$
can lead to astonishing life histories when it governs a cellular automaton as in (158).

   a) Find a way to evaluate f with a Boolean chain of 26 steps or less.
   b) Let $X_j^{(t)}$ denote row j of X at time t. Show that $X_j^{(t+1)}$ can be evaluated in at most 23 broadword steps, as a function of the three rows $X_{j-1}^{(t)}$, $X_j^{(t)}$, and $X_{j+1}^{(t)}$.

▶ **168.** [*23*] To keep an image finite, we might insist that a 3×3 cellular automaton treats a $M \times N$ bitmap as a *torus*, wrapping around seamlessly between top and bottom and between left and right. The task of simulating its actions efficiently with bitwise operations is somewhat tricky: We want to minimize references to memory, yet each new pixel value depends on old values that lie on all sides. Furthermore the shifting of bits between neighboring words tends to be awkward, taxing the capacity of a register.

   Show that such difficulties can be surmounted by maintaining an array of n-bit words A_{jk} for $0 \le j \le M$ and $0 \le k \le N' = \lceil N/(n-2)\rceil$. If $j \ne M$ and $k \ne 0$, word A_{jk} should contain the pixels of row j and columns $(k-1)(n-2)$ through $k(n-2)+1$, inclusive; the other words A_{Mk} and A_{j0} provide auxiliary buffer space. (Notice that some bits of the raster appear twice.)

169. [*22*] Continuing the previous two exercises, what happens to the Cheshire cat of Fig. 17(a) when it is subjected to the vicissitudes of Life, in a 26×31 torus?

▶ **170.** [*21*] What result does the Guo–Hall thinning automaton produce when given a solid black rectangle of M rows and N columns? How long does it take?

171. [*24*] Find a Boolean chain of length ≤ 25 to evaluate the local thinning function $g(x_{\text{NW}}, x_{\text{N}}, x_{\text{NE}}, x_{\text{W}}, x_{\text{E}}, x_{\text{SW}}, x_{\text{S}}, x_{\text{SE}})$ of (159), with or without the extra cases in (160).

172. [*M29*] Prove or disprove: If a pattern contains three black pixels that are king-neighbors of each other, the Guo–Hall procedure extended by (160) will reduce it, unless none of those pixels can be removed without destroying the connectivity.

▶ **173.** [*M30*] Raster images often need to be cleaned up if they contain noisy data. For example, accidental specks of black or white may well spoil the results when a thinning algorithm is used for optical character recognition.

   Say that a bitmap X is *closed* if every white pixel is part of a 2×2 square of white pixels, and *open* if every black pixel is part of a 2×2 square of black pixels. Let
$$X^D = \mathrel{\&} \{Y \mid Y \supseteq X \text{ and } Y \text{ is closed}\}; \qquad X^L = \mid \{Y \mid Y \subseteq X \text{ and } Y \text{ is open}\}.$$
A bitmap is called *clean* if it equals X^{DL} for some X. We might, for example, have
$$X = \blacksquare\text{\tiny\textbullet}\,; \qquad X^D = \blacksquare\text{\tiny\textbullet}\,; \qquad X^{DL} = \blacksquare\,.$$
In general X^D is "darker" than X, while X^L is "lighter": $X^D \supseteq X \supseteq X^L$.

   a) Prove that $(X^{DL})^{DL} = X^{DL}$. *Hint:* $X \subseteq Y$ implies $X^D \subseteq Y^D$ and $X^L \subseteq Y^L$.
   b) Show that X^D can be computed with one step of a 3×3 cellular automaton.

174. [*M46*] (M. Minsky and S. Papert.) Is there a three-dimensional shrinking algorithm that preserves connectivity, analogous to (161)?

175. [*15*] How many *rookwise* connected black components does the Cheshire cat have?

176. [*M24*] Let G be the graph whose vertices are the black pixels of a given bitmap X, with $u \!-\! v$ when u and v are a king move apart. Let G' be the corresponding graph after the shrinking transformation (161) has been applied. The purpose of this exercise is to show that the number of connected components of G' is the number of components of G minus the number of isolated vertices of G.

Let $N_{(i,j)} = \{(i,j), (i{-}1,j), (i{-}1,j{+}1), (i,j{+}1)\}$ be pixel (i,j) together with its north and/or east neighbors. For each $v \in G$ let $S(v) = \{v' \in G' \mid v' \in N_v\}$.

   a) Prove that $S(v)$ is empty if and only if v is isolated in G.
   b) If $u \!-\! v$ in G, $u' \in S(u)$, and $v' \in S(v)$, prove that $u' \!-\!\!\!-^{*}\, v'$ in G'.
   c) For each $v' \in G'$ let $S'(v') = \{v \in G \mid v' \in N_v\}$. Is $S'(v')$ always nonempty?
   d) If $u' \!-\! v'$ in G', $u \in S'(u')$, and $v \in S'(v')$, prove that $u \!-\!\!\!-^{*}\, v$ in G.
   e) Hence there's a one-to-one correspondence between the nontrivial components of G and the components of G'.

177. [*M22*] Continuing exercise 176, prove an analogous result for the white pixels.

178. [*20*] If X is an $M \times N$ bitmap, let X^{*} be the $M \times (2N+1)$ bitmap $X \ddagger (X \mid (X \ll 1))$. Show that the kingwise connected components of X^{*} are also rookwise connected, and that bitmap X^{*} has the same "surroundedness tree" (162) as X.

▶ **179.** [*34*] Design an algorithm that constructs the surroundedness tree of a given $M \times N$ bitmap, scanning the image one row at a time as discussed in the text. (See (162) and (163).)

▶ **180.** [*M24*] Digitize the hyperbola $y^2 = x^2 + 13$ by hand, for $0 < y \le 7$.

181. [*HM20*] Explain how to subdivide a general conic (168) with rational coefficients into monotonic parts so that Algorithm T applies.

182. [*M31*] Why does the three-register method (Algorithm T) digitize correctly?

▶ **183.** [*M29*] (G. Rote.) Explain why Algorithm T might fail if condition (v) is false.

▶ **184.** [*M22*] Find a quadratic form $Q'(x,y)$ so that, when Algorithm T is applied to (x',y'), (x,y), and Q', it produces exactly the same edges as it does from (x,y), (x',y'), and Q, but in the reverse order.

▶ **185.** [*22*] Design an algorithm that properly digitizes a straight line from (ξ, η) to (ξ', η'), when ξ, η, ξ', and η' are rational numbers, by simplifying Algorithm T.

186. [*HM22*] Given three complex numbers (z_0, z_1, z_2), consider the curve traced out by

$$B(t) = (1-t)^2 z_0 + 2(1-t)t z_1 + t^2 z_2, \qquad \text{for } 0 \le t \le 1.$$

   a) What is the approximate behavior of $B(t)$ when t is near 0 or 1?
   b) Let $S(z_0, z_1, z_2) = \{B(t) \mid 0 \le t \le 1\}$. Prove that all points of $S(z_0, z_1, z_2)$ lie on or inside the triangle whose vertices are z_0, z_1, and z_2.
   c) True or false? $S(w + \zeta z_0, w + \zeta z_1, w + \zeta z_2) = w + \zeta S(z_0, z_1, z_2)$.
   d) Prove that $S(z_0, z_1, z_2)$ is part of a straight line if and only if z_0, z_1, and z_2 are collinear; otherwise it is part of a parabola.

e) Prove that if $0 \leq \theta \leq 1$, we have the recurrence

$$S(z_0, z_1, z_2) = S(z_0, (1-\theta)z_0 + \theta z_1, B(\theta)) \cup S(B(\theta), (1-\theta)z_1 + \theta z_2, z_2).$$

187. [*M29*] Continuing exercise 186, show how to digitize $S(z_0, z_1, z_2)$ using the three-register method (Algorithm T). For best results, the digitizations of $S(z_2, z_1, z_0)$ and $S(z_0, z_1, z_2)$ should produce the same edges, but in reverse order.

188. [*25*] Given a 64×64 bitmap, what's a good way (a) to transpose it, or (b) to rotate it by $90°$, using operations on 64-bit numbers?

▶ **189.** [*25*] Bitmap images can often be viewed conveniently using pixels that are *shades of gray* instead of just black or white. Such gray levels typically are 8-bit values that range from 0 (black) to 255 (white); notice that the black/white convention is traditionally *reversed* with respect to the 1-bit case. An $m \times n$ bitmap whose resolution is 600 dots per inch corresponds nicely to the $(m/8) \times (n/8)$ grayscale image with 75 pixels per inch that is obtained by mapping each 8×8 subarray of 1-bit pixels into the gray level $\lfloor 255(1 - k/64)^{1/\gamma} + \frac{1}{2} \rfloor$, where $\gamma = 1.3$ and k is the number of 1s in the subarray.

Write an `MMIX` routine that converts a given $m \times n$ array `BITMAP` into the corresponding $(m/8) \times (n/8)$ image `GRAYMAP`, assuming that $m = 8m'$ and $n = 64n'$.

190. [*23*] A *parity pattern* of length m and width n is an $m \times n$ matrix of 0s and 1s with the property that each element is the sum of its neighbors, mod 2. For example,

$$
\begin{array}{ccccc}
\begin{matrix} 1\,1 \\ 0\,0, \\ 1\,1 \end{matrix}
&
\begin{matrix} 0\,0\,1\,1 \\ 0\,1\,0\,0 \\ 1\,1\,0\,1 \\ 0\,1\,0\,1 \end{matrix}
&
\begin{matrix} 0\,1\,0\,1\,0 \\ 1\,1\,0\,1\,1, \\ 0\,1\,0\,1\,0 \end{matrix}
&
\begin{matrix} 1\,0\,0 \\ 1\,1\,0 \\ 1\,0\,1, \\ 0\,1\,1 \\ 0\,0\,1 \end{matrix}
&
\text{and}
&
\begin{matrix} 0\,1\,1\,1\,0 \\ 1\,0\,1\,0\,1 \\ 1\,1\,0\,1\,1 \\ 1\,0\,1\,0\,1 \\ 0\,1\,1\,1\,0 \end{matrix}
\end{array}
$$

are parity patterns of sizes 3×2, 4×4, 3×5, 5×3, and 5×5.

a) If the binary vectors $\alpha_1, \alpha_2, \ldots, \alpha_m$ are the rows of a parity pattern, show that $\alpha_2, \ldots, \alpha_m$ can all be computed from the top row α_1 by using bitwise operations. Thus at most one $m \times n$ parity pattern can begin with any given bit vector.

b) True or false: The sum (mod 2) of two $m \times n$ parity patterns is a parity pattern.

c) A parity pattern is called *perfect* if it contains no all-zero row or column. For example, three of the matrices above are perfect, but the 3×2 and 3×5 examples are not. Show that every $m \times n$ parity pattern contains a perfect parity pattern as a submatrix. Furthermore, all such submatrices have the same size, $m' \times n'$, where $m' + 1$ is a divisor of $m + 1$ and $n' + 1$ is a divisor $n + 1$.

d) There's a perfect parity pattern whose first row is 0011, but there is no such pattern beginning with 01010. Is there a simple way to decide whether a given binary vector is the top row of a perfect parity pattern?

e) Prove that there's a unique perfect parity pattern that begins with $1\,\overbrace{0\ldots0}^{n-1}$.

191. [*M30*] A *wraparound parity pattern* is analogous to the parity patterns of exercise 190, except that the leftmost and rightmost elements of each row are also neighbors.

a) Find a simple relation between the parity pattern of width n that begins with α and the wraparound parity pattern of width $2n + 2$ that begins with $0\alpha 0\alpha^R$.

b) The Fibonacci polynomials $F_j(x)$ are defined by the recurrence

$$F_0(x) = 0, \qquad F_1(x) = 1, \qquad \text{and} \qquad F_{j+1}(x) = x F_j(x) + F_{j-1}(x) \quad \text{for } j \geq 1.$$

Show that there's a simple relation between the wraparound parity patterns that begin with $10\ldots0$ ($N-1$ zeros) and the Fibonacci polynomials modulo $x^N + 1$. *Hint:* Consider $F_j(x^{-1} + 1 + x)$, and do arithmetic mod 2 as well as mod $x^N + 1$.

c) If α is the binary string $a_1 \ldots a_n$, let $f_\alpha(x) = a_1 x + \cdots + a_n x^n$. Show that

$$f_{(\alpha_j 0 \alpha_j^R)}(x) = (f_\alpha(x) + f_\alpha(x^{-1})) F_j(x^{-1}+1+x) \bmod (x^N + 1) \text{ and } \bmod 2,$$

when $N = 2n + 2$ and α_j is row j of a width-n parity pattern that begins with α.

d) Consequently we can compute α_j from α in only $O(n^2 \log j)$ steps. *Hints:* See exercise 4.6.3–26; and use the identity $F_{m+n}(x) = F_m(x) F_{n+1}(x) + F_{m-1}(x) F_n(x)$, which generalizes Eq. 1.2.8–(6).

192. [*HM38*] The shortest parity pattern that begins with a given string can be quite long; for example, it turns out that the perfect pattern of width 120 whose first row is $10 \ldots 0$ has length $36{,}028{,}797{,}018{,}963{,}966(!)$. The purpose of this exercise is to consider how to calculate the interesting function

$$c(q) = 1 + \max\{m \mid \text{there exists a perfect parity pattern of length } m \text{ and width } q-1\},$$

whose initial values $(1, 3, 4, 6, 5, 24, 9, 12, 28)$ for $1 \le q \le 9$ are easy to compute by hand.

a) Characterize $c(q)$ algebraically, using the Fibonacci polynomials of exercise 191.

b) Explain how to calculate $c(q)$ if we know a number M such that $c(q)$ divides M, and if we also know the prime factors of M.

c) Prove that $c(2^e) = 3 \cdot 2^{e-1}$ when $e > 0$. *Hint:* $F_{2^e}(y)$ has a simple form, mod 2.

d) Prove that when q is odd and not a multiple of 3, $c(q)$ is a divisor of $2^{2e} - 1$, where e is the order of 2 modulo q. *Hint:* $F_{2^e-1}(y)$ has a simple form, mod 2.

e) What happens when q is an odd multiple of 3?

f) Finally, explain how to handle the case when q is even.

▶ **193.** [*M21*] If a perfect $m \times n$ parity pattern exists, when m and n are odd, show that there's also a perfect $(2m+1) \times (2n+1)$ parity pattern. (Intricate fractals arise when this observation is applied repeatedly; for example, the 5×5 pattern in exercise 190 leads to Fig. 20.)

194. [*M24*] Find all $n \le 383$ for which there exists a perfect $n \times n$ parity pattern with 8-fold symmetry, such as the example in Fig. 20. *Hint:* The diagonal elements of all such patterns must be zero.

Fig. 20. A perfect 383×383 parity pattern.

▶ **195.** [*HM25*] Let A be a binary matrix having rows $\alpha_1, \ldots, \alpha_m$ of length n. Explain how to use bitwise operations to compute the rank $m - r$ of A over the binary field $\{0, 1\}$, and to find linearly independent binary vectors $\theta_1, \ldots, \theta_r$ of length m such that $\theta_j A = 0 \ldots 0$ for $1 \le j \le r$. *Hint:* See the "triangularization" algorithm for null spaces, Algorithm 4.6.2N.

196. [*21*] (K. Thompson, 1992.) Integers in the range $0 \le x < 2^{31}$ can be encoded as a string of up to six bytes $\alpha(x) = \alpha_1 \ldots \alpha_l$ in the following way: If $x < 2^7$, set $l \leftarrow 1$ and $\alpha_1 \leftarrow x$. Otherwise let $x = (x_5 \ldots x_1 x_0)_{64}$; set $l \leftarrow \lceil (\lambda x)/5 \rceil$, $\alpha_1 \leftarrow 2^8 - 2^{8-l} + x_{l-1}$, and $\alpha_j = 2^7 + x_{l-j}$ for $2 \le j \le l$. Notice that $\alpha(x)$ contains a zero byte if and only if $x = 0$.

a) What are the encodings of $\#\mathtt{a}$, $\#\mathtt{3a3}$, $\#\mathtt{7b97}$, and $\#\mathtt{1d141}$?

b) If $x \le x'$, prove that $\alpha(x) \le \alpha(x')$ in lexicographic order.

c) Suppose a sequence of values $x^{(1)} x^{(2)} \ldots x^{(n)}$ has been encoded as a byte string $\alpha(x^{(1)}) \alpha(x^{(2)}) \ldots \alpha(x^{(n)})$, and let α_k be the kth byte in that string. Show that it's easy to determine the value $x^{(i)}$ from which α_k came, by looking at a few of the neighboring bytes if necessary.

197. [*22*] The Universal Character Set (UCS), also known as Unicode, is a standard mapping of characters to integer codepoints x in the range $0 \le x < 2^{20} + 2^{16}$. An encoding called UTF-16 represents such integers as one or two wydes $\beta(x) = \beta_1$ or $\beta(x) = \beta_1\beta_2$, in the following way: If $x < 2^{16}$ then $\beta(x) = x$; otherwise

$$\beta_1 = {}^{\#}\text{d800} + \lfloor y/2^{10} \rfloor \text{ and } \beta_2 = {}^{\#}\text{dc00} + (y \bmod 2^{10}), \text{ where } y = x - 2^{16}.$$

Answer questions (a), (b), and (c) of exercise 196 for this encoding.

▶ **198.** [*21*] Unicode characters are often represented as strings of bytes using a scheme called UTF-8, which is the encoding of exercise 196 restricted to integers in the range $0 \le x < 2^{20} + 2^{16}$. Notice that UTF-8 efficiently preserves the standard ASCII character set (the codepoints with $x < 2^7$), and that it is quite different from UTF-16.

Let α_1 be the first byte of a UTF-8 string $\alpha(x)$. Show that there are reasonably small integer constants a, b, and c such that only four bitwise operations

$$(a \gg ((\alpha_1 \gg b) \mathbin{\&} c)) \mathbin{\&} 3$$

suffice to determine the number $l - 1$ of bytes between α_1 and the end of $\alpha(x)$.

▶ **199.** [*23*] A person might try to encode $^{\#}$a as $^{\#}$c08a or $^{\#}$e0808a or $^{\#}$f080808a in UTF-8, because the obvious decoding algorithm produces the same result in each case. But such unnecessarily long forms are illegal, because they could lead to security holes.

Suppose α_1 and α_2 are bytes such that $\alpha_1 \ge {}^{\#}$80 and $^{\#}$80 $\le \alpha_2 < {}^{\#}$c0. Find a branchless way to decide whether α_1 and α_2 are the first two bytes of at least one legitimate UTF-8 string $\alpha(x)$.

200. [*20*] Interpret the contents of register \$3 after the following three MMIX instructions have been executed: MOR \$1,\$0,#94; MXOR \$2,\$0,#94; SUBU \$3,\$1,\$2.

201. [*20*] Suppose $x = (x_{15} \dots x_1 x_0)_{16}$ has sixteen hexadecimal digits. What one MMIX instruction will change each nonzero digit to f, while leaving zeros untouched?

202. [*20*] What two instructions will change an octabyte's nonzero wydes to $^{\#}$ffff?

203. [*22*] Suppose we want to convert a tetrabyte $x = (x_7 \dots x_1 x_0)_{16}$ to the octabyte $y = (y_7 \dots y_1 y_0)_{256}$, where y_j is the ASCII code for the hexadecimal digit x_j. For example, if $x = {}^{\#}$1234abcd, y should represent the 8-character string "1234abcd". What clever choices of five constants a, b, c, d, and e will make the following MMIX instructions do the job?

MOR t,x,a;   SLU s,t,4;   XOR t,s,t;   AND t,t,b;

ADD t,t,c;   MOR s,d,t;   ADD t,t,e;   ADD y,t,s.

▶ **204.** [*22*] What are the amazing constants p, q, r, m that achieve a perfect shuffle with just six MMIX commands? (See (175)–(178).)

▶ **205.** [*22*] How would you perfectly *unshuffle* on MMIX, going from w in (175) back to z?

206. [*20*] The perfect shuffle (175) is sometimes called an "outshuffle," by comparison with the "inshuffle" that takes $z \mapsto y \ddagger x = (y_{31}x_{31} \dots y_1 x_1 y_0 x_0)_2$; the outshuffle preserves the leftmost and rightmost bits of z, but the inshuffle has no fixed points. Can an inshuffle be performed as efficiently as an outshuffle?

207. [*22*] Use MOR to perform a 3-way perfect shuffle or "triple zip," taking $(x_{63} \dots x_0)_2$ to $(x_{21}x_{42}x_{63}x_{20} \dots x_2 x_{23}x_{44}x_1 x_{22}x_{43}x_0)_2$, as well as the inverse of this shuffle.

▶ **208.** [*23*] What's a fast way for MMIX to transpose an 8×8 Boolean matrix?

▶ **209.** [*21*] Is the suffix parity operation $x^{\oplus}$ of exercise 36 easy to compute with MXOR?

210. [*22*] A puzzle: Register x contains a number $8j+k$, where $0 \le j, k < 8$. Registers a and b contain arbitrary octabytes $(a_7 \ldots a_1 a_0)_{256}$ and $(b_7 \ldots b_1 b_0)_{256}$. Find a sequence of four MMIX instructions that will put a_j & b_k into register x.

▶ **211.** [*M25*] The truth table of a Boolean function $f(x_1, \ldots, x_6)$ is essentially a 64-bit number $f = \big(f(0,0,0,0,0,0) \ldots f(1,1,1,1,1,0)f(1,1,1,1,1,1)\big)_2$. Show that two MOR instructions will convert f to the truth table of the least monotone Boolean function, $\hat{f}$, that is greater than or equal to f at each point.

212. [*M32*] Suppose $a = (a_{63} \ldots a_1 a_0)_2$ represents the polynomial

$$a(x) = (a_{63} \ldots a_1 a_0)_x = a_{63}x^{63} + \cdots + a_1 x + a_0.$$

Discuss using MXOR to compute the product $c(x) = a(x)b(x)$, modulo x^{64} and mod 2.

▶ **213.** [*HM26*] Implement the CRC procedure (183) on MMIX.

▶ **214.** [*HM28*] (R. W. Gosper.) Find a short, branchless MMIX computation that computes the inverse of any given 8×8 matrix X of 0s and 1s, modulo 2, if $\det X$ is odd.

▶ **215.** [*21*] What's a quick way for MMIX to test if a 64-bit number is a multiple of 3?

▶ **216.** [*M26*] Given n-bit integers $x_1, \ldots, x_m \ge 0$, $n \ge \lambda m$, compute in $O(m)$ steps the least $y > 0$ such that $y \notin \{a_1 x_1 + \cdots + a_m x_m \mid a_1, \ldots, a_m \in \{0,1\}\}$, if λx takes unit time.

217. [*40*] Explore the processing of long strings of text by packing them in a "transposed" or "sliced" manner: Represent 64 consecutive characters as a sequence of eight octabytes $w_0 \ldots w_7$, where w_k contains all 64 of their kth bits.

> *In popular usage, the term **BDD** almost always refers to*
> *Reduced Ordered Binary Decision Diagram (ROBDD in the literature,*
> *used when the ordering and reduction aspects need to be emphasized).*
> — WIKIPEDIA, *The Free Encyclopedia* (7 July 2007)

7.1.4. Binary Decision Diagrams

Let's turn now to an important family of data structures that have rapidly become the method of choice for representing and manipulating Boolean functions inside a computer. The basic idea is a divide-and-conquer scheme somewhat like the binary tries of Section 6.3, but with several new twists.

Figure 21 shows the binary decision diagram for a simple Boolean function of three variables, the median function $\langle x_1 x_2 x_3 \rangle$ of Eq. 7.1.1–(43). We can understand it as follows: The node at the top is called the *root*. Every internal node ⓙ, also called a *branch node*, is labeled with a name or index $j = V(ⓙ)$ that designates a variable; for example, the root node ① in Fig. 21 designates x_1. Branch nodes have two successors, indicated by descending lines. One of the successors is drawn as a dashed line and called LO; the other is drawn as a solid line and called HI. These branch nodes define a path in the diagram for any values of the Boolean variables, if we start at the root and take the LO branch from node ⓙ when $x_j = 0$, the HI branch when $x_j = 1$. Eventually this path leads to a *sink node*, which is either ⊥ (denoting FALSE) or ⊤ (denoting TRUE).

Fig. 21. The binary decision diagram (BDD)
for the majority or median function $\langle x_1 x_2 x_3 \rangle$.

In Fig. 21 it's easy to verify that this process yields the function value FALSE
when at least two of the variables $\{x_1, x_2, x_3\}$ are 0, otherwise it yields TRUE.

Many authors use $\boxed{0}$ and $\boxed{1}$ to denote the sink nodes. We use $\boxed{\perp}$ and $\boxed{\top}$
instead, hoping to avoid any confusion with the branch nodes $\textcircled{0}$ and $\textcircled{1}$.

Inside a computer, Fig. 21 would be represented as a set of four nodes in
arbitrary memory locations, where each node has three fields $\boxed{\text{V} \mid \text{LO} \mid \text{HI}}$.
The V field holds the index of a variable, while the LO and HI fields each point
to another node or to a sink:

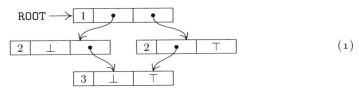

(1)

With 64-bit words, we might for example use 8 bits for V, then 28 bits for LO
and the other 28 bits for HI.

Such a structure is called a "binary decision diagram," or BDD for short.
Small BDDs can readily be drawn as actual diagrams on a piece of paper
or a computer screen. But in essence each BDD is really an abstract set of
linked nodes, which might more properly be called a "binary decision dag" — a
binary tree with shared subtrees, a directed acyclic graph in which exactly two
distinguished arcs emanate from every nonsink node.

We shall assume that every BDD obeys two important restrictions. First, it
must be *ordered*: Whenever a LO or HI arc goes from branch node $\textcircled{i}$ to branch
node $\textcircled{j}$, we must have $i < j$. Thus, in particular, no variable x_j will ever be
queried twice when the function is evaluated. Second, a BDD must be *reduced*,
in the sense that it doesn't waste space. This means that a branch node's LO
and HI pointers must never be equal, and that no two nodes are allowed to have
the same triple of values (V, LO, HI). Every node should also be accessible from
the root. For example, the diagrams

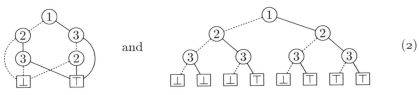

and

(2)

are not BDDs, because the first one isn't ordered and the other one isn't reduced.

Many other flavors of decision diagrams have been invented, and the literature of computer science now contains a rich alphabet soup of acronyms like

EVBDD, FBDD, IBDD, OBDD, OFDD, OKFDD, PBDD, ..., ZDD. In this book we shall always use the unadorned code name "BDD" to denote a binary decision diagram that is ordered and reduced as described above, just as we generally use the word "tree" to denote an ordered (plane) tree, because such BDDs and such trees are the most common in practice.

Recall from Section 7.1.1 that every Boolean function $f(x_1, \ldots, x_n)$ corresponds to a *truth table*, which is the 2^n-bit binary string that starts with the function value $f(0, \ldots, 0)$ and continues with $f(0, \ldots, 0, 1)$, $f(0, \ldots, 0, 1, 0)$, $f(0, \ldots, 0, 1, 1)$, ..., $f(1, \ldots, 1, 1, 1)$. For example, the truth table of the median function $\langle x_1 x_2 x_3 \rangle$ is 00010111. Notice that this truth table is the same as the sequence of leaves in the unreduced decision tree of (2), with $0 \mapsto \boxed{\bot}$ and $1 \mapsto \boxed{\top}$. In fact, there's an important relationship between truth tables and BDDs, which is best understood in terms of a class of binary strings called "beads."

A truth table of order n is a binary string of length 2^n. A *bead* of order n is a truth table β of order n that is not a square; that is, β doesn't have the form $\alpha\alpha$ for any string α of length 2^{n-1}. (Mathematicians would say that a bead is a "primitive string of length 2^n.") There are two beads of order 0, namely 0 and 1; and there are two of order 1, namely 01 and 10. In general there are $2^{2^n} - 2^{2^{n-1}}$ beads of order n when $n > 0$, because there are 2^{2^n} binary strings of length 2^n and $2^{2^{n-1}}$ of them are squares. The $16 - 4 = 12$ beads of order 2 are

$$0001, 0010, 0011, 0100, 0110, 0111, 1000, 1001, 1011, 1100, 1101, 1110; \qquad (3)$$

these are also the truth tables of all functions $f(x_1, x_2)$ that depend on x_1, in the sense that $f(0, x_2)$ is not the same function as $f(1, x_2)$.

Every truth table τ is a power of a unique bead, called its root. For if τ has length 2^n and isn't already a bead, it's the square of another truth table τ'; and by induction on the length of τ, we must have $\tau' = \beta^k$ for some root β. Hence $\tau = \beta^{2k}$, and β is the root of τ as well as τ'. (Of course k is a power of 2.)

A truth table τ of order $n > 0$ always has the form $\tau_0 \tau_1$, where τ_0 and τ_1 are truth tables of order $n - 1$. Clearly τ represents the function $f(x_1, x_2, \ldots, x_n)$ if and only if τ_0 represents $f(0, x_2, \ldots, x_n)$ and τ_1 represents $f(1, x_2, \ldots, x_n)$. These functions $f(0, x_2, \ldots, x_n)$ and $f(1, x_2, \ldots, x_n)$ are called *subfunctions* of f; and their truth tables, τ_0 and τ_1, are called *subtables* of τ.

Subtables of a subtable are also considered to be subtables, and a table is considered to be a subtable of itself. Thus, in general, a truth table of order n has 2^k subtables of order $n - k$, for $0 \le k \le n$, corresponding to 2^k possible settings of the first k variables $(x_1, \ldots, x_k)$. Many of these subtables often turn out to be identical; in such cases we're able to represent τ in a compressed form.

The *beads* of a Boolean function are the subtables of its truth table that happen to be beads. For example, let's consider again the median function $\langle x_1 x_2 x_3 \rangle$, with its truth table 00010111. The distinct subtables of this truth table are $\{00010111, 0001, 0111, 00, 01, 11, 0, 1\}$; and all of them except 00 and 11 are beads. Therefore the beads of $\langle x_1 x_2 x_3 \rangle$ are

$$\{00010111, 0001, 0111, 01, 0, 1\}. \qquad (4)$$

And now we get to the point: *The nodes of a Boolean function's BDD are in one-to-one correspondence with its beads.* For example, we can redraw Fig. 21 by placing the relevant bead inside of each node:

$$\text{(00010111)}$$
$$\text{(0001)} \quad \text{(0111)}.$$
$$\text{(01)}$$
$$\boxed{0} \qquad \boxed{1}$$

(5)

In general, a function's truth tables of order $n + 1 - k$ correspond to its sub-functions $f(c_1, \ldots, c_{k-1}, x_k, \ldots, x_n)$ of that order; so its beads of order $n + 1 - k$ correspond to those subfunctions that depend on their first variable, x_k. There-fore every such bead corresponds to a branch node (k) in the BDD. And if (k) is a branch node corresponding to the truth table $\tau' = \tau'_0 \tau'_1$, its LO and HI branches point respectively to the nodes that correspond to the roots of τ'_0 and τ'_1.

This correspondence between beads and nodes proves that *every Boolean function has one and only one representation as a BDD.* The individual nodes of that BDD might, of course, be placed in different locations inside a computer.

If f is any Boolean function, let $B(f)$ denote the number of beads that it has. This is the size of its BDD — the total number of nodes, including the sinks. For example, $B(f) = 6$ when f is the median-of-three function, because (5) has size 6.

To fix the ideas, let's work out another example, the "more-or-less random" function of 7.1.1–(22) and 7.1.2–(6). Its truth table, 1100100100001111, is a bead, and so are the two subtables 11001001 and 00001111. Thus we know that the root of its BDD will be a (1) branch, and that the LO and HI nodes below the root will both be (2)s. The subtables of length 4 are $\{1100, 1001, 0000, 1111\}$; here the first two are beads, but the others are squares. To get to the next level, we break the beads in half and carry over the square roots of the nonbeads, identifying duplicates; this leaves us with $\{11, 00, 10, 01\}$. Again there are two beads, and a final step produces the desired BDD:

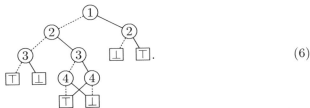

(6)

(In this diagram and others below, it's convenient to repeat the sink nodes $\boxed{\perp}$ and $\boxed{\top}$ in order to avoid excessively long connecting lines. Only one $\boxed{\perp}$ node and one $\boxed{\top}$ node are actually present; so the size of (6) is 9, not 13.)

An alert reader might well be thinking at this point, "Very nice, but what if the BDD is huge?" Indeed, functions can easily be constructed whose BDD is impossibly large; we'll study such cases later. But the wonderful thing is that a great many of the Boolean functions that are of practical importance turn out to have reasonably small values of $B(f)$. So we shall concentrate on the good news first, postponing the bad news until we've seen why BDDs have proved to be so popular.

BDD virtues. If $f(x) = f(x_1, \ldots, x_n)$ is a Boolean function whose BDD is reasonably small, we can do many things quickly and easily. For example:

• We can *evaluate* $f(x)$ in at most n steps, given any input vector $x = x_1 \ldots x_n$, by simply starting at the root and branching until we get to a sink.

• We can *find the lexicographically smallest* x such that $f(x) = 1$, by starting at the root and repeatedly taking the LO branch unless it goes directly to $\boxed{\perp}$. The solution has $x_j = 1$ only when the HI branch was necessary at (j). For example, this procedure gives $x_1 x_2 x_3 = 011$ in the BDD of Fig. 21, and $x_1 x_2 x_3 x_4 = 0000$ in (6). (It locates the value of x that corresponds to the leftmost 1 in the truth table for f.) Only n steps are needed, because every branch node corresponds to a nonzero bead; we can always find a downward path to $\boxed{\top}$ without backing up. Of course this method fails when the root itself is $\boxed{\perp}$. But that happens only when f is identically zero.

• We can *count the number of solutions* to the equation $f(x) = 1$, using Algorithm C below. That algorithm does $B(f)$ operations on n-bit numbers; so its running time is $O(nB(f))$ in the worst case.

• After Algorithm C has acted, we can speedily *generate random solutions* to the equation $f(x) = 1$, in such a way that every solution is equally likely.

• We can also *list all solutions* x to the equation $f(x) = 1$. The algorithm in exercise 16 does this in $O(nN)$ steps when there are N solutions.

• We can *solve the linear Boolean programming problem*: Find x such that

$$w_1 x_1 + \cdots + w_n x_n \text{ is maximum, subject to } f(x_1, \ldots, x_n) = 1, \qquad (7)$$

given constants $(w_1, \ldots, w_n)$. Algorithm B (below) does this in $O(n+B(f))$ steps.

• We can *compute the generating function* $a_0 + a_1 z + \cdots + a_n z^n$, where there are a_j solutions to $f(x_1, \ldots, x_n) = 1$ with $x_1 + \cdots + x_n = j$. (See exercise 25.)

• We can *calculate the reliability polynomial* $F(p_1, \ldots, p_n)$, which is the probability that $f(x_1, \ldots, x_n) = 1$ when each x_j is independently set to 1 with a given probability p_j. Exercise 26 does this in $O(B(f))$ steps.

Moreover, we will see that BDDs can be combined and modified efficiently. For example, it is not difficult to form the BDDs for $f(x_1, \ldots, x_n) \wedge g(x_1, \ldots, x_n)$ and $f(x_1, \ldots, x_{j-1}, g(x_1, \ldots, x_n), x_{j+1}, \ldots, x_n)$ from the BDDs for f and g.

Algorithms for solving basic problems with BDDs are often described most easily if we assume that the BDD is given as a sequential list of branch instructions $I_{s-1}, I_{s-2}, \ldots, I_1, I_0$, where each I_k has the form $(\bar{v}_k? \, l_k : h_k)$. For example, (6) might be represented as a list of $s = 9$ instructions

$$
\begin{array}{lll}
I_8 = (\bar{1}? \, 7{:}6), & I_5 = (\bar{3}? \, 1{:}0), & I_2 = (\bar{4}? \, 0{:}1), \\
I_7 = (\bar{2}? \, 5{:}4), & I_4 = (\bar{3}? \, 3{:}2), & I_1 = (\bar{5}? \, 1{:}1), \qquad (8) \\
I_6 = (\bar{2}? \, 0{:}1), & I_3 = (\bar{4}? \, 1{:}0), & I_0 = (\bar{5}? \, 0{:}0),
\end{array}
$$

with $v_8 = 1$, $l_8 = 7$, $h_8 = 6$, $v_7 = 2$, $l_7 = 5$, $h_7 = 4$, $\ldots$, $v_0 = 5$, $l_0 = h_0 = 0$. In general the instruction '$(\bar{v}? \, l : h)$' means, "If $x_v = 0$, go to I_l, otherwise go to I_h," except that the last cases I_1 and I_0 are special. We require that the LO and HI branches l_k and h_k satisfy

$$l_k < k, \qquad h_k < k, \qquad v_{l_k} > v_k, \quad \text{and} \quad v_{h_k} > v_k, \qquad \text{for } s > k \geq 2; \qquad (9)$$

in other words, all branches move downward, to variables of greater index. But the sink nodes $\boxed{\top}$ and $\boxed{\bot}$ are represented by dummy instructions I_1 and I_0, in which $l_k = h_k = k$ and the "variable index" v_k has the impossible value $n + 1$.

These instructions can be numbered in any way that respects the topological ordering of the BDD, as required by (9). The root node must correspond to I_{s-1}, and the sink nodes must correspond to I_1 and I_0, but the other index numbers aren't so rigidly prescribed. For example, (6) might also be expressed as

$$\begin{aligned}
I_8' &= (\bar{1}?\,7\!:\!2), & I_5' &= (\bar{4}?\,0\!:\!1), & I_2' &= (\bar{2}?\,0\!:\!1), \\
I_7' &= (\bar{2}?\,4\!:\!6), & I_4' &= (\bar{3}?\,1\!:\!0), & I_1' &= (\bar{5}?\,1\!:\!1), \\
I_6' &= (\bar{3}?\,3\!:\!5), & I_3' &= (\bar{4}?\,1\!:\!0), & I_0' &= (\bar{5}?\,0\!:\!0),
\end{aligned} \qquad (10)$$

and in 46 other isomorphic ways. Inside a computer, the BDD need not actually appear in consecutive locations; we can readily traverse the nodes of any acyclic digraph in topological order, when the nodes are linked as in (1). But we will imagine that they've been arranged sequentially as in (8), so that various algorithms are easier to understand.

One technicality is worth noting: If $f(x) = 1$ for all x, so that the BDD is simply the sink node $\boxed{\top}$, we let $s = 2$ in this sequential representation. Otherwise s is the size of the BDD. Then the root is always represented by I_{s-1}.

Algorithm C (*Count solutions*). Given the BDD for a Boolean function $f(x) = f(x_1, \ldots, x_n)$, represented as a sequence I_{s-1}, $\ldots$, I_0 as described above, this algorithm determines $|f|$, the number of binary vectors $x = x_1 \ldots x_n$ such that $f(x) = 1$. It also computes the table $c_0, c_1, \ldots, c_{s-1}$, where c_k is the number of 1s in the bead that corresponds to I_k.

C1. [Loop over k.] Set $c_0 \leftarrow 0$, $c_1 \leftarrow 1$, and do step C2 for $k = 2, 3, \ldots, s - 1$. Then return the answer $2^{v_{s-1}-1}c_{s-1}$.

C2. [Compute c_k.] Set $l \leftarrow l_k$, $h \leftarrow h_k$, and $c_k \leftarrow 2^{v_l - v_k - 1}c_l + 2^{v_h - v_k - 1}c_h$. ∎

For example, when presented with (8), this algorithm computes

$$c_2 \leftarrow 1, \ c_3 \leftarrow 1, \ c_4 \leftarrow 2, \ c_5 \leftarrow 2, \ c_6 \leftarrow 4, \ c_7 \leftarrow 4, \ c_8 \leftarrow 8;$$

the total number of solutions to $f(x_1, x_2, x_3, x_4) = 1$ is 8.

The integers c_k in Algorithm C satisfy

$$0 \leq c_k < 2^{n+1-v_k}, \qquad \text{for } 2 \leq k < s, \qquad (11)$$

and this upper bound is best possible. Therefore multiprecision arithmetic may be needed when n is large. If extra storage space for high precision is problematic, one could use modular arithmetic instead, running the algorithm several times and computing $c_k \bmod p$ for various single-precision primes p; then the final answer would be deducible with the Chinese remainder algorithm, Eq. 4.3.2–(24). On the other hand, floating point arithmetic is usually sufficient in practice.

Let's look at some examples that are more interesting than (6). The BDDs

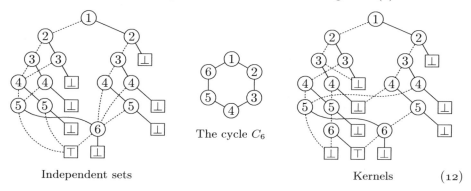

Independent sets   Kernels   (12)

The cycle C_6

represent functions of six variables that correspond to subsets of vertices in the
cycle graph C_6. In this setup a vector such as $x_1 \ldots x_6 = 100110$ stands for the
subset $\{1, 4, 5\}$; the vector 000000 stands for the empty subset; and so on. On the
left is the BDD for which we have $f(x) = 1$ when x is *independent* in C_6; on the
right is the BDD for *maximal* independent subsets, also called the *kernels* of C_6
(see exercise 12). In general, the independent subsets of C_n correspond to arrangements of 0s and 1s in a circle of length n, with no two 1s in a row; the kernels
correspond to such arrangements in which there also are no three consecutive 0s.

Algorithm C decorates a BDD with counts c_k, working from bottom to top,
where c_k is the number of paths from node k to $\boxed{\top}$. When we apply that
algorithm to the BDDs in (12) we get

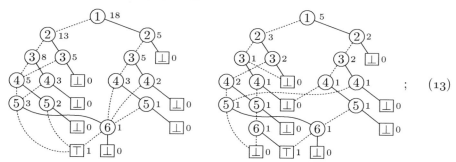

;   (13)

hence C_6 has 18 independent sets and 5 kernels.

These counts make it easy to generate uniformly *random* solutions. For
example, to get a random independent set vector $x_1 \ldots x_6$, we know that 13 of
the solutions in the left-hand BDD have $x_1 = 0$, while the other 5 have $x_1 = 1$.
So we set $x_1 \leftarrow 0$ with probability $13/18$, and take the LO branch; otherwise we
set $x_1 \leftarrow 1$ and take the HI branch. In the latter case, $x_1 = 1$ forces $x_2 \leftarrow 0$, but
then x_3 could go either way.

Suppose we've chosen to set $x_1 \leftarrow 1$, $x_2 \leftarrow 0$, $x_3 \leftarrow 0$, and $x_4 \leftarrow 0$; this case
occurs with probability $\frac{5}{18} \cdot \frac{5}{5} \cdot \frac{3}{5} \cdot \frac{2}{3} = \frac{2}{18}$. Then there's a branch from ④ to
⑥, so we flip a coin and set x_5 to a completely random value. In general, a

branch from (i) to (j) means that the $j - i - 1$ intermediate bits $x_{i+1} \ldots x_{j-1}$ should independently become 0 or 1 with equal probability. Similarly, a branch from (i) to $\boxed{\top}$ should assign random values to $x_{i+1} \ldots x_n$.

Of course there are simpler ways to make a random choice between 18 solutions to a combinatorial problem. Moreover, the right-hand BDD in (13) is an embarrassingly complex way to represent the five kernels of C_6: We could simply have listed them, 001001, 010010, 010101, 100100, 101010! But the point is that this same method will yield the independent sets and kernels of C_n when n is much larger. For example, the 100-cycle C_{100} has 1,630,580,875,002 kernels, yet the BDD describing them has only 855 nodes. One hundred simple steps will therefore generate a fully random kernel from this vast collection.

Boolean programming and beyond. A bottom-up algorithm analogous to Algorithm C is also able to find optimum *weighted* solutions (7) to the Boolean equation $f(x) = 1$. The basic idea is that it's easy to deduce an optimum solution for any bead of f, once we know optimum solutions for the LO and HI beads that lie directly below it.

Algorithm B (*Solutions of maximum weight*). Let $I_{s-1}, \ldots, I_0$ be a sequence of branch instructions that represents the BDD for a Boolean function f, as in Algorithm C, and let $(w_1, \ldots, w_n)$ be an arbitrary sequence of integer weights. This algorithm finds a binary vector $x = x_1 \ldots x_n$ such that $w_1 x_1 + \cdots + w_n x_n$ is maximum, over all x with $f(x) = 1$. We assume that $s > 1$; otherwise $f(x)$ is identically 0. Auxiliary integer vectors $m_1 \ldots m_{s-1}$ and $W_1 \ldots W_{n+1}$ are used in the calculations, as well as an auxiliary bit vector $t_2 \ldots t_{s-1}$.

B1. [Initialize.] Set $W_{n+1} \leftarrow 0$ and $W_j \leftarrow W_{j+1} + \max(w_j, 0)$ for $n \geq j \geq 1$.

B2. [Loop on k.] Set $m_1 \leftarrow 0$ and do step B3 for $2 \leq k < s$. Then do step B4.

B3. [Process I_k.] Set $v \leftarrow v_k$, $l \leftarrow l_k$, $h \leftarrow h_k$, $t_k \leftarrow 0$. If $l \neq 0$, set $m_k \leftarrow m_l + W_{v+1} - W_{v_l}$. Then if $h \neq 0$, compute $m \leftarrow m_h + W_{v+1} - W_{v_h} + w_v$; and if $l = 0$ or $m > m_k$, set $m_k \leftarrow m$ and $t_k \leftarrow 1$.

B4. [Compute the x's.] Set $j \leftarrow 0$, $k \leftarrow s - 1$, and do the following operations until $j = n$: While $j < v_k - 1$, set $j \leftarrow j + 1$ and $x_j \leftarrow [w_j > 0]$; if $k > 1$, set $j \leftarrow j + 1$ and $x_j \leftarrow t_k$ and $k \leftarrow (t_k = 0?\ l_k : h_k)$. ∎

A simple case of this algorithm is worked out in exercise 18. Step B3 does technical maneuvers that may look a bit scary, but their net effect is just to compute

$$m_k \leftarrow \max(m_l + W_{v+1} - W_{v_l}, m_h + W_{v+1} - W_{v_h} + w_v), \tag{14}$$

and to record in t_k whether l or h is better. In fact, v_l and v_h are usually both equal to $v + 1$; then the calculation simply sets $m_k \leftarrow \max(m_l, m_h + w_v)$, corresponding to the cases $x_v = 0$ and $x_v = 1$. Technicalities arise only because we want to avoid fetching m_0, which is $-\infty$, and because v_l or v_h might exceed $v+1$.

With this algorithm we can, for example, quickly find an optimum set of kernel vertices in an n-cycle C_n, using weights based on the "Thue–Morse" sequence,

$$w_j = (-1)^{\nu j}; \tag{15}$$

here νj denotes sideways addition, Eq. 7.1.3–(59). In other words, w_j is -1 or $+1$, depending on whether j has odd parity or even parity when expressed as a binary number. The maximum of $w_1 x_1 + \cdots + w_n x_n$ occurs when the even-parity vertices 3, 5, 6, 9, 10, 12, 15, ... most strongly outnumber the odd-parity vertices 1, 2, 4, 7, 8, 11, 13, ... that appear in a kernel. It turns out that

$$\{1, 3, 6, 9, 12, 15, 18, 20, 23, 25, 27, 30, 33, 36, 39, 41, 43, 46, 48,$$
$$51, 54, 57, 60, 63, 66, 68, 71, 73, 75, 78, 80, 83, 86, 89, 92, 95, 97, 99\} \quad (16)$$

is an optimum kernel in this sense when $n = 100$; only five vertices of odd parity, namely $\{1, 25, 41, 73, 97\}$, need to be included in this set of 38 to satisfy the kernel conditions, hence $\max(w_1 x_1 + \cdots + w_{100} x_{100}) = 28$. Thanks to Algorithm B, a few thousand computer instructions are sufficient to select (16) from more than a trillion possible kernels, because the BDD for all those kernels happens to be small.

Mathematically pristine problems related to combinatorial objects like cycle kernels could also be resolved efficiently with more traditional techniques, which are based on recurrences and induction. But the beauty of BDD methods is that they apply also to real-world problems that don't have any elegant structure. For example, let's consider the graph of 49 "united states" that appeared in 7–(17) and 7–(61). The Boolean function that represents all the maximal independent sets of that graph (all the kernels) has a BDD of size 780 that begins as follows:

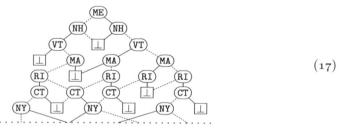

$$(17)$$

Algorithm B quickly discovers the following kernels of minimum and maximum weight, when each state vertex is simply weighted according to the sum of letters in its postal code ($w_{CA} = 3 + 1$, $w_{DC} = 4 + 3$, ..., $w_{WY} = 23 + 25$):

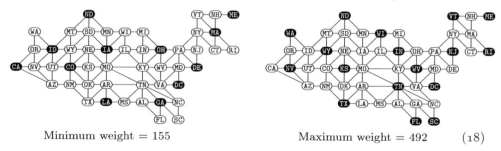

Minimum weight = 155   Maximum weight = 492   (18)

This graph has 266,137 kernels; but with Algorithm B, we needn't generate them all. In fact, the right-hand example in (18) could also be obtained with a smaller BDD of size 428, which characterizes the *independent sets*, because all weights are positive. (A kernel of maximum weight is the same thing as an independent set of maximum weight, in such cases.) There are 211,954,906 independent sets in this graph, many more than the number of kernels; yet we can find an independent set of maximum weight more quickly than a kernel of maximum weight, because the BDD is smaller.

Fig. 22. The grid $P_3 \mathbin{\square} P_3$, and a BDD for its connected subgraphs.

A quite different sort of graph-related BDD is shown in Fig. 22. This one is based on the 3×3 grid $P_3 \square P_3$; it characterizes the sets of edges that connect all vertices of the grid together. Thus, it's a function $f(x_{12}, x_{13}, \ldots, x_{89})$ of the twelve edges $1 \mathbin{—} 2$, $1 \mathbin{—} 3$, $\ldots$, $8 \mathbin{—} 9$ instead of the nine vertices $\{1, \ldots, 9\}$. Exercise 55 describes one way to construct it. When Algorithm C is applied to this BDD, it tells us that exactly 431 of the $2^{12} = 4096$ spanning subgraphs of $P_3 \square P_3$ are connected.

A straightforward extension of Algorithm C (see exercise 25) will refine this total and compute the *generating function* of these solutions, namely

$$G(z) = \sum_x z^{\nu x} f(x) = 192z^8 + 164z^9 + 62z^{10} + 12z^{11} + z^{12}. \qquad (19)$$

Thus $P_3 \square P_3$ has 192 spanning trees, plus 164 spanning subgraphs that are connected and have nine edges, and so on. Exercise 7.2.1.6–106(a) gives a formula for the number of spanning trees in $P_m \square P_n$ for general m and n; but the full generating function $G(z)$ contains considerably more information, and it probably has no simple formula unless $\min(m, n)$ is small.

Suppose each edge $u \mathbin{—} v$ is present with probability p_{uv}, independent of all other edges of $P_3 \square P_3$. What is the probability that the resulting subgraph is connected? This is the *reliability polynomial*, which also goes by a variety of other names because it arises in many different applications. In general, as discussed in exercise 7.1.1–12, every Boolean function $f(x_1, \ldots, x_n)$ has a unique representation as a polynomial $F(x_1, \ldots, x_n)$ with the properties that

   i) $F(x_1, \ldots, x_n) = f(x_1, \ldots, x_n)$ whenever each x_j is 0 or 1;

   ii) $F(x_1, \ldots, x_n)$ is multilinear: Its degree in x_j is ≤ 1 for all j.

This polynomial F has integer coefficients and satisfies the basic recurrence

$$F(x_1, \ldots, x_n) = (1 - x_1)F_0(x_2, \ldots, x_n) + x_1 F_1(x_2, \ldots, x_n), \qquad (20)$$

where F_0 and F_1 are the integer multilinear representations of $f(0, x_2, \ldots, x_n)$ and $f(1, x_2, \ldots, x_n)$. Indeed, (20) is George Boole's "law of development."

Two important things follow from recurrence (20). First, F is precisely the reliability polynomial $F(p_1, \ldots, p_n)$ mentioned earlier, because the reliability polynomial obviously satisfies the same recurrence. Second, F is easily calculated from the BDD for f, working upward from the bottom and using (20) to compute the reliability of each bead. (See exercise 26.)

The connectivity function for an 8×8 grid $P_8 \square P_8$ is, of course, much more complicated than the one for $P_3 \square P_3$; it is a Boolean function of 112 variables and its BDD has 43790 nodes, compared to only 37 in Fig. 22. Still, computations with this BDD are quite feasible, and in a second or two we can compute

$$G(z) = 12623132291249853968259481 6z^{63}$$
$$+ 10066111400354110626007613 44z^{64}$$
$$+ \cdots + 6212z^{110} + 112z^{111} + z^{112},$$

as well as the probability $F(p)$ of connectedness and its derivative $F'(p)$, when each of the edges is present with probability p (see exercise 29):

$$F(p): \qquad ; \qquad F'(p): \qquad . \qquad (21)$$
$$0 \quad p \quad 1 \qquad\qquad\qquad 0 \quad p \quad 1$$

*A sweeping generalization. Algorithms B and C and the algorithms we've been discussing for bottom-up BDD scanning are actually special cases of a much more general scheme that can be exploited in many additional ways. Consider an abstract algebra with two associative binary operators $\circ$ and $\bullet$, satisfying the distributive laws

$$\alpha \bullet (\beta \circ \gamma) = (\alpha \bullet \beta) \circ (\alpha \bullet \gamma), \qquad (\beta \circ \gamma) \bullet \alpha = (\beta \bullet \alpha) \circ (\gamma \bullet \alpha). \qquad (22)$$

Every Boolean function $f(x_1, \ldots, x_n)$ corresponds to a *fully elaborated truth table* involving the symbols $\circ$, $\bullet$, $\perp$, and $\top$, together with $\bar{x}_j$ and x_j for $1 \leq j \leq n$, in a way that's best understood by considering a small example: When $n = 2$ and when the ordinary truth table for f is 0010, the fully elaborated truth table is

$$(\bar{x}_1 \bullet \bar{x}_2 \bullet \perp) \circ (\bar{x}_1 \bullet x_2 \bullet \perp) \circ (x_1 \bullet \bar{x}_2 \bullet \top) \circ (x_1 \bullet x_2 \bullet \perp). \qquad (23)$$

The meaning of such an expression depends on the meanings that we attach to the symbols $\circ$, $\bullet$, $\perp$, $\top$, and to the literals $\bar{x}_j$ and x_j; but whatever the expression means, we can compute it directly from the BDD for f.

For example, let's return to Fig. 21, the BDD for $\langle x_1 x_2 x_3 \rangle$. The elaborations of nodes ⊥ and ⊤ are $\alpha_\perp = \perp$ and $\alpha_\top = \top$, respectively. Then the elaboration of ③ is $\alpha_3 = (\bar{x}_3 \bullet \alpha_\perp) \circ (x_3 \bullet \alpha_\top)$; the elaborations of the nodes labeled ② are $\alpha_2^l = (\bar{x}_2 \bullet (\bar{x}_3 \circ x_3) \bullet \alpha_\perp) \circ (x_2 \bullet \alpha_3)$ on the left and $\alpha_2^r = (\bar{x}_2 \bullet \alpha_3) \circ (x_2 \bullet (\bar{x}_3 \circ x_3) \bullet \alpha_\top)$ on the right; and the elaboration of node ① is $\alpha_1 = (\bar{x}_1 \bullet \alpha_2^l) \circ (x_1 \bullet \alpha_2^r)$. (Exercise 31 discusses the general procedure.) Expanding these formulas via the distributive laws (22) leads to a full elaboration with $2^n = 8$ "terms":

$$\alpha_1 = (\bar{x}_1 \bullet \bar{x}_2 \bullet \bar{x}_3 \bullet \perp) \circ (\bar{x}_1 \bullet \bar{x}_2 \bullet x_3 \bullet \perp) \circ (\bar{x}_1 \bullet x_2 \bullet \bar{x}_3 \bullet \perp) \circ (\bar{x}_1 \bullet x_2 \bullet x_3 \bullet \top)$$
$$\circ (x_1 \bullet \bar{x}_2 \bullet \bar{x}_3 \bullet \perp) \circ (x_1 \bullet \bar{x}_2 \bullet x_3 \bullet \top) \circ (x_1 \bullet x_2 \bullet \bar{x}_3 \bullet \top) \circ (x_1 \bullet x_2 \bullet x_3 \bullet \top). \qquad (24)$$

Algorithm C is the special case where 'o' is addition, '•' is multiplication, '⊥' is 0, '⊤' is 1, '$\bar{x}_j$' is 1, and 'x_j' is also 1. Algorithm B arises when 'o' is the *maximum operator* and '•' is addition; the distributive laws

$$\alpha + \max(\beta, \gamma) = \max(\alpha+\beta, \alpha+\gamma), \quad \max(\beta, \gamma) + \alpha = \max(\beta+\alpha, \gamma+\alpha) \quad (25)$$

are easily checked. We interpret '⊥' as $-\infty$, '⊤' as 0, '$\bar{x}_j$' as 0, and 'x_j' as w_j. Then, for example, (24) becomes

$$\max(-\infty, -\infty, -\infty, w_2 + w_3, -\infty, w_1 + w_3, w_1 + w_2, w_1 + w_2 + w_3);$$

and in general the full elaboration under this interpretation is equivalent to the expression $\max\{w_1 x_1 + \cdots + w_n x_n \mid f(x_1, \ldots, x_n) = 1\}$.

Friendly functions. Many families of functions are known to have BDDs of modest size. If f is, for example, a symmetric function of n variables, it's easy to see that $B(f) = O(n^2)$. Indeed, when $n = 5$ we can start with the triangular pattern

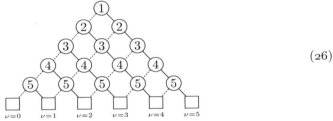

$$(26)$$

and set the leaves to ⊥ or ⊤ depending on the respective values of f when the value of $\nu x = x_1 + \cdots + x_5$ equals 0, 1, 2, 3, 4, or 5. Then we can remove redundant or equivalent nodes, always obtaining a BDD whose size is $\binom{n+2}{2}$ or less.

Suppose we take any function $f(x_1, \ldots, x_n)$ and make two adjacent variables equal:

$$g(x_1, \ldots, x_n) = f(x_1, \ldots, x_{k-1}, x_k, x_k, x_{k+2}, \ldots, x_n). \quad (27)$$

Exercise 40 proves that $B(g) \le B(f)$. And by repeating this condensation process, we find that a function such as $f(x_1, x_1, x_3, x_3, x_3, x_6)$ has a small BDD whenever $B(f)$ is small. In particular, the threshold function $[2x_1 + 3x_3 + x_6 \ge t]$ must have a small BDD for any value of t, because it's a condensed version of the symmetric function $f(x_1, \ldots, x_6) = [x_1 + \cdots + x_6 \ge t]$. This argument shows that *any* threshold function with nonnegative integer weights,

$$f(x_1, x_2, \ldots, x_n) = [w_1 x_1 + w_2 x_2 + \cdots + w_n x_n \ge t], \quad (28)$$

can be obtained by condensing a symmetric function of $w_1 + w_2 + \cdots + w_n$ variables, so its BDD size is $O(w_1 + w_2 + \cdots + w_n)^2$.

Threshold functions often turn out to be easy even when the weights grow exponentially. For example, suppose $t = (t_1 t_2 \ldots t_n)_2$ and consider

$$f_t(x_1, x_2, \ldots, x_n) = [2^{n-1} x_1 + 2^{n-2} x_2 + \cdots + x_n \ge t]. \quad (29)$$

This function is true if and only if the binary string $x_1 x_2 \ldots x_n$ is lexicographically greater than or equal to $t_1 t_2 \ldots t_n$, and its BDD always has exactly $n + 2$ nodes when $t_n = 1$. (See exercise 170.)

Another kind of function with small BDD is the 2^m-way multiplexer of Eq. 7.1.2–(31), a function of $n = m + 2^m$ variables:

$$M_m(x_1, \ldots, x_m; x_{m+1}, \ldots, x_n) = x_{m+1+(x_1\ldots x_m)_2}. \tag{30}$$

Its BDD begins with 2^{k-1} branch nodes $\textcircled{k}$ for $1 \le k \le m$. But below that complete binary tree, there's just one $\textcircled{k}$ for each x_k in the main block of variables with $m < k \le n$. Hence $B(M_m) = 1 + 2 + \cdots + 2^{m-1} + 2^m + 2 = 2^{m+1} + 1 < 2n$.

A linear network model of computation, illustrated in Fig. 23, helps to clarify the cases where a BDD is especially efficient. Consider an arrangement of computational modules $M_1, M_2, \ldots, M_n$, in which the Boolean variable x_k is input to module M_k; there also are wires between neighboring modules, each carrying a Boolean signal, with a_k wires from M_k to M_{k+1} and b_k wires from M_{k+1} to M_k for $1 \le k \le n$. A special wire out of M_n contains the output of the function, $f(x_1, \ldots, x_n)$. We define $a_0 = b_0 = b_n = 0$ and $a_n = 1$, so that module M_k has exactly $c_k = 1 + a_{k-1} + b_k$ input ports and exactly $d_k = a_k + b_{k-1}$ output ports for each k. It computes d_k Boolean functions of its c_k inputs.

The individual functions computed by each module can be arbitrarily complicated, but they must be *well defined* in the sense that their joint values are completely determined by the x's: Every choice of $(x_1, \ldots, x_n)$ must lead to exactly one way to set the signals on all the wires, consistent with all of the given functions.

Theorem M. *If f can be computed by such a network, then $B(f) \le \sum_{k=0}^{n} 2^{a_k 2^{b_k}}$.*

Proof. We will show that the BDD for f has at most $2^{a_{k-1} 2^{b_{k-1}}}$ branch nodes $\textcircled{k}$, for $1 \le k \le n$. This is clear if $b_{k-1} = 0$, because at most $2^{a_{k-1}}$ subfunctions are possible when x_1 through x_{k-1} have any given values. So we will show that any network that has a_{k-1} forward wires and b_{k-1} backward wires between M_{k-1} and M_k can be replaced by an equivalent network that has $a_{k-1} 2^{b_{k-1}}$ forward wires and none that run backward.

For convenience, let's consider the case $k = 4$ in Fig. 23, with $a_3 = 4$ and $b_3 = 2$; we want to replace those 6 wires by 16 that run only forward. Suppose Alice is in charge of M_3 and Bob is in charge of M_4. Alice sends a 4-bit signal, a, to Bob while he sends a 2-bit signal, b, to her. More precisely, for any fixed value of $(x_1, \ldots, x_n)$, Alice computes a certain function A and Bob computes a function B, where

$$A(b) = a \quad \text{and} \quad B(a) = b. \tag{31}$$

Alice's function A depends on (x_1, x_2, x_3), so Bob doesn't know what it is; Bob's function B is, similarly, unknown to Alice, since it depends on $(x_4, \ldots, x_n)$. But those unknown functions have the key property that, for every choice of $(x_1, \ldots, x_n)$, there's exactly one solution (a, b) to the equations (31).

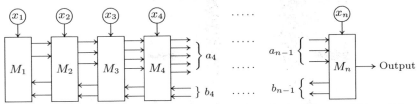

Fig. 23. A generic network of Boolean modules for which Theorem M is valid.

So Alice changes the behavior of module M_3: She sends Bob *four* 4-bit values, $A(00)$, $A(01)$, $A(10)$, and $A(11)$, thereby revealing her A function. And Bob changes the behavior of M_4: Instead of sending any feedback, he looks at those four values, together with his other inputs (namely x_4 and the b_4 bits received from M_5), and discovers the unique a and b that solve (31). His new module uses this value of a to compute the a_4 bits that he outputs to M_5. ∎

Theorem M says that the BDD size will be reasonably small if we can construct such a network with small values of a_k and b_k. Indeed, $B(f)$ will be $O(n)$ if the a's and b's are bounded, although the constant of proportionality might be huge. Let's work an example by considering the *three-in-a-row function*,

$$f(x_1, \ldots, x_n) = x_1 x_2 x_3 \vee x_2 x_3 x_4 \vee \cdots \vee x_{n-2} x_{n-1} x_n \vee x_{n-1} x_n x_1 \vee x_n x_1 x_2, \quad (32)$$

which is true if and only if a circular necklace labeled with bits $x_1, \ldots, x_n$ has three consecutive 1s. One way to implement it via Boolean modules is to give M_k three inputs (u_k, v_k, w_k) from M_{k-1} and two inputs (y_k, z_k) from M_{k+1}, where

$$u_k = x_{k-1}, \quad v_k = x_{k-2} x_{k-1}, \quad w_k = x_{n-1} x_n x_1 \vee \cdots \vee x_{k-3} x_{k-2} x_{k-1};$$
$$y_k = x_n, \quad z_k = x_{n-1} x_n. \quad (33)$$

Here subscripts are treated modulo n, and appropriate changes are made at the left or right when $k = 1$ or $k \geq n - 1$. Then M_k computes the functions

$$u_{k+1} = x_k, \quad v_{k+1} = u_k x_k, \quad w_{k+1} = w_k \vee v_k x_k, \quad y_{k-1} = y_k, \quad z_{k-1} = z_k \quad (34)$$

for nearly all values of k; exercise 45 has the details. With this construction we have $a_k \leq 3$ and $b_k \leq 2$ for all k, hence Theorem M tells us that $B(f) \leq 2^{12} n = 4096n$. In fact, the truth is much sweeter: $B(f)$ is actually $< 9n$ (see exercise 46).

Shared BDDs. We often want to deal with several Boolean functions at once, and related functions often have common subfunctions. In such cases we can work with the "BDD base" for $\{f_1(x_1, \ldots, x_n), \ldots, f_m(x_1, \ldots, x_n)\}$, which is a directed acyclic graph that contains one node for every bead that occurs within the truth tables of any of the functions. The BDD base also has m "root pointers," F_j, one for each function f_j; the BDD for f_j is then the set of all nodes reachable from node F_j. Notice that node F_j itself is reachable from node F_i if and only if f_j is a subfunction of f_i.

For example, consider the problem of computing the $n + 1$ bits of the sum of two n-bit numbers,

$$(f_{n+1} f_n f_{n-1} \ldots f_1)_2 = (x_1 x_3 \ldots x_{2n-1})_2 + (x_2 x_4 \ldots x_{2n})_2. \quad (35)$$

The BDD base for those $n + 1$ bits looks like this when $n = 4$:

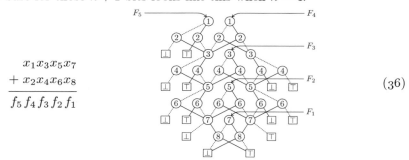

$$\begin{array}{c} x_1 x_3 x_5 x_7 \\ +\ x_2 x_4 x_6 x_8 \\ \hline f_5\, f_4\, f_3\, f_2\, f_1 \end{array} \qquad\qquad (36)$$

The way we've numbered the x's in (35) is important here (see exercise 51). In general there are exactly $B(f_1, \ldots, f_{n+1}) = 9n - 5$ nodes, when $n > 1$. The node just to the left of F_j, for $1 \le j \le n$, represents the subfunction for a *carry* c_j out of the jth bit position from the right; the node just to the right of F_j represents the complement of that carry, $\bar{c}_j$; and node F_{n+1} represents the final carry c_n.

Operations on BDDs. We've been talking about lots of things to do when a BDD is given. But how do we get a BDD into the computer in the first place?

One way is to start with an ordered binary decision diagram such as (26) or the right-hand example in (2), and to reduce it so that it becomes a true BDD. The following algorithm, based on ideas of D. Sieling and I. Wegener [*Information Processing Letters* **48** (1993), 139–144], shows that an arbitrary N-node binary decision diagram whose branches are properly ordered can be reduced to a BDD in $O(N + n)$ steps when there are n variables.

Of course we need some extra memory space in order to decide whether two nodes are equivalent, when doing such a reduction. Having only the three fields $(\mathtt{V}, \mathtt{LO}, \mathtt{HI})$ in each node, as in (1), would give us no room to maneuver. Fortunately, only one additional pointer-size field, called $\mathtt{AUX}$, is needed, together with two additional state bits. We will assume for convenience that the state bits are implicitly present in the *signs* of the $\mathtt{LO}$ and $\mathtt{AUX}$ fields, so that the algorithm needs to deal with only four fields: $(\mathtt{V}, \mathtt{LO}, \mathtt{HI}, \mathtt{AUX})$. The fact that the sign is preempted does mean that a 28-bit $\mathtt{LO}$ field will accommodate only 2^{27} nodes at most — about 134 million — instead of 2^{28}. (On a computer like $\mathtt{MMIX}$, we might prefer to assume that all node addresses are even, and to add 1 to a field instead of complementing it as done here.)

Algorithm R (*Reduction to a BDD*). Given a binary decision diagram that is ordered but not necessarily reduced, this algorithm transforms it into a valid BDD by removing unnecessary nodes and rerouting all pointers appropriately. Each node is assumed to have four fields $(\mathtt{V}, \mathtt{LO}, \mathtt{HI}, \mathtt{AUX})$ as described above, and $\mathtt{ROOT}$ points to the diagram's top node. The $\mathtt{AUX}$ fields are initially irrelevant, except that they must be nonnegative; they will again be nonnegative at the end of the process. All deleted nodes are pushed onto a stack addressed by $\mathtt{AVAIL}$, linked together by the $\mathtt{HI}$ fields of its nodes. (The $\mathtt{LO}$ fields of these nodes will be negative; their complements point to equivalent nodes that have *not* been deleted.)

The V fields of branch nodes are assumed to run from $V(\texttt{ROOT})$ up to $v_{\max}$, in increasing order from the top downwards in the given dag. The sink nodes $\boxed{\bot}$ and $\boxed{\top}$ are assumed to be nodes 0 and 1, respectively, with nonnegative LO and HI fields. They are never deleted; in fact, they are left untouched except for their AUX fields. An auxiliary array of pointers, $\texttt{HEAD}[v]$ for $V(\texttt{ROOT}) \leq v \leq v_{\max}$, is used to create temporary lists of all nodes that have a given value of V.

R1. [Initialize.] Terminate immediately if $\texttt{ROOT} \leq 1$. Otherwise, set $\texttt{AUX}(0) \leftarrow \texttt{AUX}(1) \leftarrow \texttt{AUX}(\texttt{ROOT}) \leftarrow -1$, and $\texttt{HEAD}[v] \leftarrow -1$ for $V(\texttt{ROOT}) \leq v \leq v_{\max}$. (We use the fact that $-1 = \sim 0$ is the bitwise complement of 0.) Then set $s \leftarrow \texttt{ROOT}$ and do the following operations while $s \neq 0$:

> Set $p \leftarrow s$, $s \leftarrow \sim\texttt{AUX}(p)$, $\texttt{AUX}(p) \leftarrow \texttt{HEAD}[V(p)]$, $\texttt{HEAD}[V(p)] \leftarrow \sim p$.
> If $\texttt{AUX}(\texttt{LO}(p)) \geq 0$, set $\texttt{AUX}(\texttt{LO}(p)) \leftarrow \sim s$ and $s \leftarrow \texttt{LO}(p)$.
> If $\texttt{AUX}(\texttt{HI}(p)) \geq 0$, set $\texttt{AUX}(\texttt{HI}(p)) \leftarrow \sim s$ and $s \leftarrow \texttt{HI}(p)$.

(We've essentially done a depth-first search of the dag, temporarily marking all nodes reachable from ROOT by making their AUX fields negative.)

R2. [Loop on v.] Set $\texttt{AUX}(0) \leftarrow \texttt{AUX}(1) \leftarrow 0$, and $v \leftarrow v_{\max}$.

R3. [Bucket sort.] (At this point all remaining nodes whose V field exceeds v have been properly reduced, and their AUX fields are nonnegative.) Set $p \leftarrow \sim\texttt{HEAD}[v]$, $s \leftarrow 0$, and do the following steps while $p \neq 0$:

> Set $p' \leftarrow \sim\texttt{AUX}(p)$.
> Set $q \leftarrow \texttt{HI}(p)$; if $\texttt{LO}(q) < 0$, set $\texttt{HI}(p) \leftarrow \sim\texttt{LO}(q)$.
> Set $q \leftarrow \texttt{LO}(p)$; if $\texttt{LO}(q) < 0$, set $\texttt{LO}(p) \leftarrow \sim\texttt{LO}(q)$ and $q \leftarrow \texttt{LO}(p)$.
> If $q = \texttt{HI}(p)$, set $\texttt{LO}(p) \leftarrow \sim q$, $\texttt{HI}(p) \leftarrow \texttt{AVAIL}$, $\texttt{AUX}(p) \leftarrow 0$, $\texttt{AVAIL} \leftarrow p$;
> otherwise if $\texttt{AUX}(q) \geq 0$, set $\texttt{AUX}(p) \leftarrow s$, $s \leftarrow \sim q$, and $\texttt{AUX}(q) \leftarrow \sim p$;
> otherwise set $\texttt{AUX}(p) \leftarrow \texttt{AUX}(\sim\texttt{AUX}(q))$ and $\texttt{AUX}(\sim\texttt{AUX}(q)) \leftarrow p$.
> Then set $p \leftarrow p'$.

R4. [Clean up.] (Nodes with $\texttt{LO} = x \neq \texttt{HI}$ have now been linked together via their AUX fields, beginning with $\sim\texttt{AUX}(x)$.) Set $r \leftarrow \sim s$, $s \leftarrow 0$, and do the following while $r \geq 0$:

> Set $q \leftarrow \sim\texttt{AUX}(r)$ and $\texttt{AUX}(r) \leftarrow 0$.
> If $s = 0$ set $s \leftarrow q$; otherwise set $\texttt{AUX}(p) \leftarrow q$.
> Set $p \leftarrow q$; then while $\texttt{AUX}(p) > 0$, set $p \leftarrow \texttt{AUX}(p)$.
> Set $r \leftarrow \sim\texttt{AUX}(p)$.

R5. [Loop on p.] Set $p \leftarrow s$. Go to step R9 if $p = 0$. Otherwise set $q \leftarrow p$.

R6. [Examine a bucket.] Set $s \leftarrow \texttt{LO}(p)$. (At this point $p = q$.)

R7. [Remove duplicates.] Set $r \leftarrow \texttt{HI}(q)$. If $\texttt{AUX}(r) \geq 0$, set $\texttt{AUX}(r) \leftarrow \sim q$; otherwise set $\texttt{LO}(q) \leftarrow \texttt{AUX}(r)$, $\texttt{HI}(q) \leftarrow \texttt{AVAIL}$, and $\texttt{AVAIL} \leftarrow q$. Then set $q \leftarrow \texttt{AUX}(q)$. If $q \neq 0$ and $\texttt{LO}(q) = s$, repeat step R7.

R8. [Clean up again.] If $\texttt{LO}(p) \geq 0$, set $\texttt{AUX}(\texttt{HI}(p)) \leftarrow 0$. Then set $p \leftarrow \texttt{AUX}(p)$, and repeat step R8 until $p = q$.

R9. [Done?] If $p \neq 0$, return to R6. Otherwise, if $v > V(\texttt{ROOT})$, set $v \leftarrow v - 1$ and return to R3. Otherwise, if $\texttt{LO}(\texttt{ROOT}) < 0$, set $\texttt{ROOT} \leftarrow \sim\texttt{LO}(\texttt{ROOT})$. ∎

The intricate link manipulations of Algorithm R are easier to program than to explain, but they are highly instructive and not really difficult. The reader is urged to work through the example in exercise 53.

Algorithm R can also be used to compute the BDD for any *restriction* of a given function, namely for any function obtained by "hardwiring" one or more variables to a constant value. The idea is to do a little extra work between steps R1 and R2, setting $\mathtt{HI}(p) \leftarrow \mathtt{LO}(p)$ if variable $\mathtt{V}(p)$ is supposed to be fixed at 0, or $\mathtt{LO}(p) \leftarrow \mathtt{HI}(p)$ if $\mathtt{V}(p)$ is to be fixed at 1. We also need to recycle all nodes that become inaccessible after restriction. Exercise 57 fleshes out the details.

Synthesis of BDDs. We're ready now for the most important algorithm on binary decision diagrams, which takes the BDD for one function, f, and combines it with the BDD for another function, g, in order to obtain the BDD for further functions such as $f \wedge g$ or $f \oplus g$. Synthesis operations of this kind are the principal way to build up the BDDs for complex functions, and the fact that they can be done efficiently is the main reason why BDD data structures have become popular. We will discuss several approaches to the synthesis problem, beginning with a simple method and then speeding it up in various ways.

The basic notion that underlies synthesis is a product operation on BDD structures that we shall call *melding*. Suppose $\alpha = (v, l, h)$ and $\alpha' = (v', l', h')$ are BDD nodes, each containing the index of a variable together with LO and HI pointers. The "meld" of α and α', written $\alpha \diamond \alpha'$, is defined as follows when α and α' are not both sinks:

$$\alpha \diamond \alpha' = \begin{cases} (v,\, l \diamond l',\, h \diamond h'), & \text{if } v = v'; \\ (v,\, l \diamond \alpha',\, h \diamond \alpha'), & \text{if } v < v'; \\ (v',\, \alpha \diamond l',\, \alpha \diamond h'), & \text{if } v > v'. \end{cases} \qquad (37)$$

For example, Fig. 24 shows how two small but typical BDDs are melded. The one on the left, with branch nodes $(\alpha, \beta, \gamma, \delta)$, represents $f(x_1, x_2, x_3, x_4) = (x_1 \vee x_2) \wedge (x_3 \vee x_4)$; the one in the middle, with branch nodes $(\omega, \psi, \chi, \varphi, \upsilon, \tau)$, represents $g(x_1, x_2, x_3, x_4) = (x_1 \oplus x_2) \vee (x_3 \oplus x_4)$. Nodes δ and τ are essentially the same, so we would have $\delta = \tau$ if f and g were part of a single BDD base; but melding can be applied also to BDDs that do not have common nodes. At the right of Fig. 24, $\alpha \diamond \omega$ is the root of a decision diagram that has eleven branch nodes, and it essentially represents the *ordered pair* (f, g).

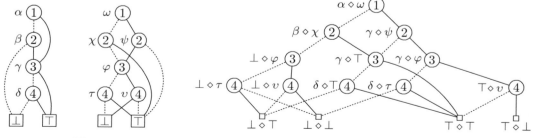

Fig. 24. Two BDDs can be melded together with the $\diamond$ operation (37).

An ordered pair of two Boolean functions can be visualized by placing the truth table of one above the truth table of the other. With this interpretation, $\alpha \diamond \omega$ stands for the ordered pair $\frac{0000011101110111}{0110111111110110}$, and $\beta \diamond \chi$ stands for $\frac{00000111}{01101111}$, etc. The melded BDD of Fig. 24 corresponds to the diagram

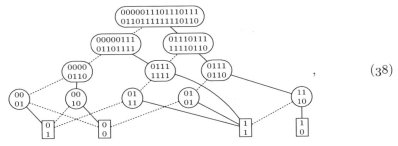

$$(38)$$

which is analogous to (5) except that each node denotes an ordered pair of functions instead of a single function. Beads and subtables are defined on ordered pairs just as before. But now we have four possible sinks instead of two, namely

$$\bot \diamond \bot, \qquad \bot \diamond \top, \qquad \top \diamond \bot, \qquad \text{and} \qquad \top \diamond \top, \qquad (39)$$

corresponding to the ordered pairs $\frac{0}{0}$, $\frac{0}{1}$, $\frac{1}{0}$, and $\frac{1}{1}$.

To compute the conjunction $f \wedge g$, we AND together the truth tables of f and g. This operation corresponds to replacing $\frac{0}{0}$, $\frac{0}{1}$, $\frac{1}{0}$, and $\frac{1}{1}$ by 0, 0, 0, and 1, respectively; so we get the BDD for $f \wedge g$ from $f \diamond g$ by replacing the respective sink nodes of (39) by $\boxed{\bot}$, $\boxed{\bot}$, $\boxed{\bot}$, and $\boxed{\top}$, then reducing the result. Similarly, the BDD for $f \oplus g$ is obtained if we replace the sinks (39) by $\boxed{\bot}$, $\boxed{\top}$, $\boxed{\top}$, and $\boxed{\bot}$. (In this particular case $f \oplus g$ turns out to be the symmetric function $S_{1,4}(x_1, x_2, x_3, x_4)$, as computed in Fig. 9 of Section 7.1.2.) The melded diagram $f \diamond g$ contains all the information needed to compute *any* Boolean combination of f and g; and the BDD for every such combination has at most $B(f \diamond g)$ nodes.

Clearly $B(f \diamond g) \leq B(f)B(g)$, because each node of $f \diamond g$ corresponds to a node of f and a node of g. Therefore the meld of small BDDs cannot be extremely large. Usually, in fact, melding produces a result that is considerably smaller than this worst-case upper bound, with something like $B(f) + B(g)$ nodes instead of $B(f)B(g)$. Exercise 60 discusses a sharper bound that sheds some light on why melds often turn out to be small. But exercises 59(b) and 63 present interesting examples where quadratic growth does occur.

Melding suggests a simple algorithm for synthesis: We can form an array of $B(f)B(g)$ nodes, with node $\alpha \diamond \alpha'$ in row α and column α' for every α in the BDD for f and every α' in the BDD for g. Then we can convert the four sink nodes (39) to $\boxed{\bot}$ or $\boxed{\top}$ as desired, and apply Algorithm R to the root node $f \diamond g$. Voilà — we've got the BDD for $f \wedge g$ or $f \oplus g$ or $f \vee \bar{g}$ or whatever.

The running time of this algorithm is clearly of order $B(f)B(g)$. We can reduce it to order $B(f \diamond g)$, because there's no need to fill in all of the matrix entries $\alpha \diamond \alpha'$; only the nodes that are reachable from $f \diamond g$ are relevant, and we can generate them on the fly when necessary. But even with this improvement in the running time, the simple algorithm is unsatisfactory because of the requirement for $B(f)B(g)$ nodes in memory. When we deal with BDDs, time is cheap but space is expensive: Attempts to solve large problems tend to fail more often because of "spaceout" than because of "timeout." That's why Algorithm R was careful to perform its machinations with only one auxiliary link field per node.

The following algorithm solves the synthesis problem with working space of order $B(f \diamond g)$; in fact, it needs only about sixteen bytes per element of the BDD for $f \diamond g$. The algorithm is designed to be used as the main engine of a "Boolean function calculator," which represents functions as BDDs in compressed form on a sequential stack. The stack is maintained at the lower end of a large array called the *pool*. Each BDD on the stack is a sequence of *nodes*, which each have three fields (V, LO, HI). The rest of the pool is available to hold temporary results called *templates*, which each have four fields (L, H, LEFT, RIGHT). A node typically occupies one octabyte of memory, while a template occupies two.

The purpose of Algorithm S is to examine the top two Boolean functions on the stack, f and g, and to replace them by the Boolean combination $f \circ g$, where $\circ$ is one of the 16 possible binary operators. This operator is identified by its 4-bit truth table, *op*. For example, Algorithm S will form the BDD for $f \oplus g$ when *op* is $(0110)_2 = 6$; it will deliver $f \wedge g$ when $op = 1$.

When the algorithm begins, operand f appears in locations $[f_0 \mathinner{\ldotp\ldotp} g_0)$ of the pool, and operand g appears in locations $[g_0 \mathinner{\ldotp\ldotp} \mathtt{NTOP})$. All higher locations $[\mathtt{NTOP} \mathinner{\ldotp\ldotp} \mathtt{POOLSIZE})$ are available for storing the templates that the algorithm needs. Those templates will appear in locations $[\mathtt{TBOT} \mathinner{\ldotp\ldotp} \mathtt{POOLSIZE})$ at the high end of the pool; the boundary markers $\mathtt{NTOP}$ and $\mathtt{TBOT}$ will change dynamically as the algorithm proceeds. The resulting BDD for $f \circ g$ will eventually be placed in locations $[f_0 \mathinner{\ldotp\ldotp} \mathtt{NTOP})$, taking over the space formerly occupied by f and g. We assume that a template occupies the space of two nodes. Thus, the assignments "$t \leftarrow \mathtt{TBOT} - 2$, $\mathtt{TBOT} \leftarrow t$" allocate space for a new template, pointed to by t; the assignments "$p \leftarrow \mathtt{NTOP}$, $\mathtt{NTOP} \leftarrow p + 1$" allocate a new node p. For simplicity of exposition, Algorithm S does not check that the condition $\mathtt{NTOP} \le \mathtt{TBOT}$ remains valid throughout the process; but of course such tests are essential in practice. Exercise 69 remedies this oversight.

The input functions f and g are specified to Algorithm S as sequences of instructions $(I_{s-1}, \ldots, I_1, I_0)$ and $(I'_{s'-1}, \ldots, I'_1, I'_0)$, as in Algorithms B and C above. The lengths of these sequences are $s = B^+(f)$ and $s' = B^+(g)$, where

$$B^+(f) = B(f) + [f \text{ is identically } 1] \tag{40}$$

is the number of BDD nodes when the sink $\boxed{\perp}$ is forced to be present. For example, the two BDDs at the left of Fig. 24 could be specified by the instructions

$$
\begin{aligned}
&I_5 = (\bar{1}? \ 4\!: 3), \quad I_3 = (\bar{3}? \ 2\!: 1), &&I'_7 = (\bar{1}? \ 5\!: 6), \quad I'_4 = (\bar{3}? \ 2\!: 3),\\
&I_4 = (\bar{2}? \ 0\!: 3), \quad I_2 = (\bar{4}? \ 0\!: 1); &&I'_6 = (\bar{2}? \ 1\!: 4), \quad I'_3 = (\bar{4}? \ 1\!: 0), \quad (41)\\
& &&I'_5 = (\bar{2}? \ 4\!: 1), \quad I'_2 = (\bar{4}? \ 0\!: 1);
\end{aligned}
$$

as usual, I_1, I_0, I'_1, and I'_0 are the sinks. These instructions are packed into nodes, so that if $I_k = (\bar{v}_k? \ l_k\!: h_k)$ we have $\mathtt{V}(f_0 + k) = v_k$, $\mathtt{LO}(f_0 + k) = l_k$, and

$\mathrm{HI}(f_0 + k) = h_k$ for $2 \le k < s$ when Algorithm S begins. Similar conventions apply to the instructions I'_k that define g. Furthermore

$$\mathrm{V}(f_0) = \mathrm{V}(f_0 + 1) = \mathrm{V}(g_0) = \mathrm{V}(g_0 + 1) = v_{\max} + 1, \qquad (42)$$

where we assume that f and g depend only on the variables x_v for $1 \le v \le v_{\max}$.

Like the simple but space-hungry algorithm described earlier, Algorithm S proceeds in two phases: First it builds the BDD for $f \diamond g$, constructing templates so that every important meld $\alpha \diamond \alpha'$ is represented as a template t for which

$$\mathrm{LEFT}(t) = \alpha, \ \ \mathrm{RIGHT}(t) = \alpha', \ \ \mathrm{L}(t) = \mathrm{LO}(\alpha \diamond \alpha'), \ \ \mathrm{H}(t) = \mathrm{HI}(\alpha \diamond \alpha'). \quad (43)$$

(The L and H fields point to templates, not nodes.) Then the second phase reduces these templates, using a procedure similar to Algorithm R; it changes template t from (43) to

$$\begin{aligned} \mathrm{LEFT}(t) = {\sim}\kappa(t), \ \ \mathrm{RIGHT}(t) &= \tau(t), \\ \mathrm{L}(t) = \tau(\mathrm{LO}(\alpha \diamond \alpha')), \ \ \mathrm{H}(t) &= \tau(\mathrm{HI}(\alpha \diamond \alpha')), \end{aligned} \qquad (44)$$

where $\tau(t)$ is the unique template to which t has been reduced, and where $\kappa(t)$ is the "clone" of t if $\tau(t) = t$. Every reduced template t corresponds to an instruction node in the BDD of $f \circ g$, and $\kappa(t)$ is the index of this node relative to position f_0 in the stack. (Setting $\mathrm{LEFT}(t)$ to ${\sim}\kappa(t)$ instead of $\kappa(t)$ is a sneaky trick that makes steps S7–S10 run faster.) Special overlapping templates are permanently reserved for sinks at the *bottom* of the pool, so that we always have

$$\mathrm{LEFT}(0) = {\sim}0, \ \ \mathrm{RIGHT}(0) = 0, \ \ \mathrm{LEFT}(1) = {\sim}1, \ \ \mathrm{RIGHT}(1) = 1, \qquad (45)$$

in accord with the conventions of (42) and (44).

We needn't make a template for $\alpha \diamond \alpha'$ when the value of $\alpha \circ \alpha'$ is obviously constant. For example, if we're computing $f \wedge g$, we know that $\alpha \diamond \alpha'$ will eventually reduce to $\boxed{\bot}$ if $\alpha = 0$ or $\alpha' = 0$. Such simplifications are discovered by a subroutine called *find_level*(f, g), which returns the positive integer j if the root of $f \diamond g$ begins with the branch (j), unless $f \circ g$ clearly has a constant value; in the latter case, *find_level*(f, g) returns the value $-(f \circ g)$, which is 0 or -1. The procedure is slightly technical, but simple, using the global truth table *op*:

Subroutine *find_level*(f, g), with local variable t:
If $f \le 1$ and $g \le 1$, return $-((op \gg (3 - 2f - g))$ & $1)$, which is $-(f \circ g)$.
If $f \le 1$ and $g > 1$, set $t \leftarrow (f? \ op$ & $3: op \gg 2)$; return 0 if $t = 0$, -1 if $t = 3$.
If $f > 1$ and $g \le 1$, set $t \leftarrow (g? \ op: op \gg 1)$ & 5; return 0 if $t = 0$, -1 if $t = 5$.
Otherwise return $\min(\mathrm{V}(f_0 + f), \mathrm{V}(g_0 + g))$. $\qquad (46)$

The main difficulty that faces us, when generating a template for a descendant of $\alpha \diamond \alpha'$ according to (37), is to decide whether or not such a template already exists — and if so, to link to it. The best way to solve such problems is usually to use a hash table; but then we must decide where to put such a table, and how much extra space to devote to it. Alternatives such as binary search trees would be much easier to adapt to our purposes, but they would add an unwanted factor of $\log B(f \diamond g)$ to the running time. The synthesis problem can actually be solved in worst-case time and space $O(B(f \diamond g))$ by using a bucket sort method analogous to Algorithm R (see exercise 72); but that solution is complicated and somewhat awkward.

Fortunately there's a nice way out of this dilemma, requiring almost no extra memory and only modestly complex code, if we generate the templates one level at a time. Before generating the templates for level l, we'll know the number N_l of templates to be requested on that level. So we can temporarily allocate space for 2^b templates at the top of the currently free area, where $b = \lceil \lg N_l \rceil$, and put new templates there while hashing into the same area. The idea is to use chaining with separate lists, as in Fig. 38 of Section 6.4; the H and L fields of our templates and potential templates play the roles of heads and links in that illustration, while the keys appear in (LEFT, RIGHT). Here's the logic, in detail:

Subroutine $make\_template(f, g)$, with local variable t:

Set $h \leftarrow$ HBASE $+ 2(((314159257f + 271828171g) \bmod 2^d) \gg (d - b))$, where d is a convenient upper bound on the size of a pointer (usually $d = 32$). Then set $t \leftarrow$ H(h). While $t \neq \Lambda$ and either LEFT$(t) \neq f$ or RIGHT$(t) \neq g$, set $t \leftarrow$ L(t). If $t = \Lambda$, set $t \leftarrow$ TBOT $- 2$, TBOT $\leftarrow t$, LEFT$(t) \leftarrow f$, RIGHT$(t) \leftarrow g$, L$(t) \leftarrow$ H(h), and H$(h) \leftarrow t$. Finally, return the value t.   (47)

The calling routine in steps S4 and S5 ensures that NTOP $\leq$ HBASE $\leq$ TBOT.

This breadth-first, level-at-a-time strategy for constructing the templates has an added payoff, because it promotes "locality of reference": Memory accesses tend to be confined to nearby locations that have recently been seen, hence controlled in such a way that cache misses and page faults are significantly reduced. Furthermore, the eventual BDD nodes placed on the stack will also appear in order, so that all branches on the same variable appear consecutively.

Algorithm S (*Breadth-first synthesis of BDDs*). This algorithm computes the BDD for $f \circ g$ as described above, using subroutines (46) and (47). Auxiliary arrays LSTART$[l]$, LCOUNT$[l]$, LLIST$[l]$, and HLIST$[l]$ are used for $0 \leq l \leq v_{\max}$.

S1. [Initialize.] Set $f \leftarrow g_0 - 1 - f_0$, $g \leftarrow$ NTOP $- 1 - g_0$, and $l \leftarrow find\_level(f, g)$. See exercise 66 if $l \leq 0$. Otherwise set LSTART$[l - 1] \leftarrow$ POOLSIZE, and LLIST$[k] \leftarrow$ HLIST$[k] \leftarrow \Lambda$, LCOUNT$[k] \leftarrow 0$ for $l < k \leq v_{\max}$. Set TBOT $\leftarrow$ POOLSIZE $- 2$, LEFT(TBOT) $\leftarrow f$, and RIGHT(TBOT) $\leftarrow g$.

S2. [Scan the level-l templates.] Set LSTART$[l] \leftarrow$ TBOT and $t \leftarrow$ LSTART$[l - 1]$. While $t >$ TBOT, schedule requests for future levels by doing the following:

Set $t \leftarrow t-2$, $f \leftarrow$ LEFT(t), $g \leftarrow$ RIGHT(t), $vf \leftarrow$ V(f_0+f), $vg \leftarrow$ V(g_0+g),

$ll \leftarrow find\_level((vf \leq vg?$ LO$(f_0 + f): f), (vf \geq vg?$ LO$(g_0 + g): g))$,
$lh \leftarrow find\_level((vf \leq vg?$ HI$(f_0 + f): f), (vf \geq vg?$ HI$(g_0 + g): g))$.

If $ll \leq 0$, set L$(t) \leftarrow -ll$; otherwise set L$(t) \leftarrow$ LLIST$[ll]$, LLIST$[ll] \leftarrow t$, LCOUNT$[ll] \leftarrow$ LCOUNT$[ll] + 1$. If $lh \leq 0$, set H$(t) \leftarrow -lh$; otherwise set H$(t) \leftarrow$ HLIST$[lh]$, HLIST$[lh] \leftarrow t$, LCOUNT$[lh] \leftarrow$ LCOUNT$[lh] + 1$.

S3. [Done with phase one?] Go to S6 if $l = v_{\max}$. Otherwise set $l \leftarrow l + 1$, and return to S2 if LCOUNT$[l] = 0$.

S4. [Initialize for hashing.] Set $b \leftarrow \lceil \lg \text{LCOUNT}[l] \rceil$, $\text{HBASE} \leftarrow \text{TBOT} - 2^{b+1}$, and $\text{H}(\text{HBASE} + 2k) \leftarrow \Lambda$ for $0 \leq k < 2^b$.

S5. [Make the level-l templates.] Set $t \leftarrow \text{LLIST}[l]$. While $t \neq \Lambda$, set $s \leftarrow \text{L}(t)$, $f \leftarrow \text{LEFT}(t)$, $g \leftarrow \text{RIGHT}(t)$, $vf \leftarrow \text{V}(f_0 + f)$, $vg \leftarrow \text{V}(g_0 + g)$, $\text{L}(t) \leftarrow \textit{make\_template}((vf \leq vg? \text{ LO}(f_0+f): f), (vf \geq vg? \text{ LO}(g_0+g): g))$, $t \leftarrow s$. (We're half done.) Then set $t \leftarrow \text{HLIST}[l]$. While $t \neq \Lambda$, set $s \leftarrow \text{H}(t)$, $f \leftarrow \text{LEFT}(t)$, $g \leftarrow \text{RIGHT}(t)$, $vf \leftarrow \text{V}(f_0 + f)$, $vg \leftarrow \text{V}(g_0 + g)$, $\text{H}(t) \leftarrow \textit{make\_template}((vf \leq vg? \text{ HI}(f_0+f): f), (vf \geq vg? \text{ HI}(g_0+g): g))$, $t \leftarrow s$. (Now the other half is done.) Go back to step S2.

S6. [Prepare for phase two.] (At this point it's safe to obliterate the nodes of f and g, because we've built all the templates (43). Now we'll convert them to form (44). Note that $\text{V}(f_0) = \text{V}(f_0 + 1) = v_{\max} + 1$.) Set $\text{NTOP} \leftarrow f_0 + 2$.

S7. [Bucket sort.] Set $t \leftarrow \text{LSTART}[l - 1]$. Do the following while $t > \text{LSTART}[l]$:

> Set $t \leftarrow t - 2$, $\text{L}(t) \leftarrow \text{RIGHT}(\text{L}(t))$, and $\text{H}(t) \leftarrow \text{RIGHT}(\text{H}(t))$.
> If $\text{L}(t) = \text{H}(t)$, set $\text{RIGHT}(t) \leftarrow \text{L}(t)$. (This branch is redundant.)
> Otherwise set $\text{RIGHT}(t) \leftarrow -1$, $\text{LEFT}(t) \leftarrow \text{LEFT}(\text{L}(t))$, $\text{LEFT}(\text{L}(t)) \leftarrow t$.

S8. [Restore clone addresses.] If $t = \text{LSTART}[l - 1]$, set $t \leftarrow \text{LSTART}[l] - 2$ and go to S9. Otherwise, if $\text{LEFT}(t) < 0$, set $\text{LEFT}(\text{L}(t)) \leftarrow \text{LEFT}(t)$. Set $t \leftarrow t + 2$ and repeat step S8.

S9. [Done with level?] Set $t \leftarrow t+2$. If $t = \text{LSTART}[l - 1]$, go to S12. Otherwise, if $\text{RIGHT}(t) \geq 0$ repeat step S9.

S10. [Examine a bucket.] (Suppose $\text{L}(t_1) = \text{L}(t_2) = \text{L}(t_3)$, where $t_1 > t_2 > t_3 = t$ and no other templates on level l have this L value. Then at this point we have $\text{LEFT}(t_3) = t_2$, $\text{LEFT}(t_2) = t_1$, $\text{LEFT}(t_1) < 0$, and $\text{RIGHT}(t_1) = \text{RIGHT}(t_2) = \text{RIGHT}(t_3) = -1$.) Set $s \leftarrow t$. While $s > 0$, do the following: Set $r \leftarrow \text{H}(s)$, $\text{RIGHT}(s) \leftarrow \text{LEFT}(r)$; if $\text{LEFT}(r) < 0$, set $\text{LEFT}(r) \leftarrow s$; and set $s \leftarrow \text{LEFT}(s)$. Finally set $s \leftarrow t$ again.

S11. [Make clones.] If $s < 0$, go back to step S9. Otherwise if $\text{RIGHT}(s) \geq 0$, set $s \leftarrow \text{LEFT}(s)$. Otherwise set $r \leftarrow \text{LEFT}(s)$, $\text{LEFT}(\text{H}(s)) \leftarrow \text{RIGHT}(s)$, $\text{RIGHT}(s) \leftarrow s$, $q \leftarrow \text{NTOP}$, $\text{NTOP} \leftarrow q + 1$, $\text{LEFT}(s) \leftarrow \sim(q - f_0)$, $\text{LO}(q) \leftarrow \sim\text{LEFT}(\text{L}(s))$, $\text{HI}(q) \leftarrow \sim\text{LEFT}(\text{H}(s))$, $\text{V}(q) \leftarrow l$, $s \leftarrow r$. Repeat step S11.

S12. [Loop on l.] Set $l \leftarrow l - 1$. Return to S7 if $\text{LSTART}[l] < \text{POOLSIZE}$. Otherwise, if $\text{RIGHT}(\text{POOLSIZE} - 2) = 0$, set $\text{NTOP} \leftarrow \text{NTOP} - 1$ (because $f \circ g$ is identically 0). ∎

As usual, the best way to understand an algorithm like this is to trace through an example. Exercise 67 discusses what Algorithm S does when it is asked to compute $f \wedge g$, given the BDDs in (41).

Algorithm S can be used, for example, to construct the BDDs for interesting functions such as the "monotone-function function" $\mu_n(x_1, \ldots, x_{2^n})$, which is true if and only if $x_1 \ldots x_{2^n}$ is the truth table of a monotone function:

$$\mu_n(x_1, \ldots, x_{2^n}) = \bigwedge_{0 \leq i \subseteq j < 2^n} [x_{i+1} \leq x_{j+1}]. \tag{48}$$

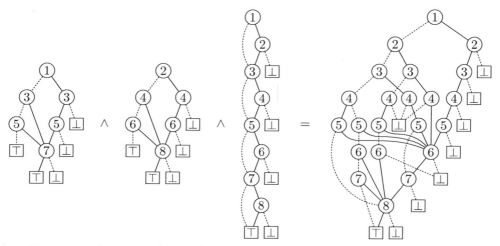

Fig. 25. $\mu_2(x_1, x_3, x_5, x_7) \wedge \mu_2(x_2, x_4, x_6, x_8) \wedge G_8(x_1, \ldots, x_8) = \mu_3(x_1, \ldots, x_8)$, as computed by Algorithm S.

Starting with $\mu_0(x_1) = 1$, this function satisfies the recursion relation

$$\mu_n(x_1, \ldots, x_{2^n}) =$$
$$\mu_{n-1}(x_1, x_3, \ldots, x_{2^n-1}) \wedge \mu_{n-1}(x_2, x_4, \ldots, x_{2^n}) \wedge G_{2^n}(x_1, \ldots, x_{2^n}), \quad (49)$$

where $G_{2^n}(x_1, \ldots, x_{2^n}) = [x_1 \leq x_2] \wedge [x_3 \leq x_4] \wedge \cdots \wedge [x_{2^n-1} \leq x_{2^n}]$. So its BDD is easy to obtain with a BDD calculator like Algorithm S: The BDDs for $\mu_{n-1}(x_1, x_3, \ldots, x_{2^n-1})$ and $\mu_{n-1}(x_2, x_4, \ldots, x_{2^n})$ are simple variants of the one for $\mu_{n-1}(x_1, x_2, \ldots, x_{2^n-1})$, and G_{2^n} has an extremely simple BDD (see Fig. 25).

Repeating this process six times will produce the BDD for μ_6, which has 103,924 nodes. There are exactly 7,828,354 monotone Boolean functions of six variables (see exercise 5.3.4–31); this BDD nicely characterizes them all, and we need only about 4.8 million memory accesses to compute it with Algorithm S. Furthermore, 6.7 billion mems will suffice to compute the BDD for μ_7, which has 155,207,320 nodes and characterizes 2,414,682,040,998 monotone functions.

We must stop there, however; the size of the next case, $B(\mu_8)$, turns out to be a whopping 69,258,301,585,604 (see exercise 77).

Synthesis in a BDD base. Another approach is called for when we're dealing with many functions at once instead of computing a single BDD on the fly. The functions of a BDD base often share common subfunctions, as in (36). Algorithm S is designed to take disjoint BDDs and to combine them efficiently, afterwards destroying the originals; but in many cases we would rather form combinations of functions whose BDDs overlap. Furthermore, after forming a new function $f \wedge g$, say, we might want to keep f and g around for future use; indeed, the new function might well share nodes with f or g or both.

Let's therefore consider the design of a general-purpose toolkit for manipulating a collection of Boolean functions. BDDs are especially attractive for this purpose because most of the necessary operations have a simple recursive formulation. We know that every nonconstant Boolean function can be written

$$f(x_1, x_2, \ldots, x_n) = (\bar{x}_v? \ f_l: f_h), \tag{50}$$

where $v = f_v$ indexes the first variable on which f depends, and where we have

$$f_l = f(0, \ldots, 0, x_{v+1}, \ldots, x_n); \quad f_h = f(1, \ldots, 1, x_{v+1}, \ldots, x_n). \tag{51}$$

This rule corresponds to branch node (v) at the top of the BDD for f; and the rest of the BDD follows by using (50) and (51) recursively, until we reach constant functions that correspond to $\boxed{\perp}$ or $\boxed{\top}$. A similar recursion defines any combination of two functions, $f \circ g$: For if f and g aren't both constant, we have

$$f(x_1, \ldots, x_n) = (\bar{x}_v? \ f_l: f_h) \quad \text{and} \quad g(x_1, \ldots, x_n) = (\bar{x}_v? \ g_l: g_h), \tag{52}$$

where $v = \min(f_v, g_v)$ and where f_l, f_h, g_l, g_h are given by (51). Then, presto,

$$f \circ g = (\bar{x}_v? \ f_l \circ g_l: f_h \circ g_h). \tag{53}$$

This important formula is another way of stating the rule by which we defined melding, Eq. (37).

Caution: The notations above need to be understood carefully, because the subfunctions f_l and f_h in (50) might not be the same as the f_l and f_h in (52). Suppose, for example, that $f = x_2 \vee x_3$ while $g = x_1 \oplus x_3$. Then Eq. (50) holds with $f_v = 2$ and $f = (\bar{x}_2? \ f_l: f_h)$, where $f_l = x_3$ and $f_h = 1$. We also have $g_v = 1$ and $g = (\bar{x}_1? \ x_3: \bar{x}_3)$. But in (52) we use the same branch variable x_v for both functions, and $v = \min(f_v, g_v) = 1$ in our example; so Eq. (52) holds with $f = (\bar{x}_1? \ f_l: f_h)$ and $f_l = f_h = x_2 \vee x_3$.

Every node of a BDD base represents a Boolean function. Furthermore, a BDD base is reduced; therefore two of its functions or subfunctions are equal if and only if they correspond to exactly the same node. (This convenient uniqueness property was *not* true in Algorithm S.)

Formulas (51)–(53) immediately suggest a recursive way to compute $f \wedge g$:

$$\text{AND}(f, g) = \begin{cases} \text{If } f \wedge g \text{ has an obvious value, return it.} \\ \text{Otherwise represent } f \text{ and } g \text{ as in (52);} \\ \text{compute } r_l \leftarrow \text{AND}(f_l, g_l) \text{ and } r_h \leftarrow \text{AND}(f_h, g_h); \\ \text{return the function } (\bar{x}_v? \ r_l: r_h). \end{cases} \tag{54}$$

(Recursions always need to terminate when a sufficiently simple case arises. The "obvious" values in the first line correspond to the terminal cases $f \wedge 1 = f$, $1 \wedge g = g$, $f \wedge 0 = 0 \wedge g = 0$, and $f \wedge g = f$ when $f = g$.) When f and g are the functions in our example above, (54) reduces $f \wedge g$ to the computation of $(x_2 \vee x_3) \wedge x_3$ and $(x_2 \vee x_3) \wedge \bar{x}_3$. Then $(x_2 \vee x_3) \wedge x_3$ reduces to $x_3 \wedge x_3$ and $1 \wedge x_3$; etc.

But (54) is problematic if we simply implement it as stated, because every nonterminal step launches two more instances of the recursion. The computation explodes, with 2^k instances of AND when we're k levels deep!

Fortunately there's a good way to avoid that blowup. Since f has only $B(f)$ different subfunctions, at most $B(f)B(g)$ distinctly different calls of AND can arise. To keep a lid on the computations, we just need to remember what we've done before, by making a *memo* of the fact that $f \wedge g = r$ just before returning r as the computed value. Then when the same subproblem occurs later, we can retrieve the memo and say, "Hey, we've already been there and done that." Previously solved cases thereby become terminal; only distinct subproblems can generate new ones. (Chapter 8 will discuss this memoization technique in detail.)

The algorithm in (54) also glosses over another problem: It's not so easy to "return the function $(\bar{x}_v? \; r_l: r_h)$," because we must keep the BDD base reduced. If $r_l = r_h$, we should return the node r_l; and if $r_l \neq r_h$, we need to decide whether the branch node $(\bar{x}_v? \; r_l: r_h)$ already exists, before creating a new one.

Thus we need to maintain additional information, besides the BDD nodes themselves. We need to keep memos of problems already solved; we also need to be able to find a node by its content, instead of by its address. The search algorithms of Chapter 6 now come to our rescue by telling us how to do both of these things, for example by hashing. To record a memo that $f \wedge g = r$, we can hash the key '$(f, \wedge, g)$' and associate it with the value r; to record the existence of an existing node $(\mathrm{V}, \mathrm{LO}, \mathrm{HI})$, we can hash the key '$(\mathrm{V}, \mathrm{LO}, \mathrm{HI})$' and associate it with that node's memory address.

The dictionary of all existing nodes $(\mathrm{V}, \mathrm{LO}, \mathrm{HI})$ in a BDD base is traditionally called the *unique table*, because we use it to enforce the all-important uniqueness criterion that forbids duplication. Instead of putting all that information into one giant dictionary, however, it turns out to be better to maintain a collection of smaller unique tables, one for each variable V. With such separate tables we can efficiently find all nodes that branch on a particular variable.

The memos are handy, but they aren't as crucial as the unique table entries. If we happen to forget the isolated fact that $f \wedge g = r$, we can always recompute it again later. Exponential blowup won't be worrisome, if the answers to the subproblems $f_l \wedge g_l$ and $f_h \wedge g_h$ are still remembered with high probability. Therefore we can use a less expensive method to store memos, designed to do a pretty-good-but-not-perfect job of retrieval: After hashing the key '$(f, \wedge, g)$' to a table position p, we need look for a memo only in that one position, not bothering to consider collisions with other keys. If several keys all share the same hash address, position p will record only the most recent relevant memo. This simplified scheme will still be adequate in practice, as long as the hash table is large enough. We shall call such a near-perfect table the *memo cache*, because it is analogous to the hardware caches by which a computer tries to remember significant values that it has dealt with in relatively slow storage units.

Okay, let's flesh out algorithm (54) by explicitly stating how it interacts with the unique tables and the memo cache:

$$\mathrm{AND}(f, g) = \begin{cases} \text{If } f \wedge g \text{ has an obvious value, return it.} \\ \text{Otherwise, if } f \wedge g = r \text{ is in the memo cache, return } r. \\ \text{Otherwise represent } f \text{ and } g \text{ as in (52);} \\ \text{compute } r_l \leftarrow \mathrm{AND}(f_l, g_l) \text{ and } r_h \leftarrow \mathrm{AND}(f_h, g_h); \\ \text{set } r \leftarrow \mathrm{UNIQUE}(v, r_l, r_h), \text{ using Algorithm U;} \\ \text{put } `f \wedge g = r\text{' into the memo cache, and return } r. \end{cases} \quad (55)$$

Algorithm U (*Unique table lookup*). Given (v, p, q), where v is an integer while p and q point to nodes of a BDD base with variable rank $> v$, this algorithm returns a pointer to a node $\text{UNIQUE}(v, p, q)$ that represents the function $(\bar{x}_v? \, p\!: q)$. A new node is added to the base if that function wasn't already present.

U1. [Easy case?] If $p = q$, return p.

U2. [Check the table.] Search variable x_v's unique table using the key (p, q). If the search successfully finds the value r, return r.

U3. [Create a node.] Allocate a new node r, and set $\text{V}(r) \leftarrow v$, $\text{LO}(r) \leftarrow p$, $\text{HI}(r) \leftarrow q$. Put r into x_v's unique table using the key (p, q). Return r. ∎

Notice that we needn't zero out the memo cache after finishing a top-level computation of $\text{AND}(f, g)$. Each memo that we have made states a relationship between nodes of the structure; those facts are still valid, and they might be useful later when we want to compute $\text{AND}(f, g)$ for new functions f and g.

A refinement of (55) will enhance that method further, namely to swap $f \leftrightarrow g$ if we discover that $f > g$ when $f \wedge g$ isn't obvious. Then we won't have to waste time computing $f \wedge g$ when we've already computed $g \wedge f$.

With simple changes to (55), the other binary operators $\text{OR}(f, g)$, $\text{XOR}(f, g)$, $\text{BUTNOT}(f, g)$, $\text{NOR}(f, g)$, ... can also be computed readily; see exercise 81.

The combination of (55) and Algorithm U looks considerably simpler than Algorithm S. Thus one might well ask, why should anybody bother to learn the other method? Its breadth-first approach seems quite complex by comparison with the "depth-first" order of computation in the recursive structure of (55); yet Algorithm S is able to deal only with BDDs that are disjoint, while Algorithm U and recursions like (55) apply to any BDD base.

Appearances can, however, be deceiving: Algorithm S has been described at a low level, with every change to every element of its data structures spelled out explicitly. By contrast, the high-level descriptions in (55) and Algorithm U assume that a substantial infrastructure exists behind the scenes. The memo cache and the unique tables need to be set up, and their sizes need to be carefully adjusted as the BDD base grows or contracts. When all is said and done, the total length of a program that implements Algorithms (55) and U properly "from scratch" is roughly ten times the length of a similar program for Algorithm S.

Indeed, the maintenance of a BDD base involves interesting questions of dynamic storage allocation, because we want to free up memory space when nodes are no longer accessible. Algorithm S solves this problem in a last-in-first-out manner, by simply keeping its nodes and templates on sequential stacks, and by making do with a single small hash table that can easily be integrated with the other data. A general BDD base, however, requires a more intricate system.

The best way to maintain a dynamic BDD base is probably to use *reference counters*, as discussed in Section 2.3.5, because BDDs are acyclic by definition. Therefore let's assume that every BDD node has a REF field, in addition to V, LO, and HI. The REF field tells us how many references exist to this node, either from LO or HI pointers in other nodes or from external root pointers F_j as in (36). For example, the REF fields for the nodes labeled ③ in (36) are respectively 4,

1, and 2; and all of the nodes labeled ② or ④ or ⑥ in that example have REF = 1. Exercise 82 discusses the somewhat tricky issue of how to increase and decrease REF counts properly in the midst of a recursive computation.

A node becomes *dead* when its reference count becomes zero. When that happens, we should decrease the REF fields of the two nodes below it; and then they too might die in the same manner, recursively spreading the plague.

But a dead node needn't be removed from memory immediately. It still represents a potentially useful Boolean function, and we might discover that we need that function again as our computation proceeds. For example, we might find a dead node in step U2, because pointers from the unique table don't get counted as references. Likewise, in (55), we might accidentally stumble across a cache memo telling us that $f \wedge g = r$, when r is currently dead. In such cases, node r comes back to life. (And we must increase the REF counts of its LO and HI descendants, possibly resurrecting them recursively in the same fashion.)

Periodically, however, we will want to reclaim memory space by removing the deadbeats. Then we must do two things: We must purge all memos from the cache for which either f, g, or r is dead; and we must remove all dead nodes from memory and from their unique tables. See exercise 84 for typical heuristic strategies by which an automated system might decide when to invoke such cleanups and when to resize the tables dynamically.

Because of the extra machinery that is needed to support a BDD base, Algorithm U and top-down recursions like (55) cannot be expected to match the efficiency of Algorithm S on one-shot examples such as the monotone-function function μ_n in (49). The running time is approximately quadrupled when the more general approach is applied to this example, and the memory requirement grows by a factor of about 2.4.

But a BDD base really begins to shine in numerous other applications. Suppose, for example, that we want the formulas for each bit of the product of two binary numbers,

$$(z_1 \ldots z_{m+n})_2 = (x_1 \ldots x_m)_2 \times (y_1 \ldots y_n)_2. \tag{56}$$

Clearly $z_1 \ldots z_m = 0 \ldots 0$ when $n = 0$, and the simple recurrence

$$(x_1 \ldots x_m)_2 \times (y_1 \ldots y_n y_{n+1})_2 = (z_1 \ldots z_{m+n}0)_2 + (x_1 \ldots x_m)_2 y_{n+1} \tag{57}$$

allows us to increase n by 1. This recurrence is easy to code for a BDD base. Here's what we get when $m = n = 3$, with subscripts chosen to match the analogous diagram for binary addition in (36):

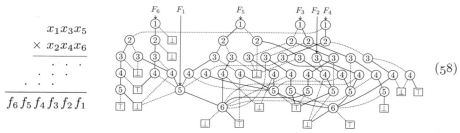

$$\begin{array}{l} x_1 x_3 x_5 \\ \times\ x_2 x_4 x_6 \\ \hline \quad\ \cdot\ \cdot\ \cdot \\ \cdot\ \cdot\ \cdot \\ \hline f_6 f_5 f_4 f_3 f_2 f_1 \end{array} \tag{58}$$

Clearly multiplication is much more complicated than addition, bitwise. (Indeed, if it weren't, factorization wouldn't be so hard.) The corresponding BDD base for binary multiplication when $m = n = 16$ is huge, with $B(f_1, \ldots, f_{32}) = 136{,}398{,}751$ nodes. It can be found after doing about 56 gigamems of calculation with Algorithm U, in 6.3 gigabytes of memory — including some 1.9 billion invocations of recursive subroutines, with hundreds of dynamic resizings of the unique tables and the memo cache, plus dozens of timely garbage collections. A similar calculation with Algorithm S would be almost unthinkable, although the individual functions in this particular example do not share many common subfunctions: It turns out that $B(f_1) + \cdots + B(f_{32}) = 168{,}640{,}131$, with the maximum occurring at the "middle bit," $B(f_{16}) = 38{,}174{,}143$.

*Ternary operations. Given three Boolean functions $f = f(x_1, \ldots, x_n)$, $g = g(x_1, \ldots, x_n)$, and $h = h(x_1, \ldots, x_n)$, not all constant, we can generalize (52) to

$$f = (\bar{x}_v?\ f_l\colon f_h) \quad \text{and} \quad g = (\bar{x}_v?\ g_l\colon g_h) \quad \text{and} \quad h = (\bar{x}_v?\ h_l\colon h_h), \qquad (59)$$

by taking $v = \min(f_v, g_v, h_v)$. Then, for example, (53) generalizes to

$$\langle fgh \rangle \;=\; \bigl(\bar{x}_v?\ \langle f_l g_l h_l \rangle\colon \langle f_h g_h h_h \rangle\bigr); \qquad (60)$$

and similar formulas hold for *any* ternary operation on f, g, and h, including

$$(\bar{f}?\ g\colon h) \;=\; \bigl(\bar{x}_v?\ (\bar{f}_l?\ g_l\colon h_l)\colon (\bar{f}_h?\ g_h\colon h_h)\bigr). \qquad (61)$$

(The reader of these formulas will please forgive the two meanings of 'h' in 'h_h'.)

Now it's easy to generalize (55) to ternary combinations like multiplexing:

$$\mathrm{MUX}(f,g,h) = \begin{cases} \text{If } (\bar{f}?\ g\colon h) \text{ has an obvious value, return it.} \\ \text{Otherwise, if } (\bar{f}?\ g\colon h) = r \text{ is in the memo cache, return } r. \\ \text{Otherwise represent } f,\ g, \text{ and } h \text{ as in (59);} \\ \text{compute } r_l \leftarrow \mathrm{MUX}(f_l, g_l, h_l) \text{ and } r_h \leftarrow \mathrm{MUX}(f_h, g_h, h_h); \\ \text{set } r \leftarrow \mathrm{UNIQUE}(v, r_l, r_h), \text{ using Algorithm U;} \\ \text{put } `(\bar{f}?\ g\colon h) = r' \text{ into the memo cache, and return } r. \end{cases} \qquad (62)$$

(See exercises 86 and 87.) The running time is $O\bigl(B(f)B(g)B(h)\bigr)$. The memo cache must now be consulted with a more complex key than before, including *three* pointers (f, g, h) instead of two, together with a code for the relevant operation. But each memo (op, f, g, h, r) can still be represented conveniently in, say, two octabytes, if the number of distinct pointer addresses is at most 2^{31}.

The ternary operation $f \wedge g \wedge h$ is an interesting special case. We could compute it with two invocations of (55), either as $\mathrm{AND}(f, \mathrm{AND}(g, h))$ or as $\mathrm{AND}(g, \mathrm{AND}(h, f))$ or as $\mathrm{AND}(h, \mathrm{AND}(f, g))$; or we could use a ternary subroutine, $\mathrm{ANDAND}(f, g, h)$, analogous to (62). This ternary routine first sorts the operands so that the pointers satisfy $f \le g \le h$. Then if $f = 0$, it returns 0; if $f = 1$ or $f = g$, it returns $\mathrm{AND}(g, h)$; if $g = h$ it returns $\mathrm{AND}(f, g)$; otherwise $1 < f < g < h$ and the operation remains ternary at the current level of recursion.

Suppose, for example, that $f = \mu_5(x_1, x_3, \ldots, x_{63})$, $g = \mu_5(x_2, x_4, \ldots, x_{64})$, and $h = G_{64}(x_1, \ldots, x_{64})$, as in Eq. (49). The computation $\mathrm{AND}(f, \mathrm{AND}(g, h))$

costs $0.2 + 6.8 = 7.0$ megamems in the author's experimental implementation; $\text{AND}(g, \text{AND}(h, f))$ costs $0.1 + 7.0 = 7.1$; $\text{AND}(h, \text{AND}(f, g))$ costs $24.4 + 5.6 = 30.0$ (!); and $\text{ANDAND}(f, g, h)$ costs 7.5. So in this instance the all-binary approach wins, if we don't choose a bad order of computation. But sometimes ternary ANDAND beats all three of its binary competitors (see exercise 88).

*Quantifiers. If $f = f(x_1, \ldots, x_n)$ is a Boolean function and $1 \leq j \leq n$, logicians traditionally define *existential and universal quantification* by the formulas

$$\exists x_j\, f(x_1, \ldots, x_n) = f_0 \vee f_1 \quad \text{and} \quad \forall x_j\, f(x_1, \ldots, x_n) = f_0 \wedge f_1, \quad (63)$$

where $f_c = f(x_1, \ldots, x_{j-1}, c, x_{j+1}, \ldots, x_n)$. Thus the quantifier '$\exists x_j$', pronounced "there exists x_j," changes f to the function of the remaining variables $(x_1, \ldots, x_{j-1}, x_{j+1}, \ldots, x_n)$ that is true if and only if at least one value of x_j satisfies $f(x_1, \ldots, x_n)$; the quantifier '$\forall x_j$', pronounced "for all x_j," changes f to the function that is true if and only if *both* values of x_j satisfy f.

Several quantifiers are often applied simultaneously. For example, the formula $\exists x_2\, \exists x_3\, \exists x_6\, f(x_1, \ldots, x_n)$ stands for the OR of eight terms, representing the eight functions of $(x_1, x_4, x_5, x_7, \ldots, x_n)$ that are obtained when we plug the values 0 or 1 into the variables x_2, x_3, and x_6 in all possible ways. Similarly, $\forall x_2\, \forall x_3\, \forall x_6\, f(x_1, \ldots, x_n)$ stands for the AND of those same eight terms.

One common application arises when the function $f(i_1, \ldots, i_l; j_1, \ldots, j_m)$ denotes the value in row $(i_1 \ldots i_l)_2$ and column $(j_1 \ldots j_m)_2$ of a $2^l \times 2^m$ Boolean matrix F. Then the function $h(i_1, \ldots, i_l; k_1, \ldots, k_n)$ given by

$$\exists j_1 \ldots \exists j_m \big(f(i_1, \ldots, i_l; j_1, \ldots, j_m) \wedge g(j_1, \ldots, j_m; k_1, \ldots, k_n) \big) \quad (64)$$

represents the matrix H that is the Boolean product $F\,G$.

A convenient way to implement multiple quantification in a BDD base has been suggested by R. L. Rudell: Let $g = x_{j_1} \wedge \cdots \wedge x_{j_m}$ be a conjunction of positive literals. Then we can regard $\exists x_{j_1} \ldots \exists x_{j_m} f$ as the binary operation $f\,\text{E}\,g$, implemented by the following variant of (55):

$$\text{EXISTS}(f, g) = \begin{cases} \text{If } f\,\text{E}\,g \text{ has an obvious value, return it.} \\ \text{Otherwise represent } f \text{ and } g \text{ as in (52);} \\ \text{if } v \neq f_v, \text{ return EXISTS}(f, g_h). \\ \text{Otherwise, if } f\,\text{E}\,g = r \text{ is in the memo cache, return } r. \\ \text{Otherwise, } r_l \leftarrow \text{EXISTS}(f_l, g_h) \text{ and } r_h \leftarrow \text{EXISTS}(f_h, g_h); \\ \text{if } v \neq g_v, \text{ set } r \leftarrow \text{UNIQUE}(v, r_l, r_h) \text{ using Algorithm U,} \\ \text{otherwise compute } r \leftarrow \text{OR}(r_l, r_h); \\ \text{put } `f\,\text{E}\,g = r\text{' into the memo cache, and return } r. \end{cases} \quad (65)$$

(See exercise 94.) The E operation is undefined when g does *not* have the stated form. Notice how the memo cache nicely remembers existential computations that have gone before.

The running time of (65) is highly variable — not like (55) where we know that $O(B(f)B(g))$ is the worst possible case — because m OR operations are invoked when g specifies m-fold quantification. The worst case now can be as bad as order $B(f)2^m$, if all of the quantification occurs near the root of the BDD for f; this is only $O(B(f)^2)$ if $m = 1$, but it might become unbearably large as m grows. On the other hand, if all of the quantification occurs near the sinks, the running time is simply $O(B(f))$, regardless of the size of m. (See exercise 97.)

Several other quantifiers are worthy of note, and equally easy, although they aren't as famous as $\exists$ and $\forall$. The *Boolean difference* and the *yes/no quantifiers* are defined by formulas analogous to (63):

$$\mathsf{D} x_j\, f = f_0 \oplus f_1; \qquad \mathsf{A} x_j\, f = \bar{f}_0 \wedge f_1; \qquad \mathsf{N} x_j\, f = f_0 \wedge \bar{f}_1. \qquad (66)$$

The Boolean difference, D, is the most important of these: $\mathsf{D} x_j\, f$ is true for all values of $\{x_1, \ldots, x_{j-1}, x_{j+1}, \ldots, x_n\}$ such that f depends on x_j. If the multilinear representation of f is $f = (x_j g + h) \bmod 2$, where g and h are multilinear polynomials in $\{x_1, \ldots, x_{j-1}, x_{j+1}, \ldots, x_n\}$, then $\mathsf{D} x_j\, f = g \bmod 2$. (See Eq. 7.1.1–(19).) Thus D acts like a derivative in calculus, over a finite field.

A Boolean function $f(x_1, \ldots, x_n)$ is monotone (nondecreasing) if and only if $\bigvee_{j=1}^{n} \mathsf{N} x_j\, f = 0$, which is the same as saying that $\mathsf{N} x_j\, f = 0$ for all j. However, exercise 105 presents a faster way to test a BDD for monotonicity.

Let's consider now a detailed example of existential quantification that is particularly instructive. If G is any graph, we can form Boolean functions $\mathrm{IND}(x)$ and $\mathrm{KER}(x)$ for its independent sets and kernels as follows, where x is a bit vector with one entry x_v for each vertex v of G:

$$\mathrm{IND}(x) = \neg \bigvee_{u - v} (x_u \wedge x_v); \qquad \mathrm{KER}(x) = \mathrm{IND}(x) \wedge \bigwedge_v \Big(x_v \vee \bigvee_{u - v} x_u\Big). \qquad (67)$$

We can form a new graph $\mathcal{G}$ whose vertices are the kernels of G, namely the vectors x such that $\mathrm{KER}(x) = 1$. Let's say that two kernels x and y are *adjacent* in $\mathcal{G}$ if they differ in just the two entries for u and v, where $(x_u, x_v) = (1, 0)$ and $(y_u, y_v) = (0, 1)$ and $u - v$. In other words, kernels can be considered as certain ways to place markers on vertices of G; moving a marker from one vertex to a neighboring vertex produces an adjacent kernel. Formally we define

$$a(x) = [\nu(x) = 2] \wedge \neg\mathrm{IND}(x); \qquad (68)$$

$$\mathrm{ADJ}(x, y) = a(x \oplus y) \wedge \mathrm{KER}(x) \wedge \mathrm{KER}(y). \qquad (69)$$

Then $x - y$ in $\mathcal{G}$ if and only if $\mathrm{ADJ}(x, y) = 1$.

Notice that, if $x = x_1 \ldots x_n$, the function $[\nu(x) = 2]$ is the symmetric function $S_2(x_1, \ldots, x_n)$. Furthermore $a(x \oplus y)$ has at most 3 times as many nodes as $a(x)$, if we interleave the variables zipperwise so that the branching order is $(x_1, y_1, \ldots, x_n, y_n)$. Thus $B(a)$ and $B(\mathrm{ADJ})$ will not be extremely large unless $B(\mathrm{IND})$ or $B(\mathrm{KER})$ is large. It's now easy to express the condition that x is an *isolated vertex* of $\mathcal{G}$ (a vertex of degree 0):

$$\mathrm{ISO}(x) \;=\; \mathrm{KER}(x) \wedge \neg \exists y\, \mathrm{ADJ}(x, y). \qquad (70)$$

For example, suppose G is the graph of contiguous states in the USA, as in (18). Then each kernel vector x has 49 entries x_v for $v \in \{\texttt{ME}, \texttt{NH}, \ldots, \texttt{CA}\}$. The graph $\mathcal{G}$ has 266,137 vertices, and we have observed earlier that the BDD sizes for $\mathrm{IND}(x)$ and $\mathrm{KER}(x)$ are respectively 428 and 780 (see (17)). In this case the BDD sizes for $a(x)$ and $\mathrm{ADJ}(x,y)$ in (68) and (69) turn out to be only 286 and 7260, respectively, even though $\mathrm{ADJ}(x,y)$ is a function of 98 Boolean variables. The BDD for $\exists y\, \mathrm{ADJ}(x,y)$, which describes all kernels x of G that have at least one neighbor, turns out to have 842 nodes; and the one for $\mathrm{ISO}(x)$ has only 77. The latter BDD proves that graph G has exactly three isolated kernels, namely

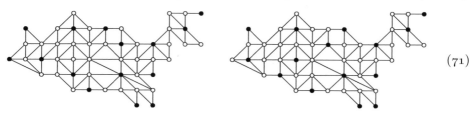

$$(71)$$

and another that is a blend of these two. Using the algorithms above, this entire calculation, starting from a list of the vertices and edges of G (not $\mathcal{G}$), can be carried out with a total cost of about 4 megamems, in about 1.6 megabytes of memory; that's only about 15 memory accesses per kernel of G.

In a similar fashion we can use BDDs to work with other "implicit graphs," which have more vertices than could possibly be represented in memory, if those vertices can be characterized as the solution vectors of Boolean functions. When the functions aren't too complicated, we can answer queries about those graphs that could never be answered by representing the vertices and arcs explicitly.

*Functional composition. The *pièce de résistance* of recursive BDD algorithms is a general procedure to compute $f(g_1, g_2, \ldots, g_n)$, where f is a given function of $\{x_1, x_2, \ldots, x_n\}$ and so is each argument g_j. Suppose we know a number $m \geq 0$ such that $g_j = x_j$ for $m < j \leq n$; then the procedure can be expressed as follows:

$$\mathrm{COMPOSE}(f, g_1, \ldots, g_n) = \begin{cases} \text{If } f = 0 \text{ or } f = 1, \text{ return } f. \\ \text{Otherwise suppose } f = (\bar{x}_v? \ f_l: f_h), \text{ as in (50);} \\ \text{if } v > m, \text{ return } f; \text{ otherwise, if } f(g_1, \ldots, g_n) = r \\ \quad \text{is in the memo cache, return } r. \\ \text{Compute } r_l \leftarrow \mathrm{COMPOSE}(f_l, g_1, \ldots, g_n) \\ \quad \text{and } r_h \leftarrow \mathrm{COMPOSE}(f_h, g_1, \ldots, g_n); \\ \text{set } r \leftarrow \mathrm{MUX}(g_v, r_l, r_h) \text{ using (62);} \\ \text{put } `f(g_1, \ldots, g_n) = r\text{'} \text{ into the cache, and return } r. \end{cases} \quad (72)$$

The representation of cache memos like '$f(g_1, \ldots, g_n) = r$' in this algorithm is a bit tricky; we will discuss it momentarily.

Although the computations here look basically the same as those we've been seeing in previous recursions, there is in fact a huge difference: The functions r_l and r_h in (72) can now involve *all* variables $\{x_1, \ldots, x_n\}$, not just the x's near the bottom of the BDDs. So the running time of (72) might actually be huge. But there also are many cases when everything works together harmoniously and efficiently. For example, the computation of $a(x \oplus y)$ in (69) is no problem.

The key of a memo like '$f(g_1, \ldots, g_n) = r$' should not be a completely detailed specification of $(f, g_1, \ldots, g_n)$, because we want to hash it efficiently. Therefore we store only '$f[G] = r$', where G is an identification number for the sequence of functions $(g_1, \ldots, g_n)$. Whenever that sequence changes, we can use a new number G; and we can remember the G's for special sequences of functions that occur repeatedly in a particular computation, as long as the individual functions g_j don't die. (See also the alternative scheme in exercise 102.)

Let's return to the graph of contiguous states for one more example. That graph is planar; suppose we want to color it with four colors. Since the colors can be given 2-bit codes $\{00, 01, 10, 11\}$, it's easy to express the valid colorings as a Boolean function of 98 variables that is true if and only if the color codes ab are different for each pair of adjacent states:

$$\text{COLOR}(a_{\text{ME}}, b_{\text{ME}}, \ldots, a_{\text{CA}}, b_{\text{CA}}) =$$
$$\text{IND}(a_{\text{ME}} \wedge b_{\text{ME}}, \ldots, a_{\text{CA}} \wedge b_{\text{CA}}) \wedge \text{IND}(a_{\text{ME}} \wedge \bar{b}_{\text{ME}}, \ldots, a_{\text{CA}} \wedge \bar{b}_{\text{CA}}) \qquad (73)$$
$$\wedge \text{IND}(\bar{a}_{\text{ME}} \wedge b_{\text{ME}}, \ldots, \bar{a}_{\text{CA}} \wedge b_{\text{CA}}) \wedge \text{IND}(\bar{a}_{\text{ME}} \wedge \bar{b}_{\text{ME}}, \ldots, \bar{a}_{\text{CA}} \wedge \bar{b}_{\text{CA}}).$$

Each of the four INDs has a BDD of 854 nodes, which can be computed via (72) with a cost of about 70 kilomems. The COLOR function turns out to have only 25,579 BDD nodes. Algorithm C now quickly establishes that the total number of ways to 4-color this graph is exactly 25,623,183,458,304 — or, if we divide by 4! to remove symmetries, about 1.1 trillion. The total time needed for this computation, starting from a description of the graph, is less than 3.5 megamems, in 2.2 megabytes of memory. (We can also find *random* 4-colorings, etc.)

Nasty functions. Of course there also are functions of 98 variables that aren't nearly so nice as COLOR. Indeed, the total number of 98-variable functions is $2^{2^{98}}$; exercise 108 proves that at most $2^{2^{46}}$ of them have a BDD size less than a trillion, and that almost all Boolean functions of 98 variables actually have $B(f) \approx 2^{98}/98 \approx 3.2 \times 10^{27}$. There's just no way to compress 2^{98} bits of data into a small space, unless that data happens to be highly redundant.

What's the worst case? If f is a Boolean function of n variables, how large can $B(f)$ be? The answer isn't hard to discover, if we consider the *profile* of a given BDD, which is the sequence $(b_0, \ldots, b_{n-1}, b_n)$ when there are b_k nodes that branch on variable x_{k+1} and b_n sinks. Clearly

$$B(f) = b_0 + \cdots + b_{n-1} + b_n. \qquad (74)$$

We also have $b_0 \le 1$, $b_1 \le 2$, $b_2 \le 4$, $b_3 \le 8$, and in general

$$b_k \le 2^k, \qquad (75)$$

because each node has only two branches. Furthermore $b_n = 2$ whenever f isn't constant; and $b_{n-1} \le 2$, because there are only two legal choices for the LO and HI branches of $\textcircled{n}$. Indeed, we know that b_k is the number of *beads* of order $n - k$ in the truth table for f, namely the number of distinct subfunctions of $(x_{k+1}, \ldots, x_n)$ that depend on x_{k+1} after the values of $(x_1, \ldots, x_k)$ have been specified. Only $2^{2^m} - 2^{2^{m-1}}$ beads of order m are possible, so we must have

$$b_k \le 2^{2^{n-k}} - 2^{2^{n-k-1}}, \qquad \text{for } 0 \le k < n. \qquad (76)$$

When $n = 11$, for instance, (75) and (76) tell us that $(b_0, \ldots, b_{11})$ is at most

$$(1, 2, 4, 8, 16, 32, 64, 128, 240, 12, 2, 2). \qquad (77)$$

Thus $B(f) \leq 1 + 2 + \cdots + 128 + 240 + \cdots + 2 = 255 + 256 = 511$ when $n = 11$. This upper bound is in fact obtained with the truth table

$$00000000\ 00000001\ 00000010\ \ldots\ 11111110\ 11111111, \qquad (78)$$

or with any string of length 2^{11} that is a permutation of the 256 possible 8-bit bytes, because all of the 8-bit beads are clearly present, and because all of the subtables of lengths 16, 32, ..., 2^{11} are clearly beads. Similar examples can be constructed for all n (see exercise 110). Therefore the worst case is known:

Theorem U. *Every Boolean function $f(x_1, \ldots, x_n)$ has $B(f) \leq U_n$, where*

$$U_n = 2 + \sum_{k=0}^{n-1} \min(2^k, 2^{2^{n-k}} - 2^{2^{n-k-1}}) = 2^{n-\lambda(n-\lambda n)} + 2^{2^{\lambda(n-\lambda n)}} - 1. \qquad (79)$$

Furthermore, explicit functions f_n with $B(f_n) = U_n$ exist for all n. ∎

If we replace λ by lg, the right-hand side of (79) becomes $2^n/(n - \lg n) + 2^n/n - 1$. In general, U_n is u_n times $2^n/n$, where the factor u_n lies between 1 and $2 + O(\frac{\log n}{n})$. A BDD with about $2^{n+1}/n$ nodes needs about $n + 1 - \lg n$ bits for each of two pointers in every node, plus $\lg n$ bits to indicate the variable for branching. So the total amount of memory space taken up by the BDD for any function $f(x_1, \ldots, x_n)$ is never more than about 2^{n+2} bits, which is four times the number of bits in its truth table, even if f happens to be one of the worst possible functions from the standpoint of BDD representation.

The average case turns out to be almost the same as the worst case, if we choose the truth table for f at random from among all 2^{2^n} possibilities. Again the calculations are straightforward: The average number of $(k{+}1)$ nodes is exactly

$$\hat{b}_k = \left(2^{2^{n-k}} - 2^{2^{n-k-1}}\right)\left(2^{2^n} - (2^{2^{n-k}} - 1)^{2^k}\right)/2^{2^n}, \qquad (80)$$

because there are $2^{2^{n-k}} - 2^{2^{n-k-1}}$ beads of order $n - k$ and $(2^{2^{n-k}} - 1)^{2^k}$ truth tables in which any particular bead does not occur. Exercise 112 shows that this complicated-looking quantity $\hat{b}_k$ always lies extremely close to the worst-case estimate $\min(2^k, 2^{2^{n-k}} - 2^{2^{n-k-1}})$, except for two values of k. The exceptional levels occur when $k \approx 2^{n-k}$ and the "min" has little effect. For example, the average profile $(\hat{b}_0, \ldots, \hat{b}_{n-1}, \hat{b}_n)$ when $n = 11$ is approximately

$$(1.0, 2.0, 4.0, 8.0, 16.0, 32.0, 64.0, 127.4, 151.9, 12.0, 2.0, 2.0) \qquad (81)$$

when rounded to one decimal place, and these values are virtually indistinguishable from the worst case (77) except when $k = 7$ or 8.

A related concept called a *quasi-BDD*, or "QDD," is also important. Every function has a unique QDD, which is similar to its BDD except that the root node is always ①, and every ⓚ node for $k < n$ branches to two $(k{+}1)$ nodes; thus every path from the root to a sink has length n. To make this possible, we allow the LO and HI pointers of a QDD node to be identical. But the QDD must still be reduced, in the sense that different nodes cannot have the same two pointers (LO, HI). For example, the QDD for $\langle x_1 x_2 x_3 \rangle$ is

$$(82)$$

it has two more nodes than the corresponding BDD in Fig. 21. Notice that the V fields are redundant in a QDD, so they needn't be present in memory.

The *quasi-profile* of a function is $(q_0, \ldots, q_{n-1}, q_n)$, where q_{k-1} is the number of $\textcircled{k}$ nodes in the QDD. It's easy to see that q_k is also the number of distinct *subtables* of order $n - k$ in the truth table, just as b_k is the number of distinct beads. Every bead is a subtable, so we have

$$q_k \geq b_k, \qquad \text{for } 0 \leq k \leq n. \tag{83}$$

Furthermore, exercise 115 proves that

$$q_k \leq 1 + b_0 + \cdots + b_{k-1} \text{ and } q_k \leq b_k + \cdots + b_n, \quad \text{for } 0 \leq k \leq n. \tag{84}$$

Consequently each element of the quasi-profile is a lower bound on the BDD size:

$$B(f) \geq 2q_k - 1, \qquad \text{for } 0 \leq k \leq n. \tag{85}$$

Let $Q(f) = q_0 + \cdots + q_{n-1} + q_n$ be the total size of the QDD for f. We obviously have $Q(f) \geq B(f)$, by (83). On the other hand $Q(f)$ can't be too much bigger than $B(f)$, because (84) implies that

$$Q(f) \leq \frac{n+1}{2}(B(f) + 1). \tag{86}$$

Exercises 116 and 117 explore other basic properties of quasi-profiles.

The worst-case truth table (78) actually corresponds to a familiar function that we've already seen, the 8-way multiplexer

$$M_3(x_9, x_{10}, x_{11}; x_1, \ldots, x_8) = x_{1+(x_9 x_{10} x_{11})_2}. \tag{87}$$

But we've renumbered the variables perversely so that the multiplexing now occurs with respect to the *last* three variables (x_9, x_{10}, x_{11}), instead of the first three as in Eq. (30). This simple change to the ordering of the variables raises the BDD size of M_3 from 17 to 511; and an analogous change when $n = 2^m + m$ would cause $B(M_m)$ to make a colossal leap from $2n - 2m + 1$ to $2^{n-m+1} - 1$.

R. E. Bryant has introduced an interesting "navel-gazing" multiplexer called the *hidden weighted bit function*, defined as follows:

$$h_n(x_1, \ldots, x_n) = x_{x_1 + \cdots + x_n} = x_{\nu x}, \tag{88}$$

with the understanding that $x_0 = 0$. For example, $h_4(x_1, x_2, x_3, x_4)$ has the truth table 0000 0111 1001 1011. He proved [*IEEE Trans.* **C-40** (1991), 208–210] that h_n has a large BDD, regardless of how we might try to renumber its variables.

With the standard ordering of variables, the profile $(b_0, \ldots, b_{11})$ of h_{11} is

$$(1, 2, 4, 8, 15, 27, 46, 40, 18, 7, 2, 2); \qquad (89)$$

hence $B(h_{11}) = 172$. The first half of this profile is actually the Fibonacci sequence in slight disguise, with $b_k = F_{k+4} - k - 2$. In general, h_n always has this value of b_k for $k < n/2$; thus its initial profile counts grow with order ϕ^k instead of the worst-case rate of 2^k. This growth rate slackens after k surpasses $n/2$, so that, for example, $B(h_{32})$ is only a modest 86,636. But exponential growth eventually takes over, and $B(h_{100})$ is out of sight: 17,530,618,296,680. (When $n = 100$, the maximum profile element is $b_{59} = 2,947,635,944,748$, which dwarfs $b_0 + \cdots + b_{49} = 139,583,861,115$.) Exercise 125 proves that $B(h_n)$ is asymptotically $c\chi^n + O(n^2)$, where

$$\chi = \frac{\sqrt[3]{27 - \sqrt{621}} + \sqrt[3]{27 + \sqrt{621}}}{\sqrt[3]{54}}$$

$$= 1.32471\ 79572\ 44746\ 02596\ 09088\ 54478\ 09734\ 07344+ \qquad (90)$$

is the so-called "plastic constant," the positive root of $\chi^3 = \chi + 1$, and the coefficient c is $7\chi - 1 + 14/(3 + 2\chi) \approx 10.75115$.

On the other hand we can do substantially better if we change the order in which the variables are tested in the BDD. If $f(x_1, \ldots, x_n)$ is any Boolean function and if π is any permutation of $\{1, \ldots, n\}$, let us write

$$f^\pi(x_1, \ldots, x_n) = f(x_{1\pi}, \ldots, x_{n\pi}). \qquad (91)$$

For example, if $f(x_1, x_2, x_3, x_4) = (x_3 \vee (x_1 \wedge x_4)) \wedge (\bar{x}_2 \vee \bar{x}_4)$ and if $(1\pi, 2\pi, 3\pi, 4\pi) = (3, 2, 4, 1)$, then $f^\pi(x_1, x_2, x_3, x_4) = (x_4 \vee (x_3 \wedge x_1)) \wedge (\bar{x}_2 \vee \bar{x}_1)$; and we have $B(f) = 10$, $B(f^\pi) = 6$ because the BDDs are

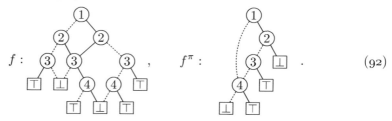

$$(92)$$

The BDD for f^π corresponds to a BDD for f that has a nonstandard ordering, in which a branch is permitted from $\textcircled{i}$ to $\textcircled{j}$ only if $i\pi < j\pi$:

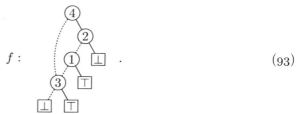

$$(93)$$

The root is $\textcircled{i}$, where $i = 1\pi^-$ is the index for which $i\pi = 1$. When the branch variables are listed from the top down, we have $(4\pi, 2\pi, 1\pi, 3\pi) = (1, 2, 3, 4)$.

Applying these ideas to the hidden weighted bit function, we have

$$h_n^\pi(x_1, \ldots, x_n) = x_{(x_1 + \cdots + x_n)\pi}, \tag{94}$$

with the understanding that $0\pi = 0$ and $x_0 = 0$. For example, $h_3^\pi(0, 0, 1) = 1$ if $(1\pi, 2\pi, 3\pi) = (3, 1, 2)$, because $x_{(x_1 + x_2 + x_3)\pi} = x_3 = 1$. (See exercise 120.)

Element q_k of the quasi-profile counts the number of distinct subfunctions that arise when the values of x_1 through x_k are known. Using (94), we can represent all such subfunctions by means of a *slate of options* $[r_0, \ldots, r_{n-k}]$, where r_j is the result of the subfunction when $x_{k+1} + \cdots + x_n = j$. Suppose $x_1 = c_1, \ldots, x_k = c_k$, and let $s = c_1 + \cdots + c_k$. Then $r_j = c_{(s+j)\pi}$ if $(s+j)\pi \le k$; otherwise $r_j = x_{(s+j)\pi}$. However, we set $r_0 \leftarrow 0$ if $s\pi > k$, and $r_{n-k} \leftarrow 1$ if $(s + n - k)\pi > k$, so that the first and last options of every slate are constant.

For example, calculations show that the following permutation $1\pi \ldots 100\pi$ reduces the BDD size of h_{100} from 17.5 trillion to $B(h_{100}^\pi) = 1{,}124{,}432{,}105$:

$$
\begin{array}{cccccccccccccccccccc}
2 & 4 & 6 & 8 & 10 & 12 & 14 & 16 & 18 & 20 & 97 & 57 & 77 & 37 & 87 & 47 & 67 & 27 & 92 & 52 \\
72 & 32 & 82 & 42 & 62 & 22 & 100 & 60 & 80 & 40 & 90 & 50 & 70 & 30 & 95 & 55 & 75 & 35 & 85 & 45 \\
65 & 25 & 98 & 58 & 78 & 38 & 88 & 48 & 68 & 28 & 93 & 53 & 73 & 33 & 83 & 43 & 63 & 23 & 99 & 59 \\
79 & 39 & 89 & 49 & 69 & 29 & 94 & 54 & 74 & 34 & 84 & 44 & 64 & 24 & 96 & 56 & 76 & 36 & 86 & 46 \\
66 & 26 & 91 & 51 & 71 & 31 & 81 & 41 & 61 & 21 & 19 & 17 & 15 & 13 & 11 & 9 & 7 & 5 & 3 & 1
\end{array}
\tag{95}
$$

Such calculations can be based on an enumeration of all slates that can arise, for $0 \le s \le k \le n$. Suppose we've tested $x_1, \ldots, x_{83}$ and found that $x_j = [j \le 42]$, say, for $1 \le j \le 83$. Then $s = 42$; and the subfunction of the remaining 17 variables $(x_{84}, \ldots, x_{100})$ is given by the slate $[r_0, \ldots, r_{17}] = [c_{25}, x_{98}, c_{58}, c_{78}, c_{38}, x_{88}, c_{48}, c_{68}, c_{28}, x_{93}, c_{53}, c_{73}, c_{33}, c_{83}, c_{43}, c_{63}, c_{23}, x_{99}]$, which reduces to

$$[1, x_{98}, 0, 0, 1, x_{88}, 0, 0, 1, x_{93}, 0, 0, 1, 0, 0, 0, 1, 1]. \tag{96}$$

This is one of the 2^{14} subfunctions counted by q_{83} when $s = 42$. Exercise 124 explains how to deal similarly with the other values of k and s.

We're ready now to prove Bryant's theorem:

Theorem B. *The BDD size of h_n^π exceeds $2^{\lfloor n/5 \rfloor}$, for all permutations π.*

Proof. Observe first that two subfunctions of h_n^π are equal if and only if they have the same slate. For if $[r_0, \ldots, r_{n-k}] \ne [r'_0, \ldots, r'_{n-k}]$, suppose $r_j \ne r'_j$. If both r_j and r'_j are constant, the subfunctions differ when $x_{k+1} + \cdots + x_n = j$. If r_j is constant but $r'_j = x_i$, we have $0 < j < n - k$; the subfunctions differ because $x_{k+1} + \cdots + x_n$ can equal j with $x_i \ne r_j$. And if $r_j = x_i$ but $r'_j = x_{i'}$ with $i \ne i'$, we can have $x_{k+1} + \cdots + x_n = j$ with $x_i \ne x_{i'}$. (The latter case can arise only when the slates correspond to different offsets s and s'.)

Therefore q_k is the number of different slates $[r_0, \ldots, r_{n-k}]$. Exercise 123 proves that this number, for any given k, n, and s as described above, is exactly

$$\binom{w}{w-s} + \binom{w}{w-s+1} + \cdots + \binom{w}{k-s} = \binom{w}{s+w-k} + \cdots + \binom{w}{s-1} + \binom{w}{s}, \tag{97}$$

where w is the number of indices j such that $s \le j \le s + n - k$ and $j\pi \le k$.

Now consider the case $k = \lfloor 3n/5 \rfloor + 1$, and let $s = k - \lceil n/2 \rceil$, $s' = \lfloor n/2 \rfloor + 1$. (Think of $n = 100$, $k = 61$, $s = 11$, $s' = 51$. We may assume that $n \ge 10$.) Then

$w + w' = k - w''$, where w'' counts the indices with $j\pi \leq k$ and either $j < s$ or $j > s' + n - k$. Since $w'' \leq (s-1) + (k - s') = 2k - 2 - n$, we must have $w + w' \geq n + 2 - k = \lceil 2n/5 \rceil + 1$. Hence either $w > \lfloor n/5 \rfloor$ or $w' > \lfloor n/5 \rfloor$; and in both cases (97) exceeds $2^{\lfloor n/5 \rfloor - 1}$. The theorem follows from (85). ∎

Conversely, there's always a permutation π such that $B(h_n^\pi) = O(2^{0.2029n})$, although the constant hidden by O-notation is quite large. This result was proved by B. Bollig, M. Löbbing, M. Sauerhoff, and I. Wegener, *Theoretical Informatics and Applications* **33** (1999), 103–115, using a permutation like (95): The first indices, with $j\pi \leq n/5$, come alternately from $j > 9n/10$ and $j \leq n/10$; the others are ordered by reading the binary representation of $9n/10 - j$ from right to left (*colex order*).

Let's also look briefly at a much simpler example, the *permutation function* $P_m(x_1, \ldots, x_{m^2})$, which equals 1 if and only if the binary matrix with $x_{(i-1)m+j}$ in row i and column j is a permutation matrix:

$$P_m(x_1, \ldots, x_{m^2}) = \bigwedge_{i=1}^{m} S_1(x_{(i-1)m+1}, x_{(i-1)m+2}, \ldots, x_{(i-1)m+m})$$

$$\wedge \bigwedge_{j=1}^{m} S_1(x_j, x_{m+j}, \ldots, x_{m^2-m+j}). \quad (98)$$

In spite of its simplicity, this function cannot be represented with a small BDD, under any reordering of its variables:

Theorem K. *The BDD size of P_m^π exceeds $m2^{m-1}$, for all permutations π.*

Proof. [See I. Wegener, *Branching Programs and Binary Decision Diagrams* (SIAM, 2000), Theorem 4.12.3.] Given the BDD for P_m^π, notice that each of the $m!$ vectors x such that $P_m^\pi(x) = 1$ traces a path of length $n = m^2$ from the root to $\boxed{\top}$; every variable must be tested. Let $v_k(x)$ be the node from which the path for x takes its kth HI branch. This node branches on the value in row i and column j of the given matrix, for some pair $(i, j) = (i_k(x), j_k(x))$.

Suppose $v_k(x) = v_{k'}(x')$, where $x \neq x'$. Construct x'' by letting it agree with x up to $v_k(x)$ and with x' thereafter. Then $f(x'') = 1$; consequently we must have $k = k'$. In fact, this argument shows that we must also have

$$\{(i_1(x), j_1(x)), (i_2(x), j_2(x)), \ldots, (i_{k-1}(x), j_{k-1}(x))\}$$
$$= \{(i_1(x'), j_1(x')), (i_2(x'), j_2(x')), \ldots, (i_{k-1}(x'), j_{k-1}(x'))\}. \quad (99)$$

Imagine m colors of tickets, with $m!$ tickets of each color. Place a ticket of color k on node $v_k(x)$, for all k and all x. Then no node gets tickets of different colors; and no node of color k gets more than $(k-1)!\,(m-k)!$ tickets altogether, by Eq. (99). Therefore at least $m!/((k-1)!\,(m-k)!) = k\binom{m}{k}$ different nodes must receive tickets of color k. Summing over k gives $m2^{m-1}$ non-sink nodes. ∎

Exercise 184 shows that $B(P_m)$ is less than $m2^{m+1}$, so the lower bound in Theorem K is nearly optimum except for a factor of 4. Although the size grows exponentially, the behavior isn't hopelessly bad, because $m = \sqrt{n}$. For example, $B(P_{20})$ is only 38,797,317, even though P_{20} is a Boolean function of 400 variables.

*Optimizing the order. Let $B_{\min}(f)$ and $B_{\max}(f)$ denote the smallest and largest values of $B(f^\pi)$, taken over all permutations π that can prescribe an ordering of the variables. We've seen several cases where $B_{\min}$ and $B_{\max}$ are dramatically different; for example, the 2^m-way multiplexer has $B_{\min}(M_m) \approx 2n$ and $B_{\max}(M_m) \approx 2^n/n$, when $n = 2^m + m$. And indeed, simple functions for which a good ordering is crucial are not at all unusual. Consider, for instance,

$$f(x_1, x_2, \ldots, x_n) \;=\; (\bar{x}_1 \vee x_2) \wedge (\bar{x}_3 \vee x_4) \wedge \cdots \wedge (\bar{x}_{n-1} \vee x_n), \quad n \text{ even}; \quad (100)$$

this is the important *subset function* $[x_1 x_3 \ldots x_{n-1} \subseteq x_2 x_4 \ldots x_n]$, and we have $B(f) = B_{\min}(f) = n + 2$. But the BDD size explodes to $B(f^\pi) = B_{\max}(f) = 2^{n/2+1}$ when π is "organ-pipe order," namely the ordering for which

$$f^\pi(x_1, x_2, \ldots, x_n) \;=\; (\bar{x}_1 \vee x_n) \wedge (\bar{x}_2 \vee x_{n-1}) \wedge \cdots \wedge (\bar{x}_{n/2} \vee x_{n/2+1}). \quad (101)$$

And the same bad behavior occurs for the ordering $[x_1 \ldots x_{n/2} \subseteq x_{n/2+1} \ldots x_n]$. In these orderings the BDD must "remember" the states of $n/2$ variables, while the original formulation (100) needs very little memory.

Every Boolean function f has a *master profile chart*, which encapsulates the set of all its possible sizes $B(f^\pi)$. If f has n variables, this chart has 2^n vertices, one for each subset of the variables; and it has $n2^{n-1}$ edges, one for each pair of subsets that differ in just one element. For example, the master profile chart for the function in (92) and (93) is

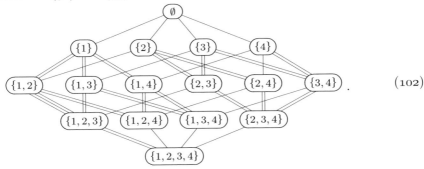

$$(102)$$

Every edge has a weight, illustrated here by the number of lines; for example, the weight between $\{1, 2\}$ and $\{1, 2, 3\}$ is 3. The chart has the following interpretation: *If X is a subset of k variables, and if $x \notin X$, then the weight between X and $X \cup x$ is the number of subfunctions of f that depend on x when the variables of X have been replaced by constants in all 2^k possible ways.* For example, if $X = \{1, 2\}$, we have $f(0, 0, x_3, x_4) = x_3$, $f(0, 1, x_3, x_4) = f(1, 1, x_3, x_4) = x_3 \wedge \bar{x}_4$, and $f(1, 0, x_3, x_4) = x_3 \vee x_4$; all three of these subfunctions depend on x_3, but only two of them depend on x_4, as shown in the weights below $\{1, 2\}$.

There are $n!$ paths of length n from $\emptyset$ to $\{1, \ldots, n\}$, and we can let the path $\emptyset \to \{a_1\} \to \{a_1, a_2\} \to \cdots \to \{a_1, \ldots, a_n\}$ correspond to the permutation π if $a_1\pi = 1$, $a_2\pi = 2$, $\ldots$, $a_n\pi = n$. Then the sum of the weights on path π is $B(f^\pi)$, if we add 2 for the sink nodes. For example, the path $\emptyset \to \{4\} \to \{2, 4\} \to \{1, 2, 4\} \to \{1, 2, 3, 4\}$ yields the only way to achieve $B(f^\pi) = 6$ as in (93).

Notice that the master profile chart is a familiar graph, the n-cube, whose edges have been decorated so that they count the number of beads in various sets of subfunctions. The graph has exponential size, $n2^{n-1}$; yet it is much smaller than the total number of permutations, $n!$. When n is, say, 25 or less, exercise 138 shows that the entire chart can be computed without great difficulty, and we can find an optimum permutation for any given function. For example, the hidden weighted bit function turns out to have $B_{\min}(h_{25}) = 2090$ and $B_{\max}(h_{25}) = 35441$; the minimum is achieved with $(1\pi, \ldots, 25\pi) = (3, 5, 7, 9, 11, 13, 15, 17, 25, 24, 23, 22, 21, 20, 19, 18, 16, 14, 12, 10, 8, 6, 4, 2, 1)$, while the maximum results from a strange permutation $(22, 19, 17, 25, 15, 13, 11, 10, 9, 8, 7, 24, 6, 5, 4, 3, 2, 12, 1, 14, 23, 16, 18, 20, 21)$ that tests many "middle" variables first.

Instead of computing the entire master profile chart, we can sometimes save time by learning just enough about it to determine a path of least weight. (See exercise 140.) But when n grows and functions get more weird, we are unlikely to be able to determine $B_{\min}(f)$ exactly, because the problem of finding the best ordering is NP-complete (see exercise 137).

We've defined the profile and quasi-profile of a single Boolean function f, but the same ideas apply also to an arbitrary BDD base that contains m functions $\{f_1, \ldots, f_m\}$. Namely, the profile is $(b_0, \ldots, b_n)$ when there are b_k nodes on level k, and the quasi-profile is $(q_0, \ldots, q_n)$ when there are q_k nodes on level k of the corresponding QDD base; the truth tables of the functions have b_k different beads of order $n - k$, and q_k different subtables. For example, the profile of the $(4 + 4)$-bit addition functions $\{f_1, f_2, f_3, f_4, f_5\}$ in (36) is $(2, 4, 3, 6, 3, 6, 3, 2, 2)$, and the quasi-profile is worked out in exercise 144. Similarly, the concept of master profile chart applies to m functions whose variables are reordered simultaneously; and we can use it to find $B_{\min}(f_1, \ldots, f_m)$ and $B_{\max}(f_1, \ldots, f_m)$, the minimum and maximum of $b_0 + \cdots + b_n$ taken over all profiles.

*Local reordering. What happens to a BDD base when we decide to branch on x_2 first, then on x_1, x_3, ..., x_n? Figure 26 shows that the structure of the top two levels can change dramatically, but all other levels remain the same.

A closer analysis reveals, in fact, that this level-swapping process isn't difficult to understand or to implement. The (1) nodes before swapping can be divided into two kinds, "tangled" and "solitary," depending on whether they have (2) nodes as descendants; for example, there are three tangled nodes at the left of Fig. 26, pointed to by s_1, s_2, and s_3, while s_4 points to a solitary node. Similarly, the (2) nodes before swapping are either "visible" or "hidden," depending on whether they are independent source functions or accessible only from (1) nodes; all four of the (2) nodes at the left of Fig. 26 are hidden.

After swapping, the solitary (1) nodes simply move down one level, but the tangled nodes are transmogrified according to a process that we shall explain shortly. The hidden (2) nodes disappear, and the visible ones simply move up to the top level. Additional nodes might also arise during the transmogrification process; such nodes, labeled (1), are called "newbies." For example, two newbies appear at the right of Fig. 26. This process decreases the total number of nodes if and only if the hidden nodes outnumber the newbies.

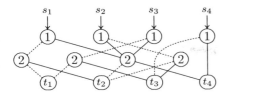
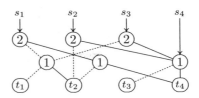

Fig. 26. Interchanging the top two levels of a BDD base. Here (s_1, s_2, s_3, s_4) are source functions; (t_1, t_2, t_3, t_4) are target nodes, representing subfunctions at lower levels.

The reverse of a swap is, of course, the same as a swap, but with the roles of ① and ② interchanged. If we begin with the diagram at the right of Fig. 26, we see that it has three tangled nodes (labeled ②) and one that's visible (labeled ①); two of its nodes are hidden, none are solitary. The swapping process in general sends (tangled, solitary, visible, hidden) nodes into (tangled, visible, solitary, newbie) nodes, respectively — after which newbies would become hidden in a reverse swap, and the originally hidden nodes would reappear as newbies.

Transmogrification is easiest to understand if we treat all nodes below the top two levels as if they were sinks, having constant values. Then every source function $f(x_1, x_2)$ depends only on x_1 and x_2; hence it takes on four values $a = f(0,0)$, $b = f(0,1)$, $c = f(1,0)$, and $d = f(1,1)$, where a, b, c, and d represent sinks. We may suppose that there are q sinks, $\boxed{1}$, $\boxed{2}$, ..., $\boxed{q}$, and that $1 \le a, b, c, d \le q$. Then $f(x_1, x_2)$ is fully described by its *extended truth table*, $f(0,0)f(0,1)f(1,0)f(1,1) = abcd$. And after swapping, we're left with $f(x_2, x_1)$, which has the extended truth table $acbd$. For example, Fig. 26 can be redrawn as follows, using extended truth tables to label its nodes:

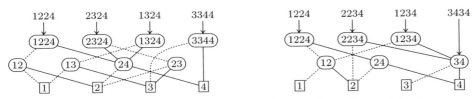

Fig. 27. Another way to represent the transformations in Fig. 26.

In these terms, the source function $abcd$ points to a solitary node when $a = b \ne c = d$, and to a visible node when $a = c \ne b = d$; otherwise it points to a tangled node (unless $a = b = c = d$, when it points directly to a sink). The tangled node $abcd$ usually has LO = ab and HI = cd, unless $a = b$ or $c = d$; in the exceptional cases, LO or HI is a sink. After transmogrification it will have LO = ac and HI = bd in a similar way, where latter nodes will be either newbies or visibles or sinks (but not both sinks). One interesting case is 1224, whose children 12 and 24 on the left are hidden nodes, while the 12 and 24 on the right are newbies.

Exercise 147 discusses an efficient implementation of this transformation, which was introduced by Richard Rudell in *IEEE/ACM International Conf. Computer-Aided Design* **CAD-93** (1993), 42–47. It has the important property that no pointers need to change, except within the nodes on the top two levels:

All source nodes s_j still point to the same place in computer memory, and all sinks retain their previous identity. We have described it as a swap between ①s and ②s, but in fact the same transformation will swap ⓙs and ⓚs whenever the variables x_j and x_k correspond to branching on adjacent levels. The reason is that the upper levels of any BDD base essentially define source functions for the lower levels, which constitute a BDD base in their own right.

We know from our study of sorting that *any* reordering of the variables of a BDD base can be produced by a sequence of swaps between adjacent levels. In particular, we can use adjacent swaps to do a "jump-up" transformation, which brings a given variable x_k to the top level without disturbing the relative order of the other variables. It's easy, for instance, to jump x_4 up to the top: We simply swap ④ ↔ ③, then ④ ↔ ②, then ④ ↔ ①, because x_4 will be adjacent to x_1 after it has jumped past x_2.

Since repeated swaps can produce any ordering, they are sometimes able to make a BDD base grow until it is too big to handle. How bad can a single swap be? If exactly (s, t, v, h, ν) nodes are solitary, tangled, visible, hidden, and newbie, the top two levels end up with $s + t + v + \nu$ nodes; and this is at most $m + \nu \leq m + 2t$ when there are m source functions, because $m \geq s + t + v$. Thus the new size can't exceed twice the original, plus the number of sources.

If a single swap can double the size, a jump-up for x_k threatens to increase the size exponentially, because it does $k - 1$ swaps. Fortunately, however, jump-ups are no worse than single swaps in this regard:

Theorem J$^+$. $B(f_1^\pi, \ldots, f_m^\pi) < m + 2B(f_1, \ldots, f_m)$ after a jump-up operation.

Proof. Let $a_1 a_2 \ldots a_{2^k-1} a_{2^k}$ be the extended truth table for a source function $f(x_1, \ldots, x_k)$, with lower-level nodes regarded as sinks. After the jump-up, the extended truth table for $f^\pi(x_1, \ldots, x_k) = f(x_{1\pi}, \ldots, x_{k\pi}) = f(x_2, \ldots, x_k, x_1)$ is $a_1 a_3 \ldots a_{2^k-1} a_2 a_4 \ldots a_{2^k}$, which incidentally can be written $a_1 \ldots a_{2^k} \,\text{·}\!\text{·}\, \mu_{k,0}$ in the "sheep-and-goats" notation of 7.1.3–(81). Thus we can see that each bead on level j of f^π is derived from some bead on level $j - 1$ of f, for $1 \leq j < k$; but every such bead spawns at most two beads of half the size in f^π. Therefore, if the respective profiles of $\{f_1, \ldots, f_m\}$ and $\{f_1^\pi, \ldots, f_m^\pi\}$ are $(b_0, \ldots, b_n)$ and $(b_0', \ldots, b_n')$, we must have $b_0' \leq m$, $b_1' \leq 2b_0$, $\ldots$, $b_{k-1}' \leq 2b_{k-2}$, $b_k' = b_k$, $\ldots$, $b_n' = b_n$. The total is therefore $\leq m + B(f_1, \ldots, f_m) + b_0 + \cdots + b_{k-2} - b_{k-1}$. ∎

The opposite of a jump-up is a "jump-down," which demotes the topmost variable by $k - 1$ levels. As before, this operation can be implemented with $k - 1$ swaps. But we have to settle for a much weaker upper bound on the resulting size:

Theorem J$^-$. $B(f_1^\pi, \ldots, f_m^\pi) < B(f_1, \ldots, f_m)^2$ after a jump-down operation.

Proof. Now the extended truth table in the previous proof changes from $a_1 \ldots a_{2^k}$ to $a_1 \ldots a_{2^{k-1}} \ddagger a_{2^{k-1}+1} \ldots a_{2^k} = a_1 a_{2^{k-1}+1} \ldots a_{2^{k-1}} a_{2^k}$, the "zipper function" 7.1.3–(76). In this case we can identify every bead after the jump with an ordered pair of original subfunctions, as in the melding operation (37) and (38). For example, when $k = 3$ the truth table 12345678 becomes 15263748, whose bead 1526 can be regarded as the meld 12 ⋄ 56. ∎

This proof indicates why quadratic growth might occur. If, for example,

$$f(x_1,\ldots,x_n) = x_1?\, M_m(x_2,\ldots,x_{m+1};x_{2m+2},\ldots,x_n):$$
$$M_m(x_{m+2},\ldots,x_{2m+1};\bar{x}_{2m+2},\ldots,\bar{x}_n), \qquad (103)$$

where $n = 1 + 2m + 2^m$, a jump-down of $2m$ levels changes $B(f) = 4n - 8m - 3$ to $B(f^\pi) = 2n^2 - 8m(n-m) - 2(n-2m) + 1 \approx \frac{1}{2}B(f)^2$.

Since jump-up and jump-down are inverse operations, we can also use Theorems J$^+$ and J$^-$ in reverse: *A jump-up operation might conceivably decrease the BDD size to something like its square root, but a jump-down cannot reduce the size to less than about half.* That's bad news for fans of jump-down, although they can take comfort from the knowledge that jump-downs are sometimes the only decent way to get from a given ordering to an optimum one.

Theorems J$^+$ and J$^-$ are due to B. Bollig, M. Löbbing, and I. Wegener, *Inf. Processing Letters* **59** (1996), 233–239. (See also exercise 149.)

*Dynamic reordering. In practice, a natural way to order the variables often suggests itself, based on the modules-in-a-row perspective of Fig. 23 and Theorem M. But sometimes no suitable ordering is apparent, and we can only hope to be lucky; perhaps the computer will come to our rescue and find one. Furthermore, even if we do know a good way to begin a computation, the ordering of variables that works best in the first stages of the work might turn out to be unsatisfactory in later stages. Therefore we can get better results if we don't insist on a fixed ordering. Instead, we can try to tune up the current order of branching whenever a BDD base becomes unwieldy.

For example, we might try to swap $x_{j-1} \leftrightarrow x_j$ in the order, for $1 < j \le n$, undoing the swap if it increases the total number of nodes but letting it ride otherwise; we could keep this up until no such swap makes an improvement. That method is easy to implement, but unfortunately it's too weak; it doesn't give much of a reduction. A much better reordering technique was proposed by Richard Rudell at the same time as he introduced the swap-in-place algorithm of exercise 147. His method, called "sifting," has proved to be quite successful. The idea is simply to take a variable x_k and to try jumping it up or down to all other levels — that is, essentially to remove x_k from the ordering and then to insert it again, choosing a place for insertion that keeps the BDD size as small as possible. All of the necessary work can be done with a sequence of elementary swaps:

Algorithm J (*Sifting a variable*). This algorithm moves variable x_k into an optimum position with respect to the current ordering of the other variables $\{x_1,\ldots,x_{k-1},x_{k+1},\ldots,x_n\}$ in a given BDD base. It works by repeatedly calling the procedure of exercise 147 to swap adjacent variables $x_{j-1} \leftrightarrow x_j$. Throughout this algorithm, S denotes the current size of the BDD base (the total number of nodes); the swapping operation usually changes S.

J1. [Initialize.] Set $p \leftarrow 0$, $j \leftarrow k$, and $s \leftarrow S$. If $k > n/2$, go to J5.

J2. [Sift up.] While $j > 1$, swap $x_{j-1} \leftrightarrow x_j$ and set $j \leftarrow j-1$, $s \leftarrow \min(S, s)$.

J3. [End the pass.] If $p = 1$, go to J4. Otherwise, while $j \neq k$, set $j \leftarrow j+1$ and swap $x_{j-1} \leftrightarrow x_j$; then set $p \leftarrow 1$ and go to J5.

J4. [Finish downward.] While $s \neq S$, set $j \leftarrow j+1$ and swap $x_{j-1} \leftrightarrow x_j$. Stop.

J5. [Sift down.] While $j < n$, set $j \leftarrow j+1$, swap $x_{j-1} \leftrightarrow x_j$, and set $s \leftarrow \min(S, s)$.

J6. [End the pass.] If $p = 1$, go to J7. Otherwise, while $j \neq k$, swap $x_{j-1} \leftrightarrow x_j$ and set $j \leftarrow j-1$; then set $p \leftarrow 1$ and go to J2.

J7. [Finish upward.] While $s \neq S$, swap $x_{j-1} \leftrightarrow x_j$ and set $j \leftarrow j-1$. Stop. ∎

Whenever Algorithm J swaps $x_{j-1} \leftrightarrow x_j$, the variable that is currently called x_j is the original variable x_k. The total number of swaps varies from about n to about $2.5n$, depending on k and the optimum final position of x_k. But we can improve the running time substantially, without seriously affecting the outcome, if steps J2 and J5 are modified to proceed immediately to J3 and J6, respectively, whenever S becomes larger than, say, $1.2s$ or even $1.1s$ or even $1.05s$. In such cases, further sifting in the same direction is unlikely to decrease s.

Rudell's sifting procedure consists of applying Algorithm J exactly n times, once for each variable that is present; see exercise 151. We could continue sifting again and again until there is no more improvement; but the additional gain is usually not worth the extra effort.

Let's look at a detailed example, in order to make these ideas concrete. We've observed that when the contiguous United States are arranged in the order

$$
\begin{array}{l}
\text{ME NH VT MA RI CT NY NJ PA DE MD DC VA NC SC GA FL AL TN KY WV OH MI IN} \\
\text{IL WI MN IA MO AR MS LA TX OK KS NE SD ND MT WY CO NM AZ UT ID WA OR NV CA}
\end{array} \quad (104)
$$

as in (17), they lead to a BDD of size 428 for the independent-set function

$$
\neg\big((x_{\mathsf{AL}} \wedge x_{\mathsf{FL}}) \vee (x_{\mathsf{AL}} \wedge x_{\mathsf{GA}}) \vee (x_{\mathsf{AL}} \wedge x_{\mathsf{MS}}) \vee \cdots \vee (x_{\mathsf{UT}} \wedge x_{\mathsf{WY}}) \vee (x_{\mathsf{VA}} \wedge x_{\mathsf{WV}})\big). \quad (105)
$$

The author chose the ordering (104) by hand, starting with the historical/geographical listing of states that he had been taught as a child, then trying to minimize the size of the boundary between states-already-listed and states-to-come, so that the BDD for (105) would not need to "remember" too many partial results at any level. The resulting size, 428, is pretty good for a function of 49 variables; but sifting is able to make it even better. For example, consider WV: Some of the possibilities for altering its position, with varying sizes S, are

$$
\begin{array}{ccccccccccccccccccc}
|\text{RI}&|\text{CT}&|\text{NY}&|\text{NJ}&|\text{PA}&|\text{DE}&|\text{MD}&|\text{DC}&|\text{VA}&|\text{NC}&|\text{SC}&|\text{GA}&|\text{FL}&|\text{AL}&|\text{TN}&|\text{KY}&|\text{OH}&|\text{MI}&|\text{IN}&|\text{IL}| \\
424&422&417&415&414&412&411&410&412&412&415&420&421&426&425&427&428&428&436&442\ 453
\end{array}
$$

so we can save $428 - 410 = 18$ nodes by jumping WV up to a position between MD and DC. By using Algorithm J to sift on all the variables — first on ME, then on NH, then ..., then on CA — we end up with the ordering

$$
\begin{array}{l}
\text{VT MA ME NH CT RI NY NJ DE PA MD WV VA DC KY OH NC GA SC AL FL MS TN IN} \\
\text{IL MI AR TX LA OK MO IA WI MN CO NE KS MT ND WY SD UT AZ NM ID CA OR WA NV}
\end{array} \quad (106)
$$

and the BDD size has been reduced to 345(!). That sifting process involves a total of 4663 swaps, requiring less than 4 megamems of computation altogether.

Instead of choosing an ordering carefully, let's consider a lazier alternative:
We might begin with the states in alphabetic order

$$\begin{array}{l}\text{AL AR AZ CA CO CT DC DE FL GA IA ID IL IN KS KY LA MA MD ME MI MN MO MS}\\ \text{MT NC ND NE NH NJ NM NV NY OH OK OR PA RI SC SD TN TX UT VA VT WA WI WV WY}\end{array} \quad (107)$$

and proceed from there. Then the BDD for (105) turns out to have 306,214
nodes; it can be computed either via Algorithm S (with about 380 megamems of
machine time) or via (55) and Algorithm U (with about 565 megamems). In this
case sifting makes a dramatic difference: Those 306,214 nodes become only 2871,
at a cost of 430 additional megamems. Furthermore, the sifting cost goes down
from 430 Mμ to 210 Mμ if the loops of Algorithm J are aborted when $S > 1.1s$.
(The more radical choice of aborting when $S > 1.05s$ would reduce the cost of
sifting to 155 Mμ; but the BDD size would be reduced only to 2946 in that case.)

And we can actually do much, much better, if we sift the variables *while*
evaluating (105), instead of waiting until that whole long sequence of disjunctions
been entirely computed. For example, suppose we invoke sifting automatically
whenever the BDD size surpasses twice the number of nodes that were present
after the previous sift. Then the evaluation of (105), starting from the alphabetic
ordering (107), runs like a breeze: It automatically churns out a BDD that has
only 419 nodes, after only about 60 megamems of calculation! Neither human
ingenuity nor "geometric understanding" are needed to discover the ordering

$$\begin{array}{l}\text{NV OR ID WA AZ CA UT NM WY CO MT OK TX NE MO KS LA AR MS TN IA ND MN SD}\\ \text{GA FL AL NC SC KY WI MI IL OH IN WV MD VA DC PA NJ DE NY CT RI NH ME VT MA}\end{array} \quad (108)$$

which beats the author's (104). For this one, the computer just decided to invoke
autosifting 39 times, on smaller BDDs.

What is the *best* ordering of states for the function (105)? The answer to
that question will probably never be known for sure, but we can make a pretty
good guess. First of all, a few more sifts of (108) will yield a still-better ordering

$$\begin{array}{l}\text{OR ID NV WA AZ CA UT NM WY CO MT SD MN ND IA NE OK KS TX MO LA AR MS TN}\\ \text{GA FL AL NC SC KY WI MI IL OH IN WV MD DC VA PA NJ DE NY CT RI NH ME VT MA}\end{array} \quad (109)$$

with BDD size 354. Sifting will not improve (109) further; but sifting has only
limited power, because it explores only $(n-1)^2$ alternative orderings, out of
$n!$ possibilities. (Indeed, exercise 134 exhibits a function of only four variables
whose BDD cannot be improved by sifting, even though the ordering of its
variables is not optimum.) There is, however, another arrow in our quiver: We
can use *master profile charts* to optimize every window of, say, 16 consecutive
levels in the BDD. There are 34 such windows; and the algorithm of exercise 139
optimizes each of them rather quickly. After about 9.6 gigamems of computation,
that algorithm discovers a new champion

$$\begin{array}{l}\text{OR ID NV WA AZ CA UT NM WY CO MT SD MN ND IA NE OK KS TX MO LA AR MS WI}\\ \text{KY MI IN IL AL TN FL NC SC GA WV OH MD DC VA PA NJ DE NY CT RI NH ME VT MA}\end{array} \quad (110)$$

by cleverly rearranging 16 states within (109). This ordering, for which the BDD
size is only 339, might well be optimum, because it cannot be improved either
by sifting or by optimizing any window of width 25. However, such a conjecture

rests on shaky ground: The ordering

$$
\begin{array}{l}
\text{AL GA FL TN NC SC VA MS AR TX LA OK KY MO NM WV MD DC PA NJ DE OH IL MI} \\
\text{IN IA NE KS WI SD WY ND MN MT UT CO ID CA AZ OR WA NV NY CT RI NH ME VT MA}
\end{array} \quad (111)
$$

also happens to be unimprovable by sifting and by width-25 window optimization, yet its BDD has 606 nodes and is far from optimum.

   With the improved ordering (110), the 98-variable COLOR function of (73)
needs only 22037 BDD nodes, instead of 25579. Sifting reduces it to 16098.

*Read-once functions. Boolean functions such as $(x_1 \supset x_2) \oplus ((x_3 \equiv x_4) \wedge x_5)$,
which can be expressed as formulas in which each variable occurs exactly once,
form an important class for which optimum orderings of variables can easily be
computed. Formally, let us say that $f(x_1, \ldots, x_n)$ is a *read-once function* if either
(i) $n = 1$ and $f(x_1) = x_1$; or (ii) $f(x_1, \ldots, x_n) = g(x_1, \ldots, x_k) \circ h(x_{k+1}, \ldots, x_n)$,
where $\circ$ is one of the binary operators $\{\wedge, \vee, \overline{\wedge}, \overline{\vee}, \supset, \subset, \overline{\supset}, \overline{\subset}, \oplus, \equiv\}$ and where
both g and h are read-once functions. In case (i) we obviously have $B(f) = 3$.
And in case (ii), exercise 163 proves that

$$
B(f) = \begin{cases} B(g) + B(h) - 2, & \text{if } \circ \in \{\wedge, \vee, \overline{\wedge}, \overline{\vee}, \supset, \subset, \overline{\supset}, \overline{\subset}\}; \\ B(g) + B(h, \bar{h}) - 2, & \text{if } \circ \in \{\oplus, \equiv\}. \end{cases} \quad (112)
$$

In order to get a recurrence, we also need the similar formulas

$$
B(f, \bar{f}) = \begin{cases} 4, & \text{if } n = 1; \\ 2B(g) + B(h, \bar{h}) - 4, & \text{if } \circ \in \{\wedge, \vee, \overline{\wedge}, \overline{\vee}, \supset, \subset, \overline{\supset}, \overline{\subset}\}; \\ B(g, \bar{g}) + B(h, \bar{h}) - 2, & \text{if } \circ \in \{\oplus, \equiv\}. \end{cases} \quad (113)
$$

A particularly interesting family of read-once functions arises when we define

$$
\begin{aligned}
u_{m+1}(x_1, \ldots, x_{2^{m+1}}) &= v_m(x_1, \ldots, x_{2^m}) \wedge v_m(x_{2^m+1}, \ldots, x_{2^{m+1}}), \\
v_{m+1}(x_1, \ldots, x_{2^{m+1}}) &= u_m(x_1, \ldots, x_{2^m}) \oplus u_m(x_{2^m+1}, \ldots, x_{2^{m+1}}),
\end{aligned} \quad (114)
$$

and $u_0(x_1) = v_0(x_1) = x_1$; for example, $u_3(x_1, \ldots, x_8) = \big((x_1 \wedge x_2) \oplus (x_3 \wedge x_4)\big) \wedge \big((x_5 \wedge x_6) \oplus (x_7 \wedge x_8)\big)$. Exercise 165 shows that the BDD sizes for these functions,
calculated via (112) and (113), involve Fibonacci numbers:

$$
\begin{aligned}
B(u_{2m}) &= 2^m F_{2m+2} + 2, & B(u_{2m+1}) &= 2^{m+1} F_{2m+2} + 2; \\
B(v_{2m}) &= 2^m F_{2m+2} + 2, & B(v_{2m+1}) &= 2^m F_{2m+4} + 2.
\end{aligned} \quad (115)
$$

Thus u_m and v_m are functions of $n = 2^m$ variables whose BDD sizes grow as

$$
\Theta(2^{m/2} \phi^m) = \Theta(n^\beta), \qquad \text{where } \beta = 1/2 + \lg \phi \approx 1.19424. \quad (116)
$$

   In fact, the BDD sizes in (115) are optimum for the u and v functions,
under all permutations of the variables, because of a fundamental result due to
M. Sauerhoff, I. Wegener, and R. Werchner:

Theorem W. *If $f(x_1, \ldots, x_n) = g(x_1, \ldots, x_k) \circ h(x_{k+1}, \ldots, x_n)$ is a read-
once function, there is a permutation π that minimizes $B(f^\pi)$ and $B(f^\pi, \bar{f}^\pi)$
simultaneously, and in which the variables $\{x_1, \ldots, x_k\}$ occur either first or last.*

Proof. Any permutation $(1\pi, \ldots, n\pi)$ leads naturally to an "unshuffled" permutation $(1\sigma, \ldots, n\sigma)$ in which the first k elements are $\{1, \ldots, k\}$ and the last $n - k$ elements are $\{k + 1, \ldots, n\}$, retaining the π order within each group. For example, if $k = 7$, $n = 9$, and $(1\pi, \ldots, 9\pi) = (3, 1, 4, 5, 9, 2, 6, 8, 7)$, we have $(1\sigma, \ldots, 9\sigma) = (3, 1, 4, 5, 2, 6, 7, 9, 8)$. Exercise 166 proves that, in appropriate circumstances, we have $B(f^\sigma) \leq B(f^\pi)$ and $B(f^\sigma, \bar{f}^\sigma) \leq B(f^\pi, \bar{f}^\pi)$. ∎

Using this theorem together with (112) and (113), we can readily optimize the ordering of variables for the BDD of any given read-once function. Consider, for example, $(x_1 \vee x_2) \oplus (x_3 \wedge x_4 \wedge x_5) = g(x_1, x_2) \oplus h(x_3, x_4, x_5)$. We have $B(g) = 4$ and $B(g, \bar{g}) = 6$; $B(h) = 5$ and $B(h, \bar{h}) = 8$. For the overall formula $f = g \oplus h$, Theorem W says that there are two candidates for a best ordering $(1\pi, \ldots, 5\pi)$, namely $(1, 2, 3, 4, 5)$ and $(4, 5, 1, 2, 3)$. The first of these gives $B(f^\pi) = B(g) + B(h, \bar{h}) - 2 = 10$; the other one excels, with $B(f^\pi) = B(h) + B(g, \bar{g}) - 2 = 9$.

The algorithm in exercise 167 finds an optimum π for any read-once function $f(x_1, \ldots, x_n)$ in $O(n)$ steps. Moreover, a careful analysis proves that $B(f^\pi) = O(n^\beta)$ in the best ordering, where β is the constant in (116). (See exercise 168.)

*Multiplication. Some of the most interesting Boolean functions, from a mathematical standpoint, are the $m + n$ bits that arise when an m-bit number is multiplied by an n-bit number:

$$(x_m \ldots x_2 x_1)_2 \times (y_n \ldots y_2 y_1)_2 = (z_{m+n} \ldots z_2 z_1)_2. \tag{117}$$

In particular, the "leading bit" z_{m+n}, and the "middle bit" z_n when $m = n$, are especially noteworthy. To remove the dependence of this notation on m and n, we can imagine that $m = n = \infty$ by letting $x_i = y_j = 0$ for all $i > m$ and $j > n$; then each z_k is a function of $2k$ variables, $z_k = Z_k(x_1, \ldots, x_k; y_1, \ldots, y_k)$, namely the middle bit of the product $(x_k \ldots x_1)_2 \times (y_k \ldots y_1)_2$.

The middle bit turns out to be difficult, BDDwise, even when y is constant. Let $Z_{n,a}(x_1, \ldots, x_n) = Z_n(x_1, \ldots, x_n; a_1, \ldots, a_n)$, where $a = (a_n \ldots a_1)_2$.

Theorem X. *There is a constant a such that $B_{\min}(Z_{n,a}) > \frac{5}{288} \cdot 2^{\lfloor n/2 \rfloor} - 2$.*

Proof. [P. Woelfel, *J. Computer and System Sci.* **71** (2005), 520–534.] We may assume that $n = 2t$ is even, since $Z_{2t+1,2a} = Z_{2t,a}$. Let $x = (x_n \ldots x_1)_2$ and $m = ([n\pi \leq t] \ldots [1\pi \leq t])_2$. Then $x = p + q$, where $q = x \,\&\, m$ represents the "known" bits of x after t branches have been taken in a BDD for $Z_{n,y}$ with the ordering π, and $p = x \,\&\, \bar{m}$ represents the bits yet unknown. Let

$$P = \{x \,\&\, \bar{m} \mid 0 \leq x < 2^n\} \quad \text{and} \quad Q = \{x \,\&\, m \mid 0 \leq x < 2^n\}. \tag{118}$$

For any fixed a, the function $Z_{n,a}$ has 2^t subfunctions

$$f_q(p) = ((pa + qa) \gg (n - 1)) \,\&\, 1, \qquad q \in Q. \tag{119}$$

We want to show that some n-bit number a will make many of these subfunctions differ; in other words we want to find a large subset $Q^* \subseteq Q$ such that

$$q \in Q^* \text{ and } q' \in Q^* \text{ and } q \neq q' \text{ implies } f_q(p) \neq f_{q'}(p) \text{ for some } p \in P. \tag{120}$$

Exercise 176 shows in detail how this can be done. ∎

Table 1

BEST AND WORST ORDERINGS FOR THE MIDDLE BIT z_n OF MULTIPLICATION

$$x_{11}x_{10}x_9x_7x_8x_6x_{13}x_{15}$$
$$\times\ x_{16}x_{14}x_{12}x_5x_4x_3x_2x_1$$
$$B_{\min}(Z_8) = 756$$

$$x_{10}x_{11}x_9x_8x_7x_{16}x_6x_{15}$$
$$\times\ x_5x_4x_3x_{12}x_{13}x_2x_1x_{14}$$
$$B_{\max}(Z_8) = 6791$$

$$x_{24}x_{20}x_{18}x_{16}x_9x_8x_{10}x_{11}x_7x_{12}x_{14}x_{21}$$
$$\times\ x_{22}x_{19}x_{17}x_{15}x_6x_5x_4x_3x_2x_1x_{13}x_{23}$$
$$B_{\min}(Z_{12}) = 21931$$

$$x_{16}x_{17}x_{15}x_{14}x_{24}x_{13}x_{12}x_{11}x_{20}x_{10}x_9x_{23}$$
$$\times\ x_8x_7x_6x_5x_{18}x_4x_{22}x_3x_2x_{19}x_1x_{21}$$
$$B_{\max}(Z_{12}) = 866283$$

Table 2

BEST AND WORST ORDERINGS FOR ALL BITS $\{z_1,\ldots,z_{m+n}\}$ OF MULTIPLICATION

$$x_{11}x_{16}x_{15}x_{14}x_{13}x_{12}x_{10}x_9$$
$$\times\ x_8x_7x_6x_5x_4x_3x_2x_1$$
$$B_{\min}(Z_{8,8}^{(1)},\ldots,Z_{8,8}^{(16)}) = 9700$$

$$x_{10}x_8x_9x_{13}x_2x_1x_{11}x_7$$
$$\times\ x_{16}x_5x_{15}x_6x_4x_{14}x_3x_{12}$$
$$B_{\max}(Z_{8,8}^{(1)},\ldots,Z_{8,8}^{(16)}) = 28678$$

$$x_{15}x_{17}x_{24}x_{23}x_{22}x_{21}x_{20}x_{19}x_{18}x_{16}x_{14}x_{13}$$
$$\times\ x_1x_2x_3x_4x_5x_6x_7x_8x_9x_{10}x_{11}x_{12}$$
$$B_{\min}(Z_{12,12}^{(1)},\ldots,Z_{12,12}^{(24)}) = 648957$$

$$x_{17}x_{22}x_{14}x_{13}x_{16}x_{10}x_{20}x_3x_2x_1x_{19}x_{12}$$
$$\times\ x_{24}x_{15}x_9x_8x_{21}x_7x_6x_{11}x_{23}x_5x_4x_{18}$$
$$B_{\max}(Z_{12,12}^{(1)},\ldots,Z_{12,12}^{(24)}) = 4224195$$

$$x_{17}x_{16}x_{10}x_9x_{11}x_{12}\ldots x_{15}x_{18}x_{19}x_{24}x_{23}\ldots x_{20}$$
$$\times\ x_1x_2x_3x_4x_5x_6x_7x_8$$
$$B_{\min}(Z_{16,8}^{(1)},\ldots,Z_{16,8}^{(24)}) = 157061$$

$$x_{13}x_{14}x_{12}x_{15}x_{16}x_{17}x_{22}x_{10}x_8x_7x_{18}x_9x_2x_1x_{19}x_6$$
$$\times\ x_{24}x_{11}x_{21}x_5x_4x_{23}x_3x_{20}$$
$$B_{\max}(Z_{16,8}^{(1)},\ldots,Z_{16,8}^{(24)}) = 1236251$$

A good upper bound for the BDD size of the middle bit function when neither operand is constant has been found by K. Amano and A. Maruoka, *Discrete Applied Math.* **155** (2007), 1224–1232:

Theorem A. *Let* $f(x_1,\ldots,x_{2n}) = Z_n(x_1,x_3,\ldots,x_{2n-1};x_2,x_4,\ldots,x_{2n})$. *Then*

$$B(f) \ \leq \ Q(f) \ < \ \tfrac{19}{7} 2^{\lceil 6n/5 \rceil}. \tag{121}$$

Proof. Consider two n-bit numbers $x = 2^k x_h + x_l$ and $y = 2^k y_h + y_l$, with $n-k$ unknown bits in each of their high parts (x_h,y_h), while their k-bit low parts (x_l,y_l) are both known. Then the middle bit of xy is determined by adding together three $(n-k)$-bit quantities when $k \geq n/2$, namely $x_h y_l \bmod 2^{n-k}$, $x_l y_h \bmod 2^{n-k}$, and $(x_l y_l \gg k) \bmod 2^{n-k}$. Hence level $2k$ of the QDD needs to "remember" only the least significant $n-k$ bits of each of the prior quantities x_l, y_l, and $x_l y_l \gg k$, a total of $3n-3k$ bits, and we have $q_{2k} \leq 2^{3n-3k}$ in f's quasi-profile. Exercise 177 completes the proof. ∎

Amano and Maruoka also discovered another important upper bound. Let $Z_{m,n}^{(p)}(x_1,\ldots,x_m;y_1,\ldots,y_n)$ denote the pth bit z_p of the product (117).

Theorem Y. *For all constants* $(a_m \ldots a_1)_2$ *and for all* p, *the BDD and QDD for the function* $Z_{m,n}^{(p)}(a_1,\ldots,a_m;x_1,\ldots,x_n)$ *have fewer than* $3 \cdot 2^{n/2}$ *nodes.*

Proof. Exercise 180 proves that $q_k \leq 2^{n+1-k}$ for this function. The theorem follows when we combine that result with the obvious upper bound $q_k \leq 2^k$. ∎

Theorem Y shows that the lower bound of Theorem X is best possible, except for a constant factor. It also shows that the BDD base for all $m + n$ product functions $Z_{m,n}^{(p)}(x_1, \ldots, x_m; x_{m+1}, \ldots, x_{m+n})$ is not nearly as large as $\Theta(2^{m+n})$, which we get for almost all instances of $m + n$ functions of $m + n$ variables:

Corollary Y. *If* $m \leq n$, $B(Z_{m,n}^{(1)}, \ldots, Z_{m,n}^{(m+n)}) < 3(m+n)2^{m+(n+1)/2}$. ∎

The best orderings of variables for the middle-bit function Z_n and for the complete BDD base remain mysterious, but empirical results for small m and n give reason to conjecture that the upper bounds of Theorem A and Corollary Y are not far from the truth; see Tables 1 and 2. Here, for example, are the optimum results of Z_n when $n \leq 12$:

$n =$	1	2	3	4	5	6	7	8	9	10	11	12
$B_{\min}(Z_n) =$	4	8	14	31	63	136	315	756	1717	4026	9654	21931
$2^{6n/5} \approx$	2	5	12	28	64	147	338	776	1783	4096	9410	21619

The ratios $B_{\max}/B_{\min}$ with respect to the full BDD base $\{Z_{m,n}^{(1)}, \ldots, Z_{m,n}^{(m+n)}\}$ are surprisingly small in Table 2. Therefore all orderings for that problem might turn out to be roughly equivalent.

Zero-suppressed BDDs: A combinatorial alternative. When BDDs are applied to combinatorial problems, a glance at the data in memory often reveals that most of the HI fields simply point to ⊥. In such cases, we're better off using a variant data structure called a *zero-suppressed binary decision diagram*, or "ZDD" for short, introduced by Shin-ichi Minato [*ACM/IEEE Design Automation Conf.* **30** (1993), 272–277]. A ZDD has nodes like a BDD, but its nodes are interpreted differently: When an $\textcircled{i}$ node branches to a $\textcircled{j}$ node for $j > i+1$, it means that the Boolean function is false unless $x_{i+1} = \cdots = x_{j-1} = 0$.

For example, the BDDs for independent sets and kernels in (12) have many nodes with HI = ⊥. Those nodes go away in the corresponding ZDDs, although a few new nodes must also be added:

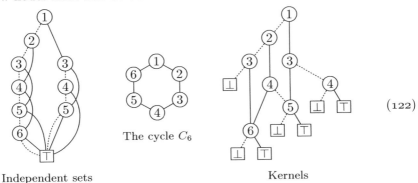

(122)

Independent sets   The cycle C_6 Kernels

Notice that we might have LO = HI in a ZDD, because of the new conventions. Furthermore, the example on the left shows that a ZDD need not contain ⊥ at all! About 40% of the nodes in (12) have been eliminated from each diagram.

One good way to understand a ZDD is to regard it as a condensed representation of a *family of sets*. Indeed, the ZDDs in (122) represent respectively the families of all independent sets and all kernels of C_6. The root node of a ZDD names the smallest element that appears in at least one of the sets; its HI and LO branches represent the residual subfamilies that do and don't contain that element; and so on. At the bottom, $\boxed{\perp}$ represents the empty family '$\emptyset$', and $\boxed{\top}$ represents '$\{\emptyset\}$'. For example, the rightmost ZDD in (122) represents the family $\{\{1,3,5\}, \{1,4\}, \{2,4,6\}, \{2,5\}, \{3,6\}\}$, because the HI branch of the root represents $\{\{3,5\}, \{4\}\}$ and the LO branch represents $\{\{2,4,6\}, \{2,5\}, \{3,6\}\}$.

Every Boolean function $f(x_1, \ldots, x_n)$ is, of course, equivalent to a family of subsets of $\{1, \ldots, n\}$, and vice versa. But the family concept gives us a different perspective from the function concept. For example, the family $\{\{1,3\}, \{2\}, \{2,5\}\}$ has the same ZDD for all $n \geq 5$; but if, say, $n = 7$, the BDD for the function $f(x_1, \ldots, x_7)$ that defines this family needs additional nodes to ensure that $x_4 = x_6 = x_7 = 0$ when $f(x) = 1$.

Almost every notion that we've discussed for BDDs has a counterpart in the theory of ZDDs, although the actual data structures are often strikingly different. We can, for example, take the truth table for any given function $f(x_1, \ldots, x_n)$ and construct its unique ZDD in a straightforward way, analogous to the construction of its BDD as illustrated in (5). We know that the BDD nodes for f correspond to the "beads" of f's truth table; the ZDD nodes, similarly, correspond to *zeads*, which are binary strings of the form $\alpha\beta$ with $|\alpha| = |\beta|$ and $\beta \neq 0 \ldots 0$, or with $|\alpha| = |\beta| - 1$. Any binary string corresponds to a unique zead, obtained by lopping off the right half repeatedly, if necessary, until the string either has odd length or its right half is nonzero.

Dear reader, please take a moment now to work exercise 187. (Really.)

The *z-profile* of $f(x_1, \ldots, x_n)$ is $(z_0, \ldots, z_n)$, where z_k is the number of zeads of order $n - k$ in f's truth table, for $0 \leq k < n$, namely the number of $\boxed{k+1}$ nodes in the ZDD; also z_n is the number of sinks. We write $Z(f) = z_0 + \cdots + z_n$ for the total number of nodes. For example, the functions in (122) have z-profiles $(1,1,2,2,2,1,1)$ and $(1,1,2,2,1,1,2)$, respectively, so $Z(f) = 10$ in each case.

The basic relations (83)–(85) between profiles and quasi-profiles hold true also for z-profiles:

$$q_k \geq z_k, \qquad \text{for } 0 \leq k \leq n; \tag{123}$$

$$q_k \leq 1 + z_0 + \cdots + z_{k-1} \text{ and } q_k \leq z_k + \cdots + z_n, \quad \text{for } 0 \leq k \leq n; \tag{124}$$

$$Z(f) \geq 2q_k - 1, \qquad \text{for } 0 \leq k \leq n. \tag{125}$$

Consequently the BDD size and the ZDD size can never be wildly different:

$$Z(f) \leq \frac{n+1}{2}\big(B(f) + 1\big) \qquad \text{and} \qquad B(f) \leq \frac{n+1}{2}\big(Z(f) + 1\big). \tag{126}$$

On the other hand, a factor of 50 when $n = 100$ is nothing to sneeze at.

When ZDDs are used to find independent sets and kernels of the contiguous USA, using the original order of (17), the BDD sizes of 428 and 780 go down to 177 and 385, respectively. Sifting reduces these ZDD sizes to 160 and 335. Is anybody sneezing? That's amazingly good, for complicated functions of 49 variables.

When we know the ZDDs for f and g, we can synthesize them to obtain the ZDDs for $f \wedge g$, $f \vee g$, $f \oplus g$, etc., using algorithms that are very much like the methods we've used for BDDs. Furthermore we can count and/or optimize the solutions of f, with analogs of Algorithms C and B; in fact, ZDD-based techniques for counting and optimization turn out to be a bit easier than the corresponding BDD-based algorithms are. With slight modifications of BDD methods, we can also do dynamic variable reordering via sifting. Exercises 197–209 discuss the nuts and bolts of all the basic ZDD procedures.

In general, a ZDD tends to be better than a BDD when we're dealing with functions whose solutions are *sparse*, in the sense that νx tends to be small when $f(x) = 1$. And if $f(x)$ itself happens to be sparse, in the sense that it has comparatively few solutions, so much the better.

For example, ZDDs are well suited to *exact cover problems*, defined by an $m \times n$ matrix of 0s and 1s: We want to find all ways to choose rows that sum to $(1, 1, \ldots, 1)$. Our goal might be, say, to cover a chessboard with 32 dominoes, like

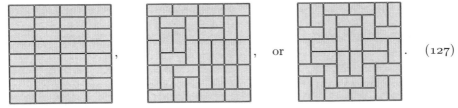

$$\begin{matrix} , & , & \text{or} & . \end{matrix} \qquad (127)$$

This is an exact cover problem whose matrix has $8 \times 8 = 64$ columns, one for each cell; there are $2 \times 7 \times 8 = 112$ rows, one for each pair of adjacent cells:

$$\begin{pmatrix} 1\,1\,0\,0\,0\,0\,0\,0\,0\,0\,0\,0 \ldots 0\,0\,0\,0\,0\,0\,0\,0\,0\,0\,0 \\ 1\,0\,0\,0\,0\,0\,0\,0\,1\,0\,0\,0 \ldots 0\,0\,0\,0\,0\,0\,0\,0\,0\,0\,0 \\ 0\,1\,1\,0\,0\,0\,0\,0\,0\,0\,0\,0 \ldots 0\,0\,0\,0\,0\,0\,0\,0\,0\,0\,0 \\ 0\,1\,0\,0\,0\,0\,0\,0\,0\,1\,0\,0 \ldots 0\,0\,0\,0\,0\,0\,0\,0\,0\,0\,0 \\ \vdots \qquad\qquad\qquad \vdots \\ 0\,0\,0\,0\,0\,0\,0\,0\,0\,0\,0\,0 \ldots 0\,0\,0\,0\,0\,0\,0\,1\,1\,0\,0 \\ 0\,0\,0\,0\,0\,0\,0\,0\,0\,0\,0\,0 \ldots 0\,0\,0\,0\,0\,0\,0\,0\,1\,1\,0 \\ 0\,0\,0\,0\,0\,0\,0\,0\,0\,0\,0\,0 \ldots 0\,0\,0\,0\,0\,0\,0\,0\,0\,1\,1 \end{pmatrix} . \qquad (128)$$

Let variable x_j represent the choice (or not) of row j. Thus the three solutions in (127) have $(x_1, x_2, x_3, x_4, \ldots, x_{110}, x_{111}, x_{112}) = (1, 0, 0, 0, \ldots, 1, 0, 1)$, $(1, 0, 0, 0, \ldots, 1, 0, 1)$, and $(0, 1, 0, 1, \ldots, 1, 0, 0)$, respectively. In general, the solutions to an exact cover problem are represented by the function

$$f(x_1, \ldots, x_m) = \bigwedge_{j=1}^{n} S_1(X_j) = \bigwedge_{j=1}^{n} [\nu X_j = 1], \qquad (129)$$

where $X_j = \{x_i \mid a_{ij} = 1\}$ and (a_{ij}) is the given matrix.

The dominoes-on-a-chessboard ZDD turns out to have only $Z(f) = 2300$ nodes, even though f has $m = 112$ variables in this case. We can use it to prove that there are exactly 12,988,816 coverings such as (127).

Similarly, we can investigate more exotic kinds of covering. In

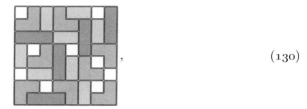

$$(130)$$

for instance, a chessboard has been covered with monominoes, dominoes, and/or trominoes — that is, with rookwise-connected pieces that each have either one, two, or three cells. There are exactly 92,109,458,286,284,989,468,604 ways to do this(!); and we can compute that number almost instantly, doing only about 75 megamems of calculation, by forming a ZDD of size 512,227 on 468 variables.

A special algorithm could be devised to find the ZDD for any given exact cover problem; or we can synthesize the result using (129). See exercise 212.

Incidentally, the problem of domino covering as in (127) is equivalent to finding the perfect matchings of the grid graph $P_8 \mathbin{\square} P_8$, which is bipartite. We will see in Section 7.5.1 that efficient algorithms are available by which perfect matchings can be studied on graphs that are far too large to be treated with BDD/ZDD techniques. In fact, there's even an explicit formula for the number of domino coverings of an $m \times n$ grid. By contrast, general coverings such as (130) fall into a wider category of hypergraph problems for which polynomial-time methods are unlikely to exist as $m, n \to \infty$.

An amusing variant of domino covering called the "mutilated chessboard" was considered by Max Black in his book *Critical Thinking* (1946), pages 142 and 394: Suppose we remove opposite corners of the chessboard, and try to cover the remaining cells with 31 dominoes. It's easy to place 30 of them, for example as shown here; but then we're stuck. Indeed, if we consider the corresponding 108×62 exact cover problem, but leave out the last

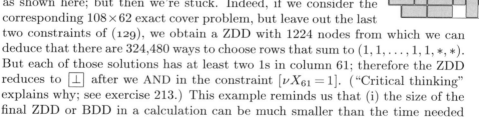

two constraints of (129), we obtain a ZDD with 1224 nodes from which we can deduce that there are 324,480 ways to choose rows that sum to $(1, 1, \ldots, 1, 1, *, *)$. But each of those solutions has at least two 1s in column 61; therefore the ZDD reduces to $\boxed{\perp}$ after we AND in the constraint $[\nu X_{61} = 1]$. ("Critical thinking" explains why; see exercise 213.) This example reminds us that (i) the size of the final ZDD or BDD in a calculation can be much smaller than the time needed to compute it; and (ii) using our brains can save oodles of computer cycles.

ZDDs as dictionaries. Let's switch gears now, to note that ZDDs are advantageous also in applications that have an entirely different flavor. We can use them, for instance, to represent the *five-letter words of English*, the set WORDS(5757) from the Stanford GraphBase that is discussed near the beginning of this chapter. One way to do this is to consider the function $f(x_1, \ldots, x_{25})$ that is defined to be 1 if and only if the five numbers $(x_1 \ldots x_5)_2$, $(x_6 \ldots x_{10})_2$, $\ldots$, $(x_{21} \ldots x_{25})_2$ encode the letters of an English word, where $\mathtt{a} = (00001)_2$, $\ldots$, $\mathtt{z} = (11010)_2$.

For example, $f(0, 0, 1, 1, 1, 0, 1, 1, 1, 1, 0, 1, 1, 1, 1, 0, 0, 1, 1, 0, 1, 1, 0, 0, x_{25}) = x_{25}$. This function of 25 variables has $Z(f) = 6233$ nodes — which isn't bad, since it represents 5757 words.

Of course we've studied many other ways to represent 5757 words, in Chapter 6. The ZDD approach is no match for binary trees or tries or hash tables, when we merely want to do simple searches. But with ZDDs we can also retrieve data that is only partially specified, or data that is only supposed to match a key approximately; many complex queries can be handled with ease.

Furthermore, we don't need to worry very much about having lots of variables when ZDDs are being used. Instead of working with the 25 variables x_j considered above, we can also represent those five-letter words as a sparse function $F(a_1, \ldots, z_1, a_2, \ldots, z_2, \ldots, a_5, \ldots, z_5)$ that has $26 \times 5 = 130$ variables, where variable a_2 (for example) controls whether the second letter is 'a'. To indicate that crazy is a word, we make F true when $c_1 = r_2 = a_3 = z_4 = y_5 = 1$ and all other variables are 0. Equivalently, we consider F to be a family consisting of the 5757 subsets $\{w_1, h_2, i_3, c_4, h_5\}$, $\{t_1, h_2, e_3, r_4, e_5\}$, etc. With these 130 variables the ZDD size $Z(F)$ turns out to be only 5020 instead of 6233.

Incidentally, $B(F)$ is 46,189 — more than nine times as large as $Z(F)$. But $B(f)/Z(f)$ is only $8870/6233 \approx 1.4$ in the 25-variable case. The ZDD world is different from the BDD world in many ways, in spite of having similar algorithms and a similar theory.

One consequence of this difference is a need for new primitive operations by which complex families of subsets can readily be constructed from elementary families. Notice that the simple subset $\{f_1, u_2, n_3, n_4, y_5\}$ is actually an extremely long-winded Boolean function:

$$\bar{a}_1 \wedge \cdots \wedge \bar{e}_1 \wedge f_1 \wedge \bar{g}_1 \wedge \cdots \wedge \bar{t}_2 \wedge u_2 \wedge \bar{v}_2 \wedge \cdots \wedge \bar{x}_5 \wedge y_5 \wedge \bar{z}_5, \qquad (131).$$

a minterm of 130 Boolean variables. Exercise 203 discusses an important *family algebra*, by which that subset is expressed more naturally as '$f_1 \sqcup u_2 \sqcup n_3 \sqcup n_4 \sqcup y_5$'. With family algebra we can readily describe and compute many interesting collections of words and word fragments (see exercise 222).

ZDDs to represent simple paths. An important connection between arbitrary directed, acyclic graphs (dags) and a special class of ZDDs is illustrated in Fig. 28. When every source vertex of the dag has out-degree 1 and every sink vertex has in-degree 1, the ZDD for all oriented paths from a source to a sink has essentially the same "shape" as the original dag. The variables in this ZDD are the *arcs* of the dag, in a suitable topological order. (See exercise 224.)

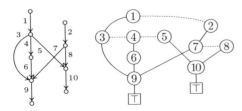

Fig. 28. A dag, and the ZDD for its source-to-sink paths. Arcs of the dag correspond to vertices of the ZDD. All branches to ⊥ have been omitted from the ZDD in order to show the structural similarities more clearly.

We can also use ZDDs to represent simple paths in an *undirected* graph.
For example, there are 12 ways to go from the upper left corner of a 3×3
grid to the lower right corner, without visiting any point twice:

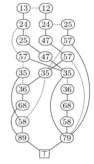

$$\text{(132)}$$

These paths can be represented by the ZDD shown at the right, which characterizes all sets of suitable edges. For example, we get the first path by taking
the HI branches at ⑬, ㊱, ⑱, and ⑧⑨ of the ZDD. (As in Fig. 28,
this diagram has been simplified by omitting all of the uninteresting
LO branches that merely go to ⊥.) Of course this ZDD isn't a truly
great way to represent (132), because that family of paths has only 12
members. But on the larger grid $P_8 \mathbin{\square} P_8$, the number of simple paths
from corner to corner turns out to be 789,360,053,252; and they can all
be represented by a ZDD that has at most 33580 nodes. Exercise 225
explains how to construct such a ZDD quickly.

A similar algorithm, discussed in exercise 226, constructs a ZDD
that represents all *cycles* of a given graph. With a ZDD of size 22275,
we can deduce that $P_8 \mathbin{\square} P_8$ has exactly 603,841,648,931 simple cycles.
This ZDD may well provide the best way to represent all of those cycles within
a computer, and the best way to generate them systematically if desired.

The same ideas work well with graphs from the "real world" that don't
have a neat mathematical structure. For example, we can use them to answer
a question posed to the author in 2008 by Randal Bryant: "Suppose I wanted
to take a driving tour of the Continental U.S., visiting all of the state capitols,
and passing through each state only once. What route should I take to minimize
the total distance?" The following diagram shows the shortest distances between
neighboring capital cities, when restricted to local itineraries that each cross only
one state boundary:

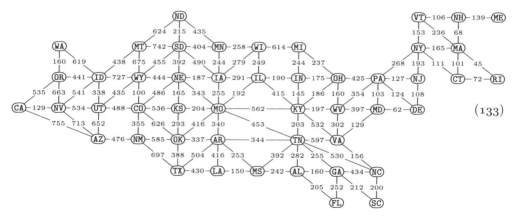

$$\text{(133)}$$

The problem is to choose a subset of these edges that form a Hamiltonian path
of smallest total length.

Every Hamiltonian path in this graph must clearly either start or end at Augusta, Maine (ME). Suppose we start in Sacramento, California (CA). Proceeding as above, we can find a ZDD that characterizes all paths from CA to ME; this ZDD turns out to have only 7850 nodes, and it quickly tells us that exactly 437,525,772,584 simple paths from CA to ME are possible. In fact, the generating function by number of edges turns out to be

$$4z^{11} + 124z^{12} + 1539z^{13} + \cdots + 33385461z^{46} + 2707075z^{47}; \qquad (134)$$

so the longest such paths are Hamiltonian, and there are exactly 2,707,075 of them. Furthermore, exercise 227 shows how to construct a smaller ZDD, of size 4726, which describes just the Hamiltonian paths from CA to ME.

We could repeat this experiment for each of the states in place of California. (Well, the starting point had better be outside of New England, if we are going to get past New York, which is an articulation point of this graph.) For example, there are 483,194 Hamiltonian paths from NJ to ME. But exercise 228 shows how to construct a *single* ZDD of size 28808 for the family of all Hamiltonian paths from ME to *any* other final state — of which there are 68,656,026. The answer to Bryant's problem now pops out immediately, via Algorithm B. (The reader may like to try finding a minimum route by hand, before turning to exercise 230 and discovering the absolutely optimum answer.)

*ZDDs and prime implicants. Finally, let's look at an instructive application in which BDDs and ZDDs are both used simultaneously.

According to Theorem 7.1.1Q, every monotone Boolean function f has a unique shortest two-level representation as an OR of ANDs, called its "disjunctive prime form" — the disjunction of all of its prime implicants. The prime implicants correspond to the minimal points where $f(x) = 1$, namely the binary vectors x for which we have $f(x') = 1$ and $x' \subseteq x$ if and only if $x' = x$. If

$$f(x_1, x_2, x_3) = x_1 \vee (x_2 \wedge x_3), \qquad (135)$$

for example, the prime implicants of f are x_1 and $x_2 \wedge x_3$, while the minimal solutions are $x_1 x_2 x_3 = 100$ and 011. These minimal solutions can also be expressed conveniently as e_1 and $e_2 \sqcup e_3$, using family algebra (see exercise 203).

In general, $x_{i_1} \wedge \cdots \wedge x_{i_s}$ is a prime implicant of a monotone function f if and only if $e_{i_1} \sqcup \cdots \sqcup e_{i_s}$ is a minimal solution of f. Thus we can consider f's prime implicants $PI(f)$ to be its family of minimal solutions. Notice, however, that $x_{i_1} \wedge \cdots \wedge x_{i_s} \subseteq x_{j_1} \wedge \cdots \wedge x_{j_t}$ if and only if $e_{i_1} \sqcup \cdots \sqcup e_{i_s} \supseteq e_{j_1} \sqcup \cdots \sqcup e_{j_t}$; so it's confusing to say that one prime implicant "contains" another. Instead, we say that the shorter one "absorbs" the longer one.

A curious phenomenon shows up in example (135): The diagram is not only the BDD for f, it's also the ZDD for $PI(f)$! Similarly, Fig. 21 at the beginning of this section illustrates not only the BDD for $\langle x_1 x_2 x_3 \rangle$ but also the ZDD for $PI(\langle x_1 x_2 x_3 \rangle)$. On the other hand, let $g = (x_1 \wedge x_3) \vee x_2$. Then the BDD for g is but the ZDD for $PI(g)$ is . What's going on here?

The key to resolving this mystery lies in the recursive structure on which BDDs and ZDDs are based. Every Boolean function can be represented as

$$f(x_1, \ldots, x_n) = (\bar{x}_1?\ f_0\colon f_1) = (\bar{x}_1 \wedge f_0) \vee (x_1 \wedge f_1), \qquad (136)$$

where f_c is the value of f when x_1 is replaced by c. When f is monotone we also have $f = f_0 \vee (x_1 \wedge f_1)$, because $f_0 \subseteq f_1$. If $f_0 \neq f_1$, the BDD for f is obtained by creating a node ① whose LO and HI branches point to the BDDs for f_0 and f_1. Similarly, it's not difficult to see that the prime implicants of f are

$$\mathrm{PI}(f) = \mathrm{PI}(f_0) \cup \big(e_1 \sqcup (\mathrm{PI}(f_1) \setminus \mathrm{PI}(f_0))\big). \qquad (137)$$

(See exercise 253.) This is the recursion that defines the ZDD for $\mathrm{PI}(f)$, when we add the termination conditions for constant functions: The ZDDs for $\mathrm{PI}(0)$ and $\mathrm{PI}(1)$ are ⊥ and ⊤.

Let's say that a Boolean function is *sweet* if it is monotone and if the ZDD for $\mathrm{PI}(f)$ is exactly the same as the BDD for f. Constant functions are clearly sweet. And nonconstant sweetness is easily characterized:

Theorem S. *A Boolean function that depends on x_1 is sweet if and only if its prime implicants are $P \cup (x_1 \sqcup Q)$, where P and Q are sweet and independent of x_1, and every member of P is absorbed by some member of Q.*

Proof. See exercise 246. (To say that "P and Q are sweet" means that they each are families of prime implicants that define a sweet Boolean function.) ∎

Corollary S. *The connectedness function of any graph is sweet.*

Proof. The prime implicants of the connectedness function f are the spanning trees of the graph. Every spanning tree that does not include arc x_1 has at least one subtree that will be spanning when arc x_1 is added to it. Furthermore, all subfunctions of f are the connectedness functions of smaller graphs. ∎

Thus, for example, the BDD in Fig. 22, which defines all 431 of the connected subgraphs of $P_3 \square P_3$, also is the ZDD that defines all 192 of its spanning trees.

Whether f is sweet or not, we can use (137) to compute the ZDD for $\mathrm{PI}(f)$ whenever f is monotone. When we do this we can actually let the BDD nodes and the ZDD nodes *coexist* in the same big base of data: Two nodes with identical (V, LO, HI) fields might as well appear only once in memory, even though they might have complete different meanings in different contexts. We use one routine to synthesize $f \wedge \bar{g}$ when f and g point to BDDs, and another routine to form $f \setminus g$ when f and g point to ZDDs; no trouble will arise if these routines happen to share nodes, as long as the variables aren't being reordered. (Of course the cache memos must distinguish BDD facts from ZDD facts when we do this.)

For example, exercise 7.1.1–67 defines an interesting class of self-dual functions called the Y functions, and the BDD for Y_{12} (which is a function of 91 variables) has 748,416 nodes. This function has 2,178,889,774 prime implicants; yet $Z(\mathrm{PI}(Y_{12}))$ is only 217,388. (We can find this ZDD with a computational cost of about 13 gigamems and 660 megabytes.)

A brief history. The seeds of binary decision diagrams were implicitly planted by Claude Shannon [*Trans. Amer. Inst. Electrical Engineers* **57** (1938), 713–723], in his illustrations of relay-contact networks. Section 4 of that paper showed that any symmetric Boolean function of n variables has a BDD with at most $\binom{n+1}{2}$ branch nodes. Shannon preferred to work with Boolean algebra; but C. Y. Lee, in *Bell System Tech. J.* **38** (1959), 985–999, pointed out several advantages of what he called "binary-decision programs," because any n-variable function could be evaluated by executing at most n branch instructions in such a program.

S. Akers coined the name "binary decision diagrams" and pursued the ideas further in *IEEE Trans.* **C-27** (1978), 509–516. He showed how to obtain a BDD from a truth table by working bottom-up, or from algebraic subfunctions by working top-down. He explained how to count the paths from a root to $\boxed{\top}$ or $\boxed{\bot}$, and observed that these paths partition the n-cube into disjoint subcubes.

Meanwhile a very similar model of Boolean computation arose in theoretical studies of automata. For example, A. Cobham [*FOCS* **7** (1966), 78–87] related the minimum sizes of branching programs for a sequence of functions $f_n(x_1, \ldots, x_n)$ to the space complexity of nonuniform Turing machines that compute this sequence. More significantly, S. Fortune, J. Hopcroft, and E. M. Schmidt [*Lecture Notes in Comp. Sci.* **62** (1978), 227–240] considered "free B-schemes," now known as FBDDs, in which no Boolean variable is tested twice on any path (see exercise 35). Among other results, they gave a polynomial-time algorithm to test whether $f = g$, given FBDDs for f and g, provided that at least one of those FBDDs is ordered consistently as in a BDD. The theory of finite-state automata, which has intimate connections to BDD structure, was also being developed; thus several researchers worked on problems that are equivalent to analyzing the size, $B(f)$, for various functions f. (See exercise 261.)

All of this work was conceptual, not implemented in computer programs, although programmers had found good uses for binary tries and Patrician trees — which are similar to BDDs except that they are trees instead of dags (see Section 6.3). But then Randal E. Bryant discovered that binary decision diagrams are significantly important in practice when they are required to be both *reduced* and *ordered*. His introduction to the subject [*IEEE Trans.* **C-35** (1986), 677–691] became for many years the most cited paper in all of computer science, because it revolutionized the data structures used to represent Boolean functions.

In his paper, Bryant pointed out that the BDD for any function is essentially unique under his conventions, and that most of the functions encountered in practice had BDDs of reasonable size. He presented efficient algorithms to synthesize the BDDs for $f \wedge g$ and $f \oplus g$, etc., from the BDDs for f and g. He also showed how to compute the lexicographically least x such that $f(x) = 1$, etc.

Lee, Akers, and Bryant all noted that many functions can profitably coexist in a BDD base, sharing their common subfunctions. A high-performance "package" for BDD base operations, developed by K. S. Brace, R. L. Rudell, and R. E. Bryant [*ACM/IEEE Design Automation Conf.* **27** (1990), 40–45], has strongly influenced all subsequent implementations of BDD toolkits. Bryant summarized the early uses of BDDs in *Computing Surveys* **24** (1992), 293–318.

Shin-ichi Minato introduced ZDDs in 1993, as noted above, to improve performance in combinatorial work. He gave a retrospective account of early ZDD applications in *Software Tools for Technology Transfer* **3** (2001), 156–170.

The use of Boolean methods in graph theory was pioneered by K. Maghout [*Comptes Rendus Acad. Sci.* **248** (Paris, 1959), 3522–3523], who showed how to express the maximal independent sets and the minimal dominating sets of any graph or digraph as the prime implicants of a monotone function. Then R. Fortet [*Cahiers du Centre d'Etudes Recherche Operationelle* **1**, 4 (1959), 5–44] considered Boolean approaches to a variety of other problems; for example, he introduced the idea of 4-coloring a graph by assigning two Boolean variables to each vertex, as we have done in (73). P. Camion, in that same journal [**2** (1960), 234–289], transformed integer programming problems into equivalent problems in Boolean algebra, hoping to resolve them via techniques of symbolic logic. This work was extended by others, notably P. L. Hammer and S. Rudeanu, whose book *Boolean Methods in Operations Research* (Springer, 1968) summarized the ideas. Unfortunately, however, their approach foundered, because no good techniques for Boolean calculation were available at the time. The proponents of Boolean methods had to wait until the advent of BDDs before the general Boolean programming problem (7) could be resolved, thanks to Algorithm B. The special case of Algorithm B in which all weights satisfying $w_i \geq 0$ was introduced by B. Lin and F. Somenzi [*IEEE/ACM International Conf. Computer-Aided Design* **CAD-90** (1990), 88–91]. S. Minato [*Formal Methods in System Design* **10** (1999), 221–242] developed software that automatically converts linear inequalities between integer variables into BDDs that can be manipulated conveniently, somewhat as the researchers of the 1960s had hoped would be possible.

The classic problem of finding a minimum size DNF for a given function also became spectacularly simpler when BDD methods became understood. The latest techniques for that problem are beyond the scope of this book, but Olivier Coudert has given an excellent overview in *Integration* **17** (1994), 97–140.

A fine book by Ingo Wegener, *Branching Programs and Binary Decision Diagrams* (SIAM, 2000), surveys the vast literature of the subject, develops the mathematical foundations carefully, and discusses many ways in which the basic ideas have been generalized and extended.

Caveat. We've seen dozens of examples in which the use of BDDs and/or ZDDs has made it possible to solve a wide variety of combinatorial problems with amazing efficiency, and the exercises below contain dozens of additional examples where such methods shine. But BDD and ZDD structures are by no means a panacea; they're only two of the weapons in our arsenal. They apply chiefly to problems that have more solutions than can readily be examined one by one, problems whose solutions have a local structure that allows our algorithms to deal with only relatively few subproblems at a time. In later sections of *The Art of Computer Programming* we shall be studying additional techniques by which other kinds of combinatorial problems can be tamed.

EXERCISES

▶ **1.** [20] Draw the BDDs for all 16 Boolean functions $f(x_1, x_2)$. What are their sizes?

▶ **2.** [21] Draw a planar dag with sixteen vertices, each of which is the root of one of the 16 BDDs in exercise 1.

3. [16] How many Boolean functions $f(x_1, \ldots, x_n)$ have BDD size 3 or less?

4. [21] Suppose three fields $\boxed{\text{V} \mid \text{LO} \mid \text{HI}}$ have been packed into a 64-bit word x, where V occupies 8 bits and the other two fields occupy 28 bits each. Show that five bitwise instructions will transform $x \mapsto x'$, where x' is equal to x except that a LO or HI value of 0 is changed to 1 and vice versa. (Repeating this operation on every branch node x of a BDD for f will produce the BDD for the complementary function, $\bar{f}$.)

5. [20] If you take the BDD for $f(x_1, \ldots, x_n)$ and interchange the LO and HI pointers of every node, and if you also swap the two sinks $\boxed{\bot} \leftrightarrow \boxed{\top}$, what do you get?

6. [10] Let $g(x_1, x_2, x_3, x_4) = f(x_4, x_3, x_2, x_1)$, where f has the BDD in (6). What is the truth table of g, and what are its beads?

7. [21] Given a Boolean function $f(x_1, \ldots, x_n)$, let

$$g_k(x_0, x_1, \ldots, x_n) = f(x_0, \ldots, x_{k-2}, x_{k-1} \vee x_k, x_{k+1}, \ldots, x_n) \qquad \text{for } 1 \le k \le n.$$

Find a simple relation between (a) the truth tables and (b) the BDDs of f and g_k.

8. [22] Solve exercise 7 with $x_{k-1} \oplus x_k$ in place of $x_{k-1} \vee x_k$.

9. [16] Given the BDD for a function $f(x) = f(x_1, \ldots, x_n)$, represented sequentially as in (8), explain how to determine the lexicographically largest x such that $f(x) = 0$.

▶ **10.** [21] Given two BDDs that define Boolean functions f and f', represented sequentially as in (8) and (10), design an algorithm that tests $f = f'$.

11. [20] Does Algorithm C give the correct answer if it is applied to a binary decision diagram that is (a) ordered but not reduced? (b) reduced but not ordered?

▶ **12.** [M21] A *kernel* of a digraph is a set of vertices K such that

$$v \in K \quad \text{implies} \quad v \not\to u \text{ for all } u \in K;$$
$$v \notin K \quad \text{implies} \quad v \longrightarrow u \text{ for some } u \in K.$$

a) Show that when the digraph is an ordinary graph (that is, when $u \longrightarrow v$ if and only if $v \longrightarrow u$), a kernel is the same as a maximal independent set.

b) Describe the kernels of the *oriented* cycle $\vec{C_n}$.

c) Prove that an acyclic digraph has a *unique* kernel.

13. [M15] How is the concept of a graph kernel related to the concept of (a) a maximal clique? (b) a minimal vertex cover?

14. [M24] How big, exactly, are the BDDs for (a) all independent sets of the cycle graph C_n, and (b) all kernels of C_n, when $n \ge 3$? (Number the vertices as in (12).)

15. [M23] How many (a) independent sets and (b) kernels does C_n have, when $n \ge 3$?

▶ **16.** [22] Design an algorithm that successively generates all vectors $x_1 \ldots x_n$ for which $f(x_1, \ldots, x_n) = 1$, when a BDD for f is given.

17. [32] If possible, improve the algorithm of exercise 16 so that its running time is $O(B(f)) + O(N)$ when there are N solutions.

18. [13] Play through Algorithm B with the BDD (8) and $(w_1, \ldots, w_4) = (1, -2, -3, 4)$.

19. [*20*] What are the largest and smallest possible values of variable m_k in Algorithm B, based only on the weights $(w_1, \ldots, w_n)$, not on any details of the function f?

20. [*15*] Devise a fast way to compute the Thue–Morse weights (15) for $1 \le j \le n$.

21. [*05*] Can Algorithm B *minimize* $w_1 x_1 + \cdots + w_n x_n$, instead of maximizing it?

▶ **22.** [*M21*] Suppose step B3 has been simplified so that '$W_{v+1} - W_{v_l}$' and '$W_{v+1} - W_{v_h}$' are eliminated from the formulas. Prove that the algorithm will still work, when applied to BDDs that represent kernels of graphs.

▶ **23.** [*M20*] All paths from the root of the BDD in Fig. 22 to $\boxed{\mathsf{T}}$ have exactly eight solid arcs. Why is this not a coincidence?

24. [*M22*] Suppose twelve weights $(w_{12}, w_{13}, \ldots, w_{89})$ have been assigned to the edges of the grid in Fig. 22. Explain how to find a minimum spanning tree in that graph (namely, a spanning tree whose edges have minimum total weight), by applying Algorithm B to the BDD shown there.

25. [*M20*] Modify Algorithm C so that it computes the generating function for the solutions to $f(x_1, \ldots, x_n) = 1$, namely $G(z) = \sum_{x_1=0}^{1} \cdots \sum_{x_n=0}^{1} z^{x_1 + \cdots + x_n} f(x_1, \ldots, x_n)$.

26. [*M20*] Modify Algorithm C so that it computes the reliability polynomial for given probabilities, namely

$$F(p_1, \ldots, p_n) = \sum_{x_1=0}^{1} \cdots \sum_{x_n=0}^{1} (1 - p_1)^{1-x_1} p_1^{x_1} \ldots (1 - p_n)^{1-x_n} p_n^{x_n} f(x_1, \ldots, x_n).$$

▶ **27.** [*M26*] Suppose $F(p_1, \ldots, p_n)$ and $G(p_1, \ldots, p_n)$ are the reliability polynomials for Boolean functions $f(x_1, \ldots, x_n)$ and $g(x_1, \ldots, x_n)$, where $f \ne g$. Let q be a prime number, and choose independent random integers $q_1, \ldots, q_n$, uniformly distributed in the range $0 \le q_k < q$. Prove that $F(q_1, \ldots, q_n) \bmod q \ne G(q_1, \ldots, q_n) \bmod q$ with probability $\ge (1 - 1/q)^n$. (In particular, if $n = 1000$ and $q = 2^{31} - 1$, different functions lead to different "hash values" under this scheme with probability at least 0.9999995.)

28. [*M16*] Let $F(p)$ be the value of the reliability polynomial $F(p_1, \ldots, p_n)$ when $p_1 = \cdots = p_n = p$. Show that it's easy to compute $F(p)$ from the generating function $G(z)$.

29. [*HM20*] Modify Algorithm C so that it computes the reliability polynomial $F(p)$ of exercise 28 and also its derivative $F'(p)$, given p and the BDD for f.

▶ **30.** [*M21*] The reliability polynomial is the sum, over all solutions to $f(x_1, \ldots, x_n) = 1$, of contributions from all "minterms" $(1 - p_1)^{1-x_1} p_1^{x_1} \ldots (1 - p_n)^{1-x_n} p_n^{x_n}$. Explain how to find a solution $x_1 \ldots x_n$ whose contribution to the total reliability is maximum, given a BDD for f and a sequence of probabilities $(p_1, \ldots, p_n)$.

31. [*M21*] Modify Algorithm C so that it computes the fully elaborated truth table of f, formalizing the procedure by which (24) was obtained from Fig. 21.

▶ **32.** [*M20*] What interpretations of '∘', '•', '⊥', '⊤', '$\bar{x}_j$', and 'x_j' will make the general algorithm of exercise 31 specialize to the algorithms of exercises 25, 26, 29, and 30?

▶ **33.** [*M22*] Specialize exercise 31 so that we can efficiently compute

$$\sum_{f(x)=1} (w_1 x_1 + \cdots + w_n x_n) \quad \text{and} \quad \sum_{f(x)=1} (w_1 x_1 + \cdots + w_n x_n)^2$$

from the BDD of a Boolean function $f(x) = f(x_1, \ldots, x_n)$.

34. [*M25*] Specialize exercise 31 so that we can efficiently compute

$$\max\{\max_{1\le k\le n}(w_1x_1+\cdots+w_{k-1}x_{k-1}+w'_kx_k+w_{k+1}x_{k+1}+\cdots+w_nx_n+w''_k)\mid f(x)=1\}$$

from the BDD of f, given $3n$ arbitrary weights $(w_1,\ldots,w_n,w'_1,\ldots,w'_n,w''_1,\ldots,w''_n)$.

▶ **35.** [*22*] A *free binary decision diagram* (FBDD) is a binary decision diagram such as

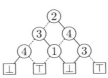

where the branch variables needn't appear in any particular order, but no variable is allowed to occur more than once on any downward path from the root. (An FBDD is "free" in the sense that every path in the dag is possible: No branch constrains another.)

a) Design an algorithm to verify that a supposed FBDD is really free.

b) Show that it's easy to compute the reliability polynomial $F(p_1,\ldots,p_n)$ of a Boolean function $f(x_1,\ldots,x_n)$, given $(p_1,\ldots,p_n)$ and an FBDD that defines f, and to compute the number of solutions to $f(x_1,\ldots,x_n)=1$.

36. [*25*] By extending exercise 31, explain how to compute the elaborated truth table for any given FBDD, if the abstract operators $\circ$ and $\bullet$ are commutative as well as distributive and associative. (Thus we can find optimum solutions as in Algorithm B, or solve problems such as those in exercises 30 and 33, with FBDDs as well as with BDDs.)

37. [*M20*] (R. L. Rivest and J. Vuillemin.) A Boolean function $f(x_1,\ldots,x_n)$ is called *evasive* if every FBDD for f contains a downward path of length n. Let $G(z)$ be the generating function for f, as in exercise 25. Prove that f is evasive if $G(-1)\ne 0$.

▶ **38.** [*27*] Let I_{s-1}, $\ldots$, I_0 be branch instructions that define a nonconstant Boolean function $f(x_1,\ldots,x_n)$ as in (8) and (10). Design an algorithm that computes the status variables $t_1\ldots t_n$, where

$$t_j = \begin{cases} +1, & \text{if } f(x_1,\ldots,x_n)=1 \text{ whenever } x_j=1; \\ -1, & \text{if } f(x_1,\ldots,x_n)=1 \text{ whenever } x_j=0; \\ 0, & \text{otherwise.} \end{cases}$$

(If $t_1\ldots t_n\ne 0\ldots 0$, the function f is therefore *canalizing* as defined in Section 7.1.1.) The running time of your algorithm should be $O(n+s)$.

39. [*M20*] What is the size of the BDD for the threshold function $[x_1+\cdots+x_n\ge k]$?

▶ **40.** [*22*] Let g be the "condensation" of f obtained by setting $x_{k+1}\leftarrow x_k$ as in (27).

a) Prove that $B(g)\le B(f)$. [*Hint:* Consider subtables and beads.]

b) Suppose h is obtained from f by setting $x_{k+2}\leftarrow x_k$. Is $B(h)\le B(f)$?

41. [*M25*] Assuming that $n\ge 4$, find the BDD size of the Fibonacci threshold functions (a) $\langle x_1^{F_1}x_2^{F_2}\ldots x_{n-2}^{F_{n-2}}x_{n-1}^{F_{n-1}}x_n^{F_{n-2}}\rangle$ and (b) $\langle x_n^{F_1}x_{n-1}^{F_2}\ldots x_3^{F_{n-2}}x_2^{F_{n-1}}x_1^{F_{n-2}}\rangle$.

42. [*22*] Draw the BDD base for all symmetric Boolean functions of 3 variables.

▶ **43.** [*22*] What is $B(f)$ when (a) $f(x_1,\ldots,x_{2n})=[x_1+\cdots+x_n=x_{n+1}+\cdots+x_{2n}]$? (b) $f(x_1,\ldots,x_{2n})=[x_1+x_3+\cdots+x_{2n-1}=x_2+x_4+\cdots+x_{2n}]$?

▶ **44.** [*M32*] Determine the maximum possible size, S_n, of $B(f)$ when f is a symmetric Boolean function of n variables.

45. [*22*] Give precise specifications for the Boolean modules that compute the three-in-a-row function as in (33) and (34), and show that the network is well defined.

46. [*M23*] What is the true BDD size of the three-in-a-row function?

47. [*M21*] Devise and prove a *converse* of Theorem M: Every Boolean function f with a small BDD can be implemented by an efficient network of modules.

48. [*M22*] Implement the hidden weighted bit function with a network of modules like Fig. 23, using $a_k = 2 + \lambda k$ and $b_k = 1 + \lambda(n - k)$ connecting wires for $1 \le k < n$. Conclude from Theorem B that the upper bound in Theorem M cannot be improved to $\sum_{k=0}^{n} 2^{p(a_k, b_k)}$ for any polynomial p.

49. [*20*] Draw the BDD base for the following sets of symmetric Boolean functions: (a) $\{S_{\ge k}(x_1, x_2, x_3, x_4) \mid 1 \le k \le 4\}$; (b) $\{S_k(x_1, x_2, x_3, x_4) \mid 0 \le k \le 4\}$.

50. [*22*] Draw the BDD base for the functions of the 7-segment display (7.1.2–(42)).

51. [*22*] Describe the BDD base for binary addition when the input bits are numbered from right to left, namely $(f_{n+1} f_n f_{n-1} \ldots f_1)_2 = (x_{2n-1} \ldots x_3 x_1)_2 + (x_{2n} \ldots x_4 x_2)_2$, instead of from left to right as in (35) and (36).

52. [*20*] There's a sense in which the BDD base for m functions $\{f_1, \ldots, f_m\}$ isn't really very different from a BDD with just one root: Consider the *junction function* $J(u_1, \ldots, u_n; v_1, \ldots, v_n) = (u_1? \; v_1: u_2? \; v_2: \cdots u_n? \; v_n: 0)$, and let

$$f(t_1, \ldots, t_{m+1}, x_1, \ldots, x_n) = J(t_1, \ldots, t_{m+1}; f_1(x_1, \ldots, x_n), \ldots, f_m(x_1, \ldots, x_n), 1),$$

where $(t_1, \ldots, t_{m+1})$ are new "dummy" variables, placed ahead of $(x_1, \ldots, x_n)$ in the ordering. Show that $B(f)$ is almost the same as the size of the BDD base for $\{f_1, \ldots, f_m\}$.

▶ **53.** [*23*] Play through Algorithm R, when it is applied to the binary decision diagram with seven branch nodes in (2).

54. [*17*] Construct the BDD of $f(x_1, \ldots, x_n)$ from f's truth table, in $O(2^n)$ steps.

55. [*M30*] Explain how to construct the "connectedness BDD" of a graph (like Fig. 22).

56. [*20*] Modify Algorithm R so that, instead of pushing any unnecessary nodes onto an AVAIL stack, it creates a brand new BDD, consisting of consecutive instructions $I_{s-1}, \ldots, I_1, I_0$ that have the compact form $(\bar{v}_k? \; l_k: h_k)$ assumed in Algorithms B and C. (The original nodes input to the algorithm can then all be recycled en masse.)

57. [*25*] Specify additional actions to be taken between steps R1 and R2 when Algorithm R is extended to compute the restriction of a function. Assume that FIX[v] = $t \in \{0, 1\}$ if variable v is to be given the fixed value t; otherwise FIX[v] < 0.

58. [*20*] Prove that the "melded" diagram defined by recursive use of (37) is reduced.

▶ **59.** [*M28*] Let $h(x_1, \ldots, x_n)$ be a Boolean function. Describe the melded BDD $f \diamond g$ in terms of the BDD for h, when (a) $f(x_1, \ldots, x_{2n}) = h(x_1, \ldots, x_n)$ and $g(x_1, \ldots, x_{2n}) = h(x_{n+1}, \ldots, x_{2n})$; (b) $f(x_1, x_2, \ldots, x_{2n}) = h(x_1, x_3, \ldots, x_{2n-1})$ and $g(x_1, x_2, \ldots, x_{2n}) = h(x_2, x_4, \ldots, x_{2n})$. [In both cases we obviously have $B(f) = B(g) = B(h)$.]

60. [*M22*] Suppose $f(x_1, \ldots, x_n)$ and $g(x_1, \ldots, x_n)$ have the profiles $(b_0, \ldots, b_n)$ and $(b'_0, \ldots, b'_n)$, respectively, and let their respective quasi-profiles be $(q_0, \ldots, q_n)$ and $(q'_0, \ldots, q'_n)$. Show that their meld $f \diamond g$ has $B(f \diamond g) \le \sum_{j=0}^{n}(q_j b'_j + b_j q'_j - b_j b'_j)$ nodes.

▶ **61.** [*M27*] If α and β are nodes of the respective BDDs for f and g, prove that

$$\text{in-degree}(\alpha \diamond \beta) \; \le \; \text{in-degree}(\alpha) \cdot \text{in-degree}(\beta)$$

in the melded BDD $f \diamond g$. (Imagine that the root of a BDD has in-degree 1.)

▶ **62.** [*M21*] If $f(x) = \bigvee_{j=1}^{\lfloor n/2 \rfloor} (x_{2j-1} \wedge x_{2j})$ and $g(x) = (x_1 \wedge x_n) \vee \bigvee_{j=1}^{\lceil n/2 \rceil - 1} (x_{2j} \wedge x_{2j+1})$, what are the asymptotic values of $B(f)$, $B(g)$, $B(f \diamond g)$, and $B(f \vee g)$ as $n \to \infty$?

63. [*M27*] Let $f(x_1, \ldots, x_n) = M_m(x_1 \oplus x_2, x_3 \oplus x_4, \ldots, x_{2m-1} \oplus x_{2m}; x_{2m+1}, \ldots, x_n)$ and $g(x_1, \ldots, x_n) = M_m(x_2 \oplus x_3, \ldots, x_{2m-2} \oplus x_{2m-1}, x_{2m}; \bar{x}_{2m+1}, \ldots, \bar{x}_n)$, where $n = 2m + 2^m$. What are $B(f)$, $B(g)$, and $B(f \wedge g)$?

64. [*M21*] We can compute the median $\langle f_1 f_2 f_3 \rangle$ of three Boolean functions by forming

$$f_4 = f_1 \vee f_2, \quad f_5 = f_1 \wedge f_2, \quad f_6 = f_3 \wedge f_4, \quad f_7 = f_5 \vee f_6.$$

Then $B(f_4) = O(B(f_1)B(f_2))$, $B(f_5) = O(B(f_1)B(f_2))$, $B(f_6) = O(B(f_3)B(f_4)) = O(B(f_1)B(f_2)B(f_3))$; therefore $B(f_7) = O(B(f_5)B(f_6)) = O(B(f_1)^2 B(f_2)^2 B(f_3))$. Prove, however, that $B(f_7)$ is actually only $O(B(f_1)B(f_2)B(f_3))$, and the running time to compute it from f_5 and f_6 is also $O(B(f_1)B(f_2)B(f_3))$.

▶ **65.** [*M25*] If $h(x_1, \ldots, x_n) = f(x_1, \ldots, x_{j-1}, g(x_1, \ldots, x_n), x_{j+1}, \ldots, x_n)$, prove that $B(h) = O(B(f)^2 B(g))$. Can this upper bound be improved to $O(B(f)B(g))$ in general?

66. [*20*] Complete Algorithm S by explaining what to do in step S1 if $f \circ g$ turns out to be trivially constant.

67. [*24*] Sketch the actions of Algorithm S when (41) defines f and g, and $op = 1$.

68. [*20*] Speed up step S10 by streamlining the common case when $\mathsf{LEFT}(t) < 0$.

69. [*21*] Algorithm S ought to have one or more precautionary instructions such as "if $\mathsf{NTOP} > \mathsf{TBOT}$, terminate the algorithm unsuccessfully," in case it runs out of room. Where are the best places to insert them?

70. [*21*] Discuss setting b to $\lfloor \lg \mathsf{LCOUNT}[l] \rfloor$ instead of $\lceil \lg \mathsf{LCOUNT}[l] \rceil$ in step S4.

71. [*20*] Discuss how to extend Algorithm S to ternary operators.

72. [*25*] Explain how to eliminate hashing from Algorithm S.

▶ **73.** [*25*] Discuss the use of "virtual addresses" instead of actual addresses as the links of a BDD: Each pointer p has the form $\pi(p)2^e + \sigma(p)$, where $\pi(p) = p \gg e$ is p's "page" and $\sigma(p) = p \bmod 2^e$ is p's "slot"; the parameter e can be chosen for convenience. Show that, with this approach, only two fields (LO, HI) are needed in BDD nodes, because the variable identifier $V(p)$ can be deduced from the virtual address p itself.

▶ **74.** [*M23*] Explain how to count the number of *self-dual* monotone Boolean functions of n variables, by modifying (49).

75. [*M20*] Let $\rho_n(x_1, \ldots, x_{2^n})$ be the Boolean function that is true if and only if $x_1 \ldots x_{2^n}$ is the truth table of a *regular* function (see exercise 7.1.1–110). Show that the BDD for ρ_n can be computed by a procedure similar to that of μ_n in (49).

▶ **76.** [*M22*] A "clutter" is a family S of mutually incomparable sets; in other words, $S \not\subseteq S'$ whenever S and S' are distinct members of $\mathcal{S}$. Every set $S \subseteq \{0, 1, \ldots, n-1\}$ can be represented as an n-bit integer $s = \sum \{2^e \mid e \in S\}$; so every family of such sets corresponds to a binary vector $x_0 x_1 \ldots x_{2^n - 1}$, with $x_s = 1$ if and only if s represents a set of the family.

Show that the BDD for the function '$[x_0 x_1 \ldots x_{2^n - 1}$ corresponds to a clutter]' has a simple relation to the BDD for the monotone-function function $\mu_n(x_1, \ldots, x_{2^n})$.

▶ **77.** [*M30*] Show that there's an infinite sequence $(b_0, b_1, b_2, \ldots) = (1, 2, 3, 5, 6, \ldots)$ such that the profile of the BDD for μ_n is $(b_0, b_1, \ldots, b_{2^{n-1}-1}, b_{2^{n-1}-1}, \ldots, b_1, b_0, 2)$. (See Fig. 25.) How many branch nodes of that BDD have $\mathsf{LO} = \boxed{\perp}$?

▶ **78.** [*25*] Use BDDs to determine the number of graphs on 12 labeled vertices for which the maximum vertex degree is d, for $0 \le d \le 11$.

79. [*20*] For $0 \le d \le 11$, compute the probability that a graph on vertices $\{1, \ldots, 12\}$ has maximum degree d, if each edge is present with probability $1/3$.

80. [*23*] The recursive algorithm (55) computes $f \wedge g$ in a depth-first manner, while Algorithm S does its computation breadth-first. Do both algorithms encounter the same subproblems $f' \wedge g'$ as they proceed (but in a different order), or does one algorithm consider fewer cases than the other?

▶ **81.** [*20*] By modifying (55), explain how to compute $f \oplus g$ in a BDD base.

▶ **82.** [*25*] When the nodes of a BDD base have been endowed with REF fields, explain how those fields should be adjusted within (55) and within Algorithm U.

83. [*M20*] Prove that if f and g both have reference count 1, we needn't consult the memo cache when computing AND(f, g) by (55).

84. [*24*] Suggest strategies for choosing the size of the memo cache and the sizes of the unique tables, when implementing algorithms for BDD bases. What is a good way to schedule periodic garbage collections?

85. [*16*] Compare the size of a BDD base for the 32 functions of 16×16-bit binary multiplication with the alternative of just storing a complete table of all possible products.

▶ **86.** [*21*] The routine MUX in (62) refers to "obvious" values. What are they?

87. [*20*] If the median operator $\langle fgh \rangle$ is implemented with a recursive subroutine analogous to (62), what are its "obvious" values?

▶ **88.** [*M25*] Find functions f, g, and h for which the recursive ternary computation of $f \wedge g \wedge h$ outperforms any of the binary computations $(f \wedge g) \wedge h$, $(g \wedge h) \wedge f$, $(h \wedge f) \wedge g$.

89. [*15*] Are the following quantified formulas true or false? (a) $\exists x_1 \exists x_2 f = \exists x_2 \exists x_1 f$. (b) $\forall x_1 \forall x_2 f = \forall x_2 \forall x_1 f$. (c) $\forall x_1 \exists x_2 f \le \exists x_2 \forall x_1 f$. (d) $\forall x_1 \exists x_2 f \ge \exists x_2 \forall x_1 f$.

90. [*M20*] When $l = m = n = 3$, Eq. (64) corresponds to the MOR operation of MMIX. Is there an analogous formula that corresponds to MXOR (matrix multiplication mod 2)?

▶ **91.** [*26*] In practice we often want to simplify a Boolean function f with respect to a "care set" g, by finding a function $\hat{f}$ with small $B(\hat{f})$ such that

$$f(x) \wedge g(x) \ \le \ \hat{f}(x) \ \le \ f(x) \vee \bar{g}(x) \qquad \text{for all } x.$$

In other words, $\hat{f}(x)$ must agree with $f(x)$ whenever x satisfies $g(x) = 1$, but we don't care what value $\hat{f}(x)$ assumes when $g(x) = 0$. An appealing candidate for such an $\hat{f}$ is provided by the function $f \downarrow g$, "f constrained by g," defined as follows: If $g(x)$ is identically 0, $f \downarrow g = 0$. Otherwise $(f \downarrow g)(x) = f(y)$, where y is the first element of the sequence x, $x \oplus 1$, $x \oplus 2$, $\ldots$, such that $g(y) = 1$. (Here we think of x and y as n-bit numbers $(x_1 \ldots x_n)_2$ and $(y_1 \ldots y_n)_2$. Thus $x \oplus 1 = x \oplus 0 \ldots 01 = x_1 \ldots x_{n-1} \bar{x}_n$; $x \oplus 2 = x \oplus 0 \ldots 010 = x_1 \ldots x_{n-2} \bar{x}_{n-1} x_n$; etc.)

    a) What are $f \downarrow 1$, $f \downarrow x_j$, and $f \downarrow \bar{x}_j$?

    b) Prove that $(f \wedge f') \downarrow g = (f \downarrow g) \wedge (f' \downarrow g)$.

    c) True or false: $\bar{f} \downarrow g = \overline{f \downarrow g}$.

    d) Simplify the formula $f(x_1, \ldots, x_n) \downarrow (x_2 \wedge \bar{x}_3 \wedge \bar{x}_5 \wedge x_6)$.

    e) Simplify the formula $f(x_1, \ldots, x_n) \downarrow (x_1 \oplus x_2 \oplus \cdots \oplus x_n)$.

    f) Simplify the formula $f(x_1, \ldots, x_n) \downarrow ((x_1 \wedge \cdots \wedge x_n) \vee (\bar{x}_1 \wedge \cdots \wedge \bar{x}_n))$.

    g) Simplify the formula $f(x_1, \ldots, x_n) \downarrow (x_1 \wedge g(x_2, \ldots, x_n))$.

h) Find functions $f(x_1, x_2)$ and $g(x_1, x_2)$ such that $B(f \downarrow g) > B(f)$.

i) Devise a recursive way to compute $f \downarrow g$, analogous to (55).

92. [*M27*] The operation $f \downarrow g$ in exercise 91 sometimes depends on the ordering of the variables. Given $g = g(x_1, \ldots, x_n)$, prove that $(f^\pi \downarrow g^\pi) = (f \downarrow g)^\pi$ for all permutations π of $\{1, \ldots, n\}$ and for all functions $f = f(x_1, \ldots, x_n)$ if and only if $g = 0$ or g is a subcube (a conjunction of literals).

93. [*36*] Given a graph G on the vertices $\{1, \ldots, n\}$, construct Boolean functions f and g with the property that an approximating function $\hat{f}$ exists as in exercise 91 with small $B(\hat{f})$ if and only if G can be 3-colored. (Hence the task of minimizing $B(\hat{f})$ is NP-complete.)

94. [*21*] Explain why (65) performs existential quantification correctly.

▶ **95.** [*20*] Improve on (65) by testing if $r_l = 1$ before computing r_h.

96. [*20*] Show how to achieve (a) universal quantification $\forall x_{j_1} \ldots \forall x_{j_m} f = f \mathbin{\text{A}} g$, and (b) differential quantification $\mathbin{\text{D}} x_{j_1} \ldots \mathbin{\text{D}} x_{j_m} f = f \mathbin{\text{D}} g$, by modifying (65).

97. [*M20*] Prove that it's possible to compute arbitrary bottom-of-the-BDD quantifications such as $\exists x_{n-5} \forall x_{n-4} \mathbin{\text{D}} x_{n-3} \exists x_{n-2} \mathbin{\curlywedge} x_{n-1} \forall x_n f(x_1, \ldots, x_n)$ in $O(B(f))$ steps.

▶ **98.** [*22*] In addition to (70), explain how to define the vertices $\mathrm{ENDPT}(x)$ of $\mathcal{G}$ that have degree ≤ 1. Also characterize $\mathrm{PAIR}(x, y)$, the components of size 2.

99. [*20*] (R. E. Bryant, 1984.) Every 4-coloring of the US map considered in the text corresponds to 24 solutions of the COLOR function (73), under permutation of colors. What's a good way to remove this redundancy?

▶ **100.** [*24*] In how many ways is it possible to 4-color the contiguous USA with exactly 12 states of each color? (Eliminate DC from the graph.)

101. [*20*] Continuing exercise 100, with colors $\{1, 2, 3, 4\}$, find such a coloring that maximizes $\sum$ (state weight) $\times$ (state color), where states are weighted as in (18).

102. [*23*] Design a method to cache the results of functional composition using the following conventions: The system maintains at all times an array of functions $[g_1, \ldots, g_n]$, one for each variable x_j. Initially g_j is simply the projection function x_j, for $1 \leq j \leq n$. This array can be changed only by the subroutine $\mathrm{NEWG}(j, g)$, which replaces g_j by g. The subroutine $\mathrm{COMPOSE}(f)$ always performs functional composition with respect to the current array of replacement functions.

▶ **103.** [*20*] Mr. B. C. Dull wanted to evaluate the formula

$$\exists y_1 \ldots \exists y_m ((y_1 = f_1(x_1, \ldots, x_n)) \wedge \cdots \wedge (y_m = f_m(x_1, \ldots, x_n)) \wedge g(y_1, \ldots, y_m)),$$

for certain functions $f_1, \ldots, f_m$, and g. But his fellow student, J. H. Quick, found a much simpler formula for the same problem. What was Quick's idea?

▶ **104.** [*21*] Devise an efficient way to decide whether $f \leq g$ or $f \geq g$ or $f \parallel g$, where $f \parallel g$ means that f and g are incomparable, given the BDDs for f and g.

105. [*25*] A Boolean function $f(x_1, \ldots, x_n)$ is called *unate* with polarities $(y_1, \ldots, y_n)$ if the function $h(x_1, \ldots, x_n) = f(x_1 \oplus y_1, \ldots, x_n \oplus y_n)$ is monotone.

a) Show that f can be tested for unateness by using the $\curlywedge$ and N quantifiers.

b) Design a recursive algorithm to test unateness in at most $O(B(f)^2)$ steps, given the BDD for f. If f is unate, your algorithm should also find appropriate polarities.

106. [*25*] Let $f\$g\$h$ denote the relation "$f(x) = g(y) = 1$ implies $h(x \wedge y) = 1$, for all x and y." Show that this relation can be evaluated in at most $O(B(f)B(g)B(h))$ steps. [*Motivation:* Theorem 7.1.1H states that f is a Horn function if and only if $f\$f\$f$; thus we can test Horn-ness in $O(B(f)^3)$ steps.]

107. [*26*] Continuing exercise 106, show that it's possible to determine whether or not f is a Krom function in $O(B(f)^4)$ steps. [*Hint:* See Theorem 7.1.1S.]

108. [*HM24*] Let $b(n, s)$ be the number of n-variable Boolean functions with $B(f) \leq s$. Prove that $(s - 3)! \, b(n, s) \leq (n(s - 1)^2)^{s-2}$ when $s \geq 3$, and explore the ramifications of this inequality when $s = \lfloor 2^n/(n + 1/\ln 2) \rfloor$. *Hint:* See the proof of Theorem 7.1.2S.

▶ **109.** [*HM17*] Continuing exercise 108, show that almost all Boolean functions of n variables have $B(f^\pi) > 2^n/(n + 1/\ln 2)$, for all permutations π of $\{1, \ldots, n\}$, as $n \to \infty$.

110. [*25*] Construct explicit worst-case functions f_n for which $f_n = U_n$ in Theorem U.

111. [*M21*] Verify the summation formula (79) in Theorem U.

112. [*HM23*] Prove that $\min(2^k, 2^{2^{n-k}} - 2^{2^{n-k-1}}) - \hat{b}_k$ is very small, where $\hat{b}_k$ is the number defined in (80), except when $n - \lg n - 1 < k < n - \lg n + 1$.

113. [*20*] Instead of having sink nodes, one for each Boolean constant, we could have 2^{16} sinks, one for each Boolean function of four variables. Then a BDD could stop four levels earlier, after branching on x_{n-4}. Would this be a good idea?

114. [*20*] Is there a function with profile $(1, 1, 1, 1, 1, 2)$ and quasi-profile $(1, 2, 3, 4, 3, 2)$?

▶ **115.** [*M22*] Prove the quasi-profile inequalities (84) and (124).

116. [*M21*] What is the (a) worst case (b) average case of a random quasi-profile?

117. [*M20*] Compare $Q(f)$ to $B(f)$ when $f = M_m(x_1, \ldots, x_m; x_{m+1}, \ldots, x_{m+2^m})$.

118. [*M23*] Show that, from the perspective of Section 7.1.2, the hidden weighted bit function has cost $C(h_n) = O(n)$. What is the exact value of $C(h_4)$?

119. [*20*] True or false: Every symmetric Boolean function of n variables is a special case of h_{2n+1}. (For example, $x_1 \oplus x_2 = h_5(0, 1, 0, x_1, x_2)$.)

120. [*18*] Explain the hidden-permuted-weighted-bit formula (94).

▶ **121.** [*M22*] If $f(x_1, \ldots, x_n)$ is any Boolean function, its *dual* f^D is $\bar{f}(\bar{x}_1, \ldots, \bar{x}_n)$, and its *reflection* f^R is $f(x_n \ldots, x_1)$. Notice that $f^{DD} = f^{RR} = f$ and $f^{DR} = f^{RD}$.
 a) Show that $h_n^{DR}(x_1, \ldots, x_n) = h_n(x_2, \ldots, x_n, x_1)$.
 b) Furthermore, the hidden weighted bit function satisfies the recurrence

$$h_1(x_1) = x_1, \quad h_{n+1}(x_1, \ldots, x_{n+1}) = (x_{n+1}?\ h_n(x_2, \ldots, x_n, x_1)\colon h_n(x_1, \ldots, x_n)).$$

 c) Define $x\psi$, a permutation on the set of all binary strings x, by the recursive rules

$$\epsilon\psi = \epsilon, \quad (x_1 \ldots x_n 0)\psi = (x_1 \ldots x_n \psi)0, \quad (x_1 \ldots x_n 1)\psi = (x_2 \ldots x_n x_1)\psi 1.$$

 For example, $1101\psi = (101\psi)1 = (01\psi)11 = (0\psi)111 = (\psi)0111 = 0111$; and we also have $0111\psi = 1101$. Is ψ an involution?
 d) Show that $h_n(x) = \hat{h}_n(x\psi)$, where the function $\hat{h}_n$ has a very small BDD.

122. [*27*] Construct an FBDD for h_n that has fewer than n^2 nodes, when $n > 1$.

123. [*M20*] Prove formula (97), which enumerates all slates of offset s.

▶ **124.** [*27*] Design an efficient algorithm to compute the profile and quasi-profile of h_n^π, given a permutation π. *Hint:* When does the slate $[r_0, \ldots, r_{n-k}]$ correspond to a bead?

▶ **125.** [*HM34*] Prove that $B(h_n)$ can be expressed exactly in terms of the sequences

$$A_n = \sum_{k=0}^{n} \binom{n-k}{2k}, \qquad B_n = \sum_{k=0}^{n} \binom{n-k}{2k+1}.$$

126. [*HM42*] Analyze $B(h_n^\pi)$ for the organ-pipe permutation $\pi = (2, 4, \ldots, n, \ldots, 3, 1)$.

127. [*46*] Find a permutation π that minimizes $B(h_{100}^\pi)$.

▶ **128.** [*25*] Given a permutation π of $\{1, \ldots, m + 2^m\}$, explain how to compute the profile and quasi-profile of the permuted 2^m-way multiplexer

$$M_m^\pi(x_1, \ldots, x_m; x_{m+1}, \ldots, x_{m+2^m}) = M_m(x_{1\pi}, \ldots, x_{m\pi}; x_{(m+1)\pi}, \ldots, x_{(m+2^m)\pi}).$$

129. [*M25*] Define $Q_m(x_1, \ldots, x_{m^2})$ to be 1 if and only if the 0–1 matrix $(x_{(i-1)m+j})$ has no all-zero row and no all-zero column. Prove that $B(Q_m^\pi) = \Omega(2^m/m^2)$ for all π.

130. [*HM31*] The adjacency matrix of an undirected graph G on vertices $\{1, \ldots, m\}$ consists of $\binom{m}{2}$ variable entries $x_{uv} = [u \text{ --- } v \text{ in } G]$, for $1 \le u < v \le m$. Let $C_{m,k}$ be the Boolean function $[G$ has a k-clique$]$, for some ordering of those $\binom{m}{2}$ variables.

  a) If $1 < k \le \sqrt{m}$, prove that $B(C_{m,k}) \ge \binom{s+t}{s}$, where $s = \binom{k}{2} - 1$ and $t = m + 2 - k^2$.

  b) Consequently $B(C_{m,\lceil m/2 \rceil}) = \Omega(2^{m/3}/\sqrt{m})$, regardless of the variable ordering.

131. [*M28*] (*The covering function.*) The Boolean function

$$C(x_1, x_2, \ldots, x_p; y_{11}, y_{12}, \ldots, y_{1q}, y_{21}, \ldots, y_{2q}, \ldots, y_{p1}, y_{p2}, \ldots, y_{pq})$$
$$= ((x_1 \wedge y_{11}) \vee (x_2 \wedge y_{21}) \vee \cdots \vee (x_p \wedge y_{p1})) \wedge \cdots \wedge ((x_1 \wedge y_{1q}) \vee (x_2 \wedge y_{2q}) \vee \cdots \vee (x_p \wedge y_{pq}))$$

is true if and only if all columns of the matrix product

$$x \cdot Y = (x_1 x_2 \ldots x_p) \begin{pmatrix} y_{11} & y_{12} & \cdots & y_{1q} \\ y_{21} & y_{22} & \cdots & y_{2q} \\ \vdots & \vdots & \ddots & \vdots \\ y_{p1} & y_{p2} & \cdots & y_{pq} \end{pmatrix}$$

are positive, i.e., when the rows of Y selected by x "cover" every column of that matrix. The reliability polynomial of C is important in the analysis of fault-tolerant systems.

  a) When a BDD for C tests the variables in the order

$$x_1, y_{11}, y_{12}, \ldots, y_{1q}, x_2, y_{21}, y_{22}, \ldots, y_{2q}, \ldots, x_p, y_{p1}, y_{p2}, \ldots, y_{pq},$$

    show that the number of nodes is asymptotically $pq2^{q-1}$ for fixed q as $p \to \infty$.

  b) Find an ordering for which the size is asymptotically $pq2^{p-1}$ for fixed p as $q \to \infty$.

  c) Prove, however, that $B_{\min}(C) = \Omega(2^{\min(p,q)/2})$ in general.

132. [*32*] What Boolean functions $f(x_1, x_2, x_3, x_4, x_5)$ have the largest $B_{\min}(f)$?

133. [*20*] Explain how to compute $B_{\min}(f)$ and $B_{\max}(f)$ from f's master profile chart.

134. [*24*] Construct the master profile chart, analogous to (102), for the Boolean function $x_1 \oplus ((x_2 \oplus (x_1 \vee (\bar{x}_2 \wedge x_3))) \wedge (x_3 \oplus x_4))$. What are $B_{\min}(f)$ and $B_{\max}(f)$? *Hint:* The identity $f(x_1, x_2, x_3, x_4) = f(x_1, x_2, \bar{x}_4, \bar{x}_3)$ saves about half the work.

135. [*M27*] For all $n \ge 4$, find a Boolean function $\theta_n(x_1, \ldots, x_n)$ that is *uniquely thin*, in the sense that $B(\theta_n^\pi) = n + 2$ for exactly one permutation π. (See (93) and (102).)

▶ **136.** [*M34*] What is the master profile chart of the median-of-medians function

$$\langle\langle x_{11}x_{12}\ldots x_{1n}\rangle\langle x_{21}x_{22}\ldots x_{2n}\rangle\ldots\langle x_{m1}x_{m2}\ldots x_{mn}\rangle\rangle,$$

when m and n are odd integers? What is the best ordering? (There are mn variables.)

137. [*M38*] Given a graph, the *optimum linear arrangement problem* asks for a permutation π of the vertices that minimizes $\sum_{u-v}|u\pi - v\pi|$. Construct a Boolean function f for which this minimum value is characterized by the optimum BDD size $B_{\min}(f)$.

▶ **138.** [*M36*] The purpose of this exercise is to develop an attractive algorithm that computes the master profile chart for a function f, given f's QDD (not its BDD).

    a) Explain how to find $\binom{n+1}{2}$ weights of the master profile chart from a single QDD.

    b) Show that the jump-up operation can be performed easily in a QDD, without garbage collection or hashing. *Hint:* See the "bucket sort" in Algorithm R.

    c) Consider the 2^{n-1} orderings of variables in which the $(i+1)$st is obtained from the ith by a jump-up from depth $\rho i + \nu i$ to depth $\nu i - 1$. For example, we get

12345 21345 32145 31245 43125 41325 42135 42315 54231 52431 53241 53421 51342 51432 51243 51234

    when $n = 5$. Show that every k-element subset of $\{1,\ldots,n\}$ occurs at the top k levels of one of these orderings.

    d) Combine these ideas to design the desired chart-construction algorithm.

    e) Analyze the space and time requirements of your algorithm.

139. [*22*] Generalize the algorithm of exercise 138 so that (i) it computes a common profile chart for all functions of a BDD base, instead of a single function; and (ii) it restricts the chart to variables $\{x_a, x_{a+1},\ldots, x_b\}$, preserving $\{x_1,\ldots,x_{a-1}\}$ at the top and $\{x_{b+1},\ldots,x_n\}$ at the bottom.

140. [*27*] Explain how to find $B_{\min}(f)$ without knowing all of f's master profile chart.

141. [*30*] True or false: If $X_1, X_2, \ldots, X_m$ are disjoint sets of variables, then an optimum BDD ordering for the variables of $g(h_1(X_1), h_2(X_2),\ldots, h_m(X_m))$ can be found by restricting consideration to cases where the variables of each X_j are consecutive.

▶ **142.** [*HM32*] The representation of threshold functions by BDDs is surprisingly mysterious. Consider the self-dual function $f(x) = \langle x_1^{w_1}\ldots x_n^{w_n}\rangle$, where each w_j is a positive integer and $w_1+\cdots+w_n$ is odd. We observed in (28) that $B(f) = O(w_1+\cdots+w_n)^2$; and $B(f)$ is often $O(n)$ even when the weights grow exponentially, as in (29) or exercise 41.

    a) Prove that when $w_1 = 1$, $w_k = 2^{k-2}$ for $1 < k \le m$, and $w_k = 2^m - 2^{n-k}$ for $m < k \le 2m = n$, $B(f)$ grows exponentially as $n \to \infty$, but $B_{\min}(f) = O(n^2)$.

    b) Find weights $\{w_1,\ldots,w_n\}$ for which $B_{\min}(f) = \Omega(2^{\sqrt{n}/2})$.

143. [*24*] Continuing exercise 142(a), find an optimum ordering of variables for the function $\langle x_1 x_2 x_3^2 x_4^4 x_5^8 x_6^{16} x_7^{32} x_8^{64} x_9^{128} x_{10}^{256} x_{11}^{512} x_{12}^{768} x_{13}^{896} x_{14}^{960} x_{15}^{992} x_{16}^{1008} x_{17}^{1016} x_{18}^{1020} x_{19}^{1022} x_{20}^{1023}\rangle$.

144. [*16*] What is the quasi-profile of the addition functions $\{f_1, f_2, f_3, f_4, f_5\}$ in (36)?

145. [*24*] Find $B_{\min}(f_1, f_2, f_3, f_4, f_5)$ and $B_{\max}(f_1, f_2, f_3, f_4, f_5)$ of those functions.

▶ **146.** [*M22*] Let $(b_0,\ldots,b_n)$ and $(q_0,\ldots,q_n)$ be a BDD base profile and quasi-profile.

    a) Prove that $b_0 \le \min(q_0, (b_1 + q_2)(b_1 + q_2 - 1))$, $b_1 \le \min(b_0 + q_0, q_2(q_2 - 1))$, and $b_0 + b_1 \ge q_0 - q_2$.

    b) Conversely, if b_0, b_1, q_0, and q_2 are nonnegative integers that satisfy those inequalities, there is a BDD base with such a profile and quasi-profile.

▶ **147.** [*27*] Flesh out the details of Rudell's swap-in-place algorithm, using the conventions of Algorithm U and the reference counters of exercise 82.

148. [*M21*] True or false: $B(f_1^\pi, \ldots, f_m^\pi) \le 2B(f_1, \ldots, f_m)$, after swapping (1) ↔ (2).

149. [*M20*] (Bollig, Löbbing, and Wegener.) Show that, in addition to Theorem J⁻, we also have $B(f_1^\pi, \ldots, f_m^\pi) \le (2^k - 2)b_0 + B(f_1, \ldots, f_m)$ after a jump-down operation of $k - 1$ levels, when $(b_0, \ldots, b_n)$ is the profile of $\{f_1, \ldots, f_m\}$.

150. [*30*] When repeated swaps are used to implement jump-up or jump-down, the intermediate results might be much larger than the initial or final BDD. Show that variable jumps can actually be done more directly, with a method whose worst-case running time is $O(B(f_1, \ldots, f_m) + B(f_1^\pi, \ldots, f_m^\pi))$.

151. [*20*] Suggest a way to invoke Algorithm J so that each variable is sifted just once.

152. [*25*] The hidden weighted bit function h_{100} has more than 17.5 trillion nodes in its BDD. By how much does sifting reduce this number? *Hint:* Use exercise 124, instead of actually constructing the diagrams.

153. [*30*] Put the tic-tac-toe functions $\{y_1, \ldots, y_9\}$ of exercise 7.1.2–65 into a BDD base. How many nodes are present when variables are tested in the order $x_1, x_2, \ldots, x_9$, $o_1, o_2, \ldots, o_9$, from top to bottom? What is $B_{\min}(y_1, \ldots, y_9)$?

154. [*20*] By comparing (104) to (106), can you tell how far each state was moved when it was sifted?

▶ **155.** [*25*] Let f_1 be the independent-set function (105) of the contiguous USA, and let f_2 be the corresponding kernel function (see (67)). Find orderings π of the states so that (a) $B(f_2^\pi)$ and (b) $B(f_1^\pi, f_2^\pi)$ are as small as you can make them. (Note that the ordering (110) gives $B(f_1^\pi) = 339$, $B(f_2^\pi) = 795$, and $B(f_1^\pi, f_2^\pi) = 1129$.)

156. [*30*] Theorems J⁺ and J⁻ suggest that we could save reordering time by only jumping up when sifting, not bothering to jump down. Then we could eliminate steps J3, J5, J6, and J7 of Algorithm J. Would that be wise?

157. [*M24*] Show that if the $m + 2^m$ variables of the 2^m-way multiplexer M_m are arranged in any order such that $B(M_m^\pi) > 2^{m+1} + 1$, then sifting will reduce the BDD size.

158. [*M24*] When a Boolean function $f(x_1, \ldots, x_n)$ is symmetrical in the variables $\{x_1, \ldots, x_p\}$, it's natural to expect that those variables will appear consecutively in at least one of the reorderings $f^\pi(x_1, \ldots, x_n)$ that minimize $B(f^\pi)$. Show, however, that if

$$f(x_1, \ldots, x_n) = [x_1 + \cdots + x_p = \lfloor p/3 \rfloor] + [x_1 + \cdots + x_p = \lceil 2p/3 \rceil] g(x_{p+1}, \ldots, x_{p+m}),$$

where $p = n - m$ and $g(y_1, \ldots, y_m)$ is any nonconstant Boolean function, then $B(f^\pi) = \frac{1}{3}n^2 + O(n)$ as $n \to \infty$ when $\{x_1, \ldots, x_p\}$ are consecutive in π, but $B(f^\pi) = \frac{1}{4}n^2 + O(n)$ when π places about half of those variables at the beginning and half at the end.

159. [*20*] John Conway's basic rule for Life, exercise 7.1.3–167, is a Boolean function $L(x_{\mathrm{NW}}, x_{\mathrm{N}}, x_{\mathrm{NE}}, x_{\mathrm{W}}, x, x_{\mathrm{E}}, x_{\mathrm{SW}}, x_{\mathrm{S}}, x_{\mathrm{SE}})$. What ordering of those nine variables will make the BDD as small as possible?

▶ **160.** [*24*] (*Chess Life.*) Consider an 8×8 matrix $X = (x_{ij})$ of 0s and 1s, bordered by infinitely many 0s on all sides. Let $L_{ij}(X) = L(x_{(i-1)(j-1)}, \ldots, x_{ij}, \ldots, x_{(i+1)(j+1)})$ be Conway's basic rule at position (i, j). Call X "tame" if $L_{ij}(X) = 0$ whenever $i \notin [1 .. 8]$ or $j \notin [1 .. 8]$; otherwise X is "wild," because it activates cells outside the matrix.

a) How many tame configurations X vanish in one Life step, making all $L_{ij} = 0$?
b) What is the maximum weight $\sum_{i=1}^{8} \sum_{j=1}^{8} x_{ij}$ among all such solutions?
c) How many wild configurations vanish *within* the matrix after one Life step?
d) What are the minimum and maximum weight, among all such solutions?
e) How many configurations X make $L_{ij}(X) = 1$ for $1 \le i, j \le 8$?

f) Investigate the tame 8×8 predecessors of the following patterns:

(1)   (2)   (3)   (4)   (5)

(Here, as in Section 7.1.3, black cells denote 1s in the matrix.)

161. [*28*] Continuing exercise 160, write $L(X) = Y = (y_{ij})$ if X is a tame matrix such that $L_{ij}(X) = y_{ij}$ for $1 \le i, j \le 8$.

a) How many X's satisfy $L(X) = X$ ("still Life")?

b) Find an 8×8 still Life with weight 35.

c) A "flip-flop" is a pair of distinct matrices with $L(X)=Y$, $L(Y)=X$. Count them.

d) Find a flip-flop for which X and Y both have weight 28.

▶ **162.** [*30*] (*Caged Life.*) If X and $L(X)$ are tame but $L(L(X))$ is wild, we say that X "escapes" its cage after three steps. How many 6×6 matrices escape their 6×6 cage after exactly k steps, for $k = 1, 2, \ldots$?

163. [*23*] Prove formulas (112) and (113) for the BDD sizes of read-once functions.

▶ **164.** [*M27*] What is the maximum of $B(f)$, over all read-once functions $f(x_1, \ldots, x_n)$?

165. [*M21*] Verify the Fibonacci-based formulas (115) for $B(u_m)$ and $B(v_m)$.

166. [*M29*] Complete the proof of Theorem W.

167. [*21*] Design an efficient algorithm that computes a permutation π for which both $B(f^\pi)$ and $B(f^\pi, \bar{f}^\pi)$ are minimized, given any read-once function $f(x_1, \ldots, x_n)$.

▶ **168.** [*HM40*] Consider the following binary operations on ordered pairs $z = (x, y)$:

$$z \circ z' = (x, y) \circ (x', y') = (x + x', \min(x + y', x' + y));$$
$$z \bullet z' = (x, y) \bullet (x', y') = (x + x' + \min(y, y'), \max(y, y')).$$

(These operations are associative and commutative.) Let $S_1 = \{(1, 0)\}$, and

$$S_n = \bigcup_{k=1}^{n-1} \{z \circ z' \mid z \in S_k,\ z' \in S_{n-k}\} \cup \bigcup_{k=1}^{n-1} \{z \bullet z' \mid z \in S_k,\ z' \in S_{n-k}\} \text{ for } n > 1.$$

Thus $S_2 = \{(2, 0), (2, 1)\}$; $S_3 = \{(3, 0), (3, 1), (3, 2)\}$; $S_4 = \{(4, 0), \ldots, (4, 3), (5, 1)\}$; etc.

a) Prove that there exists a read-once function $f(x_1, \ldots, x_n)$ for which we have $\min_\pi B(f^\pi) = c$ and $\min_\pi B(f^\pi, \bar{f}^\pi) = c'$ if and only if $(\frac{1}{2}c' - 1, c - \frac{1}{2}c' - 1) \in S_n$.

b) True or false: $0 \le y < x$ for all $(x, y) \in S_n$.

c) If $z^T = (x + y, x - y)/\sqrt{2}$, show that $z^T \circ z'^T = (z \bullet z')^T$ and $z^T \bullet z'^T = (z \circ z')^T$.

d) Prove that $x^2 + y^2 \le n^{2\beta}$ for all $(x, y) \in S_n$, if β is the constant in (116). *Hints:* Let $|z|^2 = x^2 + y^2$; it suffices to prove that $|z \bullet z'| \le 2^\beta = \sqrt{2}\phi$ whenever $0 \le y \le x$, $0 \le y' \le x'$, $|z| = r = (1-\delta)^\beta$, $|z'| = r' = (1+\delta)^\beta$, and $0 \le \delta \le 1$. If also $y = y'$, $z \bullet z'$ lies inside the ellipse $(a \cos \theta + b \sin \theta, b \sin \theta)$, where $a = r + r'$ and $b = \sqrt{rr'}$.

169. [*M46*] Is $\min_\pi B(f^\pi) \le B(v_{2m+1})$ for every read-once function f of 2^{2m+1} variables?

▶ **170.** [*M25*] Let's say that a Boolean function is "skinny" if its BDD involves all the variables in the simplest possible way: A skinny BDD has exactly one branch node (j) for each variable x_j, and either LO or HI is a sink node at every branch.

a) How many Boolean functions $f(x_1, \ldots, x_n)$ are skinny in this sense?

b) How many of them are monotone?

c) Show that $f_t(x_1, \ldots, x_n) = [(x_1 \ldots x_n)_2 \ge t]$ is skinny when $0 < t < 2^n$ and t is odd.

d) What is the *dual* of the function f_t in part (c)?

e) Explain how to find the shortest CNF and DNF formulas for f_t, given t.

171. [*M26*] Continuing exercise 170, show that a function is *read-once* and *regular* if and only if it is skinny and monotone.

172. [*M27*] How many skinny functions $f(x_1, \ldots, x_n)$ are also Horn functions? How many of them have the property that f and $\bar{f}$ *both* satisfy Horn's condition?

▶ **173.** [*HM28*] Exactly how many Boolean functions $f(x_1, \ldots, x_n)$ are skinny after some reordering of the variables, $f(x_{1\pi}, \ldots, x_{n\pi})$?

▶ **174.** [*M39*] Let S_n be the number of Boolean functions $f(x_1, \ldots, x_n)$ whose BDD is "thin" in the sense that it has exactly one node labeled ⓙ for $1 \leq j \leq n$. Show that S_n is also the number of combinatorial objects of the following types:

a) *Dellac permutations of order* $2n$ (namely, permutations $p_1 p_2 \ldots p_{2n}$ such that $\lceil k/2 \rceil \leq p_k \leq n + \lceil k/2 \rceil$ for $1 \leq k \leq 2n$).

b) *Genocchi derangements of order* $2n + 2$ (namely, permutations $q_1 q_2 \ldots q_{2n+2}$ such that $q_k > k$ if and only if k is odd, for $1 \leq k \leq 2n+2$; also $q_k \neq k$ in a derangement).

c) *Irreducible Dumont pistols of order* $2n + 2$ (namely, sequences $r_1 r_2 \ldots r_{2n+2}$ such that $k \leq r_k \leq 2n + 2$ for $1 \leq k \leq 2n+2$ and $\{r_1, r_2, \ldots, r_{2n+2}\} = \{2, 4, 6, \ldots, 2n, 2n + 2\}$, with the special property that $2k \in \{r_1, \ldots, r_{2k-1}\}$ for $1 \leq k \leq n$).

d) Paths from $(1, 0)$ to $(2n + 2, 0)$ in the directed graph

$$
\begin{array}{l}
 (7,3) \to (8,3) \to \cdots \\
 (5,2) \to (6,2) \to (7,2) \to (8,2) \to \cdots \\
 (3,1) \to (4,1) \to (5,1) \to (6,1) \to (7,1) \to (8,1) \to \cdots \\
(1,0) \to (2,0) \to (3,0) \to (4,0) \to (5,0) \to (6,0) \to (7,0) \to (8,0) \to \cdots
\end{array}
$$

(Notice that objects of type (d) are very easy to count.)

175. [*M30*] Continuing exercise 174, find a way to enumerate the Boolean functions whose BDD contains exactly b_{j-1} nodes labeled ⓙ, given a profile $(b_0, \ldots, b_{n-1}, b_n)$.

176. [*M35*] To complete the proof of Theorem X, we will use exercise 6.4–78, which states that $\{h_{a,b} \mid a \in A \text{ and } b \in B\}$ is a universal family of hash functions from n bits to l bits, when $h_{a,b}(x) = ((ax + b) \gg (n - l)) \bmod 2^l$, $A = \{a \mid 0 < a < 2^n, a \text{ odd}\}$, $B = \{b \mid 0 \leq b < 2^{n-l}\}$, and $0 \leq l \leq n$. Let $I = \{h_{a,b}(p) \mid p \in P\}$ and $J = \{h_{a,b}(q) \mid q \in Q\}$.

a) Show that if $2^l - 1 \leq 2^{l-1} \epsilon / (1 - \epsilon)$, there are constants $a \in A$ and $b \in B$ for which $|I| \geq (1 - \epsilon) 2^l$ and $|J| \geq (1 - \epsilon) 2^l$.

b) Given such an a, let $J = \{j_1, \ldots, j_{|J|}\}$ where $0 = j_1 < \cdots < j_{|J|}$, and choose $Q' = \{q_1, \ldots, q_{|J|}\} \subseteq Q$ so that $h_{a,b}(q_k) = j_k$ for $1 \leq k \leq |J|$. Let $g(q)$ denote the middle $l - 1$ bits of aq, namely $(aq \gg (n - l + 1)) \bmod 2^{l-1}$. Prove that $g(q) \neq g(q')$ whenever q and q' are distinct elements of the set $Q'' = \{q_1, q_3, \ldots, q_{2\lceil |J|/2 \rceil - 1}\}$.

c) Prove that the following set Q^* satisfies condition (120), when $l \geq 3$ and $y = a$:

$$ Q^* = \{q \mid q \in Q'', g(q) \text{ is even, and } g(p) + g(q) = 2^{l-1} \text{ for some } p \in P\}. $$

d) Finally, show that $|Q^*|$ is large enough to prove Theorem X.

177. [*M22*] Complete the proof of Theorem A by bounding the entire quasi-profile.

178. [*M24*] (Amano and Maruoka.) Improve the constant in (121) by using a better variable ordering: $Z_n(x_{2n-1}, x_1, x_3, \ldots, x_{2n-3}; x_{2n}, x_2, x_4, \ldots, x_{2n-2})$.

179. [*M47*] Does the middle bit of multiplication satisfy $B_{\min}(Z_n) = \Theta(2^{6n/5})$?

180. [*M27*] Prove Theorem Y, using the hint given in the text.

181. [*M21*] Let $L_{m,n}$ be the *leading bit function* $Z_{m,n}^{(m+n)}(x_1,\ldots,x_m;y_1,\ldots,y_n)$. Prove that $B_{\min}(L_{m,n}) = O(2^m n)$ when $m \leq n$.

182. [*M38*] (I. Wegener.) Does $B_{\min}(L_{n,n})$ grow exponentially as $n \to \infty$?

▶ **183.** [*M25*] Draw the first few levels of the BDD for the "limiting leading bit function"

$$[(.x_1 x_3 x_5 \ldots)_2 \cdot (.x_2 x_4 x_6 \ldots)_2 \geq \tfrac{1}{2}],$$

which has infinitely many Boolean variables. How many nodes b_k are there on level k? (We don't allow $(.x_1 x_3 x_5 \ldots)_2$ or $(.x_2 x_4 x_6 \ldots)_2$ to end with infinitely many 1s.)

184. [*M23*] What are the BDD and ZDD profiles of the permutation function P_m?

185. [*M25*] How large can $Z(f)$ be, when f is a symmetric Boolean function of n variables? (See exercise 44.)

186. [*10*] What Boolean function of $\{x_1, x_2, x_3, x_4, x_5, x_6\}$ has the ZDD '③'?

▶ **187.** [*20*] Draw the ZDDs for all 16 Boolean functions $f(x_1, x_2)$ of two variables.

188. [*16*] Express the 16 Boolean functions $f(x_1, x_2)$ as families of subsets of $\{1, 2\}$.

189. [*18*] What functions $f(x_1,\ldots,x_n)$ have a ZDD equal to their BDD?

190. [*20*] Describe all functions f for which (a) $Q(f) = B(f)$; (b) $Q(f) = Z(f)$.

▶ **191.** [*HM25*] How many functions $f(x_1,\ldots,x_n)$ have no $\boxed{\perp}$ in their ZDD?

192. [*M20*] Define the *Z-transform* of binary strings as follows: $\epsilon^Z = \epsilon$, $0^Z = 0$, $1^Z = 1$, and

$$(\alpha\beta)^Z = \begin{cases} \alpha^Z \alpha^Z, & \text{if } |\alpha| = n \text{ and } \beta = 0^n; \\ \alpha^Z 0^n, & \text{if } |\alpha| = n \text{ and } \beta = \alpha; \\ \alpha^Z \beta^Z, & \text{if } |\alpha| = |\beta| - 1, \text{ or if } |\alpha| = |\beta| = n \text{ and } \alpha \neq \beta \neq 0^n. \end{cases}$$

a) What is 11001001000011111^Z?

b) True or false: $(\tau^Z)^Z = \tau$ for all binary strings τ.

c) If $f(x_1,\ldots,x_n)$ is a Boolean function with truth table τ, let $f^Z(x_1,\ldots,x_n)$ be the Boolean function whose truth table is τ^Z. Show that the profile of f is almost identical to the z-profile of f^Z, and vice versa. (Therefore Theorem U holds for ZDDs as well as for BDDs, and statistics such as (80) are valid also for z-profiles.)

193. [*M21*] Continuing exercise 192, what is $S_k^Z(x_1,\ldots,x_n)$ when $0 \leq k \leq n$?

194. [*M25*] How many $f(x_1,\ldots,x_n)$ have the z-profile $(1,\ldots,1)$? (See exercise 174.)

195. [*24*] Find $Z(M_2)$, $Z_{\min}(M_2)$, and $Z_{\max}(M_2)$, where M_2 is the 4-way multiplexer.

196. [*M21*] Find a function $f(x_1,\ldots,x_n)$ for which $Z(f) = O(n)$ and $Z(\bar{f}) = \Omega(n^2)$.

197. [*25*] Modify the algorithm of exercise 138 so that it computes the "master z-profile chart" of f. (Then $Z_{\min}(f)$ and $Z_{\max}(f)$ can be found as in exercise 133.)

▶ **198.** [*23*] Explain how to compute $\text{AND}(f, g)$ with ZDDs instead of BDDs (see (55)).

199. [*21*] Similarly, implement (a) $\text{OR}(f, g)$, (b) $\text{XOR}(f, g)$, (c) $\text{BUTNOT}(f, g)$.

200. [*21*] And similarly, implement $\text{MUX}(f, g, h)$ for ZDDs (see (62)).

201. [*22*] The projection functions x_j each have a simple 3-node BDD, but their ZDD representations are more complicated. What's a good way to implement these functions in a general-purpose ZDD toolkit?

202. [*24*] What changes are needed to the swap-in-place algorithm of exercise 147, when levels $\textcircled{u} \leftrightarrow \textcircled{v}$ are being interchanged in a ZDD base instead of a BDD base?

▶ **203.** [*M24*] (*Family algebra.*) The following algebraic conventions are useful for dealing with finite families of finite subsets of positive integers, and with their representation as ZDDs. The simplest such families are the *empty family*, denoted by $\emptyset$ and represented by $\boxed{\perp}$; the *unit family* $\{\emptyset\}$, denoted by ϵ and represented by $\boxed{\top}$; and the *elementary families* $\{\{j\}\}$ for $j \geq 1$, denoted by e_j and represented by a branch node $\textcircled{j}$ with LO $= \boxed{\perp}$ and HI $= \boxed{\top}$. (Exercise 186 illustrates the ZDD for e_3.)

Two families f and g can be combined with the usual set operations:

- The *union* $f \cup g = \{\alpha \mid \alpha \in f \text{ or } \alpha \in g\}$ is implemented by OR(f, g);
- The *intersection* $f \cap g = \{\alpha \mid \alpha \in f \text{ and } \alpha \in g\}$ is implemented by AND(f, g);
- The *difference* $f \setminus g = \{\alpha \mid \alpha \in f \text{ and } \alpha \notin g\}$ is implemented by BUTNOT(f, g);
- The *symmetric difference* $f \oplus g = (f \setminus g) \cup (g \setminus f)$ is implemented by XOR(f, g).

And we also define three new ways to construct families of subsets:

- The *join* $f \sqcup g = \{\alpha \cup \beta \mid \alpha \in f \text{ and } \beta \in g\}$, sometimes written just fg;
- The *meet* $f \sqcap g = \{\alpha \cap \beta \mid \alpha \in f \text{ and } \beta \in g\}$;
- The *delta* $f \boxplus g = \{\alpha \oplus \beta \mid \alpha \in f \text{ and } \beta \in g\}$.

All three are commutative and associative: $f \sqcup g = g \sqcup f$, $f \sqcup (g \sqcup h) = (f \sqcup g) \sqcup h$, etc.

a) Suppose $f = \{\emptyset, \{1, 2\}, \{1, 3\}\} = \epsilon \cup (e_1 \sqcup (e_2 \cup e_3))$ and $g = \{\{1, 2\}, \{3\}\} = (e_1 \sqcup e_2) \cup e_3$. What are $f \sqcup g$ and $(f \sqcap g) \setminus (f \boxplus e_1)$?

b) Any family f can also be regarded as a Boolean function $f(x_1, x_2, \ldots)$, where $\alpha \in f \iff f([1 \in \alpha], [2 \in \alpha], \ldots) = 1$. Describe the operations $\sqcup$, $\sqcap$, and $\boxplus$ in terms of Boolean logical formulas.

c) Which of the following formulas hold for all families f, g, and h? (i) $f \sqcup (g \cup h) = (f \sqcup g) \cup (f \sqcup h)$; (ii) $f \sqcap (g \cup h) = (f \sqcap g) \cup (f \sqcap h)$; (iii) $f \sqcup (g \sqcap h) = (f \sqcup g) \sqcap (f \sqcup h)$; (iv) $f \cup (g \sqcup h) = (f \sqcup g) \sqcup (f \cup h)$; (v) $f \boxplus \emptyset = \emptyset \sqcap g = h \sqcup \emptyset$; (vi) $f \sqcap \epsilon = \epsilon$.

d) We say that f and g are *orthogonal*, written $f \perp g$, if $\alpha \cap \beta = \emptyset$ for all $\alpha \in f$ and all $\beta \in g$. Which of the following statements is true for all families f and g? (i) $f \perp g \iff f \sqcap g = \epsilon$; (ii) $f \perp g \implies |f \sqcup g| = |f||g|$; (iii) $|f \sqcup g| = |f||g| \implies f \perp g$; (iv) $f \perp g \iff f \sqcup g = f \boxplus g$.

e) Describe all families f for which the following statements hold: (i) $f \cup g = g$ for all g; (ii) $f \sqcup g = g$ for all g; (iii) $f \sqcap g = g$ for all g; (iv) $f \sqcup (e_1 \sqcup e_2) = f$; (v) $f \sqcup (e_1 \cup e_2) = f$; (vi) $f \boxplus ((e_1 \sqcup e_2) \cup e_3) = f$; (vii) $f \boxplus f = \epsilon$; (viii) $f \sqcap f = f$.

▶ **204.** [*M25*] Continuing exercise 203, two further operations are also important:

- the *quotient* $f/g = \{\alpha \mid \alpha \cup \beta \in f \text{ and } \alpha \cap \beta = \emptyset, \text{ for all } \beta \in g\}$.
- the *remainder* $f \bmod g = f \setminus (g \sqcup (f/g))$.

The quotient is sometimes also called the "cofactor" of f with respect to g.

a) Prove that $f/(g \cup h) = (f/g) \cap (f/h)$.

b) Suppose $f = \{\{1, 2\}, \{1, 3\}, \{2\}, \{3\}, \{4\}\}$. What are f/e_2 and $f/(f/e_2)$?

c) Simplify the expressions $f/\emptyset$, f/ϵ, f/f, and $(f \bmod g)/g$, for arbitrary f and g.

d) Show that $f/g = f/(f/(f/g))$. *Hint:* Start with the relation $g \subseteq f/(f/g)$.

e) Prove that f/g can also be defined as $\bigcup \{h \mid g \sqcup h \subseteq f \text{ and } g \perp h\}$.

f) Given f and j, show that f has a unique representation $(e_j \sqcup g) \cup h$ with $e_j \perp (g \cup h)$.

g) True or false: $(f \sqcup g) \bmod e_j = (f \bmod e_j) \sqcup (g \bmod e_j)$; $(f \sqcap g)/e_j = (f/e_j) \sqcap (g/e_j)$.

205. [*M25*] Implement the five basic operations of family algebra, namely (a) $f \sqcup g$, (b) $f \sqcap g$, (c) $f \boxplus g$, (d) f/g, and (e) $f \bmod g$, using the conventions of exercise 198.

206. [*M46*] What are the worst-case running times of the algorithms in exercise 205?

▸ **207.** [*M25*] When one or more projection functions x_j are needed in applications, as in exercise 201, the following "symmetrizing" operation turns out to be very handy:

$$(e_{i_1} \cup e_{i_2} \cup \cdots \cup e_{i_l}) \,\S\, k \;=\; S_k(x_{i_1}, x_{i_2}, \ldots, x_{i_l}), \qquad \text{integer } k \geq 0.$$

For example, $e_j \,\S\, 1 = x_j$; $e_j \,\S\, 0 = \bar{x}_j$; $(e_i \cup e_j) \,\S\, 1 = x_i \oplus x_j$; $(e_2 \cup e_3 \cup e_5) \,\S\, 2 = (x_2 \wedge x_3 \wedge \bar{x}_5) \vee (x_2 \wedge \bar{x}_3 \wedge x_5) \vee (\bar{x}_2 \wedge x_3 \wedge x_5)$. Show that it's easy to implement this operation. (Notice that $e_{i_1} \cup \cdots \cup e_{i_l}$ has a very simple ZDD of size $l + 2$, when $l > 0$.)

▸ **208.** [*16*] By modifying Algorithm C, show that all solutions of a Boolean function can readily be counted when its ZDD is given instead of its BDD.

209. [*M21*] Explain how to compute the fully elaborated truth table of a Boolean function from its ZDD representation. (See exercise 31.)

▸ **210.** [*23*] Given the ZDD for f, show how to construct the ZDD for the function

$$g(x) = [f(x) = 1 \text{ and } \nu x = \max\{\nu y \mid f(y) = 1\}].$$

211. [*M20*] When f describes the solutions to an exact cover problem, is $Z(f) \leq B(f)$?

▸ **212.** [*25*] What's a good way to compute the ZDD for an exact cover problem?

213. [*16*] Why can't the mutilated chessboard be perfectly covered with dominoes?

▸ **214.** [*21*] When some shape is covered by dominoes, we say that the covering is *faultfree* if every straight line that passes through the interior of the shape also passes through the interior of some domino. For example, the right-hand covering in (127) is faultfree, but the middle one isn't; and the left-hand one has faults galore.

How many domino coverings of a chessboard are faultfree?

215. [*21*] Japanese tatami mats are 1×2 rectangles that are traditionally used to cover rectangular floors in such a way that no four mats meet at any corner. For example, Fig. 29(a) shows a 6×5 pattern from the 1641 edition of Mitsuyoshi Yoshida's *Jinkōki*, a book first published in 1627.

Find all domino coverings of a chessboard that are also tatami tilings.

Fig. 29. Two nice examples:
(a) A 17th-century tatami tiling;   (a) 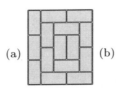   (b)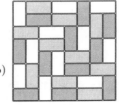
(b) a tricolored domino covering.

▸ **216.** [*30*] Figure 29(b) shows a chessboard covered with red, white, and blue dominoes, in such a way that no two dominoes of the same color are next to each other.

a) In how many ways can this be done?

b) How many of the 12,988,816 domino coverings are 3-colorable?

217. [*29*] The monomino/domino/tromino covering illustrated in (130) happens to satisfy an additional constraint: *No two congruent pieces are adjacent.* How many of the 92 sextillion coverings mentioned in the text are "separated," in this sense?

▸ **218.** [*24*] Apply BDD and ZDD techniques to the problem of Langford pairs, discussed at the beginning of this chapter.

219. [*20*] What is $Z(F)$ when F is the family (a) `WORDS(1000)`; ...; (e) `WORDS(5000)`?

▸ **220.** [*21*] The z-profile of the 5757 SGB words, represented with 130 variables $a_1 \ldots z_5$ as discussed in (131), is (1, 1, 1, ..., 1, 1, 1, 23, 3, ..., 6, 2, 0, 3, 2, 1, 1, 2).

    a) Explain the entries 23 and 3, which correspond to the variables a_2 and b_2.

    b) Explain the final entries 0, 3, 2, 1, 1, 2, which correspond to v_5, w_5, x_5, etc.

▸ **221.** [*M27*] Only 5020 nodes are needed to represent the 5757 most common five-letter words of English, using the 130-variable representation, because of special linguistic properties. But there are $26^5 = 11{,}881{,}376$ possible five-letter words. Suppose we choose 5757 of them at random; how big will the ZDD be then, on average?

▸ **222.** [*27*] When family algebra is applied to five-letter words as in (131), the 130 variables are called a_1, b_1, ..., z_5 instead of x_1, x_2, ..., x_{130}; and the corresponding elementary families are denoted by the symbols a_1, b_1, ..., z_5 instead of e_1, e_2, ..., e_{130}. Thus the family $F = $ `WORDS(5757)` can be constructed by synthesizing the formula

$$F = (\mathsf{w}_1 \sqcup \mathsf{h}_2 \sqcup \mathsf{i}_3 \sqcup \mathsf{c}_4 \sqcup \mathsf{h}_5) \cup \cdots \cup (\mathsf{f}_1 \sqcup \mathsf{u}_2 \sqcup \mathsf{n}_3 \sqcup \mathsf{n}_4 \sqcup \mathsf{y}_5) \cup \cdots \cup (\mathsf{p}_1 \sqcup \mathsf{u}_2 \sqcup \mathsf{p}_3 \sqcup \mathsf{a}_4 \sqcup \mathsf{l}_5).$$

    a) Let $\wp$ denote the *universal family* of all subsets of $\{a_1, \ldots, z_5\}$, also called the "power set." What does the formula $F \sqcap \wp$ signify?

    b) Let $X = X_1 \sqcup \cdots \sqcup X_5$, where $X_j = \{\mathsf{a}_j, \mathsf{b}_j, \ldots, \mathsf{z}_j\}$. Interpret the formula $F \sqcap X$.

    c) Find a simple formula for all words of F that match the pattern `t*u*h`.

    d) Find a formula for all SGB words that contain exactly k vowels, for $0 \le k \le 5$ (considering only a, e, i, o, and u to be vowels). Let $V_j = \mathsf{a}_j \cup \mathsf{e}_j \cup \mathsf{i}_j \cup \mathsf{o}_j \cup \mathsf{u}_j$.

    e) How many patterns in which exactly three letters are specified are matched by at least one SGB word? (For example, `m*tc*` is such a pattern.) Give a formula.

    f) How many of those patterns are matched at least twice (e.g., `*atc*`)?

    g) Express all words that remain words when a 'b' is changed to 'o'.

    h) What's the significance of the formula F/V_2?

    i) Contrast $(X_1 \sqcup V_2 \sqcup V_3 \sqcup V_4 \sqcup X_5) \cap F$ with $(X_1 \sqcup X_5) \setminus ((\wp \setminus F)/(V_2 \sqcup V_3 \sqcup V_4))$.

223. [*28*] A "median word" is a five-letter word $\mu = \mu_1 \ldots \mu_5$ that can be obtained from three words $\alpha = \alpha_1 \ldots \alpha_5$, $\beta = \beta_1 \ldots \beta_5$, $\gamma = \gamma_1 \ldots \gamma_5$ by the rule $[\alpha_i = \mu_i] + [\beta_i = \mu_i] + [\gamma_i = \mu_i] = 2$ for $1 \le i \le 5$. For example, `mixed` is a median of the words $\{$`fixed`, `mixer`, `mound`$\}$, and also of $\{$`mated`, `mixup`, `nixed`$\}$. But `noted` is not a median of $\{$`notes`, `voted`, `naked`$\}$, because each of those words has e in position 4.

    a) Show that $\{d(\alpha, \mu), d(\beta, \mu), d(\gamma, \mu)\}$ is either $\{1, 1, 3\}$ or $\{1, 2, 2\}$ whenever μ is a median of $\{\alpha, \beta, \gamma\}$. (Here d denotes Hamming distance.)

    b) How many medians can be obtained from `WORDS`(n), when $n = 100$? 1000? 5757?

    c) How many of those medians belong to `WORDS`(m), when $m = 100$? 1000? 5757?

▸ **224.** [*20*] Suppose we form the ZDD for all source-to-sink paths in a dag, as in Fig. 28, when the dag happens to be a forest; that is, assume that every non-source vertex of the dag has in-degree 1. Show that the corresponding ZDD is essentially the same as the binary tree that represents the forest under the "natural correspondence between forests and binary trees," Eqs. 2.3.2–(1) through 2.3.2–(3).

▸ **225.** [*30*] Design an algorithm that will produce a ZDD for all sets of edges that form a simple path from s to t, given a graph and two distinct vertices $\{s, t\}$ of the graph.

▸ **226.** [*20*] Modify the algorithm of exercise 225 so that it yields a ZDD for all of the simple *cycles* in a given graph.

227. [*20*] Similarly, modify it so that it considers only *Hamiltonian paths* from s to t.

228. [*21*] And mutate it once more, for Hamiltonian paths from s to *any* other vertex.

229. [*15*] There are 587,218,421,488 paths from CA to ME in the graphs (18), but only 437,525,772,584 such paths in (133). Explain the discrepancy.

230. [*25*] Find the Hamiltonian paths of (133) that have minimum and maximum total length. What is the *average* length, if all Hamiltonian paths are equally likely?

231. [*23*] In how many ways can a king travel from one corner of a chessboard to the opposite corner, never occupying the same cell twice? (These are the simple paths from corner to corner of the graph $P_8 \boxtimes P_8$.)

▶ **232.** [*23*] Continuing exercise 231, a *king's tour* of the chessboard is an oriented Hamiltonian cycle of $P_8 \boxtimes P_8$. Determine the exact number of king's tours. What is the longest possible king's tour, in terms of Euclidean distance traveled?

▶ **233.** [*25*] Design an algorithm that builds a ZDD for the family of all *oriented cycles* of a given digraph. (See exercise 226.)

234. [*22*] Apply the algorithm of exercise 233 to the directed graph on the 49 postal codes AL, AR, ..., WY of (18), with XY ⟶ YZ as in exercise 7–54(b). For example, one such oriented cycle is NC ⟶ CT ⟶ TN ⟶ NC. How many oriented cycles are possible? What are the minimum and maximum cycle lengths?

235. [*22*] Form a digraph on the five-letter words of English by saying that $x \longrightarrow y$ when the last three letters of x match the first three letters of y (e.g., crown ⟶ owner). How many oriented cycles does this digraph have? What are the longest and shortest?

▶ **236.** [*M25*] Many extensions to the family algebra of exercise 203 suggest themselves when ZDDs are applied to combinatorial problems, including the following five operations on families of sets:

- The *maximal elements* $f^\uparrow = \{\alpha \in f \mid \beta \in f \text{ and } \alpha \subseteq \beta \text{ implies } \alpha = \beta\}$;
- The *minimal elements* $f^\downarrow = \{\alpha \in f \mid \beta \in f \text{ and } \alpha \supseteq \beta \text{ implies } \alpha = \beta\}$;
- The *nonsubsets* $f \nearrow g = \{\alpha \in f \mid \beta \in g \text{ implies } \alpha \not\subseteq \beta\}$;
- The *nonsupersets* $f \searrow g = \{\alpha \in f \mid \beta \in g \text{ implies } \alpha \not\supseteq \beta\}$;
- The *minimal hitting sets* $f^\sharp = \{\alpha \mid \beta \in f \text{ implies } \alpha \cap \beta \neq \emptyset\}^\downarrow$.

For example, when f and g are the families of exercise 203(a) we have $f^\uparrow = e_1 \sqcup (e_2 \sqcup e_3)$, $f^\downarrow = \epsilon$, $f^\sharp = \emptyset$, $g^\uparrow = g^\downarrow = g$, $g^\sharp = (e_1 \sqcup e_2) \sqcup e_3$, $f \nearrow g = e_1 \sqcup e_3$, $f \searrow g = \epsilon$, $g \nearrow f = g \searrow f = \emptyset$.

a) Prove that $f \nearrow g = f \setminus (f \sqcap g)$, and give a similar formula for $f \searrow g$.

b) Let $f^C = \{\bar{\alpha} \mid \alpha \in f\} = f \oplus U$, where $U = e_1 \sqcup e_2 \sqcup \cdots$ is the "universal set." Clearly $f^{CC} = f$, $(f \cup g)^C = f^C \cup g^C$, $(f \cap g)^C = f^C \cap g^C$, $(f \setminus g)^C = f^C \setminus g^C$. Show that we also have the duality laws $f^{\uparrow C} = f^{C\downarrow}$, $f^{\downarrow C} = f^{C\uparrow}$; $(f \sqcup g)^C = f^C \sqcap g^C$, $(f \sqcap g)^C = f^C \sqcup g^C$; $(f \nearrow g)^C = f^C \searrow g^C$, $(f \searrow g)^C = f^C \nearrow g^C$; $f^\sharp = (\wp \nearrow f^C)^\downarrow$.

c) True or false? (i) $x_1^\downarrow = e_1$; (ii) $x_1^\uparrow = e_1$; (iii) $x_1^\sharp = e_1$; (iv) $(x_1 \vee x_2)^\downarrow = e_1 \cup e_2$; (v) $(x_1 \wedge x_2)^\downarrow = e_1 \sqcup e_2$.

d) Which of the following formulas hold for all families f, g, and h? (i) $f^{\uparrow\uparrow} = f^\uparrow$; (ii) $f^{\uparrow\downarrow} = f^\downarrow$; (iii) $f^{\uparrow\downarrow} = f^\uparrow$; (iv) $f^{\downarrow\uparrow} = f^\downarrow$; (v) $f^{\sharp\downarrow} = f^\sharp$; (vi) $f^{\sharp\uparrow} = f^\sharp$; (vii) $f^{\downarrow\sharp} = f^\sharp$; (viii) $f^{\uparrow\sharp} = f^\sharp$; (ix) $f^{\sharp\sharp} = f^\sharp$; (x) $f \nearrow (g \cup h) = (f \nearrow g) \cap (f \nearrow h)$; (xi) $f \searrow (g \cup h) = (f \searrow g) \cap (f \searrow h)$; (xii) $f \searrow (g \cup h) = (f \searrow g) \searrow h$; (xiii) $f \nearrow g^\uparrow = f \nearrow g$; (xiv) $f \searrow g^\uparrow = f \searrow g$; (xv) $(f \sqcup g)^\sharp = (f^\sharp \cup g^\sharp)^\downarrow$; (xvi) $(f \cup g)^\sharp = (f^\sharp \sqcup g^\sharp)^\downarrow$.

e) Suppose $g = \bigcup_{u-v}(e_u \sqcup e_v)$ is the family of all edges in a graph, and let f be the family of all the independent sets. Using the operations of extended family algebra, find simple formulas that express (i) f in terms of g; (ii) g in terms of f.

237. [25] Implement the five operations of exercise 236, in the style of exercise 205.

▶ **238.** [22] Use ZDDs to compute the *maximal induced bipartite subgraphs* of the contiguous-USA graph G in (18), namely the maximal subsets U such that $G \mid U$ has no cycles of odd length. How many such sets U exist? Give examples of the smallest and largest. Consider also the maximal induced *tripartite* (3-colorable) subgraphs.

▶ **239.** [21] Explain how to compute the *maximal cliques* of a graph G using family algebra, when G is specified by its edges g as in exercise 236(e). Find the maximal sets of vertices that can be covered by k cliques, for $k = 1, 2, \ldots$, when G is the graph (18).

▶ **240.** [22] A set of vertices U is called a *dominating set* of a graph if every vertex is at most one step away from U.
  a) Prove that every kernel of a graph is a minimal dominating set.
  b) How many minimal dominating sets does the USA graph (18) have?
  c) Find seven vertices of (18) that dominate 36 of the others.

▶ **241.** [28] The *queen graph* Q_8 consists of the 64 squares of a chessboard, with $u \!-\! v$ when squares u and v lie in the same row, column, or diagonal. How large are the ZDDs for its (a) kernels? (b) maximal cliques? (c) minimal dominating sets? (d) minimal dominating sets that are also cliques? (e) maximal induced bipartite subgraphs?
  Illustrate each of these five categories by exhibiting smallest and largest examples.

242. [24] Find all of the maximal ways to choose points on an 8×8 grid so that no three points lie on a straight line of any slope.

243. [M23] The *closure* $f^{\cap}$ of a family f of sets is the family of all sets that can be obtained by intersecting one or more members of f.
  a) Prove that $f^{\cap} = \{\alpha \mid \alpha = \bigcap \{\beta \mid \beta \in f \text{ and } \beta \supseteq \alpha\}\}$.
  b) What's a good way to compute the ZDD for $f^{\cap}$, given the ZDD for f?
  c) Find the generating function for $F^{\cap}$ when $F = \texttt{WORDS(5757)}$ as in exercise 222.

244. [25] What is the ZDD for the connectedness function of $P_3 \square P_3$ (Fig. 22)? What is the BDD for the spanning tree function of the same graph? (See Corollary S.)

▶ **245.** [M22] Show that the *prime clauses* of a monotone function f are $\text{PI}(f)^{\sharp}$.

246. [M21] Prove Theorem S, assuming that (137) is true.

▶ **247.** [M27] Determine the number of sweet Boolean functions of n variables for $n \leq 7$.

248. [M22] True or false: If f and g are sweet, so is $f(x_1, \ldots, x_n) \wedge g(x_1, \ldots, x_n)$.

249. [HM31] The connectedness function of a graph is "ultrasweet," in the sense that it is sweet under all permutations of its variables. Is there a nice way to characterize ultrasweet Boolean functions?

250. [28] There are 7581 monotone Boolean functions $f(x_1, x_2, x_3, x_4, x_5)$. What are the average values of $B(f)$ and $Z(\text{PI}(f))$ when one of them is chosen at random? What is the probability that $Z(\text{PI}(f)) > B(f)$? What is the maximum of $Z(\text{PI}(f))/B(f)$?

251. [M46] Is $Z(\text{PI}(f)) = O(B(f))$ for all monotone Boolean functions f?

252. [M30] When a Boolean function isn't monotone, its prime implicants involve negative literals; for example, the prime implicants of $(x_1? \ x_2 \colon x_3)$ are $x_1 \wedge x_2$, $\bar{x}_1 \wedge x_3$, and $x_2 \wedge x_3$. In such cases we can conveniently represent them with ZDDs if we consider them to be words in the $2n$-letter alphabet $\{e_1, e_1', \ldots, e_n, e_n'\}$. A "subcube" such as $01\!*\!0\!*$ is then $e_1' \sqcup e_2 \sqcup e_4'$ in family algebra (see 7.1.1–(29)); and $\text{PI}(x_1? \ x_2 \colon x_3) = (e_1 \sqcup e_2) \cup (e_1' \sqcup e_3) \cup (e_2 \sqcup e_3)$.

Exercise 7.1.1–116 shows that symmetric functions of n variables might have $\Omega(3^n/n)$ prime implicants. How large can $Z(\mathrm{PI}(f))$ be when f is symmetric?

▶ **253.** [*M26*] Continuing exercise 252, prove that if $f = (\bar{x}_1 \wedge f_0) \vee (x_1 \wedge f_1)$ we have $\mathrm{PI}(f) = A \cup (e'_1 \sqcup B) \cup (e_1 \sqcup C)$, where $A = \mathrm{PI}(f_0 \wedge f_1)$, $B = \mathrm{PI}(f_0) \setminus A$, and $C = \mathrm{PI}(f_2) \setminus A$. (Equation (137) is the special case when f is monotone.)

▶ **254.** [*M23*] Let the functions f and g of (52) be monotone, with $f \subseteq g$. Prove that

$$\mathrm{PI}(g) \setminus \mathrm{PI}(f) = (\mathrm{PI}(g_l) \setminus \mathrm{PI}(f_l)) \cup (\mathrm{PI}(g_h) \setminus \mathrm{PI}(f_h \cup g_l)).$$

▶ **255.** [*25*] A *multifamily* of sets, in which members of f are allowed to occur more than once, can be represented as a sequence of ZDDs $(f_0, f_1, f_2, \dots)$ in which f_k is the family of sets that occur $(\dots a_2 a_1 a_0)_2$ times in f where $a_k = 1$. For example, if α appears exactly $9 = (1001)_2$ times in the multifamily, α would be in f_3 and f_0.

a) Explain how to insert and delete items from this representation of a multifamily.

b) Implement the multiset union $h = f \uplus g$ for multifamilies.

256. [*M32*] Any nonnegative integer x can be represented as family of subsets of the binary powers $U = \{2^{2^k} \mid k \geq 0\} = \{2^1, 2^2, 2^4, 2^8, \dots\}$, in the following way: If $x = 2^{e_1} + \dots + 2^{e_t}$, where $e_1 > \dots > e_t \geq 0$ and $t \geq 0$, the corresponding family has t sets $E_j \subseteq U$, where $2^{e_j} = \prod\{u \mid u \in E_j\}$. Conversely, every finite family of finite subsets of U corresponds in this way to a nonnegative integer x. For example, the number $41 = 2^5 + 2^3 + 1$ corresponds to the family $\{\{2^1, 2^4\}, \{2^1, 2^2\}, \emptyset\}$.

a) Find a simple connection between the binary representation of x and the truth table of the Boolean function that corresponds to the family for x.

b) Let $Z(x)$ be the size of the ZDD for the family that represents x, when the elements of U are tested in reverse order $\dots, 2^4, 2^2, 2^1$ (with highest exponents nearest to the root); for example, $Z(41) = 5$. Show that $Z(x) = O(\log x / \log \log x)$.

c) The integer x is called "sparse" if $Z(x)$ is substantially smaller than the upper bound in (b). Prove that the sum of sparse integers is sparse, in the sense that $Z(x + y) = O(Z(x)Z(y))$.

d) Is the saturating difference of sparse integers, $x \mathbin{\dot-} y$, always sparse?

e) Is the product of sparse integers always sparse?

257. [*40*] (S. Minato.) Explore the use of ZDDs to represent polynomials with nonnegative integer coefficients. *Hint:* Any such polynomial in x, y, and z can be regarded as a family of subsets of $\{2, 2^2, 2^4, \dots, x, x^2, x^4, \dots, y, y^2, y^4, \dots, z, z^2, z^4, \dots\}$; for example, $x^3 + 3xy + 2z$ corresponds naturally to the family $\{\{x, x^2\}, \{x, y\}, \{2, x, y\}, \{2, z\}\}$.

▶ **258.** [*25*] Given a positive integer n, what is the minimum size of a BDD that has exactly n solutions? Answer this question also for a ZDD of minimum size.

▶ **259.** [*25*] A sequence of *parentheses* can be can be encoded as a binary string by letting 0 represent '(' and 1 represent ')'. For example, ())(() is encoded as 011001.

Every forest of n nodes corresponds to a sequence of $2n$ parentheses that are properly *nested*, in the sense that left and right parentheses match in the normal way. (See, for example, 2.3.3–(1) or 7.2.1.6–(1).) Let

$$N_n(x_1, \dots, x_{2n}) = [x_1 \dots x_{2n} \text{ represents properly nested parentheses}].$$

For example, $N_3(0, 1, 1, 0, 0, 1) = 0$ and $N_3(0, 0, 1, 0, 1, 1) = 1$; in general, N_n has $C_n \approx 4^n/(\sqrt{\pi}\,n^{3/2})$ solutions, where C_n is a Catalan number. What are $B(N_n)$ and $Z(N_n)$?

▶ **260.** [*M27*] We will see in Section 7.2.1.5 that every partition of $\{1, \ldots, n\}$ into disjoint subsets corresponds to a "restricted growth sequence" $a_1 \ldots a_n$, which is a sequence of nonnegative integers with

$$a_1 = 0 \quad \text{and} \quad a_{j+1} \leq 1 + \max(a_1, \ldots, a_j) \text{ for } 1 \leq j < n.$$

Elements j and k belong to the same subset of the partition if and only if $a_j = a_k$.

a) Let $x_{j,k} = [a_j = k]$ for $0 \leq k < j \leq n$, and let R_n be the function of these $\binom{n+1}{2}$ variables that is true if and only if $a_1 \ldots a_n$ is a restricted growth sequence. (By studying this Boolean function we can study the family of all set partitions, and by placing further restrictions on R_n we can study set partitions with special properties. There are $\varpi_{100} \approx 5 \times 10^{115}$ set partitions when $n = 100$.) Calculate $B(R_{100})$ and $Z(R_{100})$. Approximately how large are $B(R_n)$ and $Z(R_n)$ as $n \to \infty$?

b) Show that, with a proper ordering of the variables $x_{j,k}$, the BDD base for $\{R_1, \ldots, R_n\}$ has the same number of nodes as the BDD for R_n alone.

c) We can also use fewer variables, approximately $n \lg n$ instead of $\binom{n+1}{2}$, if we represent each a_k as a binary integer with $\lceil \lg k \rceil$ bits. How large are the BDD and ZDD bases in *this* representation of set partitions?

261. [*HM21*] "The deterministic finite-state automaton with fewest states that accepts any given regular language is unique." What is the connection between this famous theorem of automata theory and the theory of binary decision diagrams?

262. [*M26*] The determination of optimum Boolean chains in Section 7.1.2 was greatly accelerated by restricting consideration to Boolean functions that are *normal*, in the sense that $f(0, \ldots, 0) = 0$. (See Eq. 7.1.2–(10).) Similarly, we could restrict BDDs so that each of their nodes denotes a normal function.

a) Explain how to do this by introducing "complement links," which point to the complement of a subfunction instead of to the subfunction itself.

b) Show that every Boolean function has a unique normalized BDD.

c) Draw the normalized BDDs for the 16 functions in exercise 1.

d) Let $B^0(f)$ be the size of the normalized BDD for f. Find the average and worst case of $B^0(f)$, and compare $B^0(f)$ to $B(f)$. (See (80) and Theorem U.)

e) The BDD base for 3×3 multiplication in (58) has $B(F_1, \ldots, F_6) = 52$ nodes. What is $B^0(F_1, \ldots, F_6)$?

f) How do (54) and (55) change, when AND is implemented with complement links?

263. [*HM25*] A *linear block code* is the set of binary column vectors $x = (x_1, \ldots, x_n)^T$ such that $Hx = 0$, where H is a given $m \times n$ "parity check matrix."

a) The linear block code with $n = 2^m - 1$, whose columns are the nonzero binary m-tuples from $(0, \ldots, 0, 1)^T$ to $(1, \ldots, 1, 1)^T$, is called the *Hamming code*. Prove that the Hamming code is 1-error correcting in the sense of exercise 7–23.

b) Let $f(x) = [Hx = 0]$, where H is an $m \times n$ matrix with no all-zero columns. Show that the BDD profile of f has a simple relation to the ranks of submatrices of H mod 2, and compute $B(f)$ for the Hamming code.

c) In general we can let $f(x) = [x \text{ is a codeword}]$ define *any* block code. Suppose some codeword $x = x_1 \ldots x_n$ has been transmitted through a possibly noisy channel, and that we've received the bits $y = y_1 \ldots y_n$, where the channel delivers $y_k = x_k$ with probability p_k for each k independently. Explain how to determine the most likely codeword x, given y, p_1, $\ldots$, p_n, and the BDD for f.

264. [*M46*] The text's "sweeping generalization" of Algorithms B and C, based on (22), embraces many important applications; but it does not appear to include quantities such as

$$\max_{f(x)=1} \left(\sum_{k=1}^{n} w_k x_k + \sum_{k=1}^{n-1} w'_k x_k x_{k+1} \right) \quad \text{or} \quad \max_{f(x)=1} \sum_{j=0}^{n-1} \left(w_j \sum_{k=1}^{n-j} x_k \ldots x_{k+j} \right),$$

which also can be computed efficiently from the BDD or ZDD for f.

Develop a generalization that is even more sweeping.

> We dare not lengthen this book much more,
> lest it be out of due proportion,
> and repel men by its size.
> — ÆLFRIC, *Catholic Homilies II* (c. 1000)

> There are a thousand hacking at the branches of evil
> to one who is striking at the root.
> — HENRY D. THOREAU, *Walden; or, Life in the Woods* (1854)

SECTION 7.1.3

1. These operations interchange the bits of x and y in positions where m is 1. (In particular, if $m = -1$, the step '$y \leftarrow y \oplus (x \,\&\, m)$' becomes just '$y \leftarrow y \oplus x$', and the three assignments will swap $x \leftrightarrow y$ without needing an auxiliary register. H. S. Warren, Jr., has located this trick in vintage-1961 IBM programming course notes.)

2. All three hold when x and y are nonnegative, or if we regard x and y as "unsigned 2-adic integers" in which $0 < 1 < 2 < \cdots < -3 < -2 < -1$. But if negative integers are less than nonnegative integers, (i) fails if and only if $x < 0$ and $y < 0$; (ii) and (iii) fail if and only if $x \oplus y < 0$, namely, if and only if $x < 0$ and $y \geq 0$ or $x \geq 0$ and $y < 0$.

3. Note that $x - y = (x \oplus y) - 2(\bar{x} \,\&\, y)$ (see exercise 93). By removing bits common to x and y at the left, we may assume that $x_{n-1} = 1$ and $y_{n-1} = 0$. Then $2(\bar{x} \,\&\, y) \leq 2((x \oplus y) - 2^{n-1}) = (x \oplus y) - (x \oplus y)^M - 1$.

4. $x^{CN} = x + 1 = x^S$, by (16). Hence $x^{NC} = x^{NCSP} = x^{NCCNP} = x^{NNP} = x^P$.

5. (a) Disproof: Let $x = (\ldots x_2 x_1 x_0)_2$. Then digit l of $x \ll k$ is $x_{l-k}[l \geq k]$. So digit l of the left-hand side is $x_{l-k-j}[l \geq k][l - k \geq j]$, while digit l of the right-hand side is $x_{l-j-k}[l \geq j + k]$. These expressions agree if $j \geq 0$ or $k \leq 0$. But if $j < 0 < k$, they differ when $l = \max(0, j + k)$ and $x_{l-j-k} = 1$.

(We do, however, have $(x \ll j) \ll k \subseteq x \ll (j + k)$ in all cases.)

(b) Proof: Digit l in all three formulas is $x_{l+j}[l \geq -j] \wedge y_{l-k}[l \geq k]$.

6. Since $x \ll y \geq 0$ if and only if $x \geq 0$, we must have $x \geq 0$ if and only if $y \geq 0$. Obviously $x = y$ is always a solution. The solutions with $x > y$ are (a) $x = -1$ and $y = -2$, or $2^y > x > y > 0$; (b) $x = 2$ and $y = 1$, or $2^{-x} \geq -y > -x > 0$.

7. Set $x' \leftarrow (x + \bar{\mu}_0) \oplus \bar{\mu}_0$, where μ_0 is the constant in (47). Then $x' = (\ldots x_2' x_1' x_0')_2$, since $(x' \oplus \bar{\mu}_0) - \bar{\mu}_0 = (\ldots \bar{x}_3 x_2' \bar{x}_1' x_0')_2 - (\ldots 1010)_2 = (\ldots 0 x_2' 0 x_0')_2 - (\ldots x_3' 0 x_1' 0)_2 = x$.

[This is Hack 128 in HAKMEM; see answer 20 below. An alternative formula, $x' \leftarrow (\mu_0 - x) \oplus \mu_0$, has also been suggested by D. P. Agrawal, *IEEE Trans.* **C-29** (1980), 1032–1035. The results are correct modulo 2^n for all n, but overflow or underflow can occur. For example, two's complement binary numbers in an n-bit register range from -2^{n-1} to $2^{n-1} - 1$, inclusive, but negabinary numbers range from $-\frac{2}{3}(2^n - 1)$ to $\frac{1}{3}(2^n - 1)$ when n is even. In general the formula $x' \leftarrow (x + \mu) \oplus \mu$ converts from binary notation to the general number system with binary basis $\langle 2^n (-1)^{m_n} \rangle$ discussed in exercise 4.1–30(c), when $\mu = (\ldots m_2 m_1 m_0)_2$.]

8. First, $x \oplus y \notin (S \oplus y) \cup (x \oplus T)$. Second, suppose that $0 \leq k < x \oplus y$, and let $x \oplus y = (\alpha 1 \alpha')_2$, $k = (\alpha 0 \alpha'')_2$, where α, α', and α'' are strings of 0s and 1s with $|\alpha'| = |\alpha''|$. Assume by symmetry that $x = (\beta 1 \beta')_2$ and $y = (\gamma 0 \gamma')_2$, where $|\alpha| = |\beta| = |\gamma|$. Then $k \oplus y = (\beta 0 \gamma'')_2$ is less than x. Hence $k \oplus y \in S$, and $k = (k \oplus y) \oplus y \in S \oplus y$. [See R. P. Sprague, *Tôhoku Math. J.* **41** (1936), 438–444; P. M. Grundy, *Eureka* **2** (1939), 6–8.]

9. The Sprague–Grundy theorem in the previous exercise shows that two piles of x and y sticks are equivalent in play to a single pile of $x \oplus y$ sticks. (There is a nonnegative integer $k < x \oplus y$ if and only if there either is a nonnegative $i < x$ with $i \oplus y < x \oplus y$ or a nonnegative $j < y$ with $x \oplus j < x \oplus y$.) So the k piles are equivalent to a single pile of size $a_1 \oplus \cdots \oplus a_k$. [See C. L. Bouton, *Annals of Math.* (2) **3** (1901–1902), 35–39.]

10. For clarity and brevity we shall write simply xy for $x \otimes y$ and $x + y$ for $x \oplus y$, *in parts (i) through (iv) of this answer only.*

(i) Clearly $0y = 0$ and $x + y = y + x$ and $xy = yx$. Also $1y = y$, by induction on y.

(ii) If $x \neq x'$ and $y \neq y'$ then $xy + xy' + x'y + x'y' \neq 0$, because the definition of xy says that $xy' + x'y + x'y' < xy$ when $x' < x$ and $y' < y$. In particular, if $x \neq 0$ and

$y \neq 0$ then $xy \neq 0$. Another consequence is that, if $x = \text{mex}(S)$ and $y = \text{mex}(T)$ for arbitrary finite sets S and T, we have $xy = \text{mex}\{xj + iy + ij \mid i \in S, j \in T\}$.

(iii) Consequently, by induction on the (ordinary) sum of x, y, and z, $(x + y)z$ is

$$\text{mex}\{(x + y)z' + (x' + y)z + (x' + y)z', (x + y)z' + (x + y')z + (x + y')z'$$
$$\mid 0 \le x' < x,\ 0 \le y' < y,\ 0 \le z' < z\},$$

which is $\text{mex}\{xz' + x'z + x'z' + yz, xz + yz' + y'z + y'z'\} = xz + yz$. In particular, there's a cancellation law: If $xz = yz$ then $(x + y)z = 0$, so $x = y$ or $z = 0$.

(iv) By a similar induction, $(xy)z = \text{mex}\{(xy)z' + (xy' + x'y + x'y')(z + z')\} = \text{mex}\{(xy)z' + (xy')z + (xy)z' + \cdots\} = \text{mex}\{x(yz') + x(y'z) + x(y'z') + \cdots\} = \text{mex}\{(x + x')(yz' + y'z + y'z') + x'(yz)\} = x(yz)$.

(v) If $0 \le x, y < 2^{2^n}$ we shall prove that $x \otimes y < 2^{2^n}$, $2^{2^n} \otimes y = 2^{2^n}y$, and $2^{2^n} \otimes 2^{2^n} = \frac{3}{2}2^{2^n}$. By the distributive law (iii) it suffices to consider the case $x = 2^a$ and $y = 2^b$ for $0 \le a, b < 2^n$. Let $a = 2^p + a'$ and $b = 2^q + b'$, where $0 \le a' < 2^p$ and $0 \le b' < 2^q$; then $x = 2^{2^p} \otimes 2^{a'}$ and $y = 2^{2^q} \otimes 2^{b'}$, by induction on n.

If $p < n-1$ and $q < n-1$ we've already proved that $x \otimes y < 2^{2^{n-1}}$. If $p < q = n-1$, then $x \otimes 2^{b'} < 2^{2^q}$, hence $x \otimes y < 2^{2^n}$. And if $p = q = n - 1$, we have $x \otimes y = 2^{2^p} \otimes 2^{2^p} \otimes 2^{a'} \otimes 2^{b'} = (\frac{3}{2}2^{2^p}) \otimes z$, where $z < 2^{2^p}$. Thus $x \otimes y < 2^{2^n}$ in all cases.

By the cancellation law, the nonnegative integers less than 2^{2^n} form a subfield. Hence in the formula

$$2^{2^n} \otimes y = \text{mex}\{2^{2^n}y' \oplus x'(y \oplus y') \mid 0 \le x' < 2^{2^n}, 0 \le y' < y\}$$

we can choose x' for each y' to exclude all numbers between $2^{2^n}y'$ and $2^{2^n}(y' + 1) - 1$; but $2^{2^n}y$ is never excluded.

Finally in $2^{2^n} \otimes 2^{2^n} = \text{mex}\{2^{2^n}(x' \oplus y') \oplus (x' \otimes y') \mid 0 \le x', y' < 2^{2^n}\}$, choosing $x' = y'$ will exclude all numbers up to and including $2^{2^n} - 1$, since $x \otimes x = y \otimes y$ implies that $(x \oplus y) \otimes (x \oplus y) = 0$, hence $x = y$. Choosing $x' = y' \oplus 1$ excludes numbers from 2^{2^n} to $\frac{3}{2}2^{2^n} - 1$, since $(x \otimes x) \oplus x = (y \otimes y) \oplus y$ implies that $x = y$ or $x = y \oplus 1$, and since the most significant bit of $x \otimes x$ is the same as that of x. This same observation shows that $\frac{3}{2}2^{2^n}$ is *not* excluded. QED.

Consider, for example, the subfield $\{0, 1, \ldots, 15\}$. By the distributive law we can reduce $x \otimes y$ to a sum of $x \otimes 1$, $x \otimes 2$, $x \otimes 4$, and/or $x \otimes 8$. We have $2 \otimes 2 = 3$, $2 \otimes 4 = 8$, $4 \otimes 4 = 6$; and multiplication by 8 can be done by multiplying first by 2 and then by 4 or vice versa, because $8 = 2 \otimes 4$. Thus $2 \otimes 8 = 12$, $4 \otimes 8 = 11$, $8 \otimes 8 = 13$.

In general, for $n > 0$, let $n = 2^m + r$ where $0 \le r < 2^m$. There is a $2^{m+1} \times 2^{m+1}$ matrix Q_n such that multiplication by 2^n is equivalent to applying Q_n to blocks of 2^{m+1} bits and working mod 2. For example, $Q_1 = \left(\begin{smallmatrix} 1 & 1 \\ 1 & 0 \end{smallmatrix}\right)$, and $(\ldots x_4x_3x_2x_1x_0)_2 \otimes 2^1 = (\ldots y_4y_3y_2y_1y_0)_2$, where $y_0 = x_1$, $y_1 = x_1 \oplus x_0$, $y_2 = x_3$, $y_3 = x_3 \oplus x_2$, $y_4 = x_5$, etc. The matrices are formed recursively as follows: Let $Q_0 = R_0 = (1)$ and

$$Q_{2^m + r} = \begin{pmatrix} I & R_m \\ I & 0 \end{pmatrix} \begin{pmatrix} Q_r & & 0 \\ & \ddots & \\ 0 & & Q_r \end{pmatrix}, \qquad R_{m+1} = \begin{pmatrix} R_m & R_m^2 \\ R_m & 0 \end{pmatrix} = Q_{2^{m+1}-1},$$

where Q_r is replicated enough times to make 2^{m+1} rows and columns. For example,

$$Q_2 = \begin{pmatrix} 1 & 0 & 1 & 1 \\ 0 & 1 & 1 & 0 \\ 1 & 0 & 0 & 0 \\ 0 & 1 & 0 & 0 \end{pmatrix}; \qquad Q_3 = Q_2 \begin{pmatrix} Q_1 & 0 \\ 0 & Q_1 \end{pmatrix} = \begin{pmatrix} 1 & 1 & 0 & 1 \\ 1 & 0 & 1 & 1 \\ 1 & 1 & 0 & 0 \\ 1 & 0 & 0 & 0 \end{pmatrix} = R_2.$$

If register $\mathbf{x}$ holds any 64-bit number, and if $1 \leq j \leq 7$, the MMIX instruction MXOR y,q$_j$,x will compute $\mathbf{y} = \mathbf{x} \otimes 2^j$, given the hexadecimal matrix constants

$$\mathbf{q}_1 = \texttt{c08030200c080302},$$
$$\mathbf{q}_2 = \texttt{b06080400b060804}, \quad \mathbf{q}_4 = \texttt{8d4b2c1880402010}, \quad \mathbf{q}_6 = \texttt{b9678d4bb0608040},$$
$$\mathbf{q}_3 = \texttt{d0b0c0800d0b0c08}, \quad \mathbf{q}_5 = \texttt{c68d342cc0803020}, \quad \mathbf{q}_7 = \texttt{deb9c68dd0b0c080}.$$

[J. H. Conway, *On Numbers and Games* (1976), Chapter 6, shows that these definitions actually yield an algebraically closed field over the ordinal numbers.]

11. Let $m = 2^{a_s} + \cdots + 2^{a_1}$ with $a_s > \cdots > a_1 \geq 0$ and $n = 2^{b_t} + \cdots + 2^{b_1}$ with $b_t > \cdots > b_1 \geq 0$. Then $m \otimes n = mn$ if and only if $(a_s \mid \cdots \mid a_1) \mathbin{\&} (b_t \mid \cdots \mid b_1) = 0$.

12. If $x = 2^{2^n} a + b$ where $0 \leq a, b < 2^{2^n}$, let $x' = x \otimes (x \oplus a)$. Then

$$x' = ((2^{2^n} \otimes a) \oplus b) \otimes ((2^{2^n} \otimes a) \oplus a \oplus b) = (2^{2^n - 1} \otimes a \otimes a) \oplus (b \otimes (a \oplus b)) < 2^{2^n}.$$

To nim-divide by x we can therefore nim-divide by x' and multiply by $x \oplus a$. [This algorithm is due to H. W. Lenstra, Jr.; see *Séminaire de Théorie des Nombres* (Université de Bordeaux, 1977–1978), exposé 11, exercise 5.]

13. If $a_2 \oplus \cdots \oplus a_k = a_1 \oplus a_3 \oplus \cdots \oplus ((k-2) \otimes a_k) = 0$, every move breaks this condition; we can't have $(a \otimes x) \oplus (b \otimes y) = (a \otimes x') \oplus (b \otimes y')$ when $a \neq b$ unless $(x, y) = (x', y')$.

Conversely, if $a_2 \oplus \cdots \oplus a_k \neq 0$ we can reduce some a_j with $j \geq 2$ to make this sum zero; then a_1 can be set to $a_3 \oplus \cdots \oplus ((k - 2) \otimes a_k)$. If $a_2 \oplus \cdots \oplus a_k = 0$ and $a_1 \neq a_3 \oplus \cdots \oplus ((k-2) \otimes a_k)$, we simply reduce a_1 if it is too large. Otherwise there's a $j \geq 3$ such that equality will occur if $(j - 2) \otimes a_j$ is replaced by an appropriate smaller value $((j - 2) \otimes a_j') \oplus ((i - 2) \otimes (a_j \oplus a_j'))$, for some $2 \leq i < j$ and $0 \leq a_j' < a_j$, because of the definition of nim multiplication; hence both of the desired equalities are achieved by setting $a_j \leftarrow a_j'$ and $a_i \leftarrow a_i \oplus a_j \oplus a_j'$. [This game was introduced in *Winning Ways* by Berlekamp, Conway, and Guy, at the end of Chapter 14.]

14. (a) Each $y = (\ldots y_2 y_1 y_0)_2 = x^T$ determines $x = (\ldots x_2 x_1 x_0)_2$ uniquely, since $x_0 = y_0 \oplus t$ and $\lfloor y/2 \rfloor = \lfloor x/2 \rfloor^{T_{x_0}}$.

(b) When $k > 0$, it is a branching function with labels $t_{\alpha a \beta} = a$ for $|\beta| = k - 1$, and $t_\alpha = 0$ for $|\alpha| < k$. But when $k \leq 0$, the mapping is not a permutation; in fact, it sends 2^{-k} different 2-adic integers into 0, when $k < 0$.

[The case $k = 1$ is particularly interesting: Then x^T takes nonnegative integers into nonnegative integers of even parity, negative integers into nonnegative integers of odd parity, and $-1/3 \mapsto -1$. Furthermore $\lfloor x^T/2 \rfloor$ is "Gray binary code," 7.2.1.1–(9).]

(c) If $\rho(x \oplus y) = k$ we have $T(x) \equiv T(y)$ and $x \equiv y + 2^k$ (modulo 2^{k+1}). Hence $\rho(x^T \oplus y^T) = \rho(x \oplus y \oplus T(x) \oplus T(y)) = k$. Conversely, if $\rho(x^T \oplus y^T) = k$ whenever $y = x + 2^k$, we obtain a suitable bit labeling by letting $t_\alpha = (x^T \gg |\alpha|) \bmod 2$ when $x = (\alpha^R)_2$.

(d) This statement follows immediately from (a) and (c). For if we always have $\rho(x \oplus y) = \rho(x^U \oplus y^U) = \rho(x^V \oplus y^V)$, then $\rho(x \oplus y) = \rho(x^U \oplus y^U) = \rho(x^{UV} \oplus y^{UV})$. And if $x^{TU} = x$ for all x, $\rho(x^U \oplus y^U) = \rho(x \oplus y)$ is equivalent to $\rho(x \oplus y) = \rho(x^T \oplus y^T)$.

We can also construct the labelings explicitly: If $W = UV$, note that when $a, b, c \in \{0, 1\}$ we have $W_a = U_a V_{a'}$, $W_{ab} = U_{ab} V_{a'b'}$, and $W_{abc} = U_{abc} V_{a'b'c'}$, where $a' = a \oplus u$, $b' = b \oplus u_a$, $c' = c \oplus u_{ab}$, and so on; hence $w = u \oplus v$, $w_a = u_a \oplus v_{a'}$, $w_{ab} = u_{ab} \oplus v_{a'b'}$, etc. The labeling T inverse to U is obtained by swapping left and right subtrees of all nodes labeled 1; thus $t = u$, $t_{a'} = u_a$, $t_{a'b'} = u_{ab}$, etc.

(e) The explicit constructions in (d) demonstrate that the balance condition is preserved by compositions and inverses, because $\{0', 1'\} = \{0, 1\}$ at each level.

Notes: Hendrik Lenstra observes that branching functions can profitably be viewed as the *isometries* (distance-preserving permutations) of the 2-adic integers, when we use the formula $1/2^{\rho(x \oplus y)}$ to define the "distance" between 2-adic integers x and y. Moreover, the branching functions mod 2^d turn out to be the Sylow 2-subgroup of the group of all permutations of $\{0, 1, \ldots, 2^d - 1\}$, namely the unique (up to isomorphism) subgroup that has maximum power-of-2 order among all subgroups of that group. They also are equivalent to the automorphisms of the complete binary tree with 2^d leaves.

15. Equivalently, $(x + 2a) \oplus b = (x \oplus b) + 2a$; so we might as well find all b and c such that $(x \oplus b) + c = (x + c) \oplus b$. Setting $x = 0$ and $x = -c$ implies that $b + c = b \oplus c$ and $b - c = b \oplus (-c)$; hence $b \,\&\, c = b \,\&\, (-c) = 0$ by (89), and we have $b < 2^{\rho c}$. This condition is also sufficient. Thus $0 \le b < 2^{\rho a + 1}$ is necessary and sufficient for the original problem.

16. (a) If $\rho(x \oplus y) = k$ we have $x \equiv y + 2^k$ (modulo 2^{k+1}); hence $x + a \equiv y + a + 2^k$ and $\rho((x + a) \oplus (y + a)) = k$. And $\rho((x \oplus b) \oplus (y \oplus b))$ is obviously k.

(b) The hinted labeling, call it $P(c)$, has 1s on the path corresponding to c, and 0s elsewhere; thus it is balanced. The general animating function can be written

$$x^{P(c_0)^{-a_1} P(c_1)^{-a_2} \ldots P(c_{m-1})^{-a_m}} \oplus c_m, \qquad \text{where } c_j = b_1 \oplus \cdots \oplus b_j;$$

so it is balanced if and only if $c_m = 0$.

[Incidentally, the set $S = \{P(0)\} \cup \{P(k) \oplus P(k + 2^e) \mid k \ge 0 \text{ and } 2^e > k\}$ provides an interesting *basis* for all possible balanced labelings: A labeling is balanced if and only if it is $\bigoplus \{q \mid q \in Q\}$ for some $Q \subseteq S$. This exclusive-or operation is well defined even though Q might be infinite, because only finitely many 1s appear at each node.]

(c) The function $P(c)$ in (b) has this form, because $x^{P(c)} = x \oplus \lfloor x \oplus c \rfloor$. Its inverse, $x^{S(c)} = ((x \oplus c) + 1) \oplus c$, is $x \oplus \lfloor x \oplus \bar{c} \rfloor = x^{P(\bar{c})}$. Furthermore we have $x^{P(c)P(d)} = x^{P(c)} \oplus \lfloor x^{P(c)} \oplus d \rfloor = x \oplus \lfloor x \oplus c \rfloor \oplus \lfloor x \oplus d^{S(c)} \rfloor$, because $\lfloor x \oplus y \rfloor = \lfloor x^T \oplus y^T \rfloor$ for any branching function x^T. Similarly $x^{P(c)P(d)P(e)} = x \oplus \lfloor x \oplus c \rfloor \oplus \lfloor x \oplus d^{S(c)} \rfloor \oplus \lfloor x \oplus e^{S(d)S(c)} \rfloor$, etc. After discarding equal terms we obtain the desired form. The resulting numbers p_j are unique because they are the only values of x at which the function changes sign.

(d) We have, for example, $x \oplus \lfloor x \oplus a \rfloor \oplus \lfloor x \oplus b \rfloor \oplus \lfloor x \oplus c \rfloor = x^{P(a')P(b')P(c')}$ where $a' = a$, $b' = b^{P(a')}$, and $c' = c^{P(a')P(b')}$.

[The theory of animating functions was developed by J. H. Conway in Chapter 13 of his book *On Numbers and Games* (1976), inspired by previous work of C. P. Welter in *Indagationes Math.* **14** (1952), 304–314; **16** (1954), 194–200.]

17. (Solution by M. Slanina.) Such equations are decidable even if we also allow operations such as $x \,\&\, y$, $\bar{x}$, $x \ll 1$, $x \gg 1$, $2^{\rho x}$, and $2^{\lambda x}$, and even if we allow Boolean combinations of statements and quantifications over integer variables, by translating them into formulas of second-order monadic logic with one successor (S1S). Each 2-adic variable $x = (\ldots x_2 x_1 x_0)_2$ corresponds to an S1S set variable X, where $j \in X$ means $x_j = 1$:

$$
\begin{aligned}
z &= \bar{x} & \text{becomes} \quad & \forall t (t \in Z \Leftrightarrow t \notin X); \\
z &= x \,\&\, y & \text{becomes} \quad & \forall t (t \in Z \Leftrightarrow (t \in X \wedge t \in Y)); \\
z &= 2^{\rho x} & \text{becomes} \quad & \forall t (t \in Z \Leftrightarrow (t \in X \wedge \forall s(s < t \Rightarrow s \notin X))); \\
z &= x + y & \text{becomes} \quad & \exists C \forall t (0 \notin C \wedge (t \in Z \Leftrightarrow (t \in X) \oplus (t \in Y) \oplus (t \in C)) \\
& & & \wedge (t + 1 \in C \Leftrightarrow \langle (t \in X)(t \in Y)(t \in C) \rangle))).
\end{aligned}
$$

An identity such as $x \,\&\, (-x) = 2^{\rho x}$ is equivalent to the translation of

$$\forall X \forall Y \forall Z ((\text{integer}(X) \wedge 0 = x + y \wedge z = x \,\&\, y) \Rightarrow z = 2^{\rho x}),$$

where integer(X) stands for $\exists t \forall s (s > t \Rightarrow (s \in X \Leftrightarrow t \in X))$. We can also include 2-adic constants if they are, say, ratios of integers; for example, $z = \mu_0$ is equivalent to the formula $0 \in Z \wedge \forall t(t \in Z \Leftrightarrow t + 1 \notin Z)$. But of course we cannot include arbitrary (uncomputable) constants.

J. R. Büchi proved that all formulas of S1S are decidable, in *Logic, Methodology, and Philosophy of Science: Proceedings* (Stanford, 1960), 1–11. If we restrict attention to equations, one can show in fact that exponential time suffices.

On the other hand M. Hamburg has shown that the problem would be unsolvable if ρx, λx, or $1 \ll x$ were added to the repertoire; multiplication could then be encoded.

Incidentally, many nontrivial identities exist, even if we use only the operations $x \oplus y$ and $x + 1$. For example, C. P. Welter noticed in 1952 that

$$((x \oplus (y + 1)) + 1) \oplus (x + 1) = ((((x + 1) \oplus y) + 1) \oplus x) + 1.$$

18. Of course row x is entirely blank when x is a multiple of 64. The fine details of this image are apparently "chaotic" and complex, but there is a fairly easy way to understand what happens near the points where the straight lines $x = 64\sqrt{j}$ intersect the hyperbolas $xy = 2^{11}k$, for integers $j, k \geq 1$ that aren't too large.

Indeed, when x and y are integers, the value of $x^2 y \gg 11$ is odd if and only if $x^2 y / 2^{12} \bmod 1 \geq \frac{1}{2}$. Thus, if $x = 64\sqrt{j} + \delta$ and $xy = 2^{11}(k + \epsilon)$ we have

$$\frac{x^2 y}{2^{12}} \bmod 1 = \left(\frac{128\sqrt{j}\delta + \delta^2}{4096}\right) y \bmod 1 = \left(\frac{2\delta x - \delta^2}{4096}\right) y \bmod 1 = \left((k + \epsilon)\delta - \frac{\delta^2 y}{4096}\right) \bmod 1,$$

and this quantity has a known relation to $\frac{1}{2}$ when, say, δ is close to a small integer. [See C. A. Pickover and A. Lakhtakia, *J. Recreational Math.* **21** (1989), 166–169.]

19. (a) When $n = 1$, $f(A, B, C)$ has the same value under all arrangements except when $a_0 \neq a_1$, $b_0 \neq b_1$, and $c_0 \neq c_1$; and then it cannot exceed 1. For larger values of n we argue by induction, assuming that $n = 3$ in order to avoid cumbersome notation. Let $A_0 = (a_0, a_1, a_2, a_3)$, $A_1 = (a_4, a_5, a_6, a_7)$, ..., $C_1 = (c_4, c_5, c_6, c_7)$. Then $f(A, B, C) = \sum_{j \oplus k \oplus l = 0} f(A_j, B_k, C_l) \leq \sum_{j \oplus k \oplus l = 0} f(A_j^*, B_k^*, C_l^*)$ by induction. Thus we can assume that $a_0 \geq a_1 \geq a_2 \geq a_3$, $a_4 \geq a_5 \geq a_6 \geq a_7$, ..., $c_4 \geq c_5 \geq c_6 \geq c_7$. We can also sort the subvectors $A_0' = (a_0, a_1, a_4, a_5)$, $A_1' = (a_2, a_3, a_6, a_7)$, ..., $C_1' = (c_2, c_3, c_6, c_7)$ in a similar way. Finally, we can sort $A_0'' = (a_0, a_1, a_6, a_7)$, $A_1'' = (a_2, a_3, a_4, a_5)$, ..., $C_1'' = (c_2, c_3, c_4, c_5)$, because in each term $a_j b_k c_l$ the number of subscripts $\{j, k, l\}$ with leading bits 01, 10, and 11 must satisfy $s_{01} \equiv s_{10} \equiv s_{11}$ (modulo 2). And these three sorting operations leave A, B, C fully sorted, by exercise 5.3.4–48. (Exactly three sorts on subvectors of length 2^{n-1} are needed, for all $n \geq 2$.)

(b) Suppose $A = A^*$, $B = B^*$, and $C = C^*$. Then we have $a_j = \sum_{t=0}^{2^n-1} \alpha_t [j \leq t]$, where $\alpha_j = a_j - a_{j+1} \geq 0$ and we set $a_{2^n} = 0$; similar formulas hold for b_k and c_l. Let $A_{(p)}$ denote the vector $(a_{p(0)}, \ldots, a_{p(2^n-1)})$ when p is a permutation of $\{0, 1, \ldots, 2^n-1\}$. Then by part (a) we have

$$f(A_{(p)}, B_{(q)}, C_{(r)}) = \sum_{j \oplus k \oplus l = 0} \sum_{t, u, v} \alpha_t \beta_u \gamma_v [p(j) \leq t][q(k) \leq u][r(l) \leq v]$$
$$\leq \sum_{j \oplus k \oplus l = 0} \sum_{t, u, v} \alpha_t \beta_u \gamma_v [j \leq t][k \leq u][l \leq v] = f(A, B, C).$$

[This proof is due to Hardy, Littlewood, and Pólya, *Inequalities* (1934), §10.3.]

(c) The same proof technique extends to any number of vectors. [R. E. A. C. Paley, *Proc. London Math. Soc.* (2) **34** (1932), 263–279, Theorem 15.]

20. The given steps compute the least integer y greater than x such that $\nu y = \nu x$. They're useful for generating all combinations of n objects, taken m at a time (that is, all m-element subsets of an n-element set, with elements represented by 1 bits).

[This tidbit is Hack 175 in HAKMEM, Massachusetts Institute of Technology Artificial Intelligence Laboratory Memo No. 239 (29 February 1972).]

21. Set $t \leftarrow y+1$, $u \leftarrow t \oplus y$, $v \leftarrow t \& y$, $x \leftarrow v - (v \& -v)/(u+1)$. If $y = 2^m - 1$ is the *first* m-combination, these eight operations set x to zero. (The fact that $x = \overline{f(\overline{y})}$ does not seem to yield any shorter scheme.)

22. Sideways addition avoids the division: SUBU t,x,1; ANDN u,x,t; SADD k,t,x; ADDU v,x,u; XOR t,v,x; ADDU k,k,2; SRU t,t,k; ADDU y,v,t. But we can actually save a step by judiciously using the constant mone $= -1$: SUBU t,x,1; XOR u,t,x; ADDU y,x,u; SADD k,t,y; ANDN y,y,u; SLU t,mone,k; ORN y,y,t.

23. (a) $(0\dots01\dots1)_2 = 2^m - 1$ and $(0101\dots01)_2 = (2^{2m} - 1)/3$.

(b) This solution uses the 2-adic constant $\mu_0 = (\dots010101)_2 = -1/3$:

$$t \leftarrow x \oplus \mu_0, \quad u \leftarrow (t-1) \oplus t, \quad v \leftarrow x \mid u, \quad w \leftarrow v+1, \quad y \leftarrow w + \left\lfloor \frac{v \& \overline{w}}{\sqrt{u+1}} \right\rfloor.$$

If $x = (2^{2m} - 1)/3$, the operations produce a strange result because $u = 2^{2m+1} - 1$.

(c) XOR t,x,m0; SUBU u,t,1; XOR u,t,u; OR v,x,u; SADD y,u,m0; ADDU w,v,1; ANDN t,v,w; SRU y,t,y; ADDU y,w,y. [This exercise was inspired by Jörg Arndt.]

24. It's expedient to "prime the pump" by initializing the array to the state that it should have after all multiples of 3, 5, 7, and 11 have been sieved out. We can combine 3 with 11 and 5 with 7, as suggested by E. Wada:

```
      LOC Data_Segment
qbase GREG @ ;N IS 3584 ;n GREG N ;one GREG 1
Q     OCTA #816d129a64b4cb6e                          Q₀ (little-endian)
      LOC Q+N/16
qtop  GREG @                                          End of the Q table
Init  OCTA #9249249249249249|#4008010020040080        Multiples of 3 or 11 in [129..255]
      OCTA #8421084210842108|#0408102040810204        Multiples of 5 or 7
t IS $255 ;x33 IS $0 ;x35 IS $1 ;j IS $4
      LOC #100
Main  LDOU x33,Init; LDOU x35,Init+8
      LDA j,qbase,8; SUB j,j,qtop                     Prepare to set Q₁.
1H    NOR t,x33,x33; ANDN t,t,x35; STOU t,qtop,j      Initialize 64 sieve bits.
      SLU t,x33,2; SRU x33,x33,31; OR x33,x33,t       Prepare for the next 64 values.
      SLU t,x35,6; SRU x35,x35,29; OR x35,x35,t
      ADD j,j,8; PBN j,1B                             Repeat until reaching qtop.
```

Then we cast out nonprimes p^2, $p^2 + 2p$, $\dots$, for $p = 13$, 17, $\dots$, until $p^2 > N$:

```
p IS $0 ;pp IS $1 ;m IS $2 ;mm IS $3 ;q IS $4 ;s IS $5
      LDOU q,qbase,0; LDA pp,qbase,8
      SET p,13; NEG m,13*13,n; SRU q,q,6             Begin with p = 13.
1H    SR m,m,1                                        m ← ⌊(p² − N)/2⌋.
2H    SR mm,m,3; LDOU s,qtop,mm; AND t,m,#3f;
      SLU t,one,t; ANDN s,s,t; STOU s,qtop,mm         Zero out a bit.
      ADD m,m,p; PBN m,2B                             Advance by p bits.
      SRU q,q,1; PBNZ q,3F                            Move to next potential prime.
2H    LDOU q,pp,0; INCL pp,8                          Read in another batch
      OR p,p,#7f; PBNZ q,3F                              of potential primes.
      ADD p,p,2; JMP 2B                               Skip past 128 nonprimes.
2H    SRU q,q,1
3H    ADD p,p,2; PBEV q,2B                            Set p ← p + 2 until p is prime.
      MUL m,p,p; SUB m,m,n; PBN m,1B                  Repeat until p² > N.
```

The running time, $1172\mu + 5166\upsilon$, is of course much less than the time needed for steps P1–P8 of Program 1.3.2′P, namely $10037\mu + 641543\upsilon$ (improved to $10096\mu + 215351\upsilon$ in exercise 1.3.2′–14). [See P. Pritchard, *Science of Computer Programming* **9** (1987), 17–35, for several instructive variations. In practice, a program like this one tends to slow down dramatically when the sieve is too big for the computer's cache. Better results are obtained by working with a segmented sieve, which contains bits for numbers between $N_0 + k\delta$ and $N_0 + (k + 1)\delta$, as suggested by L. J. Lander and T. R. Parkin, *Math. Comp.* **21** (1967), 483–488; C. Bays and R. H. Hudson, *BIT* **17** (1977), 121–127. Here N_0 can be quite large, but δ is limited by the cache size; calculations are done separately for $k = 0, 1, \ldots$. Segmented sieves have become highly developed; see, for example, T. R. Nicely, *Math. Comp.* **68** (1999), 1311–1315, and the references cited there. The author used such a program in 2006 to discover an unusually large gap of length 1370 between 418032645936712127 and the next larger prime.]

25. $(1 + 1 + 25 + 1 + 1 + 25 + 1 + 1 = 56)$ mm; the worm never sees pages 2–500 of Volume 1 or 1–499 of Volume 4. (Unless the books have been placed in little-endian fashion on the bookshelf; then the answer would be 106 mm.) This classic brain-teaser can be found in Sam Loyd's *Cyclopedia* (New York: 1914), pages 327 and 383.

26. We could multiply by $^\#$aa...ab instead of dividing by 12 (see exercise 1.3.1′–17); but multiplication is slow too. Or we could deal with a "flat" sequence of 12000000×5 consecutive bits ($= 7.5$ megabytes), ignoring the boundaries between words. Another possibility is to use a scheme that is neither big-endian nor little-endian but *transposed*: Put item k into octabyte $8(k \bmod 2^{20})$, where it is shifted left by $5\lfloor k/2^{20} \rfloor$. Since $k < 12000000$, the amount of shift is always less than 60. The MMIX code to put item k into register \$1 is AND \$0,k,[#fffff] ; SLU \$0,\$0,3; LDOU \$1,base,\$0; SRU \$0,k,20; 4ADDU \$0,\$0,\$0; SRU \$1,\$1,\$0; AND \$1,\$1,#1f.

[This solution uses 8 large megabytes (2^{23} bytes). *Any* convenient scheme for converting item numbers to octabyte addresses and shift amounts will work, as long as the same method is used consistently. Of course, just 'LDBU \$1,base,k' would be faster.]

27. (a) $((x{-}1) \oplus x) + x$. [This exercise is based on an idea of Luther Woodrum, who noticed that $((x{-}1)\,|\,x) + 1 = (x \mathbin{\&} -x) + x$.]

   (b) $(y + x)\,|\,y$, where $y = (x{-}1) \oplus x$.

   (c,d,e) $((z \oplus x) + x) \mathbin{\&} z$, $((z \oplus x) + x) \oplus z$, and $\overline{((z \oplus x) + x)} \mathbin{\&} z$, where $z = x{-}1$.

   (f) $x \oplus (\text{a})$; alternatively, $t \oplus (t{+}1)$, where $t = x\,|\,(x{-}1)$. [The number $(0^\infty 01^a 11^b)_2$ looks simpler, but it apparently requires *five* operations: $((t + 1) \mathbin{\&} \bar{t}) - 1$.]

   These constructions all give sensible results in the exceptional cases when $x = -2^b$.

28. A 1 bit indicates x's rightmost 0 (for example, $(101011)_2 \mapsto (000100)_2$); $-1 \mapsto 0$.

29. $\mu_k = \mu_{k+1} \oplus (\mu_{k+1} \ll 2^k)$ [see *STOC* **6** (1974), 125]. This relation holds also for the constants $\mu_{d,k}$ of (48), when $0 \le k < d$, if we start with $\mu_{d,d} = 2^{2^d} - 1$. (There is, however, no easy way to go from μ_k to μ_{k+1}, unless we use the "zip" operation; see (77).)

30. Append 'CSZ rho,x,64' to (50), thereby adding 1υ to its execution time; or replace the last two lines by SRU t,y,rho; SLU t,t,2; SRU t,[#300020104],t; AND t,t,#f; ADD rho,rho,t, saving 1υ. For (51), we simply need to make sure that *rhotab*[0] = 8.

31. In the first place, his code loops forever when $x = 0$. But even after that bug is patched, his assumption that x is a random integer is highly questionable. In many applications when we want to compute ρx for a nonzero 64-bit number x, a more reasonable assumption would be that each of the outcomes $\{0, 1, \ldots, 63\}$ is equally likely. The average and standard deviation then become 31.5 and ≈ 18.5.

32. 'NEGU y,x; AND y,x,y; MULU y,debruijn,y; SRU y,y,58; LDB rho,decode,y' has estimated cost $\mu + 14v$, although multiplication by a power of 2 might well be faster than a typical multiplication. Add $1v$ for the correction in answer 30.

33. In fact, an exhaustive calculation shows that exactly 94727 suitable constants a yield a "perfect hash function" for this problem, 90970 of which also identify the power-of-two cases $y = 2^j$; 90918 of those also distinguish the case $y = 0$. The multiplier $^\#$208b2430c8c82129 is uniquely best, in the sense that it doesn't need to refer to table entries above $decode[32400]$ when y is known to be a valid input.

34. Identity (a) fails when $x = 5$, $y = 6$; but (b) is true, also when $xy = 0$. Proof of (c): If $x \neq y$ and $\rho x = \rho y = k$ we have $x = \alpha 10^k$ and $y = \beta 10^k$; hence $x \oplus y = (\alpha \oplus \beta)00^k = (x-1) \oplus (y-1)$. If $\rho x > \rho y = k$ we have $(x \oplus y) \bmod 2^{k+2} \neq ((x-1) \oplus (y-1)) \bmod 2^{k+2}$.

35. Let $f(x) = x \oplus 3x$. Clearly $f(2x) = 2f(x)$, and $f(4x + 1) = 4f(x) + 2$. We also have $f(4x - 1) = 4f(x) + 2$, by exercise 34(c). The hinted identity follows.

Given n, set $u \leftarrow n \gg 1$, $v \leftarrow u + n$, $t \leftarrow u \oplus v$, $n^+ \leftarrow v \mathbin{\&} t$, and $n^- \leftarrow u \mathbin{\&} t$. Clearly $u = \lfloor n/2 \rfloor$ and $v = \lfloor 3n/2 \rfloor$, so $n^+ - n^- = v - u = n$. And this is Reitwiesner's representation, because $n^+ \,|\, n^-$ has no consecutive 1s. [H. Prodinger, *Integers* **0** (2000), paper a8, 14 pp. Incidentally we also have $f(-x) = f(x)$.]

36. (i) The commands $x \leftarrow x \oplus (x \ll 1)$, $x \leftarrow x \oplus (x \ll 2)$, $x \leftarrow x \oplus (x \ll 4)$, $x \leftarrow x \oplus (x \ll 8)$, $x \leftarrow x \oplus (x \ll 16)$, $x \leftarrow x \oplus (x \ll 32)$ change x to $x^\oplus$. (ii) $x^\& = x \mathbin{\&} \sim(x + 1)$.
(See exercises 66, 70, and 117 for applications of $x^\oplus$; see also exercise 209.)

37. Insert 'CSZ y,x,half' after the FLOTU in (55), where half $= {}^\#$3fe0000000000000; note that (55) says 'SR' (not 'SRU'). No change is needed to (56), if $lamtab[0] = -1$.

38. 'SRU t,x,1; OR y,x,t; SRU t,y,2; OR y,y,t; SRU t,y,4; OR y,y,t; ...; SRU t,y,32; OR y,y,t; SRU y,y,1; CMPU t,x,0; ADDU y,y,t' takes $15v$.

39. (Solution by H. S. Warren, Jr.) Let $\sigma(x)$ denote the result of smearing x to the right, as in the first line of (57). Compute $x \mathbin{\&} \sigma((x \gg 1) \mathbin{\&} \bar{x})$.

40. Suppose $\lambda x = \lambda y = k$. If $x = y = 0$, (58) certainly holds, regardless of how we define $\lambda 0$. Otherwise $x = (1\alpha)_2$ and $y = (1\beta)_2$, for some binary strings α and β with $|\alpha| = |\beta| = k$; and $x \oplus y < 2^k \leq x \mathbin{\&} y$. On the other hand if $\lambda x < \lambda y = k$, we have $x \oplus y \geq 2^k > x \mathbin{\&} y$. And H. S. Warren, Jr., notes that $\lambda x < \lambda y$ if and only if $x < y \mathbin{\&} \bar{x}$.

41. (a) $\sum_{n=1}^{\infty} (\rho n) z^n = \sum_{k=1}^{\infty} z^{2^k}/(1 - z^{2^k}) = z/(1-z) - \sum_{k=0}^{\infty} z^{2^k}/(1 + z^{2^k})$. The Dirichlet generating function is simpler: $\sum_{n=1}^{\infty} (\rho n)/n^z = \zeta(z)/(2^z - 1)$.
(b) $\sum_{n=1}^{\infty} (\lambda n) z^n = \sum_{k=1}^{\infty} z^{2^k}/(1 - z)$.
(c) $\sum_{n=1}^{\infty} (\nu n) z^n = \sum_{k=0}^{\infty} z^{2^k}/((1 - z)(1 + z^{2^k})) = \sum_{k=0}^{\infty} z^{2^k} \mu_k(z)$, where $\mu_k(z) = (1 + z + \cdots + z^{2^k - 1})/(1 - z^{2^{k+1}})$. (The "magic masks" of (47) correspond to $\mu_k(2)$.)
[See *Automatic Sequences* by J.-P. Allouche and J. Shallit (2003), Chapter 3, for further information about the functions ρ and ν, which they denote by ν_2 and s_2.]

42. $e_1 2^{e_1 - 1} + (e_2 + 2)2^{e_2 - 1} + \cdots + (e_r + 2r - 2)2^{e_r - 1}$, by induction on r. [D. E. Knuth, *Proc. IFIP Congress* (1971), **1**, 19–27. The fractal aspects of this sum are illustrated in Figs. 3.1 and 3.2 of the book by Allouche and Shallit.] Consider also $S_n'(1)$ where

$$S_n(z) = \sum_{k=0}^{n-1} z^{\nu k} = (1 + z)^{e_1} + z(1 + z)^{e_2} + \cdots + z^{r-1}(1 + z)^{e_r}.$$

43. The straightforward implementation of (63), 'SET nu,0; SET y,x; BZ y,Done; 1H ADD nu,nu,1; SUBU t,y,1; AND y,y,t; PBNZ y,1B' costs $(5 + 4\nu x)v$; it beats the implementation of (62) when $\nu x < 4$, ties when $\nu x = 4$, and loses when $\nu x > 4$.

But we can save $4v$ from the implementation of (62) if we replace the final multiplication-and-shift by '$y \leftarrow y + (y \gg 8)$, $y \leftarrow y + (y \gg 16)$, $y \leftarrow y + (y \gg 32)$, $\nu \leftarrow y \mathbin{\&} {}^\#\mathtt{ff}$'. [Of course, MMIX's single instruction 'SADD nu,x,0' is much better.]

44. Let this sum be $\nu^{(2)}x$. If we can solve the problem for 2^d-bit numbers, we can solve it for 2^{d+1}-bit numbers, because $\nu^{(2)}(2^{2^d}x+x') = \nu^{(2)}x+\nu^{(2)}x'+2^d\nu x$. Therefore a solution analogous to (62) suggests itself, on a 64-bit machine:

Set $z \leftarrow (x \gg 1) \mathbin{\&} \mu_0$ and $y \leftarrow x - z$.
Set $z \leftarrow ((z + (z \gg 2)) \mathbin{\&} \mu_1) + ((y \mathbin{\&} \bar{\mu}_1) \gg 1)$ and $y \leftarrow (y \mathbin{\&} \mu_1) + ((y \gg 2) \mathbin{\&} \mu_1)$.
Set $z \leftarrow ((z + (z \gg 4)) \mathbin{\&} \mu_2) + ((y \mathbin{\&} \bar{\mu}_2) \gg 2)$ and $y \leftarrow (y + (y \gg 4)) \mathbin{\&} \mu_2$.
Finally $\nu^{(2)} \leftarrow (((Az) \bmod 2^{64}) \gg 56) + ((((By) \bmod 2^{64}) \gg 56) \ll 3)$,
    where $A = (11111111)_{256}$ and $B = (01234567)_{256}$.

But another approach is better on MMIX, which has sideways addition built in:

SADD nu2,x,m0	SADD t,x,m2	8ADDU nu2,t,nu2	SADD t,x,m5
SADD t,x,m1	4ADDU nu2,t,nu2	SADD t,x,m4	SLU t,t,5
2ADDU nu2,t,nu2	SADD t,x,m3	16ADDU nu2,t,nu2	ADD nu2,nu2,t

[In general, $\nu^{(2)}x = \sum_k 2^k \nu(x \mathbin{\&} \bar{\mu}_k)$. See *Dr. Dobb's Journal* **8**, 4 (April 1983), 24–37.]

45. Let $d = (x - y) \mathbin{\&} (y - x)$; test if $d \mathbin{\&} y \neq 0$. [Rokicki found that this idea, which is called *colex ordering*, can be used with node addresses to near-randomize binary search trees or Cartesian trees as if they were treaps, without needing an additional random "priority key" in each node. See *U.S. Patent 6347318* (12 February 2002).]

46. SADD t,x,m; NXOR y,x,m; CSOD x,t,y; the mask m is ~(1<<i|1<<j). (In general, these instructions complement the bits specified by $\bar{m}$ if those bits have odd parity.)

47. $y \leftarrow (x \gg \delta) \mathbin{\&} \theta$, $z \leftarrow (x \mathbin{\&} \theta) \ll \delta$, $x \leftarrow (x \mathbin{\&} m) \mid y \mid z$, where $\bar{m} = \theta \mid (\theta \ll \delta)$.

48. Given δ, there are $s_\delta = \prod_{j=0}^{\delta-1} F_{\lfloor(n+j)/\delta\rfloor+1}$ different δ-swaps, including the identity permutation. (See exercise 4.5.3–32.) Summing over δ gives $1+\sum_{\delta=1}^{n-1}(s_\delta-1)$ altogether.

49. (a) The set $S = \{a_1\delta_1+\cdots+a_m\delta_m \mid \{a_1,\ldots,a_m\} \subseteq \{-1,0,+1\}\}$ for displacements $\delta_1,\ldots,\delta_m$ must contain $\{n-1,n-3,\ldots,1-n\}$, because the kth bit must be exchanged with the $(n+1-k)$th bit for $1 \leq k \leq n$. Hence $|S| \geq n$. And S contains at most 3^m numbers, at most $2 \cdot 3^{m-1}$ of which are odd.

(b) Clearly $s(mn) \leq s(m) + s(n)$, because we can reverse m fields of n bits each. Thus $s(3^m) \leq m$ and $s(2 \cdot 3^m) \leq m + 1$. Furthermore the reversal of 3^m bits uses only δ-swaps with even values of δ; the corresponding $(\delta/2)$-swaps prove that we have $s((3^m \pm 1)/2) \leq m$. These upper bounds match the lower bounds of (a) when $m > 1$.

(c) The string $\alpha a\beta\theta\psi z\omega$ with $|\alpha| = |\beta| = |\theta| = |\psi| = |\omega| = n$ can be changed to $\omega z\psi\theta\beta a\alpha$ with a $(3n+1)$-swap followed by an $(n+1)$-swap. Then $s(n)$ further swaps reverse all. Hence $s(32) \leq s(6) + 2 = 4$, and $s(64) \leq 5$. Again, equality holds by (a). Incidentally, $s(63) = 4$ because $s(7) = s(9) = 2$. The lower bound in (a) turns out to be the exact value of $s(n)$ for $1 \leq n \leq 22$, except that $s(16) = 4$.

50. Express $n = (t_m \ldots t_1 t_0)_3$ in balanced ternary notation. Let $n_j = (t_m \ldots t_j)_3$ and $\delta_j = 2n_j + t_{j-1}$, so that $n_{j-1} - \delta_j = n_j$ and $2\delta_j - n_{j-1} = n_j + t_{j-1}$ for $1 \leq j \leq m$. Let $E_0 = \{0\}$ and $E_{j+1} = E_j \cup \{t_j - x \mid x \in E_j\}$ for $0 \leq j < m$. (Thus, for example, $E_1 = \{0,t_0\}$ and $E_2 = \{0,t_0,t_1,t_1 - t_0\}$.) Notice that $\varepsilon \in E_j$ implies $|\varepsilon| \leq j$.

Assume by induction on j that δ-swaps for $\delta = \delta_1, \ldots, \delta_j$ have changed the n-bit word $\alpha_1 \ldots \alpha_{3j}$ to $\alpha_{3j} \ldots \alpha_1$, where each subword α_k has length $n_j+\varepsilon_k$ for some $\varepsilon_k \in E_j$. If $n_{j+1} > j$, a δ_{j+1}-swap within each subword will preserve this assumption. Otherwise each subword α_k has $|\alpha_k| \le n_j + j \le 3n_{j+1} + 1 + j \le 4j + 1 < 4m$. Therefore 2^k-swaps for $\lfloor \lg 4m \rfloor \ge k \ge 0$ will reverse them all. (Note that a 2^k-swap on a subword of size t, where $2^k < t \le 2^{k+1}$, reduces it to three subwords of sizes $t - 2^k$, $2^{k+1} - t$, $t - 2^k$.)

51. (a) If $c = (c_{d-1} \dots c_0)_2$, we must have $\theta_{d-1} = c_{d-1}\mu_{d,d-1}$. But for $0 \le k < d - 1$ we can take $\theta_k = c_k\mu_{d,k} \oplus \hat{\theta}_k$, where $\hat{\theta}_k$ is *any* mask $\subseteq \mu_{d,k}$.

(b) Let $\Theta(d, c)$ be the set of all such mask sequences. Clearly $\Theta(1, c) = \{c\}$. When $d > 1$ we will have, recursively,

$$\Theta(d, c) = \{(\theta_0, \dots, \theta_{d-2}, \theta_{d-1}, \hat{\theta}_{d-2}, \dots, \hat{\theta}_0) \mid \theta_k = \theta'_{k-1} \ddagger \theta''_{k-1}, \ \hat{\theta}_k = \hat{\theta}'_{k-1} \ddagger \hat{\theta}''_{k-1}\},$$

by "zipping together" two sequences $(\theta'_0, \dots, \theta'_{d-3}, \theta'_{d-2}, \hat{\theta}'_{d-3}, \dots, \hat{\theta}'_0) \in \Theta(d-1, c')$ and $(\theta''_0, \dots, \theta''_{d-3}, \theta''_{d-2}, \hat{\theta}''_{d-3}, \dots, \hat{\theta}''_0) \in \Theta(d-1, c'')$ for some appropriate θ_0, $\hat{\theta}_0$, c', and c''.

When c is odd, the bigraph corresponding to (75) has only one cycle; so $(\theta_0, \hat{\theta}_0, c', c'')$ is either $(\mu_{d,0}, 0, \lceil c/2 \rceil, \lfloor c/2 \rfloor)$ or $(0, \mu_{d,0}, \lfloor c/2 \rfloor, \lceil c/2 \rceil)$. But when c is even, the bigraph has 2^{d-1} double bonds; so $\theta_0 = \hat{\theta}_0$ is any mask $\subseteq \mu_{d,0}$, and $c' = c'' = c/2$. [Incidentally, $\lg |\Theta(d,c)| = 2^{d-1}(d-1) - \sum_{k=1}^{d-1}(2^{d-k} - 1)(2^{k-1} - |2^{k-1} - c \bmod 2^k|)$.]

In both cases we can therefore let $\hat{\theta}_{d-2} = \dots = \hat{\theta}_0 = 0$ and omit the second half of (71) entirely. Of course in case (b) we would also do the cyclic shift directly, instead of using (71) at all. But exercise 58 proves that many other useful permutations, such as selective reversal followed by cyclic shift, can also be handled by (71) with $\hat{\theta}_k = 0$ for all k. The *inverses* of those permutations can be handled with $\theta_k = 0$ for $0 \le k < d - 1$.

52. The following solutions make $\hat{\theta}_j = 0$ whenever possible. We shall express the θ masks in terms of the μ's, for example by writing $\mu_{6,5} \ \& \ \mu_0$ instead of stating the requested hexadecimal form $^\#55555555$; the μ form is shorter and more instructive.

(a) $\theta_k = \mu_{6,k} \ \& \ \mu_5$ and $\hat{\theta}_k = \mu_{6,k} \ \& \ (\mu_{k+1} \oplus \mu_{k-1})$ for $0 \le k < 5$; $\theta_5 = \theta_4$. (Here $\mu_{-1} = 0$. To get the "other" perfect shuffle, $(x_{31}x_{63} \dots x_1 x_{33} x_0 x_{32})_2$, let $\hat{\theta}_0 = \mu_{6,0} \& \bar{\mu}_1$.)

(b) $\theta_0 = \theta_3 = \hat{\theta}_0 = \mu_{6,0} \ \& \ \mu_3$; $\theta_1 = \theta_4 = \hat{\theta}_1 = \mu_{6,1} \ \& \ \mu_4$; $\theta_2 = \theta_5 = \hat{\theta}_2 = \mu_{6,2} \ \& \ \mu_5$; $\hat{\theta}_3 = \hat{\theta}_4 = 0$. [See J. Lenfant, *IEEE Trans.* **C-27** (1978), 637–647, for a general theory.]

(c) $\theta_0 = \mu_{6,0} \ \& \ \mu_4$; $\theta_1 = \mu_{6,1} \ \& \ \mu_5$; $\theta_2 = \theta_4 = \mu_{6,2} \ \& \ \mu_4$; $\theta_3 = \theta_5 = \mu_{6,3} \ \& \ \mu_5$; $\hat{\theta}_0 = \mu_{6,0} \ \& \ \mu_2$; $\hat{\theta}_1 = \mu_{6,1} \ \& \ \mu_3$; $\hat{\theta}_2 = \hat{\theta}_0 \oplus \theta_2$; $\hat{\theta}_3 = \hat{\theta}_1 \oplus \theta_3$; $\hat{\theta}_4 = 0$.

(d) $\theta_k = \mu_{6,k} \ \& \ \mu_{5-k}$ for $0 \le k \le 5$; $\hat{\theta}_k = \theta_k$ for $0 \le k \le 2$; $\hat{\theta}_3 = \hat{\theta}_4 = 0$.

53. We can write ψ as a product of $d - t$ transpositions, $(u_1 v_1) \dots (u_{d-t} v_{d-t})$ (see exercise 5.2.2–2). The permutation induced by a single transposition (uv) on the index digits, when $u < v$, corresponds to a $(2^v - 2^u)$-swap with mask $\mu_{d,v} \ \& \ \bar{\mu}_u$. We should do such a swap for $(u_1 v_1)$ first, $\dots$, $(u_{d-1} v_{d-1})$ last.

In particular, the perfect shuffle in a 2^d-bit register corresponds to the case where $\psi = (01 \dots (d-1))$ is a one-cycle; so it can be achieved by doing such $(2^v - 2^u)$-swaps for $(u, v) = (0, 1)$, $\dots$, $(0, d-1)$. For example, when $d = 3$ the two-step procedure is $12345678 \mapsto 13245768 \mapsto 15263748$. [Guy Steele suggests an alternative $(d-1)$-step procedure: We can do a 2^k-swap with mask $\mu_{d,k+1} \ \& \ \bar{\mu}_k$ for $d-1 > k \ge 0$. When $d = 3$ his method takes $12345678 \mapsto 12563478 \mapsto 15263748$.]

The matrix transposition in exercise 52(b) corresponds to $d = 6$ and $(u, v) = (0, 3)$, $(1, 4)$, $(2, 5)$. These operations are the 7-swap, 14-swap, and 28-swap steps for 8×8 matrix transposition illustrated in the text; they can be done in any order.

For exercise 52(c), use $d = 6$ and $(u, v) = (0, 2)$, $(1, 3)$, $(0, 4)$, $(1, 5)$. Exercise 52(d) is as easy as 52(b), with $(u, v) = (0, 5)$, $(1, 4)$, $(2, 3)$.

54. Transposition amounts to reversing the bits of the minor diagonals. Successive elements of those diagonals are $m - 1$ apart in the register. Simultaneous reversal of all diagonals corresponds to simultaneous reversal of subwords of sizes $1, \ldots, m$, which can be done with 2^k-swaps for $0 \le k < \lceil \lg m \rceil$ (because such transposition is easy when m is a power of 2, as illustrated in the text). Here's the procedure for $m = 7$:

Given	6-swap	12-swap	24-swap
00 01 02 03 04 05 06	00 **10** 02 **12** 04 **14** 06	00 10 **20 30** 04 14 **24**	00 10 20 30 **40 50 60**
10 11 12 13 14 15 16	**01** 11 **03** 13 **05** 15 **25**	01 11 **21 31** 05 15 25	01 11 21 31 **41 51 61**
20 21 22 23 24 25 26	20 **30** 22 **32** 24 **16** 26	**02 12** 22 32 **06** 16 26	02 12 22 32 **42 52 62**
30 31 32 33 34 35 36	**21** 31 **23** 33 **43** 35 **45**	**03 13** 23 33 43 **53 63**	03 13 23 33 43 53 63
40 41 42 43 44 45 46	40 **50** 42 **34** 44 **36** 46	40 50 **60** 34 44 **54 64**	**04 14 24** 34 44 54 64
50 51 52 53 54 55 56	**41** 51 **61** 53 **63** 55 **65**	41 51 61 **35 45** 55 65	**05 15 25** 35 45 55 65
60 61 62 63 64 65 66	60 **52** 62 **54** 64 **56** 66	**42** 52 62 **36 46** 56 66	**06 16 26** 36 46 56 66

55. Given x and y, first set $x \leftarrow x \mid (x \ll 2^k)$ and $y \leftarrow y \mid (y \ll 2^k)$ for $2d \le k < 3d$. Then set $x \leftarrow (2^{2d+k} - 2^k)$-swap of x with mask $\mu_{2d+k} \& \bar{\mu}_k$ and $y \leftarrow (2^{2d+k} - 2^{d+k})$-swap of y with mask $\mu_{2d+k} \& \bar{\mu}_{d+k}$ for $0 \le k < d$. Finally set $z \leftarrow x \& y$, then either $z \leftarrow z \mid (z \gg 2^k)$ or $z \leftarrow z \oplus (z \gg 2^k)$ for $2d \le k < 3d$, and $z \leftarrow z \& (2^{n^2} - 1)$. [The idea is to form two $n \times n \times n$ arrays $x = (x_{000} \ldots x_{(n-1)(n-1)(n-1)})_2$ and $y = (y_{000} \ldots y_{(n-1)(n-1)(n-1)})_2$ with $x_{ijk} = a_{jk}$ and $y_{ijk} = b_{jk}$, then transpose coordinates so that $x_{ijk} = a_{ji}$ and $y_{ijk} = b_{ik}$; now $x \& y$ does all n^3 bitwise multiplications at once. This method is due to V. R. Pratt and L. J. Stockmeyer, *J. Computer and System Sci.* **12** (1976), 210–213.]

56. Use (71) with $\theta_0 = \hat{\theta}_0 = 0$, $\theta_1 = {}^\#\text{0010201122113231}$, $\theta_2 = {}^\#\text{00080e0400080c06}$, $\theta_3 = {}^\#\text{00000092008100a2}$, $\theta_4 = {}^\#\text{0000000000000f16}$, $\theta_5 = {}^\#\text{0000000003199c26}$, $\hat{\theta}_4 = {}^\#\text{00000c9f0000901a}$, $\hat{\theta}_3 = {}^\#\text{003a00b50015002b}$, $\hat{\theta}_2 = {}^\#\text{000103080c0d0f0c}$, and $\hat{\theta}_1 = {}^\#\text{0020032033233333}$.

57. The two choices for each cycle when $d > 1$ have complementary settings. So we can choose a setting in which at least half of the crossbars are inactive, except in the middle column. (See exercise 5.3.4–55 for more about permutation networks.)

58. (a) Every different setting of the crossbars gives a different permutation, because there is exactly one path from input line i to output line j for all $0 \le i, j < N$. (A network with that property is called a "banyan.") The unique such path carries input i on line $l(i, j, k) = ((i \gg k) \ll k) + (j \bmod 2^k)$ after k swapping steps have been made.

(b) We have $l(i\varphi, i, k) = l(j\varphi, j, k)$ if and only if $i \bmod 2^k = j \bmod 2^k$ and $i\varphi \gg k = j\varphi \gg k$; so $(*)$ is necessary. And it is also sufficient, because a mapping φ that satisfies $(*)$ can always be routed in such a way that $j\varphi$ appears on line $l = l(j\varphi, j, k)$ after k steps: If $k > 1$, $j\varphi$ will appear on line $l(j\varphi, j, k - 1)$, which is one of the inputs to l. Condition $(*)$ says that we can route it to l without conflict, even if l is $l(i\varphi, i, k)$. [In *IEEE Transactions* **C-24** (1975), 1145–1155, Duncan Lawrie proved that condition $(*)$ is necessary and sufficient for an arbitrary *mapping* φ of the set $\{0, 1, \ldots, N-1\}$ into itself, when the crossbar modules are allowed to be general 2×2 mapping modules as in exercise 75. Furthermore the mapping φ might be only partially specified, with $j\varphi = *$ ("wild card" or "don't-care") for some values of j. The proof that appears in the previous paragraph actually demonstrates Lawrie's more general theorem.]

(c) $i \bmod 2^k = j \bmod 2^k$ if and only if $k \le \rho(i \oplus j)$; $i \gg k = j \gg k$ if and only if $k > \lambda(i \oplus j)$; and $i\varphi = j\varphi$ if and only if $i = j$, when φ is a permutation.

(d) $\lambda(i\varphi \oplus j\varphi) \ge \rho(i \oplus j)$ for all $i \ne j$ if and only if $\lambda(i\tau\varphi \oplus j\tau\varphi) \ge \rho(i\tau \oplus j\tau) = \rho(i \oplus j)$ for all $i \ne j$, because τ is a permutation. [Note that the notation can be confusing: Bit $j\tau\phi$ appears in bit position j if permutation ϕ is applied first, *then* τ.]

(e) Since $l(j, j, k) = j$ for $0 \le k \le d$, a permutation of Ω fixes j if and only if each of its swaps fixes j. Thus the swaps performed by φ and by ψ operate on disjoint elements. The union of these swaps gives $\varphi\psi$.

59. It is $2^{M_d(a,b)}$, where $M_d(a,b)$ is the number of crossbars that have both endpoints in $[a\,..\,b]$. To count them, let $k = \lambda(a\oplus b)$, $a' = a \bmod 2^k$, and $b' = b \bmod 2^k$; notice that $b - a = 2^k + b' - a'$, and $M_d(a,b) = M_{k+1}(a', 2^k + b')$. Counting the crossbars in the top half and bottom half, plus those that jump between halves, gives $M_{k+1}(a', 2^k + b') = M_k(a', 2^k - 1) + M_k(0, b') + ((b' + 1) \doteq a')$. Finally, we have $M_k(0, b') = S(b' + 1)$; and $M_k(a', 2^k - 1) = M_k(0, 2^k - 1 - a') = S(2^k - a') = k2^{k-1} - ka' + S(a')$, where $S(n)$ is evaluated in exercise 42.

60. A cycle of length $2l$ corresponds to a pattern $u_0 \leftarrow v_0 \leftrightarrow v_1 \rightarrow u_1 \leftrightarrow u_2 \leftarrow v_2 \leftrightarrow \cdots \leftrightarrow v_{2l-1} \rightarrow u_{2l-1} \leftrightarrow u_{2l}$, where $u_{2l} = u_0$ and '$u \leftarrow v$' or '$v \rightarrow u$' means that the permutation sends u to v, '$x \leftrightarrow y$' means that $x = y \oplus 1$.

We can generate a random permutation as follows: Given u_0, there are $2n$ choices for v_0, then $2n - 1$ choices for u_1 only one of which causes $u_2 = u_0$, then $2n - 2$ choices for v_2, then $2n - 3$ choices for u_3 only one of which closes a cycle, etc.

Consequently the generating function is $G(z) = \prod_{j=1}^{n} \frac{2n-2j+z}{2n-2j+1}$. The expected number of cycles, k, is $G'(1) = H_{2n} - \frac{1}{2}H_n = \frac{1}{2}\ln n + \ln 2 + \frac{1}{2}\gamma + O(n^{-1})$. The mean of 2^k is $G(2) = (2^n n!)^2/(2n)! = \sqrt{\pi n} + O(n^{-1/2})$; and the variance is $G(4) - G(2)^2 = (n + 1 - G(2))G(2) = \sqrt{\pi}n^{3/2} + O(n)$.

62. The crossbar settings in $P(2^d)$ can be stored in $(2d-1)2^{d-1} = Nd - \frac{1}{2}N$ bits. To get the inverse permutation proceed from right to left. [See P. Heckel and R. Schroeppel, *Electronic Design* **28**, 8 (12 April 1980), 148–152. Note that *any* way to represent an arbitrary permutation requires at least $\lg N! > Nd - N/\ln 2$ bits of memory; so this representation is nearly optimum, spacewise.]

63. (i) $x = y$. (ii) Either z is even or $x \oplus y < 2^{\max(0, (z-1)/2)}$. (When z is odd we have $(x \updownarrow y) \gg z = (y \gg \lceil z/2 \rceil) \updownarrow (x \gg \lfloor z/2 \rfloor)$, even when $z < 0$.) (iii) This identity holds for all w, x, y, and z (and also with any other bitwise Boolean operator in place of &).

64. $(((z \mathbin{\&} \mu_0) + (z' \mid \bar{\mu}_0)) \mathbin{\&} \mu_0) \mid (((z \mathbin{\&} \bar{\mu}_0) + (z' \mid \mu_0)) \mathbin{\&} \bar{\mu}_0)$. (See (86).)

65. $xu(x^2) + v(x^2) = xu(x)^2 + v(x)^2$.

66. (a) $v(x) = (u(x)/(1+x^\delta)) \bmod x^n$; it's the unique polynomial of degree less than n such that $(1+x^\delta)v(x) \equiv u(x)$ (modulo x^n). (Equivalently, v is the unique n-bit integer such that $(v \oplus (v \ll \delta)) \bmod 2^n = u$.)

(b) We may as well assume that $n = 64m$, and that $u = (u_{m-1} \ldots u_1 u_0)_{2^{64}}$, $v = (v_{m-1} \ldots v_1 v_0)_{2^{64}}$. Set $c \leftarrow 0$; then, using exercise 36, set $v_j \leftarrow u_j^{\oplus} \oplus (-c)$ and $c \leftarrow v_j \gg 63$ for $j = 0, 1, \ldots, m-1$.

(c) Set $c \leftarrow v_0 \leftarrow u_0$; then $v_j \leftarrow u_j \oplus c$ and $c \leftarrow v_j$, for $j = 1, 2, \ldots, m-1$.

(d) Start with $c \leftarrow 0$ and do the following for $j = 0, 1, \ldots, m-1$: Set $t \leftarrow u_j$, $t \leftarrow t \oplus (t \ll 3)$, $t \leftarrow t \oplus (t \ll 6)$, $t \leftarrow t \oplus (t \ll 12)$, $t \leftarrow t \oplus (t \ll 24)$, $t \leftarrow t \oplus (t \ll 48)$, $v_j \leftarrow t \oplus c$, $c \leftarrow (t \gg 61) \times {}^{\#}9249249249249249$.

(e) Start with $v \leftarrow u$. Then, for $j = 1, 2, \ldots, m-1$, set $v_j \leftarrow v_j \oplus (v_{j-1} \ll 3)$ and (if $j < m - 1$) $v_{j+1} \leftarrow v_{j+1} \oplus (v_{j-1} \gg 61)$.

67. Let $n = 2l - 1$ and $m = n - 2d$. If $\frac{1}{2}n < k < n$ we have $x^{2k} \equiv x^{m+t} + x^t$ (modulo $x^n + x^m + 1$), where $t = 2k - n$ is odd. Consequently, if $v = (v_{n-1} \ldots v_1 v_0)_2$, the number

$$w = u \oplus \big(((u \gg d) \oplus (u \gg 2d) \oplus (u \gg 3d) \oplus \cdots) \mathbin{\&} -2^{l-d}\big)$$

turns out to equal $(v_{n-2} \ldots v_3 v_1 v_{n-1} \ldots v_2 v_0)_2$. For example, when $l = 4$ and $d = 2$, the square of $u_6 x^6 + \cdots + u_1 x + u_0$ modulo $(x^7 + x^3 + 1)$ is $u_6 x^5 + u_5 x^3 + (u_6 \oplus u_4)x^1 + (u_5 \oplus u_3)x^6 + (u_6 \oplus u_4 \oplus u_2)x^4 + u_1 x^2 + u_0$. To compute v, we therefore do a perfect shuffle, $v = \lfloor w/2^l \rfloor \ddagger (w \bmod 2^l)$. The number w can be calculated by methods like those of the previous exercise. [See R. P. Brent, S. Larvala, and P. Zimmermann, *Math. Comp.* **72** (2003), 1443–1452; **74** (2005), 1001–1002.]

68. `SRU t,x,delta; PUT rM,theta; MUX x,t,x.`

69. Notice that the procedure might fail if we attempt to do the 2^{d-1}-shift first instead of last. The key to proving that a small-shift-first strategy works correctly is to watch the spaces *between* selected bits; we will prove that the lengths of these spaces are multiples of 2^{k+1} after the 2^k-shift.

Consider the infinite string $\chi_k = \ldots 1^{t_4} 0^{2^k} 1^{t_3} 0^{2^k} 1^{t_2} 0^{2^k} 1^{t_1} 0^{2^k} 1^{t_0}$, which represents the situation where $t_l \geq 0$ items need to move $2^k l$ places to the right. A 2^k-shift with any mask of the form $\theta_k = \ldots 0^{t_4} *^{2^{k+1}} 1^{t_3} 0^{t_2} *^{2^{k+1}} 1^{t_1} 0^{t_0}$ leaves us with the situation represented by the string $\chi_{k+1} = \ldots 1^{T_2} 0^{2^{k+1}} 1^{T_1} 0^{2^{k+1}} 1^{T_0}$, where exactly $T_l = t_{2l} + t_{2l+1}$ items need to move right $2^{k+1} l$ places. So the claim holds by induction on k.

70. Let $\psi_k = \theta_k \oplus (\theta_k \ll 1)$, so that $\theta_k = \psi_k^{\oplus}$ in the notation of exercise 36. If we take $*^{2^{k+1}} = 0^{2^k} 1^{2^k}$ in the previous answer, we have $\psi_0 = \bar{\chi}$ and $\psi_{k+1} = (\psi_k \,\&\, \bar{\theta}_k) \gg 2^k$. Therefore we can proceed as follows:

Set $\psi \leftarrow \bar{\chi}$, $k \leftarrow 0$, and repeat the following steps while $\psi \neq 0$: Set $x \leftarrow \psi$, then $x \leftarrow x \oplus (x \ll 2^l)$ for $0 \leq l < d$, then $\theta_k \leftarrow x$, $\psi \leftarrow (\psi \,\&\, \bar{x}) \gg 2^k$, and $k \leftarrow k+1$.

The computation ends with $k = \lambda\nu\bar{\chi} + 1$; the remaining masks θ_k, ..., θ_{d-1}, if any, are zero and those steps can be omitted from (80). Sometimes this procedure gives nonzero masks θ_k that actually do nothing useful, because $t_1 = t_3 = \cdots = 0$. To avoid such redundancy, change '$\theta_k \leftarrow x$' to '$\theta_k \leftarrow x \,\&\, (x + (x \,\&\, \psi \,\&\, (\psi \gg 2^k)))$'.

[See *compress* in H. S. Warren, Jr., *Hacker's Delight* (Addison–Wesley, 2002), §7–4; also G. L. Steele Jr., *U.S. Patent 6715066* (30 March 2004).]

71. Start with $x \leftarrow y$. Do a (-2^k)-shift of x with mask θ_k, for $k = d-1$, ..., 1, 0, using the masks of exercise 70. Finally set $z \leftarrow x$ (or $z \leftarrow x \,\&\, \chi$, if you want a "clean" result).

72. $2^{2^{d-1}} x + y$.

73. Equivalently, d sheep-and-goats operations must be able to transform the word $x^{\pi} = (x_{(2^d-1)\pi} \ldots x_{1\pi} x_{0\pi})_2$ into $(x_{2^d-1} \ldots x_1 x_0)_2$, for any permutation π of $\{0, 1, \ldots, 2^d-1\}$. And this can be done by radix-2 sorting (Algorithm 5.2.5R): First bring the odd numbered bits to the left, then bring the bits j for odd $\lfloor j/2 \rfloor$ left, and so on. For example, when $d = 3$ and $x^{\pi} = (x_3 x_1 x_0 x_7 x_5 x_2 x_6 x_4)_2$, the three operations yield successively $(x_3 x_1 x_7 x_5 x_0 x_2 x_6 x_4)_2$, $(x_3 x_7 x_2 x_6 x_1 x_5 x_0 x_4)_2$, $(x_7 x_6 x_5 x_4 x_3 x_2 x_1 x_0)_2$. [See Z. Shi and R. Lee, *Proc. IEEE Conf. ASAP'00* (IEEE CS Press, 2000), 138–148.]

Historical note: The BESM-6 computer, designed in 1965, implemented half of the sheep-and-goats operation: Its «сборка» ("gather" or "pack") command produced $(z \,\&\, \chi) \cdot \mid \cdot \bar{\chi}$, and its «разборка» command ("scatter" or "unpack") went the other way.

74. If $\left| \sum c_{2l} - \sum c_{2l+1} \right| = 2\Delta > 0$, we must rob Δ from the rich half and give it to the poor. There's a position l in the poor half with $c_l = 0$; otherwise that half would sum to at least 2^{d-1}. A cyclic 1-shift that modifies positions l through $(l + t) \bmod 2^d$ makes $c'_{l+k} = c_{l+k+1}$ for $0 \leq k < t$, $c'_{l+t} = c_{l+t+1} - \delta$, $c'_{l+t+1} = \delta$, and $c'_{l+k} = c_{l+k}$ for all other k; here δ can be any desired value in the range $0 \leq \delta \leq c_{l+t+1}$. (We've treated all subscripts modulo 2^d in these formulas.) So we can use the smallest even t such that $c_{l+1} + c_{l+3} + \cdots + c_{l+t+1} = c_l + c_{l+2} + \cdots + c_{l+t} + \Delta + \delta$ for some $\delta \geq 0$.

(The 1-shift need not be cyclic, if we allow ourselves to shift left instead of right. But the cyclic property may be needed in subsequent steps.)

75. Equivalently, given indices $0 \le i_0 < i_1 < \cdots < i_{s-1} < i_s = 2^d$ and $0 = j_0 < j_1 < \cdots < j_{s-1} < j_s = 2^d$, we want to map $(x_{2^d-1} \ldots x_1 x_0)_2 \mapsto (x_{(2^d-1)\varphi} \ldots x_{1\varphi} x_{0\varphi})_2$, where $j\varphi = i_r$ for $j_r \le j < j_{r+1}$ and $0 \le r < s$. If $d = 1$, a mapping module does this.

When $d > 1$, we can set the left-hand crossbars so that they route input i_r to line $i_r \oplus ((i_r + r) \bmod 2)$. If s is even, we recursively ask one of the networks $P(2^{d-1})$ inside $P(2^d)$ to solve the problem for indices $\lfloor \{i_0, i_2, \ldots, i_s\}/2 \rfloor$ and $\lfloor \{j_0, j_2, \ldots, j_s\}/2 \rfloor$, while the other solves it for $\lfloor \{i_1, i_3, \ldots, i_{s-1}, 2^d\}/2 \rfloor$ and $\lceil \{j_0, j_2, \ldots, j_s\}/2 \rceil$. At the right of $P(2^d)$, one can now check that when $j_r \le j < j_{r+1}$, the mapping module for lines j and $j \oplus 1$ has input i_r on line j if $j \equiv r$ (modulo 2), otherwise i_r is on line $j \oplus 1$. A similar proof works when s is odd.

Notes: This network is a slight improvement over a construction by Yu. P. Ofman, *Trudy Mosk. Mat. Obshchestva* **14** (1965), 186–199. We can implement the corresponding network by substituting a "δ-map" for a δ-swap; instead of (69), we use two masks and do seven operations instead of six: $y \leftarrow x \oplus (x \gg \delta)$, $x \leftarrow x \oplus (y \,\&\, \theta) \oplus ((y \,\&\, \theta') \ll \delta)$. This extension of (71) therefore takes only d additional units of time.

76. When a mapping network realizes a permutation, all of its modules must act as crossbars; hence $G(n) \ge \lg n!$. Ofman proved that $G(n) \le 2.5 n \lg n$, and remarked in a footnote that the constant 2.5 could be improved (without giving any details). We have seen that in fact $G(n) \le 2n \lg n$. Note that $G(3) = 3$.

77. Represent an n-network by $(x_{2^n-1} \ldots x_1 x_0)_2$, where $x_k = $ [the binary representation of k is a possible configuration of 0s and 1s when the network has been applied to all 2^n sequences of 0s and 1s], for $0 \le k < 2^n$. Thus the empty network is represented by $2^{2^n} - 1$, and a sorting network for $n = 3$ is represented by $(10001011)_2$. In general, x represents a sorting network for n elements if and only if it represents an n-network and $\nu x = n + 1$, if and only if $x = 2^0 + 2^1 + 2^3 + 2^7 + \cdots + 2^{2^n-1}$.

If x represents α according to these conventions, the representation of $\alpha[i:j]$ is $(x \oplus y) \mid (y \gg (2^{n-i} - 2^{n-j}))$, where $y = x \,\&\, \bar{\mu}_{n-i} \,\&\, \mu_{n-j}$. [See V. R. Pratt, M. O. Rabin, and L. J. Stockmeyer, *STOC* **6** (1974), 122–126.]

78. If $k \ge \lg(m-1)$ the test is valid, because we always have $x_1 + x_2 + \cdots + x_m \ge x_1 \mid x_2 \mid \cdots \mid x_m$, with equality if and only if the sets are disjoint. Moreover, we have $(x_1 + \cdots + x_m) - (x_1 \mid \cdots \mid x_m) \le (m-1)(2^{n-k-1} + \cdots + 1) < (m-1)2^{n-k} \le 2^n$.

Conversely, if $m \ge 2^k + 2$ and $n > 2k$, the test is invalid. We might have, for example, $x_1 + \cdots + x_m = (2^k+1)(2^{n-k} - 2^{n-2k-1}) + 2^{n-k-1} = 2^n + (2^{n-k} - 2^{n-2k-1})$.

But if $n \le 2k$ the test is still valid when $m = 2^k + 2$, because our proof shows that $x_1 + \cdots + x_m - (x_1 \mid \cdots \mid x_m) \le (2^k+1)(2^{n-k} - 1) < 2^n$ in that case.

79. $x_\mathit{l} = (x - 1) \,\&\, \chi$. (And the formula $x_\mathit{l} = ((x - b - 1) \,\&\, a) + b$ corresponds to (85).) These recipes for x' and x_l are part of Jörg Arndt's "bit wizardry" routines (2001); their origin is unknown.

80. Perhaps the nicest way is to start with $x \leftarrow \chi - 1$ as a signed number; then while $x \ge 0$, set $x \leftarrow x \,\&\, \chi$, visit x, and set $x \leftarrow 2x - \chi$. (The operation $2x - \chi$ can in fact be performed with a single MMIX instruction, '2ADDU x,x,minuschi'.)

But that trick fails if χ is so large as to be *already* "negative." A slightly slower but more general method starts with $x \leftarrow \chi$ and does the following while $x \ne 0$: Set $t \leftarrow x \,\&\, -x$, visit $\chi - t$, and set $x \leftarrow x - t$.

81. $((z \,\&\, \chi) - (z' \,\&\, \chi)) \,\&\, \chi$. (One way to verify this formula is to use (18).)

82. Yes, by letting $z = z'$ in (86): $w \mid (z \,\&\, \bar{\chi})$, where $w = ((z \,\&\, \chi) + (z \mid \bar{\chi})) \,\&\, \chi$.

83. (The following iteration propagates bits of y to the right, in the gaps of a scattered accumulator t. Auxiliary variables u and v respectively mark the left and right of each gap; they double in size until being wiped out by w.) Set $t \leftarrow z \,\&\, \chi$, $u' \leftarrow (\chi \gg 1) \,\&\, \bar\chi$, $v \leftarrow ((\chi \ll 1) + 1) \,\&\, \bar\chi$, $w \leftarrow 3(u' \,\&\, v)$, $u \leftarrow 3u'$, $v \leftarrow 3v$, and $k \leftarrow 1$. Then, while $u \neq 0$, do the following steps: $t \leftarrow t \,|\, ((t \gg k) \,\&\, u')$, $k \leftarrow k \ll 1$, $u \leftarrow u \,\&\, \overline w$, $v \leftarrow v \,\&\, \overline w$, $w \leftarrow ((u \,\&\, (u \gg 1)) \,\&\, \bar u) \ll (k+1)) - ((u \,\&\, (v \ll 1) \,\&\, \bar v) \gg k)$, $u' \leftarrow (u \,\&\, \bar v) \gg k$, $v \leftarrow v + ((u \,\&\, \bar u) \ll k)$, $u \leftarrow u + u'$. Finally return the answer $((t \gg 1) \,\&\, \chi) \,|\, (z \,\&\, \bar\chi)$.

84. $z \,\leftarrow\, \chi = w - (z \,\&\, \chi)$, where $w = (((z \,\&\, \chi) \ll 1) + \bar\chi) \,\&\, \chi$ appears in answer 82; $z \rightarrow \chi$ is the quantity t computed (with more difficulty) in the answer to exercise 83.

85. (a) If $x = \mathtt{LOC}(a[i,j,k])$ is the drum location corresponding to interleaved bits as stated, then $\mathtt{LOC}(a[i+1,j,k]) = x \oplus ((x \oplus ((x \,\&\, \chi) - \chi)) \,\&\, \chi)$ and $\mathtt{LOC}(a[i-1,j,k]) = x \oplus ((x \oplus ((x \,\&\, \chi) - 1)) \,\&\, \chi)$, where $\chi = (11111)_8$, by (8_4) and answer 79. The formulas for $\mathtt{LOC}(a[i,j\pm1,k])$ and $\mathtt{LOC}(a[i,j,k\pm1])$ are similar, with masks 2χ and 4χ.

(b) For random access, let's hope there is room for a table of length 32 giving $f[(i_4 i_3 i_2 i_1 i_0)_2] = (i_4 i_3 i_2 i_1 i_0)_8$. Then $\mathtt{LOC}(a[i,j,k]) = (((f[k] \ll 1) + f[j]) \ll 1) + f[i]$. (On a vintage machine, bitwise computation of f would be much worse than table lookup, because register operations used to be as slow as fetches from memory.)

(c) Let p be the location of the page currently in fast memory, and let $z = -128$. When accessing location x, if $x \,\&\, z \neq p$ it is necessary to read 128 words from drum location $x \,\&\, z$ (after saving the current data to drum location p if it has changed); then set $p \leftarrow x \,\&\, z$. [See *J. Royal Stat. Soc.* **B-16** (1954), 53–55. This scheme of array allocation for external storage was devised independently by E. W. Dijkstra, circa 1960, who called it the "zip-fastener" method. It has often been rediscovered, for example in 1966 by G. M. Morton and later by developers of quadtrees; see Hanan Samet, *Applications of Spatial Data Structures* (Addison–Wesley, 1990). See also R. Raman and D. S. Wise, *IEEE Trans.* **C57** (2008), 567–573, for a contemporary perspective. Georg Cantor had considered interleaving the digits of decimal fractions in *Crelle* **84** (1878), 242–258, §7; but he observed that this idea does *not* lead to an easy one-to-one correspondence between the unit interval $[0\,..\,1]$ and the unit square $[0\,..\,1] \times [0\,..\,1]$.]

86. If (p', q', r') rightmost bits and (p'', q'', r'') other bits of (i, j, k) are in the part of the address that does not affect the page number, the total number of page faults is $2((2^{p-p'} - 1)2^{q+r} + (2^{q-q'} - 1)2^{p+r} + (2^{r-r'} - 1)2^{p+q})$. Hence we want to minimize $2^{-p'} + 2^{-q'} + 2^{-r'}$ over nonnegative integers $(p', q', r', p'', q'', r'')$ with $p' + p'' \le p$, $q' + q'' \le q$, $r' + r'' \le r$, $p' + q' + r' + p'' + q'' + r'' = s$. Since $2^a + 2^b > 2^{a-1} + 2^{b+1}$ when a and b are integers with $a > b+1$, the minimum (for all s) occurs when we select bits from right to left cyclically until running out. For example, when $(p, q, r) = (2, 6, 3)$ the addressing function would be $(j_5 j_4 j_3 k_2 j_2 k_1 j_1 i_1 k_0 j_0 i_0)_2$. In particular, Tocher's scheme is optimal.

[But such a mapping is not necessarily best when the page size isn't a power of 2. For example, consider a 16×16 matrix; the addressing function $(j_3 i_3 i_2 i_1 i_0 j_2 j_1 j_0)_2$ is better than $(j_3 i_3 j_2 i_2 j_1 i_1 j_0 i_0)_2$ for all page sizes from 17 to 62, except for size 32 when they are equally good.]

87. Set $x \leftarrow x \,\&\, {\sim}((x \,\&\, \mathtt{"@@@@@@@@"}) \gg 1)$; each byte $(a_7 \ldots a_0)_2$ is thereby changed to $(a_7 a_6 (a_5 \wedge \bar a_6) a_4 \ldots a_0)_2$. The same transformation works also on 30 additional letters in the Latin-1 supplement to ASCII (for example, æ ↦ Æ); but there's one glitch, ÿ ↦ ß.

[Don Woods used this trick in his original program for the game of Adventure (1976), uppercasing the user's input words before looking them up in a dictionary.]

88. Set $z \leftarrow (x \oplus \bar y) \,\&\, h$, then $z \leftarrow ((x \,|\, h) - (y \,\&\, \bar h)) \oplus z$.

89. $t \leftarrow x \,|\, \bar{y}, t \leftarrow t \,\&\, (t \gg 1), z \leftarrow (x \,\&\, \bar{y} \,\&\, \bar{\mu}_0) \,|\, (t \,\&\, \mu_0)$. [From the "**nasty**" test program for H. G. Dietz and R. J. Fisher's SWARC compiler (1998), optimized by T. Dahlheimer.]

90. Insert '$z \leftarrow z \,|\, ((x \oplus y) \,\&\, l)$' either before or after '$z \leftarrow (x \,\&\, y) + z$'. (The ordering makes no difference, because $x + y \equiv x \oplus y$ (modulo 4) when $x + y$ is odd. Therefore MMIX can round to odd at no additional cost, using MOR. Rounding to even in the ambiguous cases is more difficult, and with fixed point arithmetic it is not advantageous.)

91. If $\frac{1}{2}[x, y]$ denotes the average as in (88), the desired result is obtained by repeating the following operations seven times, then concluding with $z \leftarrow \frac{1}{2}[x, y]$ once more:

$$z \leftarrow \frac{1}{2}[x, y], \quad t \leftarrow \alpha \,\&\, h, \quad m \leftarrow (t \ll 1) - (t \gg 7),$$

$$x \leftarrow (m \,\&\, z) \,|\, (\overline{m} \,\&\, x), \quad y \leftarrow (\overline{m} \,\&\, z) \,|\, (m \,\&\, y), \quad \alpha \leftarrow \alpha \ll 1.$$

Although rounding errors accumulate through eight levels, the resulting absolute error never exceeds $807/255$. Moreover, it is ≈ 1.13 if we average over all 256^3 cases, and it is less than 2 with probability $\approx 94.2\%$. If we round to odd as in exercise 90, the maximum and average error are reduced to $616/255$ and ≈ 0.58; the probability of error < 2 rises to $\approx 99.9\%$. Therefore the following MMIX code uses such unbiased rounding:

```
x GREG ;y GREG ;z GREG                    ⎛ XOR  t,x,y      MOR m,ffhi,alf ⎞
alf GREG ;m GREG ;t IS $255               ⎜ MOR  z,rodd,t   PUT rM,m       ⎟
ffhi GREG -1<<56     repeat seven times:  ⎨ AND  t,x,y      MUX x,z,x       ⎬
1    GREG #0101010101010101               ⎜ ADDU z,z,t      MUX y,y,z       ⎟
rodd GREG #4020100804020101               ⎝                 SLU alf,alf,1   ⎠
```

after which the first four instructions are repeated again. The total time for eight α-blends (67υ) is less than the cost of eight multiplications.

92. We get $z_j = \lceil (x_j + y_j)/2 \rceil$ for each j. (This fact, noticed by H. S. Warren, Jr., follows from the identity $x + y = ((x \,|\, y) \ll 1) - (x \oplus y)$. See also the next exercise.)

93. $x - y = (x \oplus y) - ((\bar{x} \,\&\, y) \ll 1)$. ("Borrows" instead of "carries.")

94. $(x - l)_j = (x_j - 1 - b_j) \bmod 256$, where b_j is the "borrow" from fields to the right. So t_j is nonzero if and only if $(x_j \ldots x_0)_{256} < (1 \ldots 1)_{256} = (256^{j+1} - 1)/255$. (The answers to the stated questions are therefore "yes" and "no.")

In general if the constant l is allowed to have *any* value $(l_7 \ldots l_1 l_0)_{256}$, operation (90) makes $t_j \neq 0$ if and only if $(x_j \ldots x_0)_{256} < (l_j \ldots l_0)_{256}$ and $x_j < 128$.

95. Use (90): Test if $h \,\&\, (t(x \oplus ((x \gg 8) + (x \ll 56))) \,|\, t(x \oplus ((x \gg 16) + (x \ll 48))) \,|\, t(x \oplus ((x \gg 24) + (x \ll 40))) \,|\, t(x \oplus ((x \gg 32) + (x \ll 32)))) = 0$, where $t(x) = (x - l) \,\&\, \bar{x}$. (These 28 steps reduce to 20 if cyclic shift is available, or to 11 with MXOR and BDIF.)

96. Suppose $0 \leq x, y < 256$, $x_h = \lfloor x/128 \rfloor$, $x_l = x \bmod 128$, $y_h = \lfloor y/128 \rfloor$, $y_l = y \bmod 128$. Then $[x < y] = \langle \bar{x}_h y_h [x_l < y_l] \rangle$; see exercise 7.1.1–106. And $[x_l < y_l] = [y_l + 127 - x_l \geq 128]$. Hence $[x < y] = \lfloor \langle \bar{x} y z \rangle /128 \rfloor$, where $z = (\bar{x} \,\&\, 127) + (y \,\&\, 127)$.

It follows that $t = h \,\&\, \langle \bar{x} y z \rangle$ has the desired properties, when $z = (\bar{x} \,\&\, \bar{h}) + (y \,\&\, \bar{h})$. This formula can also be written $t = h \,\&\, {\sim}\langle x \bar{y} \bar{z} \rangle$, where $\bar{z} = {\sim}((\bar{x} \,\&\, \bar{h}) + (y \,\&\, \bar{h})) = (x \,|\, h) - (y \,\&\, \bar{h})$ by (18).

To get a similar test function for $[x_j \leq y_j] = 1 - [y_j < x_j]$, we just interchange $x \leftrightarrow y$ and take the complement: $t \leftarrow h \,\&\, {\sim}\langle x \bar{y} z \rangle = h \,\&\, \langle \bar{x} y \bar{z} \rangle$, where $z = (x \,\&\, \bar{h}) + (\bar{y} \,\&\, \bar{h})$.

97. Set $x' \leftarrow x \oplus$ "`********`", $y' \leftarrow x \oplus y$, $t \leftarrow h \,\&\, (x \,|\, ((x \,|\, h) - l)) \,\&\, (y' \,|\, ((y' \,|\, h) - l))$, $m \leftarrow (t \ll 1) - (t \gg 7)$, $t \leftarrow t \,\&\, (x' \,|\, ((x' \,|\, h) - l))$, $z \leftarrow (m \,\&\,$ "`********`"$) \,|\, (\overline{m} \,\&\, y)$. (20 steps.)

98. Set $u \leftarrow x \oplus y$, $z \leftarrow (\bar{x} \,\&\, \bar{h}) + (y \,\&\, \bar{h})$, $t \leftarrow h \,\&\, (x \oplus (u \,|\, (x \oplus z)))$, $v \leftarrow ((t \ll 1) - (t \gg 7)) \,\&\, u$, $z \leftarrow x \oplus v$, $w \leftarrow y \oplus v$. [This 14-step procedure invokes answer 96 to compute $t =$

h & $\langle \bar{x}yz \rangle$, using the footprint method of Section 7.1.2 to evaluate the median in only three steps when $x \oplus y$ is known. Of course the MMIX solution is much quicker, if available: BDIF t,x,y; ADDU z,y,t; SUBU w,x,t.]

99. In this potpourri, each of the eight bytes appears to be solving a different kind of problem; we must recast the conditions so that they fit into a common framework: $f_0 = [x_0 \oplus \text{'!'} \leq 0]$, $f_1 = [x_1 \oplus \text{'*'} > 0]$, $f_2 = [x_2 \leq \text{'A'} - 1]$, $f_3 = [x_3 > \text{'z'}]$, $f_4 = [x_4 > \text{'a'} - 1]$, $f_5 = [x_5 \oplus \text{'0'} \leq 9]$, $f_6 = [x_6 \oplus 255 > 86]$, $f_7 = [x_7 \oplus \text{'?'} \leq 3]$. Aha! We can use the formulas in answer 96, adjusting d to switch between $\leq$ and $>$ as needed: $a = (\text{'?'}(255)\text{'0'000'*''!'})_{256} = {}^{\#}\text{3fff300000002a21}$; $b = \bar{h} = {}^{\#}\text{7f7f7f7f7f7f7f7f}$; $c = \bar{h}\ \&\ {\sim}(3(86)9(\text{'a'} - 1)\text{'z'}(\text{'A'} - 1)00)_{256} = {}^{\#}\text{7c29761f053f7f7f}$ (the hardest one); $d = {}^{\#}\text{8000800000800080}$; and $e = h = {}^{\#}\text{8080808080808080}$.

100. We want $u_j = x_j + y_j + c_j - 10c_{j+1}$ and $v_j = x_j - y_j - b_j + 10b_{j+1}$, where c_j and b_j are the "carry" and "borrow" into digit position j. Set $u' \leftarrow (x + y + (6\ldots 66)_{16}) \bmod 2^{64}$ and $v' \leftarrow (x - y) \bmod 2^{64}$. Then we find $u'_j = x_j + y_j + c_j + 6 - 16c_{j+1}$ and $v'_j = x_j - y_j - b_j + 16b_{j+1}$ for $0 \leq j < 16$, by induction on j. Hence u' and v' have the same pattern of carries and borrows as if we were working in radix 10, and we have $u = u' - 6(\bar{c}_{16}\ldots \bar{c}_2\bar{c}_1)_{16}$, $v = v' - 6(b_{16}\ldots b_2b_1)_{16}$. The following computation schemes therefore provide the desired results (10 operations for addition, 9 for subtraction):

$$y' \leftarrow y + (6\ldots 66)_{16}, \quad u' \leftarrow x + y', \qquad\qquad v' \leftarrow x - y,$$
$$t \leftarrow \langle \bar{x}\bar{y}'u' \rangle\ \&\ (8\ldots 88)_{16}, \qquad\qquad t \leftarrow \langle \bar{x}yv' \rangle\ \&\ (8\ldots 88)_{16},$$
$$u \leftarrow u' - t + (t \gg 2); \qquad\qquad\qquad v \leftarrow v' - t + (t \gg 2).$$

101. For subtraction, set $z \leftarrow x - y$; for addition, set $z \leftarrow x + y + {}^{\#}\text{e8c4c4fc18}$, where this constant is built from $256 - 24 = {}^{\#}\text{e8}$, $256 - 60 = {}^{\#}\text{c4}$, and $65536 - 1000 = {}^{\#}\text{fc18}$. Borrows and carries will occur between fields as if mixed-radix subtraction or addition were being performed. The remaining task is to correct for cases in which borrows occurred or carries did not; we can do this easily by inspecting individual digits, because the radices are less than half of the field sizes: Set $t \leftarrow z\ \&\ {}^{\#}\text{8080808000}$, $t \leftarrow (t \ll 1) - (t \gg 7) - ((t \gg 15)\ \&\ 1)$, $z \leftarrow z - (t\ \&\ {}^{\#}\text{e8c4c4fc18})$. [See Stephen Soule, *CACM* **6** (1975), 344–346. We're lucky that the 'c' in 'fc18' is even.]

102. (a) We assume that $x = (x_{15}\ldots x_0)_{16}$ and $y = (y_{15}\ldots y_0)_{16}$, with $0 \leq x_j, y_j < 5$; the goal is to compute $u = (u_{15}\ldots u_0)_{16}$ and $v = (v_{15}\ldots v_0)_{16}$, with components $u_j = (x_j + y_j) \bmod 5$ and $v_j = (x_j - y_j) \bmod 5$. Here's how:

$$u \leftarrow x + y, \qquad\qquad\qquad\qquad\qquad v \leftarrow x - y + 5l,$$
$$t \leftarrow (u + 3l)\ \&\ h, \qquad\qquad\qquad\qquad t \leftarrow (v + 3l)\ \&\ h,$$
$$u \leftarrow u - ((t - (t \gg 3))\ \&\ 5l); \qquad\quad v \leftarrow v - ((t - (t \gg 3))\ \&\ 5l).$$

Here $l = (1\ldots 1)_{16} = (2^{64} - 1)/15$, $h = 8l$. (Addition in 7 operations, subtraction in 8.)

(b) Now $x = (x_{20}\ldots x_0)_8$, etc., and we must be more careful to confine carries:

$$t \leftarrow x + \bar{h},$$
$$z \leftarrow (t\ \&\ \bar{h}) + (y\ \&\ \bar{h}), \qquad\qquad z \leftarrow (x \mid h) - (y\ \&\ \bar{h}),$$
$$t \leftarrow (y \mid z)\ \&\ t\ \&\ h, \qquad\qquad\qquad t \leftarrow (y \mid \bar{z})\ \&\ \bar{x}\ \&\ h,$$
$$u \leftarrow x + y - (t + (t \gg 2)); \qquad\qquad v \leftarrow x - y + t + (t \gg 2).$$

Here $h = (4\ldots 4)_8 = (2^{65} - 4)/7$. (Addition in 11 operations, subtraction in 10.)

     Similar procedures work, of course, for other moduli. In fact we can do multibyte arithmetic on the coordinates of toruses in general, with different moduli in each component (see 7.2.1.3–(66)).

103. Let h and l be the constants in (87) and (88). Addition is easy: $u \leftarrow x \,|\, ((x \& \bar{h}) + y)$. For subtraction, take away 1 and add $x_j \& (1 - y_j)$: $t \leftarrow (x \& \bar{l}) \gg 1$, $v \leftarrow t \,|\, (t + (x \& (y \oplus l)))$.

104. Yes, in 19: Let $a = (((1901 \ll 4) + 1) \ll 5) + 1$, $b = (((2099 \ll 4) + 12) \ll 5) + 28$. Set $m \leftarrow (x \gg 5) \& \,{}^\#\mathtt{f}$ (the month), $c \leftarrow {}^\#\mathtt{10} \& \sim((x \,|\, (x \gg 1)) \gg 5)$ (the leap year correction), $u \leftarrow b + {}^\#\mathtt{3} \& (({}^\#\mathtt{3bbeecc} + c) \gg (m + m))$ (the *max_day* adjustment), and $t \leftarrow ((x \oplus a \oplus (x - a)) \,|\, (x \oplus u \oplus (u - x))) \& \,{}^\#\mathtt{1000220}$ (the test for unwanted carries).

105. Exercise 98 explains how to compute bytewise min and max; a simple modification will compute min in some byte positions and max in others. Thus we can "sort by perfect shuffles" as in Section 5.3.4, Fig. 57, if we can permute bytes between x and y appropriately. And such permutation is easy, by exercise 1. [Of course there are much simpler and faster ways to sort 16 bytes. But see S. Albers and T. Hagerup, *Inf. and Computation* **136** (1997), 25–51, and M. Thorup, *J. Algorithms* **42** (2002), 205–230, for asymptotic implications of this approach.]

106. The n bits are regarded as g fields of g bits each. First the nonzero fields are detected (t_1), and we form a word y that has $(y_{g-1} \ldots y_0)_2$ in each g-bit field, where $y_j = [\text{field } j \text{ of } x \text{ is nonzero}]$. Then we compare each field with the constants 2^{g-1}, $\ldots$, 2^0 (t_2), and form a mask m that identifies the most significant nonzero field of x. After putting g copies of that field into z, we test z as we tested y (t_3). Finally an appropriate sideways addition of t_2 and t_3 (g-bit-wise) yields λ. (Try the case $g = 4$, $n = 16$.)

To compute 2^λ without shifting left, replace '$t_2 \ll 1$' by '$t_2 + t_2$', and replace the final line by $w \leftarrow (((a \cdot (t_3 \oplus (t_3 \gg g))) \bmod 2^n) \gg (n - g)) \cdot l$; then $w \& m$ is $2^{\lambda x}$.

107.
```
     h   GREG #8000800080008000      SLU  q,t,16          OR   t,t,y
     ms  GREG #00ff0f0f33335555      ADDU t,t,q           AND  t,t,h
     1H  SRU  q,x,32                 SLU  q,t,32      5H   SLU  q,t,15
         ZSNZ lam,q,32               ADDU t,t,q           ADDU t,t,q
         ADD  t,lam,16          3H   ANDN y,t,ms           SLU  q,t,30
         SRU  q,x,t             4H   XOR  t,t,y            ADDU t,t,q
         CSNZ lam,q,t                OR   q,y,h       6H   SRU  q,t,60
     2H  SRU  t,x,lam                SUBU t,q,t            ADDU lam,lam,q
```

The total time is 22υ (and no mems). [There's also a mem-less version of (56), costing only 16υ, if its last line is replaced by `ADD t,lam,4; SRU y,x,t; CSNZ lam,y,t; SRU y,x,lam; SLU t,y,1; SRU t,[#ffffaa50],t; AND t,t,3; ADD lam,lam,t`.]

108. For example, let e be minimum so that $n \leq 2^e \cdot 2^{2^e}$. If n is a multiple of 2^e, we can use 2^e fields of size $n/2^e$, with e reductions in step B1; otherwise we can use 2^e fields of size $2^{\lceil \lg n \rceil - e - 1}$, with $e + 1$ reductions in step B1. In either case there are e iterations in steps B2 and B5, so the total running time is $O(e) = O(\log \log n)$.

109. Start with $x \leftarrow x \& -x$ and apply Algorithm B. (Step B4 of that algorithm can be slightly simplified in this special case, using a constant l instead of $x \oplus y$.)

110. Let $s = 2^d$ where $d = 2^e - e$. We will use s-bit fields in n-bit words.

K1. [Stretch $x \bmod s$.] Set $y \leftarrow x \& (s - 1)$. Then set $t \leftarrow y \& \bar{\mu}_j$ and $y \leftarrow y \oplus t \oplus (t \ll 2^j (s - 1))$ for $e > j \geq 0$. Finally set $y \leftarrow (y \ll s) - y$. [If $x = (x_{2^e - 1} \ldots x_0)_2$ we now have $y = (y_{2^e - 1} \ldots y_0)_{2^s}$, where $y_j = (2^s - 1) x_j [j < d]$.]

K2. [Set up minterms.] Set $y \leftarrow y \oplus (a_{2^e - 1} \ldots a_0)_{2^s}$, where $a_j = \mu_{d,j}$ for $0 \leq j < d$ and $a_j = 2^s - 1$ for $d \leq j < 2^e$.

K3. [Compress.] Set $y \leftarrow y \& (y \gg 2^j s)$ for $e > j \geq 0$. [Now $y = 1 \ll (x \bmod s)$. This is the key point that makes the algorithm work.]

K4. [Finish.] Set $y \leftarrow y \mid (y \ll 2^j s)$ for $0 \leq j < e$. Finally set $y \leftarrow y \mathbin{\&} (\mu_{2^e,j} \oplus -((x \gg j) \mathbin{\&} 1))$ for $d \leq j < 2^e$. ∎

111. The n bits are divided into fields of s bits each, although the leftmost field might be shorter. First y is set to flag the all-1 fields. Then $t = (\ldots t_1 t_0)_{2^s}$ contains candidate bits for q, including "false drops" for certain patterns 01^k with $s \leq k < r$. We always have $\nu t_j \leq 1$, and $t_j \neq 0$ implies $t_{j-1} = 0$. The bits of u and v subdivide t into two parts so that we can safely compute $m = (t \gg 1) \mid (t \gg 2) \mid \cdots \mid (t \gg r)$, before making a final test to eliminate the false drops.

112. Notice that if $q = x \mathbin{\&} (x \ll 1) \mathbin{\&} \cdots \mathbin{\&} (x \ll (r-1)) \mathbin{\&} {\sim}(x \ll r)$ then we have $x \mathbin{\&} \overline{x+q} = x \mathbin{\&} (x \ll 1) \mathbin{\&} \cdots \mathbin{\&} (x \ll (r-1))$.

If we can solve the stated problem in $O(1)$ steps, we can also extract the most significant bit of an r-bit number in $O(1)$ steps: Apply the case $n = 2r$ to the number $2^n - 1 - x$. Conversely, a solution to the extraction problem can be shown to yield a solution to the $1^r 0$ problem. Exercise 110 therefore implies a solution in $O(\log \log r)$ steps.

113. Let $0' = 0$, $x_0' = x_0$, and construct $x_{i'}' = x_i$ for $1 \leq i \leq r$ as follows: If $x_i = a \circ_i b$ and $\circ_i \notin \{+, -, \ll\}$, let $i' = (i-1)' + 1$ and $x_{i'}' = a' \circ_i b'$, where $a' = x_{j'}'$ if $a = x_j$ and $a' = a$ if $a = c_i$. If $x_i = a \ll c$, let $i' = (i-1)' + 2$ and $(x_{i'-1}', x_{i'}') = (a' \mathbin{\&} (\lceil 2^{n-c} \rceil - 1), x_{i'-1}' \ll c)$. If $x_i = a+b$, let $i' = (i-1)'+6$ and let $(x_{(i-1)'+1}', \ldots, x_{i'}')$ compute $((a' \mathbin{\&} \bar{h}) + (b' \mathbin{\&} \bar{h})) \oplus ((a' \oplus b') \mathbin{\&} h)$, where $h = 2^{n-1}$. And if $x_i = a - b$, do the similar computation $((a' \mid h) - (b' \mathbin{\&} \bar{h})) \oplus ((a' \equiv b') \mathbin{\&} h)$. Clearly $r' \leq 6r$.

114. Simply let $X_i = X_{j(i)} \circ_i X_{k(i)}$ when $x_i = x_{j(i)} \circ_i x_{k(i)}$, $X_i = C_i \circ_i X_{k(i)}$ when $x_i = c_i \circ_i x_{k(i)}$, and $X_i = X_{j(i)} \circ_i C_i$ when $x_i = x_{j(i)} \circ_i c_i$, where $C_i = c_i$ when c_i is a shift amount, otherwise $C_i = (c_i \ldots c_i)_{2^n} = (2^{mn} - 1)c_i/(2^n - 1)$. This construction is possible thanks to the fact that variable-length shifts are prohibited.

[Notice that if $m = 2^d$, we can use this idea to simulate 2^d instances of $f(x, y_i)$; then $O(d)$ further operations allow "quantification."]

115. (a) $z \leftarrow (\bar{x} \ll 1) \mathbin{\&} (x \ll 2)$, $y \leftarrow x \mathbin{\&} (x + z)$. [This problem was posed to the author by Vaughan Pratt in 1977.]

(b) First find $x_l \leftarrow (x \ll 1) \mathbin{\&} \bar{x}$ and $x_r \leftarrow x \mathbin{\&} (\bar{x} \ll 1)$, the left and right ends of x's blocks; and set $x_r' \leftarrow x_r \mathbin{\&} (x_r - 1)$. Then $z_e \leftarrow x_r' \mathbin{\&} (x_r' - (x_l \mathbin{\&} \bar{\mu}_0))$ and $z_o \leftarrow x_r' \mathbin{\&} (x_r' - (x_l \mathbin{\&} \mu_0))$ are the right ends that are followed by a left end in even or odd position, respectively. The answer is $y \leftarrow x \mathbin{\&} (x + (z_e \mathbin{\&} \bar{\mu}_0) + (z_o \mathbin{\&} \mu_0))$; it can be simplified to $y \leftarrow x \mathbin{\&} (x + (z_e \oplus (x_r' \mathbin{\&} \mu_0)))$.

(c) This case is impossible, by Corollary I.

116. The language L is well defined, by Lemma A (except that the presence or absence of the empty string is irrelevant). A language is regular if and only if it can be defined by a finite-state automaton, and a 2-adic integer is rational if and only if it can be defined by a finite-state automaton that ignores its inputs. The identity function corresponds to the language $L = 1(0 \cup 1)^*$, and a simple construction will define an automaton that corresponds to the sum, difference, or Boolean combination of the numbers defined by any two given automata acting on the sequence $x_0 x_1 x_2 \ldots$. Hence L is regular.

In exercise 115, L is (a) $11^*(000^*1(0 \cup 1)^* \cup 0^*)$; (b) $11^*(00(00)^*1(0 \cup 1)^* \cup 0^*)$.

117. Incidentally, the stated language L corresponds to an inverse Gray binary code: It defines a function with the property that $f(2x) = {\sim}f(2x+1)$, and $g(f(2x)) = g(f(2x+1)) = x$, where $g(x) = x \oplus (x \gg 1)$ (see Eq. 7.2.1.1–(9)).

118. If $x = (x_{n-1} \ldots x_1 x_0)_2$ and $0 \leq a_j \leq 2^j$ for $0 \leq j < n$, we have $\sum_{j=0}^{n-1} a_j x_j = \sum_{j=0}^{n-1} (a_j \mathbin{\dot-} (\bar{x} \mathbin{\&} 2^j))$. Take $a_j = \lfloor 2^{j-1} \rfloor$ to get $x \gg 1$.

Conversely, the following argument by M. S. Paterson proves that monus must be used at least $n - 1$ times: Consider any chain for $f(x)$ that uses addition, subtraction, bitwise Booleans, and k occurrences of the "underflow" operation $y \triangleleft z = (2^n - 1)[y < z]$. If $k < n-1$ there must be two n-bit numbers x' and x'' such that $x' \bmod 2 = x'' \bmod 2 = 0$ and such that all k of the $\triangleleft$'s yield the same result for both x' and x''. Then $f(x') \bmod 2^j = f(x'') \bmod 2^j$ when $j = \rho(x' \oplus x'')$. So $f(x)$ is not the function $x \gg 1$.

119. $z \leftarrow x \oplus y$, $f \leftarrow 2^p \mathbin{\&} \bar{z} \mathbin{\&} (z - 1)$. (See (90).)

120. Generalizing Corollary W, these are the functions such that $f(x_1, \ldots, x_m) \equiv f(y_1, \ldots, y_m)$ (modulo 2^k) whenever $x_j \equiv y_j$ (modulo 2^k) for $1 \le j \le m$, for $0 \le k \le n$. The least significant bit is a binary function of m variables, so it has 2^{2^m} possibilities. The next-to-least is a binary function of $2m$ variables, namely the bits of $(x_1 \bmod 4, \ldots, x_m \bmod 4)$, so it has $2^{2^{2m}}$; and so on. Thus the answer is $2^{2^m + 2^{2m} + \cdots + 2^{nm}}$.

121. (a) If f has a period of length pq, where $q > 1$ is odd, its p-fold iteration $f^{[p]}$ has a period of length q, say $y_0 \mapsto y_1 \mapsto \cdots \mapsto y_q = y_0$ where $y_{j+1} = f^{[p]}(y_j)$ and $y_1 \ne y_0$. But then, by Corollary W, we must have $y_0 \bmod 2^{n-1} \mapsto y_1 \bmod 2^{n-1} \mapsto \cdots \mapsto y_q \bmod 2^{n-1}$ in the corresponding $(n-1)$-bit chain. Consequently $y_1 \equiv y_0$ (modulo 2^{n-1}), by induction on n. Hence $y_1 = y_0 \oplus 2^{n-1}$, and $y_2 = y_0$, etc., a contradiction.

(b) $x_1 = x_0 + x_0$, $x_2 = x_0 \gg (p-1)$, $x_3 = x_1 \mid x_2$; a period of length p starts with the value $x_0 = (1 + 2^p + 2^{2p} + \cdots) \bmod 2^n$.

122. Subtraction is analogous to addition; Boolean operations are even simpler; and constants have only one bit pattern. The only remaining case is $x_r = x_j \gg c$, where we have $S_r = S_j + c$; the shift goes left when $c < 0$. Then $V_{pqr} = V_{(p+c)(q+c)j}$, and

$$x_r \mathbin{\&} \lfloor 2^p - 2^q \rfloor = ((x_j \mathbin{\&} \lfloor 2^{p+c} - 2^{q+c} \rfloor) \gg c) \mathbin{\&} (2^n - 1).$$

Hence $|X_{pqr}| \le |X_{(p+c)(q+c)j}| \le B_j = B_r$ by induction.

123. If $x = (x_{g-1} \ldots x_0)_2$, note first that $t = 2^{g-1}(x_0 \ldots x_{g-1})_{2^g}$ in (104); hence $y = (x_0 \ldots x_{g-1})_2$ as claimed. Theorem P now implies that $\lfloor \frac{1}{3} \lg g \rfloor$ broadword steps are needed to multiply by a_{g+1} and by a_{g-1}. At least one of those multiplications must require $\lfloor \frac{1}{6} \lg g \rfloor$ or more steps.

124. Initially $t \leftarrow 0$, $x_0 = x$, $U_0 = \{1, 2, \ldots, 2^{n-1}\}$, and $1' \leftarrow 0$. When advancing $t \leftarrow t + 1$, if the current instruction is $r_i \leftarrow r_j \pm r_k$ we simply define $x_t = x_{j'} \pm x_{k'}$ and $i' \leftarrow t$. The cases $r_i \leftarrow r_j \circ r_k$ and $r_i \leftarrow c$ are similar.

If the current instruction branches when $r_i \le r_j$, define $x_t = x_{t-1}$ and let $V_1 = \{x \in U_{t-1} \mid x_{i'} \le x_{j'}\}$, $V_0 = U_{t-1} \setminus V_1$. Let U_t be the larger of V_0 and V_1; branch if $U_t = V_1$. Notice that $|U_t| \ge |U_{t-1}|/2$ in this case.

If the current instruction is $r_i \leftarrow r_j \gg r_k$, let $W = \{x \in U_{t-1} \mid x \mathbin{\&} \lfloor 2^{\lg n + s} - 2^s \rfloor \ne 0$ for some $s \in S_{k'}\}$, and note that $|W| \le |S_{k'}| \lg n \le 2^{t-1+e+f}$. Let $V_c = \{x \in U_{t-1} \setminus W \mid x_{k'} = c\}$ for $|c| < n$, and $V_n = U_{t-1} \setminus W \setminus \bigcup_{|c| < n} V_c$. Lemma B tells us that at most $B_{k'} + 1 \le 2^{2^{t-1}-1} + 1$ of the sets V_c are nonempty. Let U_t be the largest; and if it is V_c, define $x_t = x_{j'} \gg c$, $i' \leftarrow t$. In this case $|U_t| \ge (|U_{t-1}| - 2^{t-1+e+f})/(2^{2^{t-1}-1} + 1)$.

Similarly for $r_i \leftarrow M[r_j \bmod 2^m]$ or $M[r_j \bmod 2^m] \leftarrow r_i$, let $W = \{x \in U_{t-1} \mid x \mathbin{\&} \lfloor 2^{m+s} - 2^s \rfloor \ne 0$ for some $s \in S_{j'}\}$, and $V_z = \{x \in U_{t-1} \setminus W \mid x_{j'} \bmod 2^m = z\}$, for $0 \le z < 2^m$. By Lemma B, at most $B_{j'} \le 2^{2^{t-1}-1}$ of the sets V_z are nonempty; let $U_t = V_z$ be the largest. To write r_i in $M[z]$, define $x_t = x_{t-1}$, $z'' \leftarrow i'$; to read r_i from $M[z]$, set $i' \leftarrow t$ and put $x_t = x_{z''}$ if z'' is defined, otherwise let x_t be the precomputed constant $M[z]$. In both cases $|U_t| \ge (|U_{t-1}| - 2^{t-1}m)/2^{2^{t-1}-1}$ is sufficiently large.

If $t < f$ we cannot be sure that $r_1 = \rho x$. The reason is that the set $W = \{x \in U_t \mid x \mathbin{\&} \lfloor 2^{\lg n + s} - 2^s \rfloor \ne 0$ for some $s \in S_{1'}\}$ has size $|W| \le |S_{1'}| \lg n \le 2^{t+e+f}$, and $|U_t \setminus W| \geq 2^{2^{e+f}-2^t+1} - 2^{t+e+f} > 2^{2^t-1} \geq |\{x_{1'} \mathbin{\&} \lfloor 2^{\lg n} - 1 \rfloor \mid x_0 \in U_t \setminus W\}|$. Two elements of $U_t \setminus W$ cannot have the same value of $\rho x = x_{1'} \mathbin{\&} \lfloor 2^{\lg n} - 1 \rfloor$.

[The same lower bound applies even if we allow the RAM to make arbitrary 2^{2^t-1}-way branches based on the contents of $(r_1, \ldots, r_l)$ at time t.]

125. Start as in answer 124, but with $U_0 = [0 .. 2^g)$. Simplifying that argument by eliminating the sets W will yield sets such that $|U_t| \geq 2^g / \max(2^m, 2n)^t$; for example, at most $2n$ different shift instructions can occur.

Suppose we can stop at time t with $t < \lfloor \lg(h+1) \rfloor$. The proof of Theorem P yields p and q with $x^R \mathbin{\&} \lfloor 2^p - 2^q \rfloor$ independent of $x \mathbin{\&} \lfloor 2^{p+s} - 2^{q+s} \rfloor$. Hence the hinted extension of Lemma B shows that x^R takes on at most $2^{2^t-1} \leq 2^{(h-1)/2}$ different values, for every setting of the other bits $\{x \mathbin{\&} \lfloor 2^{p+s} - 2^{q+s} \rfloor \mid s \in S_t\}$. Consequently $r_1 = x_{1'}$ can be the correct value of x^R for at most $2^{(h-1)/2+g-h}$ values of x. But $2^{(h-1)/2+g-h}$ is less than $|U_t|$, by (106).

126. M. S. Paterson has proposed a related (but different) conjecture: For every 2-adic chain with k addition-subtraction operations, there is a (possibly huge) integer x with $\nu x = k+1$ such that the chain does not calculate $2^{\lambda x}$.

127. Johan Håstad [*Advances in Computing Research* **5** (1989), 143–170] has shown that every polynomial-size circuit that computes the parity function from the inputs $\{x_1, \ldots, x_n, \bar{x}_1, \ldots, \bar{x}_n\}$ with AND and OR gates of unlimited fanin must have depth $\Omega(\log n / \log \log n)$.

128. (Note also that the suffix parity function $x^{\oplus}$ is considered in exercises 36 and 117.)

130. If the answer is "no," the analogous question with *variable* a suggests itself.

131. This program does a typical "breadth-first search," keeping $\text{LINK}(q) = r$. Register u is the vertex currently being examined; v is one of its successors.

OH LDOU r,q,link	1	$r \leftarrow \text{LINK}(q)$.	STOU v,q,link $\|R\|-\|Q\|$ $\text{LINK}(q) \leftarrow v$.
SET u,r	1	$u \leftarrow r$.	STOU r,v,link $\|R\|-\|Q\|$ $\text{LINK}(v) \leftarrow r$.
1H LDOU a,u,arcs	$\|R\|$	$a \leftarrow \text{ARCS}(u)$.	SET q,v $\|R\|-\|Q\|$ $q \leftarrow v$.
BZ a,4F	$\|R\|$	Is $S[u] = \emptyset$?	3H PBNZ a,2B S Loop on a.
2H LDOU v,a,tip	S	$v \leftarrow \text{TIP}(a)$.	4H LDOU u,u,link $\|R\|$ $u \leftarrow \text{LINK}(u)$.
LDOU a,a,next	S	$a \leftarrow \text{NEXT}(a)$.	CMPU t,u,r $\|R\|$ Is $u \neq r$?
LDOU t,v,link	S	$t \leftarrow \text{LINK}(v)$.	PBNZ t,1B $\|R\|$ If so, continue.
PBNZ t,3F	S	Is $v \in R$?	∎

132. (a) We always have $\tau(U) \subseteq \mathbin{\&}_{u \notin U} \delta_u = \sigma(U)$. And equality holds if and only if $2^u \subseteq \rho(u')$ for all $u \in U$ and $u' \in U$.

(b) We've proved that $\tau(U) \subseteq \sigma(U)$; hence $T \subseteq U$. And if $t \in T$ we have $2^t \subseteq \rho_u$ for all $u \in U$. Therefore $\sigma(T) \subseteq \tau(T)$.

(c) Parts (a) and (b) prove that the elements of C_n represent the cliques.

(d) If $u \subseteq v$ then $u \mathbin{\&} \rho_k \subseteq v \mathbin{\&} \rho_k$ and $u \mathbin{\&} \delta_k \subseteq v \mathbin{\&} \delta_k$; so we can work entirely with maximal entries. The following algorithm uses cache-friendly sequential (rather than linked) allocation, in a manner analogous to radix exchange sort (Algorithm 5.2.2R).

We assume that $w_1 \ldots w_s$ is a workspace of s unsigned words, bounded by $w_0 = 0$ and $w_{s+1} = 2^n - 1$. The elements of C_{k-1}^{+} appear initially in positions $w_1 \ldots w_m$, and our goal is to replace them by the elements of C_k^{+}.

M1. [Initialize.] Terminate if $\rho_k = 2^n - 1$. Otherwise set $v \leftarrow 2^k$, $i \leftarrow 1$, $j \leftarrow m$.

M2. [Partition on v.] While w_i & $v = 0$, set $i \leftarrow i + 1$. While w_j & $v \neq 0$, set $j \leftarrow j - 1$. Then if $i > j$, go to M3; otherwise swap $w_i \leftrightarrow w_j$, set $i \leftarrow i + 1$, $j \leftarrow j - 1$, and repeat this step.

M3. [Split $w_i \ldots w_m$.] Set $l \leftarrow j$, $p \leftarrow s + 1$. While $i \leq m$, do subroutine Q with $u = w_i$ and set $i \leftarrow i + 1$.

M4. [Combine maximal elements.] Set $m \leftarrow l$. While $p \leq s$, set $m \leftarrow m + 1$, $w_m \leftarrow w_p$, and $p \leftarrow p + 1$. ∎

Subroutine Q uses global variables j, k, l, p, and v. It essentially replaces the word u by $u' = u$ & ρ_k and $u'' = u$ & δ_k, retaining them if they are still maximal. If so, u' goes into the upper workspace $w_p \ldots w_s$ but u'' stays below.

Q1. [Examine u'.] Set $w \leftarrow u$ & ρ_k and $q \leftarrow s$. If $w = u$, go to Q4.

Q2. [Is it comparable?] If $q < p$, go to Q3. Otherwise if w & $w_q = w$, go to Q7. Otherwise if w & $w_q = w_q$, go to Q4. Otherwise set $q \leftarrow q - 1$ and repeat Q2.

Q3. [Tentatively accept u'.] Set $p \leftarrow p - 1$ and $w_p \leftarrow w$. Memory overflow occurs if $p \leq m + 1$. Otherwise go to Q7.

Q4. [Prepare for loop.] Set $r \leftarrow p$ and $w_{p-1} \leftarrow 0$.

Q5. [Remove nonmaximals.] While $w \mid w_q \neq w$, set $q \leftarrow q - 1$. While $w \mid w_r = w$, set $r \leftarrow r + 1$. Then if $q < r$, go to Q6; otherwise set $w_q \leftarrow w_r$, $w_r \leftarrow 0$, $q \leftarrow q - 1$, $r \leftarrow r + 1$, and repeat this step.

Q6. [Reset p.] Set $w_q \leftarrow w$ and $p \leftarrow q$. Terminate the subroutine if $w = u$.

Q7. [Examine u''.] Set $w \leftarrow u$ & $\bar{v}$. If $w = w_q$ for some q in the range $1 \leq q \leq j$, do nothing. Otherwise set $l \leftarrow l + 1$ and $w_l \leftarrow w$. ∎

In practice this algorithm performs reasonably well; for example, when it is applied to the 8×8 queen graph (exercise 7–129), it finds the 310 maximal cliques after 306,513 mems of computation, using 397 words of workspace. It finds the 10188 maximal independent sets of that same graph after about 310 megamems, using 15090 words; there are respectively $(728, 6912, 2456, 92)$ such sets of sizes $(5, 6, 7, 8)$, including the 92 famous solutions to the eight queens problem.

Reference: N. Jardine and R. Sibson, *Mathematical Taxonomy* (Wiley, 1971), Appendix 5. Many other algorithms for listing maximal cliques have also been published. See, for example, W. Knödel, *Computing* **3** (1968), 239–240, **4** (1969), 75; C. Bron and J. Kerbosch, *CACM* **16** (1973), 575–577; S. Tsukiyama, M. Ide, H. Ariyoshi, and I. Shirakawa, *SICOMP* **6** (1977), 505–517; E. Loukakis, *Computers and Math. with Appl.* **9** (1983), 583–589; D. S. Johnson, M. Yannakakis, and C. H. Papadimitriou, *Inf. Proc. Letters* **27** (1988), 119–123. See also exercise 5–23.

133. (a) An independent set is a clique of $\overline{G}$; so complement G. (b) A vertex cover is the complement of an independent set; so complement G, then complement the outputs.

134. $a \mapsto 00$, $b \mapsto 01$, $c \mapsto 11$ is the first mapping of class II.

135. The unary operators are simple: $\neg(x_l x_r) = \bar{x}_r \bar{x}_l$; $\diamond(x_l x_r) = x_r x_r$; $\square(x_l x_r) = x_l x_l$. And $x_l x_r \Leftrightarrow y_l y_r = (z_l \wedge z_r)(z_l \vee z_r)$, where $z_l = (x_l \equiv y_l)$ and $z_r = (x_r \equiv y_r)$.

136. (a) Classes II, III, IV_a, and IV_c all have the optimum cost 4. Curiously the functions $z_l = x_l \vee y_l \vee (x_r \wedge y_r)$, $z_r = x_r \vee y_r$ work for the mapping $(a, b, c) \mapsto (00, 01, 11)$ of class II as well as for the mapping $(a, b, c) \mapsto (00, 01, 1*)$ of class IV_c. [This operation is equivalent to saturating addition, when $a = 0$, $b = 1$, and c stands for "more than 1."]

(b) The symmetry between a, b, and c implies that we need only try classes I, IV_a, and V_a; and those classes turn out to cost 6, 7, and 8. One winner for class I, with

$(a, b, c) \mapsto (00, 01, 10)$, is $z_l = v_r \wedge \bar{u}_l$, $z_r = v_l \wedge \bar{u}_r$, where $u_l = x_l \oplus y_l$, $u_r = x_r \oplus y_r$, $v_l = y_r \oplus u_l$, and $v_r = y_l \oplus u_r$. [See exercise 7.1.2–60, which gives the same answer but with $z_l \leftrightarrow z_r$. The reason is that we have $(x + y + z) \bmod 3 = 0$ in this problem but $(x + y - z) \bmod 3 = 0$ in that one; and $z_l \leftrightarrow z_r$ is equivalent to negation. The binary operation $z = x \circ y$ in this case can also be characterized by the fact that the elements (x, y, z) are all the same or all different; thus it is familiar to people who play the game of SET. It is the only binary operation on n-element sets that has $n!$ automorphisms and differs from the trivial examples $x \circ y = x$ or $x \circ y = y$.]

(c) Cost 3 is achieved only with class I: Let $(a, b, c) \mapsto (00, 01, 10)$ and $z_l = (x_l \vee x_r) \wedge y_l$, $z_r = \bar{x}_r \wedge y_r$.

137. In fact, $z = (x + 1) \mathbin{\&} y$ when $(a, b, c) \mapsto (00, 01, 10)$. [It's a contrived example.]

138. The simplest case known to the author requires the calculation of *two* binary operations, such as

$$\begin{pmatrix} a & b & b \\ a & b & b \\ c & a & a \end{pmatrix} \quad \text{and} \quad \begin{pmatrix} a & b & a \\ a & b & a \\ c & a & c \end{pmatrix};$$

each has cost 2 in class V_a, but the costs are $(3, 2)$ and $(2, 3)$ in classes I and II.

139. The calculation of z_2 is essentially equivalent to exercise 136(b); so the natural representation (111) wins. Fortunately this representation also is good for z_1, with $z_{1l} = x_l \wedge y_l$, $z_{1r} = x_r \wedge y_r$.

140. With representation (111), first use full binary adders to compute $(a_1 a_0)_2 = x_l + y_l + z_l$ and $(b_1 b_0)_2 = x_r + y_r + z_r$ in $5 + 5 = 10$ steps. Now the "greedy footprint" method shows how to compute the four desired functions of (a_1, a_0, b_1, b_0) in eight further steps: $u_l = a_1 \wedge \bar{b}_0$, $u_r = a_0 \wedge \bar{b}_1$; $t_1 = a_1 \oplus b_0$, $t_2 = a_0 \oplus b_1$, $t_3 = a_1 \oplus t_2$, $t_4 = a_0 \oplus t_1$, $v_l = t_3 \wedge \bar{t}_1$, $v_r = t_4 \wedge \bar{t}_2$. [Is this method optimum?]

141. Suppose we've computed bits $a = a_0 a_1 \ldots a_{2m-1}$ and $b = b_0 b_1 \ldots b_{2m-1}$ such that

$$a_s = [s = 1 \text{ or } s = 2 \text{ or } s \text{ is a sum of distinct Ulam numbers} \leq m \text{ in exactly one way}],$$
$$b_s = [s \text{ is a sum of distinct Ulam numbers} \leq m \text{ in more than one way}],$$

for some integer $m = U_n \geq 2$. For example, when $m = n = 2$ we have $a = 0111$ and $b = 0000$. Then $\{s \mid s \leq m \text{ and } a_s = 1\} = \{U_1, \ldots, U_n\}$; and $U_{n+1} = \min\{s \mid s > m \text{ and } a_s = 1\}$. (Notice that $a_s = 1$ when $s = U_{n-1} + U_n$.) The following simple bitwise operations preserve these conditions: $n \leftarrow n + 1$, $m \leftarrow U_n$, and

$$(a_m \ldots a_{2m-1}, b_m \ldots b_{2m-1}) \leftarrow ((a_m \ldots a_{2m-1} \oplus a_0 \ldots a_{m-1}) \mathbin{\&} \overline{b_m \ldots b_{2m-1}},$$
$$(a_m \ldots a_{2m-1} \mathbin{\&} a_0 \ldots a_{m-1}) \mid b_m \ldots b_{2m-1}),$$

where $a_s = b_s = 0$ for $2U_{n-1} \leq s < 2U_n$ on the right side of this assignment.

[See M. C. Wunderlich, *BIT* **11** (1971), 217–224; *Computers in Number Theory* (1971), 249–257. These mysterious numbers, which were first defined by S. Ulam in *SIAM Review* **6** (1964), 348, have baffled number theorists for many years. The ratio U_n/n appears to converge to a constant, ≈ 13.52; for example, $U_{20000000} = 270371127$ and $U_{40000000} = 540752349$. Furthermore, D. W. Wilson has observed empirically that the numbers form quasi-periodic "clusters" whose centers differ by multiples of another constant, ≈ 21.6016. Calculations by Jud McCranie and the author for $U_n < 640000000$ indicate that the largest gap $U_n - U_{n-1}$ may occur between $U_{24576523} = 332250401$ and $U_{24576524} = 332251032$; the smallest gap $U_n - U_{n-1} = 1$ apparently occurs only when $U_n \in \{2, 3, 4, 48\}$. Certain small gaps like 6, 11, 14, and 16 have never been observed.]

142. Algorithm E in that exercise performs the following operations on subcubes: (i) Count the $*$s in a given subcube c. (ii) Given c and c', test if $c \subseteq c'$. (iii) Given c and c', compute $c \sqcup c'$ (if it exists). Operation (i) is simple with sideways addition; let's see which of the nine classes of two-bit encodings (119), (123), (124) works best for (ii) and (iii). Suppose $a = 0$, $b = 1$, $c = *$; the symmetry between 0 and 1 means that we need only examine classes I, III, IV_a, IV_c, V_a, and V_c.

For the asterisks-and-bits mapping $(0, 1, *) \mapsto (00, 01, 10)$, which belongs to class I, the truth table for $c \not\subseteq c'$ is 010*100*110***** in each component. (For example, $0 \subseteq *$ and $* \not\subseteq 1$. The $*$s in this truth table are don't-cares for the unused codes 11.) The methods of Section 7.1.2 tell us that the cheapest such functions have cost 3; for example, $c \subseteq c'$ if and only if $((b \oplus b') \mid a) \,\&\, \bar{a}' = 0$. Furthermore the consensus $c \sqcup c' = c''$ exists if and only if $\nu z = 1$, where $z = (b \oplus b') \,\&\, {\sim}(a \oplus a')$. And in that case, $a'' = (a \oplus b \oplus b') \,\&\, {\sim}(a \oplus a')$, $b'' = (b \mid b') \,\&\, \bar{z}$. [The asterisk and bit codes were used for this purpose by M. A. Breuer in *Proc. ACM Nat. Conf.* **23** (1968), 241–250.]

But class III works out better, with $(0, 1, *) \mapsto (01, 10, 00)$. Then $c \subseteq c'$ if and only if $(\bar{c}_l \,\&\, c'_l) \mid (\bar{c}_r \,\&\, c'_r) = 0$; $c \sqcup c' = c''$ exists if and only if $\nu z = 1$ where $z = x \,\&\, y$, $x = c_l \mid c'_l$, $y = c_r \mid c'_r$; and $c''_l = x \oplus z$, $c''_r = y \oplus z$. We save two operations for each consensus, with respect to class I, compensating for an extra step when counting asterisks.

Classes IV_a, V_a, and V_c turn out to be far inferior. Class IV_c has some merit, but class III is best.

143. $f(x) = ((x \,\&\, m_1) \ll 17) \mid ((x \gg 17) \,\&\, m_1) \mid ((x \,\&\, m_2) \ll 15) \mid ((x \gg 15) \,\&\, m_2) \mid ((x \,\&\, m_3) \ll 10) \mid ((x \gg 10) \,\&\, m_3) \mid ((x \,\&\, m_4) \ll 6) \mid ((x \gg 6) \,\&\, m_4)$, where $m_1 = {}^\#\texttt{7f7f7f7f7f7f}$, $m_2 = {}^\#\texttt{fefefefefefe}$, $m_3 = {}^\#\texttt{3f3f3f3f3f3f3f}$, $m_4 = {}^\#\texttt{fcfcfcfcfcfc}$. [See, for example, *Chess Skill in Man and Machine*, edited by Peter W. Frey (1977), page 59. Five steps suffice to compute $f(x)$ on MMIX (four MOR operations and one OR), since $f(x) = q \cdot x \cdot q' \mid q' \cdot x \cdot q$ with $q = {}^\#\texttt{40a05028140a0502}$ and $q' = {}^\#\texttt{2010884422110804}$.]

144. Node $j \oplus (k \ll 1)$, where $k = j \,\&\, {-}j$.

145. It names the ancestor of the leaf node $j \mid 1$ at height h.

146. By (136) we want to show that $\lambda(j \,\&\, {-}i) = \rho l$ when $l - 2^{\rho l} < i \le l \le j < l + 2^{\rho l}$. The desired result follows from (35) because $-l \le -i < -l + 2^{\rho l}$.

147. (a) $\pi v_j = \beta v_j = j$, $\alpha v_j = 1 \ll \rho j$, and $\tau j = \Lambda$, for $1 \le j \le n$.

(b) Suppose $n = 2^{e_1} + \cdots + 2^{e_t}$ where $e_1 > \cdots > e_t \ge 0$, and let $n_k = 2^{e_1} + \cdots + 2^{e_k}$ for $0 \le k \le t$. Then $\pi v_j = j$ and $\beta v_j = \alpha v_j = n_k$ for $n_{k-1} < j \le n_k$. Also $\tau n_k = v_{n_{k-1}}$ for $1 \le k \le t$, where $v_0 = \Lambda$; all other $\tau j = \Lambda$.

148. Yes, if $\pi y_1 = 010000$, $\pi y_2 = 010100$, $\pi x_1 = 010101$, $\pi x_2 = 010110$, $\pi x_3 = 010111$, $\beta x_3 = 010111$, $\beta y_2 = 010100$, $\beta x_2 = 011000$, $\beta y_1 = 010000$, and $\beta x_1 = 100000$.

149. We assume that $\text{CHILD}(v) = \text{SIB}(v) = \text{PARENT}(v) = \Lambda$ initially for all vertices v (including $v = \Lambda$), and that there is at least one nonnull vertex.

S1. [Make triply linked tree.] For each of the n arcs $u \longrightarrow v$ (perhaps $v = \Lambda$), set $\text{SIB}(u) \leftarrow \text{CHILD}(v)$, $\text{CHILD}(v) \leftarrow u$, $\text{PARENT}(u) \leftarrow v$. (See exercise 2.3.3–6.)

S2. [Begin first traversal.] Set $p \leftarrow \text{CHILD}(\Lambda)$, $n \leftarrow 0$, and $\lambda 0 \leftarrow -1$.

S3. [Compute β in the easy case.] Set $n \leftarrow n + 1$, $\pi p \leftarrow n$, $\tau n \leftarrow \Lambda$, and $\lambda n \leftarrow 1 + \lambda(n \gg 1)$. If $\text{CHILD}(p) \ne \Lambda$, set $p \leftarrow \text{CHILD}(p)$ and repeat this step; otherwise set $\beta p \leftarrow n$.

S4. [Compute τ, bottom-up.] Set $\tau \beta p \leftarrow \text{PARENT}(p)$. Then if $\text{SIB}(p) \ne \Lambda$, set $p \leftarrow \text{SIB}(p)$ and return to S3; otherwise set $p \leftarrow \text{PARENT}(p)$.

S5. [Compute β in the hard case.] If $p \neq \Lambda$, set $h \leftarrow \lambda(n \mathbin{\&} -\pi p)$, then $\beta p \leftarrow ((n \gg h) \mid 1) \ll h$, and go back to S4.

S6. [Begin second traversal.] Set $p \leftarrow \mathtt{CHILD}(\Lambda)$, $\lambda 0 \leftarrow \lambda n$, $\pi\Lambda \leftarrow \beta\Lambda \leftarrow \alpha\Lambda \leftarrow 0$.

S7. [Compute α, top-down.] Set $\alpha p \leftarrow \alpha(\mathtt{PARENT}(p)) \mid (\beta p \mathbin{\&} -\beta p)$. Then if $\mathtt{CHILD}(p) \neq \Lambda$, set $p \leftarrow \mathtt{CHILD}(p)$ and repeat this step.

S8. [Continue to traverse.] If $\mathtt{SIB}(p) \neq \Lambda$, set $p \leftarrow \mathtt{SIB}(p)$ and go to S7. Otherwise set $p \leftarrow \mathtt{PARENT}(p)$, and repeat step S8 if $p \neq \Lambda$.   ∎

150. We may assume that the elements A_j are distinct, by regarding them as ordered pairs (A_j, j). The hinted binary search tree, which is a special case of the "Cartesian trees" introduced by Jean Vuillemin [*CACM* **23** (1980), 229–239], has the property that $k(i, j)$ is the nearest common ancestor of i and j. Indeed, the ancestors of any given node j are precisely the nodes k such that A_k is a right-to-left minimum of $A_1 \ldots A_j$ or A_k is a left-to-right minimum of $A_j \ldots A_n$.

The algorithm of the preceding answer does the desired preprocessing, except that we need to set up a triply linked tree differently on the nodes $\{0, 1, \ldots, n\}$. Start as before with $\mathtt{CHILD}(v) = \mathtt{SIB}(v) = \mathtt{PARENT}(v) = 0$ for $0 \leq v \leq n$, and let $\Lambda = 0$. Assume that $A_0 \leq A_j$ for $1 \leq j \leq n$. Set $t \leftarrow 0$ and do the following steps for $v = n$, $n - 1$, ..., 1: Set $u \leftarrow 0$; then while $A_v < A_t$ set $u \leftarrow t$ and $t \leftarrow \mathtt{PARENT}(t)$. If $u \neq 0$, set $\mathtt{SIB}(v) \leftarrow \mathtt{SIB}(u)$, $\mathtt{SIB}(u) \leftarrow 0$, $\mathtt{PARENT}(u) \leftarrow v$, $\mathtt{CHILD}(v) \leftarrow u$; otherwise simply set $\mathtt{SIB}(v) \leftarrow \mathtt{CHILD}(t)$. Also set $\mathtt{CHILD}(t) \leftarrow v$, $\mathtt{PARENT}(v) \leftarrow t$, $t \leftarrow v$.

Continue with step S2 after the tree has been built. The running time is $O(n)$, because the operation $t \leftarrow \mathtt{PARENT}(t)$ is performed at most once for each node t. [This beautiful way to reduce the range minimum query problem to the nearest common ancestor problem was discovered by H. N. Gabow, J. L. Bentley, and R. E. Tarjan, *STOC* **16** (1984), 137–138, who also suggested the following exercise.]

151. For node v with k children u_1, ..., u_k, define the node sequence $S(v) = v$ if $k = 0$; $S(v) = vS(u_1)$ if $k = 1$; and $S(v) = S(u_1)v \ldots vS(u_k)$ if $k > 1$. (Consequently v appears exactly $\max(k-1, 1)$ times in $S(v)$.) If there are k trees in the forest, rooted at u_1, ..., u_k, write down the node sequence $S(u_1)\Lambda \ldots \Lambda S(u_k) = V_1 \ldots V_N$. (The length of this sequence will satisfy $n \leq N < 2n$.) Let A_j be the depth of node V_j, for $1 \leq j \leq N$, where Λ has depth 0. (For example, consider the forest (141), but add another child $K \longrightarrow D$ and an isolated node L. Then $V_1 \ldots V_{15} = CFAGJDHDK\Lambda BEI\Lambda L$ and $A_1 \ldots A_{15} = 231342323012301$.) The nearest common ancestor of u and v, when $u = V_i$ and $v = V_j$, is then $V_{k(i,j)}$ in the range minimum query problem. [See J. Fischer and V. Heun, *Lecture Notes in Comp. Sci.* **4009** (2006), 36–48.]

152. Step V1 finds the level above which αx and αy have bits that apply to both of their ancestors. (See exercise 148.) Step V2 increases h, if necessary, to the level where they have a common ancestor, or to the top level λn if they don't (namely if $k = 0$). If $\beta x \neq \beta z$, step V4 finds the topmost level among x's ancestors that leads to level h; hence it knows the lowest ancestor $\hat{x}$ for which $\beta\hat{x} = \beta z$ (or $\hat{x} = \Lambda$). Finally in V5, preorder tells us which of $\hat{x}$ or $\hat{y}$ is an ancestor of the other.

153. That pointer has ρj bits, so it ends after $\rho 1 + \rho 2 + \cdots + \rho j = j - \nu j$ bits of the packed string, by (61). [Here j is even. Navigation piles were introduced in *Nordic Journal of Computing* **10** (2003), 238–262.]

154. The gray lines define $36°$-$36°$-$90°$ triangles, ten of which make a pentagon with $72°$ angles at each vertex. These pentagons tile the hyperbolic plane in such a way that *five* of them meet at each vertex.

155. Observe first that $0 \le (\alpha 0)_{1/\phi} < \phi^{-1} + \phi^{-3} + \phi^{-5} + \cdots = 1$, since there are no consecutive 1s. Observe next that $F_{-n}\phi \equiv \phi^{-n}$ (modulo 1), by exercise 1.2.8–11. Now add $F_{k_1}\phi + \cdots + F_{k_r}\phi$. For example, $(4\phi) \bmod 1 = \phi^{-5} + \phi^{-2}$; $(-2\phi) \bmod 1 = \phi^{-4} + \phi^{-1}$. This argument also proves the interesting formula $\lfloor N(\alpha)\phi \rfloor = -N(\alpha 0)$.

156. (a) Start with $y \leftarrow 0$, and with k large enough that $|x| < F_{k+1}$. If $x < 0$, set $k \leftarrow (k-1) \mid 1$, and while $x + F_k > 0$ set $k \leftarrow k - 2$; then set $y \leftarrow y + (1 \ll k)$, $x \leftarrow x + F_{k+1}$; repeat. Otherwise if $x > 1$, set $k \leftarrow k \mathbin{\&} -2$, and while $x - F_k \le 0$ set $k \leftarrow k - 2$; then set $y \leftarrow y + (1 \ll k)$, $x \leftarrow x - F_{k+1}$; repeat. Otherwise set $y \leftarrow y + x$ and terminate with $y = (\alpha)_2$.

(b) The operations $x_1 \leftarrow a_1$, $y_1 \leftarrow -a_1$, $x_k \leftarrow y_{k-1} + a_k$, $y_k \leftarrow x_{k-1} - x_k$ compute $x_k = N(a_1 \ldots a_k)$ and $y_k = N(a_1 \ldots a_k 0)$. [Does *every* broadword chain for $N(a_1 \ldots a_n)$ require $\Omega(n)$ steps?]

157. The laws are obvious except for the two cases involving $(\alpha-)$. For those we have $N((\alpha-)0^k) = N(\alpha 0^k) + F_{-k-2}$ for all $k \ge 0$, because decrementation never "borrows" at the right. (But the analogous formula $N((\alpha+)0^k) = N(\alpha 0^k) + F_{-k-1}$ does *not* hold.)

158. Incrementation satisfies the rules $(\alpha 00)+ = \alpha 01$, $(\alpha 10)+ = (\alpha+)00$, $(\alpha 1)+ = (\alpha+)0$. It can be achieved with six 2-adic operations on the integer $x = (\alpha)_2$ by setting $y \leftarrow x \mid (x \gg 1)$, $z \leftarrow y \mathbin{\&} \sim(y+1)$, $x \leftarrow (x \mid z) + 1$.

Decrementation of a nonzero codeword is more difficult. It satisfies $(\alpha 10^{2k})- = \alpha 0(10)^k$, $(\alpha 10^{2k+1})- = \alpha(01)^{k+1}$; hence by Corollary I it cannot be computed by a 2-adic chain. Yet six operations suffice, if we allow monus: $y \leftarrow x - 1$, $z \leftarrow y \mathbin{\&} \bar{x}$, $w \leftarrow z \mathbin{\&} \mu_0$, $x \leftarrow y - w + (w \mathbin{\dot-} (z - w))$.

159. Besides the Fibonacci number system (146) and the negaFibonacci number system (147), there's also an *odd Fibonacci number system*: *Every positive integer x can be written uniquely in the form*

$$x = F_{l_1} + F_{l_2} + \cdots + F_{l_s}, \qquad \text{where } l_1 \ggg l_2 \ggg \cdots \ggg l_s > 0 \text{ and } l_s \text{ is odd.}$$

Given a negaFibonacci code α, the following 20-step 2-adic chain converts $x = (\alpha)_2$ to $y = (\beta)_2$ to $z = (\gamma)_2$, where β is the odd codeword with $N(\alpha) = F(\beta)$ and γ is the standard codeword with $F(\beta) = F(\gamma 0)$: $x^+ \leftarrow x \mathbin{\&} \mu_0$, $x^- \leftarrow x \oplus x^+$; $d \leftarrow x^+ - x^-$; $t \leftarrow d \mid x^-$, $t \leftarrow t \mathbin{\&} \sim(t \ll 1)$; $y \leftarrow (d \mathbin{\&} \bar{\mu}_0) \oplus t \oplus ((t \mathbin{\&} x^-) \gg 1)$; $z \leftarrow (y + 1) \gg 1$; $w \leftarrow z \oplus (4\mu_0)$; $t \leftarrow w \mathbin{\&} \sim(w+1)$; $z \leftarrow z \oplus (t \mathbin{\&} (z \oplus ((w+1) \gg 1)))$.

Corresponding negaFibonacci and odd representations satisfy the remarkable law

$$F_{k_1+m} + \cdots + F_{k_r+m} = (-1)^m (F_{l_1-m} + \cdots + F_{l_s-m}), \qquad \text{for all integers } m.$$

For example, if $N(\alpha) < 0$ the steps above will convert $x = (\alpha 0)_2$ to $y = (\beta)_2$, where $F((\beta \gg 2)0) = -N(\alpha)$. Furthermore β is the odd code for negaFibonacci α if and only if α^R is the odd code for negaFibonacci β^R, when $|\alpha| = |\beta|$ is odd and $N(\alpha) > 0$.

No finite 2-adic chain will go the other way, by Corollary I, because the Fibonacci code 10^k corresponds to negaFibonacci 10^{k+1} when k is odd, $(10)^{k/2}1$ when k is even. But if γ is a standard Fibonacci codeword we can compute $y = (\beta)_2$ from $z = (\gamma)_2$ by setting $y \leftarrow z \ll 1$, $t \leftarrow y \mathbin{\&} (y-1) \mathbin{\&} \bar{\mu}_0$, $y \leftarrow y - t + [t \ne 0]((t-1) \mathbin{\&} \mu_0)$. And then the method above will compute α^R from β^R. The overall running time for conversion to negaFibonacci form will then be of order $\log |\gamma|$, for two string reversals.

160. The text's rules are actually incomplete: They should also define the orientation of each neighbor. Let us stipulate that $\alpha_{sn} = \alpha$; $\alpha_{en} = \alpha$; $(\alpha 0)_{wn} = \alpha 0$, $(\alpha 1)_{wo} = \alpha 1$; $(\alpha 00)_{ns} = \alpha 00$, $(\alpha 10)_{nw} = \alpha 10$, $(\alpha 1)_{ne} = \alpha 1$; $(\alpha 0)_{oo} = \alpha 0$, $(\alpha 101)_{oo} = \alpha 101$,

$(\alpha 1001)_{oo} = \alpha 1001$, $(\alpha 0001)_{ow} = \alpha 0001$. Then a case analysis proves that all cells within d steps of the starting cell have a consistent labeling and orientation, by induction on the graph distance d. (Note the identity $\alpha + = ((\alpha 0)-) \gg 1$.) Furthermore the labeling remains consistent when we attach y coordinates and move when necessary from one strip to another via the δ-rules of (153).

161. Yes, it is bipartite, because all of its edges are defined by the set of boundary lines. (The hyperbolic *cylinder* cannot be bicolored; but two adjacent strips can.)

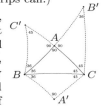

162. It's convenient to view the hyperbolic plane through another lens, by mapping its points to the upper halfplane $\Im z > 0$. Then the "straight lines" become semicircles centered on the x-axis, together with vertical halflines as a limiting case. In this representation, the edges $|z - 1| = \sqrt{2}$, $|z| = r$, and $\Re z = 0$ define a 36°-45°-90° triangle if $r^2 = \phi + \sqrt{\phi}$. Every triangle ABC has three neighbors CBA', ACB', and BAC', obtained by "reflecting" two of its edges about the third, where the reflection of $|z - c'| = r'$ about $|z - c| = r$ is $|z - c - \frac{1}{2}(x_1 + x_2)| = \frac{1}{2}|x_1 - x_2|$, $x_j = r^2/(c' \pm r' - c)$.

The mapping $z \mapsto (z - z_0)/(z - \bar{z}_0)$ takes the upper halfplane into the unit circle; when $z_0 = \frac{1}{2}(\sqrt{\phi} - 1/\phi)(1 + 5^{1/4}i)$ the central pentagon will be symmetric. Repeated reflections of the initial triangle, using breadth-first search until reaching triangles that are invisible, will lead to Fig. 14. To get just the pentagons (without the gray lines), one can begin with just the central cell and perform reflections about *its* edges, etc.

163. (This figure can be drawn as in exercise 162, starting with vertices that project to the three points ir, $ir\omega$, and $ir\omega^2$, where $r^2 = \frac{1}{2}(1 + \sqrt{2})(4 - \sqrt{2} - \sqrt{6})$ and $\omega = e^{2\pi i/3}$. Using a notation devised by L. Schläfli in 1852, it can be described as the infinite tiling with parameters $\{3, 8\}$, meaning that eight triangles meet at every vertex; see Schläfli's *Gesammelte Mathematische Abhandlungen* **1** (1950), 212. Similarly, the pentagrid and the tiling of exercise 154 have Schläfli symbols $\{5, 4\}$ and $\{5, 5\}$, respectively.)

164. The original definition requires more computation, even though it can be factored:
$$\text{custer}'(X) = X \mathbin{\&} \sim(Y_{\mathrm{N}} \mathbin{\&} Y \mathbin{\&} Y_{\mathrm{S}}), \qquad Y = X_{\mathrm{W}} \mathbin{\&} X \mathbin{\&} X_{\mathrm{E}}.$$

But the main reason for preferring (157) is that it produces a thinner, kingwise connected border. The rookwise connected border that results from the 1957 definition is less attractive, because it's noticeably darker when the border travels diagonally than when it travels horizontally or vertically. (Try some experiments and you'll see.)

165. The first image $X^{(1)}$ is the "outer" border of the original black pixels. Fingerprint-like whorls are formed thereafter. For example, starting with Fig. 15(a) we get

in a 120 × 120 bitmap, eventually alternating endlessly between two bizarre patterns. (Does *every* nonempty $M \times N$ bitmap lead to such a 2-cycle?)

166. If $X = \text{custer}(X)$, the sum of the elements of $X + (X \mathbin{\wedge} 1) + (X \ll 1) + (X \gg 1) + (X \mathbin{\vee} 1)$ is at most $4MN + 2M + 2N$, since it is at most 4 in each cell of the rectangle and at most 1 in the adjacent cells. This sum is also five times the number of black pixels. Hence $f(M, N) \leq \frac{4}{5}MN + \frac{2}{5}M + \frac{2}{5}N$. Conversely we get $f(M, N) \geq \frac{4}{5}MN - \frac{2}{5}$ by letting the pixel in row i and column j be black unless $(i + 2j) \bmod 5 = 2$. (This problem is equivalent to finding a minimum dominating set of the $M \times N$ grid.)

167. (a) With 17 steps we can construct a half adder and three full adders (see 7.1.2–(23)) so that $(z_1 z_2)_2 = x_{\mathrm{NW}} + x_{\mathrm{W}} + x_{\mathrm{SW}}$, $(z_3 z_4)_2 = x_{\mathrm{N}} + x_{\mathrm{S}}$, $(z_5 z_6)_2 = x_{\mathrm{NE}} + x_{\mathrm{E}} + x_{\mathrm{SE}}$, and $(z_7 z_8)_2 = z_2 + z_4 + z_6$. Then $f = S_1(z_1, z_3, z_5, z_7) \land (x \lor z_8)$, where the symmetric function f_1 needs seven operations by Fig. 9 in Section 7.1.2. [This solution is based on ideas of W. F. Mann and D. Sleator.]

(b) Given $x^- = X_{j-1}^{(t)}$, $x = X_j^{(t)}$, and $x^+ = X_{j+1}^{(t)}$, compute $a \leftarrow x^- \,\&\, x^+ \ (= z_3)$, $b \leftarrow x^- \oplus x^+ \ (= z_4)$, $c \leftarrow x \oplus b$, $d \leftarrow c \gg 1 \ (= z_6)$, $c \leftarrow c \ll 1 \ (= z_2)$, $e \leftarrow c \oplus d$, $c \leftarrow c \,\&\, d$, $f \leftarrow b \,\&\, e$, $f \leftarrow f \mid c \ (= z_7)$, $e \leftarrow b \oplus e \ (= z_8)$, $c \leftarrow x \,\&\, b$, $c \leftarrow c \mid a$, $b \leftarrow c \ll 1 \ (= z_5)$, $c \leftarrow c \gg 1 \ (= z_1)$, $d \leftarrow b \,\&\, c$, $c \leftarrow b \mid c$, $b \leftarrow a \,\&\, f$, $f \leftarrow a \mid f$, $f \leftarrow d \mid f$, $c \leftarrow b \mid c$, $f \leftarrow f \oplus c \ (= S_1(z_1, z_3, z_5, z_7))$, $e \leftarrow e \mid x$, $f \leftarrow f \,\&\, e$.

[For excellent summaries of the joys and passions of Life, including a proof that any Turing machine can be simulated, see Martin Gardner, *Wheels, Life and Other Mathematical Amusements* (1983), Chapters 20–22; E. R. Berlekamp, J. H. Conway, and R. K. Guy, *Winning Ways* **4** (A. K. Peters, 2004), Chapter 25.]

> *At last I've got what I wanted — an apparently unpredictable law of genetics.*
> *. . . Overpopulation, like underpopulation, tends to kill.*
> *A healthy society is neither too dense nor too sparse.*
> — JOHN H. CONWAY, letter to Martin Gardner (March 1970)

168. The following algorithm, which uses four n-bit registers x^-, x, x^+, and y, works properly even when $M = 1$ or $N = 1$. It needs only about two reads and two writes per raster word to transform $X^{(t)}$ to $X^{(t+1)}$ in (158):

C1. [Loop on k.] Do step C2 for $k = 1, 2, \ldots, N'$; then go to C5.

C2. [Loop on j.] Set $x \leftarrow A_{(M-1)k}$, $x^+ \leftarrow A_{0k}$, and $A_{Mk} \leftarrow x^+$. Then perform steps C3 and C4 for $j = 0, 1, \ldots, M - 1$.

C3. [Move down.] Set $x^- \leftarrow x$, $x \leftarrow x^+$, and $x^+ \leftarrow A_{(j+1)k}$. (Now $x = A_{jk}$, and x^- holds the former value of $A_{(j-1)k}$.) Compute the bitwise function values $y \leftarrow f(x^- \gg 1, x^-, x^- \ll 1, x \gg 1, x, x \ll 1, x^+ \gg 1, x^+, x^+ \ll 1)$.

C4. [Update A_{jk}.] Set $x^- \leftarrow A_{j(k-1)} \,\&\, {-}2$, $y \leftarrow y \,\&\, (2^{n-1} - 1)$, $A_{j(k-1)} \leftarrow x^- + (y \gg (n-2))$, $A_{jk} \leftarrow y + (x^- \ll (n-2))$.

C5. [Wrap around.] For $0 \le j < M$, set $x \leftarrow A_{jN'} \,\&\, {-}2^{n-1-d}$, $A_{jN'} \leftarrow x + (A_{j1} \gg d)$, and $A_{j1} \leftarrow A_{j1} + (x \ll d)$, where $d = 1 + (N - 1) \bmod (n - 2)$. ∎

[An $M \times N$ torus is equivalent to an $(M - 1) \times (N - 1)$ array surrounded by zeros, in many cases like (157) and (159) and even (161). For exercise 173 we can clean an $(M - 2) \times (N - 2)$ array that is bordered by two rows and columns of zeros. But Life images (exercise 167) can grow without bound; they can't safely be confined to a torus.]

169. It quickly morphs into a rabbit, which proceeds to explode. Beginning at time 278, all activity stabilizes to a two-cycle formed from a set of traffic lights and three additional blinkers, together with three still lifes (tub, boat, and bee hive).

170. If $M \ge 2$ and $N \ge 2$, the first step blanks out the top row and the rightmost column. Then if $M \ge 3$ and $N \ge 3$, the next step blanks out the bottom row and the leftmost column. So in general we're left after $t = \min(M, N) - 1$ steps with a single row or column of black pixels: The first $\lceil t/2 \rceil$ rows, the last $\lceil t/2 \rceil$ columns, the last $\lfloor t/2 \rfloor$ rows, and the first $\lfloor t/2 \rfloor$ columns have been set to zero. The automaton will stop after making two more (nonproductive) cycles.

171. Without (160): $x_1 \leftarrow x_{\mathrm{SE}} \,\&\, \bar{x}_{\mathrm{N}}$, $x_2 \leftarrow x_{\mathrm{N}} \,\&\, \bar{x}_{\mathrm{SE}}$, $x_3 \leftarrow x_{\mathrm{E}} \,\&\, \bar{x}_1$, $x_4 \leftarrow x_{\mathrm{NE}} \,\&\, \bar{x}_2$, $x_5 \leftarrow x_3 \mid x_4$, $x_6 \leftarrow x_{\mathrm{W}} \,\&\, \bar{x}_5$, $x_7 \leftarrow x_1 \,\&\, \bar{x}_{\mathrm{NE}}$, $x_8 \leftarrow x_7 \,\&\, \bar{x}_{\mathrm{NW}}$, $x_9 \leftarrow x_{\mathrm{E}} \mid x_{\mathrm{SW}}$, $x_{10} \leftarrow x_8 \,\&\, x_9$, $x_{11} \leftarrow x_{10} \mid x_6$, $x_{12} \leftarrow x_{\mathrm{S}} \,\&\, x_{11}$, $x_{13} \leftarrow x_2 \,\&\, \bar{x}_{\mathrm{E}}$, $x_{14} \leftarrow x_{13} \,\&\, x_{\mathrm{W}}$, $x_{15} \leftarrow x_{\mathrm{N}} \,\&\, x_{\mathrm{NE}}$, $x_{16} \leftarrow x_{\mathrm{SW}} \,\&\, x_{\mathrm{W}}$, $x_{17} \leftarrow x_{15} \mid x_{16}$, $x_{18} \leftarrow x_{\mathrm{NE}} \,\&\, x_{\mathrm{SW}}$, $x_{19} \leftarrow x_{17} \,\&\, \bar{x}_{18}$, $x_{20} \leftarrow x_{\mathrm{E}} \mid x_{\mathrm{SE}}$, $x_{21} \leftarrow x_{20} \mid x_{\mathrm{S}}$, $x_{22} \leftarrow x_{\mathrm{NW}} \,\&\, \bar{x}_{21}$, $x_{23} \leftarrow x_{22} \,\&\, x_{19}$, $x_{24} \leftarrow x_{12} \mid x_{14}$, $g \leftarrow x_{23} \mid x_{24}$. With (160), set $x_4 \leftarrow x_{\mathrm{NE}} \,\&\, \bar{x}_{\mathrm{N}}$ and leave everything else the same.

172. The statement isn't quite true; consider the following examples:

The 'I' and 'H' at the left show that pixels are sometimes left intact where paths join, and that rotating by 90° can make a difference. The next two examples illustrate a quirky influence of left-right reflection. The diamond example demonstrates that very thick images can be unthinnable; none of its black pixels can be removed without changing the number of holes. The final examples, one of which was inspired by the answer to exercise 166, were processed first without (160), in which case they are unchanged by the transformation. But with (160) they're thinned dramatically.

173. (a) If X and Y are closed, $X \,\&\, Y$ is closed; if X and Y are open, $X \mid Y$ is open. Thus X^D is closed and X^L is open; the hinted statement follows. Furthermore $X^{DD} = X^D$ and $X^{LL} = X^L$. (In fact we have $X^L = {\sim}({\sim}X)^D$, because the definitions are dual, obtained by swapping black with white.) Now $X^{DL} \subseteq X^D$, so $X^{DLD} \subseteq X^{DD} = X^D$. And dually, $X^L \subseteq X^{LDL}$. We conclude that there's no reason to launder a clean picture: $X^{DLDL} = (X^{DLD})^L \subseteq X^{DL} \subseteq (X^D)^{LDL} = X^{DLDL}$.

(b) We have $X^D = (X \mid X_{\mathrm{W}} \mid X_{\mathrm{NW}} \mid X_{\mathrm{N}}) \,\&\, (X \mid X_{\mathrm{N}} \mid X_{\mathrm{NE}} \mid X_{\mathrm{E}}) \,\&\, (X \mid X_{\mathrm{E}} \mid X_{\mathrm{SE}} \mid X_{\mathrm{S}}) \,\&\, (X \mid X_{\mathrm{S}} \mid X_{\mathrm{SW}} \mid X_{\mathrm{W}})$. Furthermore, in analogy with answer 167(b), this function can be computed from x^-, x, and x^+ in ten broadword steps: $f \leftarrow x \mid (x \gg 1) \mid ((x^- \mid (x^- \gg 1)) \,\&\, (x^+ \mid (x^+ \gg 1)))$, $f \leftarrow f \,\&\, (f \ll 1)$. [This answer incorporates ideas of D. R. Fuchs.]

To get X^L, just interchange $\mid$ and $\&$. [For further discussion, see C. Van Wyk and D. E. Knuth, Report STAN-CS-79-707 (Stanford Univ., 1979), 15–36.]

174. Three-dimensional digital topology has been studied by R. Malgouyres, *Theoretical Computer Science* **186** (1997), 1–41.

175. There are 25 in the outline, $2 + 3$ in the eyes, $1 + 1$ in the ears, 4 in the nose, and 1 in the smile, totalling 37. (All white pixels are connected kingwise to the background.)

176. (a) If v isn't isolated, there are eight easy cases to consider, depending on what kind of neighbor v has in G.

(b) There's a vertex of G' adjacent to each vertex of $(N_u \cup N_v) \setminus G'$. (Four cases.)

(c) Yes. In fact, by definition (161), we always have $|S'(v')| \geq 2$.

(d) Let $N'_{v'} = \{v \mid v' \in N_v\}$. If v' is the east neighbor of u', call it u'_{E}, either $u' \in G$ or $u'_{\mathrm{S}} \in G$; this element is equal-or-adjacent to every vertex of $N'_{u'} \cup N'_{v'}$. A similar argument applies when $v' = u'_{\mathrm{N}}$. If $v' = u'_{\mathrm{NE}}$, there's no problem if $u' \in G$. Otherwise $u'_{\mathrm{W}} \in G$, $u'_{\mathrm{S}} \in G$, and either $u'_{\mathrm{N}} \in G$ or $u'_{\mathrm{E}} \in G$; hence $N'_{u'} \cup N'_{v'}$ is connected in G. Finally if $v' = u'_{\mathrm{SE}}$, the proof is easy if $u'_{\mathrm{S}} \in G$; otherwise $u' \in G$ and $v' \in G$.

(e) Given a nontrivial component C of G, with $v \in C$ and $v' \in S(v)$, let C' be the component of G' that contains v'. This component C' is well defined, by (a) and (b). Given a component C' of G', with $v' \in C'$ and $v \in S'(v')$, let C be the component of G that contains v. This component C is nontrivial and well defined, by (c) and (d). Finally, the correspondence $C \leftrightarrow C'$ is one-to-one.

177. Now the vertices of G are the *white* pixels, adjacent when they are *rook*-neighbors. So we define $N_{(i,j)} = \{(i,j), (i-1,j), (i,j+1)\}$. Arguments like those of answer 176, but simpler, establish a one-to-one correspondence between the nontrivial components of G and the components of G'.

178. Observe that in adjacent rows of X^*, two pixels of the same value are kingwise neighbors only if they are rookwise connected.

179. The pixels of each row $x_1 \ldots x_N$ can be "runlength encoded" as a sequence of integers $0 = c_0 < c_1 < \cdots < c_{2m+1} = N+2$ so that $x_j = 0$ for $j \in [c_0 .. c_1) \cup [c_2 .. c_3) \cup \cdots \cup [c_{2m} .. c_{2m+1})$ and $x_j = 1$ for $j \in [c_1 .. c_2) \cup \cdots \cup [c_{2m-1} .. c_{2m})$. (The number of runs per row tends to be reasonably small in most images. Notice that the background condition $x_0 = x_{N+1} = 0$ is implicitly assumed.)

The algorithm below uses a modified encoding with $a_j = 2c_j - (j \bmod 2)$ for $0 \le j \le 2m+1$. For example, the second row of the Cheshire cat has $(c_1, c_2, c_3, c_4, c_5) = (5, 8, 23, 25, 32)$; we will use $(a_1, a_2, a_3, a_4, a_5) = (9, 16, 45, 50, 63)$ instead. The reason is that white runs of adjacent rows are rookwise adjacent if and only if the corresponding intervals $[a_j .. a_{j+1})$ and $[b_k .. b_{k+1})$ overlap, and exactly the same condition characterizes when black runs of adjacent rows are kingwise adjacent. Thus the modified encoding nicely unifies both cases (see exercise 178).

We construct a triply linked tree of components, where each node has several fields: CHILD, SIB, and PARENT (tree links); DORMANT (a circular list of all children that aren't connected to the current row); HEIR (a node that has absorbed this one); ROW and COL (location of the first pixel); and AREA (the total number of pixels in the component).

The algorithm traverses the tree in *double order* (see exercise 2.3.1–18), using pairs of pointers (P, P'), where $P' = P$ when P is traversed the first time, $P' = \text{PARENT}(P)$ when P is traversed the second time. The successor of (P, P') is $(Q, Q') = \text{next}(P, P')$, determined as follows: If $P = P'$ and $\text{CHILD}(P) \ne \Lambda$, then $Q \leftarrow Q' \leftarrow \text{CHILD}(P)$; otherwise $Q \leftarrow P$ and $Q' \leftarrow \text{PARENT}(Q)$. If $P \ne P'$ and $\text{SIB}(P) \ne \Lambda$, then $Q \leftarrow Q' \leftarrow \text{SIB}(P)$; otherwise $Q \leftarrow \text{PARENT}(P)$ and $Q' \leftarrow \text{PARENT}(Q)$.

When there are m black runs, the tree will have $m+1$ nodes, not counting nodes that are dormant or have been absorbed. Moreover, the primed pointers $P'_1, \ldots, P'_{2m+1}$ of the double traversal $(P_1, P'_1), \ldots, (P_{2m+1}, P'_{2m+1})$ are precisely the components of the current row, in left-to-right order. For example, in (163) we have $m = 5$; and $(P'_1, \ldots, P'_{11})$ point respectively to ⓪, Ⓑ, ①, Ⓑ, ⓪, Ⓒ, ⓪, Ⓐ, ②, Ⓐ, ⓪.

I1. [Initialize.] Set $t \leftarrow 1$, ROOT $\leftarrow$ LOC(NODE(0)), CHILD(ROOT) $\leftarrow$ SIB(ROOT) $\leftarrow$ PARENT(ROOT) $\leftarrow$ DORMANT(ROOT) $\leftarrow$ HEIR(ROOT) $\leftarrow \Lambda$; also ROW(ROOT) $\leftarrow$ COL(ROOT) $\leftarrow 0$, AREA(ROOT) $\leftarrow N + 2$, $s \leftarrow 0$, $a_0 \leftarrow b_0 \leftarrow 0$, $a_1 \leftarrow 2N + 3$.

I2. [Input a new row.] Terminate if $s > M$. Otherwise set $b_k \leftarrow a_k$ for $k = 1, 2, \ldots$, until $b_k = 2N+3$; then set $b_{k+1} \leftarrow b_k$ as a "stopper." Set $s \leftarrow s+1$. If $s > M$, set $a_1 \leftarrow 2N + 3$; otherwise let $a_1, \ldots, a_{2m+1}$ be the modified runlength encoding of row s as discussed above. (This encoding can be obtained with the help of the ρ function; see (43).) Set $j \leftarrow k \leftarrow 1$ and $P \leftarrow P' \leftarrow$ ROOT.

I3. [Gobble up short b's.] If $b_{k+1} \ge a_j$, go to I9. Otherwise set $(Q, Q') \leftarrow \text{next}(P, P')$, $(R, R') \leftarrow \text{next}(Q, Q')$, and do a four-way branch to (I4, I5, I6, I7) according as $2[Q \ne Q'] + [R \ne R'] = (0, 1, 2, 3)$.

I4. [Case 0.] (Now $Q = Q'$ is a child of P', and $R = R'$ is the first child of Q'. Node Q will remain a child of P', but it will be preceded by any children of R.) Absorb R into P' (see below). Set CHILD(Q) $\leftarrow$ SIB(R) and $Q' \leftarrow$ CHILD(R). If $Q' \ne \Lambda$, set R ← Q′, and while R ≠ Λ set PARENT(R) ← P′, R′ ← R, R ← SIB(R); then SIB(R) ← Q, Q ← Q′. Set CHILD(P) ← Q if P = P′, SIB(P) ← Q if P ≠ P′. Go to I8.

I5. [Case 1.] (Now component Q = R is surrounded by P′ = R′.) If P = P′, set CHILD(P) ← SIB(Q); otherwise set SIB(P) ← SIB(Q). Set R ← DORMANT(R′). Then if R = Λ, set DORMANT(R′) ← SIB(Q) ← Q; otherwise SIB(Q) ← SIB(R) and SIB(R) ← Q. Go to I8.

I6. [Case 2.] (Now Q′ is the parent of both P′ and R. Either P = P′ is childless, or P is the last child of P′.) Absorb R into P′ (see below). Set SIB(P′) ← SIB(R) and R ← CHILD(R). If P = P′, set CHILD(P) ← R; otherwise SIB(P) ← R. While R ≠ Λ, set PARENT(R) ← P′ and R ← SIB(R). Go to I8.

I7. [Case 3.] (Node P′ = Q is the last child of Q′ = R, which is a child of R′.) Absorb P′ into R′ (see below). If P = P′, set P ← R. Otherwise set P′ ← CHILD(P′), and while P′ ≠ Λ set PARENT(P′) ← R′, P′ ← SIB(P′); also set SIB(P) ← SIB(Q′) and SIB(Q′) ← CHILD(Q). If Q = CHILD(R), set CHILD(R) ← Λ. Otherwise set R ← CHILD(R), then R ← SIB(R) until SIB(R) = Q, then SIB(R) ← Λ. Finally set P′ ← R′.

I8. [Advance k.] Set $k \leftarrow k + 2$ and return to step I3.

I9. [Update the area.] Set AREA(P′) ← AREA(P′) + $\lceil a_j/2 \rceil - \lceil a_{j-1}/2 \rceil$. Then go back to I2 if $a_j = 2N + 3$.

I10. [Gobble up short a.] If $a_{j+1} \geq b_k$, go to I11. Otherwise set Q ← LOC(NODE(t)) and $t \leftarrow t + 1$. Set PARENT(Q) ← P′, DORMANT(Q) ← HEIR(Q) ← Λ; also ROW(Q) ← s, COL(Q) ← $\lceil a_j/2 \rceil$, AREA(Q) ← $\lceil a_{j+1}/2 \rceil - \lceil a_j/2 \rceil$. If P = P′, set SIB(Q) ← CHILD(P) and CHILD(P) ← Q; otherwise set SIB(Q) ← SIB(P) and SIB(P) ← Q. Finally set P ← Q, $j \leftarrow j + 2$, and return to I3.

I11. [Move on.] Set $j \leftarrow j + 1$, $k \leftarrow k + 1$, (P, P′) ← next(P, P′), and go to I3. ∎

To "absorb P into Q" means to do the following things: If (ROW(P), COL(P)) is less than (ROW(Q), COL(Q)), set (ROW(Q), COL(Q)) ← (ROW(P), COL(P)). Set AREA(Q) ← AREA(P) + AREA(Q). If DORMANT(Q) = Λ, set DORMANT(Q) ← DORMANT(P); otherwise if DORMANT(P) ≠ Λ, swap SIB(DORMANT(P)) ↔ SIB(DORMANT(Q)). Finally, set HEIR(P) ← Q. (The HEIR links could be used on a second pass to identify the final component of each pixel. Notice that the PARENT links of dormant nodes are not kept up to date.)

[A similar algorithm was given by R. K. Lutz in *Comp. J.* **23** (1980), 262–269.]

180. Let $F(x, y) = x^2 - y^2 + 13$ and $Q(x, y) = F(x - \frac{1}{2}, y - \frac{1}{2}) = x^2 - y^2 - x + y + 13$. Apply Algorithm T to digitize the hyperbola from $(\xi, \eta) = (-6, 7)$ to $(\xi', \eta') = (0, \sqrt{13})$; hence $x = -6$, $y = 7$, $x' = 0$, $y' = 4$. The resulting edges are $(-6, 7) \text{---} (-5, 7) \text{---} (-5, 6) \text{---} (-4, 6) \text{---} (-4, 5) \text{---} (-3, 5) \text{---} (-3, 4) \text{---} \cdots \text{---} (0, 4)$. Then apply it again with $\xi = 0$, $\eta = \sqrt{13}$, $\xi' = 6$, $\eta' = 7$, $x = 0$, $y = 4$, $x' = 6$, $y' = 7$; the same edges are found (in reverse order), but with negated x coordinates.

181. Subdivide at points (ξ, η) where $F_x(\xi, \eta) = 0$ or $F_y(\xi, \eta) = 0$, namely at the real roots of $\{Q(-(b\eta + d)/(2a), \eta + \frac{1}{2}) = 0, \ \xi = -(b\eta + d)/(2a) - \frac{1}{2}\}$ or the real roots of $\{Q(\xi + \frac{1}{2}, -(b\xi + e)/(2c)) = 0, \ \eta = -(b\xi + e)/(2c) - \frac{1}{2}\}$, if they exist.

182. By induction on $|x' - x| + |y' - y|$. Consider, for example, the case $x > x'$ and $y < y'$. We know from (iii) that (ξ, η) lies in the box $x - \frac{1}{2} \leq \xi < x + \frac{1}{2}$ and $y - \frac{1}{2} \leq \eta < y + \frac{1}{2}$, and from (ii) that the curve travels monotonically as it moves from (ξ, η) to (ξ', η'). It must therefore exit the box at the edge $(x - \frac{1}{2}, y - \frac{1}{2}) \text{---} (x - \frac{1}{2}, y + \frac{1}{2})$ or $(x - \frac{1}{2}, y + \frac{1}{2}) \text{---} (x + \frac{1}{2}, y + \frac{1}{2})$. The latter holds if and only if $F(x - \frac{1}{2}, y + \frac{1}{2}) < 0$, because the curve can't intersect that edge twice when $x' < x$. And $F(x - \frac{1}{2}, y + \frac{1}{2})$ is the value $Q(x, y + 1)$ that is tested in step T4, because of the initialization in step T1. (We assume that the curve doesn't go *exactly* through $(x - \frac{1}{2}, y + \frac{1}{2})$, by implicitly adding a tiny positive amount to the function F behind the scenes.)

183. Consider, for example, the ellipse defined by $F(x - \frac{1}{2}, y - \frac{1}{2}) = Q(x, y) = 13x^2 + 7xy + y^2 - 2 = 0$; this ellipse is a cigar-shaped curve that extends roughly between $(-2, 5)$ and $(1, -6)$. Suppose we want to digitize its upper right boundary. Hypotheses (i)–(iv) of Algorithm T hold with

$$\xi = \sqrt{\frac{8}{3}} - \frac{1}{2}, \quad \eta = -\sqrt{\frac{98}{3}} - \frac{1}{2}, \quad \xi' = -\sqrt{\frac{98}{39}} - \frac{1}{2}, \quad \eta' = \sqrt{\frac{104}{3}} - \frac{1}{2},$$

$x = 1$, $y = -6$, $x' = -2$, $y' = 5$. Step T1 sets $Q \leftarrow Q(1, -5) = 1$, which causes step T4 to move left (L); in fact, the resulting path is L^3U^{11}, while the correct digitization according to (164) is $\text{U}^3\text{LU}^4\text{LU}^3\text{LU}$. Failure occurred because $Q(x, y) = 0$ has two roots on the edge $(1, -5)$ — $(2, -5)$, namely $((35 \pm -\sqrt{29})/26, -5)$, causing $Q(1, -5)$ to have the same sign as $Q(2, -5)$. (One of those roots is on the boundary we are *not* trying to draw, but it's still there.) Similar failure occurs with the parabola defined by $Q(x, y) = 9x^2 + 6xy + y^2 - y = 0$, $\xi = -5/12$, $\eta = -1/4$, $\xi' = -5/2$, $\eta' = -19/2$, $x = 0$, $y = 0$, $x' = -2$, $y' = 9$. Hyperbolas can fail too (consider $6x^2 + 5xy + y^2 = 1$).

Algorithms for discrete geometry are notoriously delicate; unusual cases tend to drive them berserk. Algorithm T works properly for portions of any ellipse or parabola whose maximum curvature is less than 2. The maximum curvature of an ellipse with semiaxes $\alpha \geq \beta$ is α/β^2; the cigar-shaped example has maximum curvature ≈ 42.5. The maximum curvature of the parabola $y = \alpha x^2$ is $\alpha/2$; the anomalous parabola above has maximum curvature ≈ 5.27. "Reasonable" conics don't make such sharp turns.

To make Algorithm T work correctly *without* hypothesis (v), we need to slow it down a bit, by changing the tests '$Q < 0$' to '$Q < 0$ or X', where X is a test on the sign of a derivative. Namely, X is respectively '$S > c$', '$R > a$', '$R < -a$', '$S < -c$', in steps T2, T3, T4, T5.

184. Let $Q'(x, y) = -1 - Q(x, y)$. The key point is that $Q(x, y) < 0$ if and only if $Q'(x, y) \geq 0$. (Curiously the algorithm makes the same decisions, backwards, although it probes the values of Q' and Q in different places.)

185. Find a positive integer h so that $d = (\eta - \eta')h$ and $e = (\xi' - \xi)h$ are integers and $d + e$ is even. Then carry out Algorithm T with $x = \lfloor \xi + \frac{1}{2} \rfloor$, $y = \lfloor \eta + \frac{1}{2} \rfloor$, $x' = \lfloor \xi' + \frac{1}{2} \rfloor$, $y' = \lfloor \eta' + \frac{1}{2} \rfloor$, and $Q(x, y) = d(x - \frac{1}{2}) + e(y - \frac{1}{2}) + f$, where

$$f = \lfloor (\eta'\xi - \xi'\eta)h \rfloor - [d > 0 \text{ and } (\eta'\xi - \xi'\eta)h \text{ is an integer}].$$

(The '$d > 0$' term ensures that the opposite straight line, from (ξ', η') back to (ξ, η), will have precisely the same edges; see exercise 183.) Steps T1 and T6–T9 become much simpler than they were in the general case, because $R = d$ and $S = e$ are constant.

(F. G. Stockton [*CACM* **6** (1963), 161, 450] and J. E. Bresenham [*IBM Systems Journal* **4** (1965), 25–30] gave similar algorithms, but with diagonal edges permitted.)

186. (a) $B(\epsilon) = z_0 + 2\epsilon(z_1 - z_0) + O(\epsilon^2)$; $B(1 - \epsilon) = z_2 - 2\epsilon(z_2 - z_1) + O(\epsilon^2)$.

(b) Every point of $S(z_0, z_1, z_2)$ is a convex combination of z_0, z_1, and z_2.

(c) Obviously true, since $(1 - t)^2 + 2(1 - t)t + t^2 = 1$.

(d) The collinear condition follows from (b). Otherwise, by (c), we need only consider the case $z_0 = 0$ and $z_2 - 2z_1 = 1$, where $z_1 = x_1 + iy_1$ and $y_1 \neq 0$. In that case all points lie on the parabola $4x = (y/y_1)^2 + 4yx_1/y_1$.

(e) Note that $B(u\theta) = (1-u)^2 z_0 + 2u(1-u)((1-\theta)z_0 + \theta z_1) + u^2 B(\theta)$ for $0 \leq u \leq 1$.

[S. N. Bernshteĭn introduced $B_n(z_0, z_1, \ldots, z_n; t) = \sum_k \binom{n}{k}(1 - t)^{n-k}t^k z_k$ in *Soobshcheniĭa Khar'kovskoe matematicheskoe obshchestvo* (2) **13** (1912), 1–2.]

187. We can assume that $z_0 = (x_0, y_0)$, $z_1 = (x_1, y_1)$, and $z_2 = (x_2, y_2)$, where the coordinates are (say) fixed-point numbers represented as 16-bit integers divided by 32.

If z_0, z_1, and z_2 are collinear, use the method of exercise 185 to draw a straight line from z_0 to z_2. (If z_1 doesn't lie between z_0 and z_2, the other edges will cancel out, because edges are implicitly XORed by a filling algorithm.) This case occurs if and only if $D = x_0 y_1 + x_1 y_2 + x_2 y_0 - x_1 y_0 - x_2 y_1 - x_0 y_2 = 0$.

Otherwise the points (x, y) of $S(z_0, z_1, z_2)$ satisfy $F(x, y) = 0$, where

$$F(x, y) = \big((x - x_0)(y_2 - 2y_1 + y_0) - (y - y_0)(x_2 - 2x_1 + x_0)\big)^2$$
$$- 4D\big((x_1 - x_0)(y - y_0) - (y_1 - y_0)(x - x_0)\big)$$

and D is defined above. We multiply by 32^4 to obtain integer coefficients; then negate this formula and subtract 1, if $D < 0$, to satisfy condition (iv) of Algorithm T and the reverse-order condition. (See exercise 184.)

The monotonicity condition (ii) holds if and only if $(x_1 - x_0)(x_2 - x_1) > 0$ and $(y_1 - y_0)(y_2 - y_1) > 0$. If necessary, we can use the recurrence of exercise 186(e) to break $S(z_0, z_1, z_2)$ into at most three monotonic subsquines; for example, setting $\theta = (x_0 - x_1)/(x_0 - 2x_1 + x_2)$ will achieve monotonicity in x. (A slight rounding error may occur during this fixed point arithmetic, but the recurrence can be performed in such a way that the subsquines are definitely monotonic.)

Notes: When z_0, z_1, and z_2 are near each other, a simpler and faster method based on exercise 186(e) with $\theta = \frac{1}{2}$ is adequate for most practical purposes, if one doesn't care about making the exactly correct choice between local edge sequences like "up-then-left" versus "left-then-up." In the late 1980s, Sampo Kaasila chose to use squines as the basic method of shape specification in the TrueType font format, because they can be digitized so rapidly. The METAFONT system achieves greater flexibility with cubic Bézier splines [see D. E. Knuth, *METAFONT: The Program* (Addison–Wesley, 1986)], but at the cost of extra processing time. A fairly fast "six-register algorithm" for the resulting cubic curves was, however, developed subsequently by John Hobby [*ACM Trans. on Graphics* **9** (1990), 262–277]. Vaughan Pratt introduced *conic splines*, which are sort of midway between squines and Bézier cubics, in *Computer Graphics* **9**, 3 (July 1985), 151–159. Conic spline segments can be elliptical and hyperbolic as well as parabolic, hence they require fewer intermediate points and control points than squines; furthermore, they can be handled by Algorithm T.

188. If the rows of the bitmap are $(X_0, X_1, \ldots, X_{63})$, do the following operations for $k = 0, 1, \ldots, 5$: For all i such that $0 \le i < 64$ and $i \mathbin{\&} 2^k = 0$, let $j = i + 2^k$ and either (a) set $t \leftarrow (X_i \oplus (X_j \gg 2^k)) \mathbin{\&} \mu_{6,k}$, $X_i \leftarrow X_i \oplus t$, $X_j \leftarrow X_j \oplus (t \ll 2^k)$; or (b) set $t \leftarrow X_i \mathbin{\&} \bar\mu_{6,k}$, $u \leftarrow X_j \mathbin{\&} \mu_{6,k}$, $X_i \leftarrow ((X_i \ll 2^k) \mathbin{\&} \bar\mu_{6,k}) \mid u$, $X_j \leftarrow ((X_j \gg 2^k) \mathbin{\&} \mu_{6,k}) \mid t$.
[The basic idea is to transform $2^k \times 2^k$ submatrices for increasing k, as in exercise 5–12. Speedups are possible with MMIX, using MOR and MUX as in exercise 208, and using LDTU/STTU when $k = 5$. See L. J. Guibas and J. Stolfi, *ACM Transactions on Graphics* **1** (1982), 204–207; M. Thorup, *J. Algorithms* **42** (2002), 217. Incidentally, Theorem P and answer 54 show that $\Omega(n \log n)$ operations on n-bit numbers are needed to transpose an $n \times n$ bit matrix. An application that needs frequent transpositions might therefore be better off using a redundant representation, maintaining its matrices in both normal and transposed form.]

189. The following big-endian program assumes that $n \le 74880$.

```
        LOC   Data_Segment              LDO   k,Initk
BITMAP  LOC   @+M*N/8            0H  SET   s,N/64
base    GREG  @                 1H  SET   a,h          A trick (see below)
GRAYMAP LOC   @+M*N/64              SET   r,8
GTAB    BYTE  255,252,249,246,243  2H  LDOU  t,base,k
        BYTE  240,236,233,230,227     MOR   u,c1,t
        BYTE  224,221,217,214,211     SUBU  t,t,u        (Nypwise sums)
        BYTE  208,204,201,198,194     MOR   u,c2,t
        BYTE  191,188,184,181,178     AND   t,t,mu1
        BYTE  174,171,167,164,160     ADDU  t,t,u        (Nybblewise sums)
        BYTE  157,153,150,146,142     MOR   u,c3,t
        BYTE  139,135,131,128,124     AND   t,t,mu2
        BYTE  120,116,112,108,104     ADDU  t,t,u        (Bytewise sums)
        BYTE  100,96,92,88,84         ADDU  a,a,t
        BYTE  79,75,70,66,61          INCL  k,N/8        Move to next row.
        BYTE  56,52,46,41,36          SUB   r,r,1
        BYTE  30,24,18,10,0           PBNZ  r,2B         Repeat 8 times.
Initk   OCTA  BITMAP-GRAYMAP    3H  SRU   t,a,56
corr    GREG  N-8                   LDBU  t,gtab,t
c1      GREG  #4000100004000100     SLU   a,a,8
c2      GREG  #2010000002010000     STBU  t,z,0
c3      GREG  #0804020100000000     INCL  z,1
mu1     GREG  #3333333333333333     PBN   a,3B         (The trick)
mu2     GREG  #0f0f0f0f0f0f0f0f     SUB   k,k,corr
h       GREG  #8080808080808080     SUB   s,s,1
gtab    GREG  GTAB-#80              PBNZ  s,1B         Loop on columns.
        LOC   #100                  INCL  k,7*N/8      Loop on groups
MakeGray LDA  z,GRAYMAP             PBN   k,0B         of 8 rows.  ∎
```

[Inspired by Neil Hunt's DVIPAGE, the author used such graymaps extensively when preparing new editions of *The Art of Computer Programming* in 1992–1998.]

190. (a) We must have $\alpha_{j+1} = f(\alpha_j) \oplus \alpha_{j-1}$ for $j \geq 1$, where $\alpha_0 = 0\ldots0$ and $f(\alpha) = ((\alpha \ll 1) \,\&\, 1\ldots1) \oplus \alpha \oplus (\alpha \gg 1)$. The elements of the bottom row α_m satisfy the parity condition if and only if this rule makes α_{m+1} entirely zero.

(b) True. The parity condition on matrix entries a_{ij} is $a_{ij} = a_{(i-1)j} \oplus a_{i(j-1)} \oplus a_{i(j+1)} \oplus a_{(i+1)j}$, where $a_{ij} = 0$ if $i = 0$ or $i = m + 1$ or $j = 0$ or $j = n + 1$. If two matrices (a_{ij}) and (b_{ij}) satisfy this condition, so does (c_{ij}) when $c_{ij} = a_{ij} \oplus b_{ij}$.

(c) The upper left submatrix consisting of all rows that precede the first all-zero row (if any) and all columns that precede the first all-zero column (if any) is perfect. And this submatrix determines the entire matrix, because the pattern on the other side of a row or column of zeros is the top/bottom or left/right reflection of its neighbor. For example, if $\alpha_{m'+1}$ is zero, then $\alpha_{m'+1+j} = \alpha_{m'+1-j}$ for $1 \leq j \leq m'$.

(d) Starting with a given vector α_1 and using the rule in (a) will always lead to a row with $\alpha_{m+1} = 0\ldots0$. Proof: We must have $(\alpha_j, \alpha_{j+1}) = (\alpha_k, \alpha_{k+1})$ for some $0 \leq j < k \leq 2^{2n}$, by the pigeonhole principle. If $j > 0$ we also have $(\alpha_{j-1}, \alpha_j) = (\alpha_{k-1}, \alpha_k)$, because $\alpha_{j-1} = f(\alpha_j) \oplus \alpha_{j+1} = f(\alpha_k) \oplus \alpha_{k+1} = \alpha_{k-1}$. Therefore the first repeated pair begins with a row α_k of zeros. Furthermore we have $\alpha_i = \alpha_{k-i}$ for $0 \leq i \leq k$; hence the first all-zero row α_{m+1} occurs when m is $k - 1$ or $k/2 - 1$.

Rows $\alpha_1, \ldots, \alpha_m$ will form a perfect pattern unless there is a column of 0s. There are $t > 0$ such columns if and only if $t + 1$ is a divisor of $n + 1$ and α_1 has the form $\alpha 0\alpha^R 0 \ldots 0\alpha$ (t even) or $\alpha 0\alpha^R 0 \ldots 0\alpha^R$ (t odd), where $|\alpha| + 1 = (n + 1)/(t + 1)$.

(e) This starting vector does not have the form forbidden in (d).

191. (a) The former is $\alpha_1, \alpha_2, \ldots$ if and only if the latter is $0\alpha_1 0\alpha_1^R, 0\alpha_2 0\alpha_2^R, \ldots$.

(b) Let the binary string $a_0 a_1 \ldots a_{N-1}$ correspond to the polynomial $a_0 + a_1 x + \cdots + a_{N-1} x^{N-1}$, and let $y = x^{-1}{+}1{+}x$. Then $\alpha_0 = 0 \ldots 0$ corresponds to $F_0(y)$; $\alpha_1 = 10 \ldots 0$ corresponds to $F_1(y)$; and by induction α_j corresponds to $F_j(y)$, mod $x^N + 1$ and mod 2. For example, when $N = 6$ we have $\alpha_2 = 110001 \leftrightarrow 1 + x + x^5$ because x^{-1} mod $(x^6 + 1) = x^5$, etc.

(c) Again, induction on j.

(d) The identity in the hint holds by induction on m, because it is clearly true when $m = 1$ and $m = 2$. Working mod 2, this identity yields the simple equations

$$F_{2k}(y) = y F_k(y)^2; \qquad F_{2k-1}(y) = (F_{k-1}(y) + F_k(y))^2.$$

So we can go from the pair $P_k = (F_{k-1}(y) \bmod (x^N{+}1), F_k(y) \bmod (x^N{+}1))$ to the pair P_{k+1} in $O(n)$ steps, and to the pair P_{2k} in $O(n^2)$ steps. We can therefore compute $F_j(y) \bmod (x^N + 1)$ after $O(\log j)$ iterations. Multiplying by $f_\alpha(x) + f_\alpha(x^{-1})$ and reducing mod $x^N + 1$ then allows us to read off the value of α_j.

Incidentally, $F_{n+1}(x)$ is the special case $K_n(x, x, \ldots, x)$ of a continuant polynomial; see Eq. 4.5.3–(4). We have $F_{n+1}(x) = \sum_{k=0}^{n} \binom{n-k}{k} x^{n-2k} = i^{-n} U_n(ix/2)$, where U_n is the classical Chebyshev polynomial defined by $U_n(\cos\theta) = \sin((n+1)\theta)/\sin\theta$.

192. (a) By exercise 191(c), $c(q)$ is the least $j > 0$ such that $(x{+}x^{-1}) F_j(x^{-1}{+}1{+}x) \equiv 0$ (modulo $x^{2q} + 1$), using polynomial arithmetic mod 2. Equivalently, it's the smallest positive j for which $F_j(y)$ is a multiple of $(x^{2q} + 1)/(x^2 + 1) = (1 + x + \cdots + x^{q-1})^2$, when $y = x^{-1}{+}1{+}x$.

(b) Use the method of exercise 191(d) to evaluate $((x + x^{-1}) F_j(y)) \bmod (x^{2q} + 1)$ when $j = M/p$, for all prime divisors p of M. If the result is zero, set $M \leftarrow M/p$ and repeat the process. If no such result is zero, $c(q) = M$.

(c) We want to show that $c(2^e)$ is a divisor of $3 \cdot 2^{e-1}$ but not of $3 \cdot 2^{e-2}$ or 2^{e-1}. The latter holds because $F_{2^e-1}(y) = y^{2^{e-1}-1}$ is relatively prime to $x^{2^{e+1}} + 1$. The former holds because

$$F_{3 \cdot 2^e - 1}(y) = y^{2^{e-1}-1} F_3(y)^{2^{e-1}} = y^{2^{e-1}-1}(1 + y)^{2^e} = y^{2^{e-1}-1}(x^{-1}{+}x)^{2^e},$$

which is $\equiv 0$ modulo $x^{2^{e+1}} + 1$ but not modulo $x^{2^{e+2}} + 1$.

(d) $F_{2^e-1}(y) = \sum_{k=1}^{e} y^{2^e - 2^k}$. Since $y = x^{-1}(1{+}x{+}x^2)$ is relatively prime to $x^q{+}1$, we have $y^{-1} \equiv a_0 + a_1 x + \cdots + a_{q-1} x^{q-1}$ (modulo $x^q + 1$) for some coefficients a_i; hence

$$y^{-2^k} \equiv a_0 + a_1 x^{2^k} + \cdots + a_{q-1} x^{2^k(q-1)} \equiv a_0 + a_1 x^{2^{k+e}} + \cdots + a_{q-1} x^{2^{k+e}(q-1)} \equiv y^{-2^{k+e}}$$

(modulo $x^q + 1$) for $0 \le k < e$, and it follows that $F_{2^{2e}-1}(y)$ is a multiple of $x^{2q} + 1$.

(e) In this case $c(q)$ divides $4(2^{2e} - 1)$. Proof: Let $x^q + 1 = f_1(x) f_2(x) \ldots f_r(x)$ where $f_1(x) = x + 1$, $f_2(x) = x^2 + x + 1$, and each $f_i(x)$ is irreducible mod 2. Since q is odd, these factors are distinct. Therefore, in the finite field of polynomials mod $f_j(x)$ for $j \ge 3$, we have $y^{-2^k} = y^{-2^{k+e}}$ as in (d). Consequently $F_{2^{2e}-1}(y)$ is a multiple of $f_3(x) \ldots f_r(x) = (x^q + 1)/(x^3 + 1)$. So $F_{2(2^{2e}-1)}(y) = y F_{2^{2e}-1}(y)^2$ is a multiple of $(x^{2q} + 1)/(x^2 + 1)$ as desired.

(f) If $F_{c(q)}(y)$ is a multiple of $x^{2q}{+}1$, it's easy to see that $c(2q) = 2c(q)$. Otherwise $F_{3c(q)}(y)$ is a multiple of $F_3(y) = (1 + y)^2 = x^{-2}(1 + x)^4$; hence $F_{6c(q)}(y)$ is a multiple of $x^{4q} + 1$ and $c(2q)$ divides $6c(q)$. The latter case can happen only when q is odd.

Notes: Parity patterns are related to a popular puzzle called "Lights Out," which was invented in the early 1980s by Dario Uri, also invented independently about the same time by László Meerö and called **XL25**. [See David Singmaster's *Cubic Circular*, issues 7&8 (Summer 1985), 39–42; Dieter Gebhardt, *Cubism For Fun* **69** (March 2006), 23–25.] Klaus Sutner has pursued further aspects of this theory in *Theoretical Computer Science* **230** (2000), 49–73.

193. Let $b_{(2i)(2j)} = a_{ij}$, $b_{(2i+1)(2j)} = a_{ij} \oplus a_{(i+1)j}$, $b_{(2i)(2j+1)} = a_{ij} \oplus a_{i(j+1)}$, and $b_{(2i+1)(2j+1)} = 0$, for $0 \le i \le m$ and $0 \le j \le n$, where we regard $a_{ij} = 0$ when $i = 0$ or $i = m+1$ or $j = 0$ or $j = n+1$. We don't have $(b_{(2i)1}, b_{(2i)2}, \ldots, b_{(2i)(2n+1)}) = (0, 0, \ldots, 0)$ because $(a_{i1}, \ldots, a_{in}) \ne (0, \ldots, 0)$ for $1 \le i \le m$. And we don't have $(b_{(2i+1)1}, b_{(2i+1)2}, \ldots, b_{(2i+1)(2n+1)}) = (0, 0, \ldots, 0)$ because adjacent rows $(a_{i1}, \ldots, a_{in})$ and $(a_{(i+1)1}, \ldots, a_{(i+1)n})$ always differ for $0 \le i \le m$ when m is odd.

194. Set $\beta_i \leftarrow (1 \ll (n-i)) \mid (1 \ll (i-1))$ for $1 \le i \le m$, where $m = \lceil n/2 \rceil$. Also set $\gamma_i \leftarrow (\beta_1 \,\&\, \alpha_{i1}) + (\beta_2 \,\&\, \alpha_{i2}) + \cdots + (\beta_m \,\&\, \alpha_{im})$, where α_{ij} is the jth row of the parity pattern that begins with β_i; vector γ_i records the diagonal elements of such a matrix. Then set $r \leftarrow 0$ and apply subroutine N of answer 195 for $i \leftarrow 1, 2, \ldots, m$. The resulting vectors $\theta_1, \ldots, \theta_r$ are a basis for all $n \times n$ parity patterns with 8-fold symmetry.

To test if any such pattern is perfect, let the pattern starting with θ_i first be zero in row c_i. If any $c_i = n+1$, the answer is yes. If $\operatorname{lcm}(c_1, \ldots, c_r) < n$, the answer is no. If neither of these conditions decides the matter, we can resort to brute-force examination of $2^r - 1$ nonzero linear combinations of the θ vectors.

For example, when $n = 9$ we find $\gamma_1 = 111101111$, $\gamma_2 = \gamma_3 = 010101010$, $\gamma_4 = 000000000$, $\gamma_5 = 001010100$; then $r = 0$, $\theta_1 = 011000110$, $\theta_2 = 000101000$, $c_1 = c_2 = 5$. So there is no perfect solution.

In the author's experiments for $n \le 3000$, "brute force" was needed only when $n = 1709$. Then $r = 21$ and the values of c_i were all equal to 171 or 855 except that $c_{21} = 342$. The solution $\theta_1 \oplus \theta_{21}$ was found immediately.

The answers for $1 \le n \le 383$ are 4, 5, 11, 16, 23, 29, 30, 32, 47, 59, 62, 64, 65, 84, 95, 101, 119, 125, 126, 128, 131, 154, 164, 170, 185, 191, 203, 204, 239, 251, 254, 256, 257, 263, 314, 329, 340, 341, 371, 383.

[A fractal similar to Fig. 20, called the "mikado pattern," appears in a paper by H. Eriksson, K. Eriksson, and J. Sjöstrand, *Advances in Applied Math.* **27** (2001), 365. See also S. Wolfram, *A New Kind of Science* (2002), rule 150R on page 439.]

195. Set $\beta_i \leftarrow 1 \ll (m - i)$ and $\gamma_i \leftarrow \alpha_i$ for $1 \le i \le m$; also set $r \leftarrow 0$. Then perform the following subroutine for $i = 1, 2, \ldots, m$:

N1. [Extract low bit.] Set $x \leftarrow \gamma_i \,\&\, -\gamma_i$. If $x = 0$, go to N4.

N2. [Find j.] Find the smallest $j \ge 1$ such that $\gamma_j \,\&\, x \ne 0$ and $\gamma_j \,\&\, (x - 1) = 0$.

N3. [Dependent?] If $j < i$, set $\gamma_i \leftarrow \gamma_i \oplus \gamma_j$, $\beta_i \leftarrow \beta_i \oplus \beta_j$, and return to N1. (These operations preserve the matrix equation $C = BA$.) Otherwise terminate the subroutine (because γ_i is linearly independent from $\gamma_1, \ldots, \gamma_{i-1}$).

N4. [Record a solution.] Set $r \leftarrow r + 1$ and $\theta_r \leftarrow \beta_i$. ∎

At the conclusion, the $m - r$ nonzero vectors γ_i are a basis for the vector space of all linear combinations of $\alpha_1, \ldots, \alpha_m$; they're characterized by their low bits.

196. (a) $^\#\mathtt{0a}$; $^\#\mathtt{cea3}$; $^\#\mathtt{e7ae97}$; $^\#\mathtt{f09d8581}$.

(b) If $\lambda x = \lambda x'$, the result is clear because $l = l'$. Otherwise we have either $\alpha_1 < \alpha_1'$ or $(\alpha_1 = \alpha_1'$ and $\alpha_2 < \alpha_2')$; the latter case can occur only when $x \ge 2^{16}$.

(c) Set $j \leftarrow k$; while $\alpha_j \oplus {}^\#\mathtt{80} < {}^\#\mathtt{40}$, set $j \leftarrow j - 1$. Then $\alpha(x^{(i)})$ begins with α_j.

197. (a) $^\#$000a; $^\#$03a3; $^\#$7b97; $^\#$d834dd41.

(b) Lexicographic order is *not* preserved when, say, $x = {}^\#$ffff and $x' = {}^\#$10000.

(c) To answer this question properly one needs to know that the 2048 integers in the range $^\#$d800 $\leq x < {}^\#$e000 are not legal codepoints of UCS; they are called *surrogates*. With this understanding, $\beta(x^{(i)})$ begins at β_k if $\beta_k \oplus {}^\#$dc00 $\geq {}^\#$0400, otherwise it begins at β_{k-1}.

198. $a = {}^\#$e50000, $b = 3$, $c = {}^\#$16. (We could let $b = 0$, but then a would be huge. This trick was suggested by P. Raynaud-Richard in 1997. The stated constants, suggested by R. Pournader in 2008, are the smallest possible.)

199. We want $\alpha_1 > {}^\#$c1; $2^8\alpha_1 + \alpha_2 < {}^\#$f490; and either $(\alpha_1 \,\&\, -\alpha_1) + \alpha_1 < {}^\#$100 or $\alpha_1 + \alpha_2 > {}^\#$17f. These conditions hold if and only if

$$({}^\#\text{c1} - \alpha_1) \,\&\, (2^8\alpha_1 + \alpha_2 - {}^\#\text{f490}) \,\&\, \big(((\alpha_1 \,\&\, -\alpha_1) + \alpha_1 - {}^\#\text{100}) \mid ({}^\#\text{17f} - \alpha_1 - \alpha_2)\big) \; < \; 0.$$

Markus Kuhn suggests adding the further clause '$\&\, \big({}^\#\text{20} - ((2^8\alpha_1 + \alpha_2) \oplus {}^\#\text{eda0})\big)$', to ensure that $\alpha_1\alpha_2$ doesn't begin the encoding of a surrogate.

200. If $\$0 = (x_7 \ldots x_1 x_0)_{256}$ then $\$3$ is set to the symmetric function $S_2(x_7, x_4, x_2)$.

201. MOR x,c,x, where $c = {}^\#$f0f0f0f00f0f0f0f.

202. MOR x,x,c, where $c = {}^\#$c0c030300c0c0303; then MOR x,mone,x. (See answer 209.)

203. a $= {}^\#$0008000400020001, b $= {}^\#$0f0f0f0f0f0f0f0f, c $= {}^\#$0606060606060606, d $= {}^\#$0000002700000000, e $= {}^\#$2a2a2a2a2a2a2a2a. (The ASCII code for 0 is $6 + {}^\#$2a; the ASCII code for a is $6 + {}^\#$2a $+ 10 + {}^\#$27.)

204. $p = {}^\#$8008400420021001, $q = {}^\#$8020080240100401 (the transpose of p), $r = {}^\#$4080102004080102 (a symmetric matrix), and $m = {}^\#$aa55aa55aa55aa55.

205. Shuffle, but with $p \leftrightarrow q$, $r = {}^\#$0804020180402010, $m = {}^\#$f0f0f0f00f0f0f0f.

206. Just change p to $^\#$0880044002200110. (Incidentally, these shuffles can also be defined as permutations on $z = (z_{63} \ldots z_1 z_0)_2$ in another way: The outshuffle maps $z_j \mapsto z_{(2j) \bmod 63}$, for $0 \leq j < 63$, while the inshuffle maps $z_j \mapsto z_{(2j+1) \bmod 65}$.)

207. Do MOR y,p,x; MOR y,y,p; MOR t,y,q; PUT rM,m1; MUX y,y,t; MOR t,t,q; PUT rM,m2; MUX y,y,t. In both cases $p = {}^\#$2004801002400801; for triple zip, $q = {}^\#$4020100804020180, $m_1 = {}^\#$4949494949494949, $m_2 = {}^\#$dbdbdbdbdbdbdbdb; for the inverse, $q = {}^\#$0402018040201008, $m_1 = {}^\#$0707070707070707, $m_2 = {}^\#$3f3f3f3f3f3f3f3f.

208. (Solution by H. S. Warren, Jr.) The text's 7-swap, 14-swap, 28-swap method can be implemented with only 12 instructions:

```
MOR t,x,c1;   MOR t,c1,t;   PUT rM,m1;   MUX y,x,t;
MOR t,y,c2;   MOR t,c2,t;   PUT rM,m2;   MUX y,y,t;
MOR t,y,c3;   MOR t,c3,t;   PUT rM,m3;   MUX y,y,t;
```

here c1 $= {}^\#$4080102004080102, c2 $= {}^\#$2010804002010804, c3 $= {}^\#$0804020180402010, m1 $= {}^\#$aa55aa55aa55aa55, m2 $= {}^\#$cccc3333cccc3333, m3 $= {}^\#$f0f0f0f00f0f0f0f.

209. Four instructions suffice: MXOR y,p,x; MXOR x,mone,x; MXOR x,x,q; XOR x,x,y; here p $= {}^\#$80c0e0f0f8fcfeff, mone $= -1$, and q $= \bar{\text{p}}$.

210. SLU x,one,x; MOR x,b,x; AND x,x,a; MOR x,x,#ff; here register one $= 1$.

211. In general, element ij of the Boolean matrix product AXB is $\bigvee\{x_{kl} \mid a_{ik}b_{lj} = 1\}$. For this problem we choose $a_{ik} = [i \supseteq k]$ and $b_{lj} = [l \subseteq j]$; the answer is 'MOR t,f,a; MOR t,b,t' where a $= {}^\#$80c0a0f088ccaaff and b $= {}^\#$ff5533110f050301 $= \text{a}^T$.

(Notice that this trick gives a simple test $[f = \hat{f}]$ for monotonicity. Furthermore, the 64-bit result $(t_{63} \ldots t_1 t_0)_2$ gives the coefficients of the multilinear representation

$$f(x_1, \ldots, x_6) = (t_{63} + t_{62}x_6 + \cdots + t_1 x_1 x_2 x_3 x_4 x_5 + t_0 x_1 x_2 x_3 x_4 x_5 x_6) \bmod 2,$$

if we substitute MXOR for MOR, by the result of exercise 7.1.1–11.)

212. If $\cdot$ denotes MXOR as in (183) and $b = (\beta_7 \ldots \beta_1 \beta_0)_{256}$ has bytes β_j, we can evaluate

$$c = (a \cdot B_0^L) \oplus ((a \ll 8) \cdot (B_1^L + B_0^U)) \oplus ((a \ll 16) \cdot (B_2^L + B_1^U)) \oplus \cdots \oplus ((a \ll 56) \cdot (B_7^L + B_6^U)),$$

where $B_j^U = (q\beta_j) \mathbin{\&} m$, $B_j^L = (((q\beta_j) \ll 8) + \beta_j) \mathbin{\&} \overline{m}$, $q = {}^{\#}\mathtt{0080402010080402}$, and $m = {}^{\#}\mathtt{7f3f1f0f07030100}$. (Here $q\beta_j$ denotes *ordinary* multiplication of integers.)

213. In this big-endian computation, register nn holds $-n$, and register data points to the octabyte following the given bytes $\alpha_{n-1} \ldots \alpha_1 \alpha_0$ in memory (with α_{n-1} first). The constants aa $= {}^{\#}\mathtt{8381808080402010}$ and bb $= {}^{\#}\mathtt{339bcf6530180c06}$ correspond to matrices A and B, found by computing the remainders $x^k \bmod p(x)$ for $72 \le k < 80$.

	SET	c,0	$c \leftarrow 0$.	LDOU	t,data,nn	$t \leftarrow$ next octa.
	LDOU	t,data,nn	$t \leftarrow$ next octa.	XOR	u,u,c	$u \leftarrow u \oplus c$.
	ADD	nn,nn,8	$n \leftarrow n - 8$.	SLU	c,v,56	$c \leftarrow v \ll 56$.
	BZ	nn,2F	Done if $n = 0$.	SRU	v,v,8	$v \leftarrow v \gg 8$.
1H	MXOR	u,aa,t	$u \leftarrow t \cdot A$.	XOR	u,u,v	$u \leftarrow u \oplus v$.
	MXOR	v,bb,t	$v \leftarrow t \cdot B$.	XOR	t,t,u	$t \leftarrow t \oplus u$.
	ADD	nn,nn,8	$n \leftarrow n - 8$.	PBN	nn,1B	Repeat if $n > 0$. ∎

A similar method finishes the job, with no auxiliary table needed:

2H	SET	nn,8	$n \leftarrow 8$.	SRU	v,v,8	$v \leftarrow v \gg 8$.
3H	AND	x,t,ffooo	$x \leftarrow$ high byte.	XOR	t,t,v	$t \leftarrow t \oplus v$.
	MXOR	u,aaa,x	$u \leftarrow x \cdot A'$.	SUB	nn,nn,1	$n \leftarrow n - 1$.
	MXOR	v,bbb,x	$v \leftarrow x \cdot B'$.	PBP	nn,3B	Repeat if $n > 0$.
	SLU	t,t,8	$t \leftarrow t \ll 8$.	XOR	t,t,c	$t \leftarrow t \oplus c$.
	XOR	t,t,u	$t \leftarrow t \oplus u$.	SRU	crc,t,48	Return $t \gg 48$. ∎

Here aaa $= {}^{\#}\mathtt{8381808080808080}$, bbb $= {}^{\#}\mathtt{0383c363331b0f05}$, and ffooo $= {}^{\#}\mathtt{ff00...00}$.

> *The Books of the* Big-Endians *have been long forbidden.*
> — LEMUEL GULLIVER, *Travels Into Several Remote Nations of the World* (1726)

214. By considering the irreducible factors of the characteristic polynomial of X, we must have $X^n = I$ where $n = 2^3 \cdot 3^2 \cdot 5 \cdot 7 \cdot 17 \cdot 31 \cdot 127 = 168661080$. Neill Clift has shown that $l(n - 1) = 33$ and found the following sequence of 33 MXOR instructions to compute $Y = X^{-1} = X^{n-1}$: MXOR t,x,x; MXOR \$1,t,x; MXOR \$2,t,\$1; MXOR \$3,\$2,\$2; MXOR t,\$3,\$3; S^6; MXOR t,t,\$2; S^3; MXOR \$1,t,\$1; MXOR t,\$1,\$3; S^{13}; MXOR t,t,\$1; S; MXOR y,t,x; here S stands for 'MXOR t,t,t'. To test if X is nonsingular, do MXOR t,y,x and compare t to the identity matrix ${}^{\#}\mathtt{8040201008040201}$.

215. SADD \$0,x,0; SADD \$1,x,a; NEG \$0,32,\$0; 2ADDU \$1,\$1,\$0; SLU \$0,b,\$1; then BN \$0,Yes; here $a = {}^{\#}\mathtt{aaaaaaaaaaaaaaaa}$ and $b = {}^{\#}\mathtt{2492492492492492}$.

216. Start with $s_k \leftarrow 0$ and $t_k \leftarrow -1$ for $0 \le k < m$. Then do the following for $1 \le k \le m$: If $x_k \ne 0$ and $x_k < 2^m$, set $l \leftarrow \lambda x_k$ and $s_l \leftarrow s_l + x_k$; if $t_l < 0$ or $t_l > x_k$, also set $t_l \leftarrow x_k$. Finally, set $y \leftarrow 1$ and $k \leftarrow 0$; while $y \ge t_k$ and $k < m$, set $y \leftarrow y + s_k$ and $k \leftarrow k + 1$. Double precision n-bit arithmetic is sufficient for y and s_k. [This pleasant algorithm appeared in D. Eppstein's blog, 2008.03.22.]

217. See R. D. Cameron, *U.S. Patent 7400271* (15 July 2008); *Proc. ACM Symp. Principles and Practice of Parallel Programming* **12** (2008), 91–98.

SECTION 7.1.4

1. Here are the BDDs for truth tables 0000, 0001, ..., 1111, showing the sizes below:

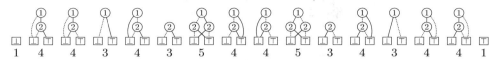

 1   4   4   3   4   3   5   4   4   5   3   4   3   4   4   1

2. (The ordering property determines the direction of each arc.)

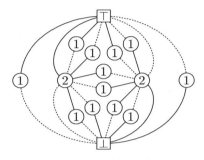

3. There are two with size 1 (namely the two constant functions); none with size 2 (because two sinks cannot both be reachable unless there's also a branch node); and $2n$ with size 3 (namely x_j and $\bar{x}_j$ for $1 \le j \le n$).

4. Set $y \leftarrow {}^{\#}\texttt{0ffffffefffffffe} \& \bar{x} + {}^{\#}\texttt{20000002}$, $y \leftarrow (y{\gg}28) \& {}^{\#}\texttt{10000001}$, $x' \leftarrow x {\oplus} y$. (See 7.1.3–(93).)

5. You get $\overline{f(\bar{x}_1, \ldots, \bar{x}_n)} = f^D(x_1, \ldots, x_n)$, the *dual* of f (see exercise 7.1.1–2).

6. The largest subtables of 1011000110010011, namely 10110001, 10010011, 1011, 0001, 1001, 0011, are all distinct beads; squares and duplicates don't appear until we look at the subtables $\{10, 11, 00, 01\}$ of length 2. So g has size 11.

7. (a) If the truth table of f is $\alpha_0\alpha_1 \ldots \alpha_{2^k-1}$, where each α_j is a binary string of length 2^{n-k}, the truth table of g_k is $\beta_0\beta_2 \ldots \beta_{2^k-2}$, where $\beta_{2j} = \alpha_{2j}\alpha_{2j+1}\alpha_{2j+1}\alpha_{2j+1}$.

(b) Thus the beads of f and g_k are closely related. We get the BDD for g_k from the BDD for f by changing (j) to $(j{-}1)$ for $1 \le j < k$, and replacing (k) by $(k{-}1)$.

8. (a) Now $\beta_{2j} = \alpha_{2j}\alpha_{2j+1}\alpha_{2j+1}\alpha_{2j}$. (b) Again change (j) to $(j{-}1)$ for $1 \le j < k$. If (k) is present in f but not (k), replace (k) by $(k{-}1)$; otherwise replace (k) (k) by

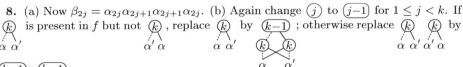

. [E. Dubrova and L. Macchiarulo, *IEEE Trans.* **C-49** (2000), 1290–1292.]

9. There is no solution if $s = 1$. Otherwise set $k \leftarrow s-1$, $j \leftarrow 1$, and do the following steps repeatedly: (i) While $j < v_k$, set $x_j \leftarrow 1$ and $j \leftarrow j+1$; (ii) stop if $k = 0$; (iii) if $h_k \ne 1$, set $x_j \leftarrow 1$ and $k \leftarrow h_k$, otherwise set $x_j \leftarrow 0$ and $k \leftarrow l_k$; (iv) set $j \leftarrow j+1$.

10. Let $I_k = (\bar{v}_k?\, l_k\!:\! h_k)$ for $0 \le k < s$ and $I'_k = (\bar{v}'_k?\, l'_k\!:\! h'_k)$ for $0 \le k < s'$. We may assume that $s = s'$; otherwise $f \ne f'$. The following algorithm either finds indices $(t_0, \ldots, t_{s-1})$ such that I_k corresponds to I'_{t_k}, or concludes that $f \ne f'$:

I1. [Initialize and loop.] Set $t_{s-1} \leftarrow s-1$, $t_1 \leftarrow 1$, $t_0 \leftarrow 0$, and $t_k \leftarrow -1$ for $2 \le k \le s-2$. Do steps I2–I4 for $k = s-1,\, s-2,\, \ldots,\, 2$ (in this order). If those steps "quit" at any point, we have $f \ne f'$; otherwise $f = f'$.

I2. [Test v_k.] Set $t \leftarrow t_k$. (Now $t \ge 0$; otherwise I_k would have no predecessor.) Quit if $v'_t \ne v_k$.

I3. [Test l_k.] Set $l \leftarrow l_k$. If $t_l < 0$, set $t_l \leftarrow l'_t$; otherwise quit if $l'_t \ne t_l$.

I4. [Test h_k.] Set $h \leftarrow h_k$. If $t_h < 0$, set $t_h \leftarrow h'_t$; otherwise quit if $h'_t \ne t_h$. ∎

11. (a) Yes, since c_k correctly counts all paths from node k to node 1. (In fact, many BDD algorithms will run correctly — but more slowly — in the presence of equivalent nodes or redundant branches. But reduction is important when, say, we want to test quickly if $f = f'$ as in exercise 10.)

(b) No. For example, suppose $I_3 = (\bar{1}?\, 2\!:\! 1)$, $I_2 = (\bar{1}?\, 0\!:\! 1)$, $I_1 = (\bar{2}?\, 1\!:\! 1)$, $I_0 = (\bar{2}?\, 0\!:\! 0)$; then the algorithm sets $c_2 \leftarrow 1$, $c_3 \leftarrow \frac{3}{2}$. (But see exercise 35(b).)

12. (a) The first condition makes K independent; the second makes it maximally so.

(b) None when n is odd; otherwise there are two sets of alternate vertices.

(c) A vertex is in the kernel if and only if it is a sink vertex or in the kernel of the graph obtained by deleting all sink vertices and their immediate predecessors.

[Kernels represent winning positions in nim-like games, and they also arise in n-person games. See J. von Neumann and O. Morgenstern, *Theory of Games and Economic Behavior* (1944), §30.1; C. Berge, *Graphs and Hypergraphs* (1973), Chapter 14.]

13. (a) A maximal clique of G is a kernel of $\bar{G}$, and vice versa. (b) A minimal vertex cover U is the complement $V \setminus W$ of a kernel W, and vice versa (see $7\text{--}(6_1)$).

14. (a) The size is $4(n - 2) + 2[n\!=\!3]$. When $n \ge 6$ these BDDs form a pattern in which there are four branch nodes for variables $4, 5, \ldots, n - 2$, together with a fixed pattern at the top and bottom. The four branches are essentially

(b) Here the numbers for $3 \le n \le 10$ are $(7, 9, 14, 17, 22, 30, 37, 45)$; then a fixed pattern at the top and bottom develops as in (a), with nine branch nodes for each variable in the middle, and the total size comes to $9(n - 5)$. The nine nodes on each middle level fall into three groups of three,

with one group for $x_1 x_2 = 00$, one for $x_1 x_2 = 01$, and one for $x_1 = 1$.

15. Both cases lead by induction to well known sequences of numbers: (a) The Lucas numbers $L_n = F_{n+1} + F_{n-1}$ [see E. Lucas, *Théorie des Nombres* (1891), Chapter 18]. (b) The Perrin numbers, defined by $P_3 = 3$, $P_4 = 2$, $P_5 = 5$, $P_n = P_{n-2} + P_{n-3}$. [See R. Perrin, *L'Intermédiaire des Mathématiciens* **6** (1899), 76–77.]

16. When the BDD isn't $\boxed{\bot}$, all solutions are generated by calling $List(1, \text{root})$, where $List(j, p)$ is the following recursive procedure: If $v(p) > j$, set $x_j \leftarrow 0$, call $List(j+1, p)$, set $x_j \leftarrow 1$, and call $List(j + 1, p)$. Otherwise if p is the sink node $\boxed{\top}$, visit the solution $x_1 \ldots x_n$. (The idea of "visiting" a combinatorial object while generating them all is discussed at the beginning of Section 7.2.1.) Otherwise set $x_j \leftarrow 0$; call $List(j + 1, \text{LO}(p))$ if $\text{LO}(p) \neq \boxed{\bot}$; set $x_j \leftarrow 1$; and call $List(j + 1, \text{HI}(p))$ if $\text{HI}(p) \neq \boxed{\bot}$.

The solutions are generated in lexicographic order. Suppose there are N of them. If the kth solution agrees with the $(k-1)$st solution in positions $x_1 \ldots x_{j-1}$ but not in x_j, let $c(k) = n - j$; and let $c(1) = n$. Then the running time is proportional to $\sum_{k=1}^{N} c(k)$, which is $O(nN)$ in general. (This bound holds because every branch node of a BDD leads to at least one solution. In fact, the running time is usually $O(N)$ in practice.)

17. That mission is impossible, because there's a function with $N = 2^{2k}$ and $B(f) = O(2^{2k})$ for which every two solutions differ in more than 2^{k-1} bit positions. The running time for any algorithm that generates all solutions for such a function must be $\Omega(2^{3k})$, because $\Omega(2^k)$ operations are needed between solutions. To construct f, first let

$$g(x_1, \ldots, x_k, y_0, \ldots, y_{2^k-1}) = \left[y_{(t_1 \ldots t_k)_2} = x_1 t_1 \oplus \cdots \oplus x_k t_k \text{ for } 0 \le t_1, \ldots, t_k \le 1\right].$$

(In other words, g asserts that $y_0 \ldots y_{2^k-1}$ is row $(x_1 \ldots x_k)_2$ of an Hadamard matrix; see Eq. 4.6.4–(38).) Now we let $f(x_1, \ldots, x_k, y_0, \ldots, y_{2^k-1}, x'_1, \ldots, x'_k, y'_0, \ldots, y'_{2^k-1}) = g(x_1, \ldots, x_k, y_0, \ldots, y_{2^k-1}) \wedge g(x'_1, \ldots, x'_k, y'_0, \ldots, y'_{2^k-1})$. Clearly $B(f) = O(2^{2k})$ when the variables are ordered in this way. Indeed, T. Dahlheimer observes that $B(f) = 2B(g) - 2$, where $B(g) = 2^k + 1 + \sum_{j=1}^{2^k} 2^{\min(k, 1 + \lceil \lg j \rceil)} = \frac{5}{3} 2^{2k-1} + 2^k + \frac{5}{3}$.

18. First, $(W_1, \ldots, W_5) = (5, 4, 4, 4, 0)$. Then $m_2 = w_4 = 4$ and $t_2 = 1$; $m_3 = t_3 = 0$; $m_4 = \max(m_3, m_2 + w_3) = 1$, $t_4 = 1$; $m_5 = W_4 - W_5 = 4$, $t_5 = 0$; $m_6 = w_2 + W_3 - W_5 = 2$, $t_6 = 1$; $m_7 = \max(m_5, m_4 + w_2) = 4$, $t_7 = 0$; $m_8 = \max(m_7, m_6 + w_1) = 4$, $t_8 = 0$. Solution $x_1 x_2 x_3 x_4 = 0001$.

19. $\sum_{j=1}^{n} \min(w_j, 0) \le \sum_{j=v_k}^{n} \min(w_j, 0) \le m_k \le \sum_{j=v_k}^{n} \max(w_j, 0) = W_{v_k} \le W_1$.

20. Set $w_1 \leftarrow -1$, then $w_{2j} \leftarrow w_j$ and $w_{2j+1} \leftarrow -w_j$ for $1 \le j \le n/2$. [This method may also compute w_{n+1}. The sequence is named for works of A. Thue, *Skrifter udgivne af Videnskabs-Selskabet i Christiania*, Mathematisk-Naturvidenskabelig Klasse (1912), No. 1, §7, and H. M. Morse, *Trans. Amer. Math. Soc.* **22** (1921), 84–100, §14.]

21. Yes; we just have to change the sign of each weight w_j. (Or we could reverse the roles of LO and HI at each vertex.)

22. If $f(x) = f(x') = 1$ when f represents a graph kernel, the Hamming distance $\nu(x \oplus x')$ cannot be 1. In such cases $v_l = v + 1$ when $l \neq 0$ and $v_h = v + 1$ when $h \neq 0$.

23. The BDD for the connectedness function of any connected graph will have exactly $n - 1$ solid arcs on every root-to-$\boxed{\top}$ path, because that many edges are needed to connect n vertices, and because a BDD has no redundant branches. (See also Theorem S.)

24. Apply Algorithm B with weights $(w'_{12}, \ldots, w'_{89}) = (-w_{12} - x, \ldots, -w_{89} - x)$, where x is large enough to make all of these new weights w'_{uv} negative. The maximum of $\sum w'_{uv} x_{uv}$ will then occur with $\sum x_{uv} = 8$, and those edges will form a spanning tree with minimum $\sum w_{uv} x_{uv}$. (We've seen a better algorithm for minimum spanning trees in exercise 2.3.4.1–11, and other methods will be studied in Section 7.5.4. However, this exercise indicates that a BDD can compactly represent the set of *all* spanning trees.)

25. The answer in step C1 becomes $(1 + z)^{v_s - 1 - 1} c_{s-1}$; the value of c_k in step C2 becomes $(1 + z)^{v_l - v_k - 1} c_l + (1 + z)^{v_h - v_k - 1} z c_h$.

26. In this case the answer in step C1 is simply c_{s-1}; and the value of c_k in step C2 is simply $(1 - p_{v_k})c_l + p_{v_k}c_h$.

27. The multilinear polynomial $H(x_1, \ldots, x_n) = F(x_1, \ldots, x_n) - G(x_1, \ldots, x_n)$ is nonzero modulo q, because it is ± 1 for some choice of integers with each $x_k \in \{0, 1\}$. If it has degree d (modulo q), we can prove that there are at least $(q-1)^d q^{n-d}$ sets of values $(q_1, \ldots, q_n)$ with $0 \le q_k < q$ such that $H(q_1, \ldots, q_n) \bmod q \ne 0$. This statement is clear when $d = 0$. And if x_k is a variable that appears in a term of degree $d > 0$, the coefficient of x_k is a polynomial of degree $d - 1$, which by induction on d is nonzero for at least $(q-1)^{d-1}q^{n-d}$ choices of $(q_1, \ldots, q_{k-1}, q_{k+1}, \ldots, q_n)$; for each of those choices there are $q - 1$ values of q_k such that $H(q_1, \ldots, q_n) \bmod q \ne 0$.

Hence the stated probability is $\ge (1 - 1/q)^d \ge (1 - 1/q)^n$. [See M. Blum, A. K. Chandra, and M. N. Wegman, *Information Processing Letters* **10** (1980), 80–82.]

28. $F(p) = (1 - p)^n G(p/(1 - p))$. Similarly, $G(z) = (1 + z)^n F(z/(1 + z))$.

29. In step C1, also set $c_0' \leftarrow 0$, $c_1' \leftarrow 0$; return c_{s-1} and c_{s-1}'. In step C2, set $c_k \leftarrow (1 - p)c_l + pc_h$ and $c_k' \leftarrow (1 - p)c_l' - c_l + pc_h' + c_h$.

30. The following analog of Algorithm B does the job (assuming exact arithmetic):

A1. [Initialize.] Set $P_{n+1} \leftarrow 1$ and $P_j \leftarrow P_{j+1} \max(1 - p_j, p_j)$ for $n \ge j \ge 1$.

A2. [Loop on k.] Set $m_1 \leftarrow 1$ and do step A3 for $2 \le k < s$. Then do step A4.

A3. [Process I_k.] Set $v \leftarrow v_k$, $l \leftarrow l_k$, $h \leftarrow h_k$, $t_k \leftarrow 0$. If $l \ne 0$, set $m_k \leftarrow m_l(1 - p_v)P_{v+1}/P_{v_l}$. Then if $h \ne 0$, compute $m \leftarrow m_h p_v P_{v+1}/P_{v_h}$; and if $l = 0$ or $m > m_k$, set $m_k \leftarrow m$ and $t_k \leftarrow 1$.

A4. [Compute the x's.] Set $j \leftarrow 0$, $k \leftarrow s - 1$, and do the following operations until $j = n$: While $j < v_k - 1$, set $j \leftarrow j + 1$ and $x_j \leftarrow [p_j > \frac{1}{2}]$; if $k > 1$, set $j \leftarrow j + 1$ and $x_j \leftarrow t_k$ and $k \leftarrow (t_k = 0? \, l_k : h_k)$. ∎

31. **C1'.** [Loop over k.] Set $\alpha_0 \leftarrow \bot$, $\alpha_1 \leftarrow \top$, and do step C2' for $k = 2, 3, \ldots, s - 1$. Then go to C3'.

C2'. [Compute α_k.] Set $v \leftarrow v_k$, $l \leftarrow l_k$, and $h \leftarrow h_k$. Set $\beta \leftarrow \alpha_l$ and $j \leftarrow v_l - 1$; then while $j > v$ set $\beta \leftarrow (\bar{x}_j \circ x_j) \bullet \beta$ and $j \leftarrow j - 1$. Set $\gamma \leftarrow \alpha_h$ and $j \leftarrow v_h - 1$; then while $j > v$ set $\gamma \leftarrow (\bar{x}_j \circ x_j) \bullet \gamma$ and $j \leftarrow j - 1$. Finally set $\alpha_k \leftarrow (\bar{x}_v \bullet \beta) \circ (x_v \bullet \gamma)$.

C3'. [Finish.] Set $\alpha \leftarrow \alpha_{s-1}$ and $j \leftarrow v_{s-1} - 1$; then while $j > 0$ set $\alpha \leftarrow (\bar{x}_j \circ x_j) \bullet \alpha$ and $j \leftarrow j - 1$. Return the answer α. ∎

This algorithm performs $\circ$ and $\bullet$ operations at most $O(nB(f))$ times. The upper bound can often be lowered to $O(n) + O(B(f))$; but shortcuts like the calculation of W_k in step B1 aren't always available. [See O. Coudert and J. C. Madre, *Proc. Reliability and Maint. Conf.* (IEEE, 1993), 240–245, §4; O. Coudert, *Integration* **17** (1994), 126–127.]

32. For exercise 25, '$\circ$' is addition, '$\bullet$' is multiplication, '$\bot$' is 0, '$\top$' is 1, '$\bar{x}_j$' is 1, 'x_j' is z. Exercise 26 is similar, but '$\bar{x}_j$' is $1 - p_j$ and 'x_j' is p_j.

In exercise 29 the objects of the algebra are pairs (c, c'), and we have $(a, a') \circ (b, b') = (a + b, a' + b')$, $(a, a') \bullet (b, b') = (ab, ab' + a'b)$. Also '$\bot$' is $(0, 0)$, '$\top$' is $(1, 0)$, '$\bar{x}_j$' is $(1 - p, -1)$, and 'x_j' is $(p, 1)$.

In exercise 30, '$\circ$' is max, '$\bullet$' is multiplication, '$\bot$' is $-\infty$, '$\top$' is 1, '$\bar{x}_j$' is $1 - p_j$, 'x_j' is p_j. Multiplication distributes over max in this case because the quantities are either nonnegative or $-\infty$; we must define $0 \bullet (-\infty) = -\infty$ in order to satisfy (22).

(Additional possibilities abound, because associative and distributive operators are ubiquitous in mathematics. The algebraic objects need not be numbers or polynomials or pairs; they can be strings, matrices, functions, sets of numbers, sets of strings, sets or multisets of matrices of pairs of functions of strings, etc., etc. We will see many further examples in Section 7.3. The min-plus algebra, with $\circ = \min$ and $\bullet = +$, is particularly important, and we could have used it in exercise 21 or 24. It is often called *tropical*, implicitly honoring the Brazilian mathematician Imre Simon.)

33. Operate on triples (c, c', c''), with $(a, a', a'') \circ (b, b', b'') = (a + b, a' + b', a'' + b'')$ and $(a, a', a'') \bullet (b, b', b'') = (ab, a'b + b'a, a''b + 2a'b' + ab'')$. Interpret '$\perp$' as $(0,0,0)$, '$\top$' as $(1,0,0)$, '$\bar{x}_j$' as $(1,0,0)$, and 'x_j' as $(1, w_j, w_j^2)$.

34. Let $x \vee y = \max(x, y)$. Operate on pairs (c, c'), with $(a, a') \circ (b, b') = (a \vee b, a' \vee b')$ and $(a, a') \bullet (b, b') = (a + b, (a' + b) \vee (a + b'))$. Interpret '$\perp$' as $(-\infty, -\infty)$, '$\top$' as $(0, -\infty)$, '$\bar{x}_j$' as $(0, w_j'')$, and 'x_j' as $(w_j, w_j' + w_j'')$. The first component of the result will agree with Algorithm B; the second component is the desired maximum.

35. (a) The supposed FBDD can be represented by instructions $I_{s-1}, \ldots, I_0$ as in Algorithm C. Start with $R_0 \leftarrow R_1 \leftarrow \emptyset$, then do the following for $k = 2, \ldots, s - 1$: Report failure if $v_k \in R_{l_k} \cup R_{h_k}$; otherwise set $R_k \leftarrow \{v_k\} \cup R_{l_k} \cup R_{h_k}$. (The set R_k identifies all variables that are reachable from I_k.)

(b) The reliability polynomial can be calculated just as in answer 26. To count solutions, we essentially set $p_1 = \cdots = p_n = \frac{1}{2}$ and multiply by 2^n: Start with $c_0 \leftarrow 0$ and $c_1 \leftarrow 2^n$, then set $c_k \leftarrow (c_{l_k} + c_{h_k})/2$ for $1 < k < s$. The answer is c_{s-1}.

36. Compute the sets R_k as in answer 35(a). Instead of looping on j as stated in step C2' of answer 31, set $\beta \leftarrow \alpha_l$ and then $\beta \leftarrow (\bar{x}_j \circ x_j) \bullet \beta$ for all $j \in R_k \setminus R_l \setminus \{v\}$; treat γ in the same manner. Similarly, in step C3' set $\alpha \leftarrow (\bar{x}_j \circ x_j) \bullet \alpha$ for all $j \notin R_{s-1}$.

37. Given any FBDD for f, the function $G(z)$ is the sum of $(1+z)^{n-\text{length}\,P} z^{\text{solid arcs in } P}$ over all paths P from the root to $\boxed{\top}$. [See *Theoretical Comp. Sci.* **3** (1976), 371–384.]

38. The key fact is that $x_j = 1$ forces $f = 1$ if and only if we have (i) $h_k = 1$ whenever $v_k = j$; (ii) $v_k = j$ in at least one step k; (iii) there are no steps with $(v_k < j < v_{l_k}$ and $l_k \neq 1)$ or $(v_k < j < v_{h_k}$ and $h_k \neq 1)$.

K1. [Initialize.] Set $t_j \leftarrow 2$ and $p_j \leftarrow 0$ for $1 \leq j \leq n$.

K2. [Examine all branches.] Do the following operations for $2 \leq k < s$: Set $j \leftarrow v_k$ and $q \leftarrow 0$. If $l_k = 1$, set $q \leftarrow -1$; otherwise set $p_j \leftarrow \max(p_j, v_{l_k})$. If $h_k = 1$, set $q \leftarrow +1$; otherwise set $p_j \leftarrow \max(p_j, v_{h_k})$. If $t_j = 2$, set $t_j \leftarrow q$; otherwise if $t_j \neq q$ set $t_j \leftarrow 0$.

K3. [Finish up.] Set $m \leftarrow v_{s-1}$, and do the following for $j = 1, 2, \ldots, n$: If $j < m$, set $t_j \leftarrow 0$; then if $p_j > m$, set $m \leftarrow p_j$. ∎

[See S.-W. Jeong and F. Somenzi, in *Logic Synthesis and Optimization* (1993), 154–156.]

39. $k(n + 1 - k) + 2$, for $1 \leq k \leq n$. (See (26).)

40. (a) Suppose the BDDs for f and g have respectively a_j and b_j branch nodes $\boxed{j}$, for $1 \leq j \leq n$. Each subtable of f of order $n + 1 - k$ has the form $\alpha\beta\gamma\delta$, where α, β, γ, and δ are subtables of order $n - 1 - k$. The corresponding subtables of g are $\alpha\alpha\delta\delta$; hence they are beads if and only if $\alpha \neq \delta$, in which case either $\alpha\beta\gamma\delta$ is a bead or $\alpha\beta = \gamma\delta$ is a bead. Consequently $b_k \leq a_k + a_{k+1}$, and $b_{k+1} = 0$. We also have $b_j \leq a_j$ for $1 \leq j < k$, because every bead of g of order $> n+1-k$ is "condensed" from at least one such bead of f. And $b_j \leq a_j$ for $j > k + 1$, because the subtables on $(x_{k+2}, \ldots, x_n)$ are identical although they might not appear in g.

(b) Not always. The simplest counterexample is $f(x_1, x_2, x_3, x_4) = x_2 \wedge (x_3 \vee x_4)$, $h(x_1, x_2, x_1, x_4) = x_2 \wedge (x_1 \vee x_4)$, when $B(f) = 5$ and $B(h) = 6$. (We do, however, always have $B(h) < 2B(f)$.)

41. (a) $3n - 3$; (b) $2n$. (The general patterns are illustrated here for $n = 6$. One can also show that the "organ-pipe ordering"
$$\langle x_n^{F_1} x_1^{F_2} x_{n-1}^{F_3} x_2^{F_4} \cdots x_{\lfloor n/2 \rfloor + [n \text{ even}]}^{F_{n-1}} x_{\lceil n/2 \rceil}^{F_{n-2}} \rangle$$
produces the profile 1, 2, 4, ..., $2\lceil n/2 \rceil - 2$, $2\lfloor n/2 \rfloor - 1$, ..., 5, 3, 1, 2, giving the total BDD size $\binom{n}{2} + 3$; this ordering appears to be the worst for the Fibonacci weights.)

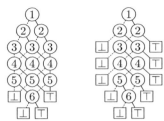

The functions $[F_n x_1 + \cdots + F_1 x_n \geq t]$ have been studied by J. T. Butler and T. Sasao, *Fibonacci Quart.* **34** (1996), 413–422.

42. (Compare with exercise 2.) The sixteen roots are the ① nodes and the two sinks:

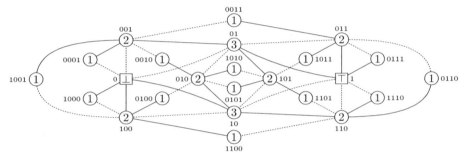

43. (a) Since $f(x_1, \ldots, x_{2n})$ is the symmetric function $S_n(x_1, \ldots, x_n, \bar{x}_{n+1}, \ldots, \bar{x}_{2n})$, we have $B(f) = 1 + 2 + \cdots + (n+1) + \cdots + 3 + 2 + 2 = n^2 + 2n + 2$.

(b) By symmetry, the size is the same for $[\sum \{x_i \mid i \in I\} = \sum \{x_i \mid i \notin I\}], |I| = n$.

44. There are at most $\min(k, 2^{n+2-k} - 2)$ nodes labeled ⓚ, for $1 \leq k \leq n$, because there are $2^{n+2-k} - 2$ symmetric functions of $(x_k, \ldots, x_n)$ that aren't constant. Thus S_n is at most $2 + \sum_{k=1}^{n} \min(k, 2^{n+2-k} - 2)$, which can be expressed in closed form as $(n+2-b_n)(n+1-b_n)/2 + 2(2^{b_n} - b_n)$, where $b_n = \lambda(n + 4 - \lambda(n+4))$ and $\lambda n = \lfloor \lg n \rfloor$.

A symmetric function that attains this worst-case bound can be constructed in the following way (related to the de Bruijn cycles constructed in exercise 3.2.2–7): Let $p(x) = x^d + a_1 x^{d-1} + \cdots + a_d$ be a primitive polynomial modulo 2. Set $t_k \leftarrow 1$ for $0 \leq k < d$; $t_k \leftarrow (a_1 t_{k-1} + \cdots + a_d t_{k-d}) \bmod 2$ for $d \leq k < 2^d + d - 2$; $t_k \leftarrow (1 + a_1 t_{k-1} + \cdots + a_d t_{k-d}) \bmod 2$ for $2^d + d - 2 \leq k < 2^{d+1} + d - 3$; and $t_{2^{d+1}+d-3} \leftarrow 1$. For example, when $p(x) = x^3 + x + 1$ we get $t_0 \ldots t_{16} = 11100101101000111$.

Then (i) the sequence $t_1 \ldots t_{2^d + d - 3}$ contains all d-tuples except 0^d and 1^d as substrings; (ii) the sequence $t_{2^d + d - 2} \ldots t_{2^{d+1} + d - 4}$ is a cyclic shift of $\bar{t}_0 \ldots \bar{t}_{2^d - 2}$; and (iii) $t_k = 1$ for $2^d - 1 \leq k \leq 2^d + d - 3$ and $2^{d+1} - 2 \leq k \leq 2^{d+1} + d - 3$. Consequently the sequence $t_0 \ldots t_{2^{d+1} + d - 3}$ contains all $(d+1)$-tuples except 0^{d+1} and 1^{d+1} as substrings. Set $f(x) = t_{\nu x}$ to maximize $B(f)$ when $2^d + d - 4 < n \leq 2^{d+1} + d - 3$.

Asymptotically, $S_n = \frac{1}{2}n^2 - n \lg n + O(n)$. [See I. Wegener, *Information and Control* **62** (1984), 129–143; M. Heap, *J. Electronic Testing* **4** (1993), 191–195.]

45. Module M_1 has only three inputs (x_1, y_1, z_1), and only three outputs $u_2 = x_1$, $v_2 = y_1 x_1$, $w_2 = z_1 x_1$. Module M_{n-1} is almost normal, but it has no input port for z_{n-1}, and it doesn't output u_n; it sets $z_{n-2} = x_{n-1}y_{n-1}$. Module M_n has only three inputs (v_n, w_n, x_n), and one output $y_{n-1} = x_n$ together with the main output, $w_n \vee v_n x_n$. With these definitions the dependencies between ports form an acyclic digraph.

(Modules could be constructed with all $b_k = 0$ and $a_k \le 5$, or even with $a_k \le 4$ as we'll see in exercise 47. But (33) and (34) are intended to illustrate backward signals in a simple example, not to demonstrate the tightest possible construction.)

46. For $6 \le k \le n-3$ there are nine branches on $\textcircled{k}$, corresponding to three cases $(\bar{x}_1, x_1\bar{x}_2, x_1 x_2)$ times three cases $(\bar{x}_{k-1}, \bar{x}_{k-2}x_{k-1}, \bar{x}_{k-3}x_{k-2}x_{k-1})$. The total BDD size turns out to be exactly $9n - 38$, if $n \ge 6$.

47. Suppose f has q_k subtables of order $n-k$, so that its QDD has q_k nodes that branch on x_{k+1}. We can encode them in $a_k = \lceil \lg q_k \rceil$ bits, and construct a module M_{k+1} with $b_k = b_{k+1} = 0$ that mimics the behavior of those q_k branch nodes. Thus by (86),

$$\sum_{k=0}^{n} 2^{a_k} 2^{b_k} = \sum_{k=0}^{n} 2^{\lceil \lg q_k \rceil} \le \sum_{k=0}^{n} (2q_k - 1) = 2Q(f) - (n+1) \le (n+1)B(f).$$

(The 2^m-way multiplexer shows that the additional factor of $(n+1)$ is necessary; indeed, Theorem M actually gives an upper bound on $Q(f)$.)

48. The sums $u_k = x_1 + \cdots + x_k$ and $v_k = x_{k+1} + \cdots + x_n$ can be represented on $1 + \lambda k$ and $1 + \lambda(n-k)$ wires, respectively. Let $t_k = x_k \wedge [u_k + v_k = k]$ and $w_k = t_1 \vee \cdots \vee t_k$. We can construct modules M_k having inputs u_{k-1} and w_{k-1} from M_{k-1} together with inputs v_k from M_{k+1}; module M_k outputs $u_k = u_{k-1} + x_k$ and $w_k = w_{k-1} \vee t_k$ to M_{k+1} as well as $v_{k-1} = v_k + x_k$ to M_{k-1}.

If p is a polynomial, $\sum_{k=0}^{n} 2^{p(a_k, b_k)} = 2^{(\log n)^{O(1)}}$ is asymptotically less than $2^{\Omega(n)}$. [See K. L. McMillan, *Symbolic Model Checking* (1993), §3.5, where Theorem M was introduced, with extensions to nonlinear layouts. The special case $b_1 = \cdots = b_n = 0$ had been noted previously by C. L. Berman, *IEEE Trans.* **CAD-10** (1991), 1059–1066.]

49.

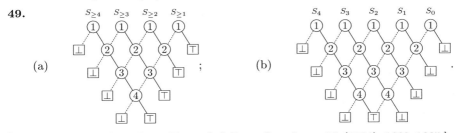

[See I. Semba and S. Yajima, *Trans. Inf. Proc. Soc. Japan* **35** (1994), 1663–1665.]

50.

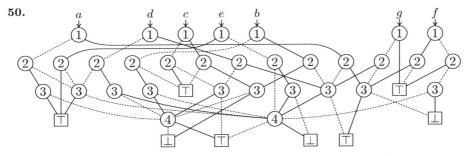

51. In this case $B(f_j) = 3j + 2$ for $1 \leq j \leq n$, and $B(f_{n+1}) = 3n + 1$; so the individual BDDs are only about $1/3$ as big as they are within (36). But almost no nodes are shared — only the sinks and one branch. So the total BDD size comes to $(3n^2 + 9n)/2$.

52. If the BDD base for $\{f_1, \ldots, f_m\}$ has s nodes, then $B(f) = s + m + 1 + [s=1]$.

53. Call the branch nodes a, b, c, d, e, f, g, with ROOT $= a$. After step R1 we have HEAD$[1] = \sim a$, AUX$(a) = \sim 0$; HEAD$[2] = \sim b$, AUX$(b) = \sim c$, AUX$(c) = \sim 0$; HEAD$[3] = \sim d$, AUX$(d) = \sim e$, AUX$(e) = \sim f$, AUX$(f) = \sim g$, AUX$(g) = \sim 0$.

After R3 with $v = 3$ we have $s = \sim 0$, AUX$(0) = \sim e$, AUX$(e) = f$, AUX$(f) = 0$; also AVAIL $= g$, LO$(g) = \sim 1$, HI$(g) = d$, LO$(d) = \sim 0$, and HI$(d) = \alpha$, where α was the initial value of AVAIL. (Nodes g and d have been recycled in favor of 1 and 0.) Then R4 sets $s \leftarrow e$ and AUX$(0) \leftarrow 0$. (The remaining nodes with V $= v$ start at s, linked via AUX.)

Now R7, starting with $p = q = e$ and $s = 0$, sets AUX$(1) \leftarrow \sim e$, LO$(f) \leftarrow \sim e$, HI$(f) \leftarrow g$, AVAIL $\leftarrow f$; and R8 resets AUX$(1) \leftarrow 0$.

Then step R3 with $v = 2$ sets LO$(b) \leftarrow 0$, LO$(c) \leftarrow e$, and HI$(c) \leftarrow 1$. No further changes of importance take place, although some AUX fields temporarily become negative. We end up with Fig. 21.

54. Create nodes j for $1 < j \leq 2^{n-1}$ by setting V$(j) \leftarrow \lceil \lg j \rceil$, LO$(j) \leftarrow 2j - 1$, and HI$(j) \leftarrow 2j$; also for $2^{n-1} < j \leq 2^n$ by setting V$(j) \leftarrow n$, LO$(j) \leftarrow f(x_1, \ldots, x_{n-1}, 0)$, and HI$(j) \leftarrow f(x_1, \ldots, x_{n-1}, 1)$ when $j = (1x_1 \ldots x_{n-1})_2 + 1$. Then apply Algorithm R with ROOT $= 2$. (We can bypass step R1 by first setting AUX$(j) \leftarrow -j$ for $4 \leq j \leq 2^n$, then HEAD$[k] \leftarrow \sim(2^k)$ and AUX$(2^{k-1} + 1) \leftarrow -1$ for $1 \leq k \leq n$.)

55. It suffices to construct an unreduced diagram, since Algorithm R will then finish the job. Number the vertices $1, \ldots, n$ in such a way that no vertex except 1 appears before all of its neighbors. Represent the edges by arcs $a_1, \ldots, a_e$, where a_k is $u_k \longrightarrow v_k$ for some $u_k < v_k$, and where the arcs having $u_k = j$ are consecutive, with $s_j \leq k < s_{j+1}$ and $1 = s_1 \leq \cdots \leq s_n = s_{n+1} = e + 1$. Define the "frontier" $V_k = \{1, v_1, \ldots, v_k\} \cap \{u_k, \ldots, n\}$ for $1 \leq k \leq e$, and let $V_0 = \{1\}$. The unreduced decision diagram will have branches on arc a_k for all partitions of V_{k-1} that correspond to connectedness relations that have arisen because of previous branches.

For example, consider $P_3 \square P_3$, where $(s_1, \ldots, s_{10}) = (1, 3, 5, 7, 8, 10, 11, 12, 13, 13)$ and $V_0 = \{1\}$, $V_1 = \{1, 2\}$, $V_2 = \{1, 2, 3\}$, $V_3 = \{2, 3, 4\}$, $\ldots$, $V_{12} = \{8, 9\}$. The branch on a_1 goes from the trivial partition 1 of V_0 to the partition $1|2$ of V_1 if $1 \not\!\!- 2$, or to the partition 12 if $1 \,\underline{\hspace{0.8em}}\, 2$. (The notation '$1|2$' stands for the set partition $\{1\} \cup \{2\}$, as in Section 7.2.1.5.) From $1|2$, the branch on a_2 goes to the partition $1|2|3$ of V_2 if $1 \not\!\!- 3$, otherwise to $13|2$; from 12, the branches go respectively to partitions $12|3$ and 123. Then from $1|2|3$, both branches on a_3 go to $\boxed{\perp}$, because vertex 1 can no longer be connected to the others. And so on. Eventually the partitions of $V_e = V_{12}$ are all identified with $\boxed{\perp}$, except for the trivial one-set partition, which corresponds to $\boxed{\top}$.

56. Start with $m \leftarrow 2$ in step R1, and $v_0 \leftarrow v_1 \leftarrow v_{\max} + 1$, $l_0 \leftarrow h_0 \leftarrow 0$, $l_1 \leftarrow h_1 \leftarrow 1$ as in (8). Assume that HI$(0) = 0$ and HI$(1) = 1$. Omit the assignments that involve AVAIL in steps R3 and R7. After setting AUX$(\text{HI}(p)) \leftarrow 0$ in step R8, also set $v_m \leftarrow v$, $l_m \leftarrow \text{HI}(\text{LO}(p))$, $h_m \leftarrow \text{HI}(\text{HI}(p))$, HI$(p) \leftarrow m$, and $m \leftarrow m + 1$. At the end of step R9, set $s \leftarrow m - [\text{ROOT} = 0]$.

57. Set LO(ROOT) $\leftarrow \sim$LO(ROOT). (We briefly complement the LO field of nodes that are still accessible after restriction.) Then for $v = $ V(ROOT), $\ldots$, $v_{\max}$, set $p \leftarrow \sim$HEAD$[v]$, HEAD$[v] \leftarrow \sim 0$, and do the following while $p \neq 0$: (i) Set $p' \leftarrow \sim$AUX(p). (ii) If LO$(p) \geq 0$, set HI$(p) \leftarrow$ AVAIL, AUX$(p) \leftarrow 0$, and AVAIL $\leftarrow p$ (node p can no longer be reached). Otherwise set LO$(p) \leftarrow \sim$LO(p); if FIX$[v] = 0$, set HI$(p) \leftarrow$ LO(p); if FIX$[v] = 1$, set

$\mathtt{LO}(p) \leftarrow \mathtt{HI}(p)$; if $\mathtt{LO}(\mathtt{LO}(p)) \geq 0$, set $\mathtt{LO}(\mathtt{LO}(p)) \leftarrow {\sim}\mathtt{LO}(\mathtt{LO}(p))$; if $\mathtt{LO}(\mathtt{HI}(p)) \geq 0$, set $\mathtt{LO}(\mathtt{HI}(p)) \leftarrow {\sim}\mathtt{LO}(\mathtt{HI}(p))$; and set $\mathtt{AUX}(p) \leftarrow \mathtt{HEAD}[v]$, $\mathtt{HEAD}[v] \leftarrow {\sim}p$. (iii) Set $p \leftarrow p'$. Finally, after finishing the loop on v, restore $\mathtt{LO}(0) \leftarrow 0$, $\mathtt{LO}(1) \leftarrow 1$.

58. Since $l \neq h$ and $l' \neq h'$, we have $l \diamond l' \neq h \diamond h'$, $l \diamond \alpha' \neq h \diamond \alpha'$, and $\alpha \diamond l' \neq \alpha \diamond h'$.

Suppose $\alpha \diamond \alpha' = \beta \diamond \beta'$, where $\beta = (v'', l'', h'')$ and $\beta' = (v''', l''', h''')$. If $v'' = v'''$ we have $v = v''$, $l \diamond l' = l'' \diamond l'''$, and $h \diamond h' = h'' \diamond h'''$. If $v'' < v'''$ we have $v = v''$, $l \diamond \alpha' = l'' \diamond \beta'$, and $h \diamond \alpha' = h'' \diamond \beta'$. Otherwise we have $v' = v'''$, $\alpha \diamond l' = \beta \diamond l'''$, and $\alpha \diamond h' = \beta \diamond h'''$. By induction, therefore, we have $\alpha = \beta$ and $\alpha' = \beta'$ in all cases.

59. (a) If h isn't constant we have $B(f \diamond g) = 3B(h) - 2$, essentially obtained by taking a copy of the BDD for h and replacing its sink nodes by two other copies.

(b) Suppose the profile and quasi-profile of h are $(b_0, \ldots, b_n)$ and $(q_0, \ldots, q_n)$, where $b_n = q_n = 2$. Then there are $b_k q_k$ branches on x_{2k+1} in $f \diamond g$, and $q_k b_{k-1}$ branches on x_{2k}, corresponding to ordered pairs of beads and subtables of h. When the BDD for h contains a branch from α to β and from α' to β', where $\mathtt{V}(\alpha) = j$, $\mathtt{V}(\beta) = k$, $\mathtt{V}(\alpha') = j'$, and $\mathtt{V}(\beta') = k'$, the BDD for $f \diamond g$ contains a corresponding branch with $\mathtt{V}(\alpha \diamond \alpha') = 2j - 1$ from $\alpha \diamond \alpha'$ to $\beta \diamond \alpha'$ when $j \leq j' < k$, and with $\mathtt{V}(\alpha \diamond \alpha') = 2j'$ from $\alpha \diamond \alpha'$ to $\alpha \diamond \beta'$ when $j' < j \leq k'$.

60. Every bead of order $n - j$ of the ordered pair (f, g) is either one of the $b_j b'_j$ ordered pairs of beads of f and g, or one of the $b_j(q'_j - b'_j) + (q_j - b_j)b'_j$ ordered pairs that have the form (bead, nonbead) or (nonbead, bead). [This upper bound is achieved in the examples of exercises 59(b) and 63.]

61. Assume that $v = V(\alpha) \leq V(\beta)$. Let $\alpha_1, \ldots, \alpha_k$ be the nodes that point to α, and let $\beta_1, \ldots, \beta_l$ be the nodes with $V(\beta_j) < v$ that point to β; an imaginary node is assumed to point to each root. (Thus $k = $ in-degree(α) and $l \leq $ in-degree(β).) Then the melded nodes that point to $\alpha \diamond \beta$ are of three types: (i) $\alpha_i \diamond \beta_j$, where $V(\alpha_i) = V(\beta_j)$ and either $(\mathtt{LO}(\alpha_i) = \alpha$ and $\mathtt{LO}(\beta_j) = \beta)$ or $(\mathtt{HI}(\alpha_i) = \alpha$ and $\mathtt{HI}(\beta_j) = \beta)$; (ii) $\alpha \diamond \beta_j$, where $V(\alpha_i) < V(\beta_j)$ for some i; or (iii) $\alpha_i \diamond \beta$, where $V(\alpha_i) > V(\beta_j)$ for some j.

62. The BDD for f has one node on each level, and the BDD for g has two, except at the top and bottom. The BDD for $f \vee g$ has four nodes on nearly every level, by exercise 14(a). The BDD for $f \diamond g$ has seven nodes (j) when $5 \leq j \leq n - 3$, corresponding to ordered pairs of subtables of (f, g) that depend on x_j when $(x_1, \ldots, x_{j-1})$ have fixed values. Thus $B(f) = n + O(1)$, $B(g) = 2n + O(1)$, $B(f \diamond g) = 7n + O(1)$, and $B(f \vee g) = 4n + O(1)$. (Also $B(f \wedge g) = 7n + O(1)$, $B(f \oplus g) = 7n + O(1)$.)

63. The profiles of f and g are respectively $(1, 2, 2, \ldots, 2^{m-1}, 2^{m-1}, 2^m, 1, 1, \ldots, 1, 2)$ and $(0, 1, 2, 2, \ldots, 2^{m-1}, 2^{m-1}, 1, 1, \ldots, 1, 2)$; so $B(f) = 2^{m+2} - 1 \approx 4n$ and $B(g) = 2^{m+1} + 2^m - 1 \approx 3n$. The profile of $f \wedge g$ begins with $(1, 2, 4, \ldots, 2^{2m-2}, 2^{2m-1} - 2^{m-1})$, because there's a unique solution $x_1 \ldots x_{2m}$ to the equations

$$((x_1 \oplus x_2)(x_3 \oplus x_4) \ldots (x_{2m-1} \oplus x_{2m}))_2 = p, ((x_2 \oplus x_3) \ldots (x_{2m-2} \oplus x_{2m-1})x_{2m})_2 = q$$

for $0 \leq p, q < 2^m$, and $p = q$ if and only if $x_1 = x_3 = \cdots = x_{2m-1} = 0$. After that the profile continues $(2^{m+1} - 2, 2^{m+1} - 2, 2^{m+1} - 4, 2^{m+1} - 6, \ldots, 4, 2, 2)$; the subfunctions are $x_{2m+j} \wedge \bar{x}_{2m+k}$ or $\bar{x}_{2m+j} \wedge x_{2m+k}$ for $1 \leq j < k \leq 2^m$, together with x_{2m+j} and $\bar{x}_{2m+j}$ for $2 \leq j \leq 2^m$. All in all, we have $B(f \wedge g) = 2^{2m+1} + 2^{m-1} - 1 \approx 2n^2$.

64. The BDD for *any* Boolean combination of f_1, f_2, and f_3 is contained in the meld $f_1 \diamond f_2 \diamond f_3$, whose size is at most $B(f_1)B(f_2)B(f_3)$.

65. $h = g$? f_1: f_0, where f_c is the restriction of f obtained by setting $x_j \leftarrow c$. The first upper bound follows as in answer 64, because $B(f_c) \leq B(f)$. The second bound fails when, for example, $n = 2^m + 3m$ and $h = M_m(x; y)$? $M_m(x'; y)$: $M_m(x''; y)$, where $x = (x_1, \ldots, x_m)$, $x' = (x'_1, \ldots, x'_m)$, $x'' = (x''_1, \ldots, x''_m)$, and $y = (y_0, \ldots, y_{2^m-1})$; but such failures appear to be rare. [See R. E. Bryant, *IEEE Trans.* **C-35** (1986), 685; J. Jain, K. Mohanram, D. Moundanos, I. Wegener, and Y. Lu, *ACM/IEEE Design Automation Conf.* **37** (2000), 681–686.]

66. Set NTOP $\leftarrow f_0 + 1 - l$ and terminate the algorithm.

67. Let t_k denote template location POOLSIZE $- 2k$. Step S1 sets LEFT$(t_1) \leftarrow 5$, RIGHT$(t_1) \leftarrow 7$, $l \leftarrow 1$. Step S2 for $l = 1$ puts t_1 into both LLIST[2] and HLIST[2]. Step S5 for $l = 2$ sets LEFT$(t_2) \leftarrow 4$, RIGHT$(t_2) \leftarrow 5$, L$(t_1) \leftarrow t_2$; LEFT$(t_3) \leftarrow 3$, RIGHT$(t_3) \leftarrow 6$, H$(t_1) \leftarrow t_3$. Step S2 for $l = 2$ sets L$(t_2) \leftarrow 0$ and puts t_2 in HLIST[3]; then it puts t_3 into LLIST[3] and HLIST[3]. And so on. Phase 1 ends with $(\text{LSTART}[0], \ldots, \text{LSTART}[4]) = (t_0, t_1, t_3, t_5, t_8)$ and

k	LEFT(t_k)	RIGHT(t_k)	L(t_k)	H(t_k)	k	LEFT(t_k)	RIGHT(t_k)	L(t_k)	H(t_k)
1	5 $[\alpha]$	7 $[\omega]$	t_2	t_3	5	3 $[\gamma]$	4 $[\varphi]$	t_6	t_8
2	4 $[\beta]$	5 $[\chi]$	0	t_4	6	2 $[\delta]$	2 $[\tau]$	0	1
3	3 $[\gamma]$	6 $[\psi]$	t_4	t_5	7	2 $[\delta]$	1 $[\top]$	0	1
4	3 $[\gamma]$	1 $[\top]$	t_7	1	8	1 $[\top]$	3 $[v]$	1	0

representing the meld $\alpha \diamond \omega$ in Fig. 24 but with $\perp \diamond x = x \diamond \perp = \perp$ and $\top \diamond \top = \top$.

Let $f_k = f_0 + k$. In phase 2, step S7 for $l = 4$ sets LEFT$(t_6) \leftarrow {\sim}0$, LEFT$(t_7) \leftarrow t_6$, LEFT$(t_8) \leftarrow {\sim}1$, and RIGHT$(t_6) \leftarrow$ RIGHT$(t_7) \leftarrow$ RIGHT$(t_8) \leftarrow -1$. Step S8 undoes the changes made to LEFT(0) and LEFT(1). Step S11 with $s = t_8$ sets LEFT$(t_8) \leftarrow {\sim}2$, RIGHT$(t_8) \leftarrow t_8$, V$(f_2) \leftarrow 4$, LO$(f_2) \leftarrow 1$, HI$(f_2) \leftarrow 0$. With $s = t_7$ that step sets LEFT$(t_7) \leftarrow {\sim}3$, RIGHT$(t_7) \leftarrow t_7$, V$(f_3) \leftarrow 4$, LO$(f_3) \leftarrow 0$, HI$(f_3) \leftarrow 1$; meanwhile step S10 has set RIGHT$(t_6) \leftarrow t_7$. Eventually the templates will be transformed to

k	LEFT(t_k)	RIGHT(t_k)	L(t_k)	H(t_k)	k	LEFT(t_k)	RIGHT(t_k)	L(t_k)	H(t_k)
1	${\sim}8$	t_1	t_2	t_3	5	${\sim}4$	t_5	t_7	t_8
2	${\sim}7$	t_2	0	t_4	6	${\sim}0$	t_7	0	1
3	${\sim}6$	t_3	t_4	t_5	7	${\sim}3$	t_7	0	1
4	${\sim}5$	t_4	t_7	1	8	${\sim}2$	t_8	1	0

(but they can then be discarded). The resulting BDD for $f \wedge g$ is

k	V(f_k)	LO(f_k)	HI(f_k)	k	V(f_k)	LO(f_k)	HI(f_k)
2	4	1	0	6	2	5	4
3	4	0	1	7	2	0	5
4	3	3	2	8	1	7	6.
5	3	3	1				

68. If LEFT$(t) < 0$ at the beginning of step S10, set RIGHT$(t) \leftarrow t$, $q \leftarrow$ NTOP, NTOP $\leftarrow q + 1$, LEFT$(t) \leftarrow {\sim}(q - f_0)$, LO$(q) \leftarrow {\sim}$LEFT(L$(t)$), HI$(q) \leftarrow {\sim}$LEFT(H$(t)$), V$(q) \leftarrow l$, and return to S9.

69. Make sure that NTOP $\leq$ TBOT at the end of step S1 and when going from S11 to S9. (It's *not* necessary to make this test inside the loop of S11.) Also make sure that NTOP $\leq$ HBASE just after setting HBASE in step S4.

70. This choice would make the hash table a bit smaller; memory overflow would therefore be slightly less likely, at the expense of slightly more collisions. But it also would slow down the action, because *make_template* would have to check that NTOP $\leq$ TBOT whenever TBOT decreases.

71. Add a new field, EXTRA$(t) = \alpha''$, to each template t (see (43)).

72. In place of steps S4 and S5, use the approach of Algorithm R to bucket-sort the elements of the linked lists that begin at LLIST[l] and HLIST[l]. This is possible if an extra one-bit hint is used within the pointers to distinguish links in the L fields from links in the H fields, because we can then determine the LO and HI parameters of t's descendants as a function of t and its "parity."

73. If the BDD profile is $(b_0, \ldots, b_n)$, we can assign $p_j = \lceil b_{j-1}/2^e \rceil$ pages to branches on x_j. Auxiliary tables of $p_1 + \cdots + p_{n+1} \leq \lceil B(f)/2^e \rceil + n$ short integers allow us to compute $V(p) = T[\pi(p)]$, $\mathrm{LO}(p) = \mathrm{LO}(M[\pi(p)] + \sigma(p))$, $\mathrm{HI}(p) = \mathrm{HI}(M[\pi(p)] + \sigma(p))$.

For example, if $e = 12$ and $n < 2^{16}$, we can represent arbitrary BDDs of up to $2^{32} - 2^{28} + 2^{16} + 2^{12}$ nodes with 32-bit virtual LO and HI pointers. Each BDD requires appropriate auxiliary T and M tables of size $\leq 2^{20}$, constructible from its profile.

[This method can significantly improve caching behavior. It was inspired by the paper of P. Ashar and M. Cheong, *Proc. International Conf. Computer-Aided Design* (IEEE, 1994), 622–627, which also introduced algorithms similar to Algorithm S.]

74. The required condition is now $\mu_n(x_1, \ldots, x_{2^n}) \wedge [\bar{x}_1 = x_{2^n}] \wedge \cdots \wedge [\bar{x}_{2^n-1} = x_{2^{n-1}+1}]$. If we set $y_1 = x_1$, $y_2 = x_3$, $\ldots$, $y_{2^{n-2}} = x_{2^{n-1}-1}$, $y_{2^{n-2}+1} = \bar{x}_{2^{n-1}}$, $y_{2^{n-2}+2} = \bar{x}_{2^{n-1}-2}$, $\ldots$, $y_{2^{n-1}} = \bar{x}_2$, (49) yields the equivalent condition $\mu_{n-1}(y_1, \ldots, y_{2^{n-1}}) \wedge [y_{2^{n-2}} \leq \bar{y}_{2^{n-2}+1}] \wedge [y_{2^{n-2}-1} \leq \bar{y}_{2^{n-2}+2}] \wedge \cdots \wedge [y_1 \leq \bar{y}_{2^{n-1}}]$, which is eminently suitable for evaluation by Algorithm S. (The evaluation should be from left to right; right-to-left would generate enormous intermediate results.)

With this approach we find that there are respectively 1, 2, 4, 12, 81, 2646, 1422564, 229809982112 monotone self-dual functions of 1, 2, $\ldots$, 8 variables. (See Table 7.1.1–3 and answer 7.1.2–88.) The 8-variable functions are characterized by a BDD of 130,305,082 nodes; Algorithm S needs about 204 gigamems to compute it.

75. Begin with $\rho_1(x_1, x_2) = [x_1 \leq x_2]$, and replace $G_{2^n}(x_1, \ldots, x_{2^n})$ in (49) by the function $H_{2^n}(x_1, \ldots, x_{2^n}) = [x_1 \leq x_2 \leq x_3 \leq x_4] \wedge \cdots \wedge [x_{2^n-3} \leq x_{2^n-2} \leq x_{2^n-1} \leq x_{2^n}]$.

(It turns out that $B(\rho_9) = 3{,}683{,}424$; about 170 megamems suffice to compute that BDD, and ρ_{10} is almost within reach. Algorithm C now quickly yields the exact numbers of regular n-variable Boolean functions for $1 \leq n \leq 9$, namely 3, 5, 10, 27, 119, 1173, 44315, 16175190, 284432730176. Similarly, we can count the self-dual ones, as in exercise 74; those numbers, whose early history is discussed in answer 7.1.1–123, are 1, 1, 2, 3, 7, 21, 135, 2470, 319124, 1214554343, for $1 \leq n \leq 10$.)

76. Say that $x_0 \ldots x_{j-1}$ *forces* x_j if $x_i = 1$ for some $i \subseteq j$ with $0 \leq i < j$. Then $x_0 x_1 \ldots x_{2^n-1}$ corresponds to a clutter if and only if $x_j = 0$ whenever $x_0 \ldots x_{j-1}$ forces x_j, for $0 \leq j < 2^n$. And $\mu_n(x_0, \ldots, x_{2^n-1}) = 1$ if and only if $x_j = 1$ whenever $x_0 \ldots x_{j-1}$ forces x_j. So we get the desired BDD from that of $\mu_n(x_1, \ldots, x_{2^n})$ by (i) changing each branch $\boxed{j}$ to $\boxed{j-1}$, and (ii) interchanging the LO and HI branches at every branch node that has LO $= \boxed{\perp}$. (Notice that, by Corollary 7.1.1Q, the prime implicants of every monotone Boolean function correspond to clutters.)

77. Continuing the previous answer, say that the bit vector $x_0 \ldots x_{k-1}$ is *consistent* if we have $x_j = 1$ whenever $x_0 \ldots x_{j-1}$ forces x_j, for $0 < j < k$. Let b_k be the number of consistent vectors of length k. For example, $b_4 = 6$ because of the vectors $\{0000, 0001, 0011, 0101, 0111, 1111\}$. Notice that exactly $c_k = b_{k+1} - b_k$ clutters $\mathcal{S}$ have the properly that k represents their "largest" set, $\max\{s \mid s \text{ represents a set of } \mathcal{S}\}$.

The BDD for $\mu_n(x_1, \ldots, x_{2^n})$ has b_{k-1} branch nodes $\boxed{k}$ when $1 \leq k \leq 2^{n-1}$. Proof: Every subfunction defined by x_1, $\ldots$, x_{k-1} is either identically false or defines a consistent vector $x_1 \ldots x_{k-1}$. In the latter case the subfunction is a bead, because it takes different values under certain settings of x_{k+1}, $\ldots$, x_{2^n}. Indeed, if $x_1 \ldots x_{k-1}$

forces x_k, we set $x_{k+1} \leftarrow \cdots \leftarrow x_{2^n} \leftarrow 1$; otherwise we set $x_j \leftarrow y_j$ for $k < j \leq 2^n$, where $y_{j+1} = [x_{i+1} = 1$ for some $i \subseteq j$ with $i + 1 < k]$, noting that $y_{2^n+k} = 0$.

On the other hand there are $b_{k'}$ branches $\overline{(k)}$ when $k = 2^n - k'$ and $0 \leq k' < 2^{n-1}$. In this case the nonconstant subfunctions arising from $x_1, \ldots, x_{k-1}$ lead to values y_j as above, where the vector $\bar{y}_{0'}\bar{y}_{1'}\ldots\bar{y}_{k'}$ is consistent. (Here $0' = 2^n$, $1' = 2^n - 1$, etc.) Conversely, every such consistent vector describes such a subfunction; we can, for example, set $x_j \leftarrow 0$ when $j < k - 2^{n-1}$ or $2^{n-1} \leq j < k$, otherwise $x_j \leftarrow y_{2^{n-1}+j}$. This subfunction is a bead if and only if $y_{k'} = 1$ or $\bar{y}_{0'}\ldots\bar{y}_{(k-1)'}$ forces $\bar{y}_{k'}$. Thus the beads correspond to consistent vectors of length k'; and different vectors define different beads.

This argument shows that there are $b_{k-1} - c_{k-1}$ branches $\overline{(k)}$ with LO $= \boxed{\perp}$ when $1 \leq k \leq 2^{n-1}$ and c_{2^n-k} such branches when $2^{n-1} < k \leq 2^n$. Hence exactly half of the $B(\mu_n) - 2$ branch nodes have LO $= \boxed{\perp}$.

78. To count graphs on n labeled vertices with maximum degree $\leq d$, construct the Boolean function of the $\binom{n}{2}$ variables in its adjacency matrix, namely $\bigwedge_{k=1}^{n} S_{\leq d}(X_k)$, where X_k is the set of variables in row k of the matrix. For example, when $n = 5$ there are 10 variables, and the function is $S_{\leq d}(x_1, x_2, x_3, x_4) \wedge S_{\leq d}(x_1, x_5, x_6, x_7) \wedge S_{\leq d}(x_2, x_5, x_8, x_9) \wedge S_{\leq d}(x_3, x_6, x_8, x_{10}) \wedge S_{\leq d}(x_4, x_7, x_9, x_{10})$. When $n = 12$ the BDDs for $d = (1, 2, \ldots, 10)$ have respectively (5960, 137477, 1255813, 5295204, 10159484, 11885884, 9190884, 4117151, 771673, 28666) nodes, so they are readily computed with Algorithm S. To count solutions with maximum degree d, subtract the number of solutions for degree $\leq d-1$ from the number for degree $\leq d$; the answers for $0 \leq d \leq 11$ are:

1	3038643940889754	29271277569846191555
140151	211677202624318662	17880057008325613629
3568119351	3617003021179405538	4489497643961740521
8616774658305	17884378201906645374	430038382710483623

[In general there are $t_n - 1$ graphs on n labeled vertices with maximum degree 1, where t_n is the number of involutions, Eq. 5.1.4–(40).]

The methods of Section 7.2.3 are superior to BDDs for enumerations such as these, when n is large, because labeled graphs have $n!$ symmetries. But when n has a moderate size, BDDs produce answers quickly, and nicely characterize all the solutions.

79. In the following counts, obtained from the BDDs in the previous answer, each graph with k edges is weighted by 2^{66-k}. Divide by 3^{66} to get probabilities.

73786976294838206464	11646725483430295546484263747584
553156749930805290074112	77677416878709243055475188038968
5985355028683152365484768	25144575345589759186086686688384
683798352205845501171675955520	4527336156360899392181933403904
138035892756457768347923329843	4596863773888180534154567673
7024096376298397076969081536512	2093195580480313818292294985

80. If the original functions f and g have no BDD nodes in common, both algorithms encounter almost exactly the same subproblems: Algorithm S deals with all nodes of $f \diamond g$ that aren't descended from nodes of the forms $\alpha \diamond \boxed{\perp}$ or $\boxed{\perp} \diamond \beta$, while (55) also avoids nodes that descend from the forms $\alpha \diamond \boxed{\top}$ or $\boxed{\top} \diamond \beta$. Furthermore, (55) takes shortcuts when it meets nontrivial subproblems $\text{AND}(f', g')$ with $f' = g'$; Algorithm S cannot recognize the fact that such cases are easy. And (55) can also win if it happens to stumble across a relevant memo left over from a previous computation.

81. Just change 'AND' to 'XOR' and '$\wedge$' to '$\oplus$' throughout. The simple cases are now $f \oplus 0 = f$, $0 \oplus g = g$, and $f \oplus g = 0$ if $f = g$. We should also swap $f \leftrightarrow g$ if $f > g \neq 0$.

Notes: The author experimentally inserted further memos '$f \oplus r = g$' and '$g \oplus r = f$' in the bottom line; but these additional cache entries seemed to do more harm than good. Considering other binary operators, there's no need to implement both BUTNOT$(f, g) = f \wedge \bar{g}$ and NOTBUT$(f, g) = \bar{f} \wedge g$, since the latter is BUTNOT(g, f). Also, XOR$(1, \text{OR}(f, g))$ may be better than an implementation of NOR$(f, g) = \neg(f \vee g)$.

82. A top-level computation of $F \leftarrow \text{AND}(f, g)$ begins with f and g in computer registers, but REF(f) and REF(g) do not include "references" such as those. (We do, however, assume that f and g are both alive.)

If (55) discovers that $f \wedge g$ is obviously r, it increases REF(r) by 1.

If (55) finds $f \wedge g = r$ in the memo cache, it increases REF(r), and recursively increases REF(LO(r)) and REF(HI(r)) in the same way if r was dead.

If step U1 finds $p = q$, it *decreases* REF(p) by 1 (believe it or not); this won't kill p.

If step U2 finds r, there are two cases: If r was alive, it sets REF$(r) \leftarrow$ REF$(r) + 1$, REF$(p) \leftarrow$ REF$(p) - 1$, REF$(q) \leftarrow$ REF$(q) - 1$. Otherwise it simply sets REF$(r) \leftarrow 1$.

When step U3 creates a new node r, it sets REF$(r) \leftarrow 1$.

Finally, after the top-level AND returns a value r that we wish to assign to F, we must first *dereference* F, if $F \neq \Lambda$; this means setting REF$(F) \leftarrow$ REF$(F) - 1$, and recursively dereferencing LO(F) and HI(F) if REF(F) has become 0. Then we set $F \leftarrow r$ (without adjusting REF(r)).

[Furthermore, in a quantification routine such as (65) or in the composition routine (72), both r_l and r_h should be dereferenced after the OR or MUX has computed r.]

83. Exercise 61 shows that the subproblem $f \wedge g$ occurs at most once per top-level call, when REF$(f) = $ REF$(g) = 1$. [This idea is due to F. Somenzi; see the paper cited in answer 84. Many nodes have reference count 1, because the average count is approximately 2, and because the sinks usually have large counts. However, such cache-avoidance did not improve the overall performance in the author's experiments, possibly because of the examples investigated, or possibly because "accidental" cache hits in other top-level operations can be useful.]

84. Many possibilities exist, and no simple technique appears to be a clear winner. The cache and table sizes should be powers of 2, to facilitate calculating the hash functions. The size of the unique table for x_v should be roughly proportional to the number of nodes that currently branch on x_v (alive or dead). It's necessary to rehash everything when a table is downsized or upsized.

In the author's experiments while writing this section, the cache size was doubled whenever the number of insertions since the beginning of the most recent top-level command exceeded $\ln 2$ times the current cache size. (At that point a random hash function will have filled about half of the slots.) After garbage collection, the cache was downsized, if necessary, so that it either had 256 slots or was at least 1/4 full.

It's easy to keep track of the current number of dead nodes; hence we know at all times how much memory a garbage collection will reclaim. The author obtained satisfactory results by inserting a new step U2$\frac{1}{2}$ between U2 and U3: "Increase C by 1, where C is a global counter. If $C \bmod 1024 = 0$, and if at least 1/8 of all current nodes are dead, collect garbage."

[See F. Somenzi, *Software Tools for Technology Transfer* **3** (2001), 171–181 for numerous further suggestions based on extensive experience.]

85. The complete table would have 2^{32} entries of 32 bits each, for a total of 2^{34} bytes (≈ 17.2 gigabytes). The BDD base discussed after (58), with about 136 million nodes using zip-ordered bits, can be stored in about 1.1 gigabyte; the one discussed in Corollary Y, which ranks all of the multiplier bits first, needs only about 400 megabytes.

86. If $f = 0$ or $g = h$, return g. If $f = 1$, return h. If $g = 0$ or $f = g$, return $\mathrm{AND}(f, h)$. If $h = 1$ or $f = h$, return $\mathrm{OR}(f, g)$. If $g = 1$, return $\mathrm{IMPLIES}(f, h)$; if $h = 0$, return $\mathrm{BUTNOT}(g, f)$. (If binary IMPLIES and/or BUTNOT aren't implemented directly, it's OK to let the corresponding cases propagate in ternary guise.)

87. Sort so that $f \leq g \leq h$. If $f = 0$, return $\mathrm{AND}(g, h)$. If $f = 1$, return $\mathrm{OR}(g, h)$. If $f = g$ or $g = h$, return g.

88. The trio of functions $(f, g, h) = (R_0, R_1, R_2)$ makes an amusing example, when

$$R_a(x_1, \ldots, x_n) = [(x_n \ldots x_1)_2 \bmod 3 \neq a] = R_{(2a + x_1) \bmod 3}(x_2, \ldots, x_n).$$

Thanks to the memos, the ternary recursion finds $f \wedge g \wedge h = 0$ by examining only one case at each level; the binary computation of, say, $f \wedge g = \bar{h}$ definitely takes longer.

More dramatically, let $f = x_1 \wedge (x_2? \; F: G)$, $g = x_2 \wedge (x_1? \; G: F)$, and $h = x_1? \; \bar{x}_2 \wedge F: x_2 \wedge G$, where F and G are functions of $(x_3, \ldots, x_n)$ such that $B(F \wedge G) = \Theta(B(F)B(G))$ as in exercise 63. Then $f \wedge g$, $g \wedge h$, and $h \wedge f$ all have large BDDs, but the ternary recursion immediately discovers that $f \wedge g \wedge h = 0$.

89. (a) True; the left side is $(f_{00} \vee f_{01}) \vee (f_{10} \vee f_{11})$, the right side is $(f_{00} \vee f_{10}) \vee (f_{01} \vee f_{11})$.
(b) Similarly true. (And ⊓'s are commutative too.)
(c) Usually false; see part (d).
(d) $\forall x_1 \exists x_2 f = (f_{00} \vee f_{01}) \wedge (f_{10} \vee f_{11}) = (\exists x_2 \forall x_1 f) \vee (f_{00} \wedge f_{11}) \vee (f_{01} \wedge f_{10})$.

90. Change $\exists j_1 \ldots \exists j_m$ to ⊓$j_1 \ldots$ ⊓j_m.

91. (a) $f \downarrow 1 = f$, $f \downarrow x_j = f_1$, and $f \downarrow \bar{x}_j = f_0$, in the notation of (63).
(b) This distributive law is obvious, by the definition of $\downarrow$. (Also true for $\vee$, $\oplus$, etc.)
(c) True if and only if g is not identically zero. (Consequently the value of $f(x_1, \ldots, x_n) \downarrow g$ for $g \neq 0$ is determined solely by the values of $x_j \downarrow g$ for $1 \leq j \leq n$.)
(d) $f(x_1, 1, 0, x_4, 0, 1, x_7, \ldots, x_n)$. This is the restriction of f with respect to $x_2 = 1$, $x_3 = 0$, $x_5 = 0$, $x_6 = 1$ (see exercise 57), also called the *cofactor* of f with respect to the subcube g. (A similar result holds when g is any product of literals.)
(e) $f(x_1, \ldots, x_{n-1}, x_1 \oplus \cdots \oplus x_{n-1} \oplus 1)$. (Consider the case $f = x_j$, for $1 \leq j \leq n$.)
(f) $x_1? \; f(1, \ldots, 1): f(0, \ldots, 0)$.
(g) $f(1, x_2, \ldots, x_n) \downarrow g(x_2, \ldots, x_n)$.
(h) If $f = x_2$ and $g = x_1 \vee x_2$ we have $f \downarrow g = \bar{x}_1 \vee x_2$.
(i) $\mathrm{CONSTRAIN}(f, g) = $ "If $f \downarrow g$ has an obvious value, return it. Otherwise, if $f \downarrow g = r$ is in the memo cache, return r. Otherwise represent f and g as in (52); set $r \leftarrow \mathrm{CONSTRAIN}(f_h, g_h)$ if $g_l = 0$, $r \leftarrow \mathrm{CONSTRAIN}(f_l, g_l)$ if $g_h = 0$, otherwise $r \leftarrow \mathrm{UNIQUE}(v, \mathrm{CONSTRAIN}(f_l, g_l), \mathrm{CONSTRAIN}(f_h, g_h))$; put '$f \downarrow g = r$' into the memo cache, and return r." Here the obvious values are $f \downarrow 0 = 0 \downarrow g = 0$; $f \downarrow 1 = f$; $1 \downarrow g = g \downarrow g = [g \neq 0]$.
[The operator $f \downarrow g$ was introduced in 1989 by O. Coudert, C. Berthet, and J. C. Madre. Examples such as the functions in (h) led them to propose also the modified operator $f \Downarrow g$, "f restricted to g," which has a similar recursion except that it uses $f \Downarrow (\exists x_v g)$ instead of $(\bar{x}_v? \; f_l \Downarrow g_l: f_h \Downarrow g_h)$ when $f_l = f_h$. See *Lecture Notes in Computer Science* **407** (1989), 365–373.]

92. See answer 91(d) for the "if" part. Notice also that (i) $x_1 \downarrow g = x_1$ if and only if $g_0 \neq 0$ and $g_1 \neq 0$, where $g_c = g(c, x_2, \ldots, x_n)$; (ii) $x_n \downarrow g = x_n$ if and only if ⊓$x_n g = 0$ and $g \neq 0$.

Suppose $f^\pi \downarrow g^\pi = (f \downarrow g)^\pi$ for all f and π. If $g \neq 0$ isn't a subcube, there's an index j such that $g_0 \neq 0$ and $g_1 \neq 0$ and $\Box x_j g \neq 0$, where $g_c = g(x_1, \ldots, x_{j-1}, c, x_{j+1}, \ldots, x_n)$. By the previous paragraph, we have (i) $x_j \downarrow g = x_j$ and (ii) $x_j \downarrow g \neq x_j$, a contradiction.

93. Let $f = J(x_1, \ldots, x_n; f_1, \ldots, f_n)$ and $g = J(x_1, \ldots, x_n; g_1, \ldots, g_n)$, where

$$f_v = x_{n+1} \vee \cdots \vee x_{5n} \vee J(x_{5n+1}, \ldots, x_{6n}; [v-1], \ldots, [v-n]),$$
$$g_v = x_{n+1} \vee \cdots \vee x_{5n} \vee J(x_{5n+1}, \ldots, x_{6n}; [v=1]+[v-1], \ldots, [v=n]+[v-n]),$$

and J is the junction function of exercise 52.

If G can be 3-colored, let $\hat{f} = J(x_1, \ldots, x_n; \hat{f}_1, \ldots, \hat{f}_n)$, where

$$\hat{f}_v = x_{n+1} \vee \cdots \vee x_{5n} \vee J(x_{5n+1}, \ldots, x_{6n}; \hat{f}_{v1}, \ldots, \hat{f}_{vn}),$$

and $\hat{f}_{vw} = [v \text{ and } w \text{ have different colors}]$. Then $B(\hat{f}) < n + 3(5n) + 2$.

Conversely, suppose there's an approximating $\hat{f}$ such that $B(\hat{f}) < 16n + 2$, and let $\hat{f}_v$ be the subfunction with $x_1 = [v=1]$, $\ldots$, $x_n = [v=n]$. At most three of these subfunctions are distinct, because every distinct $\hat{f}_v$ must branch on each of x_{n+1}, $\ldots$, x_{5n}. Color the vertices so that u and v get the same color if and only if $\hat{f}_u = \hat{f}_v$; this can happen only if $u \not\!\!\frown v$, so the coloring is legitimate.
[M. Sauerhoff and I. Wegener, *IEEE Transactions* **CAD-15** (1996), 1435–1437.]

94. *Case 1:* $v \neq g_v$. Then we aren't quantifying over x_v; hence $g = g_h$, and $f \text{ E } g = \bar{x}_v? \ f_l \text{ E } g: f_h \text{ E } g$.

Case 2: $v = g_v$. Then $g = x_v \wedge g_h$ and $f \text{ E } g = (f_l \text{ E } g_h) \vee (f_h \text{ E } g_h) = r_l \vee r_h$. In the subcase $v \neq f_v$, we have $f_l = f_h = f$; hence $r_l = r_h$, and we can directly reduce $f \text{ E } g$ to $f \text{ E } g_h$ (an instance of "tail recursion").

[Rudell observes that the order of quantification in (65) corresponds to bottom-up order of the variables. That order is convenient, but not always best; sometimes it's better to remove the $\exists$s one by one in another order, based on knowledge of the functions involved.]

95. If $r_l = 1$ and $v = g_v$, we can set $r \leftarrow 1$ and forget about r_h. (This change led to a 100-fold speedup in some of the author's experiments.)

96. For $\forall$, just change E to A and OR to AND. For $\Box$, change E to D and OR to XOR; also, if $v \neq f_v$, return 0. [Routines for the yes/no quantifiers λ and N are analogous to $\Box$. Yes/no quantifiers should be used only when $m = 1$; otherwise they make little sense.]

97. Proceeding bottom-up, the amount of work on each level is at worst proportional to the number of nodes on that level.

98. The function $\text{NOTEND}(x) = \exists y \exists z (\text{ADJ}(x, y) \wedge \text{ADJ}(x, z) \wedge [y \neq z])$ identifies all vertices of degree ≥ 2. Hence $\text{ENDPT}(x) = \text{KER}(x) \wedge \neg\text{NOTEND}(x)$. And $\text{PAIR}(x, y) = \text{ENDPT}(x) \wedge \text{ENDPT}(y) \wedge \text{ADJ}(x, y)$.

[For example, when G is the contiguous-USA graph, with the states ordered as in (104), we have $B(\text{NOTEND}) = 992$, $B(\text{ENDPT}) = 264$, and $B(\text{PAIR}) = 203$. Before applying $\exists y \exists z$ the BDD size is 50511. There are exactly 49 kernels of degree 1. The nine components of size 2 are obtained by mixing the following three solutions:

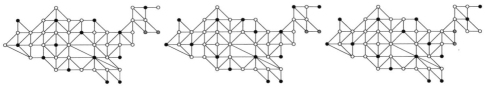

The total cost of this calculation, using the stated algorithms, is about 14 megamems, in 6.3 megabytes of memory — only about 52 memory references per kernel.]

99. Find a triangle of mutually adjacent states, and fix their colors. The BDD size also decreases substantially if we choose states of high degree in the "middle" levels. For example, by setting $a_{\text{MO}} = b_{\text{MO}} = a_{\text{TN}} = \bar{b}_{\text{TN}} = \bar{a}_{\text{AR}} = b_{\text{AR}} = 1$ we reduce the 25,579 nodes to only 4642 (and the total execution time also drops below 2 megamems).

[Bryant's original manuscript about BDDs discussed graph coloring in detail, but he decided to substitute other material when his paper was published in 1986.]

100. Replace $\text{IND}(x_{\text{ME}}, \ldots, x_{\text{CA}})$ by $\text{IND}(x_{\text{ME}}, \ldots, x_{\text{CA}}) \wedge S_{12}(x_{\text{ME}}, \ldots, x_{\text{CA}})$, to get the 12-node independent sets; this BDD has size 1964. Then use (73) as before, and the trick of answer 99, getting a COLOR function with 184,260 nodes and 12,554,677,864 solutions. (The running time is approximately 26 megamems.)

101. If a state's weight is w, assign $2w$ and w as the respective weights of its a and b variables, and use Algorithm B. (For example, variable a_{WY} gets weight $2(23 + 25) = 96$.) The solution, shown here with color codes ①②❸❹, is unique.

102. The main idea is that, when g_j changes, all results in the cache for functions with $f_v > j$ remain valid. To exploit this principle we can maintain an array of "time stamps" $G_1 \geq G_2 \geq \cdots \geq G_n \geq 0$, one for each variable. There's a master clock time $G \geq G_1$, representing the number of distinct compositions done or prepared; another variable G' records whether G has changed since COMPOSE was last invoked. Initially $G = G' = G_1 = \cdots = G_n = 0$. The subroutine $\text{NEWG}(j, g)$ is implemented as follows:

N1. [Easy case?] If $g_j = g$, exit the subroutine. Otherwise set $g_j \leftarrow g$.

N2. [Can we reset?] If $g \neq x_j$, or if $j < n$ and $G_{j+1} > 0$, go to N4.

N3. [Reset stamps.] While $j > 0$ and $g_j = x_j$, set $G_j \leftarrow 0$ and $j \leftarrow j - 1$. Then if $j = 0$, set $G \leftarrow G - G'$, $G' \leftarrow 0$, and exit.

N4. [Update G?] If $G' = 0$, set $G \leftarrow G + 1$ and $G' \leftarrow 1$.

N5. [New stamps.] While $j > 0$ and $G_j \neq G$, set $G_j \leftarrow G$ and $j \leftarrow j - 1$. Exit. ∎

(Reference counts also need to be maintained appropriately.) Before launching a top-level call of COMPOSE, set $G' \leftarrow 0$. Change the COMPOSE routine (72) to use $f[G_v]$ in references to the cache, where $v = f_v$; the test '$v > m$' becomes '$G_v = 0$'.

103. The equivalent formula $g(f_1(x_1, \ldots, x_n), \ldots, f_m(x_1, \ldots, x_n))$ can be implemented with the COMPOSE operation (72). (However, Dull was vindicated when it turned out that his formula could be evaluated more than a hundred times faster than Quick's, in spite of the fact that it uses twice as many variables! In his application, the computation of $(y_1 = f_1(x_1, \ldots, x_n)) \wedge \cdots \wedge (y_m = f_m(x_1, \ldots, x_n)) \wedge g(y_1, \ldots, y_m)$ turned out to be much easier than COMPOSE's computation of $g_j(f_1, \ldots, f_m)$ for every subfunction g_j of g; see, for example, exercise 162.)

104. The following recursive algorithm $\text{COMPARE}(f, g)$ needs at most $O(B(f)B(g))$ steps when used with a memo cache: If $f = g$, return '='. Otherwise, if $f = 0$ or $g = 1$, return '<'; if $f = 1$ or $g = 0$, return '>'. Otherwise represent f and g as in (52); compute $r_l \leftarrow \text{COMPARE}(f_l, g_l)$. If r_l is '∥', return '∥'; otherwise compute $r_h \leftarrow \text{COMPARE}(f_h, g_h)$. If r_h is '∥', return '∥'. Otherwise if r_l is '=', return r_h; if r_h is '=', return r_l; if $r_l = r_h$, return r_l. Otherwise return '∥'.

105. (a) A unate function with polarities $(y_1, \ldots, y_n)$ has $\wedge x_j f = 0$ when $y_j = 1$ and $\mathsf{N} x_j f = 0$ when $y_j = 0$, for $1 \le j \le n$. Conversely, f is unate if these conditions hold for all j. (Notice that $\wedge x_j f = \mathsf{N} x_j f = 0$ if and only if $\mathsf{d} x_j f = 0$, if and only if f doesn't depend on x_j. In such cases y_j is irrelevant; otherwise y_j is uniquely determined.)

(b) The following algorithm maintains global variables $(p_1, \ldots, p_n)$, initially zero, with the property that $p_j = +1$ if y_j must be 0 and $p_j = -1$ if y_j must be 1; p_j will remain zero if f doesn't depend on x_j. With this understanding, UNATE(f) is defined as follows: If f is constant, return *true*. Otherwise represent f as in (50). Return *false* if either UNATE(f_l) or UNATE(f_h) is *false*; otherwise set $r \leftarrow$ COMPARE(f_l, f_h) using exercise 104. If r is '$\|$', return *false*. If r is '$<$', return *false* if $p_v < 0$, otherwise set $p_v \leftarrow +1$ and return *true*. If r is '$>$', return *false* if $p_v > 0$, otherwise set $p_v \leftarrow -1$ and return *true*.

This algorithm often terminates quickly. It relies on the fact that $f(x) \le g(x)$ for all x if and only if $f(x \oplus y) \le g(x \oplus y)$ for all x, when y is fixed. If we simply want to test whether or not f is monotone, the p variables should be initialized to $+1$ instead of 0.

106. Define HORN(f, g, h) thus: If $f > g$, interchange $f \leftrightarrow g$. Then if $f = 0$ or $h = 1$, return *true*. Otherwise if $g = 1$ or $h = 0$, return *false*. Otherwise represent f, g, and h as in (59). Return *true* if HORN(f_l, g_l, h_l), HORN(f_l, g_h, h_l), HORN(f_h, g_l, h_l), and HORN(f_h, g_h, h_h) are all *true*; otherwise return *false*. [This algorithm is due to T. Horiyama and T. Ibaraki, *Artificial Intelligence* **136** (2002), 189–213, who also introduced an algorithm similar to that of answer 105(b).]

107. Let $e\$f\$g\$h$ mean that $e(x) = f(y) = g(z) = 1$ implies $h(\langle xyz \rangle) = 1$. Then f is Krom if and only if $f\$f\$f\$f$, and we can use the following recursive algorithm KROM(e, f, g, h): Rearrange $\{e, f, g\}$ so that $e \le f \le g$. Then if $e = 0$ or $h = 1$, return *true*. Otherwise if $f = 1$ or $h = 0$, return *false*. Otherwise represent e, f, g, h with the quaternary analog of (59). Return *true* if KROM(e_l, f_l, g_l, h_l), KROM(e_l, f_l, g_h, h_l), KROM(e_l, f_h, g_l, h_l), KROM(e_l, f_h, g_h, h_h), KROM(e_h, f_l, g_l, h_l), KROM(e_h, f_l, g_h, h_h), KROM(e_h, f_h, g_l, h_h), and KROM(e_h, f_h, g_h, h_h) are all *true*; otherwise return *false*.

108. Label the nodes $\{1, \ldots, s\}$ with root 1 and sinks $\{s-1, s\}$; then $(s-3)!$ permutations of the other labels give different dags for the same function. The stated inequality follows because each instruction $(\bar{v}_k? \, l_k: h_k)$ has at most $n(s-1)^2$ possibilities, for $1 \le k \le s - 2$. (In fact, it holds also for arbitrary *branching programs*, namely for binary decision diagrams in general, whether or not they are ordered and/or reduced.)

Since $1/(s-3)! < (s-1)^3/s!$ and $s! > (s/e)^s$, we have (generously) $b(n, s) < (nse)^s$. Let $s_n = 2^n/(n + \theta)$, where $\theta = \lg e = 1/\ln 2$; then $\lg b(n, s_n) < s_n \lg(ns_n e) = 2^n (1 - (\lg(1 + \theta/n))/(n + \theta)) = 2^n - \Omega(2^n/n^2)$. So the probability that a random n-variable Boolean function has $B(f) \le s_n$ is at most $1/2^{\Omega(2^n/n^2)}$. And that is really tiny.

109. $1/2^{\Omega(2^n/n^2)}$ is really tiny even when multiplied by $n!$.

110. Let $f_n = M_m(x_{n-m+1}, \ldots, x_n; 0, \ldots, 0, x_1, \ldots, x_{n-m}) \vee (\bar{x}_{n-m+1} \wedge \cdots \wedge \bar{x}_n \wedge [0 \ldots 0 x_1 \ldots x_{n-m}$ is a square]), when $2^{m-1} + m - 1 < n < 2^m + m$. Each term of this formula has $2^m + m - n$ zeros; the second term destroys all of the 2^m-bit squares. [See H.-T. Liaw and C.-S. Lin, *IEEE Transactions* **C-41** (1992), 661–664; Y. Breitbart, H. Hunt III, and D. Rosenkrantz, *Theoretical Comp. Sci.* **145** (1995), 45–69.]

111. Let $\mu n = \lambda(n - \lambda n)$, and notice that $\mu n = m$ if and only if $2^m + m \le n < 2^{m+1} + m + 1$. The sum for $0 \le k < n - \mu n$ is $2^{n - \mu n} - 1$; the other terms sum to $2^{2^{\mu n}}$.

112. Suppose $k = n - \lg n + \lg \alpha$. Then

$$\frac{(2^{2^{n-k}} - 1)^{2^k}}{2^{2^n}} = \exp\left(\frac{2^n \alpha}{n} \ln\left(1 - \frac{1}{2^{n/\alpha}} \right) \right) = \exp\left(-\frac{2^{n - n/\alpha} \alpha}{n} \left(1 + O\left(\frac{1}{2^{n/\alpha}} \right) \right) \right).$$

If $\alpha \le \frac{1}{2}$ we have $2^{n-n/\alpha}\alpha/n \le 1/(n2^{n+1})$; hence $\hat{b}_k = (2^{n/\alpha} - 2^{n/(2\alpha)})(2^{n-n/\alpha}\alpha/n) \times (1 + O(2^{-n/\alpha})) = 2^k(1 - O(2^{-n/(2\alpha)}))$. And if $\alpha \ge 2$ we have $2^{n-n/\alpha}\alpha/n \ge 2^{n/2+1}/n$; thus $\hat{b}_k = (2^{2^{n-k}} - 2^{2^{n-k-1}})(1 + O(\exp(-2^{n/2}/n)))$.

[For the variance of b_k, see I. Wegener, *IEEE Trans.* **C-43** (1994), 1262–1269.]

113. The idea looks attractive at first glance, but loses its luster when examined closely. Comparatively few nodes of a BDD base appear on the lower levels, by Theorem U; and algorithms like Algorithm S spend comparatively little of their time dealing with those levels. Furthermore, nonconstant sink nodes would make several algorithms more complicated, especially those for reordering.

114. For example, the truth table might be 01010101 00110011 00001111 00001111.

115. Let $N_k = b_0 + \cdots + b_{k-1}$ be the number of nodes (j) of the BDD for which $j \le k$. The sum of the in-degrees of those nodes is at least N_k; the sum of the out-degrees is $2N_k$; and there's an external pointer to the root. Thus at most $N_k + 1$ branches can cross from the upper k levels to lower levels. Every such branch corresponds to some subtable of order $n - k$. Therefore $q_k \le N_k + 1$.

Moreover, we must have $q_k \le b_k + \cdots + b_n$, because every subtable of order $n - k$ corresponds to a unique bead of order $\le n - k$.

For (124), change 'BDD' to 'ZDD', 'b_k' to 'z_k', 'bead' to 'zead' in these arguments.

116. (a) Let $v_k = 2^{2^k} + 2^{2^{k-1}} + \cdots + 2^{2^0}$. Then $Q(f) \le \sum_{k=1}^{n+1} \min(2^{k-1}, 2^{2^{n+1-k}}) = U_n + v_{\lambda(n-\lambda n)-1}$. Examples like (78) show that this upper bound cannot be improved.

(b) $\hat{q}_k/\hat{b}_k = 2^{2^{n-k}}/(2^{2^{n-k}} - 2^{2^{n-k-1}})$ for $0 \le k < n$; $\hat{q}_n = \hat{b}_n$.

117. $q_k = 2^k$ for $0 \le k \le m$, and $q_{m+k} = 2^m + 2 - k$ for $1 \le k \le 2^m$. Hence $Q(f) = 2^{2m-1} + 7 \cdot 2^{m-1} - 1 \approx B(f)^2/8$. (Such fs make QDDs unattractive in practice.)

118. If $n = 2^m - 1$ we have $h_n(x_1, \ldots, x_n) = M_m(z_{m-1}, \ldots, z_0; 0, x_1, \ldots, x_n)$, where $(z_{m-1} \ldots z_0)_2 = x_1 + \cdots + x_n$ is computable in $5n - 5m$ steps by exercise 7.1.2–30, and M_m takes another $2n + O(\sqrt{n})$ by exercise 7.1.2–39. Since $h_n(x_1, \ldots, x_n) = h_{n+k}(x_1, \ldots, x_n, 0, \ldots, 0)$, we have $C(h_n) \le 14n + O(\sqrt{n})$ for all n. (A little more work will bring this down to $7n + O(\sqrt{n} \log n)$; can the reader do better?)

The cost of h_4 is $6 = L(h_4)$, and $x_2 \oplus ((x_1 \oplus (x_2 \wedge x_4)) \wedge (\bar{x}_3 \oplus (\bar{x}_2 \wedge x_4)))$ is a formula of shortest length. (Also $C(h_5) = 10$ and $L(h_5) = 11$.)

119. True. For example, $S_{2,3,5}(x_1, \ldots, x_6) = h_{13}(x_1, x_2, 0, 0, 1, 1, 0, 1, 0, x_3, x_4, x_5, x_6)$.

120. We have $h_n^\pi(x_1, \ldots, x_n) = h_n(y_1, \ldots, y_n)$, where $y_j = x_{j\pi}$ for $1 \le j \le n$. And $h_n(y_1, \ldots, y_n) = y_{y_1 + \cdots + y_n} = y_{x_1 + \cdots + x_n} = x_{(x_1 + \cdots + x_n)\pi}$.

121. (a) If $y_k = \bar{x}_{n+1-k}$ we have $h_n(y_1, \ldots, y_n) = y_{\nu y} = y_{n-\nu x} = \bar{x}_{n+1-(n-\nu x)} = \bar{x}_{\nu x+1}$.

(b) If $x = (x_1, \ldots, x_n)$ and $t \in \{0, 1\}$ we have $h_{n+1}(x, t) = (t? \; x_{\nu x+1}: x_{\nu x})$.

(c) No. For example, ψ sends $0^k 11 \mapsto 0^{k-1} 101 \mapsto 0^{k-2} 10^2 1 \mapsto \cdots \mapsto 10^k 11 \mapsto 0^k 11$. (In spite of its simple definition, ψ has remarkable properties, including fixed points such as 10011010000101011000111001011 and 11101111011001011101111101111.)

(d) In fact, $\hat{h}_n(x_1 \ldots x_n) = x_1(!)$, by induction using recurrence (b).

(If $f(x_1, \ldots, x_n)$ is *any* Boolean function and τ is *any* permutation of the binary vectors $x_1 \ldots x_n$, we can write $f(x) = \hat{f}(x\tau)$, and the transformed function $\hat{f}$ may well be much easier to work with. Since $f(x) \wedge g(x) = \hat{f}(x\tau) \wedge \hat{g}(x\tau)$, the transform of the AND of two functions is the AND of their transforms, etc. The vector permutations $(x_1 \ldots x_n)\pi = x_{1\pi} \ldots x_{n\pi}$ that merely transform the indices, as considered in the text, are a simple special case of this general principle. But the principle is, in a sense, *too* general, because every function f trivially has at least one τ for which $\hat{f}$ is skinny in the sense of exercise 170; all the complexity of f can be transferred to τ. Even simple transformations like ψ have limited utility, because they don't compose well; for example, $\psi\psi$ is not a transformation of the same type. But linear transformations, which take $x \mapsto xT$ for some nonsingular binary matrix T, have proved to be useful ways to simplify BDDs. [See S. Aborhey, *IEEE Trans.* **C-37** (1988), 1461–1465; J. Bern, C. Meinel, and A. Slobodová, *ACM/IEEE Conf. Design Automation* **32** (1995), 408–413; C. Meinel, F. Somenzi, and T. Theobald, *IEEE Trans.* **CAD-19** (2000), 521–533.])

122. For example, when $n = 7$ the recurrence in answer 121(b) gives

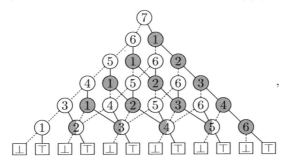

,

where shaded nodes compute the subfunction h^{DR} on the variables that haven't yet been tested. Simplifications occur at the bottom, because $h_2(x_1, x_2) = x_1$ and $h_2^{DR}(x_1, x_2) = x_2$. [See D. Sieling and I. Wegener, *Theoretical Comp. Sci.* **141** (1995), 283–310.]

123. Let $t = k - s = \bar{x}_1 + \cdots + \bar{x}_k$. There's a slate for every combination of s' 1s and t' 0s such that $s' + t' = w$, $s' \le s$, and $t' \le t$. The sum of $\binom{w}{s'} = \binom{w}{t'}$ over all such (s', t') is (97). (Notice furthermore that it equals 2^w if and only if $w \le \min(s, t)$.)

124. Let $m = n - k$. Each slate $[r_0, \ldots, r_m]$ corresponds to a function of $(x_{k+1}, \ldots, x_n)$, whose truth table is a bead except in four cases: (i) $[0, \ldots, 0] = 0$; (ii) $[1, \ldots, 1] = 1$; (iii) $[0, x_n, 1] = x_n$ (which doesn't depend on x_{n-1}); (iv) $[1, \ldots, 1, x_{k+1}, 0, \ldots, 0]$, where there are p 1s so that $x_{k+1} = r_p$, is $S_{<p}(x_{k+2}, \ldots, x_n)$.

The following polynomial-time algorithm computes $q_k = q$ and $b_k = q - q'$ by counting all slates. A subtle aspect arises when the entries of $[r_0, \ldots, r_m]$ are all 0 or 1, because such slates can occur for different values of s; we don't want to count them twice. The solution is to maintain four sets

$$C_{ab} = \{r_1 + \cdots + r_{m-1} \mid r_0 = a \text{ and } r_m = b \text{ in some slate}\}.$$

The value of 0π should be artificially set to $n + 1$, not 0. Assume that $0 \le k < n$.

H1. [Initialize.] Set $m \leftarrow n - k$, $q \leftarrow q' \leftarrow s \leftarrow 0$, $C_{00} \leftarrow C_{01} \leftarrow C_{10} \leftarrow C_{11} \leftarrow \emptyset$.

H2. [Find v and w.] Set $v = \sum_{j=1}^{m-1}[(s+j)\pi \le k]$ and $w \leftarrow v + [s\pi \le k] + [(s+m)\pi \le k]$. If $v = m - 1$, go to step H5.

H3. [Check for nonbeads.] Set $p \leftarrow -1$. If $v \ne m - 2$, go to H4. Otherwise, if $m = 2$ and $(s+1)\pi = n$, set $p \leftarrow [(s+2)\pi \le k]$. Otherwise, if $w = m$ and $(s+j)\pi = k + 1$ for some $j \in [1 .. m-1]$, set $p \leftarrow j$.

H4. [Add binomials.] For all s' and t' such that $s' + t' = w$, $0 \le s' \le s$, and $0 \le t' \le k - s$, set $q \leftarrow q + \binom{w}{s'}$ and $q' \leftarrow q' + [s' = p]$. Then go to H6.

H5. [Remember 0–1 slates.] Do the following for all s' and t' as in step H4: If $(s+m)\pi \le k$, set $C_{00} \leftarrow C_{00} \cup \{s'\}$ and $C_{01} \leftarrow C_{01} \cup \{s'-1\}$; otherwise set

$C_{01} \leftarrow C_{01} \cup \{s'\}$. If $s\pi \leq k$ and $(s+m)\pi \leq k$, set $C_{10} \leftarrow C_{10} \cup \{s'-1\}$ and $C_{11} \leftarrow C_{11} \cup \{s'-2\}$. If $s\pi \leq k$ and $(s+m)\pi > k$, set $C_{11} \leftarrow C_{11} \cup \{s'-1\}$.

H6. [Loop on s.] If $s < k$, set $s \leftarrow s+1$ and return to H2.

H7. [Finish.] For $ab = 00$, 01, 10, and 11, set $q \leftarrow q + \binom{m-1}{r}$ for all $r \in C_{ab}$. Also set $q' \leftarrow q' + [0 \in C_{00}] + [m-1 \in C_{11}]$. ∎

125. Let $S(n,m) = \binom{n}{0} + \cdots + \binom{n}{m}$. There are $S(k+1-s,s)-1$ nonconstant slates when $0 < s \leq k$ and $s \geq 2k-n+2$. The only other nonconstant slates, one each, arise when $s = 0$ and $k < (n-1)/2$. The constant slates are trickier to count, but there usually are $S(n+1-k, 2k+1-n)$ of them, appearing when $s = 2k-n$ or $s = 2k+1-n$. Taking account of nitpicky boundary conditions and nonbeads, we find

$$b_k = S(n-k, 2k-n) + \sum_{s=0}^{n-k} S(n-k-s,\, 2k+1-n+s)$$
$$- \min(k, n-k) - [n=2k] - [3k \geq 2n-1] - 1$$

for $0 \leq k < n$. Although $S(n,m)$ has no simple form, we can express $\sum_{k=0}^{n-1} b_k$ as $B_{n/2} + \sum_{0 \leq m \leq n-2k \leq n}(n+3-m-2k)\binom{k}{m} +$ (small change) when n is even, and the same expression works when n is odd if we replace $B_{n/2}$ by $A_{(n+1)/2}$. The double sum can be reduced by summing first on k, since $(k+1)\binom{k}{m} = (m+1)\binom{k+1}{m+1}$:

$$\sum_{m=0}^{n}\left((n+5-m)\binom{\lfloor(n-m+2)/2\rfloor}{m+1} - (2m+2)\binom{\lfloor(n-m+4)/2\rfloor}{m+2}\right).$$

And the remaining sum can be tackled by breaking it into four parts, depending on whether m and/or n is odd. Generating functions are helpful: Let $A(z) = \sum_{k \leq n}\binom{n-k}{2k}z^n$ and $B(z) = \sum_{k \leq n}\binom{n-k}{2k+1}z^n$. Then $A(z) = 1 + \sum_{k<n}\binom{n-k-1}{2k}z^n + \sum_{k<n}\binom{n-k-1}{2k-1}z^n = 1 + \sum_{k \leq n}\binom{n-k}{2k}z^{n+1} + \sum_{k \leq n}\binom{n-k}{2k+1}z^{n+2} = 1 + zA(z) + z^2 B(z)$. A similar derivation proves that $B(z) = zB(z) + zA(z)$. Consequently

$$A(z) = \frac{1-z}{1-2z+z^2-z^3} = \frac{1-z^2}{1-z-z^2-z^4}, \quad B(z) = \frac{z}{1-2z+z^2-z^3} = \frac{z+z^2}{1-z-z^2-z^4}.$$

Thus $A_n = 2A_{n-1} - A_{n-2} + A_{n-3} = A_{n-1} + A_{n-2} + A_{n-4}$ for $n \geq 4$, and B_n satisfies the same recurrences. In fact, we have $A_n = (3P_{2n+1} + 7P_{2n} - 2P_{2n-1})/23$ and $B_n = (3P_{2n+2} + 7P_{2n+1} - 2P_{2n})/23$, using the Perrin numbers of exercise 15.

Furthermore, setting $A^*(z) = \sum_{k \leq n} k\binom{n-k}{2k}z^n$ and $B^*(z) = \sum_{k \leq n} k\binom{n-k}{2k+1}z^n$, we find $A^*(z) = z^2 A(z)B(z)$ and $B^*(z) = z^2 B(z)^2$. Putting it all together now yields the remarkable exact formula

$$B(h_n) = \frac{56P_{n+2} + 77P_{n+1} + 47P_n}{23} - \left\lfloor\frac{n^2}{4}\right\rfloor - \left\lfloor\frac{7n+1}{3}\right\rfloor + (n \bmod 2) - 10.$$

Historical notes: The sequence $\langle A_n \rangle$ was apparently first studied by R. Austin and R. K. Guy, *Fibonacci Quarterly* **16** (1978), 84–86; it counts binary $x_1 \ldots x_{n-1}$ with each 1 next to another. The plastic constant χ was shown by C. L. Siegel to be the smallest "Pisot number," namely the smallest algebraic integer > 1 whose conjugates all lie inside the unit circle; see *Duke Math. J.* **11** (1944), 597–602.

126. When $n \geq 6$, we have $b_k = F_{\lfloor(k+7)/2\rfloor} + F_{\lceil(k+7)/2\rceil} - 4$ for $1 \leq k < 2n/3$, and $b_k = 2^{n-k+2} - 6 - [k = n-2]$ for $4n/5 \leq k < n$. But the main contributions to $B(h_n^\pi)$ come from the $2n/15$ profile elements between those two regions, and the methods of answer 125 can be extended to deal with them. The interesting sequences

$$A_n = \sum_{k=0}^{\lfloor n/2 \rfloor} \binom{n-2k}{3k}, \qquad B_n = \sum_{k=0}^{\lfloor n/2 \rfloor} \binom{n-2k}{3k+1}, \qquad C_n = \sum_{k=0}^{\lfloor n/2 \rfloor} \binom{n-2k}{3k+2}$$

have respective generating functions $(1-z)^2/p(z)$, $(1-z)z/p(z)$, $z^2/p(z)$, where $p(z) = (1-z)^3 - z^5$. These sequences arise in this problem because $\sum_{k=0}^{n} \binom{\lfloor n-2k/3 \rfloor}{k} = A_n + B_{n-1} + C_{n-2}$. They grow as α^n, where $\alpha \approx 1.7016$ is the real root of $(\alpha-1)^3\alpha^2 = 1$.

The BDD size can't be expressed in closed form, but there is a closed form in terms of $A_{\lfloor n/3 \rfloor}$ through $A_{\lfloor n/3 \rfloor + 4}$ that is accurate to $O(2^{n/4}/\sqrt{n})$. Thus $B(h_n^\pi) = \Theta(\alpha^{n/3})$.

127. (The permutation $\pi = (3, 5, 7, \ldots, 2n'-1, n, n-1, n-2, \ldots, 2n', 2n'-2, \ldots, 4, 2, 1)$, $n' = \lfloor 2n/5 \rfloor$, turns out to be optimum for h_n when $12 < n \le 24$; but it gives $B(h_{100}^\pi) = 1{,}366{,}282{,}025$. Sifting does much better, as shown in answer 152; but still better permutations almost surely exist.)

128. Consider, for example, $M_3(x_4, x_2, x_7; x_6, x_1, x_8, x_3, x_9, x_{11}, x_5, x_{10})$. The first m variables $\{x_4, x_2, x_7\}$ are called "address bits"; the other 2^m are called "targets." The subfunctions corresponding to $x_1 = c_1, \ldots, x_k = c_k$ can be described by slates of options analogous to (96). For example, when $k = 2$ there are three slates $[x_6, 0, x_9, x_{11}]$, $[x_6, 1, x_9, x_{11}]$, $[x_8, x_3, x_5, x_{10}]$, where the result is obtained by using $(x_4 x_7)_2$ to select the appropriate component. Only the third of these depends on x_3; hence $q_2 = 3$ and $b_2 = 1$. When $k = 6$ the slates are $[0, 0]$, $[0, 1]$, $[1, 0]$, $[1, 1]$, $[x_8, 0]$, $[x_8, 1]$, $[x_9, x_{11}]$, $[0, x_{10}]$, and $[1, x_{10}]$, with components selected by x_7; hence $q_6 = 9$ and $b_6 = 7$.

In general, if the variables $\{x_1, \ldots, x_k\}$ include a address bits and t targets, the slates will have $A = 2^{m-a}$ entries. Divide the set of all 2^m targets into 2^a subsets, depending on the known address bits, and suppose s_j of those subsets contain j known targets. (Thus $s_0 + s_1 + \cdots + s_A = 2^a$ and $s_1 + 2s_2 + \cdots + As_A = t$. We have $(s_0, \ldots, s_4) = (1, 1, 0, 0, 0)$ when $k = 2$ and $a = t = 1$ in the example above; and $(s_0, s_1, s_2) = (1, 2, 1)$ when $k = 6$, $a = 2$, $t = 4$.) Then the total number of slates, q_k, is $2^0 s_0 + 2^1 s_1 + \cdots + 2^{A-1} s_{A-1} + 2^A [s_A > 0]$. If x_{k+1} is an address bit, the number b_k of slates that depend on x_{k+1} is $q_k - 2^{A/2}[s_A > 0]$. Otherwise $b_k = 2^c$, where c is the number of constants that appear in the slates containing target x_{k+1}.

129. (Solution by M. Sauerhoff; see I. Wegener, *Branching Programs* (2000), Theorem 6.2.13.) Since $P_m(x_1, \ldots, x_{m^2}) = Q_m(x_1, \ldots, x_{m^2}) \wedge S_m(x_1, \ldots, x_{m^2})$ and $B(S_m) = m^3 + 2$, we have $B(P_m^\pi) \le (m^3 + 2)B(Q_m^\pi)$. Apply Theorem K.

(A stronger lower bound should be possible, because Q_m seems to have *larger* BDDs than P_m. For example, when $m = 5$ the permutation $(1\pi, \ldots, 25\pi) = (3, 1, 5, 7, 9, 2, 4, 6, 8, 10, 11, 12, 13, 14, 15, 16, 20, 23, 17, 21, 19, 18, 22, 24, 25)$ is optimum for Q_5; but $B(Q_5^\pi) = 535$, while $B(P_5^\pi) = 229$.)

130. (a) Each path that starts at the root of the BDD and takes s HI branches and t LO branches defines a subfunction that corresponds to graphs in which s adjacencies are forced and t are forbidden. We shall show that these $\binom{s+t}{s}$ subfunctions are distinct.

If subfunctions g and h correspond to different paths, we can find k vertices W with the following properties: (i) W contains vertices w and w' with $w - w'$ forced in g and forbidden in h. (ii) No adjacencies between vertices of W are forced in h or forbidden in g. (iii) If $u \in W$ and $v \notin W$ and $u - v$ is forced in h, then $u = w$ or $u = w'$. (These conditions make at most $2s + t = m - k$ vertices ineligible to be in W.)

We can set the remaining variables so that $u - v$ if and only if $\{u, v\} \subseteq W$, whenever adjacency is neither forced nor forbidden. This assignment makes $g = 1$, $h = 0$.

(b) Consider the subfunction of $C_{m,\lceil m/2\rceil}$ in which vertices $\{1,\dots,k\}$ are required to be isolated, but u — v whenever $k < u \le \lceil m/2\rceil < v \le m$. Then a k-clique on the $\lfloor m/2\rfloor$ vertices $\{\lceil m/2\rceil+1,\dots,m\}$ is equivalent to an $\lceil m/2\rceil$-clique on $\{1,\dots,m\}$. In other words, this subfunction of $C_{m,\lceil m/2\rceil}$ is $C_{\lfloor m/2\rfloor,k}$.

Now chose $k \approx \sqrt{m/3}$ and apply (a). [I. Wegener, *JACM* **35** (1988), 461–471.]

131. (a) The profile can be shown to be $(1, 1, 2, 4, \dots, 2^{q-1}, (p-2)\times(2^q-1, q\times2^{q-1}), 2^q-1, 2^{q-1}, \dots, 4, 2, 1, 2)$, where $r \times b$ denotes the r-fold repetition of b. Hence the total size is $(pq + 2p - 2q + 2)2^{q-1} - p + 2$.

(b) With the ordering $x_1, x_2, \dots, x_p, y_{11}, y_{21}, \dots, y_{p1}, \dots, y_{1q}, y_{2q}, \dots, y_{pq}$, the profile comes to $(1, 2, 4, \dots, 2^{p-1}, (q-1)p \times (2^{p-1}), 2^{p-1}, \dots, 4, 2, 1, 2)$, making the total size $(pq - p + 4)2^{p-1}$.

(c) Suppose exactly $m = \lfloor\min(p,q)/2\rfloor$ x's occur among the first k variables in some ordering; we may assume that they are $\{x_1,\dots,x_m\}$. Consider the 2^m paths in the QDD for C such that $x_j = \bar{x}_{m+j}$ for $1 \le j \le p - m$ and $y_{ij} = [i{=}j$ or $i{=}j{+}m$ or $j{>}m]$. These paths must pass through distinct nodes on level k. Hence $q_k \ge 2^m$; use (85). [See M. Nikolskaia and L. Nikolskaia, *Theor. Comp. Sci.* **255** (2001), 615–625.]

Optimum orderings for $(p,q) = (4,4)$, $(4,5)$, and $(5,4)$, via exercise 138, are:

$$x_1y_{11}x_2y_{21}x_3y_{31}y_{41}y_{12}y_{22}y_{32}y_{42}y_{13}y_{23}y_{33}y_{43}y_{14}y_{24}y_{34}y_{44}x_4 \text{ (size 108)};$$

$$x_1y_{11}x_2y_{21}x_3y_{31}y_{41}y_{12}y_{22}y_{32}y_{42}y_{13}y_{23}y_{33}y_{43}y_{14}y_{24}y_{34}y_{44}y_{15}y_{25}y_{35}y_{45}x_4 \text{ (size 140)};$$

$$x_1y_{11}x_2y_{21}y_{12}y_{22}y_{13}y_{23}y_{14}y_{24}x_3y_{31}y_{32}y_{33}y_{34}x_4y_{41}y_{42}y_{51}y_{52}y_{43}y_{53}y_{44}y_{54}x_5 \text{ (size 167)}.$$

132. There are 616,126 essentially different classes of 5-variable functions, by Table 7.1.1–5. The maximum $B_{\min}(f)$, 17, is attained by 38 of those classes. Three classes have the property that $B(f^\pi) = 17$ for *all* permutations π; one such example, $((x_2 \oplus x_4 \oplus (x_1 \wedge (x_3 \vee \bar{x}_4))) \wedge ((x_2 \oplus x_5) \vee (x_3 \oplus x_4))) \oplus (x_5 \wedge (x_3 \oplus (x_1 \vee \bar{x}_2)))$, has the interesting symmetries $f(x_1, x_2, x_3, x_4, x_5) = f(\bar{x}_2, \bar{x}_3, \bar{x}_4, \bar{x}_1, \bar{x}_5) = f(x_2, \bar{x}_5, x_1, x_3, \bar{x}_4)$.

Incidentally, the maximum difference $B_{\max}(f) - B_{\min}(f) = 10$ occurs only in the "junction function" class $x_1? \; x_2: \; x_3? \; x_4: \; x_5$, when $B_{\min} = 7$ and $B_{\max} = 17$.

(When $n = 4$ there are 222 classes; and $B_{\min}(f) = 10$ in 25 of them, including S_2 and $S_{2,4}$. The class exemplified by truth table `16ad` is uniquely hardest, in the sense that $B_{\min}(f) = 10$ and most of the 24 permutations give $B(f^\pi) = 11$.)

133. Represent each subset $X \subseteq \{1,\dots,n\}$ by the n-bit integer $i(X) = \sum_{x\in X} 2^{x-1}$, and let $b_{i(X),x}$ be the weight of the edge between X and $X \cup x$. Set $c_0 \leftarrow 0$, and for $1 \le i < 2^n$ set $c_i \leftarrow \min\{c_{i\oplus j} + b_{i\oplus j,x} \mid j = 2^{x-1}$ and $i \;\&\; j \ne 0\}$. Then $B_{\min}(f) = c_{2^n-1} + 2$, and an optimum ordering can be found by remembering which $x = x(i)$ minimizes each c_i. For $B_{\max}$, replace 'min' by 'max' in this recipe.

134.

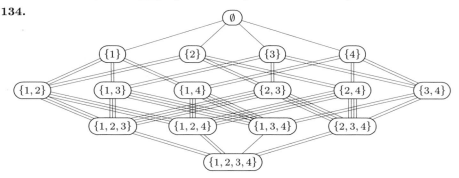

The maximum profile, $(1, 2, 4, 2, 2)$, occurs on paths such as $\emptyset \to \{2\} \to \{2,3\} \to \{2,3,4\} \to \{1,2,3,4\}$. The minimum profile, $(1, 2, 2, 1, 2)$, occurs only on the paths $\emptyset \to (\{3\} \text{ or } \{4\}) \to \{3,4\} \to \{1,3,4\} \to \{1,2,3,4\}$. (Five of the 24 possible paths have the profile $(1, 2, 3, 2, 2)$ and are unimprovable by sifting on any variable.)

135. Let $\theta_0 = 1$, $\theta_1 = x_1$, $\theta_2 = x_1 \wedge x_2$, and $\theta_n = x_n?\,\theta_{n-1}\!:\theta_{n-3}$ for $n \geq 3$. One can prove that, when $n \geq 4$, $B(\theta_n^\pi) = n+2$ if and only if $(n\pi, \ldots, 1\pi) = (1, \ldots, n)$. The key fact is that if $k < n$ and $n \geq 5$, the subfunctions obtained by setting $x_k \leftarrow 0$ or $x_k \leftarrow 1$ are distinct, and they both depend on the variables $\{x_1, \ldots, x_{k-1}, x_{k+1}, \ldots, x_n\}$, except that the subfunction for $x_{n-1} \leftarrow 0$ does not depend on x_{n-2}. Thus the weights $\{x_k\} \to \{x_k, x_l\}$ in the master profile chart are 2 except when $k = n$ or $(k, l) = (n-1, n-2)$. Below $\{x_{n-1}, x_{n-2}\}$ there are three subfunctions, namely $x_n?\,\theta_{n-4}\!:\theta_{n-3}$, $x_n?\,\theta_{n-5}\!:\theta_{n-3}$, and θ_{n-3}; all of them depend on $\{x_1, \ldots, x_{n-3}\}$, and two of them on x_n.

136. Let $n = 2n' - 1$ and $m = 2m' - 1$. The inputs form an $m \times n$ matrix, and we're computing the median of m row-medians. Let V_i be the variables in row i. If X is a subset of the mn variables, let $X_i = X \cap V_i$ and $r_i = |X_i|$. Subfunctions of type $(s_1, \ldots, s_m)$ arise when exactly s_i elements of X_i are set to 1; these subfunctions are

$$\langle S_1 S_2 \ldots S_m \rangle, \qquad \text{where } S_i = S_{\geq n' - s_i}(V_i \setminus X_i) \text{ and } 0 \leq s_i \leq r_i \text{ for } 1 \leq i \leq m.$$

When $x \notin X$, we want to count how many of these subfunctions depend on x. By symmetry we may assume that $x = x_{mn}$. Notice that the symmetric threshold function $S_{\geq t}(x_1, \ldots, x_n)$ equals 0 if $t > n$, or 1 if $t \leq 0$; it depends on all n variables if $1 \leq t \leq n$. In particular, S_m depends on x for exactly $r_m \$ n = \min(r_m + 1, n - r_m)$ choices of s_m.

Let $a_j = \sum_{i=1}^{m-1} [r_i = j]$ for $0 \leq j \leq n$. Then a_n of the functions $\{S_1, \ldots, S_{m-1}\}$ are constant, and $a_{n-1} + \cdots + a_{n'}$ of them might or might not be constant. Choosing c_i to be nonconstant gives us $(r_m \$ n)((a_n + a_{n-1} + \cdots + a_{n'} - c_{n-1} - \cdots - c_{n'})\$ m)$ times

$$\binom{a_{n-1}}{c_{n-1}} \cdots \binom{a_{n'}}{c_{n'}} 1^{a_0} 2^{a_1} \cdots (n')^{a_{n'-1}} (n'-1)^{c_{n'}} (n'-2)^{c_{n'+1}} \cdots 1^{c_{n-1}}$$

distinct subfunctions that depend on x. Summing over $\{c_{n-1}, \ldots, c_{n'}\}$ gives the answer.

When variables have the natural row-by-row order, these formulas apply with $r_m = k \bmod n$, $a_n = \lfloor k/n \rfloor$, $a_0 = m - 1 - a_n$. The profile element b_k for $0 \leq k < mn$ is therefore $(\lfloor k/n \rfloor \$ m)((k \bmod n)\$ n)$, and we have $\sum_{k=0}^{mn} b_k = (m'n')^2 + 2$. This ordering is optimum, although no easy proof is apparent; for example, some orderings can decrease b_{n+2} or b_{2n-2} from 4 to 3 while increasing b_k for other k.

Every path from top to bottom of the master chart can be represented as $\alpha_0 \to \alpha_1 \to \cdots \to \alpha_{mn}$, where each α_j is a string $r_{j1} \ldots r_{jm}$ with $0 \leq r_{j1} \leq \cdots \leq r_{jm} \leq n$, $r_{j1} + \cdots + r_{jm} = j$, one coordinate increasing at each step. For example, one path when $m = 5$ and $n = 3$ is $00000 \to 00001 \to 00011 \to 00111 \to 00112 \to 00122 \to 00123 \to 01123 \to 11123 \to 11223 \to 12223 \to 12233 \to 12333 \to 22333 \to 23333 \to 33333$. We can convert this path to the "natural" path by a series of steps that don't increase the total edge weight, as follows: In the initial segment up to the first time $r_{jm} = n$, do all transitions on the rightmost coordinate first. (Thus the first steps of the example path would become $00000 \to 00001 \to 00002 \to 00003 \to 00013 \to 00113 \to 00123$.) Then in the final segment after the last time $r_{j1} = 0$, do all transitions on the leftmost coordinate last. (The final steps would thereby become $01123 \to 01223 \to 02223 \to 02233 \to 02333 \to 03333 \to 13333 \to 23333 \to 33333$.) Then, after the first n steps, normalize the second-last coordinates in a similar fashion ($00003 \to 00013 \to 00023 \to 00033 \to 00133 \to 01133 \to 01233 \to 02233$); and before the last n steps, normalize the second coordinates ($00133 \to 00233 \to 00333 \to 01333 \to 02333 \to 03333$). Et cetera.

[This back-and-forth proof technique was inspired by the paper of Bollig and Wegener cited below. Can every nonoptimal ordering be improved by merely sifting?]

137. If we add a clique of c new vertices and $\binom{c}{2}$ new edges, the cost of the optimum arrangement increases by $\binom{c+1}{3}$. So we may assume that the given graph has m edges and n vertices $\{1, \ldots, n\}$, where m and n are odd and sufficiently large. The corresponding function f, which depends on $mn + m + 1$ variables x_{ij} and s_k for $1 \le i \le m$, $1 \le j \le n$, and $0 \le k \le m$, is $J(s_0, s_1, \ldots, s_m; h, g_1, \ldots, g_m)$, where $g_i = (x_{iu_i} \oplus x_{iv_i}) \wedge \bigwedge \{x_{iw} \mid w \notin \{u_i, v_i\}\}$ when the ith edge is $u_i \,\text{---}\, v_i$, and where $h = \langle\langle x_{11} \ldots x_{m1}\rangle \ldots \langle x_{1n} \ldots x_{mn}\rangle\rangle$ is the transpose of the function in exercise 136.

One can show that $B_{\min}(f) = \min_\pi \sum_{u-v} |u\pi - v\pi| + (\frac{m+1}{2})^2 (\frac{n+1}{2})^2 + mn + m + 2$; the optimum ordering uses $(\frac{m+1}{2})^2 (\frac{n+1}{2})^2$ nodes for h, $n + |u_i\pi - v_i\pi|$ nodes for g_i, one node for each s_k, and two sink nodes, minus one node that is shared between h and some g_i. [See B. Bollig and I. Wegener, *IEEE Trans.* **C-45** (1996), 993–1002.]

138. (a) Let $X_k = \{x_1, \ldots, x_k\}$. The QDD nodes at depth k represent the subfunctions that can arise when constants replace the variables of X_k. We can add an n-bit field DEP to each node, to specify exactly which variables of $X_n \setminus X_k$ it depends on. For example, the QDD for f in (92) has the following subfunctions and DEPs:

> depth 0: 0011001001110010 [1111];
> depth 1: 00110010 [0111], 01110010 [0111];
> depth 2: 0010 [0011], 0011 [0010], 0111 [0011];
> depth 3: 00 [0000], 01 [0001], 10 [0001], 11 [0000].

An examination of all DEP fields at depth k tells us the master profile weights between X_k and $X_k \cup x_l$, for $0 \le k < l \le n$.

(b) Represent the nodes at depth k as triples $N_{kp} = (l_{kp}, h_{kp}, d_{kp})$ for $0 \le p < q_k$, where (l_{kp}, h_{kp}) are the (LO, HI) pointers and d_{kp} records the DEP bits. If $k < n$, these nodes branch on x_{k+1}, so we have $0 \le l_{kp}, h_{kp} < q_{k+1}$; but if $k = n$, we have $l_{n0} = h_{n0} = 0$ and $l_{n1} = h_{n1} = 1$ to represent $\boxed{\bot}$ and $\boxed{\top}$. We define

$$d_{kp} = \sum \{2^{t-k-1} \mid N_{kp} \text{ depends on } x_t\};$$

hence $0 \le d_{kp} < 2^{n-k}$. For example, the QDD (82) is equivalent to $N_{00} = (0, 1, 7)$; $N_{10} = (0, 1, 3)$, $N_{11} = (1, 2, 3)$; $N_{20} = (0, 0, 0)$, $N_{21} = (0, 1, 1)$, $N_{22} = (1, 1, 0)$; $N_{30} = (0, 0, 0)$, $N_{31} = (1, 1, 0)$.

To jump up from depth b to depth a, we essentially make two copies of the nodes at depths $b - 1$, $b - 2$, $\ldots$, a, one for the case $x_{b+1} = 0$ and one for the case $x_{b+1} = 1$. Those copies are moved down to depths b, $b - 1$, $\ldots$, $a + 1$, and reduced to eliminate duplicates. Then every original node at depth a is replaced by a node that branches on x_{b+1}; its LO and HI fields point respectively to the 0-copy and the 1-copy of the original.

This process involves some simple (but cool) list processing to update DEPs while bucket sorting: Nodes are unpacked into a work area consisting of auxiliary arrays r, s, t, u, and v, initially zero. Instead of using l_{kp} and h_{kp} for LO and HI, we store HI in cell u_p of the work area, and we let v_p link to the previous node (if any) with the same LO field; furthermore we make s_l point to the last node (if any) for which LO $= l$. The algorithm below uses UNPACK(p, l, h) as an abbreviation for "$u_p \leftarrow h$, $v_p \leftarrow s_l$, $s_l \leftarrow p+1$."

When nodes of depth k have been unpacked in this way to arrays s, u, and v, the following subroutine ELIM(k) packs them back into the main QDD structure with duplicates eliminated. It also sets r_p to the new address of node p.

E1. [Loop on l.] Set $q \leftarrow 0$ and $t_h \leftarrow 0$ for $0 \leq h < q_{k+1}$. Do step E2 for $0 \leq l < q_{k+1}$. Then set $q_k \leftarrow q$ and terminate.

E2. [Loop on p.] Set $p \leftarrow s_l$ and $s_l \leftarrow 0$. While $p > 0$, do step E3 and set $p \leftarrow v_{p-1}$. Then resume step E1.

E3. [Pack node $p-1$.] Set $h \leftarrow u_{p-1}$. (The unpacked node has $(\text{LO}, \text{HI}) = (l, h)$.) If $t_h \neq 0$ and $l_{k(t_h-1)} = l$, set $r_{p-1} \leftarrow t_h - 1$. Otherwise set $l_{kq} \leftarrow l$, $h_{kq} \leftarrow h$, $d_{kq} \leftarrow ((d_{(k+1)l} \,|\, d_{(k+1)h}) \ll 1) + [l \neq h]$, $r_{p-1} \leftarrow q$, $q \leftarrow q+1$, $t_h \leftarrow q$. Resume step E2. ∎

We can now use ELIM to jump up from b to a. (i) For $k = b-1$, $b-2$, $\ldots$, a, do the following steps: For $0 \leq p < q_k$, set $l \leftarrow l_{kp}$, $h \leftarrow h_{kp}$; if $k = b-1$, UNPACK$(2p, l_{bl}, h_{bl})$ and UNPACK$(2p+1, l_{bh}, h_{bh})$, otherwise UNPACK$(2p, r_{2l}, r_{2h})$ and UNPACK$(2p+1, r_{2l+1}, r_{2h+1})$ (thereby making two copies of N_{kp} in the work area). Then ELIM$(k+1)$. (ii) For $0 \leq p < q_a$, UNPACK(p, r_{2p}, r_{2p+1}). Then ELIM(a). (iii) If $a > 0$, set $l \leftarrow l_{(a-1)p}$, $h \leftarrow h_{(a-1)p}$, $l_{(a-1)p} \leftarrow r_l$, $h_{(a-1)p} \leftarrow r_h$, for $0 \leq p < q_{a-1}$.

This jump-up procedure garbles the DEP fields above depth a, because the variables have been reordered. But we'll use it only when those fields are no longer needed.

(c) By induction, the first 2^{n-2} steps account for all subsets that do not contain n; then comes a jump-up from $n-1$ to 0, and the remaining steps account for all subsets that do contain n.

(d) Start by setting $y_k \leftarrow k$ and $w_k \leftarrow 2^k - 1$ for $0 \leq k < n$. In the following algorithm, the y array represents the current variable ordering, and the bitmap $w_k = \sum \{2^{y_j} \mid 0 \leq j < k\}$ represents the set of variables on the top k levels.

We augment the subroutine ELIM(k) so that it also computes the desired edge weights of the master profile: Counters c_j are initially 0 for $0 \leq j < n-k$; after setting d_{kq} in step E3, we set $c_j \leftarrow c_j + 1$ for each j such that $2^j \subseteq d_{kq}$; finally we set $b_{w_k, y_{k+j}+1} \leftarrow c_j$ for $0 \leq j < n-k$, using the notation of answer 133. [To speed this up, we could count bytes not bits, increasing $c_{j,(d_{kq} \gg 8j) \& \#\mathtt{ff}}$ by 1 for $0 \leq j < (n-k)/8$.]

We initialize the DEP fields by doing the following for $k = n-1$, $n-2$, $\ldots$, 0: UNPACK(p, l_{kp}, h_{kp}) for $0 \leq p < q_k$; ELIM(k); if $k > 0$, set $l \leftarrow l_{(k-1)p}$, $h \leftarrow h_{(k-1)p}$, $l_{(k-1)p} \leftarrow r_l$, and $h_{(k-1)p} \leftarrow r_h$, for $0 \leq p < q_{k-1}$.

The main loop of the algorithm now does the following for $1 \leq i < 2^{n-1}$: Set $a \leftarrow \nu i - 1$ and $b \leftarrow \nu i + \rho i$. Set $(y_a, \ldots, y_b) \leftarrow (y_b, y_a, \ldots, y_{b-1})$ and $(w_{a+1}, \ldots, w_b) \leftarrow (2^{y_b} + w_a, \ldots, 2^{y_b} + w_{b-1})$. Jump up from b to a with the procedure of part (b); but use the original (non-augmented) ELIM routine for ELIM(a) in step (ii).

(e) The space required for nodes at depth k is at most $Q_k = \min(2^k, 2^{2^{n-k}})$; we also need space for $2 \max(Q_1, \ldots, Q_n)$ elements in arrays r, u, v, plus $\max(Q_1, \ldots, Q_n)$ elements in arrays s and t. So the total is dominated by $O(2^n n)$ for the outputs $b_{w,x}$.

Subroutine ELIM(k) is called $\binom{n}{k}$ times in augmented form, for $0 \leq k < n$, and $\binom{n-1}{k+1}$ times non-augmented. Its running time in either case is $O(q_k(n-k))$. Thus the total comes to $O(\sum_k \binom{n}{k} 2^k (n-k)) = O(3^n n)$, and it will be substantially less if the QDD never gets large. (For example, it's $O((1+\sqrt{2})^n n)$ for the function h_n.)

[The first exact algorithm to determine optimum variable ordering in a BDD was introduced by S. J. Friedman and K. J. Supowit, *IEEE Trans.* **C-39** (1990), 710–713. They used extended truth tables instead of QDDs, obtaining a method for $m = 1$ that required $\Theta(3^n/\sqrt{n})$ space and $\Theta(3^n n^2)$ time, improvable to $\Theta(3^n n)$.]

139. The same algorithm applies, almost unchanged: Consider all QDD nodes that branch on x_a to be at level 0, and all nodes that branch on x_{b+1} to be sinks. Thus we do 2^{b-a} jump-ups, not 2^{n-1}. (The algorithm doesn't rely on the assumptions that $q_0 = 1$ and $q_n = 2$, except in the space and time analyses of part (e).)

140. We can find shortest paths in a network without knowing the network in advance, by generating vertices and arcs "on the fly" as needed. Section 7.3 points out that the distance $d(X, Y)$ of each arc $X \to Y$ can be changed to $d'(X, Y) = d(X, Y) - l(X) + l(Y)$ for any function $l(X)$, without changing the shortest paths. If the revised distances d' are nonnegative, $l(X)$ is a lower bound on the distance from X to the goal; the trick is to find a good lower bound that focuses the search yet isn't difficult to compute.

If $|X| = l$, and if a QDD for f with X on its top l levels has q nonconstant nodes on the next level, then $l(X) = \max(q, n - l)$ is a suitable lower bound for the $B_{\min}$ problem. [See R. Drechsler, N. Drechsler, and W. Günther, *ACM/IEEE Conf. Design Automation* **35** (1998), 200–205.] However, a stronger lower bound is needed to make this approach competitive with the algorithm of exercise 138, unless f has a relatively short BDD that cannot be attained in very many ways.

141. False. Consider $g(x_1 \vee \cdots \vee x_6, \ x_7 \vee \cdots \vee x_{12}, \ (x_{13} \vee \cdots \vee x_{16}) \oplus x_{18}, \ x_{17}, \ x_{19} \vee \cdots \vee x_{22})$, where $g(y_1, \ldots, y_5) = ((((\bar{y}_1 \vee y_5) \wedge y_4) \oplus y_3) \wedge ((y_1 \wedge y_2) \oplus y_4 \oplus y_5)) \oplus y_5$. Then $B(g) = 40 = B_{\min}(g)$ can't be achieved with $\{x_{13}, \ldots, x_{16}, x_{18}\}$ consecutive. [M. Teslenko, A. Martinelli, and E. Dubrova, *IEEE Trans.* **C-54** (2005), 236–237.]

142. (a) Suppose m is odd. The subfunctions that arise after $(x_1, \ldots, x_{m+1})$ are known are $[w_{m+2}x_{m+2} + \cdots + w_n x_n > 2^{m-1}m - 2^{m-2} - t]$, where $0 \le t \le 2^m$. The subcases $x_{m+2} + \cdots + x_n = (m-1)/2$ show that at least $\binom{m-1}{(m-1)/2}$ of these subfunctions differ.

But organ-pipe order, $\langle x_1 x_2^{2^m - 1} x_3^1 x_4^{2^m - 2} x_5^2 \ldots x_{n-2}^{2^m - 2^{m-2}} \ x_{n-1}^{2^{m-2}} \ x_n^{2^{m-1}} \rangle$, is much better: Let $t_k = x_1 + (2^m - 1)x_2 + x_3 + \cdots + (2^m - 2^{k-1})x_{2k} + 2^{k-1}x_{2k+1}$, for $1 \le k < m-1$. The remaining subfunction depends on at most $2k + 2$ different values, $\lceil t_k/2^k \rceil$.

(b) Let $n = 1 + 4m^2$. The variables are x_0 and x_{ij} for $0 \le i, j < 2m$; the weights are $w_0 = 1$ and $w_{ij} = 2^i + 2^{2m+1+j}m$. Let X_l be the first l variables in some ordering, and suppose X_l includes elements in i_l rows and j_l columns of the matrix (x_{ij}). If $\max(i_l, j_l) = m$, we will prove that $q_l \ge 2^m$; hence $B(f) > 2^m$ by (85).

Let I and J be subsets of $\{1, \ldots, 2m\}$ with $|I| = |J| = m$ and $X_l \subseteq x_0 \cup \{x_{ij} \mid i \in I, j \in J\}$; let I' and J' be the complementary subsets. Choose m elements $X' \subseteq X_l \setminus x_0$, in different rows (or, if $i_l < m$, in different columns). Consider 2^m paths in the QDD defined as follows: $x_0 = 0$, and $x_{ij} = 0$ if $x_{ij} \in X_l \setminus X'$; also $x_{i'j} = x_{ij'} = \bar{x}_{i'j'} = \bar{x}_{ij}$ for $i \in I$, $j \in J$, where $i \leftrightarrow i'$ and $j \leftrightarrow j'$ are matchings between $I \leftrightarrow I'$ and $J \leftrightarrow J'$. Then there are 2^m distinct values $t = \sum_{i \in I, j \in J} w_{ij} x_{ij}$; but $\sum_{0 \le i, j < 2m} w_{ij} x_{ij} = (2^{2m} - 1)(1 + 2^{2m+1}m)$ on each path. The paths must pass through distinct nodes on level l. Otherwise, if $t \ne t'$, one of the lower subpaths would lead to $\boxed{\bot}$, the other to $\boxed{\top}$.

[These results are due to K. Hosaka, Y. Takenaga, T. Kaneda, and S. Yajima, *Theoretical Comp. Sci.* **180** (1997), 47–60, who also proved that $|Q(f) - Q(f^R)| < n$. Do self-dual threshold functions always satisfy also $|B(f) - B(f^R)| < n$?]

143. In fact, the algorithm of exercises 133 and 138 proves that organ-pipe order is best for these weights: (1, 1023, 1, 1022, 2, 1020, 4, 1016, 8, 1008, 16, 992, 32, 960, 64, 896, 128, 768, 256, 512) gives the profile (1, 2, 2, 4, 3, 6, 4, 8, 5, 10, 4, 8, 3, 6, 2, 4, 1, 2, 2, 1, 2) and $B(f) = 80$. The worst ordering, (1022, 896, 512, 64, 8, 1, 4, 32, 1008, 1020, 768, 992, 1016, 1023, 960, 256, 128, 16, 2, 1), makes $B(f) = 1913$.

(One might think that properties of binary notation are crucial to this example. But $\langle x_1 x_2 x_3^2 x_4^4 x_5^8 x_6^{16} x_7^{31} x_8^{60} x_9^{116} x_{10}^{224} x_{11}^{224} x_{12}^{448} x_{13}^{564} x_{14}^{620} x_{15}^{649} x_{16}^{664} x_{17}^{672} x_{18}^{676} x_{19}^{678} x_{20}^{679} \rangle$ is actually the same function, by exercise 7.1.1–103(!).)

144. $(5, 7, 7, 10, 6, 9, 5, 4, 2)$; the QDD-not-BDD nodes correspond to f_1, f_2, f_3, 0, 1.

145. $B_{\min} = 31$ is attained in (36). The worst ordering for $(x_3x_2x_1x_0)_2 + (y_3y_2y_1y_0)_2$ is y_0, y_1, y_2, y_3, x_2, x_1, x_0, x_3, making $B_{\max} = 107$. Incidentally, the worst ordering for the 24 inputs of 12-bit addition, $(x_{11} \ldots x_0)_2 + (y_{11} \ldots y_0)_2$, turns out to be y_0, y_1, ..., y_{11}, x_{10}, x_8, x_6, x_4, x_3, x_5, x_2, x_7, x_1, x_9, x_0, x_{11}, yielding $B_{\max} = 39111$.

[B. Bollig, N. Range, and I. Wegener, *Lecture Notes in Comp. Sci.* **4910** (2008), 174–185, have proved that $B_{\min} = 9n - 5$ for addition of two n-bit numbers whenever $n > 1$, and also that $B_{\min}(M_m) = 2n - 2m + 1$ for the 2^m-way multiplexer.]

146. (a) Obviously $b_0 \leq q_0$; and if $q_0 = b_0 + a_0$, then $b_1 \leq 2b_0 + a_0 = b_0 + q_0$. Also $q_0 - b_0 = a_0 \leq b_1 + q_2 \leq q_2^2$, the number of strings of length 2 on a q_2-letter alphabet; similarly $b_0 + b_1 + q_2 \leq (b_1 + q_2)^2$. (The same relations hold between q_k, q_{k+2}, b_k, and b_{k+1}.)

(b) Let the subfunctions at level 2 have truth tables α_j for $1 \leq j \leq q_2$, and use them to construct beads $\beta_1, \ldots, \beta_{b_1}$ at level 1. Let $(\gamma_1, \ldots, \gamma_{q_2+b_1})$ be the truth tables $(\alpha_1\alpha_1, \ldots, \alpha_{q_2}\alpha_{q_2}, \beta_1, \ldots, \beta_{b_1})$. If $b_0 \leq b_1/2$, let the functions at level 0 have truth tables $\{\beta_{2i-1}\beta_{2i} \mid 1 \leq i \leq b_0\} \cup \{\beta_j\beta_j \mid 2b_0 < j \leq b_1\} \cup \{\gamma_j\gamma_j \mid 1 \leq j \leq b_0 + q_0 - b_1\}$. Otherwise it's not difficult to define b_0 beads that include all the β's, and use them at level 0 together with the nonbeads $\{\gamma_j\gamma_j \mid 1 \leq j \leq q_0 - b_0\}$.

147. Before doing any reordering, we clear the cache and collect all garbage. The following algorithm interchanges levels $\textcircled{u} \leftrightarrow \textcircled{v}$ when $v = u+1$. It works by creating linked lists of solitary, tangled, and hidden nodes, pointed to by variables S, T, and H (initially Λ), using auxiliary LINK fields that can be borrowed temporarily from the hash-table algorithm of the unique lists as they are being rebuilt.

T1. [Build S and T.] For each $\textcircled{u}$-node p, set $q \leftarrow \text{LO}(p)$, $r \leftarrow \text{HI}(p)$, and delete p from its hash table. If $\text{V}(q) \neq v$ and $\text{V}(r) \neq v$ (p is solitary), set $\text{LINK}(p) \leftarrow S$ and $S \leftarrow p$. Otherwise (p is tangled), set $\text{REF}(q) \leftarrow \text{REF}(q) - 1$, $\text{REF}(r) \leftarrow \text{REF}(r) - 1$, $\text{LINK}(p) \leftarrow T$, and $T \leftarrow p$.

T2. [Build H and move the visible nodes.] For each $\textcircled{v}$-node p, set $q \leftarrow \text{LO}(p)$, $r \leftarrow \text{HI}(p)$, and delete p from its hash table. If $\text{REF}(p) = 0$ (p is hidden), set $\text{REF}(q) \leftarrow \text{REF}(q) - 1$, $\text{REF}(r) \leftarrow \text{REF}(r) - 1$, $\text{LINK}(p) \leftarrow H$, and $H \leftarrow p$; otherwise (p is visible) set $\text{V}(p) \leftarrow u$ and $\text{INSERT}(u, p)$.

T3. [Move the solitary nodes.] While $S \neq \Lambda$, set $p \leftarrow S$, $S \leftarrow \text{LINK}(p)$, $\text{V}(p) \leftarrow v$, and $\text{INSERT}(v, p)$.

T4. [Transmogrify the tangled nodes.] While $T \neq \Lambda$, set $p \leftarrow T$, $T \leftarrow \text{LINK}(p)$, and do the following: Set $q \leftarrow \text{LO}(p)$, $r \leftarrow \text{HI}(p)$. If $\text{V}(q) > v$, set $q_0 \leftarrow q_1 \leftarrow q$; otherwise set $q_0 \leftarrow \text{LO}(q)$ and $q_1 \leftarrow \text{HI}(q)$. If $\text{V}(r) > v$, set $r_0 \leftarrow r_1 \leftarrow r$; otherwise set $r_0 \leftarrow \text{LO}(r)$ and $r_1 \leftarrow \text{HI}(r)$. Then set $\text{LO}(p) \leftarrow \text{UNIQUE}(v, q_0, r_0)$, $\text{HI}(p) \leftarrow \text{UNIQUE}(v, q_1, r_1)$, and $\text{INSERT}(u, p)$.

T5. [Kill the hidden nodes.] While $H \neq \Lambda$, set $p \leftarrow H$, $H \leftarrow \text{LINK}(p)$, and recycle node p. (All of the remaining nodes are alive.) ∎

The subroutine $\text{INSERT}(v, p)$ simply puts node p into x_v's unique table, using the key $(\text{LO}(p), \text{HI}(p))$; this key will not already be present. The subroutine UNIQUE in step T4 is like Algorithm U, but instead of using answer 82 it treats reference counts quite differently in steps U1 and U2: If U1 finds $p = q$, it *increases* $\text{REF}(p)$ by 1; if U2 finds r, it simply sets $\text{REF}(r) \leftarrow \text{REF}(r) + 1$.

Internally, the branch variables retain their natural order $1, 2, \ldots, n$ from top to bottom. Mapping tables ρ and π represent the current permutation from the external user's point of view, with $\rho = \pi^-$; thus the user's variable x_v appears on level $v\pi - 1$, and node UNIQUE(v, p, q) on level $v - 1$ represents the user's function $(\bar{x}_{vp}?\ p\colon q)$. To maintain these mappings, set $j \leftarrow u\rho$, $k \leftarrow v\rho$, $u\rho \leftarrow k$, $v\rho \leftarrow j$, $j\pi \leftarrow v$, $k\pi \leftarrow u$.

148. False. For example, consider six sinks and nine source functions, with extended truth tables 1156, 2256, 3356, 4456, 5611, 5622, 5633, 5644, 5656. Eight of the nodes are tangled and one is visible, but none are hidden or solitary. There are 16 newbies: 15, 16, 25, 26, 35, 36, 45, 46, 51, 61, 52, 62, 53, 63, 54, 64. So the swap takes 15 nodes into 31. (We can use the nodes of $B(x_3 \oplus x_4, x_3 \oplus \bar{x}_4)$ for the sinks.)

149. The successive profiles are bounded by $(b_0, b_1, \ldots, b_n)$, $(b_0 + b_1, 2b_0, b_2, \ldots, b_n)$, $(b_0 + b_1, 2b_0 + b_2, 4b_0, b_3, \ldots, b_n)$, $\ldots$, $(2^0 b_0 + b_1, \ldots, 2^{k-2} b_0 + b_{k-1}, 2^{k-1} b_0, b_k, \ldots, b_n)$.

Similarly, we also have $B(f_1^\pi, \ldots, f_m^\pi) \le B(f_1, \ldots, f_m) + 2(b_0 + \cdots + b_{k-1})$ in addition to Theorem J$^+$, because swaps contribute at most $2b_{k-1}, 2b_{k-2}, \ldots, 2b_0$ new nodes.

150. We may assume that $m = 1$, as in exercise 52. Suppose we want to jump x_k to the position that is jth in the ordering, where $j \ne k$. First compute the restrictions of f when $x_k = 0$ and $x_k = 1$ (see exercise 57); call them g and h. Then renumber the remaining variables: If $j < k$, change $(x_j, \ldots, x_{k-1})$ to $(x_{j+1}, \ldots, x_k)$; otherwise change $(x_{k+1}, \ldots, x_j)$ to $(x_k, \ldots, x_{j-1})$. Then compute $f \leftarrow (\bar{x}_j \wedge g) \vee (x_j \wedge h)$, using the linear-time variant of Algorithm S in exercise 72.

To show that this method has the desired running time, it suffices to prove the following: *Let $g(x_1, \ldots, x_n)$ and $h(x_1, \ldots, x_n)$ be functions such that $g(x) = 1$ implies $x_j = 0$ and $h(x) = 1$ implies $x_j = 1$. Then the meld $g \diamond h$ has at most twice as many nodes as $g \vee h$.* But this is almost obvious, when truth tables are considered: For example, if $n = 3$ and $j = 2$, the truth tables for g and h have the respective forms $ab00cd00$ and $00st00uv$. The beads β of $g \vee h$ on levels $< j$ correspond uniquely to the beads $\beta' \diamond \beta''$ of $g \diamond h$ on those levels, because $\beta = \beta' \vee \beta''$ can be "factored" in only one way by putting 0s in the appropriate places. And the beads β of $g \vee h$ on levels $\ge j$ correspond to at most two beads of $g \diamond h$, namely to $\beta \diamond \boxed{\perp}$ and/or $\boxed{\perp} \diamond \beta$.

[See P. Savický and I. Wegener, *Acta Informatica* **34** (1997), 245–256, Theorem 1.]

151. Set $t_k \leftarrow 0$ for $1 \le k \le n$, and make the swapping operation $x_{j-1} \leftrightarrow x_j$ also swap $t_{j-1} \leftrightarrow t_j$. Then set $k \leftarrow 1$ and do the following until $k > n$: If $t_k = 1$ set $k \leftarrow k + 1$; otherwise set $t_k \leftarrow 1$ and sift x_k.

(This method repeatedly sifts on the topmost variable that hasn't yet been sifted. Researchers have tried fancier strategies, such as to sift the largest level first; but no such method has turned out to dominate the simple-minded approach proposed here.)

152. Applying Algorithm J as in answer 151 yields $B(h_{100}^\pi) = 1{,}382{,}685{,}050$ after 17,179 swaps, which is almost as good as the result of the "hand-tuned" permutation (95). Another sift brings the size down to 300,451,396; and further repetitions converge down to just 231,376,264 nodes, after a total of 232,951 swaps.

If the loops of steps J2 and J5 are aborted when $S > 1.05s$, the results are even better(!), although fewer swaps are made. The first sift reduces the size to 1,342,191,700, and iteration produces $B(h_{100}^\pi) = 208{,}478{,}228$ after 139,245 swaps, where π is the following permutation:

$$
\begin{array}{cccccccccccccccccccc}
3 & 4 & 6 & 8 & 10 & 12 & 14 & 16 & 18 & 20 & 22 & 24 & 27 & 28 & 30 & 32 & 35 & 67 & 37 & 39 \\
43 & 41 & 45 & 51 & 47 & 49 & 55 & 80 & 53 & 83 & 85 & 92 & 93 & 94 & 78 & 75 & 77 & 95 & 73 & 71 \\
96 & 98 & 97 & 68 & 57 & 58 & 60 & 65 & 63 & 62 & 61 & 87 & 64 & 59 & 66 & 88 & 56 & 69 & 70 & 99 \\
100 & 72 & 76 & 91 & 79 & 74 & 90 & 89 & 86 & 84 & 52 & 82 & 81 & 48 & 54 & 50 & 46 & 44 & 42 & 40 \\
38 & 36 & 34 & 33 & 31 & 29 & 26 & 25 & 23 & 21 & 19 & 17 & 15 & 13 & 11 & 9 & 7 & 5 & 2 & 1
\end{array}
$$

Incidentally, if we sift the variables h_{100} in order of profile size, so that x_{60} is sifted first, then x_{59}, x_{61}, x_{58}, x_{57}, x_{62}, x_{56}, etc. (wherever they currently happen to be), the resulting BDD turns out to have 2,196,768,534 nodes.

Simple "downhill swapping" instead of full sifting is of no use whatever for h_{100}: The $\binom{100}{2}$ swaps $x_1 \leftrightarrow x_2$, $x_3 \leftrightarrow x_1$, $x_3 \leftrightarrow x_2$, ..., $x_{100} \leftrightarrow x_1$, ..., $x_{100} \leftrightarrow x_{99}$ completely reverse the order of all variables without changing the BDD size at any step.

153. Each gate is easily synthesized using recursions like (55). About 1 megabyte of memory and 3.5 megamems of computation suffice to construct the entire BDD base of 8242 nodes. Using exercise 138 we may conclude that the ordering x_7, x_3, x_9, x_1, o_9, o_1, o_3, o_7, x_4, x_6, o_6, o_4, o_2, o_8, x_2, x_8, o_5, x_5 is optimum, and that $B_{\min}(y_1, \ldots, y_9) = 5308$.

Reordering of variables is *not* advisable for a problem such as this, since there are only 18 variables. For example, autosifting whenever the size doubles would require more than 100 megamems of work, just to reduce 8242 nodes to about 6400.

154. Yes: CA was moved between ID and OR at the last sifting step, and we can work backwards all the way to deduce that the first sift moved ME between MA and RI.

155. The author's best attempt for (a) is

```
ME NH VT MA CT RI NY DE NJ MD PA DC VA OH WV KY NC SC GA FL AL IN MI IA
IL MO TN AR MS TX LA CO WI KS SD ND NE OK WY MN ID MT NM AZ OR CA WA UT NV
```

giving $B(f_1^\pi) = 403$, $B(f_2^\pi) = 677$, $B(f_1^\pi, f_2^\pi) = 1073$; and for (b) the ordering

```
NH ME MA VT CT RI NY DE NJ MD PA VA DC OH WV KY TN NC SC GA FL AL IN MI
IL IA AR MO MS TX LA CO KS OK WI SD NE ND MN WY ID MT AZ NM UT OR CA WA NV
```

gives $B(f_1^\pi) = 352$, $B(f_2^\pi) = 702$, $B(f_1^\pi, f_2^\pi) = 1046$.

156. One might expect two "siftups" to be at least as good as a single sifting process that goes both up and down. But in fact, benchmark tests by R. Rudell show that siftup alone is definitely unsatisfactory. Occasional jump-downs are needed to compensate for variables that temporarily jump up, although their optimum final position lies below.

157. A careful study of answer 128 shows that we always improve the size when the first address bit that follows a target bit is jumped up past all targets. [But simple swaps are too weak. For example, $M_2(x_1, x_6; x_2, x_3, x_4, x_5)$ and $M_3(x_1, x_{10}, x_{11}; x_2, x_3, \ldots, x_9)$ are locally optimal under the swapping of $x_{j-1} \leftrightarrow x_j$ for any j.]

158. Consider first the case when $m = 1$ and $n = 3t - 1 \geq 5$. Then if $n\pi = k$, the number of nodes that branch on j is a_j if $j\pi < k$, b_j if $j\pi = k$, and a_{n+2-j} if $j\pi > k$, where

$$a_j = j - 3\max(j - 2t, 0), \qquad b_j = \min(j, t, n + 1 - j).$$

The cases with $\{x_1, \ldots, x_{n-1}\}$ consecutive are $k = 1$ and $B(f^\pi) = 3t^2 + 2$; $k = n$ and $B(f^\pi) = 3t^2 + 1$. But when $k = \lceil n/2 \rceil$ we have $B(f^\pi) = \lfloor 3t/2 \rfloor (\lceil 3t/2 \rceil - 1) + n - \lfloor t/2 \rfloor + 2$.

Similar calculations apply when $m > 1$: We have $B(f^\pi) > 6\binom{p/3}{2} + B(g^\pi)$ when π makes $\{x_1, \ldots, x_p\}$ consecutive, but $B(f^\pi) \approx 2\binom{p/2}{2} + \frac{p}{3}B(g^\pi)$ when π puts $\{x_{p+1}, \ldots, x_{p+m}\}$ in the middle. Since g is fixed, $pB(g^\pi) = O(n)$ as $n \to \infty$.

[If g is a function of the same kind, we obtain examples where symmetric variables within g are best split up, and so on. But no Boolean functions are known for which the optimum $B(f^\pi)$ is less than 3/4 of the best that is obtainable under the constraint that no blocks of symmetric variables are split. See D. Sieling, *Random Structures & Algorithms* **13** (1998), 49–70.]

159. The function is almost symmetric, so there are only nine possibilities. When the center element x is placed in position $(1, 2, \ldots, 9)$ from the top, the BDD size is respectively $(43, 43, 42, 39, 36, 33, 30, 28, 28)$.

160. (a) Compute $\bigwedge_{i=0}^{9}\bigwedge_{j=0}^{9}(\neg L_{ij}(X))$, a Boolean function of 64 variables — for example, by applying COMPOSE to the relatively simple L function of exercise 159, 100 times. With the author's experimental programs, about 320 megamems and 35 megabytes are needed to find this BDD, which has 251,873 nodes with the normal ordering. Then Algorithm C quickly finds the desired answer: 21,929,490,122. (The number of 11×11 solutions, 5,530,201,631,127,973,447, can be found in the same way.)

(b) The generating function is $1+64z+2016z^2+39740z^3+\cdots+80z^{45}+8z^{46}$, and Algorithm B rapidly finds the eight solutions of weight 46. Three of them are distinct under chessboard symmetry; the most symmetric solution is shown as (A0) below.

(c) The BDD for $\bigwedge_{i=1}^{8}\bigwedge_{j=1}^{8}(\neg L_{ij}(X))$ has 305,507 nodes and 21,942,036,750 solutions. So there must be 12,546,628 wild ones.

(d) Now the generating function is $40z^{14}+936z^{15}+10500z^{16}+\cdots+16z^{55}+z^{56}$; examples of weight 14 and 56 appear below as (A1) and (A2).

(e) Exactly 28 of weight 27 and 54 of weight 28, all tame; see (A3).

(f) There are respectively (26260, 5, 347, 0, 122216) solutions, found with about (228, 3, 32, 1, 283) megamems of calculation. Among the lightest and heaviest solutions to (1) are (A4) and (A5); the nicest solution to (2) is (A6); (A7) and (A9) solve (3) lightly and (5) heavily. Pattern (4), which is based on the binary representation of π, has no 8×8 predecessor; but it does, for example, have the 9×8 in (A8):

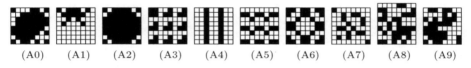

(A0)   (A1)   (A2)   (A3)   (A4)   (A5)   (A6)   (A7)   (A8)   (A9)

161. (a) With the normal row-by-row ordering $(x_{11}, x_{12}, \ldots, x_{n(n-1)}, x_{nn})$, the BDD has 380,727 nodes and characterizes 4,782,725 solutions. The computational cost is about 2 gigamems, in 100 megabytes. (Similarly, the 29,305,144,137 still Lifes of size 10×10 can be enumerated with 14,492,923 nodes, after fewer than 50 gigamems.)

(b) This solution is essentially unique; see (B1) below. There's also a unique (and obvious) solution of weight 36.

(c) Now the BDD has 128 variables, with the ordering $(x_{11}, y_{11}, \ldots, x_{nn}, y_{nn})$. We could first set up BDDs for $[L(X) = Y]$ and $[L(Y) = X]$, then intersect them; but that turns out to be a bad idea, requiring some 36 million nodes even in the 7×7 case. Much better is to apply the constraints $L_{ij}(X) = y_{ij}$ and $L_{ij}(Y) = x_{ij}$ row by row, and also to add the lexicographic constraint $X < Y$ so that still Lifes are ruled out early. The computation can then be completed with about 20 gigamems and 1.6 gigabytes; there are 978,563 nodes and 582,769 solutions.

(d) Again the solution is unique, up to rotation; see the "spark plug" (B2) $\leftrightarrow$ (B3). (And (B4) $\leftrightarrow$ (B5) is the unique 7×7 flip-flop of constant weight 26. Life is astonishing.)

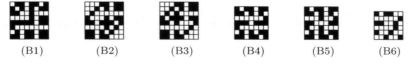

(B1)   (B2)   (B3)   (B4)   (B5)   (B6)

162. Let $T(X) = [X \text{ is tame}]$ and $E_k(X) = [X \text{ escapes after } k \text{ steps}]$. We can compute the BDD for each E_k by using the recurrence

$$E_1(X) = \neg T(X); \qquad E_{k+1}(X) = \exists Y (T(X) \wedge [L(X) = Y] \wedge E_k(Y)).$$

(Here $\exists Y$ stands for $\exists y_{11} \exists y_{12} \cdots \exists y_{66}$. As noted in answer 103, this recurrence turns out to be much more efficient than the rule $E_{k+1} = T(X) \wedge E_k(L_{11}(X), \ldots, L_{66}(X))$, although the latter looks more "elegant.") The number of solutions, $|E_k|$, is found to be $(806544 \cdot 2^{16},\ 657527179 \cdot 2^4,\ 2105885159,\ 763710262,\ 331054880,\ 201618308,$ $126169394,\ 86820176,\ 63027572,\ 41338572,\ 30298840,\ 17474640,\ 9797472,\ 5258660,$ $3058696,\ 1416132,\ 523776,\ 204192,\ 176520,\ 62456,\ 13648,\ 2776,\ 2256,\ 440,\ 104,\ 0)$ for $k = (1, 2, \ldots, 26)$; thus $\sum_{k=1}^{25} |E_k| = 67{,}166{,}017{,}379$ of the $2^{36} = 68{,}719{,}476{,}736$ possible configurations eventually escape from the 6×6 cage. (One of the 104 procrastinators in E_{25} is shown in (B6) above.)

BDD techniques are excellent for this problem when k is small; for example, $B(E_1) = 101$ and $B(E_2) = 14441$. But E_k eventually becomes a complicated "nonlocal" function: The size peaks at $B(E_6) = 28{,}696{,}866$, after which the number of solutions gets small enough to keep the size down. More than 80 million nodes are present in the formula $T(X) \wedge [L(X) = Y] \wedge E_5(Y)$ before quantification; this stretches memory limits. Indeed, the BDD for $\bigvee_{k=1}^{25} E_k(X)$ takes up more space than its 2^{33}-byte truth table. Therefore a "forward" method for this exercise would be preferable to the use of BDDs.

(Cages larger than 6×6 appear to be impossibly difficult, by *any* known method.)

163. Suppose first that $\circ$ is $\wedge$. We obtain the BDD for $f = g \wedge h$ by taking the BDD for g and replacing its $\boxed{\top}$ sink by the root of the BDD for h. To represent also $\bar{f}$, make a separate copy of the BDD for g, and use a BDD base for both h and $\bar{h}$; replace the $\boxed{\bot}$ in the copy by $\boxed{\top}$, and replace the $\boxed{\top}$ in the copy by the root of the BDD for $\bar{h}$. This decision diagram is reduced because h isn't constant.

Similarly, if $\circ$ is $\oplus$, we obtain a BDD for $f = g \oplus h$ (and possibly $\bar{f}$) from the BDD for g (and possibly $\bar{g}$) after replacing $\boxed{\bot}$ and $\boxed{\top}$ by the roots of BDDs for h and $\bar{h}$.

The other binary operations $\circ$ are essentially the same, because $B(f) = B(\bar{f})$. For example, if $f = g \supset h = \overline{g \wedge \bar{h}}$, we have $B(f) = B(\bar{f}) = B(g) + B(\bar{h}) - 2 = B(g) + B(h) - 2$.

164. Let $U_1(x_1) = V_1(x_1) = x_1$, $U_{n+1}(x_1, \ldots, x_{n+1}) = x_1 \oplus V_n(x_2, \ldots, x_{n+1})$, and $V_{n+1}(x_1, \ldots, x_{n+1}) = U_n(x_1, \ldots, x_n) \wedge x_{n+1}$. Then one can show by induction that $B(f) \le B(U_n) = 2^{\lceil (n+1)/2 \rceil} + 2^{\lfloor (n+1)/2 \rfloor} - 1$ for all read-once f, and also that we always have $B(f, \bar{f}) \le B(V_n, \bar{V}_n) = 2^{\lceil n/2 \rceil + 1} + 2^{\lfloor n/2 \rfloor + 1} - 2$. (But an optimum ordering reduces these sizes dramatically, to $B(U_n^\pi) = \lfloor \frac{3}{2}n + 2 \rfloor$ and $B(V_n^\pi, \bar{V}_n^\pi) = 2n + 2$.)

165. By induction, we prove also that $B(u_{2m}, \bar{u}_{2m}) = 2^m F_{2m+3} + 2$, $B(u_{2m+1}, \bar{u}_{2m+1}) = 2^{m+1} F_{2m+3} + 2$, $B(v_{2m}, \bar{v}_{2m}) = 2^{m+1} F_{2m+1} + 2$, $B(v_{2m+1}, \bar{v}_{2m+1}) = 2^{m+1} F_{2m+3} + 2$.

166. We may assume as in answer 163 that $\circ$ is either $\wedge$ or $\oplus$. By renumbering, we can also assume that $j\sigma = j$ for $1 \le j \le n$, hence $f^\sigma = f$. Let $(b_0, \ldots, b_n)$ be the profile of f, and $(b_0', \ldots, b_n')$ the profile of $(f, \bar{f})$; let $(c_{1\pi}, \ldots, c_{(n+1)\pi})$ and $(c_{1\pi}', \ldots, c_{(n+1)\pi}')$ be the profiles of f^π and $(f^\pi, \bar{f}^\pi)$, where $(n+1)\pi = n+1$. Then $c_{j\pi}$ is the number of subfunctions of $f^\pi = g^\pi \circ h^\pi$ that depend on $x_{j\pi}$ after setting the variables $\{x_{1\pi}, \ldots, x_{(j-1)\pi}\}$ to fixed values. Similarly, $c_{j\pi}'$ is the number of such subfunctions of f^π or $\bar{f}^\pi$. We will try to prove that $b_{j\pi-1} \le c_{j\pi}$ and $b_{j\pi-1}' \le c_{j\pi}'$ for all j.

Case 1: $\circ$ is $\wedge$. We may assume that $n\pi = n$, since $\wedge$ is commutative. *Case 1a:* $1 \le j\pi \le k$. Then $b_{j\pi-1}$ and $b_{j\pi-1}'$ count subfunctions in which only the variables $x_{i\pi}$ with $1 \le i < j$ and $1 \le i\pi \le k$ are specified. These subfunctions of $g \wedge h$ or $\bar{g} \vee \bar{h}$ have counterparts that are counted in $c_{j\pi}$ and $c_{j\pi}'$, because h^π is not constant in any subfunction when $n\pi = n$. *Case 1b:* $k < j\pi \le n$. Then $b_{j\pi-1}$ and $b_{j\pi-1}'$ count subfunctions of h or $\bar{h}$, which have counterparts counted in $c_{j\pi}$ and $c_{j\pi}'$.

Case 2: $\circ$ is $\oplus$. We may assume that $1\pi = 1$, since $\oplus$ is commutative. Then an argument analogous to Case 1 applies. [*Discrete Applied Math.* **103** (2000), 237–258.]

167. Let $f = f_{1n}$; proceed recursively to compute $c_{ij} = B_{\min}(f_{ij})$, $c'_{ij} = B_{\min}(f_{ij}, \bar{f}_{ij})$, and a permutation π_{ij} of $\{i, \ldots, j\}$ for each subfunction $f_{ij}(x_i, \ldots, x_j)$ as follows: If $i = j$, we have $f_{ij}(x_i) = x_i$; let $c_{ij} = 3$, $c'_{ij} = 4$, $\pi_{ij} = i$. Otherwise $i < j$, and we have $f_{ij}(x_i, \ldots, x_j) = f_{ik}(x_i, \ldots, x_k) \circ f_{(k+1)j}(x_{k+1}, \ldots, x_j)$ for some k and some operator $\circ$. If $\circ$ is like $\wedge$, let $c_{ij} = c_{ik} + c_{(k+1)j} - 2$, and either $(c'_{ij} = 2c_{ik} + c'_{(k+1)j} - 4$, $\pi_{ij} = \pi_{ik}\pi_{(k+1)j})$ or $(c'_{ij} = 2c_{(k+1)j} + c'_{ik} - 4$, $\pi_{ij} = \pi_{(k+1)j}\pi_{ik})$, whichever minimizes c'_{ij}. If $\circ$ is like $\oplus$, let $c'_{ij} = c'_{ik} + c'_{(k+1)j} - 2$, and either $(c_{ij} = c_{ik} + c'_{(k+1)j} - 2$, $\pi_{ij} = \pi_{ik}\pi_{(k+1)j})$ or $(c_{ij} = c_{(k+1)j} + c'_{ik} - 2$, $\pi_{ij} = \pi_{(k+1)j}\pi_{ik})$, whichever minimizes c_{ij}.

(The permutations π_{ij} represented as strings in this description would be represented as linked lists inside a computer. We could also construct an optimum BDD for f recursively in $O(B_{\min}(f))$ steps, using answer 163.)

168. (a) This statement transforms and simplifies the recurrences (112) and (113).

(b) True by induction; also $x \geq n$.

(c) Easily verified. Notice that T is a reflection about the $22\frac{1}{2}°$ line $y = (\sqrt{2}-1)x$.

(d) If $z \in S_k$ and $z' \in S_{n-k}$ we have $|z| = q^\beta$ and $|z'| = q'^\beta$, where $q \leq k$ and $q' \leq n-k$ by induction. By symmetry we may let $q = (1-\delta)t$ and $q' = (1+\delta)t$, where $t = \frac{1}{2}(q+q') \leq \frac{1}{2}n$. Then if the first hint is true, we have $|z \bullet z'| \leq (2t)^\beta \leq n^\beta$. And we also will have $|z \circ z'| \leq n^\beta$, by (c), since $|z^T| = |z|$.

To prove the first hint, we note that the maximum $|z \bullet z'|$ occurs when $y = y'$. For when $y \geq y'$ we have $|z \bullet z'|^2 = (x+x'+y')^2 + y^2 = r^2 + 2(x'+y')x + (x'+y')^2$; the largest value, given z', occurs when $y = y'$. A similar argument applies when $y' \geq y$.

Now when $y = y'$ we have $y = \sqrt{rr'} \sin\theta$ for some θ; and one can show that $x + x' \leq (r+r')\cos\theta$. Thus $z \bullet z' = (x+x'+y, y)$ lies in the ellipse of the second hint. On that ellipse we have $(a\cos\theta + b\sin\theta)^2 + (b\sin\theta)^2 = a^2/2 + b^2 + u\sin 2\theta + v\cos 2\theta = a^2/2 + b^2 + w\sin(2\theta + \tau)$, where $u = ab$, $v = \frac{1}{2}a^2 - b^2$, $w^2 = u^2 + v^2$, and $\cos\tau = u/w$. Hence $|z \bullet z'|^2 \leq \frac{1}{2}a^2 + b^2 + w$. And $4w^2 = (r+r')^4 + 4(rr')^2 \leq (r^2 + (2\sqrt{5}-2)rr' + r'^2)^2$, so

$$|z \bullet z'|^2 \leq r^2 + (\sqrt{5}+1)rr' + r'^2, \qquad r = (1-\delta)^\beta, \ r' = (1+\delta)^\beta.$$

The remaining task is to prove that this quantity is at most $2^{2\beta} = 2\phi^2$; equivalently, $f_t(2) \leq f_t(2\beta)$, where $f_t(\alpha) = (e^{t/\alpha} + e^{-t/\alpha})^\alpha - 2^\alpha$ and $t = \beta\ln((1-\delta)/(1+\delta))$. One can show, in fact, that f_t is an increasing function of α when $\alpha \geq 2$.

[The $O(n^\beta)$ bound on S_n seems to require a delicate analysis; an earlier attempt by Sauerhoff, Wegener, and Werchner was flawed. The proof given here is due to A. X. Chang and V. I. Spitkovsky in 2007.]

169. This conjecture has been verified for $m \leq 7$. [Many other curious properties also remain unexplained. A paper that describes what is known so far is currently being prepared by members of the "curious research group."]

170. (a) 2^{2n-1}. There are four choices at (j) when $1 \leq j < n$, namely LO $= \boxed{\perp}$ or LO $= \boxed{\top}$ or HI $= \boxed{\perp}$ or HI $= \boxed{\top}$; and there are two choices for (n).

(b) 2^{n-1}, since half the choices at each branch are ruled out.

(c) Indeed, if $t = (t_1 \ldots t_n)_2$ we have LO $= \boxed{\perp}$ at (j) when $t_j = 1$ and HI $= \boxed{\top}$ at (j) when $t_j = 0$. (This idea was applied to random bit generation in exercise 3.4.1–25. Since there are 2^{n-1} such values of t, we've shown that every monotone, skinny function is a threshold function, with weights $\{2^{n-1}, \ldots, 2, 1\}$. The other skinny functions are obtained by complementing individual variables.)

(d) $\bar{f}_t(\bar{x}) = [(\bar{x})_2 < t] = [(x)_2 > \bar{t}] = [(x)_2 > 2^n - 1 - t] = f_{2^n - t}(x)$.

(e) By Theorem 7.1.1Q, the shortest DNF is the OR of the prime implicants, and its general pattern is exhibited by the case $n = 10$ and $t = (1100010111)_2$: $(x_1 \wedge x_2 \wedge x_3) \vee$

$(x_1 \wedge x_2 \wedge x_4) \vee (x_1 \wedge x_2 \wedge x_5) \vee (x_1 \wedge x_2 \wedge x_6 \wedge x_7) \vee (x_1 \wedge x_2 \wedge x_6 \wedge x_8 \wedge x_9 \wedge x_{10})$. (One term for each 0 in t, and one more.) The shortest CNF is the dual of the shortest DNF of the dual, which corresponds to $2^n - t = (0011101001)_2$: $(x_1) \wedge (x_2) \wedge (x_3 \vee x_4 \vee x_5 \vee x_6) \wedge (x_3 \vee x_4 \vee x_5 \vee x_7 \vee x_8) \wedge (x_3 \vee x_4 \vee x_5 \vee x_7 \vee x_9) \wedge (x_3 \vee x_4 \vee x_5 \vee x_7 \vee x_{10})$.

171. Note that the classes of read-once, regular, skinny, and monotone functions are each closed under the operations of taking duals and restrictions. A skinny function is clearly read-once; a monotone threshold function with $w_1 \geq \cdots \geq w_n$ is regular; and a regular function is monotone. We must show that a regular read-once function is skinny.

Suppose $f(x_1, \ldots, x_n) = g(x_{i_1}, \ldots, x_{i_k}) \circ h(x_{j_1}, \ldots, x_{j_l})$, where $\circ$ is a nontrivial binary operator and we have $i_1 < \cdots < i_k$, $j_1 < \cdots < j_l$, $k + l = n$, and $\{i_1, \ldots, i_k, j_1, \ldots, j_l\} = \{1, \ldots, n\}$. (This condition is weaker than being "read-once.") We can assume that $i_1 = 1$. By taking restrictions and using induction, both g and h are skinny and monotone; thus their prime implicants have the special form in exercise 170(e). The operator $\circ$ must be monotone, so it is either $\vee$ or $\wedge$. By duality we can assume that $\circ$ is $\vee$.

Case 1: f has a prime implicant of length 1. Then x_1 is a prime implicant of f, by regularity. Hence $f(x_1, \ldots, x_n) = x_1 \vee f(0, x_2, \ldots, x_n)$, and we can use induction.

Case 2: All prime implicants of g and h have length > 1. Then $x_{j_1} \wedge \cdots \wedge x_{j_p}$ is a prime implicant, for some $p \geq 2$, but $x_{j_1-1} \wedge x_{j_2} \wedge \cdots \wedge x_{j_p}$ is not, contradicting regularity. [See T. Eiter, T. Ibaraki, and K. Makino, *Theor. Comp. Sci.* **270** (2002), 493–524.]

172. By examining the CNF for f_t in exercise 170(e), we see that when $t = (t_1 \ldots t_n)_2$ the number of Horn functions obtainable by complementing variables is one more than the number for $(t_2 \ldots t_n)_2$ when $t_1 = 0$, but twice that number when $t_1 = 1$. Thus the example $t = (1100010111)_2$ corresponds to $2 \times (2 \times (1 + (1 + (1 + (2 \times (1 + (2 \times (2 \times 2)))))))))$ Horn functions. Summing over all t gives s_n where $s_n = (2^{n-2} + s_{n-1}) + 2s_{n-1}$, where $s_1 = 2$; and the solution to this recurrence is $3^n - 2^{n-1}$.

To make both f and $\bar{f}$ Horn functions, assume (by duality) that $t \bmod 4 = 3$. Then we must complement x_j if and only if $t_j = 0$, except for the string of 1s at the right of t. For example, when $t = (1100010111)_2$, we should complement x_3, x_4, x_5, x_7, and then at most one of $\{x_8, x_9, x_{10}\}$. This gives $\rho(t+1) + 1 \geq 3$ choices related to f_t. Summing over all t with $t \bmod 4 = 3$ gives $2^n - 1$; so the answer is $2^{n+1} - 2$.

173. Consider monotone functions first. We can write $t = (0^{a_1} 1^{a_2} \ldots 0^{a_{2k-1}} 1^{a_{2k}})_2$, where $a_1 + \cdots + a_{2k} = n$, $a_1 \geq 0$, $a_j \geq 1$ for $1 < j < 2k$, and $a_{2k} \geq 2$ when $t \bmod 4 = 3$. When $t \bmod 4 = 1$, $2^n - t$ has this form. Then f_t has $a_1! a_2! \ldots a_{2k}!$ automorphisms, so it is equivalent to $n!/(a_1! a_2! \ldots a_{2k}!) - 1$ others, none of which are skinny. Summing over all t gives $2(P_n - nP_{n-1})$ monotone Boolean functions that are reorderable to skinny form, when $n \geq 2$, where P_n is the number of weak orderings (exercise 5.3.1–3). [See J. S. Beissinger and U. N. Peled, *Graphs and Combinatorics* **3** (1987), 213–219.]

Every such monotone function corresponds to 2^n different unate functions that are equally skinny, when variables are complemented. (These are the functions with the property that all of their restrictions are canalizing, known also as "unate cascades," "1-decision list functions," or "generalized read-once threshold functions.")

174. (a) Assign the numbers $0, \ldots, n-1, n, n+1$ to nodes $(1), \ldots, (n), \boxed{\top}, \boxed{\bot}$; and let the (LO, HI) branches from node k go to nodes (a_{2k+1}, a_{2k+2}) for $0 \leq k < n$. Then define p_k as follows, for $1 \leq k \leq 2n$: Let $l = \lfloor (k-1)/2 \rfloor$ and $P_l = \{p_1, \ldots, p_{2l}\}$. Set $p_k \leftarrow a_k$ if $a_k \notin P_l$; otherwise, if a_k is the mth smallest element of $P_l \cap \{l+1, \ldots, n+1\}$, set p_k to the mth smallest element of $\{n+2, \ldots, n+l+1\} \setminus P_l$. (This construction is due to T. Dahlheimer.)

(b) The inverse $p_1^{-1} \ldots p_{2n}^{-1}$ of a Dellac permutation satisfies $2(k-n) - 1 \le p_k^{-1} \le 2k$. It corresponds to a Genocchi derangement $q_1 \ldots q_{2n+2}$ when $q_2 = 1$, $q_{2n+1} = 2n+2$, and $q_{2k+2} = 1 + p_k^{-1}$, $q_{2k-1} = 1 + p_{k+n}^{-1}$ for $1 \le k \le n$.

(c) Given a permutation $q_1 \ldots q_{2n+2}$, let r_k be the first element of the sequence q_k^{-1}, q_k^{-2}, $\ldots$ that is $\ge k$. This transformation takes Genocchi permutations into Dumont pistols, and has the property that $q_k = k$ if and only if $r_k = k \notin \{r_1, \ldots, r_{k-1}\}$.

(d) Each node (j, k) represents a set of strings $r_1 \ldots r_j$, where $(1, 0) = \{1\}$ and the other sets are defined by the following transition rules: Suppose $r_1 \ldots r_j \in (j, k)$, and let $l = 2k$. If $k = 0$ then $(j+1, k)$ contains $1r_1^+ \ldots r_j^+$ when j is even, $2r_1^+ \ldots r_j^+$ when j is odd, where r^+ denotes $r + 1$. If $k > 0$ then $(j+1, k)$ contains $r_1^+ \ldots r_l^+ (l+1)r_{l+1}^+ \ldots r_j^+$ when j is even, $r_1^\pm \ldots r_{l-1}^\pm (l)r_l^\pm \ldots r_j^\pm$ when j is odd, where $r^\pm$ denotes $r + 1$ when $r \ge l$, $r - 1$ when $r < l$. Going vertically, if $l \le j - 3$ and j is odd, $(j, k+1)$ contains $r_1 \ldots r_l r_{l+2} r_{l+3} (l+3) r_{l+4} \ldots r_j$. On the other hand if $k = 1$ and j is even, $(j, 0)$ contains $r_2 r_1 r_3 \ldots r_j$. Finally if $k > 1$ and j is even, $(j, k-1)$ contains the string $r_1' \ldots r_{l-3}' (l-2) r_{l-2}' r_{l-1}' r_{l+1}' \ldots r_j'$, where r' denotes l when $r = l - 2$, otherwise $r' = r$. (One can show that the elements of $(2j, k)$ are the Dumont pistols for Genocchi permutations of order $2j$ whose largest fixed point is $2k$.)

All of these constructions are invertible. For example, the path $(1,0) \to (2,0) \to (3,0) \to (3,1) \to (4,1) \to (5,1) \to (6,1) \to (7,1) \to (7,2) \to (7,3) \to (8,3) \to (8,2) \to (8,1) \to (8,0)$ corresponds to the pistols $1 \to 22 \to 133 \to 333 \to 4244 \to 53355 \to 624466 \to 7335577 \to 7355577 \to 7355777 \to 82448688 \to 82646888 \to 82466888 \to 28466888$. The latter pistol, which can be represented by the diagram , corresponds to the Genocchi derangement $q_1 \ldots q_8 = 61537482$. And this derangement corresponds to $p_1^{-1} \ldots p_6^{-1} = 231546$ and the Dellac permutation $p_1 \ldots p_6 = 312546$. That permutation, in turn, corresponds to $a_1 \ldots a_6 = 312343$, which stands for the thin BDD

$$\textcircled{1}\!-\!\textcircled{2}\!-\!\textcircled{3}\!-\!\boxed{\top}\quad\boxed{\bot}.$$

Let d_{jk} be the number of pistols in (j, k), which is also the number of directed paths from $(1, 0)$ to (j, k). These numbers are readily found by addition, beginning with

									38227	38227	$\cdots$
							2073	2073	38227	76454	$\cdots$
					155	155	2073	4146	36154	112608	$\cdots$
			17	17	155	310	1918	6064	32008	144616	$\cdots$
		3	3	17	34	138	448	1608	7672	25944	170560	$\cdots$
	1	1	3	6	14	48	104	552	1160	8832	18272	188832	$\cdots$
1	1	1	2	2	8	8	56	56	608	608	9440	9440	198272	$\cdots$;

and the column totals $D_j = \sum_k d_{jk}$ are $(D_1, D_2, \ldots) = (1, 1, 2, 3, 8, 17, 56, 155, 608, 2073, 9440, 38227, 198272, 929569, \ldots)$. The even-numbered elements of this sequence, D_{2n}, have long been known as the Genocchi numbers G_{2n+2}. The odd-numbered elements, D_{2n+1}, have therefore been called "median Genocchi numbers." The number S_n of thin BDDs is $d_{(2n+2)0} = D_{2n+1}$.

References: L. Euler discussed the Genocchi numbers in the second volume of his *Institutiones Calculi Differentialis* (1755), Chapter 7, where he showed that the odd integers G_{2n} are expressible in terms of the Bernoulli numbers: In fact, $G_{2n} = (2^{2n+1} - 2)|B_{2n}|$, and $z \tan \frac{z}{2} = \sum_{n=1}^{\infty} G_{2n} z^{2n}/(2n)!$. A. Genocchi examined these numbers further in *Annali di Scienze Matematiche e Fisiche* **3** (1852), 395–405; and L. Seidel, in *Sitzungsberichte math.-phys. Classe, Akademie Wissen. München* **7** (1877),

157–187, discovered that they could be computed additively via the numbers d_{jk}. Their combinatorial significance was not discovered until much later; see D. Dumont, *Duke Math. J.* **41** (1974), 305–318; D. Dumont and A. Randrianarivony, *Discrete Math.* **132** (1994), 37–49. Meanwhile H. Dellac had proposed an apparently unrelated problem, equivalent to enumerating what we have called Dellac permutations; see L'*Intermédiaire des Math.* **7** (1900), 9–10, 328; *Annales de la Faculté sci. Marseille* **11** (1901), 141–164.

There's also a *direct* connection between thin BDDs and the paths of (d), discovered in 2007 by Thorsten Dahlheimer. Notice first that unrestricted Dumont pistols of order $2n + 2$ correspond to thin BDDs that are ordered but not necessarily reduced, because we can let $r_1 \ldots r_{2n}r_{2n+1}r_{2n+2} = (2a_1) \ldots (2a_{2n})(2n+2)(2n+2)$. The number of such pistols in which $\min\{i \mid r_{2i-1} = r_{2i}\} = l$ turns out to be $d_{(2n+2)(n+1-l)}$.

To prove this, we can use new transition rules instead of those in answer (d): Suppose $r_1 \ldots r_j \in (j, k)$, and let $l = j - 2k$. Then $(j+1, k)$ contains $r_1^+ \ldots r_l^+ r_l^+ \ldots r_j^+$ when j is odd, $r_1^\pm \ldots r_{l-1}^\pm (l-1)r_l^\pm \ldots r_j^\pm$ when j is even. If j is odd, $(j, k+1)$ contains $1r_1r_3 \ldots r_j$ when $l = 3$, and when $l > 3$ it contains $r_1' \ldots r_{l-4}'(l-4)r_{l-3}'r_{l-2}'r_l' \ldots r_j'$, where $r' = r + 2[r = l-4]$. Finally, if j is even and $k > 0$, $(j, k-1)$ contains $r_1 \ldots r_{l-1}qr_{l+2}r_{l+2} \ldots r_j$, where $q = l$ if $r_l = r_{l+1}$, otherwise $q = r_{l+1}$.

With these magic transitions the path above corresponds to $1 \to 22 \to 313 \to 133 \to 2244 \to 31355 \to 424466 \to 5153577 \to 5135577 \to 1535577 \to 22646688 \to 26446688 \to 26466688 \to 26466888$; so $a_1 \ldots a_6 = 132334$.

175. This problem seems to require a different approach from the methods that worked when $b_0 = \cdots = b_{n-1} = 1$. Suppose we have a BDD base of N nodes including the two sinks $\boxed{\bot}$ and $\boxed{\top}$ together with various branches labeled $\textcircled{2}, \ldots, \textcircled{n}$, and assume that exactly s of the nodes are sources (having in-degree zero). Let $c(b, s, t, N)$ be the number of ways to introduce b additional nodes labeled $\textcircled{1}$, in such a way that exactly $s+b-t$ source nodes remain. (Thus $0 \le t \le 2b$; exactly t of the old source nodes are now reachable from a $\textcircled{1}$ branch.) Then the number of nonconstant Boolean functions $f(x_1, \ldots, x_n)$ having the BDD profile $(b_0, \ldots, b_n)$ is equal to $T(b_0, \ldots, b_{n-1}; 1)$, where

$$T(b_0; s) = 2[s = b_0 = 1] + [s = 2][b_0 = 0] + [s = 2][b_0 = 2];$$

$$T(b_0, \ldots, b_{n-1}; s) = \sum_{t=\max(0, b_0 - s)}^{2b_0} c(b_0, s+t-b_0, t, b_1 + \cdots + b_{n-1}+2)\, T(b_1, \ldots, b_{n-1}; s+t-b_0).$$

One can show that $c(b, s, t, N) = \sum_{r=0}^{2b} a_{rb}p_{tr}(s, N)/b!$, where we have $(N(N-1))^{\underline{b}} = \sum_{r=0}^{2b} a_{rb}N^r$ and $p_{tr}(s, N) = \sum_k \binom{r}{k}\left\{{k \atop t}\right\}s^t(N-s)^{r-k} = \sum_k \left\{{r \atop k}\right\}\binom{k}{t}s^t(N-s)^{\underline{k-t}} = r!\,[w^t z^r]\,e^{(N-s)z}(we^z - w + 1)^s$.

176. (a) If $p \ne p'$ we have $\sum_{a \in A, b \in B}[h_{a,b}(p) = h_{a,b}(p')] \le |A||B|/2^l$, by the definition of universal hashing. Let $r_i(a, b)$ be the number of $p \in P$ such that $h_{a,b}(p) = i$. Then

$$\sum_{a \in A, b \in B}\; \sum_{0 \le i < 2^l} r_i(a, b)^2 = \sum_{a \in A, b \in B}\; \sum_{p \in P}\sum_{p' \in P}[h_{a,b}(p) = h_{a,b}(p')]$$

$$\le |P||A||B| + \sum_{p \in P}\sum_{p' \in P}[p \ne p']\frac{|A||B|}{2^l} = 2^t|A||B|\left(1 + \frac{2^t - 1}{2^l}\right).$$

On the other hand $\sum_{i=0}^{2^l-1} r_i(a, b)^2 = \sum_{i=0}^{2^l-1}(r_i(a, b) - 2^t/|I|)^2 + 2^{2t}/|I| \ge 2^{2t}/|I|$, for any a and b. Similar formulas apply when there are $s_j(a, b)$ solutions to $h_{a,b}(q) = j$.

So there must be $a \in A$ and $b \in B$ such that

$$\frac{2^{2t}}{|I|} + \frac{2^{2t}}{|J|} \leq \sum_{i \in I} r_i(a,b)^2 + \sum_{j \in J} s_j(a,b)^2 \leq 2^{t+1}\left(1 + \frac{2^t - 1}{2^l}\right) \leq \frac{2^{2t}}{2^l} + \frac{2^{2t}}{(1-\epsilon)2^l}.$$

(b) The middle l bits of $aq_k + b$ and $aq_{k+2} + b$ differ by at least 2, so the middle $l - 1$ bits of aq_k and aq_{k+2} must be different.

(c) Let q and q' be different elements of Q^* with $(g(q') - g(q)) \bmod 2^{l-1} \geq 2^{l-2}$. (Otherwise we can swap $q \leftrightarrow q'$.) If $l \geq 3$, the condition $g(p) + g(q) = 2^{l-1}$ implies that $f_q(p) = 0$. Now $(g(p) + g(q')) \bmod (2^{l-1}) = (g(q') - g(q)) \bmod (2^{l-1})$; furthermore $g(q')$ and $g(p)$ are both even. Therefore no carry can propagate to change the middle bit, and we have $f_{q'}(p) = 1$.

(d) The set Q'' has at least $(1-\epsilon)2^{l-1}$ elements, and so does the analogous set P''. At most 2^{l-2} elements of Q'' have $g(q)$ odd; and at most $2^{l-2} + 1 - |P''|$ of the elements with $g(q)$ even are not in Q^*. Thus $|Q^*| \geq (1-\epsilon)2^{l-1} - 2^{l-2} - 2^{l-1} - 1 + (1-\epsilon)2^{l-1} = (1 - 4\epsilon)2^{l-2} - 1$, and we have $B_{\min}(Z_{n,y}) \geq (1 - 4\epsilon)2^{l-1} - 2$ by (85).

Finally, choose $l = t - 4$ and $\epsilon = 1/9$. The theorem is obvious when $n < 14$.

177. Suppose $k \geq n/2$ and $x = 2^{k+1}x_h + x_l$, $y = 2^k y_h + y_l$. Then $(xy \gg k) \bmod 2^{n-k}$ depends on $2x_h y_l$, $x_l y_h$, and $x_l y_l \gg k$, modulo 2^{n-k}, so $q_{2k+1} \leq 2^{n-k-1+n-k+n-k}$.

Summing up, we get $\sum_{k=0}^{2n} q_k \leq \sum_{0 \leq k \leq 6n/5} 2^k + \sum_{6n/5 < k \leq 2n} 2^{3n-2\lfloor k/2 \rfloor - \lceil k/2 \rceil}$. If $n = 5t + (0, 1, 2, 3, 4)$ the total comes to exactly $(2^{\lceil 6n/5 \rceil} \cdot (19, 10, 12, 13, 17) - 12)/7$.

178. We can write $x = 2^k x_h + x_l$ as in the proof of Theorem A; but now $x_l = \hat{x}_l + (x \bmod 2)$, where $\hat{x}_l$ is even and $x \bmod 2$ is not yet known. Similarly $y = 2^k y_h + y_l = 2^k y_h + \hat{y}_l + (y \bmod 2)$. Let $\hat{z}_l = \hat{x}_l \hat{y}_l \bmod 2^k$. At level $2k - 2$, for $n/2 \leq k < n$, we need only "remember" three $(n-k)$-bit numbers $\hat{x}_l \bmod 2^{n-k}$, $\hat{y}_l \bmod 2^{n-k}$, $(\hat{x}_l \hat{y}_l \gg k) \bmod 2^{n-k}$, and three "carries" $c_1 = (\hat{x}_l + \hat{z}_l) \gg k$, $c_2 = (\hat{y}_l + \hat{z}_l) \gg k$, $c_3 = (\hat{x}_l + \hat{y}_l + \hat{z}_l) \gg k$. These six quantities will suffice to determine the middle bit, after x_h, y_h, $x \bmod 2$, and $y \bmod 2$ become known.

There are only six possibilities for the carries: $c_1 c_2 c_3 = 000$, 001, 011, 101, 111, or 112. Thus $q_{2k-2} \leq 6 \cdot 2^{(n-k-1)+(n-k-1)+(n-k)}$. Similarly, when $n/2 \leq k < n-1$, we have $q_{2k-1} \leq 6 \cdot 2^{(n-k-2)+(n-k-1)+(n-k)}$. With these estimates, together with $q_k \leq 2^k$, we get $\sum_{k=0}^{2n-4} q_k \leq (2^{6t} \cdot (37, 86, 184, 464, 1024) - 268)/28$ when $n = 5t + (0, 1, 2, 3, 4)$.

The actual BDD sizes, for the function f of Theorem A and the function g of this exercise, are $B(f) = $ (169, 381, 928, 2188, 5248, 12373, 29400, 68777, 162768, 377359, 879709) and $B(g) = $ (165, 352, 806, 1802, 4195, 9774, 22454, 52714, 121198, 278223, 650188) for $6 \leq n \leq 16$; so this variant appears to save about 25%. A slightly better ordering is obtained by testing (lo-bit(x), hi-bit(y), hi-bit(x), lo-bit(y)) on the last four levels, giving $B(h) = B(g) - 20$ for $n \geq 6$. Then $B(h)/B_{\min}(f) \approx$ (1.07, 1.05, 1.04, 1.04, 1.04, 1.01, 1.02) for $6 \leq n \leq 12$, so this ordering may be close to optimal as $n \to \infty$.

180. By letting $a_{m+1} = a_{m+2} = \cdots = 0$, we may assume that $m \geq p$. Let $a = (a_p \ldots a_1)_2$, and write $x = 2^k x_h + x_l$ as in the proof of Theorem A. If $p \leq n$, we have $q_k \leq 2^{p-k}$ for $0 \leq k < p$, because the given function $f = Z_{m,n}^{(p)}(a; x)$ depends only on a, x_h, and $(ax_l \gg k) \bmod 2^{p-k}$. We may therefore assume that $p > n$.

Consider the multiset $A = \{2^k x_h a \bmod 2^{p-1} \mid 0 \leq x_h < 2^{n-k}\}$. Write $A = \{2^{p-1} - \alpha_1, \ldots, 2^{p-1} - \alpha_s\}$, where $s = 2^{n-k}$ and $0 < \alpha_1 \leq \cdots \leq \alpha_s = 2^{p-1}$, and let $\alpha_{s+i} = \alpha_i + 2^{p-1}$ for $0 \leq i \leq s$. Then $q_k \leq 2s$, because f depends only on a, x_h, and the index $i \in [0..2s)$ such that $\alpha_i \leq ax_l \bmod 2^p < \alpha_{i+1}$.

Consequently $\sum_{k=0}^n q_k \leq \sum_{k=0}^n \min(2^k, 2^{n+1-k}) = 2^{\lfloor n/2 \rfloor + 1} + 2^{\lceil n/2 \rceil + 1} - 3$.

181. For every $(x_1, \ldots, x_m)$ the remaining function of $(y_1, \ldots, y_n)$ requires $O(n)$ nodes, by exercise 170.

182. Yes; B. Bollig [*Lecture Notes in Comp. Sci.* **4978** (2008), 306–317] has shown that it is $\Omega(2^{n/432})$. Incidentally, $B_{\min}(L_{12,12}) = 1158$ is obtained with the strange ordering $L_{12,12}(x_{18}, x_{17}, x_{16}, x_{15}, x_{14}, x_{12}, x_{10}, x_8, x_6, x_4, x_2, x_1; x_{19}, x_{20}, x_{21}, x_{22}, x_{23}, x_{13}, x_{11}, x_9, x_7, x_5, x_3, x_{24})$; and $B_{\max}(L_{12,12}) = 9302$ arises with $L_{12,12}(x_{24}, x_{23}, x_{20}, x_{19}, x_{22}, x_{11}, x_6, x_7, x_8, x_9, x_{10}, x_{13}; x_1, x_2, x_3, x_4, x_5, x_{21}, x_{18}, x_{17}, x_{16}, x_{15}, x_{14}, x_{12})$. Similarly $B_{\min}(L_{8,16}) = 606$ and $B_{\max}(L_{8,16}) = 3415$ aren't terribly far apart. Could $B_{\min}(L_{m,n})$ and $B_{\max}(L_{m,n})$ both conceivably be $\Theta(2^{\min(m,n)})$?

183. The profile $(b_0, b_1, \ldots)$ begins $(1, 1, 1, 2, 3, 5, 7, 11, 15, 23, 31, 47, 63, 95, \ldots)$. When $k > 0$ there's a node on level $2k$ for every pair of integers (a, b) such that $2^{k-1} \le a, b < 2^k$ and $ab < 2^{2k-1} < (a+1)(b+1)$; this node represents the function $[((a+x)/2^k)((b+y)/2^k) \ge \frac{1}{2}]$. When b is given, in the appropriate range, there are $\lceil 2^{2k-1}/b \rceil - \lfloor 2^{2k-1}/(b+1) \rfloor$ choices for a; hence
$$b_{2k} = \sum\nolimits_{2^{k-1} \le b < 2^k} (\lceil 2^{2k-1}/b \rceil - \lfloor 2^{2k-1}/(b+1) \rfloor),$$

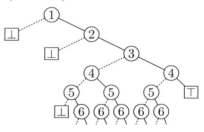

which telescopes to $2^k - 1$. A similar argument shows that $b_{2k+1} = 2^k + 2^{k-1} - 1$.

184. Two kinds of beads contribute to $b_{m(i-1)+j-1}$: One for every choice of i columns, at least one of which is $< j$; and one for every choice of $i-1$ columns, missing at least one element $\ge j$. Thus $b_{m(i-1)+j-1} = (\binom{m}{i} - \binom{m+1-j}{i}) + (\binom{m}{i-1} - \binom{j-1}{m+1-i})$. Summing over $1 \le i, j \le m$ gives $B(P_m) = (2m-3)2^m + 5$. (Incidentally, $q_k = b_k + 1$ for $2 \le k < m^2$.)

The ZDD has simply $z_{m(i-1)+j-1} = \binom{m-1}{i-1}$ for $1 \le i, j \le m$, one for every choice of $i-1$ columns $\ne j$; hence $Z(P_m) = m2^{m-1} + 2 \approx \frac{1}{4}B(P_m)$. (The lower bound of Theorem K applies also to ZDD nodes, because only such nodes get tickets; therefore the natural ordering of variables is optimum for ZDDs. The natural ordering might be optimum also for BDDs; this conjecture is known to be true for $m \le 5$.)

185. Suppose $f(x) = t_{\nu x}$ for some binary vector $t_0 \ldots t_n$. Then the subfunctions of order $d > 0$ correspond to the distinct substrings $t_i \ldots t_{i+d}$. Such substrings τ correspond to beads if and only if $\tau \ne 0^{d+1}$ and $\tau \ne 1^{d+1}$; they correspond to zeads if and only if $\tau \ne 0^{d+1}$ and $\tau \ne 10^d$.

Thus the maximum $Z(f)$ is the function S_n of answer 44. To attain this worst case we need a binary vector of length $2^{d+1} + d - 2$ that contains all $(d+1)$-tuples except 0^{d+1} and 10^d as substrings; such vectors can be characterized as the first $2^{d+1} + d - 2$ elements of any de Bruijn cycle of period 2^{d+1}, beginning with $0^d 1$.

186. $\bar{x}_1 \wedge \bar{x}_2 \wedge x_3 \wedge \bar{x}_4 \wedge \bar{x}_5 \wedge x_6$.

187. (These diagrams should be compared with the answer to exercise 1.)

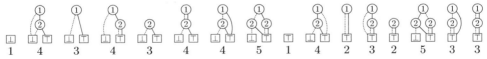

188. To avoid nested braces, let ϵ, a, b, and ab stand for the subsets $\emptyset$, $\{1\}$, $\{2\}$, and $\{1,2\}$. The families are then $\emptyset$, $\{ab\}$, $\{a\}$, $\{a, ab\}$, $\{b\}$, $\{b, ab\}$, $\{a, b\}$, $\{a, b, ab\}$, $\{\epsilon\}$, $\{\epsilon, ab\}$, $\{\epsilon, a\}$, $\{\epsilon, a, ab\}$, $\{\epsilon, b\}$, $\{\epsilon, b, ab\}$, $\{\epsilon, a, b\}$, $\{\epsilon, a, b, ab\}$, in truth-table order.

189. When $n = 0$, only the constant functions; when $n > 0$, only 0 and $x_1 \wedge \cdots \wedge x_n$. (But there are many functions, such as $x_2 \wedge (x_1 \vee \bar{x}_3)$, with $(b_0, \ldots, b_n) = (z_0, \ldots, z_n)$.)

190. (a) Only $x_1 \oplus \cdots \oplus x_n$ and $1 \oplus x_1 \oplus \cdots \oplus x_n$, for $n \geq 0$. (b) This condition holds if and only if all subtables of order 1 are either 01 or 11. So there are $2^{2^{n-1}}$ solutions when $n > 0$, namely all functions such that $f(x_1, \ldots, x_{n-1}, 1) = 1$.

191. The language L_n of truth tables for all such functions has the context-free grammar $L_0 \to 1$; $L_{n+1} \to L_n L_n \mid L_n 0^{2^n}$. The desired number $l_n = |L_n|$ therefore satisfies $l_0 = 1$, $l_{n+1} = l_n(l_n + 1)$; so $(l_0, l_1, l_2, \ldots)$ is the sequence $(1, 2, 6, 1806, 3263442, \ldots)$. Asymptotically, $l_n = \theta^{2^n} - \frac{1}{2} - \epsilon$, where $0 < \epsilon < \theta^{-2^n}/8$ and

$$\theta = 1.59791\ 02180\ 31873\ 17833\ 80701\ 18157\ 45531\ 23622 + .$$

[See *CMath* exercises 4.37 and 4.59, where $l_n + 1$ is called e_{n+1} (a "Euclid number") and θ is called E^2. The numbers $l_n + 1$ were introduced by J. J. Sylvester in connection with his study of Egyptian fractions, *Amer. J. Math.* **3** (1880), 388. Notice that a monotone decreasing function, like a function representing independent sets, always has $z_n = 1$.]

192. (a) 10101101000010110.

(b) True, by induction on $|\tau|$, because $\alpha \neq \beta \neq 0^n$ if and only if $\alpha^Z \neq \beta^Z \neq 0^n$.

(c) The beads of f of order k are the zeads of f^Z of order k, for $0 < k \leq n$. Hence the beads of f^Z are also the zeads of $(f^Z)^Z = f$. Therefore, if $(b_0, \ldots, b_n)$ and $(z_0, \ldots, z_n)$ are the profile and z-profile of f while $(b_0', \ldots, b_n')$ and $(z_0', \ldots, z_n')$ are the profile and z-profile of f^Z, we have $b_k = z_k'$ and $z_k = b_k'$ for $0 \leq k < n$.

(We also have $z_n = z_n'$, but they might both be 1 instead of 2. The *quasi-profiles* of f and f^Z may differ, but only by at most 1 at each level, because of all-0 subtables.)

193. $S_{\geq k}(x_1, \ldots, x_n)$, by induction on n. (Hence we also have $S_{\geq k}^Z(x_1, \ldots, x_n) = S_k(x_1, \ldots, x_n)$. Exercise 249 gives similar examples.)

194. Define $a_1 \ldots a_{2n}$ as in answer 174, but use the ZDD instead of the BDD. Then $(1, \ldots, 1)$ is the z-profile if and only if $(2a_1) \ldots (2a_{2n})$ is an unrestricted Dumont pistol of order $2n$. So the answer is the Genocchi number G_{2n+2}.

195. The z-profile is $(1, 2, 4, 4, 3, 2, 2)$. We get an optimum z-profile $(1, 2, 3, 2, 3, 2, 2)$ from $M_2(x_4, x_2; x_5, x_6, x_3, x_1)$, and a pessimum z-profile $(1, 2, 4, 8, 12, 2, 2)$ comes from $M_2(x_5, x_6; x_1, x_2, x_3, x_4)$ as in (78). (Incidentally, the algorithm of exercise 197 can be used to show that $Z_{\min}(M_4) = 116$ is obtained with the strikingly peculiar ordering $M_4(x_8, x_5, x_{17}, x_2; x_{20}, x_{19}, x_{18}, x_{16}, x_{15}, x_{13}, x_{14}, x_{12}, x_{11}, x_9, x_{10}, x_4, x_7, x_6, x_3, x_1)$!)

196. For example, $M_m(x_1, \ldots, x_m; e_{m+1}, \ldots, e_n)$, where $n = m + 2^m$ and e_j is the elementary function of exercise 203. Then we have $Z(f) = 2(n - m) + 1$ and $Z(\bar{f}) = (n - m + 7)(n - m)/2 - 2$.

197. The key idea is to change the significance of the DEP fields so that d_{kp} is now $\sum \{2^{t-k-1} \mid N_{kp}$ supports $x_t\}$, where we say that $g(x_1, \ldots, x_m)$ *supports* x_j if there is a solution to $g(x_1, \ldots, x_m) = 1$ with $x_j = 1$.

To implement this change, we introduce an auxiliary array $(\zeta_0, \ldots, \zeta_n)$, where we will have $\zeta_k = q$ if N_{kq} denotes the subfunction 0 and $\zeta_k = -1$ if that subfunction does not appear on level k. Initially $\zeta_n \leftarrow 0$, and we set $\zeta_k \leftarrow -1$ at the beginning of step E1. In step E3, the operation of setting d_{kq} should become the following: "If $d_{(k+1)h} \neq \zeta_{k+1}$, set $d_{kq} \leftarrow ((d_{(k+1)l} \mid d_{(k+1)h}) \ll 1) + 1$; otherwise set $d_{kq} \leftarrow d_{(k+1)l} \ll 1$. Also set $\zeta_k \leftarrow q$ if $d_{(k+1)l} = d_{(k+1)h} = \zeta_{k+1}$."

(The master z-profile chart can be used as before to minimize $z_0 + \cdots + z_{n-1}$; but additional work is needed to consider z_n if the *absolute* minimum is important.)

198. Reinterpreting (50), we represent an arbitrary family of sets f as $(\bar{x}_v ? f_l : f_h)$, where $v = f_v$ indexes the first variable that f *supports*; see answer 197. Thus f_l is the subfamily of f that doesn't support x_v, and f_h is the subfamily that does (but with x_v deleted). We also let $f_v = \infty$ if f has no support (i.e., if f is either $\emptyset$ or $\{\emptyset\}$, represented internally by $\boxed{\perp}$ or $\boxed{\top}$; see answer 200). In (52), $v = \min(f_v, g_v)$ now indexes the first variable *supported* by either f or g; thus $f_h = \emptyset$ if $f_v > g_v$, and $g_h = \emptyset$ if $f_v < g_v$.

Subroutine AND(f, g), ZDD-style, is now the following instead of (55): "Represent f and g as in (52). While $f_v \neq g_v$, return $\emptyset$ if either $f = \emptyset$ or $g = \emptyset$; otherwise set $f \leftarrow f_l$ if $f_v < g_v$, set $g \leftarrow g_l$ if $f_v > g_v$. Swap $f \leftrightarrow g$ if $f > g$. Return f if $f = g$ or $f = \emptyset$. Otherwise, if $f \wedge g = r$ is in the memo cache, return r. Otherwise compute $r_l \leftarrow$ AND(f_l, g_l) and $r_h \leftarrow$ AND(f_h, g_h); set $r \leftarrow$ ZUNIQUE(v, r_l, r_h), using an algorithm like Algorithm U except that the first step returns p when $q = \emptyset$ instead of when $q = p$; put '$f \wedge g = r$' into the memo cache, and return r." (See also the suggestion in answer 200.)

Reference counts are updated as in exercise 82, with slight changes; for example, step U1 will now decrease the reference count of $\boxed{\perp}$ (and only of this node), when $q = \emptyset$. It is important to write a "sanity check" routine that double-checks all reference counts and other redundancies in the entire BDD/ZDD base, so that subtle errors are nipped in the bud. The sanity checker should be invoked frequently until all subroutines have been thoroughly tested.

199. (a) If $f = g$, return f. If $f > g$, swap $f \leftrightarrow g$. If $f = \emptyset$, return g. If $f \vee g = r$ is in the memo cache, return r. Otherwise

set $v \leftarrow f_v$, $r_l \leftarrow$ OR(f_l, g_l), $r_h \leftarrow$ OR(f_h, g_h), if $f_v = g_v$;
set $v \leftarrow f_v$, $r_l \leftarrow$ OR(f_l, g), $r_h \leftarrow f_h$, increase REF(f_h) by 1, if $f_v < g_v$;
set $v \leftarrow g_v$, $r_l \leftarrow$ OR(f, g_l), $r_h \leftarrow g_h$, increase REF(g_h) by 1, if $f_v > g_v$.

Then set $r \leftarrow$ ZUNIQUE(v, r_l, r_h); cache it and return it as in answer 198.

(b) If $f = g$, return $\emptyset$. Otherwise proceed as in (a), but use $(\oplus, \text{XOR})$ not $(\vee, \text{OR})$.

(c) If $f = \emptyset$ or $f = g$, return $\emptyset$. If $g = \emptyset$, return f. Otherwise, if $g_v < f_v$, set $g \leftarrow g_l$ and begin again. Otherwise

set $r_l \leftarrow$ BUTNOT(f_l, g_l), $r_h \leftarrow$ BUTNOT(f_h, g_h), if $f_v = g_v$;
set $r_l \leftarrow$ BUTNOT(f_l, g), $r_h \leftarrow f_h$, increase REF(f_h) by 1, if $f_v < g_v$.

Then set $r \leftarrow$ ZUNIQUE(f_v, r_l, r_h) and finish as usual.

200. If $f = \emptyset$, return g. If $f = h$, return OR(f, g). If $g = h$, return g. If $g = \emptyset$ or $f = g$, return AND(f, h). If $h = \emptyset$, return BUTNOT(g, f). If $f_v < g_v$ and $f_v < h_v$, set $f \leftarrow f_l$ and start over. If $h_v < f_v$ and $h_v < g_v$, set $h \leftarrow h_l$ and start over. Otherwise check the cache and proceed recursively as usual.

201. In applications of ZDDs where projection functions and/or the complementation operation are permitted, it's best to fix the set of Boolean variables at the beginning, when everything is being initialized. Otherwise, *every* external function in a ZDD base must change whenever a new variable enters the fray.

Suppose therefore that we've decided to deal with functions of $(x_1, \ldots, x_N)$, where N is prespecified. In answer 198, we let $f_v = N + 1$, not ∞, when $f = \emptyset$ or $f = \{\emptyset\}$. Then the tautology function $1 = \wp$ has the $(N+1)$-node ZDD $\boxed{1} \cdots \boxed{2} \cdots \boxed{N} \boxed{\top}$, which we construct as soon as N is known. Let t_j be node $\boxed{j}$ of this structure, with $t_{N+1} = \boxed{\top}$. The ZDD for x_j is now $\boxed{1} \cdots \boxed{j} - t_{j+1} \boxed{\perp}$; thus the ZDD base for the set of all x_j will occupy $\binom{N+1}{2}$ nodes in addition to the representations of $\emptyset$ and $\wp$.

If N is small, all N projection functions can be prepared in advance. But N is large in many applications of ZDDs; and projection functions are rarely needed when "family algebra" is used to build the structures as in exercises 203–207. So it's generally best to wait until a projection function is actually required, before creating it.

Incidentally, the partial-tautology functions t_j can be used to speed up the synthesis operations of exercises 198–199: If $v = f_v \leq g_v$ and $f = t_v$, we have $\text{AND}(f, g) = g$, $\text{OR}(f, g) = f$, and (if $v \leq h_v$) also $\text{MUX}(f, g, h) = h$, $\text{MUX}(g, h, f) = \text{OR}(g, h)$.

202. In the transmogrification step T4, change '$q_0 \leftarrow q_1 \leftarrow q$' to '$q_0 \leftarrow q$, $q_1 \leftarrow \emptyset$' and '$r_0 \leftarrow r_1 \leftarrow r$' to '$r_0 \leftarrow r$, $r_1 \leftarrow \emptyset$'. Also use ZUNIQUE instead of UNIQUE; within T4, this subroutine increases $\text{REF}(p)$ by 1 if step U1 finds $q = \emptyset$.

A subtler change is needed to keep the partial-tautology functions of answer 201 up to date, because of their special meaning. Correct behavior is to keep t_u unchanged and set $t_v \leftarrow \text{LO}(t_u)$.

203. (a) $f \sqcup g = \{\{1, 2\}, \{1, 3\}, \{1, 2, 3\}, \{3\}\} = (e_1 \sqcup ((e_2 \sqcup (e_3 \cup \epsilon)) \cup e_3)) \cup e_3$; the other is $(e_1 \sqcup e_2) \cup \epsilon$, because $f \sqcap g = (e_1 \sqcup (e_2 \cup \epsilon)) \cup e_3 \cup \epsilon$ and $f \boxplus e_1 = e_1 \cup e_2 \cup e_3$.

(b) $(f \sqcup g)(z) = \exists x \, \exists y \, (f(x) \wedge g(y) \wedge (z \equiv x \vee y))$; $(f \sqcap g)(z) = \exists x \, \exists y \, (f(x) \wedge g(y) \wedge (z \equiv x \wedge y))$; $(f \boxplus g)(z) = \exists x \, \exists y \, (f(x) \wedge g(y) \wedge (z \equiv x \oplus y))$. Another formula is $(f \boxplus g)(z) = \bigvee \{f(z \oplus y) \mid g(y) = 1\} = \bigvee \{g(z \oplus x) \mid f(x) = 1\}$.

(c) Both (i) and (ii) are true; also $f \boxplus (g \cup h) = (f \boxplus g) \cup (f \boxplus h)$. Formula (iii) fails in general, although we do have $f \sqcup (g \sqcap h) \subseteq (f \sqcup g) \sqcap (f \sqcup h)$. Formula (iv) makes little sense; the right-hand side is $(f \sqcup f) \cup (f \sqcup h) \cup (g \sqcup f) \cup (g \sqcup h)$, by (i). Formula (v) is true because all three parts are $\emptyset$. And (vi) is true if and only if $f \neq \emptyset$.

(d) Only (ii) is always true. For (i), the condition should be $f \sqcap g \subseteq \epsilon$, since $f \sqcap g = \emptyset$ implies $f \perp g$. For (iii), notice that $|f \sqcup g| = |f \sqcap g| = |f \boxplus g| = 1$ whenever $|f| = |g| = 1$. Finally, in statement (iv), we do have $f \perp g \implies f \sqcup g = f \boxplus g$; but the converse fails when, say, $f = g = e_1 \cup \epsilon$.

(e) $f = \emptyset$ in (i) and $f = \epsilon$ in (ii); also $\epsilon \boxplus g = g$ for all g. There's no solution to (iii), because f would have to be $\{\{1, 2, 3, \dots\}\}$ and we are considering only finite sets. But in the finite universe of answer 201 we have $f = \{\{1, \dots, N\}\}$. (This family U has the property that $(f \boxplus U) \sqcup (g \boxplus U) = (f \sqcap g) \boxplus U$.) The general solution to (iv) is $f = e_1 \sqcup e_2 \sqcup f'$, where f' is an arbitrary family; similarly, the general solution to (v) is $f = (e_1 \sqcup f') \cup (e_2 \sqcup f'') \cup (e_1 \sqcup e_2 \sqcup (f' \cup f'' \cup f'''))$, where f', f'', and f''' are arbitrary. In (vi), $f = ((((e_1 \sqcup e_2) \cup \epsilon) \sqcup f') \cup ((e_1 \cup e_2) \sqcup f'')) \sqcup (e_3 \cup \epsilon)$, where $f' \cup f'' \perp e_1 \cup e_2 \cup e_3$; this representation follows from exercise 204(f). In (vii), $|f| = 1$. Finally, (viii) characterizes Horn functions (Theorem 7.1.1H).

204. (a) This relation is obvious from the definition. (Also $(f \cup g)/h \supseteq (f/h) \cup (g/h)$.)

(b) $f/e_2 = \{\{1\}, \emptyset\} = e_1 \cup \epsilon$; $f/e_1 = e_2 \cup e_3$; $f/\epsilon = f$; hence $f/(e_1 \cup \epsilon) = e_2 \cup e_3$.

(c) Division by $\emptyset$ gives trouble, because *all* sets α belong to $f/\emptyset$. (But if we restrict consideration to families of subsets of $\{1, \dots, N\}$, as in exercises 201 and 207, we have $f/\emptyset = \wp$; also $\wp/\wp = \epsilon$, and $f/\wp = \emptyset$ when $f \neq \wp$.) Clearly $f/\epsilon = f$. And $f/f = \epsilon$ when $f \neq \emptyset$. Finally, $(f \bmod g)/g = \emptyset$ when $g \neq \emptyset$, because $\alpha \in (f \bmod g)/g$ and $\beta \in g$ implies that $\alpha \cup \beta \in f$, $\alpha \in f/g$, and $\alpha \cup \beta \notin (f/g) \sqcup g$—a contradiction.

(d) If $\beta \in g$, we have $\beta \cup \alpha \in f$ and $\beta \cap \alpha = \emptyset$ for all $\alpha \in f/g$; this proves the hint. Hence $f/g \subseteq f/(f/(f/g))$. Also $f/h \subseteq f/g$ when $h \supseteq g$, by (a); let $h = f/(f/g)$.

(e) Let $f/\!/g$ be the family in the new definition. Then $f/g \subseteq f/\!/g$, because $g \sqcup (f/g) \subseteq f$ and $g \perp (f/g)$. Conversely, if $\alpha \in f/\!/g$ and $\beta \in g$, we have $\alpha \in h$ for some h with $g \sqcup h \subseteq f$ and $g \perp h$; consequently $\alpha \cup \beta \in f$ and $\alpha \cap \beta = \emptyset$.

(f) If f has such a representation, we must have $g = f/e_j$ and $h = f \bmod e_j$. Conversely, those families satisfy $e_j \perp g \cup h$. (This law is the fundamental recursive principle underlying ZDDs — just as the unique representation $f = (x_j?\ g\!:\ h)$, with g and h independent of x_j, underlies BDDs.)

(g) Both true. (To prove them, represent f and g as in part (f).)

[R. K. Brayton and C. McMullen introduced the quotient and remainder operations in *Proc. Int. Symp. Circuits and Systems* (IEEE, 1982), 49–54, but in a slightly different context: They dealt with families of incomparable sets of subcubes.]

205. In all cases we construct a recursion based on exercise 204(f). For example, if $f_v = g_v = v$, we have $f \sqcup g = (\bar{v}?\ f_l \sqcup g_l\!:\ (f_l \sqcup g_h) \cup (f_h \sqcup g_l) \cup (f_h \sqcup g_h));\ f \sqcap g = (\bar{v}?\ (f_l \sqcap g_l) \cup (f_l \sqcap g_h) \cup (f_h \sqcap g_l)\!:\ f_h \sqcap g_h);\ f \boxplus g = (\bar{v}?\ (f_l \boxplus g_l) \cup (f_h \boxplus g_h)\!:\ (f_h \boxplus g_l) \cup (f_l \boxplus g_h))$.

(a) If $f_v < g_v$ or ($f_v = g_v$ and $f > g$), swap $f \leftrightarrow g$. If $f = \emptyset$, return f; if $f = \epsilon$, return g. If $f \sqcup g = r$ is in the memo cache, return r. If $f_v > g_v$, set $r_l \leftarrow \text{JOIN}(f, g_l)$ and $r_h \leftarrow \text{JOIN}(f, g_h)$; otherwise set $r_l \leftarrow \text{JOIN}(f_l, g_l)$, $r_{lh} \leftarrow \text{JOIN}(f_l, g_h)$, $r_{hl} \leftarrow \text{JOIN}(f_h, g_l)$, $r_{hh} \leftarrow \text{JOIN}(f_h, g_h)$, $r_h \leftarrow \text{OROR}(r_{lh}, r_{hl}, r_{hh})$, and dereference r_{lh}, r_{hl}, r_{hh}. Finish with $r \leftarrow \text{ZUNIQUE}(g_v, r_l, r_h)$; cache it and return it as in exercise 198.

(We could also compute r_h via the formula $\text{OR}(r_{lh}, \text{JOIN}(f_h, \text{OR}(g_l, g_h)))$, or via $\text{OR}(r_{hl}, \text{JOIN}(\text{OR}(f_l, f_h), g_h))$. Sometimes one way is much better than the other two.)

The DISJOIN operation, which produces the family of *disjoint* unions $\{\alpha \cup \beta \mid \alpha \in f,\ \beta \in g,\ \alpha \cap \beta = \emptyset\}$, is similar but with r_{hh} omitted.

(b) If $f_v < g_v$ or ($f_v = g_v$ and $f > g$), swap $f \leftrightarrow g$. If $f \le \epsilon$, return f. (We consider $\emptyset < \epsilon$ and $\epsilon <$ all others.) Otherwise, if $\text{MEET}(f, g)$ hasn't been cached, there are two cases. If $f_v > g_v$, set $r_h \leftarrow \text{OR}(g_l, g_h)$, $r \leftarrow \text{MEET}(f, r_h)$, and dereference r_h; otherwise proceed analogously to (a) but with $l \leftrightarrow h$. Cache and return r as usual.

(c) This operation is similar to (a), but $r_l \leftarrow \text{OR}(r_{ll}, r_{hh})$ and $r_h \leftarrow \text{OR}(r_{lh}, r_{hl})$.

(d) First we implement the important simple cases f/e_v and $f \bmod e_v$:

$$\text{EZDIV}(f, v) = \begin{cases} \text{If } f_v = v, \text{ return } f_h; \text{ if } f_v > v, \text{ return } \emptyset. \text{ Otherwise look for} \\ f/e_v = r \text{ in the cache; if it isn't present, compute it via} \\ r \leftarrow \text{ZUNIQUE}(f_v, \text{EZDIV}(f_l, v), \text{EZDIV}(f_h, v)). \end{cases}$$

$$\text{EZMOD}(f, v) = \begin{cases} \text{If } f_v = v, \text{ return } f_l; \text{ if } f_v > v, \text{ return } f. \text{ Otherwise look for} \\ f \bmod e_v = r \text{ in the cache; if it isn't present, compute it via} \\ r \leftarrow \text{ZUNIQUE}(f_v, \text{EZMOD}(f_l, v), \text{EZMOD}(f_h, v)). \end{cases}$$

Now $\text{DIV}(f, g) = $ "If $g = \emptyset$, see below; if $g = \epsilon$, return f. Otherwise, if $f \le \epsilon$, return $\emptyset$; if $f = g$, return ϵ. If $g_l = \emptyset$ and $g_h = \epsilon$, return $\text{EZDIV}(f, g_v)$. Otherwise, if $f/g = r$ is in the memo cache, return r. Otherwise set $r_l \leftarrow \text{EZDIV}(f, g_v)$, $r \leftarrow \text{DIV}(r_l, g_h)$, and dereference r_l. If $r \ne \emptyset$ and $g_l \ne \emptyset$, set $r_h \leftarrow \text{EZMOD}(f, g_v)$ and $r_l \leftarrow \text{DIV}(r_h, g_l)$, dereference r_h, set $r_h \leftarrow r$ and $r \leftarrow \text{AND}(r_l, r_h)$, dereference r_l and r_h. Insert $f/g = r$ in the memo cache and return r." Division by $\emptyset$ returns $\wp$ if there is a fixed universe $\{1, \dots, N\}$ as in exercise 201. Otherwise it's an error (because the universal family $\wp$ doesn't exist).

(e) If $g = \emptyset$, return f. If $g = \epsilon$, return $\emptyset$. If $(g_l, g_h) = (\emptyset, \epsilon)$, return $\text{EZMOD}(f, g_v)$. If $f \bmod g = r$ is cached, return it. Otherwise set $r \leftarrow \text{DIV}(f, g)$ and $r_h \leftarrow \text{JOIN}(r, g)$, dereference r, set $r \leftarrow \text{BUTNOT}(f, r_h)$, and dereference r_h. Cache and return r.

[S. Minato gave $\text{EZDIV}(f, v)$, $\text{EZREM}(f, v)$, and $\text{DELTA}(f, e_v)$ in his original paper on ZDDs. His algorithms for $\text{JOIN}(f, g)$ and $\text{DIV}(f, g)$ appeared in the sequel, *ACM/IEEE Design Automation Conf.* **31** (1994), 420–424.]

206. The upper bound $O(Z(f)^3 Z(g)^3)$ is not difficult to prove for cases (a) and (b), as well as $O(Z(f)^2 Z(g)^2)$ for case (c). But are there examples that take such a long time? And can the running time for (d) be exponential? All five routines seem to be reasonably fast in practice.

207. If $f = e_{i_1} \cup \cdots \cup e_{i_l}$ and $k \geq 0$, let $\mathrm{SYM}(f, v, k)$ be the Boolean function that is true if and only if exactly k of the variables $\{x_{i_1}, \dots, x_{i_l}\} \cap \{x_v, x_{v+1}, \dots\}$ are 1 and $x_1 = \cdots = x_{v-1} = 0$. We compute $(e_{i_1} \cup \cdots \cup e_{i_l}) \S k$ by calling $\mathrm{SYM}(f, 1, k)$.

$\mathrm{SYM}(f, v, k) = $ "While $f_v < v$, set $f \leftarrow f_l$. If $f_v = N + 1$ and $k > 0$, return $\emptyset$. If $f_v = N + 1$ and $k = 0$, return the partial-tautology function t_v (see answer 201). If $f \S v \S k = r$ is in the cache, return r. Otherwise set $r \leftarrow \mathrm{SYM}(f, f_v + 1, k)$. If $k > 0$, set $q \leftarrow \mathrm{SYM}(f_l, f_v + 1, k - 1)$ and $r \leftarrow \mathrm{ZUNIQUE}(f_v, r, q)$. While $f_v > v$, set $f_v \leftarrow f_v - 1$, increase $\mathrm{REF}(r)$ by 1, and set $r \leftarrow \mathrm{ZUNIQUE}(f_v, r, r)$. Put $f \S v \S k = r$ in the cache, and return r." The running time is $O((k+1)N)$. Notice that $\emptyset \S 0 = \wp$.

208. Just omit the factors $2^{v_s-1}-1$, $2^{v_l-v_k-1}$, and $2^{v_h-v_k-1}$ from steps C1 and C2. (And we get the generating function by setting $c_k \leftarrow c_l + zc_h$ in step C2; see exercise 25.) *The number of solutions equals the number of paths in the ZDD from the root to* $\boxed{\top}$.

209. Initially compute $\delta_n \leftarrow \perp$ and $\delta_j \leftarrow (\bar{x}_{j+1} \circ x_{j+1}) \bullet \delta_{j+1}$ for $n > j \geq 1$. Then, where answer 31 says '$\alpha \leftarrow (\bar{x}_j \circ x_j) \bullet \alpha$', change it to '$\alpha \leftarrow (\bar{x}_j \bullet \alpha) \circ (x_j \bullet \delta_j)$'. Also make the analogous changes with β and γ in place of α.

210. In fact, when $x = x_1 \dots x_n$ we can replace νx in the definition of g by any linear function $c(x) = c_1 x_1 + \cdots + c_n x_n$, thus characterizing all of the optimal solutions to the general Boolean programming problem treated by Algorithm B.

For each branch node x of the ZDD, with fields $\mathrm{V}(x)$, $\mathrm{LO}(x)$, $\mathrm{HI}(x)$, we can compute its optimum value $\mathrm{M}(x)$ and new links $\mathrm{L}(x)$, $\mathrm{H}(x)$ as follows: Let $m_l = \mathrm{M}(\mathrm{LO}(x))$ and $m_h = c_{\mathrm{V}(x)} + \mathrm{M}(\mathrm{HI}(x))$, where $\mathrm{M}(\boxed{\perp}) = -\infty$ and $\mathrm{M}(\boxed{\top}) = 0$. Then $\mathrm{L}(x) \leftarrow \mathrm{LO}(x)$ if $m_l \geq m_h$, otherwise $\mathrm{L}(x) \leftarrow \boxed{\perp}$; $\mathrm{H}(x) \leftarrow \mathrm{HI}(x)$ if $m_l \leq m_h$, otherwise $\mathrm{H}(x) \leftarrow \boxed{\perp}$. The ZDD for g is obtained by reducing the L and H links accessible from the root. Notice that $Z(g) \leq Z(f)$, and the entire computation takes $O(Z(f))$ steps. (This nice property of ZDDs was pointed out by O. Coudert; see answer 237.)

211. Yes, unless the matrix has all-zero rows. Without such rows, in fact, the profile and z-profile of f satisfy $b_k \geq q_k - 1 \geq z_k$ for $0 \leq k < n$, because the only level-k subfunction independent of x_{k+1} is the constant 0.

212. The best alternative in the author's experiments was to make ZDDs for each term $T_j = S_1(X_j)$ in (129), using the algorithm of exercise 207, and then to AND them together. For example, in problem (128) we have $X_1 = \{x_1, x_2\}$, $X_2 = \{x_1, x_3, x_4\}$, $\dots$, $X_{64} = \{x_{105}, x_{112}\}$; to make the term $S_1(X_2) = S_1(x_1, x_3, x_4)$, whose ZDD has 115 nodes, just form the 5-node ZDD for $e_1 \cup (e_3 \cup e_4)$ and compute $T_2 \leftarrow (e_1 \cup e_3 \cup e_4) \S 1$.

But in what order should the ANDs be done, after we've got the individual terms $T_1, \dots, T_n$ of (129)? Consider problem (128). *Method 1:* $T_1 \leftarrow T_1 \wedge T_2$, $T_1 \leftarrow T_1 \wedge T_3$, $\dots$, $T_1 \leftarrow T_1 \wedge T_{64}$. This "top-down" method fills in the upper levels first, and takes about 6.2 megamems. *Method 2:* $T_{64} \leftarrow T_{64} \wedge T_{63}$, $T_{64} \leftarrow T_{64} \wedge T_{62}$, $\dots$, $T_{64} \leftarrow T_{64} \wedge T_1$. By filling in the lower levels first ("bottom-up"), the time goes down to about 1.75 megamems. *Method 3:* $T_2 \leftarrow T_2 \wedge T_1$, $T_4 \leftarrow T_4 \wedge T_3$, $\dots$, $T_{64} \leftarrow T_{64} \wedge T_{63}$; $T_4 \leftarrow T_4 \wedge T_2$, $T_8 \leftarrow T_8 \wedge T_6$, $\dots$, $T_{64} \leftarrow T_{64} \wedge T_{62}$; $T_8 \leftarrow T_8 \wedge T_4$, $T_{16} \leftarrow T_{16} \wedge T_{12}$, $\dots$, $T_{64} \leftarrow T_{64} \wedge T_{60}$; $\dots$; $T_{64} \leftarrow T_{64} \wedge T_{32}$. This "balanced" approach also takes about 1.75 megamems. *Method 4:* $T_{33} \leftarrow T_{33} \wedge T_1$, $T_{34} \leftarrow T_{34} \wedge T_2$, $\dots$, $T_{64} \leftarrow T_{64} \wedge T_{32}$; $T_{49} \leftarrow T_{49} \wedge T_{33}$, $T_{50} \leftarrow T_{50} \wedge T_{34}$, $\dots$, $T_{64} \leftarrow T_{64} \wedge T_{48}$; $T_{57} \leftarrow T_{57} \wedge T_{49}$, $T_{58} \leftarrow T_{58} \wedge T_{50}$, $\dots$, $T_{64} \leftarrow T_{64} \wedge T_{56}$; $\dots$; $T_{64} \leftarrow T_{64} \wedge T_{63}$. This is a much better way to balance the work, needing only about 850 kilomems. *Method 5:* An analogous balancing strategy that uses the ternary ANDAND operation turns out to be still better, costing just 675 kilomems. (In all five cases, add 190 kilomems for the time to form the 64 initial terms T_j.)

Incidentally, we can reduce the ZDD size from 2300 to 1995 by insisting that $x_1 = 0$ and $x_2 = 1$ in (128) and (129), because the "transpose" of every covering is another covering. This idea does not, however, reduce the running time substantially.

The rows of (128) appear in decreasing lexicographic order, and that may not be ideal. But dynamic variable ordering is unhelpful when so many variables are present. (Sifting reduces the size from 2300 to 1887, but takes a *long* time.)

Further study, with a variety of exact cover problems, would clearly be desirable.

213. It is a bipartite graph with 30 vertices in one part and 32 in the other. (Think of a chessboard as a *checkerboard*: Every domino joins a white square to a black square, and we've removed two black squares.) A row sum of $(1, \ldots, 1, 1, *, *)$ has 1s in at least 31 "white" positions, so its last two coordinates must be either $(2, 1)$ or $(3, 2)$.

214. Add further constraints to the covering condition (128), namely $\bigwedge_{j=1}^{14} S_{\geq 1}(Y_j)$, where Y_j is the set of x_i that cross the jth potential fault line. (For example, $Y_1 = \{x_2, x_4, x_6, x_8, x_{10}, x_{12}, x_{14}, x_{15}\}$ is the set of ways to place a domino vertically in the top two rows of the board; each $|Y_j| = 8$.) The resulting ZDD has 9812 nodes, and characterizes 25,506 solutions. Incidentally, the BDD size is 26,622. [Faultfree domino tilings of $m \times n$ boards exist if and only if mn is even, $m \geq 5$, $n \geq 5$, and $(m, n) \neq (6, 6)$; see R. L. Graham, *The Mathematical Gardner* (Wadsworth International, 1981), 120–126. The solution in (127) is the only 8×8 example that is symmetric under both horizontal and vertical reflection; see Fig. 29(b) for symmetry under 90° rotation.]

215. This time we add the constraints $\bigwedge_{j=1}^{49} S_{\geq 1}(Z_j)$, where Z_j is the set of four placements x_i that surround an internal corner point. (For example, $Z_1 = \{x_1, x_2, x_4, x_{16}\}$.) These constraints reduce the ZDD size to 66. There are just two solutions, one the transpose of the other, and they can readily be found by hand. [See Y. Kotani, *Puzzlers' Tribute* (A. K. Peters, 2002), 413–420.]

Conjecture: The generating function for the number of $m \times n$ tatami tilings, when $n \geq m - 2 \geq 0$ and m is even, is $(1 + z)^2 (z^{m-2} + z^m)/(1 - z^{m-1} - z^{m+1})$.

216. (a) Assign three variables (a_i, b_i, c_i) to each row of (128), corresponding to the domino's color if row i is chosen. Every branch node of the ZDD for f in (129) now becomes three branch nodes. We can take advantage of symmetry under transposition by replacing f by $f \wedge x_2$; this reduces the ZDD size from 2300 to 1995, which grows to 5981 when each branch node is triplicated.

Now we AND in the adjacency constraints, for all 682 cases $\{i, i'\}$ where rows i and i' are adjacent domino positions. Such constraints have the form $\neg((a_i \wedge a_{i'}) \vee (b_i \wedge b_{i'}) \vee (c_i \wedge c_{i'}))$, and we apply them bottom-up as in Method 2 of answer 212. This computation inflates the ZDD until it reaches more than 800 thousand nodes; but eventually it settles down and ends up with size 584,205.

The desired answer turns out to be 13,343,246,232 (which, of course, is a multiple of $3! = 6$, because each permutation of the three colors yields a different solution).

(b) This question is distinct from part (a), because many coverings (including Fig. 29(b)) can be 3-colored in several ways; we want to count them only once.

Suppose $f(a_1, b_1, c_1, \ldots, a_m, b_m, c_m) = f(x_1, \ldots, x_{3m})$ is a function with $a_i = x_{3i-2}$, $b_i = x_{3i-1}$, and $c_i = x_{3i}$, such that $f(x_1, \ldots, x_{3m}) = 1$ implies $a_i + b_i + c_i \leq 1$ for $1 \leq i \leq m$. Let's define the *uncoloring* $\$f$ of f to be

$$\$f(x_1, \ldots, x_m) = \exists y_1 \cdots \exists y_{3m} \, \big(f(y_1, \ldots, y_{3m})$$
$$\wedge \, (x_1 = y_1 + y_2 + y_3) \wedge \cdots \wedge (x_m = y_{3m-2} + y_{3m-1} + y_{3m}) \big).$$

A straightforward recursive subroutine will compute the ZDD for $\$f$ from the ZDD for f. This process transforms the 584,205 nodes obtained in part (a) into a ZDD of size 33,731, from which we deduce the answer: 3,272,232.

(The running time is 1.2 gigamems for part (a), plus 1.3 gigamems to uncolor; the total memory requirement is about 44 megabytes. A similar computation based on BDDs instead of ZDDs cost $13.6 + 1.5$ gigamems and occupied 185 megabytes.)

217. The separation condition adds 4198 further constraints of the form $\neg(x_i \wedge x_{i'})$, where rows i and i' specify adjacent placements of congruent pieces. Applying these constraints while also evaluating $\bigwedge_{j=1}^{468} S_1(X_j)$ turned out to be a bad idea, in the author's experiments; even worse was an attempt to construct a separate ZDD for the new constraints alone. Much better was to build the 512,227-node ZDD as before, then to incorporate the new constraints one by one, first constraining the variables at the lowest levels. The resulting ZDD of size 31,300,699 was finally completed after 286 gigamems of work, proving that exactly 7,099,053,234,102 separated solutions exist.

We might also ask for *strongly* separated solutions, where congruent pieces are not allowed to touch even at their corners; this requirement adds 1948 more constraints. There are 42,159,777,732 strongly separated coverings, found after 304 gigamems with a ZDD of size 20,659,124. (Other methods may well be better than ZDDs for this problem.)

218. This is an exact cover problem. For example, the matrix when $n = 3$ is

$$
\begin{array}{ll}
001001010 & (--2--2) \\
010001001 & (-3---3) \\
010010010 & (-2--2-) \\
010100100 & (-1-1--) \\
100010001 & (3---3-) \\
100100010 & (2--2--) \\
101000100 & (1-1---) \\
\end{array}
$$

and in general there are $3n$ columns and $\binom{2n-1}{2} - \binom{n}{2}$ rows. Consider the case $n = 12$: The ZDD on 187 variables has 192,636 nodes. It can be found with a cost of 300 megamems, using Method 4 of answer 212 (binary balancing); Method 5 turns out to be 25% slower than Method 4 in this case. The BDD is much larger (2,198,195 nodes) and it costs more than 900 megamems.

Thus the ZDD is clearly preferable to the BDD for this problem, and it identifies the $L_{12} = 108,144$ solutions with reasonable efficiency. (However, the "dancing links" technique of Section 7.2.2 is about four times faster, and it needs far less memory.)

219. (a) 1267; (b) 2174; (c) 2958; (d) 3721; (e) 4502. (To form the ZDD for WORDS(n) we do $n-1$ ORs of the 7-node ZDDs for $w_1 \sqcup h_2 \sqcup i_3 \sqcup c_4 \sqcup h_5$, $t_1 \sqcup h_2 \sqcup e_3 \sqcup r_4 \sqcup e_5$, etc.)

220. (a) There is one a_2 node for the descendants of each initial letter that can be followed by a in the second position (aargh, babel, ..., zappy); 23 letters qualify, all except q, u, and x. And there's one b_2 node for each initial letter that can be followed by b (abbey, ebony, oboes). However, the actual rule isn't so simple; for example, there are three z_2 nodes, not four, because of sharing between czars and tzars.

(b) There's no v_5 because no five-letter word ends with v. (The SGB collection doesn't include arxiv or webtv.) The three nodes for w_5 arise because one stands for cases where the letters $< w_5$ must be followed by w (aglo and many others); another node stands for cases where either w or y must follow (stra, or resa, or when we've seen allo but not allot); and there's also a w_5 node for the case when unse is not followed by e or t, because it must then be followed by either w or x. Similarly, the two nodes for x_5 represent the cases where x is forced, or where the last letter must be either x or y (following $\mathtt{rela}$). There's only one y_5 node, because no four letters can be followed by both y and z. Of course there's just one z_5 node, and two sinks.

221. We compute, for every possible zead ζ, the probability that ζ will occur, and sum over all ζ. For definiteness, consider a zead that corresponds to branching on r_3, and suppose it represents a subfamily of 10 three-letter suffixes. There are exactly $\binom{6084}{10} - \binom{5408}{10} \approx 1.3 \times 10^{31}$ such zeads, and by the principle of inclusion and exclusion they each arise with probability $\sum_{k \geq 1} \binom{676}{k}(-1)^{k+1}\binom{11881376-6084k}{5757-10k}/\binom{11881376}{5757} \approx 2.5 \times 10^{-32}$. [*Hint:* $|\{r, s, t, u, v, w, x, y, z\}| = 9$, $676 = 26^2$, and $6084 = 9 \times 26^2$.] Thus such zeads contribute about 0.33 to the total. The r_3-zeads for subfamilies of sizes 1, 2, 3, 4, 5, ..., contribute approximately 11.5, 32.3, 45.1, 41.9, 29.3, ..., by a similar analysis; so we expect about 188.8 branches on r_3 altogether, on average. The grand total

$$\sum_{l=1}^{5}\sum_{j=1}^{26}\sum_{s=1}^{5757}\left(\binom{26^{5-l}(27-j)}{s} - \binom{26^{5-l}(26-j)}{s}\right)$$
$$\times \sum_{k=1}^{\infty}\binom{26^{l-1}}{k}(-1)^{k+1}\binom{26^5 - 26^{5-l}(27-j)k}{5757 - sk}/\binom{26^5}{5757},$$

plus 2 for the sinks, comes to ≈ 7151.986. The average z-profile is $\approx (1.00, \ldots, 1.00; 25.99, \ldots, 25.99; 188.86, \ldots, 171.43; 86.31, \ldots, 27.32; 3.53, \ldots, 1.00; 2)$.

222. (a) It's the set of all subsets of the words of F. (There are 50,569 such subwords, out of $27^5 = 14,348,907$ possibilities. They are described by a ZDD of size 18,784, constructed from F and $\wp$ via answer 205(b) at a cost of about 15 megamems.)

(b) This formula gives the same result as $F \sqcap \wp$, because every member of F contains exactly one element of each X_j. But the computation turns out to be much slower — about 370 megamems — in spite of the fact that $Z(X) = 132$ is almost as small as $Z(\wp) = 131$. (Notice that $|\wp| = 2^{130}$ while $|X| = 26^5 \approx 2^{23.5}$.)

(c) $(F/P) \sqcup P$, where $P = \mathtt{t}_1 \sqcup \mathtt{u}_3 \sqcup \mathtt{h}_5$ is the pattern. (The words are $\mathtt{touch}$, $\mathtt{tough}$, $\mathtt{truth}$. This computation costs about 3000 mems with the algorithms of answer 205.) Other contenders for simple formulas are $F \cap Q$, where Q describes the admissible words. If we set $Q = \mathtt{t}_1 \sqcup X_2 \sqcup \mathtt{u}_3 \sqcup X_4 \sqcup \mathtt{h}_5$, we have $Z(Q) = 57$ and the cost once again is $\approx 3000\mu$. With $Q = (\mathtt{t}_1 \cup \mathtt{u}_3 \cup \mathtt{h}_5) \S 3$, on the other hand, we have $Z(Q) = 132$ and the cost rises to about 9000 mems. (Here $|Q|$ is 26^2 in the first case, but 2^{127} in the second — *reversing* any intuition gained from (a) and (b)! Go figure.)

(d) $F \cap ((V_1 \cup \cdots \cup V_5) \S k)$. The number of such words is $(24, 1974, 3307, 443, 9, 0)$ for $k = (0, \ldots, 5)$, respectively, from ZDDs of sizes $(70, 1888, 3048, 686, 34, 1)$. ("See exercise 7–34 for the words F mod $\mathtt{y}_1$ mod $\mathtt{y}_2$ mod $\cdots$ mod $\mathtt{y}_5$," said the author $\mathtt{wryly}$.)

(e) The desired patterns satisfy $P = (F \sqcap \wp) \cap Q$, where $Q = ((X_1 \cup \cdots \cup X_5) \S 3)$. We have $Z(Q) = 386$, $Z(P) = 14221$, and $|P| = 19907$.

(f) The formula for this case is trickier. First, $P_2 = F \sqcap F$ gives F together with all patterns satisfied by two distinct words; we have $Z(P_2) = 11289$, $|P_2| = 21234$, and $|P_2 \cap Q| = 7753$. But $P_2 \cap Q$ is *not* the answer; for example, it omits the pattern $\mathtt{*atc*}$, which occurs eight times but only in the context $\mathtt{*atch}$. The correct answer is given by $P_2' \cap Q$, where $P_2' = (P_2 \backslash F) \sqcap \wp$. Then $Z(P_2') = 8947$, $Z(P_2' \cap Q) = 7525$, $|P_2' \cap Q| = 10472$.

(g) $G_1 \cup \cdots \cup G_5$, where $G_j = (F/(\mathtt{b}_j \cup \mathtt{o}_j)) \sqcup \mathtt{b}_j$. The answers are $\mathtt{bared}$, $\mathtt{bases}$, $\mathtt{basis}$, $\mathtt{baths}$, $\mathtt{bobby}$, $\mathtt{bring}$, $\mathtt{busts}$, $\mathtt{herbs}$, $\mathtt{limbs}$, $\mathtt{tribs}$.

(h) Patterns that admit all vowels in second place: b*lls, b*nds, m*tes, p*cks.

(i) The first gives all words whose middle three letters are vowels. The second gives all patterns with first and last letter specified, for which there's at least one match with three vowels inserted. There are 30 solutions to the first, but only 27 to the second (because, e.g., louis and luaus yield the same pattern). Incidentally, the complementary family $\wp \setminus F$ has $2^{130} - 5757$ members, and 46316 nodes in its ZDD.

223. (a) $d(\alpha, \mu) + d(\beta, \mu) + d(\gamma, \mu) = 5$, since $d(\alpha, \mu) = [\alpha_1 \neq \mu_1] + \cdots + [\alpha_5 \neq \mu_5]$.

(b) Given families f, g, h, the family $\{\mu \mid \mu = \langle \alpha\beta\gamma \rangle$ for some $\alpha \in f$, $\beta \in g$, $\gamma \in h$ with $\alpha \neq \mu$, $\beta \neq \mu$, $\gamma \neq \mu$, and $\alpha \cap \beta \cap \gamma = \emptyset\}$ can be defined recursively to allow ZDD computation, if we consider eight variants in which subsets of the inequality constraints are relaxed. In the author's experimental system, the ZDDs for medians of WORDS(n) for $n = (100, 1000, 5757)$ have respectively $(595, 14389, 71261)$ nodes and characterize $(47, 7310, 86153)$ five-letter solutions. Among the 86153 medians when $n = 5757$ are chads, stent, blogs, ditzy, phish, bling, and tetch; in fact, tetch $= \langle$fetch teach total$\rangle$ arises already when $n = 1000$. (The running times of about $(.01, 2, 700)$ gigamems, respectively, were not especially impressive; ZDDs are probably not the best tool for this problem. Still, the programming was instructive.)

(c) When $n = 100$, exactly $(1, 14, 47)$ medians of WORDS(n) belong to WORDS(100), WORDS(1000), WORDS(5757), respectively; the solution with most common words is while $= \langle$white whole still$\rangle$. When $n = 1000$, the corresponding numbers are $(38, 365, 1276)$; and when $n = 5757$ they are $(78, 655, 4480)$. The most common English words that *aren't* medians of three other English words are their, first, and right.

224. Every arc $u \longrightarrow v$ of the dag corresponds to a vertex v of the forest. The ZDD has exactly one branch node for every arc. The LO pointer of that node leads to the right sibling of the corresponding vertex v, or to $\boxed{\bot}$ if v has no right sibling. The HI pointer leads to the left child of v, or to $\boxed{\top}$ if v is a leaf. The arcs can be ordered in many ways (e.g., preorder, postorder, level order), without changing this ZDD.

225. As in exercise 55, we try to number the vertices in such a way that the "frontier" between early and late vertices remains fairly small; then we needn't remember too much about what decisions were made on the early vertices. In the present case we also want the source vertex s to be number 1.

In answer 55, the relevant state from previous branches corresponded to an equivalence relation (a set partition); but now we express it by a table $mate[i]$ for $j \leq i \leq l$, where $j = u_k$ is the smaller vertex of the current edge $u_k - v_k$ and where $l = \max\{v_1, \ldots, v_{k-1}\}$. Let $mate[i] = i$ if vertex i is untouched so far; let $mate[i] = 0$ if vertex i has been touched twice already. Otherwise $mate[i] = r$ and $mate[r] = i$, if previous edges form a simple path with endpoints $\{i, r\}$. Initially we set $mate[i] \leftarrow i$ for $1 \leq i \leq n$, except that $mate[1] \leftarrow t$ and $mate[t] \leftarrow 1$. (If $t > l$, the value of $mate[t]$ need not be stored, because it can be determined from the values of $mate[i]$ for $j \leq i \leq l$.)

Let $j' = u_{k+1}$ and $l' = \max\{v_1, \ldots, v_k\}$ be the values of j and l after edge k has been considered; and suppose $u_k = j$, $v_k = m$, $mate[j] = \hat{j}$, $mate[m] = \hat{m}$. We cannot choose edge $j - m$ if $\hat{j} = 0$ or $\hat{m} = 0$. Otherwise, if $\hat{j} \neq m$, the new $mate$ table after choosing edge $j - m$ can be computed by doing the assignments $mate[j] \leftarrow 0$, $mate[m] \leftarrow 0$, $mate[\hat{j}] \leftarrow \hat{m}$, $mate[\hat{m}] \leftarrow \hat{j}$ (in that order).

Otherwise we have $\hat{j} = m$ and $\hat{m} = j$; we must contemplate the endgame. Let i be the smallest integer such that $i > j$, $i \neq m$, and either $i > l'$ or $mate[i] \neq 0$ and $mate[i] \neq i$. The new state after choosing edge $j - m$ is $\emptyset$ if $i \leq l'$, otherwise it is ϵ.

Whether or not the edge is chosen, the new state will be $\emptyset$ if $mate[i] \neq 0$ and $mate[i] \neq i$ for some i in the range $j \leq i < j'$.

For example, here are the first steps for paths from 1 to 9 in a 3×3 grid (see (132)):

k	j	l	m	$mate[1] \dots mate[9]$	$\hat{\jmath}$	$\hat{m}$	$mate'[1] \dots mate'[9]$
1	1	1	2	9 2 3 4 5 6 7 8 1	9	2	0 9 3 4 5 6 7 8 2
2	1	2	3	9 2 3 4 5 6 7 8 1	9	3	0 2 9 4 5 6 7 8 3
2	1	2	3	0 9 3 4 5 6 7 8 2	0	3	—
3	2	3	4	0 2 9 4 5 6 7 8 3	2	4	0 4 9 2 5 6 7 8 3
3	2	3	4	0 9 3 4 5 6 7 8 2	9	4	0 0 3 9 5 6 7 8 4

where $mate'$ describes the next state if edge j — m is chosen. The state transitions $mate_{j..l} \mapsto mate'_{j'..l'}$ are $9 \mapsto (\overline{12}?\ 92:\ 09)$; $92 \mapsto (\overline{13}?\ \emptyset:\ 29)$; $09 \mapsto (\overline{13}?\ 93:\ \emptyset)$; $29 \mapsto (\overline{24}?\ 294:\ 492)$; $93 \mapsto (\overline{24}?\ 934:\ 039)$.

After all reachable states have been found, the ZDD can be obtained by reducing equivalent states, using a procedure like Algorithm R. (In the 3×3 grid problem, 57 branch nodes are reduced to 28, plus two sinks. The 22-branch ZDD illustrated in the text was obtained by subsequently optimizing with exercise 197.)

226. Just omit the initial assignments '$mate[1] \leftarrow t$, $mate[t] \leftarrow 1$.'

227. Change the test '$mate[i] \neq 0$ and $mate[i] \neq i$' to just '$mate[i] \neq 0$' in two places. Also, change '$i \leq l'$' to '$i \leq n$'.

228. Use the previous answer with the following further changes: Add a dummy vertex $d = n + 1$, with new edges v — d for all $v \neq s$; accepting this new edge will mean "end at v." Initialize the $mate$ table with $mate[1] \leftarrow d$, $mate[d] \leftarrow 1$. Leave d out of the maximization when calculating l and l'. When beginning to examine a stored $mate$ table, start with $mate[d] \leftarrow 0$ and then, if encountering $mate[i] = d$, set $mate[d] \leftarrow i$.

229. 149,692,648,904 of the latter paths go from VA to MD; graph (133) omits DC. (However, the graphs of (18) have fewer *Hamiltonian* paths than (133), because (133) has 1,782,199 Hamiltonian paths from CA to ME that do not go from VA to MD.)

230. The unique minimum and maximum routes from ME both end at WA:

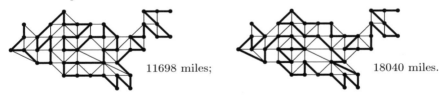

11698 miles;　　　　　　　　　　　　　　18040 miles.

Let $g(z) = \sum z^{\text{miles}(r)}$, summed over all routes r. The average cost, $g'(1)/g(1) = 1022014257375/68656026 \approx 14886.01$, can be computed rapidly as in answer 29.

(Similarly, $g''(1) = 15243164303013274$, so the standard deviation is ≈ 666.2.)

231. The algorithm of answer 225 gives a proto-ZDD with 8,062,831 branch nodes; it reduces to a ZDD with 3,024,214 branches. The number of solutions, via answer 208, is 50,819,542,770,311,581,606,906,543.

232. With answer 227 we find $h = 721,613,446,615,109,970,767$ Hamiltonian paths from a corner to its horizontal neighbor, and $d = 480,257,285,722,344,701,834$ of them to its diagonal neighbor; in both cases the relevant ZDD has about 1.3 million nodes. The number of oriented Hamiltonian cycles is $2h + d = 1,923,484,178,952,564,643,368$. (Divide by 2 to get the number of *undirected* Hamiltonian cycles.)

Essentially only two king's tours achieve the maximal length $8 + 56\sqrt{2}$:

233. A similar procedure can be used but with $mate[i] = r$ and $mate[r] = -i$ when the previous choices define an oriented path from i to r. Process all arcs $u_k \longrightarrow v_k$ and $u_k \longleftarrow v_k$ consecutively when $u_k = j < v_k = m$. Define $\hat{\jmath} = -j$ if $mate[j] = j$, otherwise $\hat{\jmath} = mate[j]$. Choosing $j \longrightarrow m$ is illegal if $\hat{\jmath} \geq 0$ or $\hat{m} \leq 0$. The updating rule for that choice, when legal, is: $mate[j] \leftarrow 0$, $mate[m] \leftarrow 0$, $mate[-\hat{\jmath}] \leftarrow \hat{m}$, $mate[\hat{m}] \leftarrow \hat{\jmath}$.

234. The 437 oriented cycles can be represented by a ZDD of ≈ 800 nodes. The shortest are, of course, $\mathtt{AL} \longrightarrow \mathtt{LA} \longrightarrow \mathtt{AL}$ and $\mathtt{MN} \longrightarrow \mathtt{NM} \longrightarrow \mathtt{MN}$. There are 37 of length 17 (the maximum), such as $(\mathtt{ALARINVTNMIDCOKSC})$ — i.e., $\mathtt{AL} \longrightarrow \mathtt{LA} \longrightarrow \cdots \longrightarrow \mathtt{SC} \longrightarrow \mathtt{CA} \longrightarrow \mathtt{AL}$.

Incidentally, the directed graph in question is the arc-digraph D^* of the digraph D on 26 vertices $\{\mathtt{A}, \mathtt{B}, \ldots, \mathtt{Z}\}$ whose 49 arcs are $\mathtt{A} \longrightarrow \mathtt{L}$, $\mathtt{A} \longrightarrow \mathtt{R}$, $\ldots$, $\mathtt{W} \longrightarrow \mathtt{Y}$. Every oriented walk of D^* is an oriented walk of D, and conversely (see exercise 2.3.4.2–21); but the oriented *cycles* of D^* are not necessarily simple in D. In fact, D has only 37 oriented cycles, the longest of which is unique: $(\mathtt{ARINMOKSDC})$.

If we extend consideration to the 62 postal codes in exercise 7–54(c), the number of oriented cycles rises to 38336, including the unique 1-cycle $(\mathtt{A})$, as well as 192 that have length 23, such as $(\mathtt{APRIALASCTNMNVINCOKSDCA})$. About 17000 ZDD nodes suffice to characterize the entire family of oriented cycles in this case.

235. The digraph has 7912 arcs; but we can prune them dramatically by removing arcs from vertices of in-degree zero, or arcs to vertices of out-degree zero. For example, $\mathtt{owner} \longrightarrow \mathtt{nerdy}$ goes away, because $\mathtt{nerdy}$ is a dead end; in fact, all successors of $\mathtt{owner}$ are likewise eliminated, so $\mathtt{crown}$ is out too. Eventually we're left with only 112 arcs among 85 words, and the problem can basically be done by hand.

There are just 74 oriented cycles. The unique shortest one, $\mathtt{slant} \longrightarrow \mathtt{antes} \longrightarrow \mathtt{tesla} \longrightarrow \mathtt{slant}$, can be abbreviated to '$(\mathtt{slante})$' as in the previous answer. The two longest are $(\alpha\omega)$ and $(\beta\omega)$, where $\alpha = \mathtt{picastepsomaso}$, $\beta = \mathtt{pointrotherema}$, and $\omega = \mathtt{nicadrearedidoserumoreliciteslabsitaresetuplenactoricedarerunichesto}$.

236. (a) Suppose $\alpha \in f$ and $\beta \in g$. If $\alpha \subseteq \beta$, then $\alpha \in f \sqcap g$. If $\alpha \cap \beta \in f$, then $\alpha \cap \beta \notin f \nearrow g$. A similar argument, or the use of part (b), shows that $f \searrow g = f \setminus (f \sqcup g)$.

Notes: The complementary operations "$f \nwarrow g = f \setminus (f \searrow g) = \{\alpha \in f \mid \alpha \supseteq \beta$ for some $\beta \in g\}$" for supersets, and "$f \swarrow g = f \setminus (f \nearrow g) = \{\alpha \in f \mid \alpha \subseteq \beta$ for some $\beta \in g\}$" for subsets, are also important in applications. They were omitted from this exercise only because five operations are already rather intimidating. The superset operation was introduced by O. Coudert, J. C. Madre, and H. Fraisse [*ACM/IEEE Design Automation Conference* **30** (1993), 625–630]. The identity $f \nwarrow g = f \cap (f \sqcup g)$ was noted by H. G. Okuno, S. Minato, and H. Isozaki [*Information Processing Letters* **66** (1998), 195–199], who also listed several of the laws in (d).

(b) Elementary set theory suffices. (The first six identities appear in pairs, each of which is equivalent to its mate. Strictly speaking, f^C involves infinite sets, and U is the AND of infinitely many variables; but the formulas hold in any finite universe. Notice that, when cast in the language of Boolean functions, $f^C(x) = f(\bar{x})$ is the complement of f^D, the Boolean dual; see exercise 7.1.1–2. Is there any use for the dual of $f^\sharp$, namely $\{\alpha \mid \beta \in f$ implies $\alpha \cup \beta \neq U\}^\uparrow$? If so, we might denote it by $f^\flat$.)

(c) All true except (ii), which should have said that $x_1^\uparrow = x_1^{C\downarrow C} = \bar{x}_1^{\downarrow C} = \epsilon^C = U$.

(d) The "identities" to cross out here are (ii), (viii), (ix), (xiv), and (xvi); the others are worth remembering. Regarding (ii)–(vi), notice that $f = f^\uparrow$ if and only if $f = f^\downarrow$, if and only if f is a clutter. Formula (xiv) should be $f \searrow g^\downarrow = f \searrow g$, the dual of (xiii). Formula (xvi) is almost right; it fails only when $f = \emptyset$ or $g = \emptyset$. Formula (ix) is perhaps the most interesting: We actually have $f^{\sharp\sharp} = f$ if and only if f is a clutter.

(e) Assuming that the universe of all vertices is finite, we have (i) $f = \wp \searrow g$ and (ii) $g = (\wp \setminus f)^\downarrow$, where $\wp$ is the universal family of exercises 201 and 222, because g is the family of minimal dependent sets. (Purists should substitute $\wp_V = \bigsqcup_{v \in V}(\epsilon \cup e_v)$ for $\wp$ in these formulas. The same relations hold in any hypergraph for which no edge is contained in another.)

237. MAXMAL$(f) =$ "If $f = \emptyset$ or $f = \epsilon$, return f. If $f^\uparrow = r$ is cached, return r. Otherwise set $r \leftarrow$ MAXMAL(f_l), $r_h \leftarrow$ MAXMAL(f_h), $r_l \leftarrow$ NONSUB(r, r_h), dereference r, and $r \leftarrow$ ZUNIQUE(f_v, r_l, r_h); cache and return r."

MINMAL$(f) =$ "If $f = \emptyset$ or $f = \epsilon$, return f. If $f^\downarrow = r$ is cached, return r. Otherwise set $r_l \leftarrow$ MINMAL(f_l), $r \leftarrow$ MINMAL(f_h), $r_h \leftarrow$ NONSUP(r, r_l), dereference r, and $r \leftarrow$ ZUNIQUE(f_v, r_l, r_h); cache and return r."

NONSUB$(f, g) =$ "If $g = \emptyset$, return f. If $f = \emptyset$ or $f = \epsilon$ or $f = g$, return $\emptyset$. If $f \nearrow g = r$ is cached, return r. Otherwise represent f and g as in (52). If $v < g_v$, set $r_l \leftarrow$ NONSUB(f_l, g), $r_h \leftarrow f_h$, and increase REF(f_h) by 1; otherwise set $r_h \leftarrow$ NONSUB(f_l, g_l), $r \leftarrow$ NONSUB(f_l, g_h), $r_l \leftarrow$ AND(r, r_h), dereference r and r_h, and set $r_h \leftarrow$ NONSUB(f_h, g_h). Finally $r \leftarrow$ ZUNIQUE(v, r_l, r_h); cache and return r."

NONSUP$(f, g) =$ "If $g = \emptyset$, return f. If $f = \emptyset$ or $g = \epsilon$ or $f = g$, return $\emptyset$. If $f_v > g_v$, return NONSUP(f, g_l). If $f \searrow g = r$ is cached, return r. Otherwise set $v = f_v$. If $v < g_v$, set $r_l \leftarrow$ NONSUP(f_l, g) and $r_h \leftarrow$ NONSUP(f_h, g); otherwise set $r_l \leftarrow$ NONSUP(f_h, g_h), $r \leftarrow$ NONSUP(f_h, g_l), $r_h \leftarrow$ AND(r, r_l), dereference r and r_l, and set $r_l \leftarrow$ NONSUP(f_l, g_l). Finally $r \leftarrow$ ZUNIQUE(v, r_l, r_h); cache and return r."

MINHIT$(f) =$ "If $f = \emptyset$, return ϵ. If $f = \epsilon$, return $\emptyset$. If $f^\sharp = r$ is cached, return r. Otherwise set $r \leftarrow$ OR(f_l, f_h), $r_l \leftarrow$ MINHIT(r), dereference r, $r \leftarrow$ MINHIT(f_l), $r_h \leftarrow$ NONSUP(r, r_l), dereference r, and $r \leftarrow$ ZUNIQUE(f_v, r_l, r_h); cache and return r."

As in exercise 206, the worst-case running times of these routines are unknown. Although NONSUB and NONSUP can be computed via JOIN or MEET and BUTNOT, by exercise 236(a), this direct implementation tends to be faster. It may be preferable to replace '$f = \epsilon$' by '$\epsilon \in f$' in MINMAL and MINHIT; also '$g = \epsilon$' by '$\epsilon \in g$' in NONSUP.

[Olivier Coudert introduced and implemented the operators $f^\uparrow$, $f \nearrow g$, and $f \searrow g$ in *Proc. Europ. Design and Test Conf.* (IEEE, 1997), 224–228. He also gave a recursive implementation of the interesting operator $f \odot g = (f \sqcup g)^\uparrow$; however, in the author's experiments, much better results have been obtained without it. For example, if f is the 177-node ZDD for the independent sets of the contiguous USA, the operation $g \leftarrow$ JOIN(f, f) costs about 350 kilomems and $h \leftarrow$ MAXMAL(g) costs about 3.6 megamems; but more than 69 *giga*mems are needed to compute $h \leftarrow$ MAXJOIN(f, f) all at once. Improved caching and garbage-collection strategies may, of course, change the picture.]

238. We can compute the 177-node ZDD for the family f of independent sets, using the ordering (104), in two ways: With Boolean algebra (67), $f = \neg \bigvee_{u-v}(x_u \wedge x_v)$; the cost is about 1.1 megamems with the algorithms of answers 198–201. With family algebra, on the other hand, we have $f = \wp \searrow \bigsqcup_{u-v}(e_u \sqcup e_v)$ by exercise 236(e); the cost, via answer 237, is less than 175 kilomems.

The subsets that give 2-colorable and 3-colorable subgraphs are $g = f \sqcup f$ and $h = g \sqcup f$, respectively; the maximal ones are $g^\uparrow$ and $h^\uparrow$. We have $Z(g) = 1009$, $Z(g^\uparrow) = 3040$, $Z(h) = 179$, $Z(h^\uparrow) = 183$, $|g| = 9{,}028{,}058{,}789{,}780$, $|g^\uparrow| = 2{,}949{,}441$, $|h| = 543{,}871{,}144{,}820{,}736$, and $|h^\uparrow| = 384$. The successive costs of computing g, $g^\uparrow$, h, and $h^\uparrow$ are approximately 350 Kμ (kilomems), 3.6 Mμ, 1.1 Mμ, and 230 Kμ. (We could compute $h^\uparrow$ by, say, $(g^\uparrow \sqcup f)^\uparrow$; but that turns out to be a bad idea.)

The maximal induced bipartite and tripartite subgraphs have the respective generating functions $7654z^{25} + \cdots + 9040z^{33} + 689z^{34}$ and $128z^{43} + 84z^{44} + 112z^{45} + 36z^{46} + 24z^{47}$. Here are typical examples of the smallest and largest:

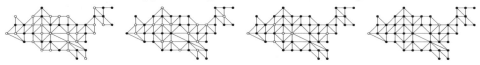

(Compare with the smallest and largest "1-partite" subgraphs in 7–(61) and 7–(62).)

Notice that the families g and h tell us exactly which induced subgraphs can be 2-colored and 3-colored, but they *don't* tell us how to color them.

239. Since $h = ((e_1 \cup \cdots \cup e_{49}) \S 2) \setminus g$ is the set of nonedges of G, the cliques are $f = \wp \setminus h$, and the maximal cliques are $f^\uparrow$. For example, we have $Z(f) = 144$ for the 214 cliques of the USA graph, and $Z(f^\uparrow) = 130$ for the 60 maximal ones. In this case the maximal cliques consist of 57 triangles (which are easily visible in (18)), together with three edges that aren't part of any triangle: AZ — NM, WI — MI, NH — ME.

Let f_k describe the sets coverable by k cliques. Then $f_1 = f$, and $f_{k+1} = f_k \sqcup f$ for $k \geq 1$. (It's not a good idea to compute f_{16} as $f_8 \sqcup f_8$; much faster is to do each join separately, even if the intermediate results are not of interest.)

The maxim*um* elements of f_k in the USA graph have sizes 3, 6, 9, ..., 36, 39, 41, 43, 45, 47, 48, 49 for $1 \leq k \leq 19$; these maxima can readily be determined by hand, in a small graph such as this. But the question of maxim*al* elements is much more subtle, and ZDDs are probably the best tool for investigating them. The ZDDs for $f_1, \ldots, f_{19}$ are quickly found after about 30 megamems of calculation, and they aren't large: $\max Z(f_k) = Z(f_{11}) = 9547$. Another 400 megamems produces the ZDDs for $f_1^\uparrow, \ldots, f_{19}^\uparrow$, which likewise are small: $\max Z(f_k^\uparrow) = Z(f_{11}^\uparrow) = 9458$.

We find, for example, that the generating function for $f_{18}^\uparrow$ is $12z^{47} + 13z^{48}$; eighteen cliques suffice to cover all but one of the 49 vertices, if we leave out CA, DC, FL, IL, LA, MI, MN, MT, SC, TN, UT, WA, or WV. There also are twelve cases where we can maximally cover 47 vertices; for example, if all but NE and NM are

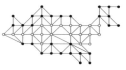

covered by 18 cliques, then neither of those states are covered. An unusual example of maximal clique covering is illustrated here: If the 29 "black" states are covered by 12 cliques, none of the "white" states will also be covered.

240. (a) In fact, the subformula $f(x) = \bigwedge_v (x_v \vee \bigvee_{u - v} x_u)$ of (67) precisely characterizes the dominating sets x. And if any element of a kernel is removed, it isn't dominated by the others. [C. Berge, *Théorie des graphes et ses applications* (1958), 44.]

(b) The Boolean formula of part (a) yields a ZDD with $Z(f) = 888$ after about 1.5 Mμ of computation; then another 1.5 Mμ with the MINMAL algorithm of answer 237 gives the minimal elements, with $Z(f^\downarrow) = 2082$.

A more clever way is to start with $h = \bigvee_v (e_v \sqcup \bigsqcup_{u-v} e_u)$, and then to compute $h^\sharp$, because $h^\sharp = f^\downarrow$. However, cleverness doesn't pay in this case: About 80 Kμ suffice to compute h, but the computation of $h^\sharp$ by the MINHIT algorithm costs about 350 Mμ.

Either way, we deduce that there are exactly 7,798,658 minimal dominating sets. More precisely, the generating function has the form $192z^{11} + 58855z^{12} + \cdots + 4170z^{18} + 40z^{19}$ (which can be compared to $80z^{11} + 7851z^{12} + \cdots + 441z^{18} + 18z^{19}$ for kernels).

(c) Proceeding as in answer 239, we can determine the sets of vertices d_k that are dominated by subsets of size $k = 1, 2, 3, \ldots$, because $d_{k+1} = d_k \sqcup d_1$. Here it's much faster to start with $d_1 = \wp \sqcap h$ instead of $d_1 = h$, even though $Z(\wp \sqcap h) = 313$ while $Z(h) = 213$, because we aren't interested in details about the small-cardinality members of d_k. Using the fact that the generating function for d_7 is $\cdots + 61z^{42} + z^{43}$, one can verify that the illustrated solution is unique. (Total cost ≈ 300 Mμ.)

241. Let g the family of all 728 edges. Then, as in previous exercises, $f = \wp \searrow g$ is the family of independent sets, and the cliques are $c = \wp \searrow (((\bigcup_v e_v) \S 2) \setminus g)$. We have $Z(g) = 699$, $Z(f) = 20244$, $Z(c) = 1882$.

(a) Among $|f| = 118969$ independent sets, there are $|f^\uparrow| = 10188$ kernels, with $Z(f^\uparrow) = 8577$ and generating function $728z^5 + 6912z^6 + 2456z^7 + 92z^8$. The 92 maximum independent sets are the famous solutions to the classic 8-queens problem, which we shall study in Section 7.2.2; example (C1) is the only solution with no three queens in a straight line, as noted by Sam Loyd in the *Brooklyn Daily Eagle* (20 December 1896). The $728 = 91 \times 8$ minimum kernels were first listed by C. F. de Jaenisch, *Traité des applications de l'analyse math. au jeu des échecs* **3** (1863), 255–259, who ascribed them to "M^r de R***." The upper left queen in (C0) can be replaced by king, bishop, or pawn, still dominating every open square [H. E. Dudeney, *The Weekly Dispatch* (3 Dec 1899)].

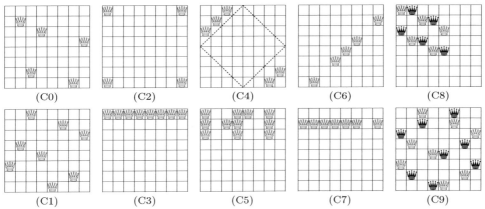

(C0)   (C2)   (C4)   (C6)   (C8)

(C1)   (C3)   (C5)   (C7)   (C9)

(b) Here $Z(c^\uparrow) = 866$; the 310 maximal cliques are described in exercise 7–129.

(c) These subsets are computationally more difficult: The ZDD for all dominating sets d has $Z(d) = 12,663,505$, $|d| = 18,446,595,708,474,987,957$; the minimal ones have $Z(d^\downarrow) = 11,363,849$, $|d^\downarrow| = 28,281,838$, and generating function $4860z^5 + 1075580z^6 + 14338028z^7 + 11978518z^8 + 873200z^9 + 11616z^{10} + 36z^{11}$. One can compute the ZDD for d in 1.5 Gμ by Boolean algebra, and then the ZDD for $d^\downarrow$ in another 680 Gμ; alternatively, the "clever" approach of answer 240 obtains $d^\downarrow$ in 775 Gμ without computing d. The 11-queen arrangement in (C5) is the only such minimal dominating set that is confined to three rows. H. E. Dudeney presented (C4), the only 5-queen solution that avoids the central diamond, in *Tit Bits* (1 Jan 1898), 257. The set of all 4860 minimum solutions was first enumerated by K. von Szily [*Deutsche Schachzeitung* **57** (1902), 199]; his complete list appears in W. Ahrens, *Math. Unterhaltungen und Spiele* **1** (1910), 313–318.

(d) Here it suffices to compute $(c \cap d)^{\downarrow}$ instead of $c \cap (d^{\downarrow})$, if we don't already know $d^{\downarrow}$, because $c \sqcap \wp = c$. We have $Z(c \cap d^{\downarrow}) = 342$ and $|c \cap d^{\downarrow}| = 92$, with generating function $20z^5 + 56z^6 + 16z^7$. Once again, Dudeney was first to discover all 20 of the 5-queen solutions [*The Weekly Dispatch* (30 July 1899)].

(e) We have $Z(f \sqcup f) = 91{,}780{,}989$ at a cost of 24 Gμ; then $Z((f \sqcup f)^{\uparrow}) = 11{,}808{,}436$ after another 290 Gμ. There are 27,567,390 maximal induced bipartite subgraphs, with generating function $109894z^{10} + 2561492z^{11} + 13833474z^{12} + 9162232z^{13} + 1799264z^{14} + 99408z^{15} + 1626z^{16}$. Any 8 independent queens can be combined with their mirror reflection to obtain a 16-queen solution, as (C1) yields (C9). But the disjoint union of minimum kernels is not always a maximal induced bipartite subgraph; for example, consider the union of (C0) with its reflection:

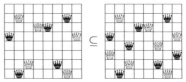

Parts (a), (b), (d), and possibly (c) can be solved just as well without the use of ZDDs; see, for example, exercise 7.1.3–132 for (a) and (b). But the ZDD approach seems best for (e). And the computation of all the maximal *tripartite* subgraphs of Q_8 may be beyond the reach of *any* feasible algorithm.

[In larger queen graphs Q_n, the smallest kernels and the minimum dominating sets are each known to have sizes either $\lceil n/2 \rceil$ or $\lceil n/2 \rceil + 1$ for $12 \leq n \leq 120$. See P. R. J. Östergård and W. D. Weakley, *Electronic J. Combinatorics* **8** (2001), #R29; D. Finozhenok and W. D. Weakley, *Australasian J. Combinatorics* **37** (2007), 295–200. The largest minimal dominating sets have been investigated by A. P. Burger, E. J. Cockayne, and C. M. Mynhardt, *Discrete Mathematics* **163** (1997), 47–66.]

242. These are the kernels of an interesting 3-regular hypergraph with 1544 edges. Its 4,113,975,079 independent subsets f (that is, its subsets with no three collinear points) have $Z(f) = 52{,}322{,}105$, computable with about 12 gigamems using family algebra as in answer 236(e). Another 575 Gμ will compute the kernels $f^{\uparrow}$, for which we have $Z(f^{\uparrow}) = 31{,}438{,}750$ and $|f^{\uparrow}| = 66{,}509{,}584$; the generating function is $228z^8 + 8240z^9 + 728956z^{10} + 9888900z^{11} + 32215908z^{12} + 20739920z^{13} + 2853164z^{14} + 73888z^{15} + 380z^{16}$.

```
oooo●●oo    oo●ooooo●    oooooooo    oooooooo    ooooooooooo
oooo●●oo    oo●oo●ooo    ooo●oooo    ooo●ooooo   oooooo●oooo
●●oooooo    ●●oooooo     oo●oooo●    ●●ooooo●    oo●ooooooooo
●●oooooo    oooo●oo●     ooooo●o●    oo●ooo●oo   o●oo●oooooo
oooooooo    o●ooooo●     o●●ooooo    oooo●●ooo   ●●ooooooooo
ooooo●●●    ●o●ooooo     ooo●oooo    ooo●●oooo   ●ooo●oooooo
ooo●oooo    ●oo●oooo     ooo●oooo    oooooooo    oooooo●oooo
oo●●oooo    ●ooooo●o     ooo●ooo●    oooooooo    ooooo●oooo●
```

[The problem of finding an independent set of size 16 was first posed by H. E. Dudeney in *The Weekly Dispatch* (29 Apr 1900 and 13 May 1900), where he gave the leftmost pattern shown above. Later, in the London *Tribune* (7 Nov 1906), Dudeney asked puzzlists to find the second pattern, which has two points in the center. The full set of maximum kernels, including 51 that are distinct under symmetry, was found by M. A. Adena, D. A. Holton, and P. A. Kelly, *Lecture Notes in Math.* **403** (1974), 6–17, who also noted the existence of an 8-point kernel. The middle pattern above is the only such kernel with all points in the central 4×4. The other two patterns yield kernels that have respectively $(8, 8, 10, 10, 12, 12, 12)$ points in $n \times n$ grids for $n = (8, 9, \ldots, 14)$; they were found by S. Ainley and described in a letter to Martin Gardner, 27 Oct 1976.]

243. (a) This result is readily verified even for infinite sets. (Notice that, as a Boolean function, $f^{\cap}$ is the least Horn function that is $\supseteq f$, by Theorem 7.1.1H.)

(b) We could form $f^{(2)} = f \sqcap f$, then $f^{(4)} = f^{(2)} \sqcap f^{(2)}$, $\ldots$, until $f^{(2^{k+1})} = f^{(2^k)}$, using exercise 205. But it's faster to devise a recurrence that goes to the limit all at once. If $f = f_0 \cup (e_1 \sqcup f_1)$ we have $f^{\cap} = f' \cup (e_1 \sqcup f_1^{\cap})$, where $f' = f_0^{\cap} \cup (f_0^{\cap} \sqcap f_1^{\cap})$.

[An alternative formula is $f' = (f_0 \cup f_1)^\cap \setminus (f_1^\cap \nearrow f_0)$; see S. Minato and H. Arimura, *Transactions of the Japanese Society for Artificial Intelligence* **22** (2007), 165–172.]

(c) With the first suggestion of (b), the computation of $F^{(2)}$, $F^{(4)}$, and $F^{(8)} = F^{(4)}$ costs about $(610 + 450 + 460)$ megamems. In this example it turns out that $F^{(4)} = F^{(3)}$, and that just three patterns belong to $F^{(3)} \setminus F^{(2)}$, namely c***f, *k*t*, and ***sp. (The words that match ***sp are clasp, crisp, and grasp.) A direct computation of $F^\cap$ using the recurrence based on $f_0^\cap \cap f_1^\cap$ costs only 320 Mμ; and in this example the alternative recurrence based on $(f_0 \cup f_1)^\cap$ costs 470 Mμ. The generating function is $1 + 124z + 2782z^2 + 7753z^3 + 4820z^4 + 5757z^5$.

244. To convert Fig. 22 from a BDD to a ZDD, we add appropriate nodes with LO = HI where links jump levels, obtaining the z-profile (1, 2, 2, 4, 4, 5, 5, 5, 5, 5, 2, 2, 2). To convert it from a ZDD to a BDD, we add nodes in the same places, but with HI = $\boxed{\perp}$, obtaining the profile (1, 2, 2, 4, 4, 5, 5, 5, 5, 5, 2, 2, 2). (In fact, the connectedness function and the spanning tree function are Z-transforms of each other; see exercise 192.)

245. See exercise 7.1.1–26. (It should be interesting to compare the performance of the Fredman–Khachiyan algorithm in exercise 7.1.1–27 with the ZDD-based algorithm MINHIT in answer 237, on a variety of different functions.)

246. If a nonconstant function doesn't depend on x_1, we can replace x_1 in the formulas by x_v, as in (50). Let P and Q be the prime implicants of functions p and q. (For example, if $P = e_2 \cup (e_3 \sqcup e_4)$ then $p = x_2 \lor (x_3 \land x_4)$.) By (137) and induction on $|f|$, the function f described in the theorem is sweet if and only if p and q are sweet and $\mathrm{PI}(f_0) \cap \mathrm{PI}(f_1) = \emptyset$. The latter equality holds if and only if $p \subseteq q$.

247. We can characterize them with BDDs as in (49) and exercise 75; but this time

$$\sigma_n(x_1, \ldots, x_{2^n}) = \sigma_{n-1}(x_1, \ldots, x_{2^n-1}) \land$$
$$\left((\bar{x}_2 \land \cdots \land \bar{x}_{2^n}) \lor \left(\sigma_{n-1}(x_2, \ldots, x_{2^n}) \land \bigwedge_{j=0}^{2^{k-1}} \left(\bar{x}_{2j+1} \lor \bigvee_{i \subset j} x_{2i+2} \right) \right) \right).$$

The answers $|\sigma_n|$ for $0 \le n \le 7$ are (2, 3, 6, 18, 106, 2102, 456774, 7108935325). (This computation builds a BDD of size $B(\sigma_7) = 7{,}701{,}683$, using about 900 megamems and 725 megabytes altogether.)

248. False; for example, $(x_1 \lor x_2) \land (x_2 \lor x_3)$ isn't sweet. (But the conjunction *is* sweet if f and g depend on disjoint sets of variables, or if x_1 is the only variable on which they both depend.)

249. (Solution by Shaddin Dughmi and Ian Post.) A nonzero monotone Boolean function is ultrasweet if and only if its prime implicants are the bases of a matroid; see Section 7.6.1. By extending answer 247 we can determine the number of ultrasweet functions $f(x_1, \ldots, x_n)$ for $0 \le n \le 7$: (2, 3, 6, 17, 69, 407, 3808, 75165).

250. Exhaustive analysis shows that ave $B(f) = 76726/7581 \approx 10.1$; ave $Z(\mathrm{PI}(f)) = 71513/7581 \approx 9.4$; $\Pr(Z(\mathrm{PI}(f)) > B(f)) = 151/7581 \approx .02$; and max $Z(\mathrm{PI}(f))/B(f) = 8/7$ occurs uniquely when f is $(x_1 \land x_4) \lor (x_1 \land x_5) \lor (x_2 \land x_3 \land x_4) \lor (x_2 \land x_5)$.

251. More strongly, could it be that $\limsup Z(\mathrm{PI}(f))/B(f) = 1$?

252. The ZDD should describe all words on $\{e_1, e_1', \ldots, e_n, e_n'\}$ that have exactly j unprimed letters and $k - j$ primed letters, and no occurrences of both e_i and e_i' in the same word, for some set of pairs (j, k). For example, if $n = 9$ and $f(x) = v_{vx}$, where $v = 110111011$, the pairs are $(0, 8)$, $(3, 6)$, and $(8, 8)$. Regardless of the set of pairs, the

z-profile elements will all be $O(n^2)$, hence $Z(\mathrm{PI}(f)) = O(n^3)$. (We order the variables so that x_i and x_i' are adjacent.) And $f(x) = S_{\lfloor n/3 \rfloor, \dots, \lfloor 2n/3 \rfloor}(x)$ has $Z(\mathrm{PI}(f)) = \Omega(n^3)$.

253. Let $\mathrm{I}(f)$ be the family of all *implicants* of f; then $\mathrm{PI}(f) = \mathrm{I}(f)^\downarrow$. The formula $\mathrm{I}(f) = \mathrm{I}(f_0 \wedge f_1) \cup (e_1' \sqcup \mathrm{I}(f_0)) \cup (e_1 \sqcup \mathrm{I}(f_1))$ is easy to verify. Thus $\mathrm{I}(f)^\downarrow = A \cup (e_1' \sqcup (\mathrm{PI}(f_0) \searrow A)) \cup (e_1 \sqcup (\mathrm{PI}(f_1) \searrow A))$, as in exercise 237. But $\mathrm{PI}(f_0) \searrow A = \mathrm{PI}(f_0) \setminus A$, since $A \subseteq \mathrm{I}(f)$.

[This recurrence for prime implicants is due to O. Coudert and J. C. Madre, *ACM/IEEE Design Automation Conf.* **29** (1992), 36–39. Partial results had previously been formulated by B. Reusch, *IEEE Trans.* **C–24** (1975), 924–930.]

254. By (53) and (137), we need to show that $\mathrm{PI}(g_h) \setminus \mathrm{PI}(f_h \cup g_l) = (\mathrm{PI}(g_h) \backslash \mathrm{PI}(g_l)) \setminus (\mathrm{PI}(f_h) \backslash \mathrm{PI}(f_l))$. But both of these are equal to $\mathrm{PI}(g_h) \setminus (\mathrm{PI}(f_h) \cup \mathrm{PI}(g_l))$, because $f_l \subseteq f_h \subseteq g_h$ and $f_l \subseteq g_l \subseteq g_h$.

[This recurrence produces a ZDD directly from the BDDs for f and g, and it yields $\mathrm{PI}(g)$ when $f = 0$. Thus it is easier to implement than (137), which requires also the set-difference operator on ZDDs. And it sometimes runs much faster in practice.]

255. (a) A typical item α like $e_2 \sqcup e_5 \sqcup e_6$ has a very simple ZDD. We can readily devise a BUMP routine that sets $g \leftarrow g \oplus \alpha$ and returns $[\alpha \in g]$, given ZDDs g and α.

To insert α into the multifamily f, start with $k \leftarrow c \leftarrow 0$; then while $c = 0$, set $c \leftarrow \mathrm{BUMP}(f_k)$ and $k \leftarrow k + 1$. To delete α, assuming that it is present, start with $k \leftarrow 0$ and $c \leftarrow 1$; while $c = 1$, set $c \leftarrow \mathrm{BUMP}(f_k)$ and $k \leftarrow k + 1$.

(b) Suppose f_k and g_k are $\emptyset$ for $k \geq m$. Set $k \leftarrow 0$ and $t \leftarrow \emptyset$ (the ZDD $\boxed{\perp}$). While $k < m$, set $h_k \leftarrow f_k \oplus g_k \oplus t$ and $t \leftarrow \langle f_k g_k t \rangle$. Finally set $h_m \leftarrow t$.

[This representation and its insertion algorithm are due to S. Minato and H. Arimura, *Proc. Workshop, Web Information Retrieval and Integration* (IEEE, 2005), 3–10.]

256. (a) Reflect the binary representation from left to right, and append 0s until the number of bits is 2^n for some n. The result is the truth table of the corresponding Boolean function $f(x_1, \dots, x_n)$, with x_k corresponding to $2^{2^{n-k}} \in U$. When $x = 41$, for example, 10010100 is the truth table of $(x_1 \wedge \bar{x}_2 \wedge x_3) \vee (\bar{x}_1 \wedge x_2 \wedge x_3) \vee (\bar{x}_1 \wedge \bar{x}_2 \wedge \bar{x}_3)$.

(b) If $x < 2^{2^n}$, we have $Z(x) \leq U_n = O(2^n/n)$, by (79) and exercise 192.

(c) There's a simple recursive routine $\mathrm{ADD}(x, y, c)$, which takes a "carry bit" c and pointers to the ZDDs for x and y and returns a pointer to the ZDD for $x + y + c$. This routine is invoked at most $4Z(x)Z(y)$ times.

(d) We cannot claim that $Z(x \mathbin{\dot{-}} y) = O(Z(x)Z(y))$, because $Z(x \mathbin{\dot{-}} y) = n + 1$ and $Z(x) = 3$ and $Z(y) = 1$ when $x = 2^{2^n}$ and $y = 1$. But by computing $x \mathbin{\dot{-}} y = (x + 1 + ((2^{2^n} - 1) \oplus y)) - 2^{2^n}$ when $y \leq x < 2^{2^n}$, we can show that $Z(x \mathbin{\dot{-}} y) = O(Z(x)Z(y) \log \log x)$. (See the ZDD nodes t_j in answer 201.) So the answer is "yes."

(e) No. For example, if $x = (2^{2^{2^k + k}} - 1)/(2^{2^k} - 1)$, we have $Z(x) = 2^k + 1$ but $Z(x^2) = 3 \cdot (2^{2^k} - 1) = U_{2^k + k + 1} - 2$, where $U_{2^k + k + 1}$ is the largest possible ZDD size for numbers with $\lg \lg x^2 < 2^k + k + 1$ (see part (b)).

[This exercise was inspired by Jean Vuillemin, who began to experiment with such sparse integers about 1993. Unfortunately the numbers that are of greatest importance in combinatorial calculations, such as Fibonacci numbers, factorials, binomial coefficients, etc., rarely turn out to be sparse in practice.]

257. See *Proc. Europ. Design and Test Conf.* (IEEE, 1995), 449–454. With signed coefficients one can use $\{-2, 4, -8, \dots\}$ instead of $\{2, 4, 8, \dots\}$, as in negabinary arithmetic.

[In the special case where the degree is at most 1 in each variable and where addition is done modulo 2, the polynomials of this exercise are equivalent to the multilinear representations of Boolean functions (see 7.1.1–(19)), and the ZDDs are equivalent to "binary moment diagrams" (BMDs). See R. E. Bryant and Y.-A. Chen, *ACM/IEEE Design Automation Conf.* **32** (1995), 535–541.]

258. If n is odd, the BDD must depend on all its variables, and there must be at least $\lceil \lg n \rceil$ of them. Thus $B(f) \geq \lceil \lg n \rceil + 2$ when $n > 1$, and the skinny functions of exercise 170(c) achieve this bound. If n is even, add an unused variable to the solution for $n/2$.

The ZDD question is easily seen to be equivalent to finding a shortest addition chain, as in Section 4.6.3. Thus the smallest $Z(f)$ for $|f| = n$ is $l(n) + 1$, including $\boxed{\top}$.

259. The theory of nested parentheses (see, for example, exercise 2.2.1–3) tells us that $N_n(x) = 1$ if and only if $\bar{x}_1 + \cdots + \bar{x}_k \geq x_1 + \cdots + x_k$ for $0 \leq k \leq 2n$, with equality when $k = 2n$. Equivalently, $k - n \leq x_1 + \cdots + x_k \leq k/2$ for $0 \leq k \leq 2n$. So the BDD for N_n is rather like the BDD for $S_n(x)$, but simpler; in fact, the profile elements are $b_k = \lfloor k/2 \rfloor + 1$ for $0 \leq k \leq n$ and $b_k = n + 1 - \lceil k/2 \rceil$ for $n \leq k < 2n$. Hence $B(N_n) = b_0 + \cdots + b_{2n-1} + 2 = \binom{n+2}{2} + 1$. The z-profile has $z_k = b_k - [k \text{ even}]$ for $0 \leq k < 2n$, because of HI branches to $\boxed{\bot}$ on even levels; hence $Z(N_n) = B(N_n) - n$.

[An interesting BDD base for the $n+1$ Boolean functions that correspond to C_{nn}, $C_{(n-1)(n+1)}$, ..., $C_{0(2n)}$ in 7.2.1.6–(21) can be constructed by analogy with exercise 49.]

260. (a,b) Arrange the variables $x_{n,0}$, $x_{n,1}$, ..., $x_{n,n-1}$, $x_{n-1,0}$, ..., $x_{1,0}$, from top to bottom. Then the HI branch from the ZDD root of R_n is the ZDD root of R_{n-1}. (This ordering actually turns out to minimize $Z(R_n)$ for $n \leq 6$, probably also for all n.) The z-profile is $1, \ldots, 1; n - 2, \ldots, 2, 1, 1; n - 3, \ldots, 2, 1, 1; \ldots$; hence $Z(R_n) = \binom{n}{3} + 2n + 1 \approx \frac{1}{6}n^3$ and $Z(R_{100}) = 161{,}901$. The ordinary profile is $1, 2, 2, 3, 4, \ldots, n - 1; n - 1, 2n - 4, 2n - 5, \ldots, n - 1; n - 2, 2n - 6, \ldots, n - 2; \ldots$; altogether $B(R_n) = 3\binom{n}{3} + \binom{n+1}{2} + 3$ for $n \geq 5$, and $B(R_{100}) = 490{,}153$.

[See I. Semba and S. Yajima, *Trans. Inf. Proc. Soc. Japan* **35** (1994), 1666–1667. Incidentally, the method of exercise 7.2.1.5–26 leads to a ZDD for set partitions that has only $\binom{n}{2}$ variables and $\binom{n}{2} + 1$ nodes. But the connection between that representation and the partitions themselves is less direct, thus harder to restrict in a natural way.]

(c) Now there are 573 variables instead of 5050 when $n = 10$; the number of variables in general is $nl - 2^l + 1$, where $l = \lceil \lg n \rceil$, by Eq. 5.3.1–(3). We examine the bits of a_n, a_{n-1}, ..., with the most significant bit first. Then $B(R'_{100}) = 31{,}861$, and one can show that $B(R'_n) = \binom{n}{2}l - \frac{1}{6}4^l - \frac{1}{2}2^l - \nu(n-1) + l + \frac{8}{3}$ for $n > 2$. The ZDD size is more complicated, and appears to be roughly 60% larger; we have $Z(R'_{100}) = 50{,}154$.

261. Given a Boolean function $f(x_1, \ldots, x_n)$, the set of all binary strings $x_1 \ldots x_n$ such that $f(x_1, \ldots, x_n) = 1$ is a finite language, so it is regular. The minimum-state deterministic automaton $\mathcal{A}$ for this language is the QDD for f. (In general, when L is regular, the state of $\mathcal{A}$ after reading $x_1 \ldots x_k$ accepts the language $\{\alpha \mid x_1 \ldots x_k \alpha \in L\}$.)

[The quoted theorem was discovered in a more general context by D. A. Huffman, *Journal of the Franklin Institute* **257** (1954), 161–190, and independently by E. F. Moore, *Annals of Mathematics Studies* **34** (1956), 129–153.]

An interesting example of the connection between this theory and the theory of BDDs can be found in early work by Yuri Breitbart that is summarized in *Doklady Akad. Nauk SSSR* **180** (1968), 1053–1055. Lemma 7 of Breitbart's paper states, in essence, that $B_{\min}(\psi) = \Omega(2^{n/4})$, where ψ is the function of $2n$ variables $x = (x_1, \ldots, x_n)$ and $y = (y_1, \ldots, y_n)$ defined by $\psi(x, y) = x_{\nu y} \oplus y_{\nu x}$, with the understanding that $x_0 = y_0 = 0$. (Notice that ψ is sort of a "two-sided" hidden weighted bit function.)

262. (a) If a denotes the function or subfunction f, we can for example let $C(a) = a \oplus 1$ denote $\bar{f}$, assuming that each node occupies an even number of bytes. Then

$C(C(a)) = a$, and a link to a denotes a nonnormal function if and only if a is odd; $a \;\&\; -2$ always points to a node, which always represents a normal function.

The LO pointer of every node is even, because a normal function remains normal when we replace any variable by 0. But the HI pointer of any node might be complemented, and an external root pointer to any function of a normalized BDD base might also be complemented. Notice that the $\boxed{\top}$ sink is now impossible.

(b) Uniqueness is obvious because of the relation to truth tables: A bead is either normal (i.e., begins with 0) or the complement of a normal bead.

(c) In diagrams, each complement link is conveniently indicated by a dot:

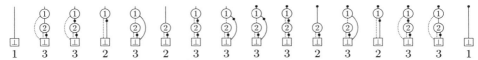

1	3	3	2	3	2	3	3	3	2	3	2	3	3	1

(d) There are $2^{2^{m}-1} - 2^{2^{m-1}-1}$ normal beads of order m. The worst case, $B^0(f) \le B^0(f_n) = 1 + \sum_{k=0}^{n-1} \min(2^k, 2^{2^{n-k}-1} - 2^{2^{n-k-1}-1}) = (U_{n+1} - 1)/2$, occurs with the functions of answer 110. For the average normalized profile, change $2^{2^{n-k}} - 1$ in (80) to $2^{2^{n-k}} - 2$, and divide the whole formula by 2; again the average case is very close to the worst case. For example, instead of (81) we have

$$(1.0, 2.0, 4.0, 8.0, 16.0, 32.0, 64.0, 127.3, 103.9, 6.0, 1.0, 1.0).$$

(e) We save $\boxed{\top}$, one $\textcircled{6}$, two $\textcircled{5}$s, and three $\textcircled{4}$s, leaving 45 normalized nodes.

(f) It's probably best to have subroutines AND, OR, BUTNOT for the case where f and g are known to be normal, together with a subroutine GAND for the general case. The routine $\text{GAND}(f,g)$ returns $\text{AND}(f,g)$ if f and g are even, $\text{BUTNOT}(f,C(g))$ if f is even but g is odd, $\text{BUTNOT}(g,C(f))$ if g is even but f is odd, $C(\text{OR}(C(f),C(g)))$ if f and g are odd. The routine $\text{AND}(f,g)$ is like (55) except that $r_h \leftarrow \text{GAND}(f_h, g_h)$; only the cases $f = 0$, $g = 0$, and $f = g$ need be tested as "obvious" values.

Notes: Complement links were proposed by S. Akers in 1978, and independently by J. P. Billon in 1987. Although such links are used by all the major BDD packages, they are hard to recommend because the computer programs become much more complicated. The memory saving is usually negligible, and never better than a factor of 2; furthermore, the author's experiments show little gain in running time.

With ZDDs instead of BDDs, a "normal family" of functions is a family that doesn't contain the empty set. Shin-ichi Minato has suggested using $C(a)$ to denote the family $f \oplus \epsilon$, instead of $\bar{f}$, in ZDD work.

263. (a) If $Hx = 0$ and $x \ne 0$, we can't have $\nu x = 1$ or 2 because the columns of H are nonzero and distinct. [R. W. Hamming, *Bell System Tech. J.* **29** (1950), 147–160.]

(b) Let r_k be the rank of the first k columns of H, and s_k the rank of the last k columns. Then $b_k = 2^{r_k + s_{n-k} - r_n}$ for $0 \le k < n$, because this is the number of elements in the intersection of the vector spaces spanned by the first k and last $n-k$ columns. In the Hamming code, $r_k = 1 + \lambda k$ and $s_k = \min(m, 2 + \lambda(k-1))$ for $k > 1$; so we find $B(f) = (n^2 + 5)/2$. [See G. D. Forney, Jr., *IEEE Trans.* **IT-34** (1988), 1184–1187.]

(c) Let $q_k = 1 - p_k$. Maximizing $\prod_{k=1}^{n} p_k^{[x_k = y_k]} q_k^{[x_k \ne y_k]}$ is the same as maximizing $\sum_{k=1}^{n} w_k x_k$, where $w_k = (2y_k - 1)\log(p_k/q_k)$, so we can use Algorithm B.

Notes: Coding theorists, beginning with unpublished work of Forney in 1967, have developed the idea of a code's so-called *trellis*. In the binary case, the trellis is the same as the QDD for f, but with all nodes for the constant subfunction 0 eliminated. (Useful codes have distance > 1; then the trellis is also the BDD for f, but with $\boxed{\bot}$

eliminated.) Forney's original motivation was to show that the decoding algorithm of A. Viterbi [*IEEE Trans.* **IT-13** (1967), 260–269] is optimum for convolutional codes. A few years later, L. R. Bahl, J. Cocke, F. Jelinek, and J. Raviv [*IEEE Trans.* **IT-20** (1974), 284–287] extended trellis structure to linear block codes and presented further optimization algorithms. See also the papers of G. B. Horn and F. R. Kschischang [*IEEE Trans.* **IT-42** (1996), 2042–2047]; J. Lafferty and A. Vardy [*IEEE Trans.* **C-48** (1999), 971–986].

264. Procedures that combine the "bottom-up" methods of Algorithm B with "top-down" methods that optimize over predecessors of a node might be more efficient than methods that go strictly in one direction.

INDEX AND GLOSSARY

Indexes need not necessarily be dry.
— HENRY B. WHEATLEY, *How to Make an Index* (1902)

When an index entry refers to a page containing a relevant exercise, see also the *answer* to that exercise for further information. An answer page is not indexed here unless it refers to a topic not included in the statement of the exercise.

Also Available from Donald E. Knuth
and Addison-Wesley

0-201-89683-4

0-201-89684-2

0-201-89685-0

0-201-85392-2

0-201-48541-9

0-321-53496-4

0-321-58050-8

0-201-85393-0

0-201-85394-9

0-321-33570-8

Fascicles from Volume 4

For more information about these books, visit us online at www.informit.com/aw.

Also Available from Donald E. Knuth and Addison-Wesley

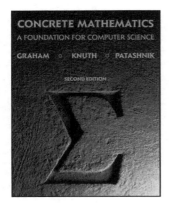

Concrete Mathematics, Second Edition:
A Foundation for Computer Science

0-201-55802-5

This book introduces the mathematics that supports advanced computer programming and the analysis of algorithms. It is an indispensable text and reference not only for computer scientists—the authors themselves rely heavily on it!—but for serious users of mathematics in virtually every discipline.

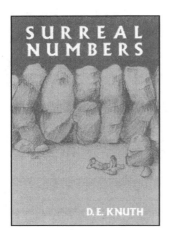

Surreal Numbers

0-201-03812-9

Some years ago John Horton Conway introduced a new way to construct numbers. Donald E. Knuth, in appreciation of this revolutionary system, wrote an introduction to Conway's method. Knuth wrote this introduction as a work of fiction—a novelette. *Surreal Numbers* will appeal to anyone who might enjoy an engaging dialogue on abstract mathematical ideas, and who might wish to experience how new mathematics is created.

Computers & Typesetting, Volumes A–E Boxed Set

0-201-73416-8

Donald E. Knuth's five volumes on *Computers & Typesetting* comprise the definitive user guides and thoroughly documented program code for the TeX and METAFONT systems. This open-source software is widely used around the world by scientists, mathematicians, and others to produce high-quality, aesthetically pleasing text, especially where technical content is included.

For more information about these books, visit us online at www.informit.com/aw.